HANDBOOK OF GENDER

The Oxford India Handbooks are an important initiative in academic publishing.
Each volume offers a comprehensive survey of research in a critical subject area
and provides facts, figures, and analyses for a well-grounded perspective.
The series provides scholars, students, and policy planners
with a balanced understanding of a wide range of issues in the social sciences.

Other Titles in the Series

HANDBOOK OF CLIMATE CHANGE AND INDIA
Development, Politics, and Governance
Navroz K. Dubash (Editor)

HANDBOOK OF MODERNITY IN SOUTH ASIA
Modern Makeovers
Saurabh Dube (Editor)

HANDBOOK OF PSYCHOLOGY IN INDIA
Girishwar Misra (Editor)

THE RIGHT TO INFORMATION ACT 2005
A Handbook
Sudhir Naib

HANDBOOK OF POPULATION AND DEVELOPMENT IN INDIA
A.K. Shiva Kumar, Pradeep Panda, and Rajani R. Ved (Editors)

GLOBALIZATION AND DEVELOPMENT
A Handbook of New Perspectives (OIP)
Ashwini Deshpande (Editor)

HANDBOOK OF MUSLIMS IN INDIA
Empirical and Policy Perspectives
Rakesh Basant and Abusaleh Shariff (Editors)

HANDBOOK OF ENVIRONMENTAL ECONOMICS IN INDIA
Kanchan Chopra and Vikram Dayal

HANDBOOK OF AGRICULTURE IN INDIA (OIP)
Shovan Ray (Editor)

HANDBOOK OF ENVIRONMENTAL LAW
P.B. Sahasranaman

HANDBOOK OF LAW, WOMEN, AND EMPLOYMENT
Policies, Issues, Legislation, and Case Law
Surinder Mediratta

HANDBOOK OF HUMAN DEVELOPMENT
Concepts, Measures, and Policies
Sakiko Fukuda-Parr and A.K. Shiva Kumar (Editors)

HANDBOOK OF ENVIRONMENTAL DECISION MAKING IN INDIA
An EIA Model
O.V. Nandimath

HANDBOOK OF URBANIZATION IN INDIA (Second Edition) (OIP)
K.C. Shivaramakrishnan, Amitabh Kundu, and B.N. Singh

MAKING NEWS
Handbook of the Media in Contemporary India (OIP)
Uday Sahay (Editor)

HANDBOOK OF INDIAN SOCIOLOGY (OIP)
Veena Das (Editor)

MANAGING BUSINESS IN THE 21ST CENTURY
A Handbook (OIP)
Anindya Sen and P.K. Sett (Editors)

HANDBOOK OF GENDER

edited by
RAKA RAY

UNIVERSITY PRESS

OXFORD
UNIVERSITY PRESS

Oxford University Press is a department of the University of Oxford.
It furthers the University's objective of excellence in research, scholarship,
and education by publishing worldwide. Oxford is a registered trademark of
Oxford University Press in the UK and in certain other countries

Published in India by
Oxford University Press
YMCA Library Building, 1 Jai Singh Road, New Delhi 110 001, India

© Oxford University Press 2012

The moral rights of the author have been asserted

First Edition published in 2012

All rights reserved. No part of this publication may be reproduced, stored in
a retrieval system, or transmitted, in any form or by any means, without the
prior permission in writing of Oxford University Press, or as expressly permitted
by law, by licence, or under terms agreed with the appropriate reprographics
rights organization. Enquiries concerning reproduction outside the scope of the
above should be sent to the Rights Department, Oxford University Press, at the
address above

You must not circulate this work in any other form
and you must impose this same condition on any acquirer

ISBN-13: 978-0-19-807147-1
ISBN-10: 0-19-807147-7

Typeset in Minion Pro 11/13.6
by Sai Graphic Design, New Delhi 110 055
Printed in India by Replika Press Pvt. Ltd

CONTENTS

List of Tables and Figure ... ix
Publisher's Acknowledgements ... xi
List of Abbreviations ... xiii

Introduction: The Politics of Knowledge—Gender Scholarship and Women's Movement in India ... 1
RAKA RAY

I. LAW

1. The Foundations of Modern Legal Structures in India ... 25
   JANAKI NAIR
2. Conjugality, Property, Morality, and Maintenance ... 52
   FLAVIA AGNES

II. SEXUALITY

3. Uneven Modernities and Ambivalent Sexualities: Women's Constructions of Puberty in Coastal Kanyakumari, Tamil Nadu ... 79
   KALPANA RAM
4. Outing Heteronormativity: Nation, Citizen, Feminist Disruptions ... 107
   NIVEDITA MENON

III. CASTE

5. Whatever Happened to the Vedic *Dasi*? Orientalism, Nationalism, and a Script for the Past ... 147
   UMA CHAKRAVARTI

6. A Cartography of Resistance: The National Federation of Dalit Women — 185
KALPANA KANNABIRAN

IV. MASCULINITY

7. Potent Protests: The Age of Consent Controversy, 1891 — 209
MRINALINI SINHA
8. Style — 249
LAWRENCE COHEN

V. LABOUR

9. Family and Factory: Women in the Bombay Cotton Textile Industry, 1919–39 — 271
RADHA KUMAR
10. Women Workers, Liberalization, and Social Citizenship in India — 304
AMRITA CHHACHHI

VI. RELIGION

11. Heroic Women, Mother Goddesses: Family and Organization in Hindutva Politics — 337
TANIKA SARKAR
12. Feminist Theory, Agency, and the Liberatory Subject: Some Reflections on the Islamic Revival in Egypt — 368
SABA MAHMOOD

VII. MEDIA

13. Dharma and Desire, Freedom and Destiny: Rescripting the Man–Woman Relationship in Popular Hindi Cinema — 403
PATRICIA UBEROI
14. Forbidden Love and Passionate Denials: A Dialogue on Domesticities and Queer Intimacy — 428
SHOHINI GHOSH

VIII. ENVIRONMENT

15. The Gender and Environment Debate: Lessons from India — 453
BINA AGARWAL

16. Genderscapes: Deepening Our Understanding of 494
    Gender–Environment Linkages
    SUMI KRISHNA

IX. WOMEN'S MOVEMENT

17. Women's Politics in India 519
    ILINA SEN
18. Feminism, Poverty, and the Emergent Social Order 539
    MARY E. JOHN

Notes on Contributors 572

TABLES AND FIGURE

TABLES

9.1	Percentages of Married, Unmarried, and Widowed to the Total Population, by Sex	275
9.2	Age, Sex, and Civil Condition: Variations in Proportions of Married Population, Bombay City, 1921–41	276
9.3	Classification of Women according to Age Groups, 1937–41	279
9.4	Children of Widowed Women Workers, 1941	279
9.5	Sex Ratio in Three Wards, 1921–31	283
9.6	Working of the Bombay Maternity Benefit Act, 1929, in Bombay City, Ahmedabad, and Sholapur, 1933–9	291
9.7	Proportion of Women Workers Claiming Maternity Benefits and Proportions of Claims Paid, 1933–9	292
9.8	Average Amount Paid per Claim, 1933–9	292
9.9	Average Earnings in Winding and Reeling Departments, 1921–37	295
9.10	Frequency of Monthly Earnings, 1926 and 1931	297
9.11	Earners in Working Class Families, 1932–44	300
15.1	Average Annual Income from Village Commons in Select Districts of India, 1982–5	464
15.2	Distribution of Privatized Village Commons in Select Districts of India	468
15.3	Time Taken and Distance Travelled for Firewood Collection	475

16.1	Approaches to Women and the Environment	498
16.2	Summation	511

FIGURE

10.1	Vulnerability/Security Index	323

PUBLISHER'S ACKNOWLEDGEMENTS

THE PUBLISHER ACKNOWLEDGES the following for permission to include articles/extracts in this volume.

Kali for Women for Janaki Nair, 'The Foundations of Modern Legal Structures in India', in Janaki Nair, *Women and Law in Colonial India: A Social History*. New Delhi, 1996, pp. 19–48; for Kalpana Ram, 'Uneven Modernities and Ambivalent Sexualities: Women's Constructions of Puberty in Coastal Kanyakumari, Tamil Nadu', in Mary E. John and Janaki Nair (eds), *A Question of Silence? The Sexual Economies of Modern India*. New Delhi, 1998, pp. 269–303; for Uma Chakravarti, 'Whatever Happened to the Vedic *Dasi*? Orientalism, Nationalism, and a Script for the Past', in Kumkum Sangari and Sudesh Vaid (eds), *Recasting Women: Essays in Indian Colonial History*. New Delhi, 1989, pp. 27–87; and for Tanika Sarkar, 'Heroic Women, Mother Goddesses: Family and Organization in Hindutva Politics', in Tanika Sarkar and Urvashi Butalia (eds), *Women and the Hindu Right*. New Delhi, 1995, pp. 181–215.

Women Unlimited and Zed Books for Nivedita Menon, 'Outing Heteronormativity: Nation, Citizen, Feminist Disruptions', in Nivedita Menon (ed.), *Sexualities*. New Delhi and London.

Sage Publications for Kalpana Kannabiran, 'A Cartography of Resistance: The National Federation of Dalit Women', in Nira Yuval-Davis, Kalpana Kannabiran, and Ulrike Vieten (eds), *Situating Contemporary Politics of Belonging*. London, 2006, pp. 54–73; and for Radha Kumar, 'Family and Factory: Women in the Bombay Cotton Textile Industry, 1919–39', *The Indian Economic and Social History Review*, 1983, 20(1), pp. 81–96.

Kali Press for Mrinalini Sinha, 'Potent Protests: The Age of Consent Controversy, 1891', in Mrinalini Sinha, *Colonial Masculinity: The 'Manly' Englishman and the 'Effeminate' Bengali in the Late Nineteenth Century*. New Delhi, 1998, pp. 138–80.

Feminist Studies for Bina Agarwal, 'The Gender and Environment Debate: Lessons from India', Spring 1992, 18(1), pp. 119–58.

ABBREVIATIONS

AICCWW	All India Coordination Committee of Working Women
AIDS	acquired immune deficiency syndrome
AIDWA	All India Democratic Women's Association
AIWC	All India Women's Conference
BGMUS	Bhopal Gas Peedit Mahila Udyog Sangathan
BJP	Bharatiya Janata Party
BTLU	Bharat Textile Labour Union
CALERI	Campaign for Lesbian Rights
CMSS	Chhattisgarh Mines Shramik Sangh
CPI	Communist Party of India
CPI (M)	Communist Party of India (Marxist)
CPI (M–L)	Communist Part of India (Marxist–Leninist)
CPSU	Communist Party of the Soviet Union
CrPC	Criminal Procedure Code
CWDS	Centre for Women's Development Activities
CYSV	Chhatra Yuva Sangharsh Vahini
DAV	Dayanand Anglo Vedic
DMC	*Divorce and Matrimonial Cases*
DWCRA	Development of Women and Children in Rural Areas
EIC	East India Company
ESI	Employees' State Insurance
GA	Gender Analysis
GAD	Gender and Development
HEAL	Health Education Health Liaison
HIV	human immunodeficiency virus
HMA	Hindu Marriage Act
IAWS	Indian Association of Women's Studies

IB	Intelligence Bureau
ICDS	Integrated Child Development Scheme
ICS	Indian Civil Service
IGLHRC	International Gay and Human Rights Commission
IIT	Indian Institute of Technology
ILGA	International Lesbian and Gay Association
ILO	International Labour Organization
IT	Information Technology
ITES	IT-enabled Services
JMS	Janwadi Mahila Samiti
JWP	Joint Women's Programme
KSSS	Kottar Social Service Society
LGBT	Lesbian, Gay, Bisexual, Transgender
LGBTHK	Lesbian, Gay, Bisexual, Transgender, Hijra, Kothi
LTTE	Liberation of Tamil Tigers Eelam
MDS	Mahila Dakshata Samiti
MMM	Mahila Mukti Morcha
MOA	Mill Owners' Association
MP	Member of Parliament
MSM	Men who have sex with men
MWA	Muslim Women's Act
NCERT	National Council of Educational Research and Training
NCEUS	National Commission for Enterprises in the Unorganised Sector
NFDW	National Federation of Dalit Women
NFIW	National Federation of Indian Women
NGO	non-governmental organization
NIFT	National Institute of Fashion Technology
NPP	National Perspective Plan
NSS	National Sample Survey
NSSO	National Sample Survey Organisation
PDS	Public Distribution System
POW	Progressive Organisation of Women
PUCL-K	People's Union for Civil Liberties-Karnataka
PWDVP	Protection of Women from Domestic Violence Act
PWO	Progressive Women's Organization
RSS	Rashtriya Swayamsevak Sangh
SALGA	South Asian Lesbian and Gay Association
SEWA	Self-employed Women's Association
SEZ	special economic zone

SHG	Self-Help Group
SMA	Samagra Mahila Aghadi
SMS	Stree Mukti Sangathana
SSMS	Shramik Stree Mukti Sangathana
SSS	Stree Shakti Sangathana
TLA	Textile Labour Organization
UCC	Uniform Civil Code
UNCED	United Nations Conference on Environment and Development
UNESCO	United Nations Educational, Scientific and Cultural Organization
UNICEF	United Nations Children's Fund
VHP	Vishwa Hindu Parishad
WAD	Women and Development
WCAR	World Conference against Racism
WDP	World Development Programme
WED	World and Environment Development
WIA	Women's Indian Association
WID	Women in Development
WPR	Worker Population Ratio
WTO	World Trade Organization
YWCA	Young Women's Christian Association

INTRODUCTION

The Politics of Knowledge—Gender Scholarship and Women's Movement in India

RAKA RAY

AT THE TURN OF THE TWENTIETH CENTURY, when women in England were fighting for suffrage, an eminent zoologist from Cambridge, named Walter Heape (famous for the first embryo transfer in the 1890s), described menstruation with the following violent words. During menstruation, he wrote, 'the entire epithelium is torn away, leaving behind a ragged wreck of tissue, torn glands, ruptured vessels, jagged edges of stroma, and masses of corpuscles, which it would seem hardly possible to heal satisfactorily without the aid of surgical treatment' (Walter Heape, quoted in Lacquer 1990: 221). What can explain this excessive description of the normal functioning of most women's bodies? According to feminist scholar Emily Martin (2001), Walter Heape was not only a scientist but also a militant anti-suffragist. He was making a point: How could we possibly trust women with the vote, given the condition to which they were reduced every month—a condition which must surely prevent any rational functioning. Heape's words are remarkable only because they are an egregious manifestation of a phenomenon with which theorists of gender have long been familiar. Knowledge is interested. Science is not value-free but comes attached to positions and worldviews. The study of gender has been instrumental in revealing not only countervailing points of view about the constitution and effects of gendered individuals and societies, but also in revealing the often vested interests behind the politics of knowledge.

The question of the status of women in India has often been the grounds over which struggles over leadership and dominance have taken place. As Lata Mani showed in the case of sati; Mrinalini Sinha in the case of Katherine Mayo's *Mother India*; and Flavia Agnes in the case of Shah Bano, the question of the status of women has consistently been about more than women (Mani 1998; Sinha 2000; and Agnes 2001). Gender has been the terrain over which communities assert their own superiority and the inferiority of others. It has been the terrain over which nations claim their own purity and the contamination of others. It is the terrain over which the West marks its development over the backwardness of others. Thus, it is not surprising that writing about gender is so political and so politicized.

Indeed, feminism has long been both an intellectual project and a political one. Though, as Saba Mahmood (2004) has argued, this conflation may be problematic, it has resulted in a vibrant and lively intellectual project in the Indian context. One of the most remarkable aspects of the field of gender scholarship is that it has been consistently willing to challenge itself. Perhaps, because it is so linked with the concept of political change, feminist theory has remained vigilant and has been willing to shift its understanding of its own foundational terms—such as women, gender, and liberation—in order to maintain the critical edge that continues to inspire both scholarship and social movements of all kinds.

The recent history of gender scholarship in India is generally thought to have begun in the 1970s due to a combination of the same two forces that kick-started the women's movement of that period. The first was the general unease and frustration with the failure of the Nehruvian state to deliver upon its promises, leading to unrest and agitation amongst many sections of society. Postcolonial India was going through the tensions and disappointments of a new country after the first flush of promise was replaced by a loss of democracy and an increase in cost of living. The vehicle for these promises, the Congress party, was seen to have failed, and with the decline in faith in the Congress came the rise of mass movements and new social movements in which women were active. The shocking revelations of *Towards Equality* (1974), the Government of India–sponsored study of the status of women in India, which laid out in the starkest possible terms just how much the Indian nation had failed its women, provided intellectuals and policymakers with a second spur to take the issue of gender seriously. Thus, the women's movement of the 1970s and the study of gender (generally called 'Women's Studies') emerged together, and this is a fundamental characteristic of gender scholarship in India.

In this brief introduction to the *Handbook of Gender*, rather than run through a chronological list of the many notable contributions, I suggest that three characteristics mark the field of gender studies in India. All three characteristics have to do with the relationship of politics to the academic study of gender: (a) the field of gender studies is marked by an imbrication with the political exigencies of the time; (b) gender studies in India has been deeply and resolutely intersectional; and (c) gender scholars have been at the forefront of critiques of Eurocentric theorization and of understanding the effects of globalization.

In this volume I have gathered together works that represent the best of feminist scholarship, taking as my point of departure the path-breaking *Recasting Women* (1989), edited by Kumkum Sangari and Sudesh Vaid, which presented the best of historical scholarship on gender in India at the time and effectively transformed the parameters of gender scholarship for the next generation. Twenty years on, the field of gender has blossomed, and we now have a wealth of scholarship in multiple fields from sexuality to labour to religion and the law on both historical and contemporary India. For this handbook, I have chosen to focus on key areas of debate and scholarship in gender, with one essay considered a classic in the field paired with one essay that reflects the state of the field or the vibrant new directions in which the field is going. The second part of the pairing is not meant to indicate a replacement for the first, but rather to reflect transformations (or not) in questions and concerns over this period of 20 years, since the publication of *Recasting Women*.

GENDER AND POLITICS

I begin with the question of the imbrication of gender studies in India within a larger political critique. In the US, Gayle Rubin, Shulamith Firestone, Angela Davis, Nancy Chodorow, and other early theorists of the second wave of the women's movement derived their ideas and questions from their activism in the women's liberation movement, the student movement, and the civil rights movement, as did Sheila Rowbotham and others in the UK. Deeply political and driven by a sense of urgency, these women tasked themselves with both documenting and trying to explain the seriousness of women's oppression in all its 'monotonous similarity and endless variety'. From the very beginning then, the point of theorizing women's oppression was to end it. The political agenda and intellectual agenda went hand in hand. Over time, however, the study of gender in the US became institutionalized and leeched of its immediate political context, and while not entirely disconnected, academia and women's movement activism have tended to follow divergent paths.

In India, however, many key scholars of gender have retained a deep connection to activism. As Mary E. John (2008: 7) reminds us, the leadership of both the women's movement and women's studies tended to be drawn from the ranks of teachers and researchers. These scholar-activists have consistently pointed their theorizing towards illuminating moments of political contention, or even persuasively arguing for a reorientation of thinking when faced with particular political crises. A significant period of such reorienting came with the Shah Bano case of 1985, the destruction of the Babri Masjid in 1992, and with the continuing debates around the uniform civil code. As the events of that period unfolded, the women's movement forced itself to rethink the unified category of 'woman' despite the threat that the absence of the unified category offered to the possibilities of activism. Through their work, both the possibilities of activism and theorizing around gender were extended.

In order to understand women's movement activism and the motivation behind gender scholarship, we must first pay attention to the trajectory of social movements in India. In the introduction to a recent volume on social movements, Mary Katzenstein and I characterized three phases in the relationship of social movements to the state in India (Ray and Katzenstein 2005). We argued that the preponderance of Indian movements in the early post-independence years was accountable to a master frame set by the postcolonial developmentalist state, which required activists to attest to an engagement with issues of class and, specifically, the poor. Social movements, whose thinking and actions were once framed by their rotation in the orbit of the Nehruvian 'sun', have had to reinvent themselves. This reinvention has been necessitated by the dramatic swing from the early post-independence symbiosis of state, party, and movement organized around democratic socialism on the left to its unravelling in the mid-1960s through the 1980s and the ascendance of its institutional mirror image on the right, the similarly synergistic nexus of state, party, and movement now organized, however, around religious nationalism and the market. In short, the shift from a postcolonial democratic quasi-socialist regime to a postcolonial neo-liberal regime has had profound consequences for social movements in India.

During the Nehruvian years, the twin discourses of poverty alleviation and development, with their attendant contradictions, came to occupy the status of a dominant social script, as the postcolonial developmental state was born. While the language of democratic socialism continued to stand in tension with the pressures of capitalist development, Nehru and the Congress were seen to speak in the name of the nation and all interest groups (Frankel 1978). Despite little actual poverty alleviation during that period, the women's movement, like most other social movements, was more or less quiescent, buying into the belief in the developmental state. This phase coincided with the height of the developmental state and its modernist hubris (dams as the new temples of India). The one force that stood outside this dominant discourse, that resisted discussion of rights and poverty, and countered it with unity of blood and the importance of the non-material was the early ideology of the Rashtriya Swayamsevak Sangh (RSS) (see the chapter by Tanika Sarkar in this volume).

Within just a few years of Nehru's death in 1964 and through the late 1980s—which can be seen as a transitional phase—the language of class and of poverty amelioration reverted to a mere strategy in the grab bag of populist/electoral resources rather than a prevailing presumption of official discourse. In accordance with a now much-rehearsed account, by 1967, the Indian state had entered what can arguably be called a crisis of deinstitutionalization. The women's movement came into its own in this phase, particularly post-1977, and gave rise to a generation of scholar-activists. Despite the fragmentation of the left and the deinstitutionalization of the Congress, or perhaps because of it, new political formations came into being during the 1970s and 1980s.[1] The organizational vehicles for these groups varied widely. Some were small, autonomous, urban groups; others were mass-based rural groups; and yet others were radical wings of political parties. Especially post-1977, women's groups such as Stree Mukti Sanghatana, Forum Against Rape, Stree Shakti Sanghatana, Stree Sangharsh, Sachetana, Vimochana, and Manushi mushroomed. So too did politically affiliated groups such as Mahila Dakshata, a rejuvenated National Federation of Indian Women (NFIW) and eventually, the

[1] The new movements whose origins post-dated the birth of the nation fostered quite a different movement politics from that of the Nehruvian era. In 1972, the Jharkhand Mukti Morcha, the All-Assam Students Union, the Self-employed Women's Association, various regional farmers' association, the Chipko movement, and the Dalit Panthers were all formed. Civil liberties organizations, people's science movements, and a range of other organizations followed, and a revolution in Indian politics was underway (Omvedt 1993: 47).

All India Democratic Women's Association (AIDWA).[2] What needs to be emphasized here is that though these movements were marked by organizational variation and innovation, they retained their connection to the master frame's commitment to the poor, as the essays by Ilina Sen and Mary E. John in this volume show. They also retained a certain ambivalent connection to the Indian state. The key issues that emerged at this time were as diverse as the organizational vehicles—the rise in the prices of essential commodities, dowry, rape, and labour activism, among others. While some issues had national resonance, others were selectively picked up by activists embedded in different political fields (Ray 1999). But with every issue, activists theorized, borrowed from existing scholarship, and built new archives of scholarship as they sought to deepen their understandings of the issues with which they worked. Most of the first of the paired essays in this volume were written in this moment.

In the third phase (from the late 1980s to the present), there is a striking change in political discourse. In the wake of Market, Mandal, and Masjid, we have a new, more fragmented institutionalization, coupled with the twin ideologies of market and Hindu nationalism. Economic liberalization has been accompanied by the massive NGO-ification of civil society, arguably crowding out some of the more protest-oriented forms of organizing within the social movement sector. In the women's movement, Mandal–Masjid marked the dissolution of the idea of the unified 'woman'. Post-Mandal saw the emergence of upper-caste women asserting gendered logics against Dalit women (as in Chunduru) and post-Masjid saw the hardening of religious lines based on the Hindu Right's opportunistic reading of Islam and gender. Mainstream Indian politics post-market and post-Mandal/Masjid has folded into itself narratives of progressiveness–backwardness such that lower-caste rural and Muslim communities stand in for backwardness while in the hands of urban Hindu upper castes lies the shining path of India's future. These changes are reflected not only in law and social movements but also in the media (see the chapters by Shohini Ghosh and Lawrence Cohen in this volume).

While many of the conditions faced by the women's movement in the 1970s and 1980s have been fundamentally altered, I suggest this is a movement which has been, in fact, able to rise to the occasion *analytically*, if not in practice. The second of the paired essays in the volume offer a window into the major rethinking and theorization of economy, politics, the social, and the intimate that the present historical conjuncture demands.

[2] Parts of the preceding section are excerpted from Katzenstein and Ray (2005).

INTERSECTIONALITY

Standing on stage at a women's studies conference at Jadavpur University in Kolkata in 1991, in what is now considered a landmark speech, feminist lawyer and activist Flavia Agnes announced that the women's movement, for all its secular pretensions, was normatively Hindu. She protested being called a 'Christian' feminist while Hindu feminists were simply feminists. It was no different, she argued, from the logic of Hindutva-vadis, who claimed Hinduism as a culture and not a religion. If Hinduism was a 'culture', she argued, a feminist from a Hindu family could keep an idol of Krishna in her house or celebrate Diwali and still be considered 'secular'. But if a feminist from a Christian family were to display a picture of Christ or celebrate Christmas, she would inevitably be considered a 'Christian feminist', and so always inadequately secular. I mark that as a moment of self-consciousness for the larger Indian feminist movement. While the awareness of this issue had begun to surface for several activists and scholars of gender, Agnes's speech was the moment of naming after which no one could plead innocence. It publicly started a debate that deepened feminist dismay at the avid participation of Hindu women in the Babri Masjid events (referred to in Ilina Sen's article in this anthology). When put together with the emergence of upper caste gendered identities and women's participation in the Hindutva movement, Agnes's words called for a reassessment of the 'secular' feminist who speaks in the name of all women, just as the emergence of lower-caste politics demanded a critique of Brahmanic Hinduism that spoke in the name of all Hindus, and the unquestioned caste- and sex-based division of labour (Rege 1998; Kalpana Kannabiran's chapter in this volume). That Agnes's speech occurred at a women's studies conference and not a women's movement conference underscores the dialectical relationship between the two, while her words point to the simultaneously political and theoretical need for intersectional analysis.

The concept of intersectionality assumed considerable importance in the studies of gender in the US in the 1990s. Early feminists such as Gayle Rubin (1975) and Catherine MacKinnon (1988) tended to isolate gender from other social forces, to analyse its specificity—as different from class and race—while marking gender as the core contradiction of society, indeed of all societies. Of the assumptions made here, the first to be challenged was that there was something unique to women and shared by all women—the assumption of universality. This challenge arose, at least in the US and Europe, out of the recognition of working class women and women of colour that the assumptions made about women's shared experiences were not in fact shared by all women. What was being considered universal to women was in fact a US- and England-based white middle-class specificity.

The theoretical move here was the rejection of middle-class white womanhood as the *normatively universal* category and an acceptance that it was a *particular* category.[3] Gender also came to be seen not as *the*, but a, major structuring principle of society whose effects and meanings came about within specific contexts. Further, gender came to be seen as a force whose effects were best understood in intersection with other elements (race, sexuality, class, and so on). Key scholars in this field include Patricia Hill Collins (2000), perhaps best known for her articulation of the intersection of race and gender; Evelyn Nakano Glenn (2002), one of the first to highlight how occupational sex segregation took different forms depending upon the ethnic category of the women and men in question; Kimberle Crenshaw (1996) to whom the term 'intersectionality' is attributed; and cultural theorists such as Bell Hooks (2000). Gender, then, came to be seen as a social relation that operates not in isolation (no more than does class or race), but as one embedded in a field of other relations, which include class, age, sexuality, race, and geo-politics. Those inspired by poststructuralists such as Joan Scott (1999) take this one step further and emphasize not just the interactive or intersectional effects of race, class, and gender, but the discursive and material *co-constitution* of gender, race, sexuality, and class within different contexts.

While certainly much work on gender in India also assumes and universalizes a middle-class Hindu subject, because much of the early theorizing came out of a Marxist tradition, class has been a primary vector of gender analysis since the 1970s, with sharp criticisms of work which focuses unreflexively on middle-class Hindu women. Scholars of gender from the 1980s on routinely worked at the intersection of class and gender (see the chapter by Radha Kumar in this volume). By the mid-1980s, the Shah Bano debate, followed by the destruction of the Babri Masjid and its aftermath in the early 1990s, brought home clearly to both women's movement activists and gender theorists that 'woman' *per se* was no longer a tenable category. Unlike in the US, this move to intersectionality—this realization that women's experiences as women were powerfully marked by

---

[3] Chakrabarty (2000) was to make a similar point later with reference to the tendency to universalize Europe's particular history.

their religion and caste such that it was not possible to assume that Muslim women and Hindu women had the same interests and thus that theorizing gender was simply inadequate without a simultaneous theorizing of caste/religion—was not kept at the margins of the field. Most serious scholarship in gender since the 1990s, examples of which are evident in this collection of essays, has assumed the irreducible importance of intersectionality.

THEORIZING POSTCOLONIALITY AND GLOBALIZATION

Both scholarship on gender and gender politics have, since they developed roots in India, had to grapple with uncomfortable questions about their relationship with the entity called 'the West'. Politically, in this period of post-liberalization, there is no way to discount the presence of transnational non-governmental organizations (NGOs), particularly in the areas of health, sexuality, and micro-finance, while economically we see its effects on the daily lives of working men and women (see the chapter by Amrita Chhachhi in this volume). The global political economy has both material and discursive effects on the flow of ideas as well.

The question of knowledge and global legibility about the construction of gender in India has been deeply problematic both in its colonial past and today. Indian feminist historians have laid out for us the extent to which the 'history' of women in India was written by the British as a story of the emergence of a group from the darkness of oppression into the light of liberation in order to justify the continuation of British rule in India (see also the chapters by Mrinalini Sinha, Janaki Nair, and Kalpana Ram in this volume).[4] We know that one nationalist reaction to this narrative was to accept the British perspective and to strive towards 'lifting' Indian womanhood up to a standard the British would deem acceptable for a civilized or civilizing society, to 'improve', 'modernize', and remove what

---

[4] After 1818, the previous British policy of tolerance and non-interference in India's society was swamped by an increasingly interventionist policy shared by the Utilitarians, the Liberals, and the Evangelicals. The condition of Indian women constituted an integral part of their civilizational critique. James Mill (1840: 309–10) famously announced:

The condition of women is one of the most remarkable circumstances in the manners of nations...The history of uncultivated nations uniformly represents the women as in a state of abject slavery, from which they slowly emerge as civilisation advances...A state of dependence more strict and humiliating than that which is ordained for the weaker sex among the Hindus cannot be easily conceived.

were considered 'inhuman' practices against women. Another reaction was to reject the British story in favour of asserting an ancient golden age when women were revered scholars with leadership positions, and attributing the 'decline' to the arrival of foreigners, namely Muslims (see the chapter by Uma Chakravarti in this volume).

Looking closely at feminist writings in the West about gender in the Third World, Chandra Mohanty (1988) was one of the first to raise the question of the importance of geo-political location in theorizing gender. Since then, postcolonial theorists located in the West, such as Gayatri Spivak (2004), have laid bare the extent to which theorizing about the condition of women in the Third World enabled women in the West to develop a sense of themselves as more liberated and enlightened. The Third World provided an alibi for Western feminists not only to understand themselves as better off but also, frequently, to collude with imperial projects in the name of saving those women.[5] Given the aforementioned, the task of knowledge production faced by Indian feminists is a difficult one. While most do continue to write embedded in and for the Indian context, many must write with an awareness that their writings do draw from and circulate in the feminist global public sphere. In addition, many who write about India are not located here and therefore must be doubly aware of the context within which their work circulates (see Saba Mahmood's chapter in this volume for an example of this dialogue in the context of Egypt).

Scholars of gender too grapple with coming to terms with this moment in history, with how to locate India in it, and how to imagine a transformational politics within it. Nivedita Menon (2004: 100) writes, 'The challenge for feminist politics is the working out of a different space for a radical politics of culture, one differentiated from both left and right-wing articulations of cultural and economic nationalism, as well as from libertarian and celebratory responses to globalization from the consuming elites'. In recent writings, several feminist scholars have claimed the term 'postnational politics'—such a term would signify that the nation no longer occupies a sovereign position in our political imaginings, or that we must

---

[5] As a scholar of gender in India and a teacher in US classrooms, Spivak (2004: 532) insists on a pedagogy that leads away from teaching corporatist benevolence, and away from having US students believe, that 'I am necessarily better, I am necessarily indispensable, I am necessarily the one to right wrongs, I am necessarily the end product for which history happened, and that New York is necessarily the capital of the world.'

think and act politically across national borders as well as 'under' them (*Economic and Political Weekly* 2009).

The workings of globalization across and under nations are complex indeed, as can be illustrated by the following case. In 2005, without fuss or fanfare, the government passport office in India quietly added a third official gender option to the application instructions on its website (see Nivedita Menon's chapter in this volume). How did one of the most marginalized groups in India achieve such a victory and what might globalization have to do with it? The global transgender movement has tended to see this as its victory. But, in fact, there is no worldwide move to add a third gender to the passport (in the US, for example, the transgender movement focuses on the circumstances under which the gender on the passport can be switched from 'M' to 'F' or from 'F' to 'M'). Is it the internationalization of a gay identity? Yet, no gay rights have been won here. On the contrary, I suggest that the appearance of 'O' on the passport is a combination of the recognition of a long-standing belief in Indian culture that there is a third gender, together with the capacity to mobilize *hijra*s indirectly via AIDS funding in India. The challenge of HIV did open up discursive spaces for different sexual practices to be talked about in the public sphere. HIV/AIDS programmes reached out to hijras who worked as sex workers and, through that, enabled their mobilization as collective actors. But I would suggest the success is also due partially to the strategy inherited from the women's movement (what I have elsewhere called the sympathetic bureaucrat strategy) and primarily due to the particular social organization (strong guru–shisya-based organizational structure) which has made hijras so mobilizable. Thus, we must indeed be able to think both across and under nations in order to understand this particular change to the Indian passport.

While the political challenges to gender issues appear from multiple directions, through their analytical work, feminist intellectuals in India, many of whom emerged out of the women's movement in India and are integral to it, have continually evolved their conception of politics, and their understanding of the changing political regimes as well as of their relationship to those regimes. Faced with the collapse of the Nehruvian paradigm, and the decline of what was then a vibrant movement, they have challenged each other to rethink the foundational premises of their theorizing. As illustrated below, the trajectory of this scholarship has been both broad and deep, and continues to reflect intellectual suppleness and flexibility.

CHAPTERS AND THEMES

Law

Law has been one of the central strategies for the women's movement and has also produced some of the finest contemporary thinkers of the movement, from Nandita Haksar to Ratna Kapur to Flavia Agnes. For the two essays in this section, I have selected one that sketches a history of the creation of the laws under which we live, and a second that represents an issue of extreme contemporary importance—the provision of legal mandates governing the dissolution of marriage. Both of these essays reflect the importance of the intersection of gender/religion/caste and class in understanding the creation and application of legal justice. In the first, Janaki Nair traces the development of codified law under the British who assumed that a lack of legality existed under the Mughal rule. In the process of codification, scriptural texts were given heightened authority, replacing non-scriptural practices such that by the time the British left India, India had more theocratic rule over more areas than it had had before the British. The understanding of the ways in which the laws under which Indians live were created by British collusion with and in accommodation to Brahminical patriarchy has been central to unravelling the legal mandates that have wracked the nation from sati to Shah Bano.

The second essay in this section is by lawyer, scholar, and activist Flavia Agnes. If Nair draws attention to the history behind the laws under which women in India live, Agnes spells out its consequences. Taking on the subject of dissolution of marriage, Agnes argues that underneath all the laws lurks a punitive morality by which women's claims for maintenance are judged. Through all the measures outlined in this essay, Hindu and Muslim men try to use laws most convenient to them through which women can be denied the right to maintenance. Since most women are less able to hire the legal help they need to make a strong case, it is often left to the judiciary to interpret the laws. In one of the most telling examples in this regard, Agnes shows that quiet judicial intervention may, under the given circumstances in India, be the best solution for women. Loud and politicized interventions, as in the case of the Shah Bano judgement, may cost women dearly.

Sexuality

It was in the late 1980s that sexuality became a specific site of exploration, first in terms of patriarchal control over the sexuality of women, and more recently in terms of queer and alternative sexualities. On the one hand, India is marked by a plurality of sexual regimes and practices. Yet, the nation-state recognizes only a few as legitimate, with others being marked as signs of a community's backwardness. Kalpana Ram's essay is a reflection on the complicated relationship between regimes of sexual control and modernity. Ram introduces her essay with a discussion of the problematic category of modernity as it is applied to countries like India, suggesting that had India been the starting point of the concept of modernity, it would have been understood as something necessarily contradictory and uneven. How, she asks, should we be able to conceive of contradictory subjectivities and different temporalities within the same moment? She investigates these questions through an ethnographic study of sexuality among Mukkuvar women of Tamil Nadu where pre-colonial coming-of-age rites co-exist with colonial and postcolonial projects of reform.

Nivedita Menon's recent essay reflects the increased attention to non-heteronormative sexualities in India, and it too, like the works of many feminists, starts with colonial erasures and projects of recuperation of gay and lesbian histories. In this essay, which exemplifies the fluid relationship between activism and intellectual work, Menon suggests that sexual identities in India must be understood as relational, situated, and political. Questioning the insistence on distinctions between 'indigenous' and 'Western' forms of sexual self-identification, she offers counter-heteronormativity as the third axis of intersectionality with gender, along with caste and community. Ultimately, her essay suggests that we must embrace a politics that is flexible enough to accommodate new experiences and identities, and must simultaneously work under the nation and above it.

Caste

One of the lasting consequences of the vast body of knowledge built up by Western Indology has been a particular and pervasive misrecognition of the caste system. Uma Chakravarti's important essay, first published in *Recasting Women*, 'Whatever Happened to the Vedic *Dasi*? Orientalism, Nationalism, and a Script for the Past', demonstrated how the rewriting of history in the nineteenth century resulted in the creation of a specifically Hindu-Aryan identity. An early example of intersectional analysis, the essay argues that the myth of the golden age of womanhood, though embedded in contemporary Indian consciousness, only emerged out of the interplay of nationalist and colonial efforts through the nineteenth century. 'Knowledge' about India's past was knowledge that was interested and vested in larger projects. On the part of the British, these larger projects included the justification of colonial rule or an indictment of Hindu culture. Indian social reformers and nationalists, both men and women, for their part, repeatedly and selectively used this new 'knowledge' to argue their case for educating women, or for controlling women's sexuality, or, ultimately, for independence. But all of them worked only with, and thus wrote into history, the hyperbolized educated and pure upper-caste woman whose status had now fallen, while the Vedic dasi, or women enslaved by the Aryans, disappeared from historical traces.

The disappearance of the dasi, or the lack of historical traces of lower-caste women, has had consequences for contemporary Indian understandings of the intersection of caste and gender even within the women's movement, with a belated recognition of Dalit women as actors. Kalpana Kannabiran's chapter reflects a more recent focus on Dalit women's theorization and agency, the interpretation of caste as race by Dalit groups, and the subsequent 'difference' politics of these organizations. Her discussion of the National Federation of Dalit Women shows how this group self-consciously distances itself both from the autonomous women's organizations, on the one hand, and progressive male-led organizations, including Dalit organizations, on the other. Her essay highlights a group in the process of becoming, trying to combat both racism/casteism and sexism, and developing their own standpoint. The reflexively intersectional nature of this group can be seen from the claim in their charter that 'Dalit women have the right to self protection in the face of dominant caste male and female aggression, of Dalit male aggression, and of aggression committed by law enforcing machineries of the State.'[6]

Masculinity

A major shift occurred in the late 1980s in the object of study from women (seen as a group or a category with shared traits) to the production and construction of gendered practices where masculinity(ies) and femininity(ies) exist in relation to one another. Thus, women and men were now seen to be interesting in as much as they usually (but not always—the slippages and alternative possibilities are important here) embody different sets of gendered practices.[7] These clusters of practices,

---

[6] See p. 203 of this volume.
[7] In other words, gender derives from what you do rather than what you are.

named masculinity and femininity, get their power from being constructed in opposition to each other. This was also the shift that legitimized the study of men through the study of practices of masculinity. In India, masculinities came to be discussed not just in relation to femininities but also in relation to each other, particularly against the backdrop of colonial history. In her now landmark discussion of colonial masculinity, Mrinalini Sinha represents the first generation of postcolonial historians who demonstrated convincingly that particular masculinities were the outcome of political struggles between elite Indians and colonial authorities. In the excerpt from her book, *Colonial Masculinity*, included in this volume, Sinha suggests that it was sympathy for patriarchal privilege that gave the colonial authorities pause during the struggle over the Age of Consent Bill of 1891. The struggles over the bill took place at a time of a perceived crisis in British patriarchy with the emergence of early feminism. The British style of ruling conceded to native men their right to rule over the domestic sphere, thus shoring up indigenous patriarchy and, as with the debate over sati, women as a group were invisible as actors in the debate. Sinha's work highlights the political contexts within which masculinity is perceived and is emboldened to act.

In Lawrence Cohen's 'Style' we look at specifically small-town non-elite masculinity in an age of global media and 'style'. Following the fortunes of young men who seek and fail to make it in Mumbai's fashion industry, Cohen shows us an emergent complex world overlain with metropolitan and non-elite, heterosexuality, metrosexuality, and homosexuality, in which new forms of male sociality obtain. Analysing both the narratives of recent films and of these men, Cohen suggests that aspirations to style can be seen as a means of upward mobility such that through behaving as if they have a cellphone, and walking and dressing a particular way, men hope to be able to achieve what government jobs never gave to their fathers. The essay is a meditation on the aspirations and fears of failure that mark a certain class of men in this historical moment.

Labour

As many scholars and activists from the women's movement came from a Marxist background, and had indeed been involved in organizing labour, it is not surprising that many of the early writings dwelt on women's labour force participation and conditions of work, especially in the informal sector where most Indian women work. Both essays in this section address the use to which the ideological weight of women's domestic work is put when trying to discipline women or remove them from the workforce. Radha Kumar's essay on women in the Bombay textile industry in the early part of the twentieth century, while not typical of early work on labour, represents a distinctively feminist analysis in which she traces how women's work came to be seen as supplementary to the family. Through a study that compares Family Budget Surveys between 1922 and 1932, Kumar shows that between the two surveys, families move from being considered simply 'self-contained units' to 'natural family' units, and the term 'family wage' (one person's wage supporting the family) first comes into use before it is a reality (at that time over 41 per cent of the working class needed two wages to survive). During this period, women started out as workers who militantly defended their rights. By the end of the period, as industry was rationalized, it was women's jobs which disappeared. Kumar suggests that the family wage declared intent, not fact. It put in place the possibility that women would withdraw their labour from the labour force and put it to use in reproducing the next generation of labour power.

In her discussion of women workers in post-liberalization India, Amrita Chhachhi continues the theme of women's militancy broached by Radha Kumar, and returns us to a new moment of labour retrenchment. Through a study of four domestic and labour regimes within which women workers in the electronics industry are located, Chhachhi explores the possibilities of 'citizenship in participation' in each. Regular employment remains an important route for women to access independent rights to social citizenship entitlements. Marking the main trend in the contemporary period as a state-sanctioned feminization of the conditions of work—that is, work that is informalized, irregular, insecure, and usually low paid—for both male and female workers, Chhachhi argues that there is a need to 'integrate both employment and citizenship entitlements', in the absence of which women will increasingly have to pay both tangible and intangible costs.

Religion

The intersection of religious identity and gender identity has yielded some of the most fraught and yet productive scholarship on gender. Precisely because religion was not a subject most progressive scholars touched, the visible emergence of the Hindu right in the late 1980s spurred them to examine closely that which had been so long neglected. Historian Tanika Sarkar was one of the first scholars to look at women of the Hindu right. In the essay reproduced here, she suggests that the women's movement of the new right reveals the new politics, culture, and resources of the Indian middle class. The RSS, the only voice that was heard outside of the Nehruvian social democratic compact in the first two decades of India's independence, has long cultivated its women's wing. These women, who are drawn from the most conservative sections of society, participate in a political project of building a Hindu patriotic order but they do so under the cover of religion. Though there is nothing emancipatory about their gender project, there is for these women, a limited but certain empowerment about their capacities as well as the power of solidarity.

Saba Mahmood directly addresses questions of empowerment and agency through the women's piety movement in Egypt. In this essay, drawn from her book *Politics of Piety: The Islamic Revival and the Feminist Subject*, Mahmood highlights the conceptual challenges women in Islamist movements offer Western feminist analysis. In particular, she suggests, women's participation in the mosque movement and their active cultivation of projects of self and morality, bring into question feminist assumptions of agency, in which agency is understood primarily through a lens of resistance. It brings into question, further, the feminist assumption (springing as it does from the conjoining of political and intellectual projects) that the desire to be free from subordination is universal. Through her analysis of key concepts of sabr and al-haya, used and cultivated by mosque women, Mahmood suggests we look for alternative models of agency, though they may be an uncomfortable fit with our own political projects.

Media

Given the immense power media exercises over our imaginations of the right and the good gender order, it is little surprise that gender scholars have long considered media an important archive in their scholarship. In India, in particular, first films and then television quickly formed a subfield of media studies within the study of gender. In this section, therefore, two essays are presented, both of which address a distinctively South Asian gendered corporal aesthetics. Patricia Uberoi reads the beloved film *Sahib, Bibi aur Ghulam* through a nationalist and gendered lens, exploring how the film expresses the limits of female desire in the Indian nation through the oppositional tropes of dharma and desire, freedom and destiny. Unpacking the four core sexual relationships in the film, she argues that only one relationship survives—the one sanctioned by society and cosmological destiny. Other relationships and, indeed, lives are destroyed either by an excess of wifely passion within marriage or passion for a courtesan outside of it. The essay shows how caste, class, and religion are inseparable in any analysis of gender in film.

The theme of forbidden love returns in Shohini Ghosh's essay on the Bengali telefilm, *Ushno Taar Jonno*, where she discusses emergent notions of intimacy, friendship, and 'family' through the first Bengali film to explicitly address same sex love and desires. Ghosh argues that with the sweep towards globalization and neo-liberalism, cultural anxieties manifested in a return to 'the family'— romanticized, neo-traditional, and filled with Hindu right iconography—as a key theme in film and television. Unlike in the utopian films of this period, she suggests, television serials offer family spaces as far more complex and fraught. In the public sphere at large, there have been debates about sex, sexuality, sex work, and sexual preferences. While the 'ambivalent discourses of popular films establish a tolerance for queer desires while eventually reaffirming the inevitability of heterosexuality', Ghosh argues, it is perhaps in readings across texts and in the spaces within them that 'thicker accounts of subaltern sexual desires' may best emerge.

Environment

It was perhaps the Chipko movement that served as a wake-up call about the relationship between women's activism and the environment. Even though women were by no means the only actors in this movement against deforestation, their tactics captured the world's imagination and served to perpetuate the somewhat romantic idea that women were naturally keepers of the environment. But is there a way to think analytically about the connection without romanticization? Bina Agarwal's 1992 essay powerfully encapsulates the various analytical strands in theorizing the relationship between gender and the environment. She offers us a more material relationship, one based on the organization, structure, and distribution of property and power along caste/class/gender lines. When processes such as environmental degradation, statization, and privatization of resources occur, Agarwal argues, the pre-existing gender division of labour together with gender differences in the distribution of subsistence resources create different effects in women's lives (in terms of time, nutrition, income, health, etc.) than they do in men's. Women's environmental activism must also be understood along those lines.

Writing in the first decade of the twenty-first century, Sumi Krishna links the strengths and weaknesses of key gender and development frameworks to parallel frameworks in theorizing the relationship between gender and the environment. Like Agarwal, Krishna too moves away from romantic or celebratory conceptualizations of women's agency, and offers us the concept of 'genderscapes' which take into account intersectionalities between gender, age, place, ethnicity, religion, caste, and class, particularly with respect to maintaining biodiversity. A 'landscape is a world produced by the people who dwell and work in/on it', Krishna suggests, and not an abstraction. It is this awareness of both the material and ideological dimensions of occupied spaces that must be brought into the understanding of the relationship between the local and the global, to enable us to better respond to global challenges.

Women's Movement

As I have noted earlier, the women's movement in India has been closely linked to the theorization of gender, the nature of politics, and indeed to a rethinking of Indian history. Chronicling the history of the women's movement in post-independence India from a perspective in the late 1980s, Ilina Sen draws attention to one of its core dimensions—the plurality of its forms of organization. Her analysis draws not exclusively on the urban women's movement, which has received much attention, but on the struggles for women's rights that emerged out of mass movements for labour rights, against environmental degradation, and for democracy. Her essay notes the disagreement and dialogue between autonomous women's organizations and those affiliated to parties of the left and mass organizations, but draws attention to the continued vibrancy of the conversation between them. Finally, she draws attention to three developments that require further thinking—the co-optation of certain issues by the state, the visibility of right-wing women's organizations, and the international funding of women's groups.

In her analysis of the movement, written over a decade later, Mary E. John highlights the effects on the women's movement of the shift from a developmentalist state to a neo-liberal one in an era of globalization. In a telling example, she draws on key struggles of poor rural women in the 1990s to show how, despite some initial successes, the Indian state's neo-liberal shift has meant that these struggles have been co-opted and moulded into issues of micro-finance and self-help. She ends her essay with a reflection on the extent to which further work is needed to better understand the effects of changes in the economy, the state, and in the political sphere (particularly women's participation in panchayats and the rise of political parties based on caste and minority status) on women, reiterating that while these are all challenges for the women's movement, it is a movement noted for its ability to respond to challenges. Her essay draws explicit links between the women's movement and academia, showing how the movement actively borrowed from academic disciplines to make its case about the past and the present of gendered arrangements in India.

REFERENCES

Agnes, Flavia (2001), 'Minority Identity and Gender Concerns', *Economic and Political Weekly*, 36(42): 3973–6.

Chakrabarty, Dipesh (2000), *Provincializing Europe: Postcolonial Thought and Historical Difference*. Princeton: Princeton University Press.

Collins, Patricia Hill (2000), *Black Feminist Thought: Knowledge, Consciousness, and the Politics of Empowerment*. New York: Routledge.

Crenshaw, Kimberle (1996), 'Mapping the Margins: Intersectionality, Identity Politics, and Violence against Women of Color', in D. Kelly Weisberg (ed.), *Applications of Feminist Legal Theory to Women's Lives*. Philadelphia: Temple University Press, pp. 363–77.

Economic and Political Weekly (2009), Special Theme—Postnational Condition, 44(10), 7 March.

Frankel, Francine (1978), *India's Political Economy, 1947–1977: The Gradual Revolution*. Princeton: Princeton University Press.

Glenn, Evelyn Nakano (2002), *Unequal Freedom: How Race and Gender Shaped American Citizenship and Labor*. Cambridge, MA: Harvard University Press.

Government of India (1974), *Toward Equality: Report of the Committee on the Status of Women in India*. New Delhi: Ministry of Education and Social Welfare, Government of India.

Hooks, Bell (2000), *Feminist Theory: From Margin to Center*, 2nd edition. Boston: South End Press.

John, Mary E. (2008), 'Introduction', in Mary E. John (ed.), *Women's Studies in India: A Reader*. New Delhi: Penguin Books, pp. 1–19.

Katzenstein, Mary and Raka Ray (2005), 'And in the Beginning There was the Nehruvian State', in Raka Ray and Mary Katzenstein (eds), *Social Movements in India: Poverty, Power, and Politics*. New York: Rowman and Littlefeld, pp. 1–31.

Lacquer, Thomas (1990), *Making Sex: Body and Gender from the Greeks to Freud*. Cambridge: Harvard University Press.

MacKinnon, Catherine A. (1988), *Feminism Unmodified: Discourses on Life and Law*. Cambridge, MA: Harvard University Press.

Mahmood, Saba (2004), *Politics of Piety: The Islamic Revival and the Feminist Subject*. Princeton: Princeton University Press.

Mani, Lata (1998), *Contentious Traditions: The Debate on Sati in Colonial India*. Berkeley and Los Angeles: University of California Press.

Martin, Emily (2001), *The Woman in the Body: A Cultural Analysis of Reproduction*. Boston, Massachusetts: Beacon Press.

Menon, Nivedita (2004), 'Refusing Globalisation and the Authentic Nation Feminist Politics in Current Conjuncture', *Economic and Political Weekly*, 39(1): 100–4.

Mill, James (1840), *The History of British India* (edited by H.H. Wilson), London: Baldwin, Cradock and Joy.

Mohanty, Chandra (1988), 'Under Western Eyes: Feminist Scholarship and Colonial Discourses', *Feminist Review*, 30: 61–88.

Omvedt, Gail (1993), *Reinventing Revolution: New Social Movements and the Socialist Tradition in India*. Armonk, NY: M.E. Sharpe.

Ray, Raka (1999), *Fields of Protest: Women's Movements in India*. Minneapolis: University of Minnesota Press.

Ray, Raka and Mary Katzenstein (eds) (2005), *Social Movements in India: Poverty, Power, and Politics*. USA: Rowman and Littlefeld Publishers, Inc.

Rege, Sharmila (1998), 'Dalit Women Talk Differently: A Critique of Difference and Towards a Dalit Feminist Standpoint', *Economic and Political Weekly*, 33(44): 39–46.

Rubin, Gayle (1975), 'The Traffic in Women: Notes on the Political Economy of Sex', in Rayna R. Reiter (ed.), *Toward an Anthropology of Women*. New York: Monthly Review Press, pp. 157–210.

Sangari, Kumkum and Sudesh Vaid (1989), *Recasting Women: Essays in Colonial History*. New Delhi: Kali for Women.

Scott, Joan W. (1999), *Gender and the Politics of History*. New York: Columbia University Press.

Sinha, Mrinalini (2000), 'Introduction', in Katherine Mayo (ed.), *Mother India: Selections from the Controversial 1927 Text*. Ann Arbor: University of Michigan Press, pp. 1–62.

Spivak, Gayatri (2004), 'Righting Wrongs', *The South Atlantic Quarterly*, 103(2/3): 523–81.

I. LAW

Chapter 1

THE FOUNDATIONS OF MODERN LEGAL STRUCTURES IN INDIA*

JANAKI NAIR

THE EAST INDIA COMPANY (EIC) first gained political and economic control over India when it was granted the revenues of Bengal in 1765. Since it was more than just the new landlord of this part of India, the Company was compelled to fashion a legal–juridical apparatus for its new dominions, primarily to ensure the steady and painless yield of revenues that it had been awarded.

When the first flush of victory had subsided, the EIC discovered that this was no easy task. For one, the British had no real understanding of the agrarian systems of India and the range of rights that existed on land, which bore no resemblance to the relatively clear-cut alienability of land in Britain, which, as E.P. Thompson (1993) has clearly shown, was itself only a recent development. Also, British experience of the administration of its other colonies hardly prepared it for the first bewildering encounter with the problems of governing India. In the colonies of North America and the Caribbean, non-state legal systems were quickly replaced by

---

* Originally published in Janaki Nair (1996), *Women and Law in Colonial India: A Social History*, New Delhi: Kali for Women, pp. 19–48.

state systems,¹ and before long they were governed by institutions that were primarily an extension of the basic political and legal institutions of Britain (Cohn 1989). These colonies, whose indigenous populations were quickly subjugated or simply massacred by earlier conquistadors, required few of the innovations that were necessary in a country like India, which appeared to have recognizable institutions and codes that were binding and had the force of law. At the same time, several of the Indian codes had no equivalents in British law. To compound the bewilderment was the almost complete lack of knowledge of the languages of governance and of law (Persian and Sanskrit).² Before long, it became clear that Indian territories could not be governed without a better knowledge of the 'traditions' and 'local usages' in addition to a detailed knowledge of the better known legal texts on which the indigenous people appeared to rely.

Any social history of law as it affected women must plot the contradictory pulls within the broader framework of social forces operating through successive periods of British rule. Simply put, India was no tabula rasa on which the interests of the colonial power could be inscribed. The process of producing a coherent reliable body of laws governing all Indian subjects was fraught with contradictions, compromises, and sometimes overwhelmed by political and economic exigencies. We shall at first consider the ideological bases for the development of legal structures in India, before concluding with a brief consideration of how these structures were related to the material transformations of Indian society.

---

[1] The distinction between 'state' and 'non-state' legal systems was used by Upendra Baxi to identify legal institutions and practices that existed before, and alongside, the legal innovations of the colonial state. See Baxi (1992: 252).

[2] (Guha 1981: 13). In his discussion of early British encounters with the Indian agrarian system, Guha says,

For most of the English officers sent out to the districts to manage the collection of revenues, it was a journey into the unknown in more than one sense. At every step they came up against quasi-feudal rights and obligations which defied any interpretation in familiar western terms. The hieroglyphics of Persian estate accounts baffled them. It was only in part a difficulty that they could not easily master the languages in which the ancient and medieval texts relating to the laws of property were written; *for tradition recorded only in memory and customs embedded in a variety of local usages wielded an authority equal to that of any written code* (emphasis added).

ORIENTALIST UNDERSTANDINGS OF INDIA AND THE LAW

As their conquests extended over various parts of the world, European colonial powers had to produce a body of knowledge about the subject people which would enable both administration and exploitation, as well as provide the ideological justification for the introduction of alien rule.[3] The attempt to forge a manageable grid through which Indian realities could be understood, and thereby controlled by the new authority, produced a breed of scholars called the Orientalists who mastered the classical languages of the subcontinent and translated what were identified as key texts (Kopf 1969; Viswanathan 1990). The first efforts in this direction were made by Warren Hastings, a successful commercial agent and later governor general of India from 1772, who encouraged a group of younger servants of the Company to devote themselves to the study of classical Indian languages, such as Sanskrit, Persian, and Arabic.

One of the enduring ironies of current historical knowledge of the Indian past is that it has been derived largely from the interpretations developed over the last 200 years, and, as a result, derived from ways of studying the past that were inaugurated by the Orientalists (Thapar 1975: 3). This reconstructed history was, however, framed as one of the benefits of colonial rule to be passed on to Indian subjects: the 'natives' were given back their own history, of which they had been previously ignorant.[4] Accustomed as they were to a reading of history which relied largely on written sources, which were also considered the most authentic ones, British Orientalists in India also began the process of privileging certain written texts in their reconstruction of the Indian past. Especially in the earlier decades of British rule in India, the administrators' search for certainty, for discovering the appropriate rule to be applied, drove them towards a study of the sacred *sastric* texts: the sources of Hindu law

---

[3] The most influential, and useful, framework for understanding the links between power and knowledge in the encounter between Western colonizing powers and the East has been provided by Said (1978). Said's use of the word Orientalism diverged sharply from conventional understanding that saw Orientalism merely as a study of Oriental pasts without noting the ways in which power constructed and defined this knowledge and produced 'truths' about the subject nation. It is in this sense that Orientalism is used throughout this discussion although 'Orientalists' still refers to the men who were actively engaged in the collection and translation of Indian texts.

[4] For a critique of Indian historiography's 'complicity with colonialist historiography', see Guha (1989).

were the *sruti*s, *smriti*s, *Dharmasastra*s, and an assortment of digests and commentaries. The dynamic interaction between textual law and non-textual custom, which had gradually evolved in pre-British India, was therefore hypostatized.[5] J.D.M. Derrett (1968: 177) says, for instance, that the 'sastra tells us little or nothing about the customs of the mlecchas, forest or hill tribes or other untouchables living on the fringe of Hindu society: the jurisprudence did not grow to include them.' Any decision to rely on sastric tradition, therefore, was a decision that overlooked the historical specificity of the text's application. For Islamic India on the other hand, from quite an early stage the texts were found to provide a reliable degree of certainty, as a result of which case law became much less important. Indeed, as we shall see, enactments to modify Islamic law were few and far between. Most jurisprudential and legislative attention was focused throughout this period on Hindu law. Finally, the reliance on scriptural texts produced an understanding of Indian society as overwhelmingly religious; religion, rather than economics or politics, was considered the prime mover of Indian society throughout history.

The scholarly efforts of the Orientalists often yielded conflicting views of the Indian past. Yet in the main part, Hastings and the scholars he encouraged as well as those who came after him, such as Nathaniel Halhed, William Jones, and H.T. Colebrooke, strove to counter the most pervasive British conception about pre-British (Mughal) India—that it was 'despotic' and arbitrary, relying directly and entirely on the power of its rulers. This, for example, was the view that had been stressed by Alexander Dow, an EIC servant and author of *Dissertation on the Origin and Nature of Despotism in Hindustan* (Guha 1981: 26ff). His understanding of despotism, which, it was claimed, sprang from the very nature of the soil and climate of India, stressed the arbitrariness of the political order. In Dow's view, before the independent and, by definition, capricious, will of the sovereign, no other law prevailed: the Mughal legal system was therefore a system of arbitrary and unchecked power (Cohn 1989: 138). Several scholars did much to dispel such deprecating knowledges of pre-British India. Nevertheless, these scholars argued that although there was a definite notion of 'authority', there was no commensurate notion of 'legality'. This view continues to retain its persuasive power even today (see, for example, Lingat 1973: 257–9). Such an interpretation of the pre-colonial past had important uses

---

[5] For a discussion of the relations between custom and sastra in the pre-British periods, see Derrett (1968: 'Custom and Law in Ancient India', 'Law and the Social Order before the Muhammedan Conquest': 148–224).

for colonial administrators, given their penchant for strong-handed rule, that is, establishing a long promised 'law and order' in India which would earn them the respect of the indigenous people.

The work of the Orientalists employed by Hastings led to a recognition of the ancient constitutional basis of Indian legal codes, which scholars believed not only had to be discovered but interpreted for use by the British administrators. It was confidently presumed that there were texts which could be interpreted and understood by British scholars in collaboration with the indigenous scholars, and which would authoritatively establish the content of Hindu law to be administered in the EIC's district courts. In this scheme of things, scriptural texts were valorised and given an authority they had never before enjoyed. Derrett has quite justifiably called the British 'the patrons of sastra', even suggesting that the British desire for explicatory law texts encouraged the production of fresh ones in the late eighteenth and early nineteenth centuries. As D.A. Washbrook (1981: 653) points out, 'With the support of British power, the Hindu law expanded its authority across large areas of society which had not known it before, or which for a very long period had possessed their own more localised and non-scriptural customs.' In their quest for an authority based on prevailing notions of power (which were nevertheless invested with new meaning), the British encouraged the interpretation of Indian scriptures as the theocratic source of all binding codes. As a result, the attempt to counter the theory of pre-colonial Indian states as despotic produced a fresh theory of theocratic regimes in its place.

THE NATIVE INTERPRETERS OF LAW

Even such organized effort could not rule out dependence on those 'subtle natives' who could 'perplex' the colonizers at every turn, especially on tricky questions of customary practices. The interpreters of the Hindu code were naturally the traditional intellectuals, Brahmins, whose monopoly of learning in a highly segmented society had ensured that they were the sole authorities conversant with the textual traditions of India.

The law as it operated when the EIC acquired the *dewani* of Bengal was fundamentally Islamic 'but explicitly recognised the jurisdiction of the Hindu referees and arbitrators to settle disputes among the Hindus according to their laws and customs, reserving to itself exclusive jurisdiction in matters of crime and constitutional and fiscal matters' (Derrett 1968: 239). Robert Lingat (1973: 262) has gone so far as to suggest that under Mughal rule, 'a law based above all on tradition and precedent attached more or less laxly to one or other of the schools of interpretation' was strengthened at the expense of the consultation of 'that ocean of texts'. This was primarily because the Muslim rulers left Hindu local bodies a great deal of autonomy, much like what Muslims themselves enjoyed under Hindu rulers.

The relative autonomy of the village assembly, caste tribunal, and the *sreni* (or guild) that had long developed before the advent of British rule was seriously undermined by the very structure of the court system as it was imagined by Warren Hastings. The colonial state absorbed some aspects of local law-ways even as it gradually transformed the meaning and content of others. From the rather narrow brief of early charters of the EIC, such as the one of 1668 which contemplated the establishment of courts on English lines for the government of Bombay and factories elsewhere, the EIC's role had considerably expanded by the end of the eighteenth century, when it was both more ambitious and had learned to be more pragmatic (see Fawcett 1934: 12). In the early years of EIC rule in India, Hastings set up an administrative structure which included a dual court system: the Presidency courts, with English judges and lawyers, offset by the mofussil courts (including the *sadr* [chief] court) which were presided over by the collector/judge who entertained Indian pleaders. The collector/judge performed two kinds of functions, adjudicating on the dewani cases relating to the revenue and civil litigation, and the faujdari cases relating to the criminal and internal legal affairs. 'Facts' were established on testimony from witnesses and documentary evidence placed before the court, for which the collector/judge was assisted by the pandits and maulvis. In an act of settlement in 1781, the Hastings plan, which made space for the operation of Hindu and Muslim law on matters pertaining to 'succession, inheritance, marriage, caste and all religious usages and institutions' and was applicable only to mofussil courts, was extended to the Supreme Court of Bengal. A specific effort was made to take customary law into consideration (Cohn 1989: 136–7). For this purpose, pandits and maulvis were directly appointed by the Supreme Court from 1777, and by the time of Cornwallis's Code of 1793, were attached to the District Courts, Provincial Courts, and the Sadr Dewani Adalat as well (Derrett 1968). The appointment of pandits and maulvis to assist judges finally ended in 1864, when it was believed the colonial authorities had achieved an adequate grasp of the mechanics of Indian legal systems and a sufficient body of case law had been developed on which future generations of judges could rely.

The new structure undid the relative autonomy at the lower levels in one major sense: the English judge made the final decision as to what was legally acceptable under what was shaping up as a new legal system, whether he followed the opinion of the pandits, in the absence of detailed personal knowledge, or relied on his own knowledge of the texts (ibid.: 263). As a result, his exteriority to the legal traditions of India was never overcome.

In contrast to the obvious admiration of the Orientalists for the classical Indian past was, as Upendra Baxi (1992: 252) notes, the reluctance on the part of the colonial authorities to 'name community adjudication as law'. Neglecting the historical processes by which 'non-state legal systems' were appropriated to the state, the British in India claimed this too as part of their civilizing mission, namely to weld the host of disparate practices that went in the name of Hindu law into a single legal code. In the process of doing so, they transformed the nature of judicial discourse. For long, the village panchayat had arbitrated and adjudicated in small face-to-face village communities on questions relating to breaches of village norms, while caste councils arbitrated and adjudicated disputes internal to castes. Through a process of consensus and compromise, vertical ties of the village community in the former instance and horizontal ties within castes were secured (Cohn 1987b). The colonial legal-juridical structure—that is, state law—effected irreversible changes in the nature and importance of local law-ways, introducing for the first time, adversarial proceedings; while disputes relating to caste and kinship rules were invariably settled within the caste councils, disputes relating to land increasingly made their way into state courts (Epstein 1962: 145–6; see also Mendelsohn 1981). Similarly, the colonial judicature occupied a centrality in disputes over temple honours and rituals (see, for instance, Presler 1987; also Appadurai 1979). This points to the multiple ways in which the colonial administration structured 'tradition' through the agency of the courts, serving to equalize structurally unequal people (such as an upper-caste landlord and his Dalit servant) in a court of law, while ensuring that in the cumbersome process of 'appeals, adjournments and counter appeals, the poorer litigant was ruined' (Cohn 1987a).

Yet the continued resilience of local law-ways over state law, right up to the present day, is an indication that colonial legal systems rarely achieved the kind of dominance they aspired to. One may therefore speak of a quest for, rather than an attainment of, certainty, consistency, and uniformity (Baxi 1986: 20). To take just one instance, the quest for a uniform legal code, which was a central concern of early colonial rule, continues to inform the actions of the independent Indian state even today.

THE FIRST MOVE TOWARDS CODIFICATION

At the beginning of the process of producing a usable Hindu legal code in the eighteenth century, the court appointments firmly established the Brahmin pandits, invariably male, at the centre of the emerging judicial discourse. The pandits themselves were hardly left to their own devices. At the Sanskrit colleges in Benares and Calcutta (now Kolkata) that were specifically set up for the purpose, they were trained in the very sastras which were considered 'little known and little read. . .'[6] The body of texts chosen for this training in the first half of the nineteenth century and probably even earlier included *Mitakshara, Dayabhaga, Daya Krama, Daya Taitva*, the *Dattaka Candrika*, the *Dattaka Mimamsa, Vivada Chintamani, Tithi Tattva, Suddhi Tattva,* and *Prayascitta Taitva*. This list, though impressive in itself, included no work from southern India until the publication of the *Malayala Vyavahara Mala* in the late nineteenth century.

The 'unreliability' of the pandit and the flood of litigation which soon overwhelmed the courts after 1772 made it imperative to forge a coherent and stable interpretation of the law which the collector/judge could master, thereby reducing reliance on the indigenous experts and avoiding corruption. The search for the earliest, authoritative text and the most reliable indigenous system of jurisprudence led the Orientalists to the Dharmasastra, which, they were told by the Brahmin interpreters, held high prestige among the peoples of India and provided actual rules for a wide variety of contexts. However, as a teaching of righteousness, it certainly included law but was not co-extensive with it, and consisted of precepts rather than legally binding statutes; *vyavastha*s were therefore quite an important source of legal interpretation. The vyavasthas of the pandits were an amalgam of customary practices, rough and ready readings of the sastras and diverse materials chosen from epics and legends, and from other treatises of relatively later date such as the *purana*s, spurious smritis, *agama*s, and *tantra*s (Derrett 1968: 230).

From this potpourri, an attempt was made to construct an abstract legal code in the late eighteenth century. Eleven pundits 'learned in the Shaster' (Halhed 1776: lxxiv) were chosen by Warren Hastings from

---

[6] 'Parliamentary Papers on Hindu Widows' (1821: 532), cited in Mani (1986: 35).

various parts of Bengal to compile precisely such a digest in 1773, in order to produce a handy tool with which to cope with the flood of cases which had inundated the courts, and to provide 'a precise idea of the customs and manners of these people which to their great injury have long been misrepresented in the western world' (ibid.: 1). The digest which emerged from the deliberations of the pandits in 1775 was appropriately called the *Vivadarnava Setu* ('Bridge across the Ocean of Litigation') and was translated into English by Nathaniel Halhed from a Persian version of the original Sanskrit. Halhed's translation, suitably entitled *A Code of Gentoo Laws or Ordinations of the Pundits*, claimed absolute fidelity to the original, which in turn, he said, 'was picked out sentence by sentence from various originals in the Shanscrit Language, neither adding nor diminishing any part of the original text' (Halhed 1776: x). Quite apart from all the slippages and theoretical difficulties of the translation process, the entire process of making available a digested form of the Dharmashastra allowed the Brahmins to secure for themselves a new status in the emerging legal order, adroitly managing the transition from the legal systems that had prevailed (Derrett 1973: 9). The pronouncements of the English judge in turn lent a fixity to Hindu law that had not previously existed.

It is also significant that it was Hindu law, rather than Muslim law, that was the focus of reform and codification throughout this period. When Muslim law did become the focus of attention, its scriptural roots were traced relatively easily by those anxious to produce administrable laws. Since the legal theory of Islam did not usually recognize custom as a formal or independent source of law, even when customary law was practised, as among the Mapillas of Malabar or the Memons of western India, it was regarded as a result of Hindu influence, and therefore un-Islamic. Just as the Brahmanization of Hindu law took place over the course of the nineteenth century, Muslim law was progressively Islamized. For Muslims, the core text that was translated for the use of officials was the *Hedaya*, chosen by maulvis, translated first from Arabic to Persian and then into English by Hamilton. The posts of *kazis*, who performed judicial as well as non-judicial functions, were abolished in 1864, and re-established by an Act of 1880, although they were confined to non-judicial private functions. Nevertheless, disputes concerning succession, marriage, divorce, and family relations were increasingly referred to muftis, functionaries who were assigned the task of conflict resolution, since the demand for Islamic institutions among the Muslim community was quite high (Baxi 1986: 18).

Sir William Jones (1746–94), who was appointed to the Crown Court in 1783, was dissatisfied with the Halhed text since it left judges at the mercy of Indian interpreters. Jones's distrust of Indian interpreters ran deep, and he was troubled by the excessive reliance on Brahmin pandits, since they had proved themselves capable of pulling out appropriate authorities from the 'ocean of sastra' (Jones et al. 1792: 91). The Brahmin's supposed infinite capacity for deception and concealment could only be avoided by a reliable, authentic version of Hindu law. It was believed that

> If the law were digested by an authoritative and independent authority, it would be easier to learn and refer to than the extensive and vague literature normally consulted. (Derrett 1968: 239)

Jones himself proposed a far more complex and complete 'digest of Hindu and Mussalman Law' analogous to the British codes, for which he appealed to Cornwallis for help (Cohn 1989: 145). The compilation of Sanskrit and Arabic texts was complete in 1794; translations were begun by Jones, and completed after his death by H.T. Colebrooke. It was as a result of these labours that *The Digest of Hindu Law on Contracts and Successions* was published in 1798. In this work, a long cherished dream of William Jones had come true: the English judge would now possess the ability to arbitrate on 'all disputes among the natives without uncertainty, which is in truth a disgrace, though satirically called a glory' (Jones et al. 1792: 91). Colebrooke devised, some believe mistakenly, conceptual distinctions between schools of Hindu law which schematically bore close resemblance to the clearly established Islamic schools of law. Hindu law was divided into Dayabhaga and Mitakshara, and the latter subdivided into the Benares, Mithila, Maharashtrian, and Dravidian schools, to parallel the distinctions between Sunni and Shia, and Hanafi, Maliki Shafai, and Hanbali laws (Cohn 1989: 146).

Colebrooke's interest in acquiring authentic texts led to the sudden flowering of new Sanskrit sastras in the period after him, especially in the 1820s. In part this was a response to the demand for new texts, but the new texts were equally a refutation of the assertions of Western scholars such as William Hay McNaghten and Thomas Strange. However, as Derrett points out, the process of procuring reliable texts for south India had barely begun in this period. One text that came conveniently to hand was the Malayalam *Vyavahara Mala*, written almost certainly in the late eighteenth century in anticipation of the British need for a usable text in the newly acquired dominions of Malabar. This was rediscovered by A.C. Burnell, a district and sessions judge of South Canara in 1877, and formed the basis of a south Indian law digest (Derrett 1968: 260–2).

Hastings had made it compulsory for the judges to consult the sastris but only on listed subjects such as inheritance, marriage, caste, and other religious usages (ibid.: 231). As far as unspecified topics were concerned, laws with which inhabitants were familiar, whether sastric or customary, were applicable, for which the consultation of the pandit by the judge was desirable but not necessary (Lingat 1973: 135). However, as the British Indian empire expanded, the difficulties of privileging textual traditions became painfully obvious. Commenting on the ways in which the Bombay Regulation of 1827, to take one example, deviated from the Bengal precedents, P.C. Ilbert wrote that by this time 'Anglo-Indian administrators had become aware that the sacred or semi-sacred text books were not such trustworthy guides as they had been supposed to be in the time of Warren Hastings and that local or personal usage played a more important part than had previously been attributed to them' (cited in Tahir Mahmood 1983: 15). As a result, the Bombay Regulation gave precedence to local usage over the written Mohammedan or Hindu law. This process of acknowledging the importance of custom and usage was well under way when Queen Victoria proclaimed her intention to honour the laws and customs of her Indian subjects, especially those grounded in religion, following the revolt of 1857. Nevertheless, the relation between law and custom remained a troublesome one and dogged British efforts at producing a uniform code.

The need for codification was increasingly felt by the 1830s since a body of substantive law had not been built up, and the task of building this was placed on courts adjudicating cases on the doctrine of 'justice, equity and good conscience'. It was precisely in order to bring some coherence to the body of laws that the idea of the Law Commission first came up. Thomas Macaulay, Law Member of the Government of India after 1833 echoed William Jones's and Thomas Strange's fears about excessive reliance on pandits and maulvis and urged immediate codification. By the 1830s, British rule was on a surer footing in almost all parts of the subcontinent and the optimism of that period was reflected in the passage of laws related to the transformation of certain social practices. Macaulay, more clearly than others, was willing to admit that the codification of the laws was imperative, and that this should be done by a small group of jurists. In 1833, he declared:

This seems to me to be precisely that point of time at which the advantage of a completely written code of laws may be easily conferred on India. It is a work which cannot be well performed in an age of barbarism and which cannot without great difficulty be performed in an age of freedom. It is the work which specially belongs to a government like that of India: to an enlightened and paternal despotism.[7]

The First Law Commission, under the leadership of Macaulay, produced the draft of the Indian Penal Code which was adopted in 1860. The Second Commission devised the Criminal Procedure Code, enacted in 1861, and reorganized the court system. The Second Law Commission, however, expressed strong reservations against the codification of Hindu and Muslim laws. Thereafter, the field of personal law was marked off as beyond the reach of colonial administrators. The most important set of laws that governed the status of women, namely Hindu and Muslim personal laws, were increasingly identified as those which only the members of the respective communities could reform. Thus, the Indian Succession Act of 1865 applied only to those other than Hindus and Muslims. That the fears of the Second Law Commission (1853–6) were not unfounded became painfully evident in the revolt of 1857.

Although the Third Law Commission drew up drafts codifying contracts, laws of evidence, negotiable instruments, and so on, it left personal laws severely alone. The fourth and last British Law Commission, appointed in 1879, attempted a further codification of substantive law but it too left personal laws untouched. Sir Courteney Ilbert, Law Member in 1882, recognized the need for codification of Hindu family law in order to enable judges to cut through the thickets of existing case law, but declared inability since the Hindus were reluctant to accept such reform.

By 1864, when the pandits and maulvis were disbanded from their employment in the courts, the process of restating Hindu or Muslim law had more or less been abandoned. The optimism of Bentinck's time had dissolved following the political challenge to British rule posed by the subject Indian people. There was a clear shift in the conception of the relation between customs and local usages of people and scriptural texts. Thus, the famous Privy Council ruling of 1868, in Collector of Madura vs Moottoo Ramalinga (12 MIA 397, 436, 1868) declared, 'Under the Hindu system of law, clear proof of usage will outweigh the written text of law' (Jain 1987: 480).

This must not be taken to mean that the British had given up their avowed aim of introducing a 'rule of law' in India. British courts continued the process of pronouncing judgement on Hindu and Muslim practices, and the colonial state even transformed some practices when enough

---

[7] *Hansard Debates* (Third Series, vol. XIX, pp. 531–3), as cited in Jain (1987: 405).

pressure was brought on it by educated Indians. If anything, the processes that were well under way by the mid-nineteenth century had transformed 'a matrix of real historical experience... into a matrix of abstract legality so that the will of the state could be made to penetrate, reorganize part by part and eventually control the will of the population' (Guha 1987: 141).

THE CODE AND WOMEN

The reference to sastras and their interpretation by the male pandits, easily drawn from the most conservative sections of Indian society, produced the first in a series of pronouncements about the scriptural standing of women in Indian society. Chapter 20 of Halhed's translation was on the duties of women. Halhed recognized that some of the precepts of that section were incommensurate with emerging bourgeois ideals of woman as companion, and felt constrained to say as a preface to the chapter that 'the Brahmins who compiled this code were men far advanced in years' by way of apology for 'the observations they have selected and the censures they have passed upon the conduct and merits of the fair sex' (Halhed 1776: ixv). In Halhed's apologetic preface we may detect the first signs of an ambiguity which would plague the colonial authorities' search for the definitive text. The colonial state had to perform a delicate balancing act, poised between its aspirations as a paramount power and the respect for Indian 'tradition' that was first elaborated by Hastings. Once British rule was more secure, one of the major planks of cultural legitimation for its continued economic and political domination of India rested on the introduction of a scale of civilization that hierarchized the position of women in various societies. On any such scale, the women of England easily constituted the top while those of India lagged far behind.

In Halhed's book, the chapter 'Of What Concerns Women' began with a prefatory statement on the relations between the sexes:

A man, both day and night, must keep his wife in so much subjection that she by no means be mistress of her own actions if the wife have her own free will notwithstanding she be sprung from a superior caste. (ibid.: 249)

This clearly marked women off as a category of people who had few rights, if any, under the existing codes of law. It was also an attempt to homogenize the category of Woman, specifying that caste (and class) could make no difference to the inherent characteristics of women, who deserved only to be subordinated and controlled.

Betraying persistent upper caste male fears about female sexuality was the assertion about the sexual proclivities of women:

> A woman is never satisfied with the copulation of man, no more than a fire is satisfied with burning fuel, or the main ocean with receiving the rivers, or the empire of death with the dying of men and animals: in this case therefore, a woman is not to be relied on (ibid.: 250).

Women's wrongs thus formed the theoretical basis for men's rights, or more properly, male duties towards moderating women's lust. Such lust was expressed by women not just for sex, but for 'jewels, fine furniture, handsome clothes and nice victuals'. It is in this context that Manu's famous injunction was understood: 'her father protects her in childhood, her husband protects her in youth, her sons protect her in old age: a woman does not deserve independence' (Embree 1988: 228).

If the natural urges of women from this description were unspeakably evil, the sastras also outlined the normative code for good women, which once more spoke of fears and fantasies rather than remaining an expression of existing material realities.

> A woman, who is of good disposition and who puts on her jewels and clothes with decorum, and is of good principles, whenever the husband is cheerful the wife is also cheerful, and if the husband is sorrowful, the wife is also sorrowful, and whenever the husband undertakes a journey, the wife puts on a careless dress, lays aside her jewels and other ornaments and abuses no person and will not expend a single dam without her husband's consent and has a son, and takes proper care of the household goods, and at the times of worship, performs her worship to the deity in the proper manner, and goes not out of the house, and is not unchaste, and makes no quarrels or disturbances, and has no greedy passions, and is always employed in some good work, and pays proper respect to all persons, such is a good woman. (Halhed 1776: 251)

Countless prescriptions for correct female behaviour, clearly intended to present an ideal notion of womanhood that would ensure the preservation of the patriarchal household, included a number of actions over which a woman had control, thereby appearing to acknowledge woman's agency. At the same time, it included several actions which were beyond her control, such as the duty of having a son. The bulk of the normative code spelt out the responsibility of women to curb their 'natural' urges which were uniformly evil and dangerous, even as it strove to produce the figure of the desirable female.

Such an essentialized conception of Indian female nature extracted from several texts and authorities would soon be deployed in another framework altogether. The new intellectual current that swept through India was that of the Utilitarians, whose reforming zeal was most evident in the early decades of the nineteenth century. James Mill, whose influential

History of British India was written in 1826 and formed the text for all those civil servants educated in Haileybury College, found the normative code an ideal one to attack in his diatribe on pre-colonial India. In his optic, as well as that of the newly ascendant Evangelical doctrines, Britain's civilizing mission in India was clearly mapped out. Mill's optimism about the transformatory power of colonial rule sprang, in part, from a new political confidence in the expanding colonial empire in India. The ideological shift from reverence for the Indian past to cultural contempt was an expression of this emerging confidence. The Indian people could now be rescued from their stultifying laws and practices by the reforming efforts of the British.

Yet, despite the extraordinary investment of early colonial energies in uncovering textual traditions, the position of women in pre-British India was by no means governed entirely by the misogynic sastric pronouncements of Manu or the commentators who followed. As Derrett (1968: 206) has pointed out, 'On the whole, the sastra turns a blind eye to the customs of the non-Aryan peoples, in particular, non-patrilineal communities....' Tensions between custom (namely unwritten law) and sastra were particularly severe in the south and among the non-Brahmanic peoples of other parts of India. Thus, the eighteenth century text *Dattaka Candrika* 'comments on the strange customs of the wicked people of Malabar amongst whom the sister's son is the heir' (ibid.: 103).[8] Indeed, at no point did the sastras acknowledge the independence or high status of women that prevailed in distinct pockets of Indian society, where women shared equal rights to matrimonial property, had access to divorce, and where the remarriage of widows was encouraged (ibid.: 206–7). For instance, adoption by women such as the Devadasis, though widely practised, was not acknowledged by the sastras. Indeed, tensions between custom and sastric law were most severe in the realm of family law, not surprising given that entire communities neglected the sastric requirements of marriage.

At the same time, by no means should the prevalence of customs that favoured women be taken to mean that customs were unequivocally

---

[8] The unwillingness to see practices in southern India as amounting to more than deviations from 'Hindu Law' has persisted even in contemporary India. Intervening in the debate on the divorce provisions of the Hindu Marriage Act in the early 1950s, S.P. Mukherjee, who opposed such provisions and was told of the long-standing practice of divorce in south India said, 'I say good luck to South India. Let South India proceed from progress to progress, from divorce to divorce...Why force it on others who do not want it?' (as cited in Som 1994: 180).

gender neutral. Customs were after all also devised and sustained by male community elders, and women were rarely consulted in such formulation. In fact, some customs could be, and were, reinstated by colonial rule in ways that disadvantaged women. But as the debates on widow immolation, widow remarriage, and child marriage revealed, British reformers, Indian liberals, and orthodox opponents all relied rather heavily on the sastric record.

THE UTILITARIAN DISCOURSE ON LAW

After war and intrigue had secured the Indian empire for the British and made their continued existence in India less uncertain than it had been in the 1770s, the colonial authorities were emboldened to undertake legislative measures which would form the basis of a whole new legal system. Law would become, in the words of Ranajit Guha, the 'state's emissary'—an instrument through which it could wield its power and deploy its disciplinary efforts. The first efforts of the nineteenth century were aimed at policing the populace and ridding it of the most 'repugnant' of practices in the eyes of the British, as is evident from the legislation against sati and 'thuggee' in the first half of the nineteenth century. Transformations of law were unique because the struggle around it had to be 'expressed in terms of general statements of principle' rather than 'in particular statements of private and discrete interest' (Washbrook 1981: 649). As such, some higher ideal had to be in position as the aim of legal reform. Therefore, initiating legislation in the name of improving the status of women was no accident.

The very study of the Indian past which was intended to provide the Indians with their own history was soon skilfully deployed in a critique of Indian society itself. The critique was supposedly based on knowledge rather than ignorance. The foremost and extremely influential of these critics was James Mill. He never set foot in India nor, unlike the Orientalists, did he study a single Indian language: nevertheless, he composed a five-volume history of India, which, as Guha has pointed out, assimilated Indian history to the history of Great Britain: 'Indian history...would henceforth be used as a comprehensive measure of difference between the peoples of these two countries' (Guha 1989: 211). In contrast to Orientalist accounts which had charted a decline in Indian civilization from great heights, Mill suggested that Indian civilization was inherently flawed and only worthy of thorough reform.

The cultural policy of the Marquess of Wellesley reflected the difference between Orientalist and Utilitarian doctrines influenced by the writings of Charles Grant and James Mill, respectively. The emerging policy also sprung from the optimism characteristic of Utilitarianism in England: the empire could be made more permanent if it successfully seized the unlimited opportunities for reform in India (Hutchins 1967). Now 'the British civil servant was to be an agent of cultural change and not an agent in the perpetuation of Hinduism' (Kopf 1969: 134).

Mill's assessment of Indian society was in part based on the position of its women. In his work, the position of women was taken as emblematic of the general state of that society. According to Mill, Hindu women were

[in] a state of dependence more strict and humiliating than which is ordained for the weaker sex.... They are held in extreme degradation, excluded from the sacred books, deprived of education, and [of a share] in the paternal property (Mill 1840: 312-13).

Although Mill was unwilling to suggest that women everywhere were ordained for anything other than a lower rung in the social hierarchy, he affirmed that there were degrees of oppression that were tolerable, even necessary, but that Indian society had plumbed the depths in this regard.

The state of 'barbarity' to which Indian women were condemned was one from which they had to be rescued: admirably poised to play the role of rescuers were the colonial authorities. The protection offered by the colonial state to Indian women was a natural corollary of its characterization of Indian men as effeminate and incapable, yet the very people from whom women had to be rescued (Chakravarti 1990: 35).[9]

The critique of the Indian past initiated by the colonial authorities had an unintended effect: the discredited past was gradually sacralized by the subject population and became the basis for the development of a new cultural identity. It is hardly surprising that early Indian cultural nationalism sprang to the defence of a tradition they believed was under fierce attack. The argument in favour of Indian tradition was made throughout

---

[9] We may speculate briefly on the consequences of that construction of Indian masculinity: if the Bengali was indeed the weak, emasculated caricature and indistinctly gendered, how were the women to be characterized? Must the British critique of Bengali society be seen as an initial step in an attempt to realign Indian society on lines that were recognizably patriarchal in a British sense? This suspicion is confirmed when we turn to ways in which those parts of pre-colonial society where women enjoyed a measure of economic and social power under matriliny were aggressively transformed and brought in line with more recognizable patriarchal formations.

the nineteenth century, and also redeployed in an anti-imperialist strategy. In order to do this, the nationalists had to address what they believed were some well-founded critiques of Indian tradition. In other words, they admitted the necessity for reforms which would restore their tradition to its former glory. Indian history, in the optic of the nationalists, began to be understood as a narrative of decline from the pinnacles of Aryan achievement.

In this, they were amply aided by the work of the Orientalists. Despite the increasing political significance of James Mill and other Anglicists, and their continued irreverence, the work of the British Orientalists prepared the way for the work of the German Indologist, Friedrich Max Mueller (1823-1900). For Max Mueller, the Vedas, of which he provided a full collation and publication, formed 'the natural basis of Indian history' (ibid.: 39). Further, he discovered and triumphantly flourished a common ancestry for the ruling European race and the subjugated Indian. The Aryan 'origins' of Indian civilization were discovered and enthroned as central to an understanding of Indian history only in the nineteenth century. The discovery of the Aryan past and the valorization of the Vedas resonated not only in the writings of the colonialists but in the dialectically constituted oppositional discourse of cultural nationalism as well. 'The Aryan,' says Uma Chakravarti, 'was an important element in the nationalist construction of a sense of identity for its association with vigour, conquest and expansion, in other words for its connotations of political and cultural achievement' (ibid.: 47).

In the cultural nationalism of the nineteenth and early twentieth centuries, the image of the Aryan woman as 'helpmate' of the man in sacrifice and war was a recurring motif which had enormous implications for emerging ideal-typical constructions of Indian women. The Aryan woman, singled out from the rich tapestry of historical choices, soon became the quintessence of India, eclipsing all other figures and speaking for all of Indian womanhood. This thoroughly de-historicized figure was present in the discourse of Ram Mohun Roy, Ishwar Chandra Vidyasagar, Mahadev Govind Ranade, Bal Gangadhar Tilak, and Vivekananda; even Gandhi's vision did little to challenge the formulation.

In the course of a century of study and reflection that was inaugurated during the colonial period, a new 'tradition' was 'invented': that of a Vedic Golden Age, replete with glowing heroines who stood shoulder to shoulder with the Aryan males. The invented tradition of the Vedic heroine would play a critical role in fortifying the nationalist challenge to imperial rule; it also homogenized Indian womanhood and ignored existing inequalities among women along the axes of caste, class, and community. The subsuming of all Indian womanhood to the idealized Indian middle-class woman translated in legal terms into instituting a Brahmanical patriarchal family form with its reproductive sexual economy at the centre. Thus, spheres of female power, customs, and practices that had long existed within pre-colonial society, such as the matrilineal communities of Kerala and south Canara, or the Devadasis and Basavis in parts of south India, were identified as 'aberrations', archipelagos of un-Hindu practices. For instance, one specific claim about 'Hindu Law', whether under the Mitakshara or Dayabhaga legal system,[10] as it was discovered and codified by the British, was that it did not grant women any rights to property. Twentieth-century Indian nationalism could then claim to represent Indian womanhood by calling for the bestowal of rights to property on Hindu women from the top down.

In its effects, ignorance of the rich plurality of Indian social forms was not benign. The invention of a golden age in Indian history also determined the emphasis of 'social reforms' through legislation even when they were initiated by Indian men. The most important aspects of reformist concern for the particular forms of oppression were those that affected the women of upper-caste, middle-class households. The effect of reformist concern for the particular forms of oppression of women in these households was to universalize them and thereby extend the reach of reform legislation to women in households that did not observe such practices. What may have been construed as progressive legislation for the women of upper-caste households, then, frequently succeeded in undermining or reversing privileges women may have enjoyed in non-upper-caste households.

---

[10] The two systems originated sometime in the twentieth century, and formed the principal basis of Hindu law, particularly as they were identified and codified by the colonial state. The Mitakshara system, which was based on the commentary on *Yagnavalkya smriti* by Vignaneswara of the south, was followed in nearly all parts of the Indian subcontinent, while the Dayabhaga system, based on a digest written by Jimutavahana of Bengal, prevailed in Bengal and Assam. There was a flowering of sub-schools under the Mitakshara system between the thirteenth and the sixteenth centuries, respectively identified as the Mithila, Bombay, Madras, and Benares schools, but as far as inheritance rights of women were concerned, there was little to substantially distinguish between them. (Kane 1946; Altekar 1956).

THE POSSIBILITY OF A 'RULE OF LAW'

The account so far lays out some of the ideological bases for the development of colonial legal systems. Yet the process by which a range of customary privileges were codified into rights throughout the nineteenth and twentieth centuries cannot be understood in isolation of the material realities which determined the success or failure of ideological developments. It was precisely in the realm of negotiating conflicting interests that the ambitions of the colonial and nationalist ideologies alike met their most serious challenges and made accommodations.

Since colonialism confers only subjecthood on the colonized, and is predicated on a denial of citizenship, the normalizing functions of its state apparatuses are historically destined to remain unrealized. The colonial state's power after all, as Partha Chatterjee reminds us, is derived from the 'rule of colonial difference', namely the preservation of the alienness of the ruling group (Chatterjee 1993: 10). In colonial societies such as India, the persuasive powers and instrumentalities of an abstract legality remained firmly subordinated to the use of naked force; as such the colonial state exercised 'dominance without hegemony' (Guha 1989).[11]

Nevertheless, one of the most enduring myths of colonialist discourse, which has outlived its use as a justificatory mechanism for the conquest and exploitation of India, was that the EIC, and the British Government thereafter, succeeded in establishing a 'Rule of Law'.[12] What accounts for the relative success with which a culturally specific (British) achievement assumes universal significance is, Guha (1989: 276) suggests, 'the pervasive power of the ideology of law in English political thought' and its dissemination worldwide in the age of capital. Yet, though the worldwide expansion of capital contained the promise of tearing down all challenges and barriers to its expansion, under colonial rule, 'the universality towards which [capital] irresistibly strives' encounters barriers that are a product of colonial rule: as such, they are only 'ideally' but never 'really' overcome (Marx 1973: 410–11). The contradictions of a partial, timid,

---

[11] Alexander Dow's conception of pre-colonial law is discussed by Cohn (1989: 138–9). Baxi (1992) points out that even such sensitive scholars as Ranajit Guha and Shahid Amin are not fully cognizant of the extent to which the notion of 'law' itself was appropriated by colonial law.

[12] Lloyd and Susan Rudolph thus do not doubt the 'intention' of the British to bring justice via a new legal system to India; they failed to do so because 'Indians did not appreciate the system's morality and logic'. See Rudolph and Rudolph (1967: 255).

and circumscribed legality on the one hand, nevertheless producing a remarkable degree of litigiousness in colonial society on the other, were therefore symptomatic of the combined and uneven development of capitalism in India.

There cannot be 'rights bearing subjects' where there are no citizens: the political conception of right after all precedes the legal conception. Under colonial rule, this was an impossibility. How then may we chart the emergence of a specific set of relations, legal relations, instituted by a colonial regime in the absence of a civil society dissolved into independent individuals? How, except in conjunction with the ideology that promised citizenship and the nation-state, namely nationalism? The mixture of administrative orders and legal regulations that constituted the totality of colonial governance were impelled by the needs of the colonial economy: revenue extraction required the introduction of a rule of property in land (Guha 1981); the exigencies of recruiting and rendering the labour force on plantations, mines, and factories stable and permanent required the introduction of rudimentary labour laws (Das 1941; Punekar and Varickayil 1989). Yet as the nineteenth century wore on, an indigenous moral–intellectual leadership, increasingly conscious of the impossibility of achieving economic 'modernity' under conditions of colonial rule, attempted the cultural regeneration of the Indian nation through recourse to a matrix of abstract legality.

Law then was the domain which starkly defined the limits of the colonial state's own transformatory capabilities, even as it opened up sites of contestation on which the indigenous elites hoped to prove theirs. Therefore, one cannot entirely agree with Washbrook's 'materialist' reading of law in agrarian Indian society, that the colonial state merely arbitrated between already existing social forces in the Indian subcontinent (1981: 668). While making the useful, if far from novel, suggestion that the British Raj cannot be viewed as a monolithic whole, Washbrook goes on to suggest that the undiluted sway of colonial power in India was restricted to a few decades of the early nineteenth century, the period of 'high colonialism'. In its previous mercantilist phase, the colonial state merely 'adapted to its own ends the state structure which it had been bequeathed'; as such, the clumsy efforts of the colonial state to develop a market in land raise doubts about whether that was ever their intention (ibid.: 658, 660, 665, 667). By 1857, according to this reading, the high colonial state had passed its prime, yielding to the phase of the 'incipient nation state' when the role of the colonial state was reduced to that of a 'broker' between existing social and economic groups (ibid.: 711). Even in that phase when the colonial state could effect significant change, in the few decades between 1820 and 1857, the Raj merely undertook a 'balancing act' of keeping control over land in the hands of agrarian corporations. We may recall, however, that this was the period when the Indian economy was restructured in such a way as to rule out all possibility of its transformation as a modern industrial power (see, for example, Bagchi 1988). Washbrook thereby continues in the realm of law what is a wider project of conjuring away the effects of colonialism; if he dismantles certain colonial myths about the autonomy of law at all, it is by effacing colonialism itself. Colonial law, as colonial power itself, rather than effecting irreversible changes in the economy while exacerbating existing cleavages in society, appears in this account to be stepping between already prevalent social forces and their antagonisms, thereby reducing the history of colonialism to one made entirely by the Indian people themselves.

Nicholas Dirks offers a slightly different optic on the role of law in colonial society. While substantially agreeing with Washbrook's analysis, he goes on to suggest that colonial law performed a cultural function that has often been overlooked, providing, for example, the little kingdoms of south India, deprived of their political power, 'a structural replacement for politics' (1992: 200). Their participation in this alternative theatre of action, however, amounted to no more than 'rituals' since they 'created [culturally] significant, if ultimately *unreal* taxonomies of power and control' (ibid.: 191; emphasis added). While law may indeed have functioned as the site onto which the political ambitions of the *palaiyakarars* were displaced, and thereby neutralized, the effects of colonial law more generally in producing, not just containing, crises, and the substantial dislocations within the social space engendered by legal initiatives cannot be confined to a framework which assigns purely symbolic value to the law.

To the extent that certain pre-colonial legal regulations embedded in kin and community networks were gradually loosened and redefined (Chowdhry 1990),[13] an attempt was made to homogenize and codify theological aspects of Indian law (Derrett 1968), and 'adversarial' proceedings were introduced where dispute settlements through consensus had been the norm, the colonial state did not function as a neutral arbiter of ongoing social struggles, nor did colonial law assume merely symbolic functions.[14] To the extent that colonial law directly thwarted social mobility instead of

---

[13] The colonial 'creation' of customary law, Francis Snyder (1981) informs us, is now widely recognized in studies of African societies as well.

[14] See Baxi (1986: 14–15).

encouraging it,[15] homogenization was in effect a Brahmanization of Indian law at the expense of customary law (see, for example, Carroll 1989), and an invidious distinction was made and retained between the spheres of 'personal' and 'public' law, to the continuing detriment of women's rights within the family (Parashar 1992: 66),[16] colonial law could not be an unqualified instrument of 'modernity'. A high cultural Brahmanism, posturing as an antique, universal 'tradition', was thus thoroughly imbricated in the articulation of colonial modernity and, as we shall see, even received a fresh lease of life.[17]

Throughout this long struggle over the shape of the legal mechanism, between colonial authorities, indigenous elites, and subaltern classes, there was a persistent tension of balancing customary and traditional forms of conflict resolution, which sought reconciliation through compromise and consensus rather than adversary proceedings so characteristic of the 'rule of (state) law'. Since racial difference was at the very root of colonial rule, rather than abstract notions of legality, it is impossible to speak of a 'rule of law', especially when no more than 30 per cent of Indians were ever enfranchised, few Indians sat in legislatures, and different legal standards were applied to Europeans and Indians in India. In effect, the deployment of a 'rule of law' in a colonial setting was inevitably despotic, and by no means contained the liberatory promises of homogenization. The mid-nineteenth century decision to support the reform of Hindu or Muslim law only if the demand came from within the respective communities was merely an indication of this. Similarly, the virulent European response to the Ilbert Bill in 1883, which proposed to remove invidious distinctions between Indian and European judges, unmistakably revealed the racist underpinnings of colonial rule.

Not surprisingly, there were many contradictions between 'the individual freedoms supposedly supported by public law and the social constraints strongly imposed by the personal law' (Washbrook 1981: 657). Though they had profound implications for all layers of Indian society,

---

[15] See, for example, the Rudolphs' (1967: 40-3) discussion of the aspirations of the Shanans to legally effect a change in caste status and the colonial judicature's refusal to endorse such caste transgressions.

[16] Parashar (1992: 76) points out that despite this distinction, 'by the time India gained independence from English rule, the personal laws of different communities were labelled religious laws, but in some cases they were actually state enactments, while in others the contents of the rules had undergone substantial changes'.

[17] In contrast, Cohn (1989: 151) cites post-1864 law's reference to 'judicial precedence' to conclude that the English search for indigenous law finally ended up producing 'English Law as the law of India'.

the contradictions were especially pronounced in definitions of the rights of women. To the extent that codification of Indian law occurred at all, it held contradictory promises for Indian women: offering an escape from oppressive social practices on the one hand, while imposing a Brahmanic code that cut into certain customary privileges on the other. As the nineteenth century wore on, it became increasingly clear that one of the colonial state's preferred modes of seeking collaborators amongst Indians was to support and buttress Indian patriarchies, rather than rescue women from them. In turn, the Indian nationalist movement fiercely resisted change in the domestic domain, which began to be regarded as an uncolonized space, one that would be guarded against any colonial intrusion.

Yet, almost a third of the Indian subcontinent remained under indigenous rulers: princely states constituted a relatively autonomous domain where legislation aimed at transforming the familial structure could be passed without risking the opposition of the people. Not surprisingly, Baroda was the earliest state to introduce provisions for divorce; Mysore introduced, and took several measures to implement, an Infant Marriage Prevention Act as early as 1894, without the bitter debates that occurred in British India over the Age of Consent Act. A bill according rights to women under Hindu law, which extended property rights and granted maintenance, adoption, and related rights, became law with relatively little opposition in 1933, a full four years before even a partial bill was passed in the central legislature.

Even so, such changes occurred under the paramountcy of the British, and the princely states were by no means isolated from the broader currents sweeping across the Indian subcontinent. Thus, both Malabar, a part of the Madras Presidency, and Travancore, a princely state, introduced and passed broadly similar bills relating to the reform of matrilineal traditions in roughly the same period. The lack of commensurable laws created its own administrative problems since the princely state was unable to prevent the violation of its laws beyond its borders. It was not uncommon, for instance, for Mysoreans to cross over into Madras Presidency in order to perform the marriage of underage children, which was illegal in Mysore after 1894. More important, on no account would the colonial state admit to reciprocality of prosecution of laws since that would dilute the very concept of British paramountcy in India. Thus, the coffee planters of Mysore in the late nineteenth and early twentieth centuries complained bitterly about their inability to prosecute contractors and labourers, who had escaped into British India, under the Mysore Breach of Contract Act (see, for instance, Gustafson 1969: 270–4). The autonomy of the princely state was therefore severely circumscribed.

Throughout this period of change, the reconceptualization of Indian tradition was aligned with the 'modernizing' consequences of India's incorporation into the capitalist world system, although the trajectory of such 'modernization' was far from linear and unambiguous given the colonial and, therefore, dependent status of the country. The contradictory circumstances of colonial rule meant that figures like Ram Mohun Roy, Vidyasagar, and Keshab Chandra Sen, who have long been considered patriarchs of the Indian renaissance, were incompletely absorbed in the very bourgeois modernity they espoused.

The transition from 'tradition' to 'modernity' was by no means unilinear, nor were the terms unambiguously antithetical. In colonial India, 'tradition' and 'custom', whether of the scriptural kind or not, were hardly subordinated to the secular, impartial operation of a 'rule of law'. Instead, all too often, traditions were given a new lease of life within the 'modern' (in the purely technical sense) institutions of the Raj. Thus, the custom of *karewa* (widow remarriage) in Punjab was reinforced by the colonial state in order to ensure that property was not alienated by widows. Even as late as 1937, the colonial state thought fit to introduce legislation that made the Shariat the basis of Muslim personal law.

It is therefore no longer sufficient to view the weight of Indian tradition (whether of caste, community, or kinship) acting as a brake on the modernizing impulse of the British colonial state. Rather it is more important to mark the co-ordinates within which the accommodation, reinvention, or alteration of traditions took place in successive periods of British rule. A social history of law cannot content itself merely with abstract legal or sociological principles and their realization, but must engage with the multiplicity of levels at which colonial society was decisively transformed.

REFERENCES

Altekar, A.S. (1956), *The Position of Women in Hindu Civilisation*. Delhi: Motilal Banarasidass.

Appadurai, Arjun (1979), *Worship and Conflict under Colonial Rule: A South Indian Case*. Cambridge: Cambridge University Press.

Bagchi, A.K. (1988), 'Colonialism and the Nature of Capitalist Enterprise in India', *Economic and Political Weekly*, 23: 38–49.

Baxi, Upendra (1986), *Towards a Sociology of Indian Law*. New Delhi: Satvahan Publications.

Baxi, Upendra (1992), 'The State's Emissary: The Place of Law in Subaltern Studies', in Partha Chatterjee and Gyan Pandey (eds), *Subaltern Studies VII*. New Delhi: Oxford University Press, pp. 247–64.

Carroll, Lucy (1989), 'Law, Custom and Statutory Social Reform: The Hindu Widow's Remarriage Act of 1856', in J. Krishnamurty (ed.), *Women in Colonial India: Essays on Survival, Work and the State*. New Delhi: Oxford University Press, pp. 1–26.

Chakravarti, Uma (1990), 'Whatever Happened to the Vedic Dasi?', in Kumkum Sangari and Sudesh Vaid (eds), *Recasting Women: Essays in Indian Colonial History*. New Brunswick: Rutgers University Press, pp. 27–87.

Chatterjee, Partha (1993), *The Nation and Its Fragments: Colonial and Post Colonial Histories*. Princeton: Princeton University Press.

Chowdhry, Prem (1990), 'Customs in a Peasant Economy', in Sangari and Vaid (eds), *Recasting Women*, pp. 302–30.

Cohn, Bernard (1987a), 'Some Notes on Law and Change in North India', in *An Anthropologist Among the Historians and Other Essays*. New Delhi: Oxford University Press, pp. 554–74.

——— (1987b), 'Notes on Disputes and Law in India', *An Anthropologist Among the Historians and Other Essays*. New Delhi: Oxford University Press, pp. 575–631.

——— (1989), 'Law and the Colonial State in India', in June Starr and Jane F. Collier (eds), *History and Power in the Study of Law: New Directions in Legal Anthropology*. Ithaca: Cornell University Press, pp. 131–52.

Das, Rajani Kanta (1941), *History of Indian Labour Legislation*. Calcutta: University of Calcutta.

Derrett, J.D.M. (1968), *Religion, Law and the State in India*. London: Faber and Faber.

——— (1973), *Dharmasastra and Juridical Literature*. Wiesbaden: Harrassowitz.

Dirks, Nicholas (1992), 'From Little Kingdom to Landlord: Colonial Discourse and Colonial Rule', in N. Dirks (ed.), *Colonialism and Culture*. Ann Arbor: University of Michigan Press.

Embree, Ainslie (ed.) (1988), *Sources of Indian Tradition* (second edition), *Vol. 1*. New York: Columbia University Press.

Epstein, T. Scarlett (1962), *Economic Development and Social Change in South India*. Manchester: Manchester University Press.

Fawcett, Charles (1934), *The First Century of British Justice in India*. Oxford: Clarendon Press.

Guha, Ranajit (1981), *A Rule of Property in Bengal*. Delhi: Orient Longman.

——— (1987), 'Chandra's Death', in Ranajit Guha (ed.), *Subaltern Studies V*. New Delhi: Oxford University Press.

——— (1989), 'Dominance without Hegemony and Its Historiography', in Ranajit Guha (ed.), *Subaltern Studies VI: Writings on South Asian History and Society*. New Delhi: Oxford University Press, pp. 210–309.

Gustafson, D.R. (1969), 'Mysore, 1881–1902: The Making of a Model State', PhD dissertation, University of Wisconsin.

Halhed, Nathaniel B. (1776), *A Code of Gentoo Laws*. Fort William.

Hutchins, Francis (1967), *The Illusion of Permanence*. Princeton: Princeton University Press.
Jain, M.P. (1987), *Outlines of Indian Legal History*. Bombay: Tripathi.
Jones, William *et al.* (1792), Dissertations and Miscellaneous Pieces Relating to the History and Antiquities, the Arts, Sciences and Literature of Asia, I. London: G. Nichol.
Kane, P.V. (1946), *History of Dharmashastra III*. Poona: Bhandarkar Oriental Research Institute.
Kopf, David (1969), *British Orientalism and the Bengal Renaissance, 1773-1835*. Berkeley: University of California Press.
Lingat, Robert (1973), *The Classical Law of India* (translated with additions by J.D.M. Derrett). Delhi: Thompson Press.
Mahmood, Tahir (1983), *Muslim Personal Law*. Nagpur: All India Reporter.
Mani, Lata (1986), 'Production of an Official Discourse on Sati in Nineteenth Century Bengal', *Economic and Political Weekly*, 26 April, 21(17).
Marx, Karl (1973), *Grundnsse: An Introduction to the Critique of Political Economy*. Harmohdsworth: Penguin Books.
Mendelsohn, Oliver (1981), 'The Pathology of the Indian Legal System', *Modern Asian Studies*, 15(4): 823-63.
Mill, James (1840), *The History of British India* (with notes by H.H. Wilson, 5th edition). London: James Madden.
Parashar, Archana (1992), *Women and Family Law Reform in India*. New Delhi: Sage Publications.
Presler, Franklin (1987), *Religion under Bureaucracy: Policy and Administrations for Hindu Temples in South India*. Cambridge: Cambridge University Press.
Punekar, S.D. and R. Varickayil (1989), *Labour Movement in India: Documents 1850-1890*. Delhi: ICHR.
Rudolph, Lloyd and Susan Rudolph (1967), *The Modernity of Tradition: Political Development in India*. Chicago: University of Chicago Press.
Said, Edward (1978), *Orientalism*. New York: Penguin Books.
Snyder, Francis (1981), 'Colonialism and Legal Form: The Creation of Customary Law in Senegal', *Journal of Legal Pluralism*, 9: 49-79.
Som, Reba (1994), 'Jawaharlal Nehru and the Hindu Code Bill: A Victory of Symbol Over Substance', *Modern Asian Studies*, 28(1): 165-94.
Thapar, Romila (1975), *The Past and Prejudice*. New Delhi: National Book Trust of India.
Thompson, E.P. (1993), 'Custom, Law and Common Rights', in *Customs in Common: Studies in Traditional Popular Culture*. New York: The New Press.
Viswanathan, Gowri (1990), *Masks of Conquest*. New York: Columbia.
Washbrook, D.A. (1981), 'Law, State and Agrarian Society in Colonial India', *Modern Asian Studies*, 15(3): 649-721.

Chapter 2

CONJUGALITY, PROPERTY, MORALITY, AND MAINTENANCE

FLAVIA AGNES

THIS CHAPTER EXAMINES THE ECONOMIC RIGHTS of married women in India today. The four basic concepts that are invoked to determine the economic entitlements of women at the time of divorce are 'title', 'fault', 'need', and 'contribution'.

Matrimonial laws of most countries have adopted the principle of 'division of matrimonial property' at the time of divorce, which abandons the concepts of 'title', 'fault', and 'need', and relies primarily upon 'contribution'. It takes into consideration a woman's non-economic contribution in acquiring assets during a marriage. In India, we lag far behind in this respect and still follow the old English system of 'separation of property' (rather than the more contemporary 'division of matrimonial property') where rights are based on 'title' or, at the most, upon economic contribution. Within these constraints, a woman's economic rights revolve around the right of maintenance, the granting of which is premised on her assessed 'need' and 'fault'. Since this is the only provision for economic claims within marriage, it is highly contested and a wide range of issues surface during legal contests. The important ingredients are the husband's 'obligation' and the wife's 'need', but situated within a patriarchal order, the right of maintenance is pitted against issues of sexuality and 'sexual purity'.

Within pluralistic traditions and customary practices which validate 'relationships in the nature of marriage', the right of maintenance comes into conflict within the mandate of a monogamous marriage under the Hindu Marriage Act. The rights of Muslim women, which are governed by a different set of rules and which have raised several controversies, have also been a matter of concern and heated debate. The claims of women as they are situated within these diverse premises are examined here.

CONJUGALITY AND MATRIMONIAL PROPERTY

When we examine the economic entitlements which arise out of a matrimonial relationship, we are confronted with a glaring void within the Indian matrimonial statutes which do not provide for division of property upon divorce. Thus, fear of poverty, destitution, or a lowering of economic standards haunts most women during divorce proceedings. As we shall see, dominant gender ideologies shape the extent to which women are punished or rewarded within these proceedings.

The husband is perceived as the primary 'breadwinner' of the family, and in order to facilitate this status, a woman is expected to sacrifice her career and dedicate herself completely to the task of looking after the well-being of her husband. Within the prevalent patrilocal tradition, marriage also results in migration for women, which in turn may necessitate resignation from a permanent job. A woman is also expected to be the homemaker with the additional responsibilities of child bearing and child rearing. In order to fulfil these obligations, most women may have to opt out of a secure job either permanently or for a limited number of years until these demands become less taxing. Even when she is required or permitted to be gainfully employed, it is mainly to augment the family income, and her earnings are treated as supplementary income of the family.

There are instances wherein the courts have penalized a woman for pursuing her career at the cost of her primary role as the caretaker of the family, as this act in itself can be construed as cruelty, which is a ground for divorce.[1] At times the choice for women seems to be to either remain married or hold on to the job. This is a concern confined not only to the private domain of marriage and family, but spills over to the public domain

---

[1] See the ruling in Suman Kapur vs Sudhir Kapur II (2008) DMC 774 SC (Supreme Court), where the Supreme Court held that pursuing a career and neglecting the family amounts to cruelty on the part of the wife.

of employment, where women were expected to tender their resignation at the time of their marriage or during their first pregnancy.[2] Though the situation has improved considerably in recent years in the public sector, within the private sector, employers may still force women to resign rather than pay them maternity benefits or provide crèche facilities. There is constant tension between the dual roles of a woman as the homemaker and wage-earner which correspond to the sharply divided 'private' and 'public' spheres of her life. It requires a fine balancing act to cope with both. This tension is specific to women and is linked to their assigned roles within marriage; men are spared these tensions as the primary breadwinners of the family.

Ironically, a woman's role as a homemaker has no economic value attached to it. Women's contribution to the domestic household during the subsistence of their marriage does not get any recognition under the matrimonial statutes. India follows the common law regime of 'separation of property'. Under this notion, property acquired by the husband is treated as his exclusive property. A wife does not acquire any right, title, or interest in the assets acquired by the husband during the subsistence of the marriage. Since marriage is not viewed as an 'economic partnership', a woman is not entitled to claim division of property at the time of divorce. Her contribution in creating these assets by performing domestic chores is not considered to be a relevant factor.

If the husband dies intestate, the widow is awarded a status no higher than that of the children, thus completely ignoring her contribution to the household and family in the form of unpaid work. She is treated as a 'beneficiary' and can be willed out of his estate, in the event the husband so desires. The only provision under the matrimonial statutes which addresses the issue of property division, S.27 of the Hindu Marriage Act (HMA), 1955, is clad in quaint and obscure language—'property presented on or about the time of marriage which may belong jointly to both the husband and the wife'. Hence, some courts have held that property acquired subsequent to marriage by the spouses through their own and which they hold jointly would not fall within the purview of S.27 of HMA. In Kamalakar Ganesh Sambhus vs Master Tejas Kamalakar Sambhus,[3] even though the wife established that she had contributed half the amount

---

[2] Even public sector undertakings followed this policy, which was challenged in the landmark case Air India vs Nergesh Meerza, All India Reporter (AIR) 1981 SC 1829, which is popularly known as the airhostess case. The policy has now been changed and airhostesses do not need to resign at the time of their marriage or first pregnancy.

[3] AIR 2004 Bombay 478.

towards the construction of the house property, the Bombay High Court held that this could not be the subject matter of an order under S.27 HMA and set aside the order of the family court on these grounds.⁴ A woman can claim a share in property which is purchased in the spouses' joint names as per the rules governing general property laws which foreground economic contributions.

The right of residence in the matrimonial home is protected by the recently enacted Protection of Women from Domestic Violence Act (PWDVA), 2005. While this is an important development, it does not provide any solace to a woman who wishes to opt out of marriage. There are no concepts such as a 'deserted wife's equity' or 'constructive trust' which are important premises of English matrimonial law. By introducing these innovative concepts, in the absence of a statutory law, an English jurist, Lord M.R. Denning, was able to protect deserted wives' rights of residence in their matrimonial homes. In a series of cases ranging from the 1940s to the 1970s, he was able to protect the rights of deserted wives not only against their husbands but also against their creditors.

For instance, in 1962 in Hine vs Hine, Denning ruled that family property had to be treated differently from other forms of property and that the judge had the discretionary power to reallocate property rights between the parties.⁵ The discretion transcends all rights, legal and equitable, and enables the court to make such an order as may be fair and just. In National Provincial Bank Ltd. vs Ainsworth, he held that the bank could not claim possession against the wife who was in possession of the matrimonial home.⁶ He ruled that since the wife has a right to remain in the matrimonial home by the notion of constructive trust, it is unlawful for the husband to enter into any agreement designed to turn her out.

Under the Indian statutes, divorced women are not protected from eviction by landlords. A Supreme Court ruling, B.P. Achala Anand vs S. Appi Reddy, makes this amply clear, despite its positive proclamations.⁷ In this judgement delivered in 2004, the judiciary broke new grounds by invoking the English concept of 'deserted wife's equity', and awarded legal recognition to the woman's right of residence by placing her in the

---

⁴ But after the Supreme Court ruling in 2004 in B.P. Achala Anand vs S. Appi Reddy I (2005) DMC 345 SC (discussed later), the situation seems to have substantially changed and it is now possible to claim division of joint property acquired subsequent to the marriage during matrimonial proceedings.

⁵ 3 All ER (All England Reporter) 345 at 347 F.

⁶ [1965] 2 All ER 472, HL (House of Lords).

⁷ I (2005) DMC 345 SC.

position of a sub-tenant. It was held that she had a right to defend herself in proceedings initiated by the landlord for eviction which would deprive her of the right of possession of the matrimonial home. The court also expanded the scope of S.27 HMA and ruled that this section could be invoked to pass orders regarding the separate property of the parties or even the tenanted premises. The decision amounted to judicial law-making and the court emphasized that it was using this power while responding to the demands of social and gender justice in order to 'do complete justice'. But all these proclamations did not benefit the woman concerned as she had already been divorced while the case was pending. Since the terms of divorce settlement did not contain a provision regarding the dwelling home, the apex court ruled that she had no right to the matrimonial home.

The Supreme Court affirmed this position in Ruma Chakraborty vs Sudha Rani Banerji, where a divorced woman and her children were evicted from their home that was rented in the husband's name, on the pretext that their right of tenancy was terminated with the divorce since this right was not negotiated during the divorce.[8] The apex court held that although the right to matrimonial home exists for a deserted woman, the same could not be extended to a divorced woman.

The trend followed by most countries runs counter to the position adopted by the Supreme Court in the cases discussed earlier. The Continental law or the civil law of Europe, introduced in the nineteenth century, is based on the premise of 'community of property'. Under this, upon marriage, the property of the spouses acquired after marriage is deemed as the joint property of the spouses, with equal powers of maintenance, management, improvement, and disposal. Upon divorce, the property is divided equally between the spouses. Most countries which had followed the common law tradition of 'separation of property', inherited from the English legal system during colonial rule, have gradually accepted the premise of 'differed community of property'. According to this, the property remains separate until divorce, with spouses having the power to manage their respective property. But upon divorce, the property acquired during marriage is deemed as 'matrimonial property' and becomes divisible on an equal basis, irrespective of title or financial contribution. The legal frameworks in the United States, Canada, Australia, and New Zealand provide examples of this shift which occurred in the 1970s when 'no fault' divorce was introduced into the matrimonial laws. English matrimonial law has also adopted this premise. While the courts initially

---

[8] AIR 2005 SC 3557.

started by awarding one-third of the assets to the wife, the principle of equal distribution is gradually being accepted under the English law.

As per the 'no fault' notion, divorce can be granted on the basis of 'breakdown of marriage' even when the other spouse is not guilty of a matrimonial fault such as cruelty, adultery, or desertion. As this concept would cause great economic hardships to innocent wives,[9] it was deemed necessary to introduce the notion of division of property.

Countries such as Singapore, Malaysia, Iran, Fiji, and Tanzania have adopted the system of division of property, or at least give recognition to a woman's unpaid domestic labour in the division. In this regard, India (and South Asia as a whole) lags far behind. Thus, while there have been attempts to introduce the notion of 'no fault' divorce through judge-mandated laws, there has not been any attempt to introduce division of property.[10] In this context, it is notable that the Law Commission Report No. 217 (March 2009), which recommends the introduction of 'no fault' divorce, contains no suggestion regarding division of property during divorce proceedings. The recommendation appears to have been made in response to popular demands, without serious attention to the potentially adverse consequences it would have upon women who have not committed any matrimonial fault that would entitle a husband to obtain a divorce.

In the Indian context, despite its derogatory connotations, the discussion on economic rights of married women must be situated within the notion of 'maintenance' as it remains the only avenue for women to stake their claim of financial entitlement upon divorce. Within Indian family law, women's economic claims arising out of a marriage contract are confined to recurring monthly maintenance or a lump sum settlement or alimony at the time of divorce. Many times, settlements are negotiated through the process of mediation. During these proceedings, if the husband is desperate to obtain a quick divorce (in order to remarry), then the wife does get some bargaining power to negotiate favourable financial settlements. But on the other hand, the husband is able to twist the arm of the wife by

---

[9] This term was used in the context of 'matrimonial guilt' or 'fault', which would entitle the other spouse to obtain a divorce. If the spouse is 'innocent', it was presumed that divorce would not be granted to the other spouse. Divorce was viewed more as a punishment for matrimonial guilt.

[10] See the Supreme Court rulings in V. Bhagat vs D. Bhagat AIR 1994 SC 710 and Romesh Chander vs Savitri I (1995) DMC 231 SC.

pressing for joint child custody or increased rights of access to the child. Afraid of the adverse consequences of such an arrangement, the wife may forego financial claims in order to negotiate exclusive custody of the child or limited access rights to the husband.

CONSTITUTIONAL CLAIMS AND MAINTENANCE RIGHTS

As a women's rights lawyer, I am often confronted with a provocative question—within the gender-neutral language of matrimonial laws, which refers to the 'husband' and 'wife' as 'spouses', how do we locate the specific claim of women to maintenance? I concede that 'maintenance' signifies a dependency which has no place in the gender-neutral terminology of modern divorce theories. It is a need-based approach which reduces the wife to a subordinate position and does not award recognition to her as an equal partner in marriage. We must also accept that despite the egalitarian terminology, marriages continue to be partnerships based on unequal premises. The roles, responsibilities, and obligations within marriage are gendered and unequal. A mere change of terminology does not transform relationships of inequality into egalitarian and equal partnerships. As per the constitutional mandate, equality can only be between equals. Treating unequals as equals only serves to widen the disparity between the two parties.

The provision of maintenance is crucial to women who are in difficult marriages and to deserted and destitute women. Although maintenance can be claimed under the personal laws of the parties, most poor and destitute women opt to claim it under the summary proceedings available under S.125 of the Criminal Procedure Code, 1973 (CrPC). This provision is a beneficial social legislation to prevent vagrancy and delinquency.

The right of a woman to maintenance needs to be located within citizenship claims enshrined in the Constitution. It is grounded within the constitutional paradigm of ensuring social justice and is reflective of a social obligation which the state casts upon economically stronger members of the family to provide shelter and sustenance to the 'weaker' members, that is, women, children, the elderly, and the disabled. The provision for additional safeguards and special privileges for disadvantaged groups is grounded in Article 15(3) of the Indian Constitution. This was affirmed by the Supreme Court in Captain Ramesh Chandra Kaushal vs Veena Kaushal in which the court commented that S.125 CrPC, which is specially enacted to protect women and children, falls within the constitutional ambit of Article 15(3).[11]

Within the patriarchal paradigm of marriage, as discussed earlier, for a vast majority of women, marriage results in economic dependency. It is in this context that statutory law and judicial interpretations must lean in favour of destitute women and vulnerable children by moving away from the rubric of formal equality of Article 14 towards substantive equality guaranteed under Article 15(3) in order to set right a historical wrong. For most women, the right of maintenance forms the central core of their matrimonial dispute. It is far easier to come to an amicable settlement regarding divorce and custody while maintenance remains a contested question.

MAINTENANCE AND MORALITY

Securing an order of adequate maintenance can be an extremely humiliating experience for women, as there is a high quotient of sexual morality that engulfs the question of maintenance. Curiously, the core of what should be an economic dispute does not revolve around questions of financial arrangements of the family unit, but hinges upon issues of sexual mores. In the context of unequal power relations prevailing within marriages, women's economic rights are determined within these codes. The morality dictates of a patriarchal marriage are deeply entangled with the economic claims.

Allegations of adultery and immorality can constantly be hurled against women. This can extend further to a denial of the marriage itself and, consequentially, the legitimacy and even paternity of children. Stipulations such as those contained in clauses 4 and 5 of S.125 of CrPC also contribute by linking maintenance to sexual morality:

(4) No woman shall be entitled to receive an allowance if she is living in adultery.
(5) On proof that any wife whose favor an order has been made under this section is living in adultery...the magistrate shall cancel the order.

This stipulation provides the armour for husbands to entangle women in vicious and dilatory litigation over what may be a pittance. A careful

[11] AIR 1978 SC 1807.

scrutiny of reported cases in any law journal reveals the extent to which allegations of sexual promiscuity are made to subvert women's claims. To give an example, *Divorce and Matrimonial Cases* (*DMC*), a popular journal widely relied upon by lawyers practising matrimonial law, reported in Volume I of 2001 approximately 45 cases under the title 'Maintenance'. In almost half of these cases, sexuality and morality were the core issues that were contested. This challenge on the ground of sexual purity entangles them in protracted litigation despite S.125 CrPC being a summary proceedings.[12]

The cases reported in law journals constitute only the tip of the iceberg since they have survived a first round of litigation in the trial courts and were appealed in the higher courts, and only thereafter merited reporting in the law journal. In each of these cases, the women were assaulted and driven out of the matrimonial home. Most of these cases also contained allegations of dowry harassment. But none of these women had filed a criminal complaint under S.498A (cruelty to wives) of the Indian Penal Code. All they did was file an application for maintenance, and it is then that the husbands lashed out with allegations of sexual promiscuity.

The layered and multiple contexts through which sexual morality surfaces, as per the norms of patriarchy, serve only one end: to challenge the legitimacy of women's claims. Scanning through the judgements, one can see a positive trend emerging, where the courts have upheld the women's claims and disallowed the husbands' contentions. But despite this change, clauses 4 and 5 of S.125, CrPC, provide the scope for husbands to engage destitute and deserted women in protracted and humiliating litigation. The false and frivolous interventions entangle women in circuitous legal rigmaroles which are time consuming, financially draining, and emotionally charged.

CONCUBINES, MISTRESSES, AND MAINTENANCE

Hindu marriages were rendered monogamous by the enactment of the Hindu Marriage Act in 1955. But husbands can flout this mandate of monogamy with impunity. To add insult to injury, during litigation, the fact of a bigamous marriage can be used as armour to defeat women's

---

[12] The term 'summary proceedings' indicates that the court is not required to conduct a full-length trial with lengthy cross-examinations and the case can be decided after arguments and examining documents. Under S.125 CrPC, it is not required to prove the marriage.

claims. In other words, a husband may claim that since the litigant is a second wife, his marriage to her is not legally binding, and hence he is not obligated to pay her maintenance. This plea is advanced so routinely that the Supreme Court in Vimala vs Veeraswamy[13] was constrained to hold that when a husband pleads that the marriage is bigamous, the previous marriage would have to be strictly proved. In a similar manner, the Bombay High Court dismissed the plea of bigamous marriage in Rajlingu vs Sayamabai[14] as a mere afterthought. This leaves us perplexed as to how matrimonial misconduct or 'guilt' can be flagrantly invoked by a husband to defeat the woman's economic claim, without any adverse criminal or civil consequences for him during court proceedings. This flouting of a legal mandate and its subsequent invocation to gain financial edge against a vulnerable person can take place only within a blatantly sexist social order.

Despite some progressive interpretations and innovative legal maxims, the path to justice has not progressed in a linear trajectory. There is a great deal of judicial latitude which allows contradictory verdicts to emerge on the same issue, not just between various high courts but also within the same court. For example, in a ruling in the Bombay High Court on the rights of a woman in a bigamous marriage, in 1976, Justice M.H. Kania held that since the Hindu Marriage Act is a social legislation, it could not have been the intention of the legislature that even in a case where a Hindu woman was duped into contracting a bigamous marriage, she should be deprived of her right to claim maintenance.[15]

Similarly, in a leading case, Vimala vs Veeraswamy,[16] the Supreme Court held:

> S.125 CrPC is meant to achieve a social purpose. The objective is to prevent vagrancy and destitution. When an attempt is made by the husband to negate the claim of the neglected wife by depicting her as a kept mistress on the plea that he was already married, the court insists on strict proof of the earlier marriage. A provision in the law which disentitles the second wife from receiving maintenance from her husband, for the sole reason that the marriage ceremony, though performed in the customary form, lacks legal sanctity, can be applied only when the husband satisfactorily proves the subsistence of a legal and valid marriage. This is so particularly when S.125 CrPC is a measure of social justice intended to protect women and children. In the absence of clear proof that the respondent is living with another woman as husband and wife, the court cannot be persuaded to hold that the marriage duly solemnised suffers from any legal infirmity.

---

[13] (1991) 2 SCC (Supreme Court Cases) 375.
[14] I (2007) DMC 396 Bombay.
[15] Govindrao vs Anandibai AIR 1976 Bombay 433.
[16] (1991) 2 SCC 375.

In a landmark ruling in 2004, Rameshchandra Daga vs Rameshwari Daga,[17] the Supreme Court upheld the maintenance rights of another woman in a similar situation. The ruling was delivered in an appeal filed by the husband against the judgement of the Bombay High Court. The husband, a widower, had married Rameshwari who had obtained a customary divorce (*chor chittee*) through a divorce deed. The wife alleged that this document was shown to the husband prior to the marriage and he had accepted its validity. Later, when disputes arose and the wife was driven out of the matrimonial home, she filed for judicial separation and claimed maintenance. During these proceedings, the husband denied the marriage on the ground that the woman had not been formally divorced. Rejecting the plea, both the Family Court at Mumbai as well as the High Court had upheld the wife's and her daughter's right of maintenance. In the final verdict, the Supreme Court upheld the woman's plea that the husband, an advocate, was aware of the customary divorce at the time of his marriage. The court went further and chastised him for denying the paternity of his daughter.

'The facts of this case tell the tragic tale of an Indian woman, who having gone through two marriages with a child born to her, apprehends destitution as both marriages have broken down', the judges commented with a note of compassion.[18] The Supreme Court appears to have accepted that Hindu marriages, like Muslim marriages, were bigamous prior to the 1955 enactment. There is also a tacit acceptance that the ground reality has not changed much since the enactment. So, though such marriages are illegal as per the statutory provisions of the codified Hindu law, the Supreme Court has ruled that they are not 'immoral' and hence a financially dependent woman cannot be denied maintenance on this ground.

In stark contrast is the Supreme Court ruling of 2005 in Savitaben Somabhai Bhatiya vs State of Gujarat.[19] Justice Arijit Pasayat and Justice S.H. Kapadia commented that however desirable it may be to take note of the plight of the unfortunate woman, the legislative intent being clearly reflected in S.125 CrPC, there is no scope for enlarging it by introducing any artificial definition to include woman not lawfully married in the expression 'wife'. The court further commented that it is inconsequential that the man was treating the woman as his wife. It is the intention of the legislation which is relevant and not the attitude of the party.

---

[17] I (2005) DMC 1 SC.
[18] Rameshchandra Daga vs Rameshwari Daga, I (2005) DMC 1 SC.
[19] AIR 2005 SC 1809: I (2005) DMC 503 SC.

A judgement of the Allahabad High Court conveys the extent of humiliation a woman goes through during such litigation:

> If the man and woman choose to live together and indulge into [sic] sex, no marital status can be conferred automatically by their so living upon such a woman. She is not entitled to the legal status of a wife in the eyes of law and society. Law and society treat such women either as concubine or a mistress....The two may agree to live together to satisfy their animal needs. But such a union is never called a marriage. A woman leading such a life cannot be bestowed with the sacrosanct honor of wife. No marital obligations accrue to such a woman against her husband. Such a wife must be termed as an adulteress.[20]

While comments about the high moral standard may appear salutary, it does seem that the price for immorality is to be paid only by the woman, while the man is left free to exploit both women.

PLURALISTIC TRADITIONS AND HARMONIOUS CONSTRUCTIONS

The advantage of the mandate of 'legal monogamy' lies with the husband as he can escape from the economic liability of maintaining his wife on the plea that the marriage suffered from a legal defect or lacked legal sanctity. Since ancient Hindu law and customary practices validated the institution of concubinage, even in present times, the plea that the woman concerned is a 'concubine' or 'mistress' and not the 'wife' can be advanced with ease in legal arguments, as can be observed from the various rulings discussed earlier. The volume of case law on the subject exemplifies the fact that husbands have taken undue advantage and grossly misappropriated this mandate. An oft-invoked legal ploy is to term the woman the domestic maid or a mistress and not the 'wife' with rights and entitlements.

After the Supreme Court ruling in Rameshchandra Daga vs Rameshwari Daga, it appeared that it would no longer be possible for a Hindu husband to escape from his liability of maintaining his wife on the plea that the wife is not formally divorced from her previous husband or on the plea that the woman is his concubine since his own previous marriage is still subsisting. But the subsequent ruling in Savitaben Somabhai Bhatiya vs State of Gujarat has again rendered the situation ambiguous.

In this context, two recent judgements by the Delhi High Court, in 2008 bear scrutiny. These judicial pronouncements have attempted to cross the stumbling block posed by the stipulation of monogamy under S.5 of the

---

[20] Malti vs State of Uttar Pradesh I (2001) DMC 104 Allahabad.

HMA by invoking innovative legal maxims to protect the rights of women. In the first case, Suresh Khullar vs Vijay Kumar Khullar,[21] the husband's first marriage was dissolved by a court of law while contracting the present marriage. The wife was innocent and oblivious of the fraudulent circumstances under which the husband had obtained an ex-parte decree of divorce against his first wife. After a few months of her marriage, the subsequent wife, Suresh, was driven out of the matrimonial home. Thereafter, the husband's ex-parte decree of divorce from the first marriage was set aside on the ground of fraud and, through this legal incident, Suresh Khullar's marriage was rendered bigamous and invalid. She filed a suit for damages against the husband and his first wife on the ground of fraud and cheating, which was decreed by a civil judge. While upholding the right of the woman, with respect to S.18 of the Hindu Adoption and Maintenance Act (HAMA), 1956, the court held that while interpreting a statute, the courts may not only take into consideration the purpose for which the statute was enacted, but also the mischief it seeks to suppress. The court invoked the legal maxim *construction ut res magis valeat quam pereat*, that is, where alternative constructions are possible, the Court must give effect to that which will be responsible for the smooth working of the system for which the statute has been enacted rather than one which will put a road block in its way. The court commented that if this interpretation is not accepted, it would amount to giving a premium to the husband for defrauding the wife. Therefore, it was held that for the purpose of claiming maintenance under S.18 of HAMA, the woman should be treated as the legally wedded wife.

The second ruling was pronounced in Narinder Pal Kaur Chawla vs Manjeet Singh Chawla.[22] The wife had approached the court for maintenance under S.18 of HAMA in 1997 and pleaded that her husband had duped her by suppressing his earlier marriage. The couple had lived together for 14 years and had two daughters. The husband pleaded that since his earlier marriage was valid and subsisting, his marriage with Narinder Pal Kaur was void. After a prolonged and contentious litigation, she was able to secure an order of interim maintenance of Rs 1,500 per month. But when the case was finally decided in 2005, the trial court dismissed her petition on the ground that she could not be treated as a 'Hindu wife' under S.18 of HAMA as she did not have the status of a legally wedded wife. In appeal, the Delhi High Court upheld the right of the wife

---

[21] I (2008) DMC 719 Delhi.
[22] I (2008) DMC 529 Delhi.

and maintained that even if the woman cannot be treated as a 'Hindu wife', she is entitled to a lump settlement by way of damages.

It appears that women who were deprived of their status and rights through the mandate of monogamy introduced by the HMA of 1955 had to suffer for 50 years before some recognition could be awarded to them. The PWDVA, 2005, does bestow some social status and legal rights on women who were once part of a prevailing social system and yet legally could be branded concubines or mistresses, transforming the concubines of yesteryear into present-day cohabitees. Their right to protection from domestic violence and rights of maintenance and residence have been awarded statutory recognition. While some may dismiss the term cohabitee as a Western or urban phenomenon, this term can now be invoked to protect the rights of thousands of women, both urban and rural, who were earlier scoffed at as 'mistresses' or 'keeps' in judicial discourse because of some technical defect in their marriage. The PWDVA does not clearly prescribe whether the new term 'cohabitee' will safeguard the rights of women who were earlier denigrated as concubines and mistresses. That is left for judicial interpretation. But it does help to bring the debate to a new plane.

ECONOMIC ENTITLEMENTS OF MUSLIM WOMEN

The economic rights of Muslim women at divorce have taken a very different trajectory as compared to other matrimonial laws. This is because under Christian and Hindu traditions, marriage was viewed as an indissoluble sacrament, while Muslim law, from its origin, viewed marriages as contractual and dissoluble.[23] The notion of a life-long dependency, which is linked to the notion of marriage permanence, has no place within Islamic jurisprudence. The right of maintenance is therefore confined to the period of the marriage. Even the codified statute, the Dissolution of Muslim Marriages Act of 1939, did not contain any provision for post-divorce maintenance.

Within this context, the economic rights of Muslim women are confined to *mehr*, which is a Quranic right. This is a unique feature of Muslim law which is not found in any other matrimonial statute. The husband is

---

[23] Subsequently, this concept was incorporated into French civil law in 1800, which rendered Christian marriages dissoluble. Later, in 1857, English family law accepted this principle. It was adopted by Hindu law in 1955 when the HMA was enacted.

bound to assure an amount as a mark of respect to the wife at the time of marriage, which provides a future security for her. The mehr stipulation forms part of the marriage contract and is an essential ingredient of a Muslim marriage. While other laws presume that the husband will provide for the wife, under Muslim law, the husband is bound to make a covenant or a contractual agreement to this effect. Mehr is viewed as a debt and an obligation of the husband towards his wife, and it can be enforced in a court of law. Mehr can either be prompt (payable upon consummation of marriage) or deferred, payable on demand during the marriage or, in any case, upon its dissolution. The high amount of mehr stipulated in the *nikahnama* was meant to act as a deterrent to unilateral and arbitrary divorce because the husband would then be obliged to settle his mehr dues to the wife. Under Shariat law, the woman has a charge over her husband's property for the payment of her mehr, even after his death.

In post-independence India, mehr has been reduced to a token amount in most Muslim communities. The protection offered by this provision has been corroded and, instead, many communities have accepted the Hindu custom of dowry; hence, mehr has ceased to be a future security or a deterrent against arbitrary divorce. But the fact that mehr amounts were high can be ascertained from the cases reported in law journals during the pre-independence period among the affluent Muslim families. The legal precedents also indicate that the rights of mehr and pre-marriage agreements (which are recognized under Muslim law but not under Hindu or other matrimonial laws) were not illusory but secured viable economic safeguards to women. A large number of Muslim women seem to have approached the British courts for enforcement of the contractual obligation of mehr.[24]

But during the post-independence period, when mehr amounts became illusory, the husbands' use of the provision of arbitrary triple talaq led women to face great hardships as they were not entitled to post-divorce maintenance. When a deserted Muslim wife approached the court for maintenance under S.125 CrPC, which is a secular provision uniformly applicable to all women, the husbands would pronounce talaq during the course of the litigation. Thereafter they would argue that their obligation towards the wife ended upon payment of the customary right of mehr and that they had no further obligation to maintain their wives.

In order to deal with this problem, when the CrPC was amended in 1973, an explanation of the word 'wife' was provided to include 'ex-wife' under

---

[24] For a detailed discussion on this issue, see Agnes (1996: 2832).

S.125 of CrPC. So even after the talaq, the courts could order maintenance to the wife under S.125 of CrPC, unless the wife had received a substantial amount as mehr, which would prevent her from destitution. Two historical rulings by the Supreme Court pronounced by Justice Krishna Iyer in 1979 and 1980 confirmed this view without creating a Muslim backlash.[25] It was held that an illusory amount under customary or personal law does not absolve a husband from the purview of this beneficial provision. In a subsequent judgement of the Supreme Court, pronounced in 1981 by Justice Murtaza Fazal Ali, it was held that the court is not bound to cancel the order of maintenance on payment of mehr.[26]

But the Shahbano judgement pronounced by a Constitutional Bench headed by Chief Justice Chandrachud in 1985, while upholding the right of a divorced Muslim woman, made certain adverse comments against Islam and also urged the state to enact a uniform civil code.[27] It must be remembered that the enactment of a compulsory civil code had been a contentious issue for the Muslim community even during the Constitutional Assembly Debates in 1947–9. It was seen as an attempt to enforce Hindu law upon an insecure Muslim minority, and hence was placed in the Directive Principles of State Policy, to be enacted when the Muslim community would feel secure enough within secular India to accept a uniform civil code.[28] Against this background, the judgement led to a backlash, with the Muslim orthodoxy demanding the exclusion of divorced Muslim women from the purview of S.125 CrPC and a separate statute that would be based on Islamic jurisprudence.

Relenting under the political pressure exerted by the Muslim religious leadership, the ruling Congress, headed by the then-Prime Minister Rajiv Gandhi, enacted the Muslim Women (Protection of Rights on Divorce) Act (hereafter the Muslim Women's Act or MWA), 1986. Through this enactment, the right of a divorced Muslim woman was taken out of the purview of the general law of maintenance under S.125 of the CrPC and placed under this new legislation.

This statute came to be viewed by secular and women's rights groups as the most glaring defeat of gender justice for Indian women as well as of secular principles within the Indian polity. It seemed that the Act would

---

[25] Bai Tahira vs Ali Hussain Fiddali Chothia AIR 1979 SC 362; and Fuzlunbi vs K. Khadir Vali AIR 1980 SC 1730.

[26] Zohra Khatoun vs Mohd Ibrahim AIR 1981 SC 1243.

[27] Mohd Ahmed Khan vs Shah Bano Begam AIR 1985 SC 945.

[28] But this did not happen. On the contrary, the situation has only gone from bad to worse for minority communities—both Muslims and Christians.

deprive divorced Muslim women of the rights granted under a secular provision, S.125 CrPC, on the basis of religion alone and thus violate the constitutional mandate of equality. The Act was a departure from the Directive Principle enshrined in Article 44 of the Indian Constitution: 'the state shall endeavour to enact a Uniform Civil Code'. The right-wing political parties such as the Bharatiya Janata Party (BJP) and the Shiv Sena used this incident to whip up anti-Muslim communal hysteria which later resulted in the demolition of the Babri Masjid in 1992 and communal riots in the country. It was projected that the partisan attitude of the ruling Congress was the cause of the anti-Muslim sentiments in the country.[29]

After the enactment, several women's rights and human rights groups filed writ petitions in the Supreme Court, challenging the constitutional validity of the Act. While the writ petitions were pending, several high courts began to interpret the Act innovatively and in women's favour. They held that a divorced Muslim woman has the right to a 'fair and reasonable settlement' for her lifetime, *in addition* to maintenance during the *iddat* period.[30] Further, the courts commented that a fair and reasonable provision for the woman's future needs (*mataaoon bil ma'aroofe*) is a Quranic injunction.

The high courts of Gujarat and Kerala were among the first to herald the new tidings. They affirmed that the new Act was to *protect* the rights of divorced Muslim women and not to *deprive* them of their rights. They further stressed that any ambiguity within its clauses must be interpreted in such a manner as to reconcile with the proclamation contained in the title of the Act, that is, an Act for the protection of divorced Muslim women. Banishing divorced women to a life of destitution would not amount to protecting their rights as stipulated by the statute, they declared.

The first significant judgement on this issue was pronounced by the Gujarat High Court on 18 February 1988, within a year-and-a-half of the enactment. But even before this, the dice were cast in women's favour

---

[29] Later there were also similar communal riots in many parts of the country, and the worst riot was in Gujarat during February–March 2002, which resulted in the killing of 3,000 Muslims. Several women were raped, disfigured, and burnt. Through a curious twist, the Shahbano judgement and the enactment of the Muslim Women's Act seemed to justify these anti-Muslim sentiments. Within a communally vitiated political atmosphere, an injustice to a Muslim woman came to be converted into a Hindu injury, justifying the riots and the killing and maiming of Muslim women.

[30] Arab Ahemadhia Abdulla vs Arab Bail Mohmuna Saiyadbhai AIR 1988 Gujarat 141; Ahmed vs Aysha II(1990) DMC 110: 1987 Cri.LJ (Criminal Law Journal) 980; K. Zunaideen vs Ameena Begum II (1997) DMC 91; Karim Abdul Rehman Shaikh vs Shehnaz Karim Shaikh 2000 Cri.LJ 3560.

by a woman judicial magistrate in Lucknow on 6 January 1988. The woman concerned, Fathima Sardar, was awarded Rs 85,000 as fair and reasonable provision and maintenance during the iddat period. Justice M.B. Shah, while presiding over the Gujarat High Court, explained: 'The determination of fair and reasonable provision and maintenance would depend upon the needs of the divorced woman, the standard of life enjoyed by her during her marriage and the means of her former Husband. The amount must include provision for her future residence, clothes, food and other articles for her livelihood.'[31] In the same year, the Kerala High Court reaffirmed this position in Ali vs Sufaira and Aliyar vs Pathu in July and August, respectively, and reaffirmed this position again in Ahmed vs Aysha in 1990.[32]

The authoritative judgement of the Supreme Court on this issue was pronounced in 2001 in Daniel Latifi vs Union of India.[33] The Supreme Court confirmed that the MWA has substituted the earlier right of recurrent maintenance under S.125 CrPC with a new right of a lump sum provision to be made and paid to the woman soon after her divorce. If the husband fails to make the settlement, a divorced Muslim woman has the right to approach the magistrate's court for enforcement of the right under S.3 of the MWA.

The court held that a Muslim husband is liable to make a reasonable and fair provision for the future of his divorced wife, which must be made within the iddat period. The court further clarified that the liability of the Muslim husband to the divorced wife to pay maintenance under the Act is not confined to the iddat period. A Muslim wife is entitled to a fair and reasonable provision with respect to her future needs. In cases where the husband is unable to pay the entire amount, the Full Bench of the Bombay High Court, in Karim Abdul Rehman Shaikh vs Shehnaz Karim Shaikh,[34] held that the amount can be paid in instalments, and until the payment is made, the magistrate can direct monthly payments to the wife even beyond the iddat period.

In Nizar vs Hyrunneessa,[35] the Kerala High Court rejected the plea that since the wife had re-married, she was not entitled to a fair and reasonable settlement for the future. The court held that the re-marriage of a divorced

---

[31] Arab Ahemadhia Abdulla vs Arab Bail Mohmuna Saiyadbhai AIR 1988 Gujarat 141.
[32] 1988 (2) KLT (Kerala Law Time) 172, 1988(2) KLT 94, and II (1990) DMC 110, respectively.
[33] 2001(7) SCC 740: 2001 Cri.LJ 4660 SC FB.
[34] 2000 Cri.LJ 3560.
[35] I (2000) DMC 229 Kerala.

woman is not a criterion in determining a 'fair and reasonable' settlement. The only aspect to be considered is the liability of the former husband to make a reasonable and fair provision to the divorced wife and fix the quantum sum as contemplated under S.3(3) of the Act. The court awarded Rs 90,000, calculating the amount on the basis of Rs 1,500 per month. The amount awarded as fair and reasonable settlement cannot be set aside on a plea that the divorced wife is leading an adulterous life.[36]

The lump sum provisions for future security, which the courts so carefully crafted out of the controversial legislation, seem to provide a better safeguard against destitution than the meagre handouts to which Muslim women were entitled under the earlier anti-vagrancy provision under S.125 CrPC. In a significant number of cases, a concerned and sensitive judiciary carved out a space for the protection of women's rights from what appeared to be an erroneously conceived, badly formulated, and blatantly discriminatory statute, without invoking a political backlash. Endorsing the spirit of Islam and the Shariat, and drawing upon the Islamic concept of *mataaoon bil ma'aroofe* (fair and reasonable provision), the courts opened a new portal for the protection of divorced Muslim women by reading into the statute notions of justice and equity. Doing precisely what the Act in its title proclaimed, that is, protection of rights of divorced Muslim women, the judiciary turned what had initially appeared to be a misnomer and a mockery into a factual reality and ushered in a silent revolution in the realm of Muslim women's rights.

A reading of the judgements indicates that the Act had rid itself of the agenda of alleviating vagrancy and destitution among divorced women (the defining feature of S.125 CrPC) and had extended itself to the claims of women from higher social strata. The statute, enacted in haste at the insistence of the conservative leadership, seemed to have boomeranged. Since the Muslim law permits bigamy, a husband cannot escape the liability of paying maintenance to the wife on the ground that the marriage is bigamous or the woman is a keep or a mistress.

While analysing the provision of a 'fair and reasonable settlement at the time of divorce' with respect to matrimonial property, it appears that the provision is based on both past 'contribution' and future 'need' but does not stretch itself to the premise of equal division of property upon divorce. It also endorses the 'clean break' theory where rights are determined upon divorce without future obligations of continued maintenance.

---

[36] M. Alavi vs T.V. Safia I (1992) DMC 62.

The economic rights of Christian and Parsi women are similar to the provisions for women under Hindu law and hence do not warrant a separate discussion, though there are some interesting cases that are reported. Here, it is relevant to mention that one of the first rulings on the issue of women's right to the matrimonial home, delivered by the Bombay High Court, was in a case under Parsi matrimonial law, the Parsi Marriage and Divorce Act, 1936, in Banoo Jal Daruwalla vs Jal C. Daruwalla.[37] The judge in this case relied upon the observations of Lord Denning in Bendall vs McWhirter (as cited in Banoo Daruwalla) that it is the duty of the court to ensure that the wife is not thrown out of the matrimonial home. Since it was not possible for the wife to reside in the matrimonial home along with the husband, the wife was awarded Rs 275 per month as maintenance.

JURISPRUDENTIAL QUESTIONS AND TOOLS OF INTERPRETATION

The Supreme Court rulings in cases such as Daniel Latifi provide us with a good example of how best to positively interpret a statute without evoking a backlash or a political controversy. These rulings endorse the spirit of Islam while upholding the human rights of women without posing the issue as 'women versus minorities', and hence serve Muslim women better than more confrontational rulings such as the Shahbano judgement. The controversy which followed this judgement ultimately led Shahbano herself to renounce her claim on the grounds that if claiming maintenance from her ex-husband was against the tenets of her religion, then she would rather be a good Muslim than claim her rights as a woman. Subsequent political events such as the Gujarat riots have taught a very painful lesson to Muslim women that they are violated, raped, maimed, and killed not only as women but also as Muslims. It is the composite identity as 'Muslim' and 'women' that they need to cope with. Their struggle must involve a composite strategy against patriarchy, community, communal forces, and the state. While interpreting statutory provisions that are enacted for their benefit, the courts must keep this composite identity of Muslim women in view. The Shahbano judgement faltered in this respect while upholding the rights of an individual woman.

[37] (1962) LXV BLR (Bombay Law Reporter) 750.

A different kind of challenge confronts the judiciary while determining the rights of women from other communities. Confronted with contradictory viewpoints regarding the criterion for determining the 'legislative intent' of a beneficial provision, what are the crutches that trial court judges have at their disposal while delivering 'constitutional justice'?

Justice A.K. Sikri and Justice Aruna Suresh attempt to provide an answer:

> Where alternative constructions are possible the court must give effect to that which will be responsible for the smooth working of the system for which the statue has been enacted rather than the one which would put hindrances in its way. If the choice is between two interpretations, the narrower of which would fail to achieve the manifest purpose of the legislation should be avoided. We should avoid a construction which would reduce the legislation to futility and should accept the bolder construction based on the view that Parliament would legislate only for the purpose of bringing about an effective result.[38]

In this tussle between the old world, feudal value systems reflected in ancient Hindu law—the law of the Smritis—alongside pluralistic traditions validated by customs at one end, and the newer statutory provisions of modern (often colonially) codified Hindu law at the other end, what are the avenues for harmonious constructions of legal principles? How do we revisit the provisions of early Hindu law in the context of its modern-day manifestations within the statutory framework of contemporary Hindu law, while delivering justice?[39] The same bench, comprised of Justice A.K. Sikri and Justice Aruna Suresh, has provided certain tools of interpretations in this respect:

> The principles of Hindu Personal Law have developed in an evolutionary way out of concern for all those subject to it so as to make fair provision against destitution. There is clear evidence to indicate that the law of maintenance stems out of the secular desire and so as to achieve the social objectives for making bare minimum provision to sustain the members of relatively smaller social groups. Organically and originally the law itself is irreligious. Its fountain spring is humanistic. In its operational field though it lays down the permissible categories under its benefaction, which are so entitled either because of the

---

[38] Suresh Khullar vs Vijay Kumar Khullar I (2008) DMC 719 Delhi.

[39] The old Hindu law was modernized through the enactment of the HMA in 1955. Under this, Hindu marriages became monogamous. Hence, women in bigamous relationships were denied their right of maintenance awarded to them under the old Hindu law. This is a violation of their human rights. The quote that follows makes the case that we should harmoniously construct the rights given under the ancient law with those under the modern law so that the rights of women in vulnerable situations like informal relationships or bigamous marriages are not trampled upon when we use the provisions of the codified law.

tenets supported by clear public policy or because of the need to subserve the social and individual morality measured for maintenance.[40]

Beyond protection of individual rights, the courts also have a mandate to develop the science of jurisprudence, as Chief Justice S.B. Sinha, Justice Ramesh Madhav Bapat, and N.V. Ramana of the Andhra Pradesh High Court suggest that '[t]he interpretation of law is not merely for the determination of a particular case but also in the interest of law as a science. As such, interpretation of law must be in accordance with justice, equity and good conscience, and more so, in furtherance of justice.'[41]

This call to move with the times and blend the ancient with the modern in pursuit of justice is the call of duty. The judicial oath mandates this. The primary aim of the courts is to 'do justice', as Justice P.N. Bhagwati and Justice Ranganath Misra (as the Lordships then were; subsequently both justices became the chief justices of India) succinctly pointed out: 'The role of the court is not that of silent spectator or of a passive agency. When a dispute is brought before the court where maintenance of a neglected wife or a minor child is in issue, the court must take genuine interest to find out the truth of the matter.'[42]

In this context, the recent ruling of the Supreme Court in D. Velusamy vs Patchaiammal[43] which denied maintenance to women who are in a marriage like relationship with married men, and termed such women as 'mistresses' and 'keeps' is a cause of concern. But the issue is still wide open as another ruling by another bench of the Supreme Court in Chanmuniya vs Virendra Kumar Singh Kushwaha[44], has upheld the right of women in technically defective marriages by holding that the term 'wife' must be given a broad and expansive interpretation and has referred the issue to a larger bench.[45]

* * *

I began this essay by discussing the importance of understanding the theoretical underpinnings of concepts of 'need' and 'contribution' that are used in assessing maintenance settlements. While 'need' presumes dependency, 'contribution' presumes equality. While lamenting the fact that we do not subscribe to the theory of 'division of property' at the time

---

[40] Narinder Pal Kaur Chawla vs Manjeet Singh Chawla I (2008) DMC 529 Delhi.
[41] P. Srinivasa Rao vs P. Indira I (2002) DMC 749.
[42] Sumitra Devi vs Bhikan Choudhary AIR 1985 SC 765.
[43] 2010 (10) SCC 469.
[44] 2011 (1) SCC 141.
[45] For a more detailed discussion, see Agnes (2011).

of divorce and while discussing the economic entitlement of maintenance which is 'need'-based, it is not my argument here that an equality model of marriage as a partnership would protect women better. The needs of women and their dependency will continue even when we accept the theory of property distribution based on the model of equality. I am arguing not for equality under Article 14 of the Constitution, but for additional protections and economic security in terms of matrimonial assets under Article 15(3) of the Constitution.

In the context of equal distribution of property in the US, feminist scholar Martha Fineman (1991: 270) argues:

> The material circumstances of divorcing women and children are being detrimentally ignored by supplanting a focus on 'contribution' as the primary distributive concept. The ascendancy of 'contribution' may represent a nice neat instance of conceptual progress to legal academics and law reformers, but for many divorcing spouses, as well as the practising professionals to whom they turn for advice, adverse material circumstances, and the needs they generate, have not been left behind.

She suggests that one source of controversy about property distribution rules is the existence of two competing, and perhaps incompatible and unrealistic, political visions of contemporary marriage. The first is the more modern view that marriage as an institution has been transformed so as to be more consistent with formalistic notions of equality between the sexes. The second is the more traditional policy stance that 'family' continues to be the solitary institution which addresses problems of dependency that inevitably arise in the context of families, such as caring for the young, the sick, and the aged, and meeting these demands as the caretaker creates further 'needs' for the primary caretaker, which in most cases is the woman. Highly sceptical of the 'contribution' model, which is based on the assumption that marriage is a partnership between equals, she argues for a 'need'-based framework (ibid.: 265).

At a conceptual level, quality standards in the distribution of property may be linked to broader ideals of placing equal value and promoting freedom of choice in marriage. Making equality the ongoing concept underlying divorce may be considered part of a series of conscious symbolic choices about how best to ensure a more just society. But when equality rhetoric is translated into specific rules governing distribution of property, the results must be measured and assessed in more than symbolic terms. Symbolic expression may be important, but Fineman argues that care should be taken so that when translated into legislation having direct impact on the lives of many people, the results also meet the standards of fairness and justice (ibid.: 276).[46] I end by emphasizing a similar approach of cautiousness and scepticism and urge that this must be reflected in our campaigns for law reforms.

REFERENCES

Agnes, Flavia (1996), 'Economic Rights of Women under the Islamic Law', *Economic and Political Weekly*, XXXI(41–2): 2832–8.

―― (2011), 'The Concubine and Notions of Constitutional Justice', *Economic and Political Weekly*, 11 June, XLVI(24): 31–3.

Fineman, M.A. (1991), 'Societal Factors Affecting the Creation of Legal Rules for Distribution of Property at Divorce', in M.A. Fineman and N.S. Thomadsen (eds), *At the Boundaries of Law—Feminism and Legal Theory*. New York: Routledge, pp. 265–79.

---

[46] For example, if the principle of 'equal division of property' is adopted, a woman who has been a homemaker and who has custody of her minor children, with little opportunity to enter the job market, may suffer. She would require extra protection. So, the principle of equality cannot be applied blindly, and at times, the principle of special protection to a disadvantaged class may suit women better.

II. SEXUALITY

Chapter 3

UNEVEN MODERNITIES AND AMBIVALENT SEXUALITIES

Women's Constructions of Puberty in Coastal Kanyakumari, Tamil Nadu*

KALPANA RAM**

I WISH TO BEGIN WITH SOME REFLECTIONS on the dilemmas and legacies that derive from debates in Marxist political economy. Tropes such as unevenness when referring to Indian modernity immediately recall debates that have been particularly well elaborated in the Indian context, producing a vocabulary of uneven development and of articulation

* Originally published in Mary E. John and Janaki Nair (eds) (1998), *A Question of Silence? The Sexual Economies of Modern India*. New Delhi: Kali for Women, pp. 269–303.
 ** I wish to acknowledge the assistance of the Australian Research Council for funding this research. I thank participants in the workshop 'Rethinking Indian Modernity: The Political Economy of Sexuality', August 1996, for their comments, some of which have generated ongoing discussions, particularly with Mary E. John and Janaki Nair. I also thank participants who heard an early version at SNDT University, October 1996, in a seminar organized by Sujata Patel. Finally, I thank Ian Bedford for his editorial assistance. The system of transliterations of Tamil words adopted here is that of the *Tamil Lexicon*, University of Madras, 1982. Certain names of individuals have been altered to make them less identifiable.

between capitalist and pre-capitalist modes of production. The debate on political economy has now shifted, in some quarters, to a debate around the cultural components of modernity (see, for example, Banerjee 1989; Niranjana et al. 1993; Panikkar 1995). Some of the characteristic dilemmas and questions, however, have not changed. The ambiguities once attendant on development, when viewed from the perspective of the 'Third World' rather than from the advanced metropoles of capitalism, are now displaced to the sphere of power (more broadly conceived than before) and subjectivity. Where once we had recourse to notions of articulation between modes of production, or various shades of 'semi-ness' (as in arrested development) in order to characterize Indian modes of production, we now wonder how to characterize a modernity that does not or cannot (depending on the perspective of the theorist) deliver the full emancipatory promise of rationalism, secularism, and freedom from the bonds of class, caste, and gender.

The problems with utilizing Eurocentric theorizations of power also persist. Foucault's pioneering insights into the capacity of discourses of power to produce and form subjects are evidently of great use, and, in this chapter, I draw inspiration particularly from his delineation of embodied sites of modernity such as bio-medicine and sexuality, which cannot be reduced to the organizational powers of the modern state. However, while his failure to interrogate the colonial construction of European modernity has been particularly noticeable to those in postcolonial locations, we have yet to trace all the theoretical effects of this failure.[1] To what extent, for example, are some of the problems that haunt his formulations of power an effect of taking the self-sufficiency of European modernity at face value? For all his insistence on the formation of resistance at the sites of power, his metaphors of power and governmentality as 'capillary-like' conjure an all-pervasive power that is all the more total for its being de-centred.

Could such a totalizing vision of modernity, so all-encompassing, have arisen from the perspective of Indian modernity? I suggest not, if only because modernity in the colonies is characteristically experienced not as a unilinear triumphant conquest over the old, but instead as a contradictory necessity to invoke tradition both as a resource for nationalism *and* as the recalcitrant material that must be opposed, reformed, and 'recast'.[2]

---

[1] See, for example, Stoler (1995). Here I wish rather to highlight problems that exist in Foucault's more general conceptualization of power itself.

[2] I allude here to the title of the pioneering text *Recasting Women: Essays in Colonial History* (Sangari and Vaid 1989).

These different subject positions in relation to modernity have in turn shaped social theory in the West and in India. Here I will concern myself with just one dimension of this vast topic, namely, with the conceptualization of time. In classical Western social theory, a certain taken-for-granted homogeneity of the time of modernity is made possible by projecting difference in time onto the colonized other. In my discipline of anthropology, the denial of a time that is co-eval, or shared between anthropologist and the people who are written about, characterizes more than the writing practice that Johannes Fabian (1983, 1991) has explored. It stems, as Fabian himself would argue, from an older colonizing structuration of time as linear, progressive, culminating in the time of European modernity, and of tradition as a time that lingers on in the non-European world. The construction of difference is allied, in this formulation, to the colonial subject's inhabiting of a time outside that of the modern, scientific enquirer/observer. The artifice of an anthropological time-present rests on such bifurcations between the time of the enquirer and the time of the subject of enquiry. Time-present in anthropology does not refer to present time, but rather to an artificial, synchronic, temporal form (Cohen 1991: 211).

It is precisely the dilemmas of subjectivity generated for the colonized by such formulations of time that have propelled historiography to the fore as one of the master disciplines for Indian nationalism and for the postcolonial state.[3] The overwhelming tendency of Indian historiography to insert Indian life into the cultural and temporal homogeneity of secular-rationalist versions of modernity may be sympathetically understood as an effort to resist colonial versions of difference. However, this effort has engendered its own problems, notably the dilemma that in this secular-rationalist narrative, Indian modernity can never be located in the present. Instead, Indian historiography and social theories of modernization have typically identified modernity as a mission yet-to-be-accomplished, endlessly deferred to a future that depends on conquering the persistence of tradition.

These differences in turn shape the divergent critiques of modernity that emerge in the West as opposed to India. Where a Foucault can only imagine sites of subversion and resistance which already presume the constitutive power of modern disciplinary formations, resistant historians in India have had no trouble in conceiving of a 'subaltern' domain, turning

---

[3] See, for example, Chatterjee's (1993: 76ff) discussion of the urgent call from Bengali nationalists, 'We must have a history'.

for their subject matter to caste, religion, and kinship as so many radical internal differences *within* Indian modernity. Where the enunciation of a *post*-modernity is a radical, if contested gesture in the West, in India an equivalent gesture would be to finally locate modernity in the present, in all its contradictoriness and messiness.

Hitherto representable only in the more imaginative world of literary fiction where a writer like Rushdie can embrace and celebrate India's richness of social relations without any sense of contradiction, a recognition of difference is moving at last into the disciplinary grids of the modernizing social sciences and humanities. Tropes of 'doubleness' and 'multiplicity' recur in recent formulations. Veena Das, for example, has argued that major institutions, whether ostensibly traditional, such as caste and religion, or modern like the law courts, are all in fact subject to a double articulation. Each is coloured and reconstituted by the other (Das 1995: 53). Kumkum Sangari (1995) pluralizes the concept of patriarchy in an effort to represent a feminist reworking of the Indian theme of unity in diversity: namely, multiple patriarchies that are operative in the one social formation.

REPRESENTING SEXUALITY

These developments in social theory represent only partial gains. Our theoretical language does not at present have the resources with which to articulate different temporalities and subjectivities while also being able to show how they are all organized, as well, to co-exist in a single time-dimension. Nevertheless, the partial openings have particular implications for our capacity to represent sexuality. For representations of sexuality, like representations of gender relations more generally, bear the marks of colonial/nationalist history, reflecting 'the shaping power of the reified polarities of capitalist versus pre-capitalist, or modernity versus tradition. Such polarities allow the rich complexity of domains such as sexuality to evaporate in the very process of achieving representation.'[4] Sexuality, and perhaps particularly female sexuality, is organized and discursively produced not through one but a number of competing discursive formulations that bear the mark of diverging social relations (caste, class) that are identifiable not only in terms of space/(region), but time (periodicities).

[4] On this point, see Seremetakis (1991, especially p. 217ff).

This chapter's ethnographic location is among the coastal women of Kanyakumari district, Tamil Nadu. Here, discourses of social reform aimed at reconstructing sexuality co-exist, albeit in uneasy fashion, alongside discourses that enjoy archaic, pre-colonial resonances. Discourses of spirit possession, for example, retain their capacity to shape subjectivity and experiences of the body (see Ram 1992: chapters 3 and 4; see also Ram 1996a). Yet, such experiences of possession co-exist with discourses of social reform that have permeated right down to the rural labouring poor, where they continue to enjoy a lively existence through the efforts of school teachers, doctors and nurses, non-governmental organizations (NGOs), and radicalized clergy.[5] These publicly circulating discourses of social reform have been imbibed and turned into the site of individual re-fashionings of the body, particularly in its gendered and sexualized dimensions. Modernity, even among the elites, is internally various, contradictory, and selective in the understandings and practices that are assembled. They emerge afresh as ambivalences and selectivities in renditions of both tradition and modernity among rural villagers.

This chapter traces the effects of the doubling and splitting of subjectivity as they are lived by women in a poor Catholic fishing village. In November/December of 1991, I conducted interviews with groups of women I had already come to know well through previous fieldwork in the 1980s. I also conducted interviews in the agricultural villages of Chengalpattu district, in order to begin some comparative fieldwork, but these interviews are, inevitably, partial, and only occasionally drawn on here. In addition, I sought out women who had attended the health classes run by the local NGO, the Kottar Social Service Society (KSSS), run by Belgian Catholics. Some of the women had been recruited as village-level animators for these classes. I also interviewed the teachers at the local village primary school. I was accompanied at my request by an old friend, Stella, who once worked as health coordinator for KSSS, and is now running her own NGO in Chengalpattu. The questions, loosely taking inspiration from Emily Martin's (1987) questionnaire in *The Woman in the Body*, asked the women (among other things) to describe their own experiences when coming of age, and also to consider how they would treat their daughter's coming of age.

What is elicited in our shared interaction is not experience as some raw datum, but the women's explicit attempts to synthesize—at the level of an orally related biography—their past, present, and future. Two discourses

[5] For a full discussion, see Ram (1996b).

emerged as particularly significant in their experience of puberty. The first concerns a ritual through which the advent of a fertile sexuality is heralded to the village but more specifically to marriageable kin. The second is a moral discourse that requires the emergent pubescent girl to become a woman through submission to a code of bodily disciplines and restrictions, which accompany her efflorescent sexuality. Before examining the women's negotiation of these discourses, their milieu needs to be situated ethnographically and historically. Responses to a puberty ritual already presume, for example, a construction of female sexuality that is specific to region and caste. I will also attempt to historicize the available ethnographic representations in order to see how the ritual is located within those wider constructions of masculine power and sexuality that have been given a new life in the politics of Dravidian cultural nationalism.

ANTHROPOLOGICAL DISCOURSES ON DRAVIDIAN KINSHIP AND SEXUALITY

Anthropological discourses on kinship suffer, as Carol Vance (1991) has argued, from a tendency to naturalize sexuality in spite of their efforts to demonstrate cultural variability. In what she terms a weak version—by far the most prevalent model—of cultural constructionism, demonstrations of variability in culture co-exist quite comfortably with the assumption of sexuality as an underlying universal substratum that is simply manifested in different ways. I suggest, however, that anthropological discourse on kinship and ritual can, if recast, provide vital sources of insight. I suggest we read these discourses not as pointing to variations on a pre-existing human essence (although I wish to leave open the question of that which precedes, and exceeds the shaping power of culture), but as active sites in which sexuality, desire, and affect, as well as gender-specific subjectivities, are produced and renegotiated. Modalities of kinship have been used in anthropological discourse to map out a very specific region in which female sexuality is produced in a relatively public, visible, and celebratory fashion in and through a ritual marking of the advent of menarche in a girl. In an extensive across-regional survey of the puberty ceremony for girls, Good (1991) maps the region as not only including the four linguistic zones of southern India, but as reaching down into Sri Lanka, and extending north as far as the Madhya Pradesh–Orissa border of central India. This regional mapping is integrally bound, in this view, with the distinctively southern system of prescriptive marriage which, as Louis Dumont (1983: 14) put it in his celebrated formulations, means that affinity is inherited, rather than made afresh at the time of marriage.

The culturalist biases of the American school of ethnography have meant that the social basis for Tamil cultural meanings regarding sexuality and gender are seen as located entirely in the sphere of kinship. In my own previous work (Ram 1992: 202ff) as in Karin Kapadia's ethnography (1996: 252, 166ff), we have argued that these symbolic constructions of female sexuality are materially grounded, insofar as they are found not simply in the south, but are particularly elaborated among those caste communities where women also work in the public sphere, as among the Mukkuvars, where women partake of the sphere of trade in fish, or among the Pallars, in rice cultivation. But even this argument, with its exclusive focus on labour and fertility, seems unduly limited to me now.

Anthropologists are being asked to confront the fact that the rituals and kinship systems they document and take to be cultural wholes are in reality nothing more than surviving and rearticulated fragments of more widely articulated systems of power and meaning in pre-colonial societies.[6] In the light of the rich ethno-historiographical work on the late pre-colonial state in south India (see, for example, Appadurai 1981; Bayly 1989; Dirks 1989; Narayana Rao *et al.* 1992), the puberty ritual seems precisely that—a fragment. It is the fragment of a pre-colonial system which constructed both female and male power simultaneously in ritual contexts that ranged from the village rituals of puberty, to the elaborate theatres of power enacted in temples and courts. Even among castes that celebrate fertility as a relatively autonomous female domain within the terms of the puberty ceremony, the mother's brother enacts a model of masculinity that reconstitutes, on a micro level, more widely employed codes of masculine honour. These codes have a historical depth in Tamil Nadu, where kinship has historically been integrated with wider processes of state formation and chiefly authority. The public display of generosity and the privilege of ruling on behalf of a superior were the central modalities through which sovereignty was multiplied, but also regularized in large-scale empires such as the Vijayanagara Kingdom, surviving into the twentieth century in princely states like Pudukottai (see Dirks 1989). Such processes were not unified, but rather, segmentary and duplicative.[7] It is, therefore, not altogether surprising to find a duplication in the ritualized codes of masculinity adopted even by agricultural labouring men who nevertheless

---

[6] See Asad (1995). Dirks (1989) argues this position for the south Indian context.

[7] See Stein (1980) on the segementary state. See also Dirks (1989).

enjoy their own little kingdom with respect to the female members of their kin group.

MASCULINE AND FEMININE SEXUALITY IN THE CONSTRUCTION OF A 'DRAVIDIAN' MODERNITY

Such constructions of kingship are not as culturally distant as the historical periodization of pre-colonial, colonial, and postcolonial suggests. Contrasts between Brahminic Hinduism and the non-Brahminic complex have consequences for the particular versions of modernity that have evolved. In Tamil Nadu, the existence of divergent constructions of kinship, sexuality, and gender, like the more conspicuous use of language itself, has provided raw materials for the making of a Dravidian modern. The construction of an anti-Brahmin, anti-colonial, avowedly Tamil modernity in this century has breathed new life into these codes of honour and kingship. In contesting the rise of Brahminic power as a professional and administrative elite class under colonial rule in Tamil Nadu,[8] the bypassed non-Brahmin castes mobilized readily available alternative codes of authority and power. Orators and filmmakers conveyed to audiences pride in the fact that the great Tamil kings had, after all, been non-Brahmin.[9] In the masculine gendering of the Tamil nation, warrior-king codes of virility, generosity, and public constructions of honour, rank, and privilege have become markers of successful party leaders, culminating in the apotheosis of 'the MGR phenomenon' (see M.S.S. Pandian 1992).

How did these redefinitions work in the sphere of femininity and feminine sexuality? The overriding construction of femininity in the Dravidian movement has been that of chaste women and heroic mothers (Lakshmi 1990; J. Pandian 1992). Women's honour has been represented in terms far more restrictive than men's, tied firmly to their status within kin groups and to the sphere of sexuality. Thus, women can only establish their honour in relation to their chastity and their virtue as mothers, while men gain yet another additional sphere in which to provide their uniquely 'Tamil' credentials as defenders of female chastity and maternal dedication. I will not enter here into the lively and ongoing debate as to whether and to

---

[8] See Irschick (1986) and Nambi Arooran (1980). On colonial Brahmin alliances as a pan-Indian phenomenon, see Mani (1989).

[9] See Price (1996). See also, Ramaswamy (1994) on wider Tamil nationalist representations of kingship.

what extent the Dravidian movement ever offered women a wider vision of subjecthood.[10] It is important to note, however, that the construction of a Tamil modernity carries within it much more than the politics of cultural nationalism. It also offers a social critique in the name of an egalitarian and rational modernity. The revitalization of codes of masculine and feminine honour reflects the impact of *both* these strands. Under E.V. Ramaswamy Naicker, *mānam* or honour became redefined as *tanmānam* or the honouring of one's own personal code of ethics; while *mariyātai* or respect became *suya-mariyātai*, or self-respect, from which the movement took its name. Such notions of a personalized code of honour departed significantly from codes of honour based on inherited status.[11]

While it is true that these redefinitions of honour still remained a largely masculinist prerogative, they have also inflected the coding of female honour as chastity. After all, the literary classics, that the Dravidian movement drew so freely from, display a far wider range of meanings for female sexuality than the motif of chastity will allow. They include, also, a strikingly overt and robust expression of female erotic ardour that was embellished and developed in the court and temple traditions of dance and song. There is, therefore, a selective narrowing in the construction of Tamil tradition. The political context in which chastity was picked out as the defining virtue of Tamil women deserves more recognition. The cultural hegemony of the Victorian–Brahmin reconstruction of patriarchy not only deprived such traditions of female sexuality of their material basis in the courtly–temple nexus, they actively made it impossible to continue a celebration of such values. The controversies around the redefinition of the devadasi tradition as a form of prostitution were complex and need not be entered into here (see Kannabiran 1995; Nair 1994; Srinivasan 1984). What is clear is that for the leaders of the non-Brahmin movement—many of whom were sons of devadasis, and, in the case of women like Moovalur Ramamirtham Ammaiyar, themselves ex-devadasis (see Anandhi 1991b)—the reclamation of honour in this politically charged context entailed affirming the chastity of non-Brahmin women. In a future move, the blame for the prostitution of non-Brahmin women was placed squarely onto the Brahminic priestly class as the upholders of such a debased religion.

---

[10] See the contributions by Pandian *et al.* (1991); Anandhi (1991a); see also Anandhi (1998).
[11] See the extended discussion on this aspect in Price (1996).

Most studies of the Dravidian movement have emphasized the emptying out of all elements of radical critique in the quest for nationalism and electoral power.[12] However, in the rural areas of Tamil Nadu, agendas of social reform continue to be fuelled by enlightenment critiques. Price (1996) finds that when one looks away from the top party leadership to the cadre living in rural Madurai, the message of the DMK continues to be identified above all with having taught certain universalist values.

THE POLITICS OF ENLIGHTENMENT: SEXUALITY IN CHRISTIAN KANYAKUMARI

It should be clear by now that I am not arguing for any one set of connections between modernity and sexuality. In some parts of Tamil Nadu, the politics of non-Brahminism encouraged wealthy mercantile castes such as the Chettiars to adopt the most elaborate versions of female puberty ceremonies (Kapadia 1996: 114). In sharp contrast, the Christian communities of Kanyakumari, the radicalized clergy, and non-governmental organizations (NGOs) (both Christian and non-Christian) keep alive the kind of peculiar blend of missionary and rationalist scientific critique of village beliefs that marks the politics of 'enlightenment in the colonies' (see Chatterjee 1986: 168). The thrust here is to modernize gender relations into a more egalitarian version of patriarchal norms, based on the mutually respectful couple rather than on the wider kin-based social organization of sexuality (Ram 1996b, 1998).

The coastal villages of Kanyakumari are located at the regional intersections of Tamil and Kerala politics. In addition to the impact of Tamil modernity, they are exposed to the activist communist traditions of Kerala, particularly notable for its interventions in literacy, health, and education. Part of the Travancore kingdom till 1956, Kanyakumari district is heir to an era of reform in public health and land reform that began with the princely rulers of the nineteenth century (Jeffrey 1992, especially p. 56f). Kerala-based social movements represented by such groups as the Kerala Shastra Sahitya Parishad include the Kanyakumari town of Nagercoil in their tours which seek to popularize scientific and rationalist values in the rural population. They find a ready response among NGOs in the district, including the radicalized Christian NGOs working in the coastal villages, such as the Kotar Social Service Society (KSSS).

---

[12] Compare M.S.S. Pandian (1993b) with J. Pandian (1992) and M.S.S. Pandian (1993a).

The contrast between tradition and modernity in these discourses of reform emerges most sharply as the opposition between science and ritual. Biomedical discourses, displaying their scientific authority, are opposed to ritual constructions of the body. This opposition radically simplifies the actual complexity of village prescriptions on the body. People refer to local medical discourses as much as ritual ones. When questioned about menstruation, for example, village women point out that without menstruation, 'we [women] would get sick, our bodies would become bloated. There would be stomach boils, related to lack of bodily balance and imbalance of heat.' As Maria Pushpam put it:

It is good to have regular periods—it is bad for the body if it does not come.

Another woman, Jeannette, said:

The blood should flow, or else we have illness.

In reformist discourses, however, such local knowledges, based on a humoral physiology culled from the practitioners of Siddha medical traditions, as well as on village cures, are all ignored. Instead, ritual comes to stand for the entirety of tradition as in the following extract from a girl's letter which is singled out for reproduction in the text of one of the reformist clergy, Fr Alphonse:

When I came of age, I was only thirteen. I was devastated by my fear and ignorance of changes in my body. My parents called everyone and had a feast, they decked me with flowers and decoration, jewellery and goodness knows what else. But about the changes in my body they told me nothing. They did not have even a little bit of *arivu* [knowledge]. (Alphonse 1991: 229)

One of the important elements in the redefinition of local discourse I wish to trace here concerns the redefinition of arivu or knowledge. This is a term which is also significant in village women's notions of moral sensibility (see later). In the hands of an enlightenment discourse, it is transformed to mean the use of physiology that will explain the inner workings of the body in a scientific way. Such modern, rationalist redefinitions of knowledge appear also among women who have had lessons from the KSSS:

Amala Urpam [says she would use menstrual charts to teach her daughters]: I have *arivu* now, which dispels fears. I feel KSSS has made changes to hygienic practices, and brought medical awareness to the coast. Girls need education.

Lourdes: I have learned some things from the KSSS health team, that the menstrual blood comes from the uterus [*karppappai*], that this is the excess, waste blood [*kaḷaivu rattam*] that comes from there.

Pamela Rose: At college I began to read books about reproduction. I even lent it out to a married woman who was too shy to approach the nuns. Since then I have introduced some element of education on family relations in the catechism class I take in the village. I teach them not only about bodily relations, but about the need for understanding and mutual acceptance of one another in a marriage, the way Father Alphonse describes it.[13] Some of the village girls show interest, others hang their heads and others never reappear.

I interviewed teachers working at the coastal primary school for their experiences of puberty. Here the impact of a scientific medical discourse was more established, but still occasionally represented by the women as a militant advance on tradition and therefore a source of pride.

Maria Pushpam: [I ask her what she thinks of the questions I am putting to her.] I think your questions are aimed at revealing what girls do and do not know. Girls do not know about their bodily makeup [*uṭal amaippu*]. I use the rhythm method for contraception, I wait for the safe period. During pregnancies I also have check ups and my children have been delivered in hospital.

Vimla (headmistress of village primary school, mother of three): I would teach a girl who has come of age that she is now mature enough to be a mother, that there are changes in the uterus. I am approaching a change now, though my periods have not stopped. These things are all part of nature [*īyarkat*], and we should take it on as such.

It is important to note the double-edged nature of the impact of modernity. On the one hand, women who have been interpellated by the discourse of social reform are empowered with a new professional identity that allows them to intervene in the practices of others and to move into a newly expanded female public sphere. On the other hand, the same process constructs women who speak in the name of older, local knowledges as traditional and superstitious.[14] The transformative qualities of these discourses of modernity are most apparent among those women who work as mediators between the leadership of NGOs and the less educated village women—known in the jargon of NGOs as animators.

Health worker Jeannette (village animator): My activities in the village involve educating people about disease, immunisations and injections, hygiene and the treatment for diarrhoea. We hold mothers' meetings, suggest writing to the BDO [block development office] about complaints. We have gone there ourselves with the women, who have broken their water pots outside his office to show they have no water, or have demanded electricity. The changes we advise for the women in the area of health is to boil the water. We get them to drink milk and eat eggs during pregnancy, which they feel might make the baby too big and give them a difficult birth. Seventy five per cent change after asking us questions. They are just superstitious [*muḍai nambikkai*], just the society speaking. My sister-in-law burnt herself and her spirit was supposed to come over me, but my tongue has been loosened since going to the KSSS and I ask them all: what ill has befallen me since I have done all the things I should not have?

---

[13] See Alphonse (1991). His text is discussed further in Ram (1996b).

[14] On conflicting knowledges and practices surrounding the medicalization of childbirth, see Ram (1994) and Ram (1998).

Victoria (NGO health worker in Chengalpattu): The sisters at the convent at Porur suggested I train for social work—my parents worked there for the nuns as servants. I was trained in speech and dress, and given a cycle, I was only fifteen then. They taught me not to giggle, but to mix with people, to work diligently. When I went out on my work, people would talk: look at her go with an umbrella, like some teacher. I would ignore them, or talk back: Did you have to pay for my umbrella? I was afraid of men when I first got married, and told my husband quite early on not to insist, or harass me when my body is not right, like during my periods. My husband has agreed. Now he also sometimes says he is tired, or not wanting to, and I feel I can say that too. We use the rhythm method. I learned in workshops, to watch my discharge and avoid the fertile period.

Such a conferral of new, activist identities on to rural women is part of a long history of mission initiatives in the Travancore region.[15] Tracing the contradictory effects of mission discourse, Haggis finds that the very activism demanded of the lady missionary and her Bible women bequeathed a legacy of female professionalism. These Bible women were, like the animators Victoria and Jeannette of our time, recruited from rural castes low in the local hierarchy. Their reports, recorded in 1897, strikingly echo Victoria's account of the taunts she endured for carrying an umbrella, signifier of high status:

For six months we walked past the mosques without getting permission to go into a single house to teach the women ... they would not allow us to carry an umbrella or a bag and sometimes snatched away our books and tore them. (Haggis 1998: 94)

The animators display exactly this mix of daring and resilience enabled by their newly gained position as educators. By contrast, women who have settled into their professional role, employed by schools and hospitals, display more of the other side of modernity. Here, the women's self-perception as bearers of a superior way of life becomes the basis for class distinction: in their self-representation as professional women whose job it is to teach the children of the coastal villagers, the discourses of science and rationalism serve not only to reinforce previously formed inequalities, but to create the means for new class differences. I have argued this elsewhere (Ram 1998), and will content myself with just one example:

Vimla: Now the villagers in the coast—they neither take pregnancies as a time to take sensible precautions, nor will they stop having children. To them, it is like eating and drinking and going to the toilet—everyday bodily functions. Yet they complain endlessly of their special burdens. They should see pregnancy as a time of special joys and responsibilities, and should not see themselves as sick patients. As for myself, I have taught at school right until the last moment, before the onset of labour in both my childbirths. I have always had a strong will in these matters.

---

[15] Robin Jeffrey (1992: 96ff) describes the particular attraction of Christian missions to Travancore who were drawn by the presence of much older Christian communities.

The bulk of the women I interviewed along with my co-interviewer Stella, belonged, however, neither to the category of professional school teachers nor to the quasi-professionalized category of mediators between NGOs and villagers. Rather, they were coastal women who either worked as fish traders, as household managers of finance, or as wives and mothers. They were also a divided stratum because of their varying levels of education. Their responses, more than any others, have inspired the title of this chapter, 'Uneven Modernities'.

RUPTURES AND AMBIVALENCES IN FEMALE BODILY HEXIS

The impact of modernity on the sexual knowledgeability and forwardness of the young was a widely shared object of commentary by older men and women in the villages (both fishing and agricultural), as well as among school teachers. When I asked women if they would give their daughters more information about menstruation and sexuality than they had themselves received, the answer was often:

Don't our kids know enough already? They see it in all the movies and read it in all the books these days.

Beatrice, the teacher, reports it thus: Today's kids know so much, they know it all. They get ideas from films and books, so that girls won't sit with boys, even as little children—they think it is too much like husband and wife.

Old women also regarded the children of today as knowing a great deal more about sexuality than in their days. While interviewing old women in an agricultural labouring village in the district of Chengalpattu, they recalled their own marriages consummated soon after puberty and contrasted themselves with today's children:

Today there is *uṇarchi* [understanding, form of knowing linked with feeling and emotion] and even kids still wearing *pāvāṭais* [that is, prepubertal] do not have any shyness.

A Nadar potter of Kanyakumari, inclined to moralism, contrasts the *verkam* or modesty of girls in the old days:

In the *paṇḍeyakālam* [the days of the Pandian king, old days], the girl coming of age would be shy, she would be kept isolated. Now there is knowledge and progress. In the old days brides would keep their eyes covered with betel leaf, so that they need not know where they were being taken—today she lifts her head even as the *tāli* is being tied, and all is considered finished once she has done a *namaskāram* to the mother-in-law!

Asked to reconstruct their experience of puberty, and to consider which elements of their treatment they would repeat for their daughters, the coastal women's responses indicated significant ruptures in some elements of generational transmission of the unquestioned, taken-for-granted reproduction of bodily habits. There was a striking selectivity in terms of the way women negotiate more dominant constructions of modernity and of tradition. Some elements were admitted through and were not only valued by the women, but were described as essential aspects they would attempt to pass on to their daughters. Others, however, were minimized, devalued, or rejected outright. The main single element of traditional culture to be minimized or rejected was the puberty ritual. This minimization took several forms, and I have grouped them under different headings.

Humorous Distancing: Then They Came and Fed Us That 'Poisonous Stuff'

Lourdes is unmarried, 26 years old, and a lively, cheeky young woman, who felt very much at ease with us, being well known to me and related to Stella. Our interview was therefore intimate and often hilarious. She is the youngest of three sisters, and talks about how she knew, from very early, what puberty entailed. She refers to the procedures as 'knowing what was in store', humorously re-describing all the main elements of the treatment of puberty. In her version, the seven days of seclusion inside the house becomes rendered as 'being shut up and left to rot indoors'. The special foods, such as the eggs and the oil brought to the girl to enhance her fertility, are rendered as 'that poison they bring you'. She derived additional mileage out of the fact that they kept up the special diet for seven days instead of three, pointing to her plump form and saying, 'Maybe that is why I am like this!' There was no public ceremony performed for her, and asked what she thinks of this, she again makes a joke of it:

Sure, I'd like one tomorrow! Next month! Get some saris, some jewellery, have some money spent on me!

Lourdes has attended classes on health and reproduction run by the KSSS, and her elder sister was one of the local women coordinating the meetings. She has been influenced by her association with the classes, and told us of the topics covered: social reform, social work, women's liberation, women's rights, sex, and reproduction. She tells us she prefers hospitalized births. 'New ways and methods are better than old time customs,' she tells us. Her elder married sister now lives in Bangalore, giving Lourdes access to the ways of the big city, and she points out that hospital medicines are just as good as village remedies. Here too she gives a characteristic light touch when talking about what she has learned from KSSS:

> If I was a knowing sort of girl before, KSSS sure spoilt me good and proper! I already knew from shared lavatories and where women wash clothes, about how pregnancy occurs: after marriage, if the flow stops for two months, accompanied by nausea and tiredness, one is pregnant. But with KSSS I was made really 'bad'!

Beatrice, the primary school teacher, also reveals a light-hearted approach in the way she talks to the young girls in her charge if they look as if they are nearing the time of menarche:

> I say to the girls: Get ready with oil and eggs! No, I don't take it too seriously, I tell the girls, get ready to wear a sari, it won't be long now!

However, such deft and spirited negotiations concerning the ritualized injunctions surrounding menstruation are not restricted to young, more modernized women. Claramma is 66 years old and talks about how she simply used to get around the restrictions on menstruating women by not telling anyone:

> I went to have a bath in Muttom, where they said it was infested with demons. I went at night, with my periods. Nothing happened—absolutely nothing. I told no one about the periods, or they would not have let me. If I wanted to go urgently to a ritual occasion, it became a nuisance. If one has to go—just don't let anyone know.

Economic Considerations

Many women expressed reservations based on the economic costs of holding a public ritual. They made distinctions between the different levels at which it could be celebrated, depending on who, outside the circle of kinship, was invited, whether or not a feast for the wider community was held, whether or not a movie was shown. For most families, holding a public ceremony (*saṭaṅku*) meant inviting only kinspeople, not making it a grand affair. The management of expenses and money is a uniquely female sphere in the fishing community, so women who expressed concern over the costs were intimately involved in making ends meet against the fluctuating cycle of the men's catch (see Ram 1992: chapter 6).

> Antoniammal: When it comes to my daughter's turn, I would rather not have the expenses of a *saṭaṅku*, I would just call the relevant kinspeople and have a simple affair, not a big feast or anything. There is simply no need for the whole village to know. It was difficult even

when I came of age—my father had just died, I did not think we should have the *saṭaṅku* because of the expenses involved. (Generally, anyway, we wait for the good fishing season before we hold the ceremony for our girls.) But then, my mother needed the support from her kinspeople, as well as the gifts they would give as part of the occasion.

Pamela Rose (27, unmarried, educated, with B.A. degree in English from Tiruvaiyaru, partly employed): I felt worried and guilty about costing my family so much, at a time when there was such poverty in our midst. I felt, couldn't this have come at another time?

Claramma redirected our discussion of sexuality towards problems of economic burden. She saw no sense in my talk of 'freedom'. I had been talking of freedom from male-dominated definitions of sexuality and beauty. She transformed this discourse into one based on economic unfreedom:

In those countries you speak of [where women experience the pressures of having to look young and attractive to men, (i.e. Australia)] there is so much money, the only problem is who to give it away to. Here, I have a handicapped son who needs care, and there is no money for facilities; one unmarried daughter and no money for dowry; and one daughter with five children, who is ill so much of the time, I have to care for the children.

This is Women's Secret, 'Peṇkaḷ Rahasyam'

The function of the ritual is precisely to render the girl's coming of age a matter of public knowledge. The ritual is a *vilambaram* or advertisement to the public. If the public sphere defined by the ritual was one specific to caste and kinship, today, with the impact of the media, the public is more widely defined as in the practice in larger cities of taking out advertisements in newspapers to announce female puberty in much the same manner as one would advertise marriages, or the death of a significant family member. For those who view the ritual with a newly modern distaste, it is precisely this vilambaram or advertising function of the ritualized construction of female sexuality that has become improper:

Lourdes: If I had a daughter, I would keep her only one day at home, and send her back to school the next day. I would not have a *saṭaṅku*—do not wish to *advertise* it. [Lourdes uses the English word here.]

Some of the respondents made it clear that the public construction of menarche was being judged in terms of its more privatized construction as a feminine secret:

Maria Pushpam (39-year-old primary school teacher): I would not have any public ceremony for my daughter's attaining age. It is a female secret [*peṇkaḷ rahasyam*]. There is simply no need to inform the whole *ūru* [village, native place] of this matter.

Others made it clear that the transition from public to privatized constructions of female sexuality had strategic value in terms of the economic and cultural shame attached to having unmarried post-pubertal daughters. This is an increasing social problem in the fishing community, and in Kanyakumari district more generally, where there is an unusually high incidence of female literacy and most women marry after they are 19 years of age.[16]

Beatrice (school teacher): People are starting to wonder about the ceremony—why should we let everyone know? Passing men can then comment and do *keli* [tease, mock]. Hindu customs are there to advertise that our girl has come of age, she is available for marriage. At the same time now if there are two such girls in a family and they are both unmarried, people will talk. So parents worry and grieve over the girls—how are we to marry them? It is better not to have any ceremony, better to keep it to ourselves.

Even the presence of girls in the classroom becomes the occasion for new clashes between the sexualized body of the puberty ritual and the ostensibly ungendered body of the school child. Girls are withdrawn abruptly from the 'modern' space of the classroom, inducted into the sexualized space of kinship and ritual, and then have to come back and negotiate the teasing from classmates and from boys.

Teacher: They get teased by the boys. They call out: Has the pot cracked then?

In addition, the church, an overwhelming presence in coastal villages (Ram 1992: chapter 2), does not support the puberty ritual—making this the only life cycle ritual that is not officiated by a Catholic priest (see also Kapadia 1996: 112). There is evidence that for some, the First Communion is beginning to replace the puberty ceremony:

Santhoos Mary: There was no *saṭaṅku*—in our family, there is no such custom. We feel it is not right for people to get to know about it. Instead, we had a grand First Communion for me. But even then, my mother resented the big fuss my father's sister made over her contribution to the communion, so we dropped all such celebrations after that.

---

[16] Ram (1992: 222ff), on the importance of an educated strata among the village women. According to statistics from the 1981 census, literacy rates are 78 per cent, as against 22 per cent for the state as a whole; less than 5 per cent of women in the age group 15–19 are married, as against 22 per cent of women for the state as a whole. See also Swaminathan (1996, especially p. 10ff).

Moral Bodily Disciplines in the Making of the Female Sexed Subject

Although the anthropological gaze has been fascinated by the ritual, an equally, if not more significant aspect of the transition from pre-pubertal to womanly status is the moral discourse of instructions on bodily disciplines and restrictions, which accompanies the transition. The reason for the neglect of this dimension is quite possibly because it is not available for the anthropological gaze in the way that the more spectacular public ritual is. Even this more limited focus on the ritual has been rendered primarily in terms of the symbolic language of the ritual itself. The subjectivity of the women who undergo the ritual has not, for the most part, been a concern of the anthropological account. The underlying assumption seems to be that this subjectivity can be assumed, as something that can be read off the language of the ritual. We have seen already that this is not necessarily the case at all. We now come to a further complexity. There is a discourse which is not public but which in fact turns out to enjoy far greater shaping power over the subjectivity of women than the public fanfare of the ritual. This discourse revolves around the concept of *kaṭappāṭu*, which may be glossed in English as disciplines, but also as the duties and obligations which are incumbent on the girl after the ritual transition to womanhood. In practice, katappatu refers to the daily schooling of the female body in keeping one's bodily motility and language under control.[17] The nature of these instructions was conveyed by the women to us in conventionalized, generalized terms:

Do not go 'here and there'. [*inge ange pōkāte*]
There is no need to go out too much any more.
From now on, learn to behave yourself.

I have noted that the semantic field around the disciplinary tutelage of katappatu is intertwined with notions of duties and obligations. This intermingling of meanings meant that katappatu became immune from criticism or resentment. Far from being equated with a loss of freedom, most women and girls saw such restraint as marking the moment at which they stood on the threshold of becoming adult, a properly social occasion. Pre-pubertal childhood is not romanticized but is seen as a time before the advent of good sense, the more conventional meaning of *arivu* and of *buddhi*. Although these are more general terms that can be applied in

---

[17] See also, Ram (1992: chapters 3 and 4); Niranjana (1997), for a convergent discussion.

a non-gender-specific way, they do carry specific meanings for women. They refer to the development of a form of 'self-consciousness', in which the female self is fashioned on the basis of an awareness of her critical role in upholding the family's reputation and honour. In some ways, this consciousness expands to cover nearly all of a woman's sense of social subjecthood.

When I asked women to describe their childhood, there was puzzlement as to what they could describe. The following description comes from Karpagam, 60-year-old agricultural labourer from Chengalpattu district:

I would eat the *puḷi* [tamarind], play under the trees and near rivers. Using a small peanut for currency, I would play, I would play at making rice with a toy stove. I *did not understand anything*. Then as my *buddhi* increased, I was sent to work for a lady in Madras where my relative was a servant [emphasis added].

Lourdes: Certain *kaṭappāṭu* does come with puberty—do not go out too much, do not talk to others too much. But I felt I now had taken no responsibilities for my family, and I must consult my elders before doing things. A girl needs these disciplines. [I ask her if she did not miss her childhood freedoms.] Well, as a child I was just playing around. Now, I had a sense of how to conduct myself with responsibility.

The moral disciplines which surround the embodied transitions from pre- to post-menarche operate in a totalizing way, to encompass physiological, moral, and cognitive development. The textual traditions elaborate this totalizing schema (see Ram 2003). What flowers at the point of menarche according to the literary, performative, and medical traditions are not merely the reproductive organs and breasts, but a number of quintessentially 'feminine' *kunam* (Skt guṇas): *accam, maṭam, nāṇam, payarippu*. These traits, listed in the chapters on reproduction found in medical Siddha texts (Venukopal 1986: chapter 2), are not obscure. On the contrary, they are readily and commonly listed by contemporary Tamils as the traits of femininity. The Tamil Lexicon, itself a thoroughly contemporary endeavour,[18] undertakes to gloss their meaning as: *accam*: dread, terror; *maṭam*: ignorance, folly, artlessness; *nāṇam*: shyness, coyness, shame, sensitive dread of evil, keen moral sense, shrinking as does a startled plant or animal when touched; *payarippu*: disgust, abhorrence, delicacy, modesty, shrinking from anything strange (*The Tamil Lexicon* 1982: 22).

---

[18] For the Tamil nationalist politics surrounding the publication of *The Tamil Lexicon*, see Nambi Arooran (1980: 110ff).

The kunam are therefore simultaneously emotion, forms of ethical conduct, and forms of cognition, all said to spontaneously flower along with the girl's sexuality. These descriptions strikingly resonate with the women's descriptions of their experiences of the transition to womanhood. In particular, the embodied construction of a specifically feminine morality and cognitive maturity (buddhi, arivu) stands out in the women's accounts.

However, there are important divergences between the dominant discourse on female sexuality and the discourses of the women. Where the dominant discourse sees female sexuality as flowering spontaneously, there is nothing spontaneous about this production as far as the women are concerned. Femininity is still integrally a morality for the women, but it is a morality produced by acceptance and internalization of a hard and rigorous disciplining of one's bodily subjectivity. An account offered by Victoria, now working for an NGO in Chenglepet, gives us a glimpse of how shame and self-awareness, supposedly spontaneously flowering in young women, are experienced by the women themselves as a shift in inter-subjectivity, as a consciousness that is produced in the knowing gaze of others:

I came of age in the hostel. Older girls had tried to tell me what this was, others just laughed. My mother said I was a big girl now, that I should not laugh, talk or move too freely. I felt shame, so this is what it was, I understood, this is how I will be misunderstood by others if I do not do what mother says.

The arrival of buddhi and arivu entails undertaking observance of these moral disciplines. The result is not only the making of the self, but the making of the self as a socially responsible being, a process whereby the woman comes to see that the family's good name depends on her. Although the advice is worded in generalizing terms 'Do not go here and there' (*Inge ange pōkāte*), the girl understands the sexual core of the injunction.

Pamela Rose: I knew what was meant—what they meant by not doing wrong involved not becoming pregnant, now that my periods had started.

In a striking demonstration of a selective rendition of modernity, the women, whether or not they expressed ambivalence about the overly sexualizing, public ritualized treatment of girls' bodies, in all cases fiercely retained the importance of the moral discourse of sexually disciplining the self. Over and over again, our questions as to whether they would educate their girls about menstruation were understood and affirmed by the women in terms of the moral discourse of *kaṭuppāṭu* in sharp variance to the model of scientific education advocated by discourses of reform.

Antoniammal: My school friends had already told me, that this is how it will come, you will find you have a new sense of wisdom, sense [*buddhi*]. *Buddhi* comes from the coming of age. At the time, I felt shy but also a little proud, not embarrassed. But the *kaṭuppāṭu* came hard to me. They said I was now a big girl, that I should not go out too much, not mix too much with other children, I should cease roaming around, going out to cinemas and such like, and generally not go too far [from the home]. I felt the passing of a period in my life. Then I came to accept it. It meant, after all, that others would see that I was a well-behaved girl, rather than a bad [*moshamāna*, immoral] one.

Antoniammal strikingly expressed the tautological nature of the system of moral reasoning which identifies coming of age with the acceptance of disciplines:

After all, *Vīṭile āna piḷḷai vīṭile tān irrukaṇam*. *The girl who has become of the house* [i.e. attained puberty] *cannot but stay in the house*. In terms of my daughter, yes, I would teach her. In those days my mother was not educated and did not, but I am educated and I would teach her. I educate her in other ways, after all, so I would in this respect as well, I would tell her not to run around any more, to mind her step.

Santi (woman in her forties): Yes I would teach girls about it beforehand, that this is what will happen, and you must not do certain things. Is it not right to instruct a child who might do the wrong thing? [She elaborates on the instruction]: 'You are a girl, others will speak ill of you, reform your ways and behave.' That is my way, to teach the young. There are those who resent my instructions to their children. But that is my way.

The theme of replacing social control over sexuality with self-control is not limited to the sphere of sexuality. It merges with a broader campaign to get subjects to take responsibility for their actions—as opposed to attributing it to *pēy*s or spirit demons. Fr John, for instance, writes tracts that ask people to see their own imagination, their fear, and guilt as the only reason for psychological problems.[19] Resonances of their messages are clearly heard in statements like the following by Lourdes. When asked whether she believes in the discourse about pēys that are attracted to girls at the time of menarche, she responds:

Well, this is what the grandmothers say—don't throw out the bloodied rags, it will bring the *pēy*. But I think—well, I am the *pēy*, I am the *pishāshu*, so why would they come to me? My mind, that is the reason for these *pēy*s.

FEMINISM AND DIVERGENT REGIMES OF SEXUALITY

I have argued that the rationalistic, secular, scientific dimensions of the non-Brahmin movement's construction of modernity continue to exercise

---

[19] See Ram (1996b: 302ff) and Ram (1998: 122ff) for a discussion of Fr John's tracts.

an important influence, thanks to the ongoing efforts of those who may be regarded, in the Gramscian sense of the term, as state intellectuals (see Ram 1996b). I have traced these effects both in the ambivalence to puberty as constructed by ritual, and in the upholding of puberty as entailing codes of chastity. Even in the upholding of chastity as female honour, the women interpret it in a specifically activist way, embracing it as a personalized code of conduct in which they as women are responsible for family honour.[20] This is the only available alternative, vastly preferable to becoming the passive objects of disciplining by the family, by the neighbours, and by society. Many women openly expressed their special pride in never having given their elders any occasion to explicitly instruct them on how to behave. For example, Beatrice said: 'There were no restraints placed on me, because my mother had utmost faith in her daughters.' Pamela Rose said: 'I did not need to be told these things—I was already a quiet type, went only to the next few houses.' This active sense of being responsible for the family's honour is in many ways an extension of coastal women's material sources of independence. Chastity becomes yet another way in which women, particularly in the fishing economy, 'look after' their families.

At the same time there are wider sources than the fishing economy for such an activist interpretation of female chastity. The poet Tiruvalluvar, writing between AD 400 and AD 500, has been widely popularized by the politics of Tamil language-nationalism. His best known work, the *Tirukkural*, is particularly popular, I would argue, due to its being constructed by the Dravidian movement as 'secular', compatible with its own preference for a secular-rational modern. In the *Tirukkural*, the poet raises the banner on behalf of women, setting the tone for the parameters of radical debate on female chastity within contemporary Tamil politics:

cirai kākkum kāppu eṇceyyum makalir
nirai kākkum kappe talai

I translate it thus:

Of what use is it to the girl to protect her by placing her and watching her in a prison-like home?
To control chastity with one's mind, is the highest form of all.

These debates, conducted exclusively with reference to the parameters of Tamil tradition, do not exhaust the meanings of modernity available to Tamil women. The pan-Indian women's movement provides a widely

---

[20] For a similar argument in relation to female interpretations of honour in the context of Bedouin women, see Abu-Lughod (1986).

circulating discourse in which a much more radical reconceptualization of women's embodied rights has been attempted. A recurring motif in these challenges to patriarchal constructions of female puberty is the contrast between the fear and ignorance in which girls experience the changes in their body, and a feminist demand for knowledge and bodily autonomy. The Marathi street theatre play written and performed in the late 1980s, *Mulgi Zhali Āhe* ('A girl child is born'), critically mimics the generalizing injunctions thrown at the girl when she comes to puberty:

Don't lose control, don't give up your woman's vow:
Don't speak while looking up, stay in the house;
Bend your head, look down;
Walk without looking above, don't let your eyes wander.[21]

A Tamil short story, written by the feminist author Ambai, highlights a girl's sense of terrified abandonment when even her mother, hitherto the source of female wisdom and nurturance, becomes the mouthpiece of patriarchal injunctions. This is experienced by her daughter as the mother's fall from a near-autonomous power (see Ambai 1992: 'My Mother, Her Crime'). The circulation of such feminist critiques, more radical than those offered by the Dravidian movement, means that when women who are already involved in NGO work are given the opportunity to reflexively reconsider codes of chastity, they are capable of shifting their position with remarkable speed. My fieldwork provided the occasion for one such renegotiation. Stella and I conducted the interviews in Kanyakumari together, and would discuss them, while transcribing, late into the night. On her return to Chengalpattu, the first thing she did was to organize a workshop for adolescent girls. Her talent, which resides particularly in language, both in written and spoken form, will hopefully come through even in my hastily translated notes of the speech I heard her deliver on that occasion:

Stella: What do your parents and elders say when they give you that *tāvaṇi*, those two metres of cloth which are handed out as soon as your body changes?
    Girl attending workshop: Do not go out too much, conduct yourself responsibly.
    Stella: In this fear we come of age. Have they told you what happens in your bodies? As a result of their ignorance we bear the brunt of folly and blame. The boy is not blamed, but we and not only us girls, but our mothers and fathers and grandparents are blamed. The restrictions start even before puberty. Boys can come home at all hours, after the second show [movies], sleep anywhere. Once we start wearing the sari, it cannot be worn anyhow, but just so, tucked in just right, only then is it modest. There are new kinds of

---

[21] Translations from Marathi to English are by Leela Dube, cited in Van Woerkens (1990: WS 11).

work responsibilities, and we are removed from school. Puberty is a time of dreaming as well as of bodily changes. Puberty is saturated with cinema and video images. Physiological maturing does not mean we are ready to have babies. The legal age is high, but in villages girls are marrying at fifteen. It is regarded as a lessening of the patent's duty, their burden is lightened by marrying us off to someone. But girls are not ready for marriage and babies and this leads to many complications as the girl does not have the maturity to deal with the enormous adjustments to the in-laws' houses.

We are seen as easily spoiled. It is as if we are the food that is cooked today—spoiled tomorrow, or like the flower that opens in the morning—spoiled by evening. Even coming late to puberty, or to marriage or to children, is regarded as a scandal. The virtues of femininity—*accam, nānam, payarippu*—only adopt them if appropriate. Only feel shame if you do wrong, not just for being female, or for saying your name to a stranger, like when I asked you all your names this morning. We blame the men. What about our own values? We take the punishment before we have done wrong, we panic and throw ourselves into wells, or take to abortifacients. If a woman questions, we ourselves tell her: sit down and be quiet. If one girl is suffering or questioning, we must all support her. We are bones, flesh, blood, spirit, human, not worms or insects. Say to yourself, I have life and I must live. We must realise we cannot blame society. Society is also us. What is it to be: to walk looking down at our feet, or with straight torso and looking ahead, as Bharatiyar[22] taught us, so that we too will know what is going on in the world?

The persistent appearance of certain sites of resistance in these feminist tracts, widely separated as they are in region and context, testifies to the existence of certain pan-Indian unities in the way that patriarchal codes have constructed the female body. At the same time, we need to remain alert to differences in emphasis and more substantial qualitative differences of style within these patriarchal codes. A good deal of feminist resistance has been directed at the values of impurity, shame, and seclusion that accompany female menstruation and menarche. Yet, in the light of the ethnographic evidence I have introduced in this chapter, many of these values emerge as specifically Brahminic and Sanskritic. The existence of alternative, more celebratory codes of female puberty needs to be recognized. The responses of the coastal Christian women do not encourage feminist romanticism about these alternative codes. Rather, these women are caught up in the construction of a different modernity, engaging the values more relevant to their caste and class location.

REFERENCES

Abu-Lughod, L. (1986), *Veiled Sentiments: Honor and Poetry in a Bedouin Society.* Berkeley and Los Angeles: University of California Press.

---

[22] Stella draws here on the familiarity of Tamils with the Tamil nationalist poet Subramania C. Bharathi (1882–1921).

Alphonse, T. (1991), *Anpu Idayankal, Inpa Utayankal*. Trichinopoly: Holy Family College.
Ambai (1992), 'My Mother, Her Crime', in Ambai, *A Purple Sea: Short Stories by Ambai*, (translated by L. Holmstrom). Madras: Affiliated East–West Press, pp. 11–21.
Anandhi, S. (1991a), 'Women's Question in the Dravidian Movement, c. 1925–1948', *Social Scientist*, 19(5–6): 24–41.
—— (1991b), 'Representing Devadasis: *Dasigal Mosavalai* as a Radical Text', *Economic and Political Weekly*, 26(11 and 12): 736–46.
—— (1998), 'Reproductive Bodies and Regulated Sexuality: Birth Control Debates in Early 20th Century Tamilnadu', in M.E. John and J. Nair (eds), *A Question of Silence? The Sexual Economies of Modern India*. New Delhi: Kali for Women, pp. 139–66.
Appadurai, A. (1981), *Worship and Conflict under Colonial Rule: A South Indian Case*. Cambridge: Cambridge University Press.
Asad, T. (1995), 'Two European Images of Non-European Rule', in T. Asad (ed.), *Anthropology and the Colonial Encounter*. London: Ithaca Press, pp. 103–18.
Banerjee, S. (1989), *The Parlour and the Streets: Elite and Popular Culture in Nineteenth Century Calcutta*. Calcutta: Seagull Books.
Bayly, S. (1989), *Saints, Goddesses and Kings: Muslims and Christians in South Indian Society 1700–1900*. Cambridge: Cambridge University Press.
Chatterjee, Partha (1986), *Nationalist Thought and the Colonial World: A Derivative Discourse?* London: Zed Press.
—— (1993), *The Nation and Its Fragments: Colonial and Postcolonial Histories*. Princeton: Princeton University Press.
Cohen, D.W. (1991), 'La Fontaine and Wamimbi: The Anthropology of "Time-Present" as the Substructure of Historical Oration', in J. Bender and D.E. Wellbery (eds), *Chronotypes: The Construction of Time*. Stanford: Stanford University Press, pp. 205–25.
Das, V. (1995), *Critical Events: An Anthropological Perspective on Contemporary India*. New Delhi: Oxford University Press.
Dirks, N. (1989), *The Hollow Crown: Ethnohistory of an Indian Kingdom*. Cambridge: Cambridge University Press.
Dumont, L. (1983), *Affinity as a Value: Marriage Alliance in South India, with Comparative Essays on Australia*. Chicago and London: The University of Chicago Press.
Fabian, J. (1983), *Time and the Other: How Anthropology Makes Its Object*. New York: Columbia University Press.
—— (1991), 'Of Dogs Alive, Birds Dead and Time to Tell a Story', in J. Bender and D.E. Wellbery (eds), *Chronotypes: The Construction of Time*. Stanford: Stanford University Press, pp. 185–204.
Good, A. (1991), *The Female Bridegroom: A Comparative Study of Life-crisis Rituals in South India and Sri Lanka*. Oxford: Oxford University Press.
Haggis, J. (1998), '"Good Wives and Mothers" or "Dedicated Workers"? Contradictions of Domesticity in the "Mission of Sisterhood", Travancore, South India', in K. Ram and M. Jolly (eds), *Maternities and Modernities: Colonial*

and *Postcolonial Experiences in Asia and the Pacific*. Cambridge: Cambridge University Press, pp. 81–113.

Irschick, E.F. (1986), *Tamil Revivalism in the 1930s*. Madras: Cre-A.

Jeffrey, Robin (1992), *Politics, Women and Well-Being: How Kerala Became a Model*. London: Macmillan Publishers Ltd.

Kannabiran, Kalpana (1995), 'Judiciary, Social Reform and Debate on Religious Prostitution', *Economic and Political Weekly*, 30(43): WS 59–69.

Kapadia, K. (1996), *Siva and Her Sisters: Gender, Caste and Class in Rural South India*. Colorado: Westview.

Lakshmi, D.S. (1990), 'Mother, Mother-Community and Mother-Politics in Tamilnadu', *Economic and Political Weekly*, 25(42 and 43): WS 72–83.

Mani, L. (1989), 'Contentious Traditions: The Debate on Sati in Colonial India', in K. Sangari and S. Vaid (eds), *Recasting Women: Essays in Colonial History*. New Delhi: Kali for Women, pp. 88–126.

Martin, Emily (1987), *The Woman in the Body: A Cultural Analysis of Reproduction*. Boston: Beacon Press.

Nair, Janaki (1994), 'The Devadasi, Dharma and the State', *Economic and Political Weekly*, 29(50): 3157–68.

Nambi Arooran, K. (1980), *Tamil Renaissance and Dravidian Nationalism 1905–1944*. Madurai: Koodal Publishers.

Narayana Rao, V., D. Shulman, and S. Subrahmanyam (1992), *Symbols of Substance: Court and State in Nayaka Period, Tamilnadu*. New Delhi: Oxford University Press.

Niranjana, Seemanthini (1997), 'Femininity, Space and the Female Body', in M. Thapan (ed.), *Embodiment: Essays on Gender and Identity*. New Delhi: Oxford University Press, pp. 107–24.

Niranjana, T., P. Sudhir, and V. Dhareshwar (eds) (1993), *Interrogating Modernity: Culture and Colonialism in India*. Calcutta: Seagull Books.

Pandian, J. (1992), 'The Goddess Kannagi: A Dominant Symbol of South Indian Tamil Society', in J.A. Preston (ed.), *Mother Worship: Theme and Variations*. Chapel Hill: University of North Carolina Press, pp. 177–91.

Pandian, M.S.S. (1992), *The Image Trap: MG Ramachandran in Film and Politics*. New Delhi: Sage Publications.

—— (1993a), 'Jayalalitha: Desire and Political Legitimation', *Seminar*, January, 401: 31–4.

—— (1993b), 'Denationalising the Past: Nation in E.V. Ramaswamy's Political Discourse', *Economic and Political Weekly*, 26(42): 2282–7.

Pandian, M.S.S., Anandhi S., and A.R. Venkatachalapathy (1991), 'Of Maltova Mothers and Other Stories', *Economic and Political Weekly*, 26(16): 1059–64.

Panikkar, K.N. (1995), *Culture, Ideology, Hegemony-Intellectuals and Social Consciousness in Colonial India*. New Delhi: Tulika.

Price, Pamela (1996), 'Revolution and Rank in Tamil Nationalism', *The Journal of Asian Studies*, 55(2): 359–83.

Ram, Kalpana (1992), *Mukkuvar Women: Gender, Hegemony and Capitalist Transformation in a South Indian Fishing Community*. New Delhi: Kali for Women.

Ram, Kalpana (1994), 'Medical Management and Giving Birth: Responses of Coastal Women in Tamilnadu', *Reproductive Health Matters*, November, 4: 20–6.

—— (1996a), 'The Female Body of Possession: A Feminist Phenomenological Perspective on Rural Tamil Women's Experiences', paper presented at Anveshi conference, 'Women and Mental Health', February.

—— (1996b), 'Rationalism, Cultural Nationalism and the Reform of Body Politics: Minority Intellectuals of the Tamil Catholic community', in P. Uberoi (ed.), *Social Reform, Sexuality and the State*. New Delhi: Sage Publications, pp. 291–318.

—— (1998), 'Maternity and the Story of Enlightenment in the Colonies: Tamil Coastal Women, South India', in K. Ram and M. Jolly (eds), *Maternities and Modernities: Colonial and Postcolonial Experiences in Asia and the Pacific*. Cambridge: Cambridge University Press, pp. 114–43.

—— (2003), 'The Female Body of Puberty: Tamil Linguistic and Ritual Perspectives on Sexuality', in P. Komesaroff (ed.), *Sexuality and Medicine: Bodies, Practices, Knowledges*. Philadelphia: Xlibris.

Ramaswamy, S. (1994), 'The Nation, the Region, and the Adventures of a Tamil Hero', *Contributions to Indian Sociology* (n.s.), 28(2): 295–322.

Sangari, K. (1995), 'Politics of Diversity: Religious Communities and Multiple Partiarchies', Parts I and II, *Economic and Political Weekly*, 30(51): 3287–310 and 30(52): 3381–9.

Sangari, K. and S. Vaid (eds) (1989), *Recasting Women: Essays in Colonial History*. New Delhi: Kali for Women.

Seremetakis, N. (1991), *The Last Word: Women, Death and Divination in Inner Mani*. Chicago and London: The University of Chicago Press.

Srinivasan, Amrit (1984), 'Temple "Prostitution" and Community Reform: An Examination of the Ethnographic, Historical and Textual Context of the Devadasi of Tamilnadu, India', unpublished PhD, Anthropology Department, Cambridge University.

Stein, Burton (1980), *Peasant State and Society in Medieval South India*. New Delhi: Oxford University Press.

Stoler, A. (1995), *Race and the Education of Desire*. Durham and London: Duke University Press.

Swaminathan, P. (1996), 'The Failures of Success? An Analysis of Tamilnadu's Recent Demographic Experience', Working Paper No. 141, Madras Institute of Development Studies, July.

The Tamil Lexicon (1982), Madras: University of Madras Press.

Van Woerkens, Martine (1990), 'Dialogues on First Menstrual Periods: Mother–Daughter Communication', *Economic and Political Weekly*, 25(17): WS 7–14.

Vance, Carol (1991), 'Anthropology Rediscovers Sexuality: A Theoretical Comment', *Social Science and Medicine*, 33(8): 875–84.

Venukopal, Du. Mu (1986), *Cul Maruttuvam*. Madras: Office of the Text Book Committee for Sidda Medicine, Tamilnadu Sidda Marutuvam Corporation.

Chapter 4

OUTING HETERONORMATIVITY
Nation, Citizen, Feminist Disruptions*

NIVEDITA MENON**

THIS CHAPTER IS AN ENGAGEMENT with a range of political assertions that I term counter-heteronormative, which acquired, during the 1990s in India, a sense of autobiography. Questions about history begin to emerge, and of course, points of origin turn out to be elastic. They can appear to stretch backwards to antiquity, or they can snap back to yesterday, depending on the name used to describe the phenomenon being traced and on the theoretical framework supporting the search. Is it anachronistic to look for something called 'feminism', 'homosexuality', or 'nation' at a time in which these terms have no meaning? Or is it impossible to look

---

* Originally published in Nivedita Menon (ed.), *Sexualities*. New Delhi: Women Limited and London: Zed Books.

** This chapter would have been quite literally impossible without the encouragement, generosity with campaign material, and serious engagements with earlier drafts that I have received from Arvind Narrain, Jaya Sharma, and V.N. Deepa. I would also like to thank Aditya Nigam, Bindu Menon, Gautam Bhan, Lakshmi Murthy, Tejaswini Ganti, Pramada Menon, and Lesley Esteves for their time and inputs. The contribution of participants at the seminar at the International Center for Advanced Studies, New York University, was invaluable. I have also been fortunate to receive thought-provoking feedback from scholars at Kitab Mandal, University of Michigan; Simmons College, Boston; Women's Studies Programme, UC Irvine; Centre for South Asia Studies, UC Berkeley.

backward in time except through the categories that we have already produced? Is it analytically correct or ethically permissible to apply our labels and descriptive terms to activities and identities that do not, or did not, identify themselves as such?

It is precisely when histories start being written that such dilemmas emerge, and we recognize the birth of a movement. That moment is the 1990s for counter-heteronormative movements in India. This chapter is not a history of such movements, but rather an attempt to destabilize feminist politics by engaging with the implications revealed by their politics.

The term 'counter-heteronormative' is used to refer to a range of political assertions that implicitly or explicitly challenge heteronormativity and the institution of monogamous patriarchal marriage. Such assertions are seen around the demand for the repeal of Section 377 of the Indian Penal Code, which penalizes 'sexual acts against the order of nature', and various kinds of political action around issues related to the lives and civil liberties of *hijra*s (a traditional community of male-to-female transgendered people), *kothi*s (a traditional identity assumed by men who perform femininity with male lovers but may also be married to women and have children), gay, lesbian, bisexual and trans people, and sex workers.

A distinction is being made here between everyday practices on the one hand, and on the other the narrativizing of these practices in a particular mode—that of modern history writing. This distinction is not between *public* and *private*, but between *political practices* (both public and private) and a certain mode of writing about these, the mode of *modern history writing*. People in their everyday practices have lived for centuries as individuals and in communities, overtly or covertly violating dominant norms. Self-identified gay and lesbian individuals appeared occasionally in the public eye, as when a glamour magazine published gay activist Ashok Row Kavi's coming-out interview in 1986. But it is in the 1990s that these histories begin to be traced and something like a movement acquires a self-identity, increasing visibility, and confidence. It is when Kavi's interview of 1986 reappears in 1999, in a 'Dateline' tracing a history of 'the lesbian, gay and bisexual peoples' movement in India', that it acquires the status of a historical fact belonging to this particular narrative.[1] In 1996 lesbian desire is traced to temple architecture in ancient India (Thadani 1996), and in 2000 a compilation is published, going back to Vedic texts of 1500

---

[1] Instances of other events included in 'Dateline' are the formation in 1989 of Delhi Group, a regular meeting of lesbian feminists, and the signature campaign by women's groups in 1987 against the discharge from service of two policewomen who got married. 'Dateline' in Fernandez (1999: 181).

BC to find same-sex love (Vanita and Kidwai 2000). A significant essay by Paola Bacchetta is critical of US-situated academics praising the fact that '*finally* queer movements emerged in the postcolonial world in the *mid-to-late 1990s*' (Bacchetta, 'Rescaling Transnational 'Queerdom'; emphasis in original). Mapping 'lesbian agentic forms in Delhi in the 1980s', Bacchetta asserts that lesbianisms in India have ancient roots, 'much prior to the US's existence as a settler colony itself'. However, this statement draws on Giti Thadani's work of 1996, while the narratives of lesbian suicides and marriages that Bacchetta traces to the late 1970s and 1980s are derived from a citizens' report on homosexuality prepared by an activist group in 1991. Until the report was published, these incidents had remained merely scattered sensational newspaper items.

The first distinction then is that between everyday practices that are not necessarily self-conscious, and their selection and welding into a historical narrative, which is a self-conscious political practice. However, a second distinction should also be made between an understanding that makes the first distinction and an understanding that is simply blind to everyday practices that do not take on the form of self-conscious political activity. From this point of view, Bacchetta's critique of the assumption that '*finally* queer movements emerged in the postcolonial world in the mid-to-late 1990s' is still valid.

Why the 1990s? From the late 1980s, growing awareness about the acquired immune deficiency syndrome (AIDS) epidemic made it increasingly legitimate to talk of sex outside the realms of law, demography, and medicine—and not only as violence against women or in terms of 'population control'. Although AIDS is a disease which also fits into medical discourse, its source made sex itself speakable. For example, a highly political, left-wing, non-funded group supporting the rights of homosexuals, which filed a petition against Section 377 in 1992 (and which produced the report that Bacchetta refers to), calls itself AIDS Bhedbhav Virodhi Andolan (ABVA; Movement Against AIDS-based Discrimination), 'AIDS' in effect acting as a code for homosexuality. Sex workers' unions such as Durbar Mahila Samanwaya Committee in Kolkata and Sampada Grameen Mahila Sanstha (SANGRAM) in Sangli, Maharashtra, both started as peer-education programmes distributing condoms as part of a human immunodeficiency virus (HIV) control project. They now function like trade unions, protecting their members in various ways, organizing street demonstrations, initiating legal action against police violence, and standing up to local criminals (Misra *et al.* 2005).

International funding for HIV/AIDS prevention played a significant role in the creation of new non-governmental organizations (NGOs) dealing with sexuality, or added sexuality programmes in old ones.[2] Once such programmes were started and telephone helplines and safe spaces established, it opened the floodgates for political articulation of non-normative sexualities. Autonomous women's groups had since the late 1970s had discussions on sexuality, including lesbian sexuality and links with international women's groups. But AIDS awareness finally helped produce a critical mass of such an understanding in the public realm in India. It provided the opening and the monetary resources for public articulation of issues around sexuality, for workshops and meetings often providing startling new perspectives, bringing together people from all over the country and international participants, and for mobilization of such politics at a country-wide level (Deepa 2005; Gupta 2005; Narrain and Bhan 2005; Rai Chowdhury 2005; Rege 1997a, 1997b; Sharma and Nath 2005). For example, when 'a few faces tired of hiding behind the mask' in a small town in West Bengal decided to form a group in 2003, they were supported by several big AIDS-work related NGOs that received international funding (Rai Chowdhury 2005: 217–18). The Bangkok Conference of the Asian Lesbian network in 1990 brought Indian delegates face to face with their other Asian counterparts—'It was like looking into a mirror.' More significantly, that conference brought together lesbian feminists from different parts of India for the first time, leading to 'more focused activities back home' (Rege 1997a: 145).

Another factor that made sexuality visible in public spaces, both elite and non-elite, was the opening up of the media in the 1990s, as part of the liberalization of the Indian economy. Sexually explicit and suggestive images from the West flowed in through private cable television channels, effecting a certain degree of banalisation of the hitherto unspeakable.

One is reminded of Foucault's interview that urged us 'to recognise the indefiniteness of the struggle...' (Foucault 1980: 56–7). Thus, while AIDS activism as it arose in the US and other Western countries was an intrinsic part of gay political activism and 'had to challenge traditional modes of empowering knowledge as well as traditional modes of authorising and legitimising power' (Halperin 1995: 28), in India AIDS prevention is, in effect, the point at which disciplinary power and biopower's normalizing techniques intersect. The official discourse of HIV/AIDS control and

---

[2] There are also groups that refuse funding on principle, such as ABVA mentioned earlier.

the funding generated by it is extremely state-centric, and is about new ways of regulating and controlling sexuality and the population as a whole. However, its effects are uncontrollable, and spill over into forms of radicalization it could not have predicted or desired. Swati Ghosh has addressed the emergence of the 'prostitute' as 'sex worker' in the context of HIV/AIDS discourse, as the point at which the sex worker is subjected to governmental technologies even as s/he emerges as Subject of other sets of political discourses (Ghosh 2004). At the same time, AIDS discourse itself as well as funding imperatives can also tame radicalism and normalize once non-normative forms of sex, with new rules and regulations. ('Sex outside marriage/homosexual sex is okay *as long as it is safe sex*'.) Counsellors and therapists now reserve for confessions of unprotected sex the guilt-inducement and opprobrium once reserved by priests for masturbation.[3] The focus on AIDS can be narrowly health-related and depoliticized. Sexual identities like kothi tend to get reified by NGOs whose continued funding depends on the numbers they have 'outreach' with, and competition for funding can splinter solidarity. Lawrence Cohen demonstrates in his textured account how NGOs compete for what he calls 'AIDS capital' and how terms like kothi get produced as a 'black box', an unquestioned and unquestionable fact (Cohen 2005).

Perhaps most disturbingly, the AIDS industrial complex with its big players, the multinational pharmaceutical companies, can be formidably anti-democratic. Vimochana, a feminist organization in Bengaluru that tried to initiate a discussion on material circulated by a Canadian feminist health group questioning dominant assumptions about the relationship between HIV and AIDS, found itself blocked, both by funders and other groups working on AIDS.[4] In non-party political circles in India this is rare,

---

[3] A new theology that Foucault defied. While David Halperin sharply attacks James Miller's biography (*The Passion of Michel Foucault*, Simon and Schuster, 1993) for its 'lurid portrayal' and pathologizing of Foucault's advocacy of a range of sexual practices, Halperin shows that for Foucault, such practices were transformative techniques of resistance, and offers us an alternative reading of his understanding of 'pleasure' in *Saint Foucault* (Halperin 1995; specifically pp. 51–125). Farber (1999: 64) writes about subcultures in the US that eroticize unprotected sex: 'What is interesting about this new phenomenon is that it breaks the holiest of AIDS pledges—to live in fear forever…You can no longer control a person who doesn't fear death.' Consider Foucault (2003: 248) on death: 'Now that power is decreasingly the power of the right to take life, and increasingly the right to intervene to make live…death becomes…the end of power too. Power can control mortality but it has no control over death.'

[4] Vimochana has been trying to set up a discussion around issues raised by Women's Health Interaction, Ottawa, in a document, *Uncommon Questions: A Feminist Exploration of AIDS*, August 1993, which draws on the dissident work of scientists like Peter Duesberg,

for every opinion, for better or worse, gets thrashed out, even if without resolution and however acrimoniously. The AIDS orthodoxy, however, has proved impossible to breach, even at the level of raising questions. One does indeed have to recognize 'the indefiniteness of the struggle'.

The presence of large numbers of NGOs receiving funding for AIDS-related work makes it necessary to maintain a distinction between political practice that is self-consciously counter-hegemonic and the increasingly acceptable discourse about homosexuality produced by the former which is restricted to AIDS prevention. And yet, it often happens that counter-hegemonic voices are able to tip the scales within a constellation produced by a range of ideas and circumstances external to themselves. Thus, by 1998, when Deepa Mehta's film *Fire*, depicting a sexual affair between sisters-in-law in a traditional Hindu household, was attacked violently by the Hindu Right, there was a sufficiently self-aware community for the attack to act as a catalyst for public demonstrations in defence of freedom of expression and against homophobia, on the streets of Mumbai and Delhi and some other cities, of a size and visibility unknown before in India (Bachman 2002; Ghosh 2003b; John and Niranjana 1999; Kapur 2000; Patel 2002). These demonstrations brought together opponents of the Hindu Right, defenders of freedom of expression, human rights activists, and gay and lesbian activists—of course, many or all of these categories overlapped.

This chapter engages with this politics, now over a decade old, from the perspective of feminism in India. What are the questions raised and challenges posed to feminist politics by seriously engaging with the worldview provided by counter-heteronormativity?...

Eleni Papadopulos-Eleopulos, and Robert Root-Bernstein, who raise questions about the link between HIV and AIDS, and advance alternative theories about the causes of AIDS. A somewhat polemical articulation of this view by Thabo Mbeki, President of South Africa, has done it much harm, but political movements must look beyond statements by politicians. In the US, 'AIDS dissidents' and gay/lesbian rights activists of AIDS Coalition to Unleash Power (ACT UP) and Health Education AIDS Liaison (HEAL) are among those who have been conducting a vigorous campaign against prevalent health policies of mandatory HIV testing of pregnant women and administering of toxic drugs like AZT to those testing positive. They argue with the help of scientific and statistical evidence that AIDS is not an epidemic, that it is not caused by a virus, and that antibody testing cannot reliably predict illness. They have been calling for a public hearing to open up orthodoxies on the cause, identification, and treatment of AIDS. 'Health Dissidents Meet Mayor of San Francisco', *Continuum*, 5(5), mid-winter, 1999, p. 6. In India, a recent study (2006) has demonstrated that methods used to estimate the number of people infected by HIV/AIDS are flawed. The actual number may be only 40 per cent of official United Nations figures ('India "Overestimates" HIV/AIDS', BBC News, 13 December 2006).

...HISTORICAL ERASURE OF HOMOEROTICISM AND NATURALIZATION OF HETEROSEXUALITY

To consider how this transformation took place in India, it is important to remember that the criminalization of same-sex activity is no ancient Indian tradition, but a legal provision introduced in the nineteenth century by the British colonial government. Vanita and Kidwai (2000) point out that in Britain itself the anti-sodomy law of 1860 was progressive insofar as it reduced the punishment for sodomy from execution to 10 years' imprisonment. But its introduction in India in 1861 as Section 377 of the Indian Penal Code criminalized practices hitherto invisible to the law. Its description is general enough to allow any sexual act to be interpreted as coming under its ambit, for it prohibits 'voluntary carnal intercourse against the order of nature, with any man, woman or animal'. The law has rarely been invoked to punish anyone for consensual sex, but its existence on the statute books enables routine police harassment of men and hijras in public places (Bhaskaran 2002; Revathi 2005; Vanita and Kidwai 2000: 195–6). The significance of the introduction of Section 377 can only be understood by revisiting the 'history of sexuality' in pre-colonial India.

There is abundant scholarship which establishes that the delegitimation of homosexual desire and the production of the naturally heterosexual, properly bi-gendered (unambiguously male *or* female) population of citizens, with the women respectably desexualized, is a process that is central to nation formation all over the globe.[5] A significant and revealing instance is the fascinating account of Iran's 'long 19th century' by Afsaneh Najmabadi who argues that it was the cultural encounter with Europe that produced in Iran 'the heteronormalisation of love and the feminisation of beauty' (Najmabadi 2005: 2). She further offers the stark conclusion that the modernist project of women's emancipation in Iran bore the 'birthmark of disavowal of male homosexuality' (ibid.: 7–8).

It is equally impossible to engage with what is called 'sexuality' in contemporary India without recognizing its passage through the complexity of the practices that were homogenized under the sign of Modernity. The polyvalence of gender identities and sexual desire prevalent even up to the nineteenth century in India was sutured in a variety of ways, through legal and social interventions that disciplined a range of non-normative sexualities and family arrangements. Ruth Vanita and Saleem Kidwai in their path-breaking collection *Same-Sex Love in India* trace from *c.* 1500 BC

---

[5] For an overview of this literature, see Stoler (2002).

up to the present, writings in Indian languages about 'love between women and love between men who are not biologically related' (Vanita and Kidwai 2000: xiii). It is only in the nineteenth century, they argue, that 'a minor homophobic voice that was largely ignored by mainstream society in pre-colonial India...becomes a dominant voice' (ibid.: 191).

It is important to insist here that the scholarship that makes this kind of argument is not an 'indigenist' critique of 'the West'—what is at issue is not discourses of Place, but of Time, leading us to the realization that the values of modernity have not been unambiguously emancipatory, have often eradicated spaces of relative autonomy, and produced new forms of subjection.

Thus, expressions of non-normative sexuality and desire, far from being 'Western' imports, as Hindu right-wing critics of feminism in India allege, have much older histories as everyday practices. Scholarship in several fields has shown that earlier forms of sexuality, family, and property arrangements that did not conform to modern bourgeois patriarchal norms were reconstituted to fit these new norms by a strange partnership of British colonial institutions on the one hand and the modernizing nationalist elites who opposed the British, on the other.[6]

Anxieties about homoeroticism circulated in a variety of spheres. Cross-dressing in theatre is a phenomenon that yields rich insights. For instance, the study of Bengali theatre by Rimli Bhattacharya shows that arguments about gender verisimilitude were made in order to end the practice of men playing women's roles (Bhattacharya 2003). However, that the perceived 'naturalness' of gendered appearance is a product of socio-historical circumstances is clear from Kathryn Hansen's work on theatre in western India, which demonstrates that female impersonation, far from appearing unnatural, in fact fashioned 'a widely circulated standard for female appearance and modified code of feminine conduct' (Hansen 1999: 128). Female viewers indeed, were instructed to model themselves on the transvestite actor. Clearly, cross-dressing produced anxieties about what Hansen terms the 'underlying homoerotic valence that linked the gazes of hero and male heroine on stage, and impersonator and male spectator in the theatre hall' (ibid.: 139). Rimli Bhattacharya, too, records that in Bengali theatre, alongside the arguments about the unsatisfactory portrayal of women by men, was a pervasive 'undercurrent of uneasiness about boys dressing up as girls/women'. An article on Bengali drama, while commenting on the choric dance of female companions in *jatras* by

---

[6] For a discussion of this work, see 'Introduction' in Menon (2007).

young boys, is also critical of their unattractiveness as female figures, their 'deformity' and 'discordant voices', but concludes with the entirely opposite fear, '...they imitate all posture and gesture calculated to soil the mind and pollute the fancy' (Bhattacharya 2003: 226–7).

Also illustrative is the controversy over a short story collection in Hindi titled *Chaklet* ('Chocolate') by Pandey Bechain Sharma (alias Ugra). In 1927, a charge of obscenity was made against the book, which purported in its eight short stories, to denounce male homosexuality. Writing about it, Charu Gupta argues that the three-pronged attack on *Chaklet*—by the colonial state, the growing nationalist movement, and the emerging high literary trends expressing a new 'Hindu' identity—despite the book's overt anti-homosexual stance, came about because by 'speaking the unspeakable' it acknowledged the prevalence of such practices. The attack on it was also part of a nationalist critique, for the 'de-gendered (Indian) male was one stereotype of colonial domination' which *Chaklet* seemed to prove, by casting doubts on 'the stability of the heterosexual regime, on procreative imperatives, and on modern monogamous ideals of marriage' (Gupta 2001: 61–3).

Ruth Vanita's view is that that while Ugra claimed that he wrote the book to denounce homosexuality, many readers, both homosexual and anti-homosexual, received from it positive representations of male–male sexual relations. Homosexual characters in the book are 'respectable' members of society, highly cultured, and educated, 'in fact, they are the mirror images of the Hindi litterateurs engaged in the controversy'. More alarmingly, these men claim Hindi, Urdu, and English literature as their own, tracing an illustrious lineage for homosexual activity, from Socrates to Surdas and Tulsidas. Although they are always defeated in debate, the ambiguity of the message of the book is acknowledged, Vanita points out, by readers' responses, divided between praising the collection and protesting its indecency (Vanita 2002: 7, chapter 9).

The significant overarching theme here is the interrelationship between colonial/European homophobia and nationalist disavowal of homoeroticism in India as it appears to have been in Iran and other parts of the non-Western world.[7]

---

[7] Some traditions that offered space for, and even valorized, gender ambiguity, still linger in practices like men dressing as women to propitiate the female deity of a temple in Kerala. In an annual pilgrimage, men not only wear women's clothes, but use make-up and accessories to please the goddess Babu (2005).

HISTORY AND NAMING

The completeness of this erasure is evident in the Hindu right-wing attack on *Fire* as a false representation of Indian reality, introducing Western and Islamic aberrations into Hindu/Indian society. As Jyoti Puri has pointed out, questions of alternative sexualities thus find themselves 'fused with questions of nationhood', and this is why one of the important strategies to counter forms of homophobia and heterosexism has been to claim histories of homosexuality and alternative sexuality as inherent to Indian (Hindu and Islamic) traditions (Puri 1999: 182–3). However, it is not accurate to characterize this strategy as she does, as a claim that an 'exemplary' tradition has degenerated. If this were the claim, then Puri's critique would be justified, that it attracts the danger of a counter-claim that the tradition has in fact righted itself, and that it is the contemporary moment which is the degeneration (ibid.: 183). But I would argue that these attempts to make visible counter-hegemonic practices of sexuality are less interested in reclaiming 'tradition' than in writing modern histories, following the codes and protocols of historiography. They do not, as the previous section has shown, valorize the pre-modern, and indeed it is the tools provided by modernity that also enable the critique made by these scholars.

Clearly, history and naming are key issues of debate within the movement. They are interrelated because the very tracing of a movement, the attribution of a history, is determined by the name given to that which is being sought out. One argument is characterized by Vanita and Kidwai, as well as Giti Thadani, despite their differences,[8] that same-sex love and eroticism have origins that go back to as far as one has the cultural/linguistic resources to go, and that they can be identified by specific historical names that are not simply derivatives of modern self-consciousness.

Ruth Vanita's critique goes further than simply arguing that everyday same-sex practices existed but were not self-conscious. Rather, she insists that both in Europe and South Asia, same-sex love and eroticism were self-identified and widely recognized for centuries. Indeed, her earlier work with Saleem Kidwai traced precisely such sources and such names in India.[9] What makes such terms unavailable to modern-day Indians are

---

[8] See Vanita and Kidwai (2000: 2).

[9] Vanita mentions several examples of such words for 'what we feel for each other'—*tritiya prakriti* (the third nature, for men who prefer sex with men) in the fourth century *Kamasutra*; *swayamvara sakhi* in an eleventh-century Sanskrit text, which suggests choosing a female friend as life partner; *dogana* and *zanakhi* in Urdu (from the work of Carla Petievich), *chapti* for female-to-female sexual activity; and *amradparast* from Urdu

the processes in operation throughout the nineteenth century, erasing histories of homoeroticism. As a result, it now appears that the English term 'homosexuality' must be literally translated into Indian languages, resulting in artificial constructs like *samlaingikta*. Vanita is right in arguing that the entire debate over using the terms homosexual or gay while writing about the past is misplaced. 'Since neither the producer/author's intention nor the "original" audience's reception can ever be definitively recovered, is it meaningful for us as readers to try to read texts not from our own perspective but from that of some imagined past reader?' She also points out that other terms such as family, marriage, slave, law, woman/man are routinely applied to past societies in non-Anglophone societies where translations of these words 'are well known to have widely different meanings from those they have today. Historians rightly consider it sufficient to point out as many of the differences as possible and then proceed to use the term currently in use' (Vanita 2002: 4).

For contemporary India too, the question arises of the relevance or otherwise of the English terms gay/lesbian. Paola Bacchetta in her study of Delhi in the 1980s makes a distinction between 'lesbians' (within quotation marks)—women who love women and do not identify with the term lesbian; and lesbians—those who do. It is notable, she points out, that the Delhi Group, which was formed precisely to study these histories and experiences, omitted from its name the term lesbian, as it was a subject of disagreement, although some women within the group felt comfortable with it. Among those who did not, a women's movement activist, who had been living with a woman for over 10 years, tells Bacchetta that the term lesbian is not politically useful in her context. Along with the women of the urban slum settlement who she worked with, she evolved the term *ekal mahila* (single woman) in order to raise the issue of women's status outside the heterosexual institution of marriage and family. The term was designed to be 'inclusive of all women who have ruptured with the heterosexual matrix: "lesbians", celibates, ascetics, unmarried and divorced women, widows ... [S]ingle women disrupt patriarchal genealogies while establishing lineage with women within and outside their families' (Bacchetta 2007).

---

poems translated by Saleem Kidwai and herself. She adds: 'Given that very little research has been done on the histories of love and friendship in South Asia, I am convinced, on the basis of conversations that I have had with people from widely varying backgrounds in India, that these and other terms found by scholars represent the tip of the iceberg' (Vanita 2002: 3).

Not surprisingly, in other contexts too, in which English is not the dominant language, the terms 'lesbian' and 'gay' circulate in very different ways. A Thai activist told a researcher that in Thailand, the term lesbian entered the local context to describe female-to-female sex in visual pornography produced for a heterosexual male audience. As a result, Thai women who love women avoid calling themselves lesbian. The same study also notes that in the Philippines, Indonesia, and Thailand, the term gay interacts in different ways with local terms for male homosexuals, transgendered, and transsexual identities, and has different valences accordingly (Jackson 2001: 23).

A distinction that has been introduced via international discourses of AIDS intervention is the term 'men who have sex with men' (MSM) in preference to 'gay'. Shivananda Khan, founder of Naz Foundation International, based in London, makes this distinction to disentangle 'male to male sexual behaviour' from 'male sexualities'. In Khan's understanding, 'sexuality' refers to self-identity in reference to sexual desire and gender, while many men who have sex with men, whom he interviewed, are not self-identified as gay. Many feel sexual desire for women, or are simply interested in the act of sex ('discharge-sex' as Khan terms it), not the gender of the person they have sex with (Khan 2001). Their sexuality, in other words, is not gay, they do not identify themselves as homosexual or bisexual—they merely have sex with men. Many men see this as simply having fun or *masti* (meaning 'fun' in Hindi) (ibid.: 101).[10] Khan suggests that in South Asia generally, male sexual behaviours exist as part of 'a broader sexual repertoire' (ibid.: 102). In addition, since most people in this region and in India in particular do not understand these English terms, Khan's concern is that the use of these terms might not yield accurate information about the extent of male-to-male sex that exists. This would lead to the understanding that HIV prevention programmes are not necessary.

But this is not his only concern. While Khan concedes that 'western understandings of lesbian and gay identities' have emerged in India, he suggests that this is limited to upper-class circles in which diasporic lesbian and gay organizations act as 'instigators of a queer India'. He likens this process to 'sexual neo-colonialism', in which Western sexual ideologies have invaded Indian discourses, so that 'indigenous histories and cultures become invisible'. However, he also argues that the diasporic urge to seek out such histories is a form of self-justification which should not be necessary:

---

[10] Khan incorrectly renders *masti* as *maasti*.

'As contemporary self-identified Indian lesbians or gay men (whatever those terms mean to us personally) we shouldn't need self-validation based on a presumptive past. Our existence is our own validation' (ibid.: 105).

Khan raises a number of issues in this account. The last assertion is certainly one we can agree with, that the fact that there are gay and lesbian Indian Americans/British Indians *today* is sufficient validation, whether or not a history of homosexuality can be traced to ancient times in India. However, Khan does not seem to recognize that to say this is to make a political statement. To address the question of *validation* is already to enter the realm of power and ethics, that is, the realm of politics. Validation by whom, of what, and why—these are political questions. However, Khan's assertions tend to hide their political nature and assume the status of factual statements such as (a) men in India who have sex with men do not identify themselves as gay, so the term has no relevance; (b) if Indians do identify as gay/lesbian, this identity is 'instigated' by diasporic Indians; and (c) this identity suppresses indigenous cultures and is a form of neo-colonialism.

These assertions assume that there is a clear inside and an outside to 'indigenous' and 'Western' worldviews and lives, and that forms of self-identification are unchanging, objective 'facts'. Any change in self-identification in this account would involve some sort of bad faith. To highlight the inconsistencies involved, let us consider a series of counter-questions: Would it be correct to say that gay and lesbian people of Indian origin living in the West were 'instigated' into these identities by American/British gay and lesbian people? Who instigated the latter? What produced the first ever self-identified gay man and lesbian woman? Is every man who has sex with men in the West self-identified as gay? Since we know this is not so, why does the term continue to have relevance there? And finally, MSM too is an English term, created by NGOs working on AIDS, and it would have to be translated into different linguistic and cultural contexts—nobody would 'naturally' identify as 'MSM', so what makes it different from 'gay/lesbian'?

My point is that identities and self-identification are (a) socially, culturally, politically, and historically contingent; (b) relational (deriving meaning with reference to what they are *not*); and (c) most importantly, a process. They are not objective, independent facts frozen in time. Although they seem to acquire fixity at particular points, they are continuously amenable to change. Identities emerge both through mechanisms of governmentality in Foucault's sense (through discourses of medicine, psychiatry, politics, and so on) as well as through processes of resistance to these mechanisms. There were and are, both in India and the West, everyday practices of counter-heteronormativity that do not identify with movements, but political action is precisely the attempt to produce particular forms of self-identification and to hegemonize common sense meanings of language. For instance, two researchers who conducted a study on violence faced by lesbians in India, deliberately, in what can be seen as a political move, define the term lesbian as: 'women who are in or desire to be in, emotional and/or sexually intimate relationships with other women. This definition therefore *does not exclude* women who are bisexual or women who do not use the word "lesbian" to describe themselves' (Fernandez and Gomathy 2003: 6).

There will continue to be some everyday practices that resist both hegemonic norms as well as attempts to translate them into self-conscious counter-hegemonic movements. However, some others will be amenable to being mobilized by movements. To charge the latter with a sort of originary bad faith is even more troubling when it is only made at Indians in India, who are apparently to be custodians of something Khan defines as 'indigenous' culture. Indians in the West, when they take on the identity of gay/lesbian, apparently display no such bad faith.

While Khan's fear is justified, that exclusively using the lens of self-identified gay men to assess the extent of HIV/AIDS will be dangerously deceptive, there is no evidence in his essay and none that I am aware of, that AIDS activism has in fact ever been limited to this form of identification. Of course, there are innumerable homophobic voices that deny the existence of homosexuality in India except as an aberration—to counter this, AIDS activism need not enter into the Gay vs MSM debate at all. It is sufficient to demonstrate evidence of large numbers of men who do have sex with men (but even more important, to show that HIV/AIDS *is not limited to MSM*—the really dangerous stereotype being that it is).

To make the distinction then is crucial both for political practice (where MSM/gay would function like the 'lesbian'/lesbian distinction that Bacchetta suggests) as well as for more narrowly focused AIDS-prevention strategies. But I disagree with Khan's delegitimizing of all forms of politicized homosexual self-identity in India, as if the only way one can be authentically homosexual is if one does not acknowledge that one is. Jeremy Seabrook, a self-defined 'mature gay man', too has argued that Indians who do not identify themselves in indigenous terms like *panthi* and kothi are elitist and complicit with Western imperialism. Both Khan (who is of South Asian origin, living in the West) and Seabrook (of Western origin who spends a lot of time in India) define themselves as 'gay' but delegitimize Indians living in India who define themselves as such. As Shohini Ghosh said in a review of Seabrook's book, while it is worth discussing the strategic usefulness of the more neutral term 'MSM' as opposed to the more politicizd term 'gay' and the gains and losses of such a strategy, his argument negates the significant contribution that self-identified gays and lesbians have made to 'an affirmative public discourse around queer sexualities' (Ghosh 2003a). Similarly, Paola Bacchetta's manner of making the distinction between lesbian and 'lesbian' is more complex, and does not attribute or deny legitimacy to one or the other. But Khan and Seabrook work with essentialist notions of 'West' and 'indigenous', and treat MSM as some sort of factual objective category actually existing 'out there', as opposed to 'gay', and thus close off possibilities of dynamic forms of self-identification.

The 'affirmative public discourse' Shohini Ghosh refers to, the subject of this chapter, insists on the potential fluidity of sexual identifications and the linking of sexuality to other forms of identities, as a politically productive stance. In this context, the term 'queer' is increasingly gaining currency among activists familiar with academic and political work in the Anglophone world, although it may be taking somewhat different forms and directions in India. I have suggested in earlier political writing that the term 'queer' enables a questioning of the supposed naturalness of the *heterosexual* identity: 'If we recognise that "normal" heterosexuality is painfully constructed and kept in place by a range of cultural, biomedical and economic controls, and that these help sustain existing hierarchies of class and caste and gender, then we would have to accept that we are all, or have the potential to be—queer' (Menon 2004b).

The term queer has, from the beginning in India, gone beyond sexuality. The editors of a volume subtitled *Queer Politics in India* hold that:

The term queer...speaks...of communities that name themselves (as gay or lesbian for example), as well as those that do not, recognising the spaces for same-sex desire and sexuality that cannot be captured in identities alone.... Queer politics does not speak of the issues of these communities as 'minority issues', but instead speaks of larger understandings of gender and sexuality in our society that affects all of us, regardless of our sexual orientation. It speaks of sexuality as a politics intrinsically and inevitably connected with the politics of class, gender, caste, religion and so on, thereby both acknowledging other movements and also demanding inclusion within them. (Narrain and Bhan 2005: 3–4)

Voices Against 377, a broad coalition formed to campaign for the abolition of Section 377, links same-sex desire to women's rights, child rights, anti-communalism, and anti-war politics. PRISM, a 'non-funded, non-registered feminist forum of individuals inclusive of all gender and sexual expressions and identities'[11] seeks to 'link sexuality with the other axes of construction and control such as gender, caste and religion. By highlighting these links, we seek to establish the need for progressive movements to engage with issues of marginalised sexualities as an intrinsic part of their mandate' (Sharma and Nath 2005: 82–3).

This knitting together of sexuality with a wider left-wing politics can, paradoxically, also be limiting for a queer politics of sexuality. Alok Gupta reflects on the reluctance of gay men in Mumbai to make a broader political commitment to the 'larger queer community', which includes, in his account, 'hijras, kothis, lesbians and women's activists' (and of course, many gay men). He points out that while Gay parties in Mumbai can attract up to 400 men, barely a handful show up for political action. Apart from caution about public political participation and inter-organizational rivalry, one of the significant reasons for this reluctance, he suggests, is Left influence on the queer movement, which is 'not a bad thing by itself, but it ends up excluding a lot of others'. As a young gay man said to Gupta, 'Just because I am gay and identify as queer, and am interested in supporting the movement, I don't want to have the same commitment for people being displaced by unruly dams or bashing America' (Gupta 2005: 138–9).

Gupta's conclusion is not that the queer movement should change its political commitment, but rather that the movement as well as gay men should be *more* aware of the operation of class, which he defines in terms of access to money and ability to speak English, a very effective working definition indeed (ibid.: 129). People who identify themselves as hijra or kothi (who have been very visible in public queer political action) are not, in this sense, of the same class as people likely to identify themselves as gay/lesbian/queer. It is significant, he points out, that while upper- and middle-class activists of the queer movement that he spoke to did not think of class as a problem, 'almost everyone I spoke to from lower class backgrounds felt class to be one of the major barriers facing the community at large'. In a society of strong and visible class differences, this is not surprising, and the temporary resolution that has apparently been worked out, he says in an insightful and troubling recognition, is to draw a line between social and political spaces—'social spaces allow us time with our own and political spaces bring us together on a common platform' (ibid.: 133).

---

[11] Self-description in invitation to a public event. The name PRISM initially was an acronym for People for the Rights of Indian Sexuality Minorities. However, the understanding of the group soon grew into an explicit rejection of a 'minority' identity for non-heteronormative sexualities. PRISM now is used as a complete name in itself, not as an acronym.

Three features of the politics of the 'queer' identity in India seem to emerge from the account so far. One, it engages with the question of biology critically, treating sexuality as fluid, not a biological or genetic given. The 'gay gene' type of theories play no significant role in queer politics in India.

Two, it does not attempt to produce a new universal, within which all sexual identities will be submerged. Rather, it sees 'queer' as a political and in some ways unstable term, enabling the continuous challenge to heteronormativity, whether through gay/lesbian/transgender, feminist, or other identities. In the West, a critique is made of queer politics by some gay theorists and lesbian-feminists, growing out of a sense that 'it despecifies the realities of lesbian and gay oppression, obscuring what is irreducibly *sexual* about these practices' (Halperin 1995: 65) or that the lesbian experience and patriarchy as such is rendered invisible by the term (Jeffreys 2003). At this point in India, such a critique may not be centre-stage for the way queer politics has developed here, although there are other concerns expressed by lesbian activists here which may be specific to India. In one lesbian activist's words:

There are two issues. One has to do with funding. Since the bulk of funding for sexual minority/LGBT (Lesbian, Gay, Bisexual, and Transgender)/queer projects is generated by the HIV/AIDS crisis, and lesbians are not perceived as a high risk group, there is more money available for supporting MSM and sex worker (male and female) interventions and movements, than there is for lesbians/queer women, who often find themselves in a position of marginalisation and dependence in relation to these larger structures. The second question has to do with the politics of visibility, mobility and the capacity of being 'out' and how that matters under patriarchy. The greater visibility of even 'feminine' gendered identities like hijras and kothis rather than lesbian women in many political and public contexts is related to this.[12]

But at the same time, her concern was to emphasize that it is a complicated issue precisely because of the tremendous marginalization experienced by people in those communities.

Three, queer politics sees itself as complicated at its point of origin by class, caste, and community identity, and is self-critical to the extent it is unable to engage with this complication.[13]

---

[12] Personal email communication.

[13] A related observation, based on conversations, is that there is not so much an attempt to translate the term queer into Indian languages (as there has been with the term homosexual or gay/lesbian) as to disseminate its meaning. Thus, the term may be simply transliterated or not even mentioned at all, while making an argument for what would essentially be a queer politics. However, I make this statement provisionally, pending a systematic study of political writing/material produced by NGOs in Indian languages.

In what has become a characteristic feature of counter-heteronormative alliances in India, nobody is identified publicly as heterosexual. Statements and petitions use the term 'we', often with the implication of LGBT identity, even when many of the signatories/participants are not publicly or privately non-heterosexual. While this has never been explicitly debated, to my knowledge, it would seem that this move is partly in order to protect LGBT people not ready to come out. More importantly, however, I suggest it has the potential for a recognition that LGBT politics is not about 'others'—it is about 'us'.

How can this last implication be drawn out to radically destabilize feminist politics? It seems that engaging seriously with the politics of counter-heteronormativity produces two questions for feminist politics.

The first is—who is the subject of feminist politics? The second is—what is the source of political identities in modern societies?

THE SUBJECT OF FEMINIST POLITICS

It is significant that counter-heteronormative movements in India should have turned to the women's movement as a natural ally. In the 1980s, the initial response of the established leadership of the women's movement was entirely homophobic, and even today the alliance is not an unproblematic one, but internal contestations have been intense. An important landmark is the Conference of Autonomous Women's Movements in Tirupati in 1994 at which an open and often acrimonious discussion on lesbianism took place, with the greatest hostility coming from leftist groups, decrying lesbianism as an elitist deviation from real political issues. A statement on sexuality acknowledging same-sex desire was finally issued at the conference. Since then the conversations have continued, with lesbian women and allies within the women's movement pressing for greater visibility. One of the arenas of confrontation has been the annual International Women's Day (8 March) rally, usually dominated by left party women's groups, in different cities. The point at issue has been whether the banners or the names of lesbian groups should be included in the marches and programmes. In cities like Pune and Mumbai, the issue has finally been resolved in favour of visible participation. Chayanika Shah writes about Mumbai:

International Women's Day, 8 March 2004.

While attending the Joint Women's Groups celebrations, some of us sit with bated breath as the names of the groups organising the programme are read out. One of the activists from a 'mainstream' women's group reads out the names one after the other and then, without any fumbling or any kind of hesitation, she reads the name of our newly renamed collective, 'Lesbians and Bisexuals in Action'... and we are elated at hearing her pronounce the L*** word'. (Shah 2005: 143)

In Delhi the discussions continue. Openly homophobic arguments are almost never made (publicly) any more within the women's movement. Rather, the objections suggest that sexuality is less urgent than bigger issues facing the women's movement. For instance, as a left party-linked women's organization put it, banners of lesbian groups in the 8th March rally would 'cause confusion about' and 'divert attention from the issues we have agreed to highlight' (that is, demolition of slums and dislocation of workers due to closures of industries). Thus, their objection was to the mere presence of the banner of Campaign for Lesbian Rights (CALERI) during the rally, even though CALERI was marching in support of the 'issues we have agreed to highlight'. The left wing women's organization accepted that groups had the right to prioritize getting 'social recognition for sexual rights and preferences' but this was not their own priority. Another left wing women's organization expressed its support for lesbian rights as part of 'the broader ambit of the struggle for civil liberties and democratic rights', but emphasized that 'in the context of building a mass movement for women's rights, there are several *more* pressing problems'.[14]

Arguments about priority and elitism have historically been made by left movements to counter feminism, and it is ironic that a new universal of Woman/Class is now being constituted by women's organizations of the left against the destabilizing implications of homosexuality.

Nevertheless, today it is clear that challenges to heteronormativity are an unshakeable part of the agenda of feminist politics in India, however internally contested it may be. At the annual conference of the Indian Association of Women's Studies (IAWS) in 2005, a resolution against Section 377 was passed after much debate. There was broad agreement that Section 377 should be abolished but disagreement on whether it was necessary to go beyond a 'human rights and equality under the law' argument to enter into the more radical endorsement that 'IAWS commits to engaging with the experiences and emerging perspectives that communities

---

[14] Written correspondence between Left women's organizations (All India Democratic Women's Association [AIDWA] and National Federation of Indian Women [NFIW]) and Campaign for Lesbian Rights before 8 March 2001 are on file with the author; emphasis in original.

perceived to deviate from the "normal" offer to the women's movement'.[15] The resolution that was finally passed acknowledged that 'deviations from the normal' enrich the perspective of the women's movement.

I see counter-heteronormativity as the third axis in my problematizing of 'gender' in the Indian context—the first two being caste and community. From my understanding of the debates on the Uniform Civil Code and on reservations for women in Parliament, I have argued that identities are created and mobilized in and through politics, they do not pre-exist politics (Menon 1998, 2004a). This argument about caste or religious identity in India, or race in the West, is by now generally accepted, for these are no longer seen as natural or primordial identities, but as identities that have taken their present forms over the course of certain historical developments.[16]

However, when it comes to 'woman', there continues to be a tendency to view the category as self-evident, when in fact the painful recognition that the women's movement has had to come to terms with is precisely that 'women' as the subject of feminist politics has to be brought into being by political practice. In other words, there are not pre-existing 'women' who may be Hindu or Muslim, upper caste or Dalit, white or black—there are 'people' who may respond in different kinds of political mobilization as 'white' or 'Muslim'—or as 'women'.

The politics of counter-heteronormativity raises similar questions for feminist politics, posing a radical challenge to the identity of woman from a different subject position than that of both religion and caste. This is the point at which the theoretical recognition of 'woman as fractured subject' is confronted in political practice. For instance, some hijras claim the right to be recognized as 'women' as exemplified by a banner, 'Hijras are Women', carried at the World Social Forum, Mumbai, 2004. Since hijras speak of themselves as being neither men nor women, although they use the feminine gender in referring to themselves, the banner needs some explanation. In 2002, two High Court judgements set aside the election of two hijras from posts reserved for women. The banner was in effect a protest at these judgements. People's Union for Civil Liberties-Karnataka

---

[15] This resolution does not necessarily mean that the majority of participants at the conference shared these views. The resolutions were passed in the last session, when most participants had left, and while there was a serious debate, it involved very few people.

[16] On race, a representative manner of posing the argument is by Hall (1988: 45): 'The fact is "black" has never been just there either. It has always been an unstable identity, psychically, culturally and politically. It, too, is a narrative, a story, a history. Something constructed, told, spoken, not simply found.'

(PUCL-K), an organization that brought out a powerful report on human rights violations of hijras in Bangalore, criticized the judgements on the grounds that they 'essentially imply that one cannot choose one's sex and that one should remain within the sex into which one is born' (PUCL 2003: 51).

The questions that arise here, however, are more complicated. The judgements were not so much reflecting on identity as on the political representation of identities. What is at stake here is: who can claim to represent a particular identity. Hijras continue to hold elected posts in general (unreserved) seats, and these judgements did not affect them. The fact highlighted by PUCL-K is not in question that hijras are today among the most marginalized communities in India, often reduced to the borders of criminal extortion (in the guise of demanding traditional 'gifts' at weddings and childbirths) to make a living. They are routinely harassed by police and physically threatened and/or assaulted under the umbrella of Section 377. Their specific needs for a dignified existence are not addressed by any political grouping, and certainly not by the women's movement. It is as sex workers that they have become politicized, and in sex workers' unions that they find some of their demands articulated. The PUCL report in fact is a study of transgender sex workers in Bangalore.

However, the question is—can hijras represent women in constituencies reserved for women? While the question of reservations for women in Parliament is still not settled, it has been implemented at local-level institutions for more than a decade and even longer in some states. But the experience has shown that the identity of 'woman' cannot be seen in isolation from the identity of 'caste'. Reservation for an undifferentiated category of 'women' in Parliament has been uniformly denounced by politicians and writers speaking for backward castes and Dalits, as an upper caste ploy to stem the rising tide of lower caste men in politics. This reaction has to be understood in the context of the decades-long experience of women's reservations in local-level institutions. Studies in several states have confirmed that the entrenched power of the dominant castes has been strengthened by women's reservations. Their demand has therefore been that there should be a further reservation for backward castes and Muslim women within the quota for women (Menon 2004a).

It is, therefore, not the biological category of 'woman' that requires reservation, but particular kinds of materially located experiences that need to find space in representative institutions. The issue is not whether one can biologically become a woman at any point in one's life, but whether *experiences* of 'women' of different 'classes' and 'castes' can somehow be written into parliamentary discourses—and these identities are not simply biological. If the experiences of hijras, among other identities, are to be similarly written in, then we must think of more radical alternatives than to divide representation simply between 'men' and 'others'. The experience of oppression of hijras is not reducible to the experience of 'women'. Thus, the possibility of alliances between hijras/trans people and the women's movement faces questions not immediately amenable to any clear resolution. Moreover, precisely because 'everyone wrestles with gender to some degree' (Sukhtankar, 'Complicating Gender'), it does not seem to take us very far to translate all political questions into the language of 'rights' for fixed and settled identities, to be fitted within the framework of existing modern state institutions.

If we are to understand 'materially located experiences' not as a given but as something produced by social/cultural/economic systems, we are recognizing, in Joan Scott's words, that

> it is not individuals who have experiences, but subjects who are constituted through experience. Experience in this definition then becomes, not the origin of our explanation, not the authoritative (because seen or felt) evidence that grounds what is known, but rather, *that which we seek to explain, that about which knowledge is produced.* (Joan Scott 1999: 779–80; emphasis added)

Any politics that seeks radical transformation would have to re-vision systems of political representation that would be potentially capable of representing newer and different kinds of experiences that produce political configurations—the anti-big dam movements, anti-nuclear energy movements, sex workers' movements, and other counter-heteronormative movements, to name only a few. Another strategy followed by hijras is more promising, the demand to be recognized as a third gender. Recently, as the result of long-term lobbying by NGOs working on sexuality and human rights, the provision was introduced on Indian passport forms, that hijras can write in the column which requires M/F for 'sex'.[17] The recognition of several genders and of multiple and shifting ways of being constituted as political entities may be able to help generate new ways of thinking about representative institutions in a democracy.

In David Scott's problematization of institutions of liberal democracy in post-colonial states, identity has become inseparable from the 'statistical principle' (David Scott 1999: 188–9). The very forms of such institutions

---

[17] However, some activists told reporters they would have preferred the new category to have been T for 'transgender', as hijras represent only one part of the transgender population. 'Third Sex Finds a Place on Indian Passport Forms', Infochange Human Rights. See http://www.infochangeindia.org/HumanItop.jsp?section_idv= 13#3801. See also Thomas (2005).

would have to be re-imagined. Political representation then becomes a more complex question than that of allocating some seats out of the existing number in an existing Parliament to certain reified identities. If identities emerge in and through political mobilization, then we must guard against the possibility that some identities may freeze into new formations of power, thus blocking the emergence of new identities and new alignments....

...ACCOMMODATING GAY/LESBIAN IDENTITIES WITHIN THE NATION

All these identities that we have discussed so far can, of course, be politicized in ways that are not counter-heteronormative, and which may even be politically conservative. This section considers an instance of gay/lesbian politics in India that attempts to claim legitimacy within the nation by producing another kind of exclusion. The pioneer of gay politics in India, and a very influential spokesperson for the movement, Ashok Row Kavi, has articulated a Hindu nationalist position very clearly.

In 2001, the premises of Bharosa (a partner of Naz Foundation International), an NGO in Lucknow working on HIV/AIDS issues, were raided by police. Employees of the organizations were arrested and charged under Section 377 as well as under sections of the Indian Penal Code that have to do with obscenity and indecent representation of women. The standard paraphernalia of a safe-sex campaign found on the premises were represented by police and by a compliant media as pornographic material, and they were alleged to be running 'gay clubs in contrast to Indian culture and ethics'.[18]

In this context, Kavi published an article highlighting the fact that Bharosa and Naz were run by Muslims (one of 'Anglo-Bangladeshi origin') (Kavi 2002). This article reproduced a report from the newspaper *The Times of India*, which he endorsed, based on an Intelligence Bureau (IB) report of 1998. The IB had 'tipped off' the government that 'the gay culture spreading its roots in parts of Uttar Pradesh' was funded by international organizations based in Canada and Europe, 'which have a chunk of Pakistani nationals residing there'.

---

[18] The quotation is from the Senior Superintendent of Police in Lucknow, B.B. Bakshi. The account of the incident is put together from leaflets and reports issued by the groups that coordinated the campaign against the police action.

Kavi points out that indeed, the partner NGOs of Naz Foundation International were present in some 'very strategic towns and cities in India'. He explains how each one is strategic; for example, Chennai is the 'capital of Dravidian sub-nationalism with close ties to LTTE in Sri Lanka'.[19] He also emphasizes what he evidently considers a damning fact regarding statements by Amnesty London and International Gay and Lesbian Human Rights Commission (IGLHRC) condemning the raid on Bharosa—that Amnesty London is headed by a Muslim woman of Bangladeshi origin and IGLHRC by a Pakistani Muslim.

This article must be read in conjunction with his general views, evident in several other public pronouncements. What Kavi is concerned with is inclusion within the Hindu nation for LGBT people. He stands for a tolerant India which, however, he believes is tolerant only because of its Hindu majority. Consequently, he denounced the groups that attacked *Fire* as Hindu Taliban (Kavi 2004), and wrote an open letter to the chief of Rashtriya Swayamsewak Sangh (RSS), the ideological front of Hindu cultural nationalism, 'pleading' for the RSS to stop the campaign against gay men and lesbians as a 'foreign lifestyle issue'. He argues that unlike Islam and Christianity (in Hindutva ideology these religions are not native to India and so their followers do not consider this land to be their sacred land, unlike Hindus), Hindu texts have never considered homosexuality to be a sin. The letter concludes, 'We'll never accept second-class citizenship and be pushed into the darkness again. If need be, we'll fight you.'[20] He makes no reference in this letter to the citizenship rights of minority communities, which are the primary target of RSS attacks. Kavi's Hindu nationalist stance ensures that while gay/lesbian people can lay claim to the Hindu Nation, the Muslim is the eternal outsider, who will always be under pressure to prove his/her loyalty to the Nation. Kavi wrote in an electronic discussion list: 'All Muslims are not terrorists, but every terrorist caught till now is a Muslim.'[21] Finally, in this worldview, Pakistan and Bangladesh (as well as Sri Lanka) will always loom menacingly over the security of

---

[19] With this, Kavi invokes the assassination of prime minister Rajiv Gandhi in 1991, by an LTTE suicide bomber. Some of the other 'strategic' cities he lists are: Lucknow, capital of the largest state in India and the (then) prime minister's constituency; Bangalore, India's Information Technology (IT) capital with strategic public sector companies like Hindustan Aeronautics; Cochin, largest naval base on the west coast, and so on. These are of course also some of the largest or fastest growing cities in India where one would expect to find HIV/AIDS work being done.

[20] Reproduced in Versey (2004).

[21] Available at arkitectindia@yahoogroups.com, 3 August 2005.

the Indian nation, aided and abetted by internal traitors (Muslims, Tamils) and, of course, the West.[22]

Indeed, the stakes in being conservative, xenophobic, nationalist, racist, casteist, are greater for those who do not conform to the one crucial standard. In the article on the Bharosa incident discussed earlier, Kavi (2002) spells it out—the 'expensive lesson' Lucknow has taught us, he concludes, is that 'gay NGOs have to learn to live with mainstream society'. At that time India was governed by the Hindu right wing-led coalition, which was to be in power for some more years, and mainstream society looked well on the way to becoming deep saffron.[23]

A feminist and queer politics of radical transformation cannot in fact 'learn to live with mainstream society,' as Kavi urges. The objective of such a politics cannot simply be that of seeking full citizenship within the nation—for some other group will always be excluded. The political agenda in the US of challenging the 'Don't Ask Don't Tell' policy regarding gay men and lesbian women in the armed forces, and seeking to be recruited *as* gay/lesbian Americans can be seen as a move similar to Row Kavi's, seeking visibility and inclusion within the nation. However, if all

[22] Kavi's position is by no means uncontested by activists in the counter-heteronormative movements, nor is it the hegemonic voice. Nevertheless, Kavi is an iconic figure and his view demonstrates one way in which LGBT identities can be accommodated within conservative discourses.

[23] Kavi's letter implicitly raises two other serious issues, though he does not reflect on them, since his concerns are very different. The first is the politics of competing for funding. He complains that the partner NGOs of Naz were elbowing out 'the older established gay groups' when it came to funding. Second, with reference to the role of organizations like IGLHRC, the more complex question is about international human rights norms and the politics of their global, funding-directed application. See, for instance, Paola Bacchetta (2007). A thought-provoking article by Joseph Massad (2002) is sharply critical of organizations like IGLHRC and International Lesbian and Gay Association (ILGA), which he characterizes as dominated by 'white western males', and their usage of 'US human rights discourses' in the Arab world. Examining scholarship and political writings on homosexuality in Muslim countries by what he terms the 'Gay International', Massad argues that it orientalizes and 'others' Muslims, misrepresents/misunderstands Islam, and 'incites discourse' on homosexuals where 'none existed before', that is, none self-identified in 'Western' terms like homosexual or gay. This produces in reaction, says Massad, Islamist and nationalist anti-gay discourses, and obliterates the spaces in which Arab men practised same-sex contact without identifying as homosexual or gay. It certainly is significant that these orientalizing or otherwise problematic sources he cites are all Westerners or Arabs based in the West, but Massad himself is based in the US. The resonances with Shivananda Khan's argument discussed earlier are inescapable, and it would be interesting to explore what the reactions, if any, by activists and scholars *located in* 'the Arab world' have been to Massad's argument which in effect characterizes any and all politicizing of gay identity as a 'western' project.

identities including that of modern citizenship are derived from patriarchal institutions establishing compulsory heterosexuality, is any feminist/queer critique of the contemporary—whether of capitalism, racism/casteism, imperialism, or patriarchy—possible without questioning all three—the family, national boundaries/citizenship, and heteronormativity?

ILLEGITIMATE DESIRE AND THE FAMILY/NATION

Discussing 'fluidity' in self-identifications, Shivananda Khan cites the example of a man who said to him that when he is cruising for sex in a park, he is gay, but outside the park he is many other things—a good Hindu, a married man with a family. From this and other examples, Khan asserts that in India and in South Asia in general, the focus of the self is not on the individual but on kinship, and 'procreative sexuality' therefore becomes a 'social compulsion, as a familial and community duty' (Khan 2001: 107). He does not explicitly note a feature of relevance to us—that 'procreative sexuality' needs also to be *legitimate*, that is, within the bounds of marriage limited by caste and community boundaries. Further, he is not interested in the gendered nature of fluid self-identification, such that women would not have the same freedom that men have to find sex outside marriage with other men or with women, and he does not need to use the term patriarchy even once in his article on sexuality. Since his objective is to focus single-mindedly on the male subject population potentially affected by HIV/AIDS, he is blind to the extent to which 'legitimate procreative sexuality' is in fact fractured and resisted. Since Khan's agenda is not political, but narrowly prophylactic, these fissures and cracks are of no interest to him.

Two phenomena over the last decade-and-a-half have thrown into startling relief such fractures in discourses of legitimate procreative sexuality. One—instances of caste panchayats,[24] political organizations based on religious community identity and family members, carrying out or ordering physical punishment, including death, for young heterosexual couples of different castes/communities who decided to marry or did get married. Each such instance of 'punishment' that reaches public attention in fact makes visible the growing challenge to caste and community norms

---

[24] Local, usually village-level caste-based councils with no formal legal standing but with informal power over their members.

of sexual propriety.[25] B.R. Ambedkar had seen the potential of inter-caste marriage for what he called 'the annihilation of caste'. In a famous passage first published in 1936, he wrote:

Where society is already well knit by other ties, marriage is an ordinary incident of life. But where society is cut asunder, marriage as a binding force becomes a matter of urgent necessity. The *real remedy for breaking caste is inter-marriage. Nothing else will serve as the solvent of caste*. (Ambedkar 1936/1979: 67; emphasis in original)

Clearly, Ambedkar's recognition of inter-caste marriage as potentially disruptive of caste identities is one that continues to be shared, and feared, by caste panchayats 70 years later. One might like to add that this potential arises not so much because marriage is a 'binding force', as Ambedkar believed, but because inter-caste marriage poses a question mark over inherited caste identities. However, the Supreme Court's 2005 judgement on inheriting the father's caste, is a chastening reminder that only the delegitimation of heterosexual patriarchal marriage itself, as the source of such identity, can ensure a sufficiently radical challenge to the caste system. As long as marriage has this authority, the question of caste identity will revolve around whether marriage has taken place or not, as it did in this case.

The second phenomenon that highlights the fissures in 'legitimate procreative sexuality' is that of lesbian suicides. Men manage to circumvent the limitations of marriage by marrying women and raising families while continuing to have sex with men. Some women too have managed to live such lives (married to men, but continuing to have sex with women). Several gay and lesbian people have entered into marriages recognized as such within the political community and/or family circles, although having no legal sanction. Two policewomen found a priest to marry them, one who believed that marriage is a union of two souls regardless of the gender of the participants. They were, however, dismissed from service. Two women from Gujarat took advantage of a quasi-legal arrangement called *Maitri Karar* (Friendship Contract) used by wealthy married men

---

[25] A recent example that made headlines was the Bombay High Court's notices to the parents of four girls from the Gujarati Patel community living in Mumbai, who had secretly married outside their community. The court was responding to petitions filed by their husbands. Soon after the marriages were made public, the parents allegedly arranged for the girls to be kidnapped and kept in an environment of physical and mental abuse, till they promised to marry Patels. The man who arranged this is allegedly the mastermind behind the Naroda-Patiya massacre during the communal violence in Gujarat in 2002—Babu Bajrangi and his organization, Navchetan Sangathan, who perform this function for a fee. See Bhattacharya (2005).

to have relationships with women who insisted on some form of security (Rege 1997a).

For most women, however, the limitations imposed by marriage are insurmountable, and lesbian suicides have become increasingly common. These are identifiable as such because they leave suicide notes that explicitly express the fear of losing women they love due to marriage or family pressure.[26]

When a 'National Consultation on Right to Marry' was planned by some NGOs and political organizations (in Lucknow in 2003), in the context of violence against inter-caste and community marriages, feminist and queer groups were able to bring pressure to change the title to 'National Consultation on If, When and Whom to Marry', in order to raise the question of same-sex relationships. PRISM made a presentation in which it contested an opinion prevalent among feminists that women who love women have considerable space in the Indian social context and that two women who choose to live together can do so easier than a man and woman trying to live together outside marriage. Such an opinion holds that the assertion of a 'lesbian' identity may jeopardize these spaces. Countering this, PRISM discussed the growing instances of violence against lesbians (particularly psychiatric interventions) and lesbian suicides, proving that such 'space' is conditional and temporary. It also urged the recognition that lesbian suicides should not be seen in the framework of minority rights but

---

[26] An illustrative case that was investigated by ABVA, referred to it by a local NGO activist, was the suicide attempt by two young women in Orissa in which one of them died, and the other, it appeared, was being charged with murder. ABVA found that after a five-year friendship, they had signed a deed of agreement before the Notary Public to remain as life partners, and when the father of one was transferred to another town, they attempted suicide. ABVA never met the survivor, who it seemed, after some psychiatric treatment, had been whisked away by her family (AIDS Bhedbhav Virodhi Andolan 1999).

Newspapers have reported attempted and successful suicides in other parts of India as well. In Tamil Nadu, three young women took poison, and left suicide notes begging their parents not to separate them at least in death; in Gujarat, two women left notes saying their marriages had been arranged, and they could not bear life without each other (PRISM 2003). Fernandez and Gomathy (2003: 121–3) list 18 suicides by lesbians reported in newspapers from all over the country from 1980 to 2001. Sahayatrika, a project developing support networks for lesbian and bisexual women in Kerala, on the basis of newspaper reports that cite a same-sex relationship as the cause for the suicide, has compiled a list of such suicides in the state comprising 24 women and four men over a period of about eight years (Deepa 2005). Sahayatrika has also begun the painful process of conducting long interviews with families and friends of lesbian women who have committed or attempted suicide, in order to map and document a history that would otherwise remain at the level of sensational stories in the media. These interviews have been transcribed and translated into English to be documented for the wider non-Malayali political community.

as a manifestation of the way in which all women's sexuality is sought to be controlled (PRISM 2003).

These two kinds of challenges to legitimate procreative sexuality need to be knit together in a feminist analysis which confronts the institution of the family head on. Feminist critique of the family is as old as feminism of course, but generally (and not only in India), feminist analysis of the family and feminist responses to LGBT/queer politics have tended to run on parallel lines. The first turns its critique towards actually existing families, addressing say, specific issues such as dowry and domestic violence, thus implicitly reinforcing the idea of a 'normal' heterosexual family free of such violence. The Indian women's movement interventions on the Uniform Civil Code too have largely taken for granted heterosexual monogamous marriage as the norm (Menon 1998).

The second, feminist responses to queer politics, at best accepts sexuality issues in terms of a framework of minority rights/privacy/civil liberties, so that the alphabets (LGBTHK—Lesbian, Gay, Bisexual, Transgender, Hijra, Kothi) continue to proliferate endlessly *outside* the unchallenged heterosexual space.

The problem with this is that feminist politics rarely confront the family as *such*, the biologically defined, heterosexual patriarchal institution that is the lynch-pin of a 'social stability' marked by injustice and oppression. It is this institution that produces 'homosexuality' as a minority issue, and naturalizes compulsory heterosexuality, delegitimizing potential flows of desire along innumerable and unpredictable dimensions. This is not to suggest that there is a natural spring of human desire that has been dammed by institutions of heteronormativity, nor that heterosexual desire is unnatural. Rather, I urge politically confronting the implications of the recognition that 'desire' can potentially take any number of forms, sexual and non-sexual, of which heterosexual desire is only one.

It is useful to consider the idea of the 'constitutive outside', in the way in which Ernesto Laclau and Chantal Mouffe have developed the Derridean notion (Laclau and Mouffe 1990: 20–3). Derrida has shown how an identity's constitution is always based on excluding something and establishing a violent hierarchy between the two resultant poles— for example: form/matter, black/white, male/female, or for that matter, heterosexual/homosexual. Laclau and Mouffe argue, therefore, that all identities are relational, they never manage to constitute themselves fully. Thus, on the one hand, the antagonizing force 'blocks' the full constitution of the identity to which it is opposed and thus shows its contingency. But on the other hand, each identity in an antagonistic pair *is part of the conditions of existence of the other*—'black' derives its meaning from not being 'white', 'male' its meaning from not being 'female', 'heterosexual' from its not being 'homosexual'.

The implication here is that the antagonistic Other of each identity is both outside it and simultaneously *constitutes* it by defining its boundary, its shape, and its outlines. Section 377 then becomes not about a homosexuality which is out there, but about *procreative heterosexuality*. It becomes revealed as one of the nails holding up the sets of the elaborate fiction that normality springs from nature. The institutions of compulsory heterosexuality are outlined and held firm by their 'outside—counter-heteronormativity in all its various forms—which must be firmly excluded but which must continue to exist for the outlines of heterosexuality to be clear and sharp. Laclau and Mouffe remind us that 'if the "constitutive outside" is present within the inside as its always real possibility, in that case the inside itself becomes a purely contingent and reversible arrangement' (Mouffe 1999).

From this perspective it becomes possible to insert the stories of violence against inter-caste/religious marriage and lesbian suicides into a history, not of inter-caste marriage and of lesbianism in India, but into the history of compulsory heterosexuality and of marriage as the institution that best represents it—its bright lights showing up even sharper against its dark underbelly.

While gay/lesbian marriages at one level do de-naturalize the institution of the family, the ambivalence towards it in queer and feminist circles is not surprising. In India, same-sex marriage, as a demand made on the state, has not so far been foregrounded on the agenda of counter-heteronormative movements. During debates on the Uniform Civil Code in the 1990s, a Mumbai-based feminist group, Forum Against Oppression of Women, came up with a proposal for marriage law reform that included legal recognition to 'homosocial relationships', but it is not a demand that figures generally in campaigns. Generally, the movement has tended towards critiques of the dominant idea in India that marriage is natural and inevitable,[27] which oppresses lesbian women in particular, rather than towards demands to extend its privileges to same-sex couples.

Judith Butler, responding to the debate in the US and France, is wary of homosexual marriage as a demand on the state. The argument in favour of legal alliance can work in tandem, she argues, 'with a state normalisation of recognisable kinship relations, a condition that extends rights of contract

---

[27] Is it only in India that this is a dominant idea?

while in no way disrupting the patrilineal assumptions of kinship or the project of the unified nation which it supports' (Butler 2004: 104). At the same time, she maintains that 'legitimation is double-edged', and resists a resolution of the dilemma, stating that it is crucial politically to lay claim to intelligibility and recognizability (ibid.: 117). However, it seems to me that for a movement to aspire to intelligibility within the terms set by the state is precisely to resolve the dilemma. The political task should surely be to redefine radically the source and nature of 'intelligibility' itself, which is impossible if the target of the demand for intelligibility continues to be the state. Indeed, it may be that the potential of gay/lesbian marriage to subvert marriage as an institution is highest when such marriage is not legal.[28]

COUNTERING THE NATION

The heterosexual patriarchal family as the cornerstone of the Nation—this is the arrangement that has successfully normalized unjust and unequal forms of identification, property ownership, and access to resources. The story of the nation-state from the eighteenth century onwards has been told as a heroic saga, of struggle against tyranny and expanding frontiers of citizenship. That narrative renders unthinkable the closures and fractures, the marginalizations, and silencings that are constitutive of the identity of the citizen. Indeed, the 'nation' can only represent dominant, majoritarian values—minorities reasserting 'their' culture can never claim the legitimacy of representing the nation, whether it is Muslims in India or Indians in the US. Further, the 'secular' nation too has constituted the citizen through equally anti-democratic measures. In the classic case of France, Eugen Weber writes of the 'acculturation' process in the nineteenth century—by which the inhabitants of the area that became France were made 'French'— that it was 'akin to colonialism' (Weber 1976: 486).

In the Indian context too, secularist discourse has been intimately tied to a notion of 'development' that is predicated on the large-scale sacrifice

---

[28] Vaid (1995), former head of the National Gay and Lesbian Task Force in the US, argued that the pursuit of mainstream integration and civil rights had led the gay and lesbian movement in the US not to genuine equality but to a status of conditional—or virtual—equality. The pursuit of civil rights, she said, does not challenge the fundamental inequalities of a system that is built upon an exploitative, inherently racist economic system, in which the family is by definition heterosexist and patriarchal. See interview with Vaid (Mathur and Das 1997).

of sectional interests in the greater interest of the 'Indian citizen'. We who would practise democratic politics cannot afford to be unreflexive of the founding moment of discursive violence that both presupposed and produced 'the nation', nor of the repressions and marginalizations on which hegemonic nationalist discourse is predicated. No project of nationalism is ever 'completed'—it is frozen at some point or the other through a coercive apparatus backed by the sanction of violence, that prevents the further articulation of other voices and identities with similar aspirations.

Any radical transformative politics today must therefore be postnational. Here the *post* of postnationalism is to be understood not in the sense of *after*, but in the sense of having *passed through*, the nation. The idea that the nation-state is a historically contingent, if enduring, institution is hardly a new one. When I use the term postnational, therefore, it is both to build on and depart from scholarship that has problematized the nation-state in various ways.[29] Etienne Balibar points out that the current discourse about the end of the nation-state is understood by some (he cites Hobsbawm) as a positive phenomenon bringing the 'great universalist project of modernity to a fitting conclusion', whereas for others, precisely because of the strong affiliation between nation and modernity, the decline of the nation-state is a symptom of regression and crisis (Balibar 2004: 13). Thus, in the contemporary moment, it seems only two kinds of reactions to corporate globalization are possible—either turning to the nation-state to reassert its old authority against Empire, or on the other hand, assuming its demise and celebrating globalization. Both reactions are entirely misplaced.

Here the insistence on an uncompromising critique of the nation, therefore, is the very obverse of the argument for postnationalism 'from above' made from two opposed positions—one, in which the sovereignty of the nation is sought to be bypassed in the interests of global capital, and the other, a Habermasian celebration of global universalism. Rather, the kind of postnationalism I refer to is better described as being 'from below'. Its politics can be represented by any idea that is counter-hegemonic, whether that hegemony refers to development, sexuality, caste/community, or any other. But equally important, it must be seen as having two dimensions— one, 'over' the nation, across national borders; and two, 'under' the nation, resisting inclusion into the 'larger' national identity, insisting on space/

---

[29] Thanks to the Postnational Collective—Malathi de Alwis, Satish Deshpande, Mary E. John, Aditya Nigam, Pradeep Jeganathan, M.S.S. Pandian, and Akbar Zaidi—discussions within which are in the process of developing this idea.

time trajectories that do not mesh with progressivist dominant narratives of nation and history.

The first dimension is easier, in a sense, to recognize as a subversive strategy, for it begins with the assumption of existing nations, which it then interrogates. For example, Black Laundry, an Israeli anti-occupation queer group, positions itself differently from other Israeli gay/lesbian groups that presented themselves as part of the mainstream. It also distinguishes itself from the Israeli Left, with its universalist understanding against which Black Laundry posed its 'concrete social positioning' as a platform for critique. Amalia Ziv, in a study of the group, suggests that Black Laundry tied together 'sexual deviance' and 'national deviance' with slogans like 'Free Condoms, Free Palestine', 'Bull Dykes, Not Missile Strikes', 'Transgender not Transfer' (forced deportation of Palestinians), which break down the hierarchies of Nation and Sex, challenging queer politics with anti-occupation politics and vice versa. Ziv argues that through the twin strategies of national betrayal and sexual depravity, Black Laundry deliberately situated itself outside the discursive community of Israel/Palestine as well as hetero/homosexual (Ziv 2005).

The diasporic location, too, is one that offers rich insights from 'over' the Nation. An instructive example is the relationship of gay and lesbian people of Indian/South Asian origin in the US, to something called 'India'. The Federation of Indian Associations, a private organization dominated by Indian businessmen in the US, refused permission for years to South Asian Lesbian and Gay Association (SALGA, formed in 1992) to march in the Indian Independence Day parade in New York city. But SALGA was not the only organization not allowed to march—initially nor was Sakhi, an organization that addressed the question of domestic violence against women in the South Asian community. SALGA and Sakhi threatened to disrupt narratives of the Indian nation in two crucial ways, as the reasons given for their exclusion attest—one, they insisted on the South Asian identity, which would have meant that Bangladeshis and Pakistanis would have marched in the Indian parade. Two, SALGA is gay and lesbian, identities that could not, by definition, be 'Indian', since homosexuality did not exist in India. Sakhi was, evidently, additionally problematic because it exposed disjunctures in the family, the cornerstone of the Indian nation. After sustained pressure, Sakhi was 'allowed' to join, but SALGA had to carry on struggling for much longer, until in 2000 it won the right to participate (Gopinath 2005: 16–17; Shah 2001). The presence of these two organizations in the India Day parade is a constant reminder that the idea of the unified and homogeneous nation has the potential to unravel through feminist, queer, and counter-nationalist politics. In the context of the South Asian diaspora, Gayatri Gopinath suggests that the critical framework of a 'queer diaspora' can challenge nationalist ideologies by restoring their 'impure, inauthentic, non-reproductive potential' and can 'denaturalise the close relationship between nationalism and heterosexuality'. Suturing queer and diaspora thus 'recuperates those desires, practices and subjectivities that are rendered impossible and unimaginable within conventional diasporic and nationalist imaginaries' (Gopinath 2005: 11).

The other dimension of postnational politics—'under' the nation—is less obvious as a strategy, because it does not assume the prior existence of the nation. More significantly, its subversive edge may lie in the exact opposite of what animates the politics of 'over' the nation—the strategy of exit and movement across borders. The interrogation of the nation from under may involve rather, the *refusal* to move, as for example, in the struggles against big dams or mining operations which involve massive relocation of populations. From the perspective of counter-heteronormative politics, this dimension may involve claiming histories that run parallel to, that do not intersect with, that of the nation. Or claiming forms of family and kinship that produce identity that are splintered and fluid, that resist inclusion into larger formations. A startling moment, de-normalizing the idea of family, is produced when hijras contesting elections claim that precisely because they cannot have children to inherit their property, they will be less selfish and corrupt.[30] Sex workers refusing to shift their work premises in the face of intimidation by local communities force a recognition of the imbrication of sex work in everyday life. This *politics of refusal* thus implies the simultaneous transformation, through practices of everyday life, of the place where you insist on staying. The potential is enormous, and the imaginative horizons expansive.

And in the meanwhile, how do we engage with actually existing nation states and borders? The dilemma here is akin to that of a politics seeking to boycott corporations because of their global monopolies. A campaign to boycott Microsoft may well circulate on computers powered by its software. But this would only be one strand. There would be those who shift to free software, and more yet who live in the grey zones of the 'pirate economies' (Sundaram 2004), where piracy as an everyday practice, not necessarily as a self-conscious act of resistance, erodes the limits of corporate power. It is

---

[30] See interviews with hijra candidates, available at http://www.thewe.cc/contents/more/archive/aruvani.html, accessed on 22 March 2006.

in these latter areas of 'porous legalities' (Liang 2005) that one may expect the roots of institutions to be nibbled away. An alliance between feminist and queer politics thus has the potential to disrupt official autobiographies of the Nation along all its dimensions.

REFERENCES

AIDS Bhedbhav Virodhi Andolan (ABVA) (1999), *For People Like Us*. New Delhi: ABVA.

Ambedkar, B.R. (1936/1979), 'Annihilation of Caste', in *B.R. Ambedkar's Writings and Speeches, Vol. 1* (compiled by Vasant Moon). Mumbai: Education Department, Government of Maharashtra.

Babu, Ramesh (2005), 'Cross-Dressing for Divine Help', *Indian Express*, 29 March.

Bacchetta, Paola (2007), 'Rescaling Transnational "Queerdom": Lesbian and "Lesbian" Identitary-Positionalities in Delhi in the 1980s', in Nivedita Menon (ed.), *Sexualities*. New Delhi: Women Unlimited, pp. 103–27.

Bachman, Monica (2002), 'After the Fire', in Ruth Vanita (ed.), *Queering India: Same-Sex Love and Eroticism in Indian Culture and Society*. New York and London: Routledge.

Balibar, Etienne (2004), *We the People of Europe? Reflections on Transnational Citizenship*. Princeton and Oxford: Princeton University Press.

Bhaskaran, Suparna (2002), 'The Politics of Penetration: Section 377 of the Indian Penal Code', in Vanita (ed.), *Queering India*, pp. 15–29.

Bhattacharya, Chandrima S. (2005), 'Love-Marriage Scourge Label on Riot Accused', *The Telegraph*, 29 December.

Bhattacharya, Rimli (2003), 'The Nautee in "the Second City of the Empire"', *The Indian Economic and Social History Review*, 40(2): 191–235.

Butler, Judith (2004), 'Is Kinship Always Already Heterosexual?' in Judith Butler, *Undoing Gender*. New York and London: Routledge.

Cohen, Lawrence (2005), 'The Kothi Wars: AIDS Cosmopolitanism and the Morality of Classification', in Vincanne Adams and Stacey Leigh Pigg (eds), *Sex in Development: Science, Sexuality and Morality in Global Perspective*. Durham and London: Duke University Press, pp. 269–303.

Deepa, V.N. (2005), 'Queering Kerala', in Arvind Narrain and Gautam Bhan (eds), *Because I Have a Voice: Queer Politics in India*. New Delhi: Yoda Press, pp. 175–96.

Farber, Celia (1999), 'Unprotected Sex', *Continuum*, 5(5): 63–4.

Fernandez, Bina (ed.) (1999), *Humjinsi: A Resource Book on Lesbian, Gay and Bisexual Rights in India*. Mumbai: Combat Law Publications.

Fernandez, Bina and N.B. Gomathy (2003), *The Nature of Violence Faced by Lesbian Women in India*. Mumbai: Research Centre on Violence against Women, Tata Institute of Social Sciences.

Foucault, Michel (1980), 'Body/Power', in *Power/Knowledge: Selected Interviews and Other Writings 1972–1977*. New York: Pantheon Books.

——— (2003), 'Lecture of 17 March 1976', in *Society Must Be Defended*. New York: Picador.

Ghosh, Shohini (2003a), 'Sex by Whatever Name', *Psychological Foundations: The Journal*, V(J), June. Review of *Love in a Different Climate: Men Who Have Sex with Men in India* by Jeremy Seabrook. London and New York: Verso.

——— (2003b), 'From the Frying Pan to the Fire: Dismantled Myths and Deviant Behaviour', in Vijaya Ramaswamy (ed.), *Re-Searching Indian Women*. Delhi: Manohar Publishers and Distributors.

Ghosh, Swati (2004), 'The Shadow Lines of Citizenship: Prostitutes' Struggle over Workers' Rights', *Identity, Culture and Politics*, 5(1 and 2): 105–23.

Gopinath, Gayatri (2005), *Impossible Desires: Queer Diasporas and South Asian Public Cultures*. Durham: Duke University Press.

Gupta, Alok (2005), '*Englishpur ki Kothi*: Class Dynamics in the Queer Movement in India', in Narrain and Bhan (eds), *Because I Have a Voice*, pp. 123–42.

Gupta, Charu (2001), *Sexuality, Obscenity, Community. Women, Muslims and the Hindu Public in Colonial India*. New Delhi: Permanent Black.

Hall, Stuart (1988), 'Minimal Selves', in L. Appignanesi (ed.), *Identity Documents: The Real Me: Postmodernism and the Question of Identity*. London: ICA Documents 6.

Halperin, David M. (1995), *Saint Foucault: Towards a Gay Hagiography*. New York and Oxford: Oxford University Press.

Hansen, Kathryn (1999), 'Making Women Visible: Gender and Race Cross-Dressing in the Parsi Theatre', *Theatre Journal*, 51(2): 127–47.

Jackson, Peter A. (2001), 'Pre-Gay, Post-Queer: Thai Perspectives on Proliferating Gender/Sex Diversity in Asia', *Journal of Homosexuality*, 40(3/4): 1–25.

John, Mary and Tejaswini Niranjana (1999), 'Mirror Politics: "Fire", Hindutva and Indian Culture', *Economic and Political Weekly*, 6–19 March, 34(10 and 11): 581–4.

Jeffreys, Sheila (2003), *Unpacking Queer Politics: A Lesbian Feminist Perspective*. London: Polity Press.

Kapur, Ratna (2000), 'Too Hot to Handle: The Cultural Politics of *Fire*', *Feminist Review*, Spring, 64: 53–64.

Kavi, Ashok Row (2002), 'Sex, Lies and Lucknow', *Bombay Dost*, March, 8(1 and 2).

——— (2004), 'Expose the Hindu Taliban', Rediff on the Net available at http://enkidu.netfirms.com/art/2004/240204/E_002_080204.htm.

Khan, Shivananda (2001), 'Culture, Sexualities, Identities: Men Who Have Sex with Men in India', *Journal of Homosexuality*, 40(3/4): 99–115.

Laclau, Ernesto and Chantal Mouffe (1990), 'Post-Marxism without Apologies', in Ernesto Laclau (ed.), *New Reflections on the Revolution of Our Time*. London: Verso.

Liang, Lawrence (2005), 'Porous Legalities and Avenues of Participation', *Bare Acts, Sarai Reader 05*. The Sarai Programme, Delhi: CSDS.

Massad, Joseph (2002), 'Re-Orienting Desire: The Gay International and the Arab World', *Public Culture*, 14(2): 361–85.

Mathur, Chandana and Aniruddha Das (1997), 'Equality, Identity and Factoring the Left Back into the Political Equation', *Samar*, Winter, 7.

Menon, Nivedita (1998), 'Women and Citizenship', in Partha Chatterjee (ed.), *Wages of Freedom*. New Delhi: Oxford University Press, pp. 241–66.

―――― (2004a), *Recovering Subversion: Feminist Politics beyond the Law*. New Delhi: Permanent Black.

―――― (2004b), *'Sexuality, Nation, Community and Women'*, Lecture at panel organized by PRISM, World Social Forum, Mumbai, published in *Scripts*, No. 4, LABIA, Mumbai.

―――― (ed.) (2007), *Sexualities*. New Delhi: Women Unlimited.

Misra, Geetanjali, Ajay Mahal, and Rima Shah (2005), 'Protecting the Rights of Sex Workers: The Indian Experience', in Geetanjali Misra and Radhika Chandiramani (eds), *Sexuality, Gender and Rights: Exploring Theory and Practice in South and Southeast Asia*. New Delhi: Sage Publications, pp. 88–115.

Mouffe, Chantal (1999), 'For a Politics of Democratic Identity', Lecture delivered at 'Globalisation and Cultural Differentiation' seminar, 19–20 March, available at http://www.macba.es/antagonismos/english/09_04.html.

Najmabadi, Afsaneh (2005), *Women with Moustaches and Men without Beards: Gender and Sexual Anxieties of Iranian Modernity*. Berkeley: University of California Press.

Narrain, Arvind and Gautam Bhan (2005), 'Introduction', in Arvind Narrain and Gautam Bhan (eds), *Because I Have a Voice: Queer Politics in India*, New Delhi: Yoda Press.

Patel, Geeta (2002), 'On Fire: Sexuality and Its Inducements', in Ruth Vanita (ed.), *Queering India: Same-Sex Love and Eroticism in Indian Culture and Society*, pp. 221–33. New York and London: Routledge.

People's Union for Civil Liberties (PUCL) (2003), *Human Rights Violations against the Transgender Community: A Study of Hijra and Kothi Sex Workers in Bangalore, India*, September. Karnataka: PUCL.

PRISM (2003), 'The Politics of Representation. Lesbian Sexuality and the Women's Movement', Presentation at National Consultation on 'If, When and Whom to Marry', Lucknow.

Puri, Jyoti (1999), *Woman, Body Desire in Post-colonial India*. London: Routledge.

Rai Chowdhury, Anis (2005), 'Amitie: Organising LGBTs in Small-Town India', in Narrain and Bhan (eds), *Because I Have a Voice*.

Rege, Arati (1997a), 'A Decade of Lesbian Hulla Gulla', in Bina Fernandez (ed.), *Humjinsi: A Resource Book on Lesbian, Gay and Bisexual Rights in India*. Mumbai: Combat Law Publications.

―――― (1997b), 'Proceedings of the Workshop on "Strategies for Furthering Lesbian, Gay, Bisexual Rights in India", Mumbai, 1997', in Bina Fernandez (ed.), *Humjinsi: A Resource Book on Lesbian, Gay and Bisexual Rights in India*. Mumbai: Combat Law Publications, pp. 143–6.

Revathi (2005), 'A Hijra's Own Story', in Narrain and Bhan (eds), *Because I Have a Voice*, pp. 225–30.

Scott, David (1999), 'Community, Number, Ethos of Democracy', in *Refashioning Futures: Criticism after Postcoloniality*. Princeton: Princeton University Press.

Scott, Joan W. (1999), 'The Evidence of Experience', *Critical Inquiry*, Summer, 17: 773–97.

Shah, Chayanika (2005), 'The Roads that E/Merged: Feminist Activism and Queer Understanding', in Narrain and Bhan (eds), *Because I Have a Voice*, pp. 143–54.

Shah, Svati P. (2001), 'Out and Out Radical. New Directions for Progressive Organizing', *Samar*, Fall/Winter, 14. Available at http://samarmagazine.org/archive/articles/60.

Sharma, Jaya and Dipika Nath (2005), 'Through the Prism of Intersectionality: Same-Sex Sexualities in India', in Geetanjali Misra and Radhika Chandiramani (eds), *Sexuality, Gender and Rights: Exploring Theory and Practice in South and Southeast Asia*. New Delhi: Sage Publications.

Stoler, Ann Laura (2002), *Carnal Knowledge and Imperial Power, Race and the Intimate in Colonial Rule*. Berkeley, Los Angeles and London: University of California Press.

Sukhtankar, Ashwini (2007), 'Complicating Gender: Rights of Transsexuals in India', in Nivedita Menon (ed.), *Sexualities*. New Delhi: Women Unlimited.

Sundaram, Ravi (2004), 'Uncanny Networks: Pirate and Urban in the New Globalisation in India', *Economic and Political Weekly*, 3 January, 39(1): 64–71.

Sunder Rajan, Rajeswari (2003), *The Scandal of the State. Women, Law and Citizenship in Post-colonial India*. Durham and London: Duke University Press.

Thadani, Giti (1996), *Sakhiyani: Lesbian Desire in Ancient and Modern India*. New York: Cassel.

Thomas, Shibu (2005), 'Column for Eunuchs in Passport Form', *Midday*, 9 March: 1.

Vaid, Urvashi (1995), *Virtual Equality: The Mainstreammg of Gay and Lesbian Liberation*. New York: Anchor Books.

Vanita, Ruth (ed.) (2002), *Queering India: Same-Sex Love and Eroticism in Indian Culture and Society*. New York and London: Routledge.

Vanita, Ruth and Saleem Kidwai (2000), *Same-Sex Love in India: Readings from Literature and History*. New York: St. Martin's Press.

Versey, Farzana (2004), 'Lesbians vs. Gays vs. Hinduism vs. Modernity?', *Chowk*, 11 June.

Weber, Eugen (1976). *Peasants into Frenchmen: The Modernisation of Rural France, 1880–1914*. Stanford University Press.

Ziv, Amalta (2005), 'Performative Politics in Israeli Queer Anti-Occupation Activism', paper presented at Centre for the Study of Gender and Sexuality, New York University, 4 October.

III. CASTE

Chapter 5

WHATEVER HAPPENED TO THE VEDIC *DASI*?
Orientalism, Nationalism, and a Script for the Past*

UMA CHAKRAVARTI

MEN AND WOMEN IN INDIA, whether or not they have formally learnt history, carry with them a sense of the past which they have internalized through the transmission of popular beliefs, mythology, tales of heroism, and folklore. Formal history also percolates down, often in a transmuted form to a wider range of people through articles in popular journals, discussions, and through what may be termed as the 'dispersal effect', so that elements of oral history may be overlaid by more serious historical conclusions forming a sort of medley of ideas. It is just such a medley of ideas that forms the basis of our understanding of the status of women in ancient times; and is also part of our deeply embedded perceptions of the past in a more general sense.

Particular elements that constitute a given community or group's sense of history are not, however, timeless and unchanging. Perceptions of the past are constantly being constituted and reconstituted anew. At specific

---

* Originally published in Kumkum Sangari and Sudesh Vaid (eds) (1989), *Recasting Women: Essays in Indian Colonial History*. New Delhi: Kali for Women, pp. 27–87.

junctures the sense of history may be heightened and the past may be dramatically reconstituted, bringing into sharp focus the need of a people for a different self-image from the one that they hold of themselves. One such juncture for India, when historical consciousness was being reshaped, came in the nineteenth century. In the new script for the past, the women's question held a key place, but it is important to bear in mind that it was only one element in a set of related elements, all of which were being constituted at the same time and through the same process, ultimately ending in the creation of a Hindu-Aryan identity. The new self-image fulfilled a growing need of the emerging middle classes since it enabled them to contend with the 'burden' of the present, especially with the loss of self-esteem following the British conquest of India.

What was gradually and carefully constituted, brick by brick, in the interaction between colonialism and nationalism is now so deeply embedded in the consciousness of the middle classes that ideas about the past have assumed the status of revealed truths. Any suggestion that we might fruitfully analyse the manner and the different stages by which this body of knowledge was built up, or how and when we came by our immediate intellectual and cultural heritage (which is often only a 150 years old) would therefore be considered quite unnecessary or even futile. But for women in particular this heritage, this perception of the past, of the 'lost glory', is almost a burden. It has led to a narrow and limiting circle in which the image of Indian womanhood has become both a shackle and a rhetorical device that nevertheless functions as a historical truth.

This chapter attempts to demonstrate the factors and the stages spanning roughly the last century-and-a-half, but focusing particularly on the second half of the nineteenth century, in the formation of the present historical consciousness. I will also outline here the different elements within a complex structure of ideas wherein knowledge about the past ultimately ended in the creation of a persuasive rhetoric, shared by Hindu liberals and conservatives alike, especially in relation to the myth of the golden age of Indian womanhood as located in the Vedic period. This image foregrounded the Aryan woman (the progenitor of the upper-caste woman) as the *only* object of historical concern. It is no wonder then that the Vedic *dasi* (woman in servitude), captured, subjugated, and enslaved by the conquering Aryans, but who also represents one aspect of Indian womanhood (Chakravarti 1985), disappeared without leaving any trace of herself in nineteenth century history. Since no one had noticed her existence, it is natural that there was no one to mourn her disappearance.

My intention in this chapter is not to rescue the Vedic dasi, which of course needs to be done and requires a separate study, but to situate the nineteenth century historiography of the women's question within the cultural and ideological encounter between England and India. This is the story of how the Aryan woman came to occupy the centre of the stage in the recounting of 'the wonder that was India', representing an amalgamation of Brahminical and Kshatriya values. In this chapter, the process of the reconstruction of the past has been divided into three phases and is dealt with in three sections. Each phase was marked by certain trends although neither the phases nor the trends were watertight or exclusive. The first section provides a brief summary of the major ideas and themes in the work of the Orientalists, Anglicists, and Evangelists, and the proto-nationalists, covering the period up to 1850; the next section deals with the succeeding group of Orientalists, namely Max Muller and two European women writers who extended his romantic reconstruction of the Aryan past to women, as well as the emergence of cultural nationalism in the period between 1850 and 1880. This was expressed in the writings of R.C. Dutt, Bankim Chandra Chatterji, and Dayananda among others, and highlighted Kshatriya/Aryan values in the reconstruction of a new identity for Indian womanhood. The third section examines the relationship between such images of womanhood and the actual experiences of women in the closing decades of the nineteenth century.

I

In the nineteenth century we recovered our long lost ancient literatures, Vedic and Buddhistic, as well as the buried architectural monuments of Hindu days. The Vedas and their commentaries had almost totally disappeared from the plains of Aryavarta where none could interpret them; none had even a complete manuscript of the texts. The English printed these ancient scriptures of the Indo-Aryans and brought them to our doors. (Sarkar: 1928/1979: 84)

The contribution of Europeans to the rediscovery of India's past was widely accepted by scholars and popular writers in the nineteenth and twentieth centuries. The perception of the past was influenced by European, more specifically British, perceptions in two separate and contradictory ways. One strand was represented by the Orientalists whose reconstruction of the glory of Indian civilization in the ancient past was taken over lock, stock, and barrel by nineteenth century Indian writers to build a picture of Indian civilization not just for a particular region like Bengal (which contributed substantially to the building of this picture, especially in the early years of writing), but for the whole of India. The other strand was the Utilitarian and Evangelical attack on contemporary Indian society, especially on the visibly low status of women. Orientalism and Utilitarianism coalesced in the works of the early nationalist writers whose most enduring and successful construction was the image of womanhood in the lost past as a counter to the real existence of women in the humiliating present.

Among the Orientalists who contributed most substantially to the notion of a 'golden age' that had existed in a remote and unchartered period of Indian history were William Jones (1746–94) and H.T. Colebrooke. Closely associated with the Asiatic Society, their researches covered a wide range of themes in Sanskrit literature, history, and philosophy which were refined and elaborated in later years. It is significant, however, that glossing over certain aspects of the past was a characteristic feature of the work of the Orientalists who did not particularly react to the specific forms of inequality of caste, class, and gender prevailing in India. In part, this may be due to the fact that status distinctions were deeply ingrained in British society, but partly the lack of concern may be explained as a natural consequence of their heavy reliance on the conservative indigenous literati, the Brahmin *pandit*s.

The women's question, notably, was not one of the themes that were foregrounded in the earliest work of the Asiatic Society. Jones, for example, did not pay any attention to *sati* (widow immolation) and made only a passing reference to Gargi, whom he described as 'eminent for her piety and learning' (Jones 1807: IV, 64). More important than Jones in influencing the actual reconstruction of the past was the work of Colebrooke whose original researches earned for him the admiration of Max Muller. With Colebrooke the Orientalists came to focus their attention directly upon the women's question by compiling evidence bearing on women from the ancient texts; predictably, the focal starting point was the ritual of sati. One of Colebrooke's first pieces of research was 'On the Duties of the Faithful Hindu Widow' (Colebrooke 1895), wherein he presented the textual position on sati. The chapter reflects all the characteristic features of the historiography of the women's question: the reference to a variety of ancient texts, the special authority given to texts over custom, the search for the 'authentic' position as contained in the older and more authoritative texts, and the confusion in reconciling contradictory evidence. However, it is significant that there is nothing in Colebrooke's chapter to suggest that the Vedas were recognized as either the oldest or the most authentic texts; the past was as yet unstratified and was perceived as one homogenous whole.

The focusing on the 'duties' of the 'faithful' Hindu widow would most likely have had a great impact on Europeans who were the main readers of the *Asiatic Researches*. For many decades thereafter, a reference to Hindus appears to have evoked the image of a burning woman as recorded by Max Muller almost 80 years later (Neufeldt 1980: 3). Whatever other research Colebrooke engaged himself with in reconstructing the 'glories' of the ancient Hindus, an unintended consequence of his essay on the 'faithful widow' was to add the weight of scholarship to the accounts of travellers and other lay writers whose descriptions of burning women came to represent an integral part of the perception of Indian reality. Colebrooke's account of sati highlighted an 'awesome' aspect of Indian womanhood, carrying both the associations of a barbaric society *and* of the mystique of the Hindu woman who 'voluntarily' and 'cheerfully' mounted the pyre of her husband.

Colebrooke's essay on the Vedas (Colebrooke 1805) was the first piece of work drawing attention to the texts as a major achievement of the ancient Aryans. Of interest to us are the references to Gargi and Maitreyi (ibid.: 443–8), two of the oft-quoted examples of the glory of ancient Indian womanhood. It is significant that Colebrooke attributes no particular importance to the account of the conversation between Maitreyi and Yajnavalkya. Gargi too appears merely as one of the contenders, neither more nor less important than the other participants in the debate with Yajnavalkya.

Jones, Colebrooke, and a whole range of students at the Fort William College who formed the earliest group of the Orientalists, saw themselves as engaged in reintroducing the Hindu elite to the 'impenetrable mystery' of its ancient lore. The Sanskritic tradition, 'locked up' till then in the hands of a closed priesthood, was being thrown open and its treasures made available to the people in its 'pristine' form (Kopf 1969: 149); the truths of indigenous traditions were being recuperated (Mani 1986: 35). In sum, the Europeans who had successfully constituted their own 'true' history were now engaged in giving to Indians the greatest gift of all—a history (Cohn 1985: 326). But the first stage of the Orientalist enterprise in reconstructing the past was hardly a case of 'giving back to the natives the truths of their own little read and less understood Shaster (sic)' (*Parliamentary Papers on Hindu Widows* 1821: 532, cited in Mani 1986: 35), as portrayed by the Orientalists. The indigenous intelligentsia were not functioning within a political and social vacuum. The natives were no passive recipients of the perception of the past, then in the process of being reconstituted. In fact, the indigenous literati were *active agents* in constructing the past and were consciously engaged in choosing particular elements from the embryonic body of knowledge flowing from their own current social and political concerns.

The implications of the British position on social and cultural questions and the possibilities of generating certain changes through legislation became fairly clear in the early nineteenth century. The reconstruction of the past thereafter assumed a practical and utilitarian function. The question was no longer one of discovering fragments of texts, or translating them, but as the movement for abolition gained momentum, stratifying the texts to establish authenticity became crucial. All this meant that apart from a general increase in historical consciousness, the past was beginning to be classified and analysed more rigorously to argue the debates of the present. What was of lasting significance from the point of view of historical consciousness was the fact that the reconstruction of the past was no longer confined to the pages of the *Asiatic Researches*, read by a few select people. The reconstructed past was increasingly appearing in pamphlets and vernacular journals, made possible with the introduction of printing, and the participants in this were the newly emerging intelligentsia composed of both traditional and modern elements who perceived themselves as interpreters of tradition in a changing situation. This intelligentsia could regard itself as a product of an 'exhausted' culture but, through the work of the Orientalists, could simultaneously feel optimistic that despite the present circumstances they were representatives of a culture which had been 'organically disrupted by historical circumstance but was capable of revitalisation' (Kopf 1969: 8). Rammohun Roy epitomizes this dominant trend among the indigenous intelligentsia in the first quarter of the nineteenth century and is best known for his crusade against sati, although his writing and thinking spanned a whole gamut of issues relating to Hinduism.

The case against sati had been argued forcefully even before Rammohun Roy by Mritunjay Vidyalankar. Together Rammohun and Mritunjay introduced into sati a highly intellectual argument, one that evoked the highest goal of religion which had never been evoked before in the case of women, except in the dissident tradition as exemplified by Buddhism. The goal for women, as spelt out by the ancient Hindu legislators, was *pativrata dharma* (devotion to the husband). But Mritunjay, and then Rammohun, argued that the ultimate goal of *all* Hindus was selfless absorption in a divine essence, a union which could not flow from an action like sati. It was in this context, in response to the exigencies of social needs, that Roy imaginatively used the Maitreyi–Yajnavalkya episode (Ghose 1885: 43) to argue against the subjection of women. He imbued the account with two features (neither of which could be seen in the Jones–Colebrooke accounts), both of which have survived into the twentieth century upper-caste Hindu perception: one was the spiritual potential of women, and the second was that in the area of spirituality women were not inferior to men. From this followed the implicit assumption that the 'status' of women in the ancient past had been quite high unlike that of contemporary women. Rammohun used the Maitreyi episode to state that Yajnavalkya had imparted divine knowledge of the most difficult nature to Maitreyi and that she had not only been able to comprehend the high philosophy but had also actually attained divine knowledge. Roy thus provided a concrete example from the earliest antiquity to reinforce Mritunjay's position that women *had* pursued the highest goal of Hindu religion, and in his view, it was the 'wicked' pandits who distorted the Shastras in subsequent times.

It is significant that the Maitreyi account should have been imbued with a normative value for Hindu womanhood during the course of the sati debate by a reformer arguing for change. While the Orientalists tried to write without taking a position, for the Indian writer that was virtually impossible. The entire series of arguments used by Mritunjay and Roy indicate their refusal to accept, albeit at an intellectual level, that the final goal of Hindu women was different from that of Hindu men. It was at the same time an implicit devaluation of the pativrata ideal, where salvation lay in unqualified devotion to the husband, until then the only legitimate aspiration conceded to women by the legislators.

Roy's search for an alternative to superstitious and ritualized Hinduism in its present degenerate form also led him to search for these strands in the glorious past which could be highlighted as providing an indigenous alternative to degenerate Hinduism in the form of the Vedanta. In scrapping everything except the Vedas and Upanishads, which were identified as the core of Hindu tradition, he thus created a precedent for the crucial nineteenth century foregrounding of the Vedas. Further, once the Upanishads were identified as the 'true' religion, the golden age was perceived as lasting up to the time the Upanishads were composed. Ultimately the golden age of Hindu womanhood would also have to be located within this era.

The emerging Indian intelligentsia in the first half of the nineteenth century were involved in a dual encounter with colonial ideology. Awareness of the past through Orientalist scholarship was countered by an equally strong negative perception of the present which missionaries, administrators, travellers, and others were engaged in writing about.

Historical consciousness and especially the women's question were crucial components in this stream of writing too. In seeking a psychological advantage over their subjects, colonial ideology felt compelled to assert the moral superiority of the rulers in many subtle and not so subtle ways. One of the not so subtle ways was in the area of gender relations. The 'higher' morality of the imperial masters could be effectively established by highlighting the low status of women among the subject population as it was an issue by which the moral 'inferiority' of the subject population could simultaneously be demonstrated. The women's question thus became a crucial tool in the colonial ideology. History, in turn, came to occupy a key position in the cultural conflict between the ruling power and the colonized subjects. This was the context for the obsessive concern with cultural questions in the reconstruction of the past.

The bulk of colonial writing in India focused on demonstrating the peculiarities of Hindu civilization, and the barbaric practices pertaining to women. The circulation of this negative perception was much wider than that of Orientalist scholarship and probably preceded and outlasted the work of the Orientalists in revealing India's 'lost glory'. While they were writing and publishing mainly in learned journals, the Anglican writers, especially Christian missionaries, were methodically building up an indictment, also in print, about the hideous state of Indian society (Philips 1961: 218). Together their best representatives, Mill, Grant, and Duff, drew up what has been termed as a 'national' account-sheet of moral lapses and strong points of Indian and Western civilization.[1]

The best known work of this genre of writing is Mill's monumental account of India and her past; its reach and impact were tremendous because it was the first comprehensive history of India. In sharp contrast to the Orientalists who had suggested that the Hindus were a people of high culture now in a state of decline, Mill deemed Hindu civilization as crude from its very beginnings, and plunged in the lowest depths of immorality and crime.

Central to the criterion by which Mill judged the level of civilization was the position it accorded to its women. According to him Hindu women were in

a state of dependence more strict and humiliating than that which is ordained for the weaker sex.... Nothing can exceed the habitual contempt which Hindus entertain for their women.... They are held in extreme degradation, excluded from the sacred books, deprived

---

[1] The casting of moral balance sheets has been called the characteristic vice of British writers on Indian history. See Ballhatchet (1956).

of education and (of a share) in the paternal property.... That remarkable barbarity, the wife held unworthy to eat with her husband, is prevalent in Hindustan.[2]

A major conclusion of Mill's was that the practice of segregating women did not come with the Mohammedans (Mill 1840: 318); rather it was a consequence of the whole spirit of Hindu society where women must be constantly guarded at all times for fear of their innate tendency towards infidelity. Quoting from an ancient text he stated that the Hindus compared women with 'a heifer on the plain that longeth for fresh grass', with reference to their uncontrollable sexuality (ibid.: 314). Thus, the conquest of Hindustan by Muslim invaders had nothing to do with the general degradation of women which, Mill argued, did not alter 'the texture of society' (ibid.: 318). Further, Mill was not concerned with taking up specific social practices in demonstrating the degradation of women. He merely makes a passing mention of sati in the notes while discussing the indissolubility of the marriage tie that bound wives to their husbands even in death (ibid.: 315).

The degeneration of Hindu civilization and the abject position of Hindu women, requiring the 'protection' and 'intervention' of the colonial state, were two aspects of colonial politics. The third aspect was the 'effeminacy' of the Hindu men who were unfit to rule themselves (Sinha 1986). On all three counts British rule in India could be justified on grounds of moral superiority.

Throughout the first half of the nineteenth century, and even before, writers like Mill, Orme, Dubois, Macaulay, and Bentinck were labouring to certify the 'natives' as a frail, cowardly, and soft-bodied little people (Rosselli 1980: 121). Reaction to the representation of Hindus as effete, and their womenfolk requiring protection from the barbarity of their customs was bound to come and it began to crystallize immediately after the banning of sati. There were three major elements that coalesced and triggered off the beginnings of cultural nationalism in the 1830s: one was the attack of the Utilitarians and Anglicists on Hindu civilization; the second was the perceived threat of the Christian missionaries as exemplified in the person of Duff whose ambition was to convert the whole of Calcutta; and the third was the abolition of sati, which was perceived as an intrusion into the Hindu family, the most sacred sphere of Hindu society. Compounding the sense of an attack was the threat from 'within' in the form of Derozio

---

[2] Mill (1840: 312–13). Subsequent references are cited in the text.

and the group called Young Bengal whose 'outrageous' behaviour included scoffing at the Gods.[3]

The explicit reaction to the attacks on Hindu civilization by the proto-nationalists in the 1840s was preceded by a growing historical consciousness of the past. As an important aspect of the ideological encounter between the West and Hinduism was contained in the writing of history, it is necessary to briefly review the early indigenous historical works and trace the subsequent shift as the century progresses.

For instance, the very first textbook published at Serampore press in 1801 was *Raja Pratapaditya Charita*, a historical sketch of the Raja of Jessore by Ramram Basu (Kopf 1969: 125). This was followed by *Rajaboli*, a story of kings, by Mritunjay Vidyalankar. Essentially anecdotal, it, however, included tales of heroes, Hindu, Muslim, and British, from the battles of Kurukshetra down to Plassey. It is significant that at this early stage, heroism was not an attribute of nationalism in particular, that the Marathas are cast as 'alien plunderers', and that valour was not associated with particular communities in India. Further, it should be noted that historical knowledge about ancient India was still not available. Vidyalankar says nothing of Ashoka, the Guptas, or Buddhist India; the rediscoveries by nineteenth century scholarship which would establish the contours of the political history of ancient India were still to come (ibid.: 124). *Rajaboli* was thus a reflection of the eighteenth century consciousness (often transmitted through the oral tradition) of the Bengali pandits *before* the birth of cultural nationalism.

It was at this embryonic stage in the writing of history that Mill published his *History of British India*, which influenced the direction historical consciousness would take. The Indian intelligentsia reacted violently to his grim picture of Hindu civilization and marshalled arguments against each of his major criticisms. In a sense, therefore, Mill defined the parameters of the nineteenth century discourse on history.

A small beginning was made by Gobind Chandra Sen between October 1840 and May 1841 to rebut Mill and resuscitate the image of Hindu civilization. His account reflected in a rudimentary form some of the stereotypes now associated with Rajputs as 'freedom lovers' and Muslims as 'marauders' (Chattopadhyaya 1965: 201). Gobind Chandra Sen wrote mainly on medieval India but the proto-nationalist Peary Chand Mitra

---

[3] One young man when asked to bow down before the goddess Kali greeted the image with a 'Good morning madam'. See Sarkar (1958: 20).

focused squarely on pre-Muslim India which he characterized as the 'state of Hindustan under the Hindus' and as the 'scene of glorious exploits and actions' (ibid.: 131). Throughout Peary Chand's account it is clear that he is addressing, and contesting, the unseen presence of Mill. There had been, he asserted, no despotism under Hindu rulers. Further, while the Hindus were as valiant as anybody else, they 'did not encroach upon the dominions of any foreign power'. This covert snipe against the British was accompanied by a reminder to his fellow countrymen that their ancestors had resisted the invasions of those who 'allured by the wealth and grandeur of the country came to bring it to subjection'. He argued that though the ignorant were branding the Indians as 'barbarians' and men who were '*naturally inferior* to the Europeans', the former achievements of the Hindus in the field of intellectual glory and moral eminence remained as 'splendid beacons' (ibid.: 94–6, 168, 176, 180–1, 277).

Apart from the general structure of Hindu civilization, the condition of women in the past was a key aspect of historical writing in the 1840s. It was not uncommon for Mill to be echoed by other writers, particularly by those who have been termed the 'nativist-evangelists'. One such example was the account of women in the past provided by M.C. Deb, a Christian convert and a member of the Young Bengal group. Deb combined elements of Mill with what was then a widely circulating perception about the Muslim interregnum as the dark ages, especially in its effects upon women. According to Deb, men in India looked upon women as household slaves and treated them with a superciliousness which even the 'Sultan of Turkestan does not show towards his meanest serf' (ibid.: 94). The primary responsibility for the 'sad and deplorable' (ibid.: 95–6) conditions was attributed to the ravages of Muslim rule.

In contrast to M.C. Deb, Peary Chand Mitra, also a member of the Young Bengal group, provided in 1842 a well-argued response to the Mill approach on the position of women in Hindu civilization. Using the Orientalists and anticipating later nationalist historians, Mitra takes up different aspects of women's status, focusing on education and female seclusion as key contemporary issues. Admitting that the status of women in contemporary Bengal was bad, he sought to provide evidence for his argument that in the past women had access to Sanskrit learning and had produced many notable philosophers and debators. He quotes from the *Mahanirban Tantra* which states that the daughter should be 'nursed and educated with care' and married to a learned man, and uses Kalidasa's plays, Tamil literature, and accounts of well-known philosophical debates to provide a series of examples of women like Leelavati and Avaiyar who were learned (ibid.: 277). The example of Avaiyar, a Tamil Bhakti poetess, is particularly striking as it indicates a familiarity with a 'great Sanskritic tradition' to which the Orientalists had contributed substantially and which was an important dimension in the ultimate crystallization of a 'national' feminine identity based on 'high' culture.

The reaction to Mill, Grant, Duff, and their kind of writing on Hindu women had been firmly set in motion by Peary Chand Mitra and it was to be developed and refined in the subsequent decades alongside the development of a nationalist ideology. The fact that this reaction to the women's question was launched by someone like Peary Chand is particularly notable as the Young Bengal group, to which he had belonged, had begun in the late 1820s and early 1830s with a severe onslaught on Hinduism. Now in the 1840s the women's question in particular seems to have touched a raw nerve and the Hindu intelligentsia was less willing to stand by and passively watch the attacks on its culture and the devaluation of its womanhood.

II

If the indigenous writing of the 1840s, broadly in the area of culture, represents elements of proto-nationalism, the writing of the period after the 1860s is directly imbued with nationalist fervour. The nationalist consciousness which permeated the writing of historical and semi-historical literature was greatly facilitated by an extension of British Orientalism through the work of Friedrich Max Muller (1823–1900) who more than any other of the Orientalists focused upon the achievements of the 'Aryans' as contained in their ancient text of the Vedas. Under Max Muller the word 'Aryan' acquired such a range of normative connotations that it has left a permanent impress upon the collective consciousness of the upper strata of Indian society.

A product of the German Romantic movement (which departed from the eighteenth century Enlightenment and rationalism) and a sympathetic witness to the 1848 Paris revolt in his student days, Max Muller was initially part of the liberal tendency within Germany. However, like other liberals in Germany, he grew politically conservative about German nationalism and became a staunch admirer of Bismarck (Max Muller: 1902: 72; Voigt 1967: xi, 53–8). His initial interest in Sanskrit came as much from a romantic childhood interest in India[4] as from a pragmatic decision that he would have better career prospects in this area than in the already heavily saturated field of classical European studies.

The core of Max Muller's work which he himself valued most was his collation and publication of the full text of the Vedas.[5] According to him, it was the only 'natural basis of Indian history', which could throw light over the whole historical development of the Indian mind, and therefore the task of fixing its age was of paramount significance (Max Muller 1892: 57). Like the earlier Orientalists, Max Muller saw the recovery of the Vedas as bringing to Hindus the truths of their ancient tradition. He believed that the Veda is 'the root of their religion, and to show what that root is, I feel sure, the only way of uprooting all that has sprung from it during the last 3,000 years' (quoted in Choudhari 1974: 90). Since the Veda was also the root of all religion, law, and philosophy, it was to trace the origin of these that one needed to reconstruct the Veda.

So great an influence has the Vedic age ... exercised upon all succeeding periods of Indian history, so deeply have the religious and moral ideas of that primitive era taken root in the mind of the Indian nation, so minutely has almost every private and public act of Indian life been regulated by old traditionary precepts that it is impossible to find the right point of view for judging of Indian religion, morals, and literature without a knowledge of the literary remains of the Vedic age. (Choudhari 1974: 135)

Regarding the Veda as the 'Bible' of the Aryans resulted in a great deal of importance being attributed to the term Aryan; although it was already well-known and often used, it gained tremendous currency following Max Muller's work. Starting from the researches on comparative philology, Max Muller extended the meaning of the term Aryan to apply it to the unknown people who 'spoke the assumed Indo-European original language common to all members of this language group'. Sanskrit was the closest language to this unknown language group (Max Muller 1892: 13). Later, the

---

[4] Max Muller's romantic interest in India was awakened when at the age of 10 he saw a picture of Benares in one of his school books which showed men and women on the banks of the Ganga stepping down to bathe in it. Until then he knew of India only as a place where the 'people were black' and they 'burnt their widows'. On his book, however, they were represented as 'tall and beautiful', certainly not like 'niggers'. The mosques and temples on the banks of the river were so impressive that they looked more majestic than the churches and palaces in his home-town. The young boy was moved enough by the sight to remember it almost 50 years later (Neufeldt 1980: 3).

[5] The attention drawn to the Vedas was almost entirely due to their popularization initially by Max Muller and later by R.C. Dutt and Dayananda. When first published by Colebrooke in 1805, it was dismissed as a damp squib. See Dutt (1888/1972: viii).

emphasis shifted from language to race and the 'unknown' Aryans were then described as the 'true ancestors of our race' (F. Max Muller, *Chips from a German Workshop*, I: 4, cited in Voigt 1967: 6). For his European audience, Max Muller attempted to establish the relationship between the Aryans in India who had, in their primitive glory, composed the Veda and the Aryans who now inhabited Europe; making a distinction between two major 'races', the Aryan (or the Indo-European) and the Semitic, he went on to imply that the Aryans were racially superior to the Turanian and Semitic races:

> The [Aryans] have been the prominent actors in the great drama of history, and have carried to their fullest growth all the elements of active life with which our nature is endowed. They have perfected society and morals.... In continual struggle with each other and with Semitic and Turanian races these Aryan nations have become the rulers of history and it seems to be their mission to link all parts of the world together by the chains of civilization and religion. (F. Max Muller, *Chips from a German Workshop*, I: 63, cited in Voigt 1967: 7)

The task of convincing the rulers of a nation that they were of the same race as their subjects was by no means easy, so Max Muller had to reiterate the theme of common origins in his writings: 'Though the historian may shake his head, *though the physiologist may doubt* all must yield before the facts furnished by language' (Max Muller 1859: 12; emphasis added). To bolster his argument that Europeans and Indians were of the same stock, it was necessary to highlight the great achievements of ancient Aryans in India; knowledge of 'universal history' according to Max Muller required that

> ... we should not leave out of sight our nearest intellectual relatives, the Aryas of India, the framers of the most wonderful language, the fellow workers in the constitution of the most wonderful concepts, the fathers of the most natural religions, the makers of the most transparent mythologies, the inventors of the most subtle philosophy and the givers of the most elaborate laws. (Max Muller 1892: 15)

Much of Max Muller's writing was directed at young Indian Civil Service (ICS) trainees in England with the prospect of a career in post-Mutiny India, who were to be enthused with a sense of mission and injected with a feeling of excitement and adventure. Even if the conquests of soldiers were no longer possible, there were other literary and historical conquests that were available for the asking such as retrieving the flagging Orientalist movement.

Though there are some references to women, it is significant that at no point in his writings does Muller dwell at any length upon them. In fact, there appears to be an implicit assumption that the Aryan patriarchal system did not itself pay too much attention to women and certainly did not regard them as equal. Like all writers on the Vedas, he too narrated the Maitreyi–Yajnavalkya episode but he concluded the passage with the remark that although women participated in the ritual, they were not initiated, and still less were they admitted to the highest knowledge of the *atman or brahman*. Cases like Maitreyi, according to him, were the exception, not the rule (ibid.: 33). He used Strabo's quotations on women in India in support of his views:

Indians did not communicate their metaphysical doctrines to women thinking that if their wives understood these doctrines and learned to be indifferent to pleasure and pain, and to consider life and death as the same they would no longer continue to be the slaves of others; or if they failed to understand them they would be talkative and communicate their knowledge to those who had no right to do it. (Max Muller 1859: 24)

Max Muller goes on to say that this statement by the Greek writer was fully borne out by the later Sanskrit literature; he quotes from the *Srauta* and *Grihya Sutra*s where it is stated that women were not allowed to learn the sacred songs of the Vedas. There is nothing in Max Muller's writing to suggest that he considered women to be spiritual, or learned, in the Vedic period. He himself attached little significance to the inferior position held by women.[6] Muller's contribution to nineteenth-century historiography was thus clearly not in relation to the women's question; however, everything else that he wrote about was taken up with enthusiasm, as I shall show presently. The different aspects of his work on the Vedas, Sanskrit literature more generally, and especially philosophy, had one connecting thread: all these were the achievements of the glorious Aryans. Max Muller vastly popularized a racist Aryan version of the Orientalist Hindu golden age, and it was this newly formulated golden age that became so influential in later Indian thought.

Other British/European writers used the newly emerging body of knowledge on the Aryans in distinctive and less simplistic ways and these also had a bearing on the construction of the Aryan myth. One such example is W.W. Hunter's *The Annals of Rural Bengal*, which argues that with the Aryan conquest of India there was a rigid division between the conquering Aryans and the aboriginal people which later resulted in the emergence of mixed castes (Stokes 1961: 394). Here we see a new element that was missing in the work of Max Muller who not only had concentrated

---

[6] A paternalistic concern for the misery of the widow was, however, evident in Max Muller's activities. He petitioned Queen Victoria on the need to alleviate the pathetic condition of child widows. See Voigt (1967: 49).

exclusively on the Aryans but had treated Hindus, Brahmins, Aryans, and Indians as synonymous, almost giving the impression that no other category had ever existed. Hunter's use of Aryan to show internal division, stratification, and hierarchy is thus significant. So too is his notion of the 'vigorous' Aryan conquerors as getting degenerate through mixed breeding and ending up as effete Bengali Brahmins.

The use of the term Aryan by European scholars was varied, but in all cases Aryan is clearly associated with vigour, with race, and with a conquering group who came to India from elsewhere, and in their pure form possessed nothing but positive attributes. Directly or indirectly, some of these writers, who used the term Aryan (but did not focus in particular on women), influenced the more specific European writing on Hindu women. Significantly, some of this writing was by women themselves.

An early example of such a work was published in 1856 by Mrs Speier who was stationed at Calcutta.[7] All we know about her is that she had access to the publications of the *Asiatic Researches*, may have attended the meetings of the Asiatic Society, and appears to have known the well-known scholar H.H. Wilson whom she acknowledges in her preface.

Speier was writing what appears to be one of the many historical works by Europeans in the nineteenth century. Her book titled *Life in Ancient India* fully accepts Max Muller and the common Indo-Aryan origin theory. But she warns against associating all Indians with Rammohun Roy or Dwarkanath Tagore who were as unlike typical Hindus as Robert Burns was the British ploughman. It is in her portrayal of ancient Indian womanhood that Speier is unabashedly romantic:

> A thousand years B.C. Hindu women appear to have been as free as Trojan dames or the daughters of Judaea. Hymns in the Rig Veda mention them with respect and affection.... Even in the succeeding phase when Brahmans contemplated the soul beneath the Himavat women attended their discourses.... We find in one of the Upanishads a king holding a solemn sacrifice and inviting his chief guests to state their opinions on theology. Amongst these guests a learned female named Garga is conspicuous. A more pleasing instance of women's interests in holy themes is afforded by a conversation between Yajnavalkya and Maitreyi. (Speier 1856/1973: 166–7)

Speier then goes on to transform Colebrooke's staid account of Maitreyi and Yajnavalkya (upon which her own account is admittedly based) into a more imaginative and powerful rendering in which Maitreyi *chooses* 'immortality' in place of 'mere' riches, and learns to 'contemplate the soul alone since everything is soul', the aim being to merge all thought

---

[7] Speier (1856/1973: 39). Subsequent references are cited in the text.

and feeling into the universal soul. It is in Speier's work that one notices Vedic women being epitomized by Gargi and Maitreyi; subsequently they were the stock favourites of the nationalist writers arguing about the 'high' status of women in ancient India.

Speier proceeds to recount the evidence of later Brahminical texts, such as Manu's code, to depict the changed status of women which she characterizes as 'Obedience to her husband is the beginning, and the middle, and the end of female duty', and concludes that women's rights 'were wholly ignored by the Brahmanical code'. Because 'daughters and wives are often too happy to require rights', she argues that we tend to forget that according to the code they are without rights and get taken in by other representations of 'domestic' bliss (ibid.: 166–70). Though Speier is aware of the contradictory statements in the texts about women and implicitly suggests a decline in their status from the freedom and learning they enjoyed in very early times, she nevertheless goes on to paint the most romantic and glorified picture of the heroines of literature, all focusing on the beautiful 'conjugal' love among the ancient Aryans as had existed between Nala and Damyanti, and Savitri and Satyavan (ibid.: 171–2). Speier seems to be fascinated by these models of womanhood and by the power of their love, especially the travails of couples like Nala and Damayanti who must undergo untold misery before their love is vindicated. While the Nala–Damayanti narration is titled 'Wedded Love', the Savitri–Satyavan story is called 'Woman's Love' (ibid.: 171, 181). Describing Yama's attempts at taking away the dead Satyavan which are foiled by Savitri, Speier recounts what Savitri says to the God of death:

Where he goes, my path shall be,
I will follow where thou leadest,
Listen once again to me...

Speier ends the story with 'and at length love conquers all' (ibid.: 183).

The fascination, even the mystique, of Hindu womanhood is much more explicit in Speier's reference to sati. Asserting that Brahminical law makes woman the property of man whose fate is 'death upon the funeral pyre when he dies', Speier goes on to say that nature (female nature) had not entirely succumbed to law and the 'free woman's character of the Sanskrit epics has not been universally suppressed in India' (ibid.: 454). She then cites extensively from Sleeman's account of a sati who, when prevented from mounting the pyre, refused to eat till she was permitted to fulfil her wishes, and also gives the example of Ahalya Bai's daughter who argued with her mother when she tried to prevent the daughter from mounting the pyre (ibid.: 455). Clearly, emotional accounts such as Sleeman's had left a deep impress on many European women. By this time sati had been banned for over a generation and as an issue of the past it was no longer horrifying, but rather awe-inspiring, and was seen as the ultimate power that the Hindu woman had in an otherwise powerless situation.

The glorification of Hindu womanhood in the ancient past is even more noticeable in Clarisse Bader's monograph on women in ancient India. Published in 1867, when Bader was a young girl of 22, it was directly inspired by Max Muller's romanticization of the past. Bader takes for granted the original connection between the Aryans, be they in India or in Europe, and also the moral and intellectual superiority of the Aryans in relation to the defeated Dasyus. Bader makes constant comparisons between the West and the East with the exhortation that the West should learn from the East; she bemoans the rapidly changing Western society with its superficiality and materialism. Reacting to industrialized Europe she pleaded passionately, 'Has not the time arrived to refresh ourselves from more life giving and generous sources? And only India has the honour of affording such sources.'[8] Bader's intention in her monograph was, very simply, to seek the 'part played by woman in the Hindu pantheon from the time of Aryan symbolism to the materialistic age of Krishna and his worshippers'. Her enthusiasm in pursuing her mission is evident from the way she ends her preface: 'May the Gangetic muse occupy her proper position on the domestic hearth, whose austere joys she has so worthily sung' (Bader 1925: x).

Bader notes with approval the fact that women were not excluded from 'labouring' for the sacrifice as it was women who collected the *kusa* grass for the sacred enclosure, and the plant from which *soma* juice was extracted; they had the right of offering sacrifices in their own names as well as in composing hymns. The example of Vispala who participated in battles is cited to show that women had been the recipients of the beneficence of the gods (ibid.: 8–9). The account that Bader really labours over is the Maitreyi–Yajnavalkya episode in which three of her major concerns converge, namely Aryan genius, spiritualism, and women. While introducing the episode Bader says:

In a dialogue in which the Aryan genius was displayed in all the grandeur of its spiritual tendencies and in which the great question of the immortality of the soul was debated one of the interlocutors was a woman; and it is *she* who began the solemn conversation. (ibid.: 10–12)

---

[8] Bader (1925: viii). Subsequent references are cited in the text.

Bader then proceeds to narrate the episode in the greatest detail to establish the most complete expression of belief in the universal spirit and simultaneously of the depth of the knowledge that a woman was judged capable of 'receiving, and still more, of understanding' (ibid.: 12). But alas, says Bader, the situation changed. Manu did not recognize the right of a woman to lift up her soul to God. He debased her instead by the exclusive adoration of a 'creature similar to herself'; women's zeal was now to be demonstrated in the service of the husband instead of a spiritual father; in the care of the home instead of the 'maintenance of the sacred fire' (ibid.: 17–18). The real fall for women came with the growth of the Krishna cult which was gross and materialist. The decadence continued to increase until the day came when India 'debilitated and corrupted by the cult yielded to the enervating influence of Islam and showed to what depth of physical and moral degradation the most gifted of people could fall, once it had exchanged the yoke of duty to that of passion' (ibid.: 330). In such a society, the position of women naturally plunged to the depths.

Bader, like Speier, saw sati as awe-inspiring. In her view, it was an expression of woman's ability to go beyond the 'bounds of requirement'. As she put it, 'The law commanded her to identify her life with her husband's; but she went "further" and identified her death with his' (ibid.: 332). For her, 'Ardent piety, spiritual and ascetic tenderness, complete abnegation of herself, unlimited devotion to her family, a boundless need of love, formed the character of such women' (ibid.: 333). And that sums up the power of 'Hindu–Aryan' womanhood as it was perceived by the Orientalist-inspired women of the West.

The contribution of the second round of the Orientalists and their feminine counterparts may be summed up as the transformation of the Hindu golden age into an Aryan golden age wherein the men were free, brave, vigorous, fearless, themselves civilized and civilizing others, noble, and deeply spiritual; and the women were learned, free, and highly cultured; conjointly they offer sacrifices to the gods, listening 'sweetly' to discourses, and preferring spiritual upliftment to the pursuit of 'mere' riches. Additionally, they represented the best examples of conjugal love, offering the supreme sacrifice of their lives as a demonstration of their feeling for their partners in the brief journey of life. This was to be an enduring legacy.

The researches and writings of European scholars in the second half of the nineteenth century, idealizing and giving prominence to the notion of the Aryan, were a tremendous boost to the attempts by indigenous writers to raise the morale of all Indians. The researches on philology popularized by Max Muller had highlighted the common origin of the Europeans and Indians, and the theory of shared Aryan origins came to be isolated as the most significant aspect of Sanskrit studies as far as the cultural nationalists were concerned. As used by the indigenous intelligentsia, the Aryan origin theory was, however, a double-edged weapon. On the one hand, it gave the subjugated people a sense of self-esteem, and a means by which all Indians of the upper strata could, in opposition to their colonial rulers, gain a sense of 'national' identity; on the other, it meant that the subject people could at the same time identify with the rulers as people belonging to the same stock and therefore no different from themselves. Comparative philology thus had a political utility and provided a specific character and a scholarly basis to modern Indian cultural nationalism.[9]

The Aryan was an important element in the nationalist construction of a sense of identity for its association with vigour, conquest, and expansion; in other words, for its connotations of political and cultural achievement. These aspects are to be seen in relation to the negative qualities of an effete, unmanly, slothful, and slack people as imputed by one section of European writers on India. This characterization was in a general sense applicable to all Hindus but it had a particular association with Bengalis. Many Bengalis themselves believed this to be true since they were perceived as failing to have shown sufficient resistance to Muslim power. Since the loss of independence was associated with effeteness, regeneration required the forging of a new identity. To counteract the weakness of the Bengali or the Hindu, the nationalists projected heroes from an earlier era but also constructed an alternative Hindu male. Thus, a transregional unified Hindu identity was forged using elements from history and folklore to valorise heroic action. As conceived by the nationalists, jointly they were the inheritors of a glorious Hindu–Aryan heritage, and with renewed vigour they would succeed in asserting a new Hindu identity.[10]

The foregrounding of Aryan elements in the formation of an alternative identity was accompanied by the introduction of specifically martial qualities that were associated with particular regions and groups of people such as the Marathas, Rajputs, and Sikhs. Such groups had been categorized by the British as martial races for purposes of recruitment in the army. The nationalists adapted the notion of martial races to their own ends, endowing

[9] The common origin theory worked both ways and affected British attitudes towards Indians. According to one Bengali writer, 'From being niggers at one time we have now become brethren.' See Choudhari (1974: 316–18).

[10] As S.C. Bose put it, 'The young man of the future, our heart tells us will be very different.' Cited in Rosselli (1980: 126).

them with the heroic character of resistance to foreign rule (primarily Muslim). The process was considerably helped by the publication, around the mid-nineteenth century, of the detailed works of British writers: Grant Duff (1826) on the Marathas, Tod (1920) on the Rajputs, and Cunningham (1849) on the Sikhs. These works, although widely used by Indians later on in the century, hardly excited great enthusiasm, at least initially, among the British for whom they were meant.

But in the last quarter of the nineteenth century there was a spate of more popular historical writing where the 'heroic' communities received enthusiastic coverage. While Ranade popularized the heroism of Shivaji and the Marathas (see Hatalkar 1973), works like *Rajasthaner Itihas* (Mallik 1961: 451) highlighted the chivalry, honour, and heroism of Rajputs. Similarly, *Sikh Yudher Itihasa* (ibid.: 449) circulated awareness of the great battles fought by the Sikhs against the British. A most popular work was *Arya-Kirtti* ('The Fame of the Aryans') by Rajani Kanta Gupta which ran into 15 editions and had sketches of the great historical figures of 'Hindu' India, the Rajputs, Marathas, and Sikhs, and was intended to produce national consciousness, self-respect, and a feeling of pride in one's country. The same author wrote a 700-page book in four parts on the Mutiny called *Sipahi Yudher Itihasa* (1876) which highlighted characters like the Rani of Jhansi, Kunwar Singh, and Nana Sahib for their heroic role in the Mutiny (ibid.). This process of rewriting history at a popular level provided material for novels, stories, poems, and plays, and contributed tremendously to the rise of a militant cultural nationalism (Majumdar 1961: 423).

The roots of the martial spirit valorized by the nationalist writers could be traced back to the traditional Kshatriya values of the ancient social order, as in R.C. Dutt's writing. His work is important as he contributed the first major historical account of ancient Indian civilization. At Bankim's instance (Sen 1973: 320), he also wrote novels, four of which dealt with historical themes set in the medieval period, idealized a 'Hindu' past, and regretted its loss (Chandra 1987: 5). They enabled Dutt to inspire patriotism as he effectively used the medium of Rajput and Maratha heroes to construct his images of patriotism. Apart from the symbolism of a heroic, unselfish, and relentless warrior, the Rajput hero in particular was cast as a hero who had never accepted—even in the face of the severest hardship including certain death—the overlordship of 'alien' rulers.

The Rajput warrior was linked to ancient Kshatriya warriors such as the Pandavas and other heroes whose valour had been preserved in the 'imperishable epics' (Dutt 1888/1972: 7). The Kshatriya warrior himself was then linked to the Aryans who were the original primeval conquerors in history, and whatever was good among the later Aryans, after their original vigour had declined, was associated with the Kshatriyas (ibid.: 8–9). In part, this may be explained by the belief, by now fairly strong, that it was the 'priesthood' that was responsible for the moral and material degeneration of Hindu society. Further, the ideology of martial races (Nandy 1983: 7) enabled a covert identification with the aggressor just as the common Aryan origin theory had done. Authentic Indianness in the regenerated Hindu thus lay in Kshatriyahood which combined in itself martial, Hindu, and Aryan elements of the past. As R.C. Dutt viewed it, Kshatriyahood also combined the vigour of heroic conquerors and the truly spiritual speculation and knowledge of the Upanishadic seers and philosophers.

In the wider context of cultural nationalism, Bankim too was creatively involved in forging a new national identity for both men and women which highlighted the newly regenerated Hindu–Aryan male as one who combined in himself the militancy of the martial groups and the spirituality of the *sanyasi* (renouncer). In Bankim's view, India was in a subject position because Indians were weak (*balhin*) and effeminate (*strisvabhav*) (Clark 1961: 435). He bemoaned that liberty was unknown to any Indian people except the Rajputs. According to Bankim the concept of *svadhinta* (freedom) was unknown in ancient or in medieval literature (ibid.: 436). The only people who had a consciousness of their nationhood were the ancient Aryan invaders of India but in course of time even they became divided into small and separate groups and lost the sense of nationhood (ibid.: 437). To remedy the situation, Bankim felt it was necessary to develop a strong militant race. The prerequisite for attaining this objective was the restoration of national unity and pride through a reinterpretation of the past.[11]

It was this analysis that motivated Bankim into writing his most historically significant piece of work, the *Krishnacharita*, where he constructed a Krishna for the future as a historical figure symbolizing the possibility of energetic historical action. This he achieved by cleansing the Krishna legend of its erotic dimension and by 'recovering' the earlier rationalist figure, the Krishna who was a man of action and of serious philosophic thought (see Kaviraj 1987). Bankim's newly constructed

---

[11] According to Bankim, while the British recorded even their yawns, the modesty of the Hindus meant that there was no 'Hindu' history. The writing of history was thus very important to Bankim (Clark 1961: 435).

nationalist identity, for which Krishna was the ideal model, also had other elements not contained explicitly at least in the recovery of the 'warrior'. A major element was a deep consciousness about a 'Hindu' past symbolized by the great works of art, literature, and philosophy.[12]

The aggressiveness of the new cultural nationalism marked a sharp break from the universalism of the earlier phase associated with Rammohun Roy and a section of the Brahmo Samaj. The new identity of aggressive cultural nationalism valorized select features of a Hindu past; everything related to Aryan and Kshatriya values embodying vigour and militancy was central to this new identity; so was genuine spiritualism of the world-affirming kind such as that associated with the Vedas or even with Bankim's Krishna in the *Krishnacharita* or the sanyasis in *Anandmath*. But this process of selection also meant a process of exclusion in the formation of the new national identity. First, it was clearly a new 'Hindu' identity which excluded all 'foreigners', which for Bankim meant Muslims. Further, in his view, the Hindu identity also came to be explicitly associated with a specifically Aryan identity. In his analysis there was also a connection between the un-Aryan and the Muslim. In Bengal, the awareness and pride in an Aryan identity had led to a simple dichotomization of the population into high castes comprising Aryan, and labouring groups comprising un-Aryan. Bankim extended this dichotomization by associating Aryan purity with the high castes, especially the Bengali Brahmin, and non-Aryan impurity with the low castes, especially those who had converted en-masse to Islam. Thus, Bankim's regenerated Hindu 'national' identity excluded not only the Muslims but also the lower castes as they were of non-Aryan and 'impure' extraction. This process of exclusion and inclusion was more explicit in Bankim's case but it is important to bear in mind that it was fairly representative of the nineteenth century cultural nationalists.

What was expected of women in the context of aggressive cultural nationalism and the valorization of Kshatriya values in the new national identity for men? Men must be heroic in a country that has been subjugated but what were women to do in such a situation? What kind of

---

[12] 'Thus, apart from the assertion of a warrior figure there was also a move towards a 'specific' Hindu identity forged through a recourse to history and a constant reiteration of a link between the past, the present, and the future, as in this passage by Bankim: 'Who polished the stones with such delicate artistry, was he a Hindu like any one of us? ... Who carved those female figures, were they Hindus like us? Then I remembered the Hindus, then I recollected the Upanishads, Gita, Ramayana, Mahabharata, Kumara Sambhava, Shakuntala, Panini, Katyayana, Sankhya, Patanjali, Vedanta ... all these were the achievements of Hindus. Then I thought blessed am I that I was born a Hindu.' Cited in Poddar (1976: 202).

heroism or what kind of role was required of them? From the disparate body of writing, a sub-stratum may be extracted to throw some light on the emerging ideology of womanhood.

A point to note about the problems in the formation of a 'national' identity of women was the whole question of the continuing impetus to a reform of their status, the need for a protection of their minimum rights, and a raising of their status through education. Alternative identity formation in the case of women had no single or coherent model like regenerating the Hindu male from the ignominy of effeminacy. The kind of woman required for the present and the future was much more difficult to construct, given the need for a different kind of regeneration that was necessary in her case. In such a situation it was considerably easier to construct models of womanhood in the past. The most significant historical work was R.C. Dutt's *History of Civilisation in Ancient India* where he provided a comprehensive rebuttal of James Mill's denigration of Hindu civilization and of the low position of Hindu women within it. In Dutt's work, the fully worked out version of of the myth of the Vedic woman as the highest symbol of Hindu womanhood, indicated by writers like Peary Chand Mitra, Speier, and Clarisse Bader, was finalized. His sketch of the Vedic woman is penned with a keen eye to contemporary debates on women's status (Dutt 1888/1972: 67).

Dutt takes up every debated area of the contemporary status of women and counterposes it with evidence drawn from the Vedas. Women were educated, chose their partners, and even contracted second marriages, which, according to Dutt, was a 'national' custom. Dutt's work relies on the careful researches of Sanskrit scholars from the days of Jones and Colebrooke, and also recounts the Gargi and Maitreyi instances in great detail to establish the 'high' status of women in the Aryan golden age (ibid.: 73, 169–70). He concludes:

Do not such passages as these indicate that women were honoured in ancient India, more perhaps than among any other ancient nation in the face of the globe? Considered the intellectual companions of their husbands, as their affectionate helpers in the journey of life, and as inseparable partners in their religious duties, Hindu wives received the honour and respect due to their position.... (ibid.: 170–1)

Dutt also outlined the role of women in the more recent medieval past. The Vedic 'helpmate' in the sacrifice which was so important to the early nationalist historians, was easily extendable to other helpmate roles for women. The brave warriors who would not give in to the might of alien rule were supported by the female Kshatriya values of courage and bravery which made no demands on their menfolk; indeed these values enabled the men to resist to the very end. This they did in a variety of ways including the ultimate example of the major feminine counterpart of Kshatriya value—that of choosing death rather than ravishment (Dutt 1947). In his novel *Pratap Singh*, all the women characters are of course brave, but pre-eminent among the exemplars of 'Kshatriyani' virtues are women like the wise Devi of the cave, a strong mother figure who acts as an oracle and inspiration to martial valour; the Amazonian figure as the biological progenitor of a heroic race; and the heroic Rajput mother who must perforce continue to live for the sake of her son. Dutt recounts an episode wherein a Rajput ruler dies while defending his fort against the foreign invader. Before the widow of the chieftain could mount the pyre, a neighbouring chieftain attempted to usurp the throne of the minor son. The queen then fought tooth and nail to save the ancestral kingdom for her son. She met her end when 10 men overwhelmed her but her indomitable courage and fierce resistance inspired the young son with a burning passion to avenge his parents' death (ibid.: 8–9, 64–8).

There are other instances in the narrative of 'Kshatriyani' virtues such as the resolve to mount the pyre to allow the men to go and fight without the fear of their womenfolk being ravished.[13] The high point in the narrative comes when the kingdom is surrounded by alien armies. The Rani calls all the womenfolk together and addresses them, 'Friends, we shall perform the sati today; what happier fate can destiny hold for Rajput women? Let our enemies behold the sight. Our men are heroes, our women are chaste.' The account concludes with a rhapsodic description of the event.[14] Rajput women, no less than their menfolk, were thus seen as providing models of wisdom, indomitable courage, and undying resistance.

Women of the past were valorized in two separate ways; for their spiritual potential and their role as *sahadharmini*s (partners in religious duties) in ancient times, and as heroic resisters to alien rulers who cheerfully chose death rather than dishonour. From these elements out of history and folklore, constituting images of glorious women of the golden

---

[13] The code of conduct for Rajput men in times of crisis requires that they fight to the bitter end after they have ensured that their women will not be ravished. As a young prince tells his mother, 'The Rathor fears no human foe, he will fight. But before this the honour of the Rajput ladies must be secured' (Dutt 1947: 124).

[14] 'In the morning sunlight one thousand women performed their baths, offered their prayers and assembled together. The child, the youth, the aged all stood together and with joy in their hearts chanted a prayer. And then? And then in accordance with the ancient Rajput custom the thousand women decked with jewels and ornaments with a joyful cry on their lips mounted the pyre. When defeat, dishonour, and loss of religion are inevitable Rajput women preserve their chastity in this manner' (Dutt 1947: 124–5).

past, was fashioned a new identity for women to suit the present and the future. How much and what aspects of tradition went into the construction of a new feminine identity varied from one writer to another but on many essentials there was considerable similarity; indeed the convergence on the fundamental characteristics of Hindu womanhood cut across the liberal-revivalist divide.

The most coherent early construction of a 'national' identity for women was by Bankim. The inherent tension between the womanhood of the past and the womanhood of the present was resolved in Bankim's literary portrayal of women, especially in his last novels (Bagchi 1985: 60–1). Essentially conservative on contemporary issues relating to women, his literary characters are, however, free to pursue non-conventional roles. He makes contemptuous jibes at the new type of worthless woman emerging in Bengal whose utter laziness was bound to have disastrous consequences on her own health and upon her children. Such a woman, who contributed to no one's happiness but her own, was little better than an animal and her birth was in vain (Borthwick 1984: 196). Not surprisingly, one of his female characters argues that people who recommend widow remarriage and education for women, and oppose child marriage, will not understand the 'true significance of the devotion to one's husband' (*Bankim Racnabali*, I: 374, cited in Murshid 1983: 195). In all his novels the wife never transgresses the notion of true wifehood. But in his last novels true wifehood extends to energizing the husband for the goal of regenerating the motherland. Actual questions of women's status including the problem of widowhood and the need for reform remained outside the ambit of Bankim's concerns.

In *Anandmath*, Bankim creates, according to Bagchi, a parable of nationalist confrontation in the novel. The role of women in such a situation could not thus remain what it was, or could be, in a period of stability as the golden past had been. Thus, the traditional roles of women would no longer do in a crisis of the kind that the nation had never faced in the past. Externally and internally the threatened moral and social order desperately required a new kind of woman for which the old sahadharmini model was too passive and could only apply once order had been re-established. A ravaged nation required heroic action from both men and women; if anything, it was women who could actually release the potential for such action. It was therefore incumbent upon them to energize men who might easily fall into temptation otherwise. Only women, by controlling or sublimating their sexuality, could release both men and women for the selfless sacrifices required for the liberation of the ravaged motherland. Bankim thus provided a powerful image of womanhood, one that dynamized the image of a sahadharmini of the past into a force for the present and the future. In this aspect the transformed woman 'defied the normal canons of femininity in order to join the resistance against the crisis in the order' (Bagchi 1985: 61).

Shanti in *Anandmath* is the prototype of the womanhood required by a nation in crisis. Only such a crisis justified the delinking of wifehood from the 'enclosed space' of domesticity (ibid.). Shanti performs her wife's role in the war of liberation by donning the guise of a male *sanyasi* (religious mendicant) and fighting by the side of her husband. The Vedic woman who performed sacrifices to the gods by the side of her husband as an equal partner in the offering of oblations (till then envisaged as the highest role for women by the early cultural nationalists) is here dynamized into a figure who fights shoulder to shoulder with her husband in liberating the Motherland from its shackles. Shanti has thus transcended both her sexuality and her domesticity and made it possible for her husband to do the same. She would provide a model of womanhood, which came closest to a 'national' feminine identity during the late nineteenth and twentieth centuries till India became independent.

The Aryan theme was developed somewhat differently by Dayananda. As a practical reformer he was less concerned with identity formation than the nationalist historian or the litterateur. Nevertheless, Dayananda too had a vision of the past—however, this past was to be actually recreated rather then merely remembered, and that accounts for the rather direct and fundamental way in which the Vedas became the foundation of his ideology. The Vedas in turn account for the centrality of the Aryan theme in Dayananda's writing and provide it with its most long term expression in the institution of the Arya Samaj. As the influence of the Arya Samaj spread throughout north India, the concept of an Aryan golden age and the philosophy and social institutions of the Aryans as embodied in the *Rig Veda* became part of the general consciousness of the region. Historical awareness of the past was now fully permeated with an 'Aryan' consciousness accompanied by its attendant baggage of associations such as vitality, spirituality, and high mindedness.

A core feature of Dayananda's reformed Hinduism was his insistence on the superiority of the Vedic religion over all others and this in turn made for irreconcilable differences between his thought and that of the Brahmo reformers in Bengal (Jordens 1978: 82). But there is reason to believe that it was in Calcutta that he was first exposed to the women's question which ultimately became part of his basic vision of a reformed society. He found Vidyasagar in particular a man after his own heart as someone who was steeped in tradition. Dayananda also met historians and other members of the intelligentsia who made him aware of the world of historical scholarship. Works such as Datta's *Dharma Niti*, which had attempted to answer certain questions related to the nature and function of the state, made Dayananda sensitive to the problem of statecraft in any comprehensive philosophy (ibid.: 85-7). Subsequently in the *Satyarth Prakash* (published in 1875) he proposed an overall theory of the state, and expressed his understanding of society, history, and religion.

Dayananda, like Rammohun Roy earlier, also reinterpreted the past and rewrote history. In the reinterpreted version of the Vedic religion, on which Dayananda's Arya Samaj was based, monotheism replaced polytheism, the pantheon of gods becoming merely attributes of one universal God. Idolatory, caste, child marriage, Brahminical claims of superiority, and the vast bulk of popular Hindu religious practices—all disappeared along with polytheism, leaving only a rationalist monotheism. Dayananda was looking for an overall historical explanation both of contemporary conditions and of their relationship with the Golden Age of the Aryas in the past. The *Satyarth Prakash* thus starts out with a 'panegyric of that Golden Age in the Aryavarta, the ancient land which overflowed with milk and honey, where even the poor grew rich. There the first men were born, Sanskrit, mother of all tongues was spoken, and not only did theoretical wisdom flourish but also the practical industrial sciences' (ibid.: 110).

But how was the present degeneracy of Hinduism and the fact of colonial subservience to be explained? What cataclysmic event destroyed the 'Golden Age' of Vedic truth? Dayananda found a novel answer—it was the great Mahabharata war. The titanic struggle engulfed the subcontinent, beginning a decline into ignorance from which Hinduism could not escape. War and selfishness on the part of the priestly classes destroyed the vitality of Hindu culture (Jones 1976: 32). Since Aryavarta had been ruined by Brahmins and others, Dayananda, like Vivekananda later, was struck by the need in Hindu culture for vigour, self-assertion, and courage. The loss of masculinity and cultural regression of the Hindus was due to the loss of their original Aryan qualities which they had shared with Westerners. He expected Hindus to take on European characteristics by reforming Hindu religious life through a return to Vedic faith (Nandy 1983: 25).

It was Dayananda's emphasis on a reformed Hinduism based on the *Rig Veda* that led him to use the term 'Arya' for regenerated Hinduism. While in Calcutta he had heard a great deal about the stigma attached to the term Hindu and had told his audience then that they should discard 'that derogatory name imposed by foreigners' and call themselves Aryans instead.[15] While others had used the term Aryan synonymously with Hindu, with Dayananda it came to mean a purified and reformed Hindu. However, it had by now also become clearly identified with race and this aspect certainly had a bearing in popularizing it as a term; indeed it could gain widespread currency precisely because it carried within itself such a connotation.

Dayananda's references to the women of the past were part of his wider concern for a reformed Hindu society dominated by Aryan institutions. He believed that in the ideal society of the Vedic period women lived an idyllic existence, fully participated in all areas of public life, and it was Muslim influence that taught Hindus to imprison their women inside the house. These ideas were fairly common by the latter half of the nineteenth century and were not unique to Dayananda (Jordens 1978: 117).

What was central to Dayananda's thinking was his understanding of the role of women in the maintenance of race and, inter alia, concern about their sexuality. Motherhood for Dayananda was the sole rationale of a woman's existence but what was crucial in his concept of motherhood was its specific role in the procreation and rearing of a special breed of men. For example, the *Satyarth Prakash* lays down a variety of rules and regulations for ideal conception. The birth of the child is also followed by a series of regulations on food, cleanliness, clothing, and so on, for both mother and child. Dayananda's concern for a healthy and pure stock of Aryas even leads him to advocate the appointment of a wet nurse for the child rather than that the mother should feed it. According to Dayananda the child's body is made up of elements derived from the body of the mother, which accounts for the mother getting weaker after each confinement. Thus, he says:

> It is best therefore, for the mother not to suckle her child. Plasters should be applied to the breast that will soon dry up the milk. By following this system the woman becomes strong again in about two months. Till then the husband should have thorough control over his passions and thus preserve the reproductive element. Those that will follow this plan will have children of a superior order, enjoy long life, and continually gain in strength and energy so that their children will be of a high mental calibre, strong, energetic and devout. (Dayananda 1915: 22)

What really marks Dayananda's conceptualization of womanhood is the way he deals with the sexuality of women. The general concern for the

---

[15] Nandy (1983). There was thus a political meaning in Dayananda's decision to call his organization the Arya Samaj.

propagation of race implied that both men and women were equally the objects of his attention. But since the function of the women in particular was merely to procreate healthy progeny, the sexuality of women was of fundamental importance. At one level Dayananda's thinking is related to the way in which the monastic tradition in India had perceived women's sexuality as a threat to the pursuit of salvation (Chakravarti 1987: 35). But Dayananda had one foot in the sanyasi ethos and another (the more active foot) in the overall regeneration of Hinduism. While Dayananda had imbibed the traditional hostility of the sanyasi to women he also had a dynamic view of the changed times and shared the nationalist ethos. The traditional suspicion of women's sexuality was thus tempered, and the sexuality of women was transformed into a force which could be constructively channelized to serve in the regeneration of the Aryas. This transformation was unique to Dayananda: of the nineteenth century thinkers, he alone was to grapple squarely with the question; whereas others had worked around the problem restricting themselves to merely resurrecting images of ancient womanhood, Dayananda had a theoretical framework within which he could confront the sexuality of women and successfully fit it into an ideology which was consistent within itself.

So deep seated was the anxiety to control sexuality that it occurs even in the conceptualization of the school system. Both boys and girls in this regenerated Hinduism were entitled to education but they had to be physically segregated. The structures to ensure this physical segregation were of the most stringent kind. The schools themselves were to be separated by a distance of at least three miles. Further, the preceptors and the employees in the boys' school should all be male, and in the girls' school, female. Dayananda ruled:

Not even a child of five years of the opposite sex should be allowed to enter the school. As long as they are *Brahmacaris* [in the stage of celibacy] they should abstain from the following eight kinds of sexual excitement in relation to persons of opposite sex: looking upon them with the eye of lust; embracing them; having sexual intercourse with them; intimately conversing with them; playing with them; associating with them; reading or talking of libidinous subjects; and indulging in lascivious thoughts.[16]

Dayananda's division of the traditional *ashram*s or four stages of life was suitably redesigned from the point of view of his overall ideology. There were, according to him, four stages of the human body: a period of

---

[16] Dayananda (1915: 32). The last two are described by the helpful translator as having 'mental' intercourse. Subsequent references are cited in the text.

adolescence (16–25 years), a period of manhood (25–40 years), a period of maturity which was about the 40th year when the tissues, organs, and secretions of the body reached their highest stage of perfection. Thereafter came the period of loss in which there was excess of secretions when the reproductive element began to be lost in sleep, through perspiration, and so on (Dayananda 1915: 43). The best time for marriage was the 40th or 48th year. But since this was rather too long to wait, Dayananda suggested the more flexible period of between 25 and 48 for men, and 16 and 24 for women (ibid.: 90). Once marriage is decided upon, certain categories of people should be excluded from being considered as suitable partners; this was necessary from the point of view of ensuring healthy progeny. The best form of marriage—the *svayamvara* (self-chosen partner)—itself is linked with the maximum probability of ensuring the best reproduction (ibid.: 93).

While Dayananda considered that the partners to a marriage should themselves be responsible for their choice, on no condition were the two to meet alone before marriage 'since such a meeting of young people may lead to bad consequences'. Some amount of interaction in the presence of tutors, parents, and other respectable persons was desirable (ibid.: 105). Then, 'as soon as they feel that their love for each other is strong enough to entitle them to marry', a suitable date should be fixed. Dayananda advised that the very best arrangement 'should be made with regard to their diet so that their bodies that had weakened through the practice of rigid discipline may soon gain in muscles and strength just as the new moon grows into the full moon' (ibid.: 105). Later, when they are strong enough, on the day which has been decided upon for the 'purpose of generating a new life' (that is, marriage), they should most 'cheerfully go through the ceremony of *panigrahana* (clasping of the hands)' (ibid.: 106). The ceremony should be finished by 10 pm or 12 pm, and then the couple must retire to fulfil the *summum bonum* of the wife's existence, that is, to forthwith 'generate' a new life. 'As far as possible they should never waste their reproductive elements, perfected and preserved by the practice of Brahmacharya because the children born of such a union *are of a very superior order*' (ibid.: 107). If the rules laid down are not followed carefully, 'the reproductive element is uselessly lost, the lives of the husband and wife are shortened and they are afflicted with diverse diseases' (ibid.). For the continued needs of propagating strong and healthy children, the wife and husband should be content with each other for if the wife does not love and please her husband, the husband will be unhappy; being unhappy, he will not be sexually excited and consequently no offspring will be produced.

Even if they are, the children so born are 'very wicked and of a low type' (ibid.: 109).

The management of sexuality was the key to the thorny problem of widow remarriage. Throughout the nineteenth century the most problematic category of women were widows, and reformers were attempting to resolve the problem of what to do with the widow especially since a large proportion of upper-caste women were widowed, often as a consequence of early marriage. Implicit in the whole debate on widow remarriage was the recognition of women as sexual beings and the relationship of female sexuality with prevailing family and property structures. While others had tackled the problem from a humanitarian standpoint, essentially as a response to the plight of the child widow, Dayananda came to grips with the problem within his broader philosophy of a regenerated Hinduism which required a regenerated race of people. Since motherhood played a vital role, he held that remarriage for both men and women was equally valid if there were no children from the earlier marriage. Dayananda found his solution to the remarriage question and the problem of female sexuality in the institution of the *niyoga* (levirate), associated with the early Aryans.

The practice of niyoga was suggested by Dayananda in the form of a theoretical debate between an objector and Dayananda himself in the *Satyarth Prakash* (ibid.: 129–40). The main points in the discussion are significant in tracing the development of Dayananda's position on widow marriage. Dayananda first argued that remarriage for the twice-born castes was prohibited because there would be family disputes based on property disagreements, and many families would just be blotted out of existence if a widow remarried (ibid.: 129). The objector then pointed out that family lines would die out anyway if either party died before any male issues were born. 'Besides,' says the objector, bringing up the sexuality question, if remarriage is not allowed, 'widows and widowers will resort to fornication and adultery, procure abortion, and commit wicked deeds of kindred nature' (ibid.: 130). For these reasons the objector suggested that remarriage was desirable. At this point, Dayananda ruled that the best practice for both men and women was *brahmacharya* (self-control), followed by the adoption of a boy. However, he added that for those who could not control their passions the best recourse was niyoga. Dayananda tells the objector that when people are young, 'desire for children and sexual enjoyment will drive people to the necessity of forming secret relations if the laws of the state or society disallow lawful gratification'. The only proper way of preventing adultery and illicit intimacies is to let those who require it contract niyoga relationships 'so that the chances of illicit intercourse may be greatly minimised, good children can be born, the human race improved, and the practice of foeticide put a stop to' (ibid.: 133). Dayananda interpreted a variety of texts to allow the contracting parties to practise niyoga till two children are born; however, successive niyoga relationships are permitted until 10 children are born (this is the number of children prescribed for normal marriages) after which the practice must be terminated (ibid.: 132).

Both marriage and niyoga thus share the same basis in Dayananda's view, that of begetting healthy and strong children. In recommending niyoga, Dayananda sought both to revive an institution that had been 'shunned by Hinduism for nearly two millenia, and also to greatly extend its application. From the narrow purpose of providing a son to a deceased husband it was now to solve the much wider problem of widowhood' (Jordens 1978: 119). This was one form of the nationalist resolution of women's sexuality; to use her biological potential for child-bearing in the service of the physical regeneration of what was seen as a now weakened Aryan race....

III

...As the nineteenth century closed, the women's question as an area of reform appeared to evoke less enthusiasm than it had done before. What appeared to be more important was the question of a feminine identity which continued to receive finishing touches throughout the twentieth century.

At the beginning of the twentieth century, the experience of the nineteenth century, especially of its second half, in terms of the formation of women's identity, is reflected in Vivekananda's image of Hindu womanhood. Many of his statements on women (like Ramabai's before him) were addressed to a Western audience and this might explain the context in which his picture of Hindu womanhood within the image of a spiritual East is contrasted with Western women in a materialist setting. In fact, there is a constant interplay between the West and East in Vivekananda's characterization of Hindu womanhood. On the ideal of womanhood Vivekananda held:

The ideal of womanhood centres in the Aryan race of India, the most ancient in the world's history. In that race men and women were priests 'Sabatimini' (Sahadharmini) or co-religionists as the Vedas call them. There, every family had its hearth or altar. There man and wife together offered their sacrifices.... In India it was a female sage who first found the unity of God and laid down this doctrine in one of the first hymns of the Vedas.... (Vivekananda 1958: II, 504-5)

> The Aryan and Semitic ideals of woman have always been diametrically opposed. Amongst the Semites the presence of a woman is considered dangerous to devotion ... According to the Aryan, man cannot perform a religious action without a wife. (ibid.: V, 229)

On the materialism of the West and the spiritualism of the East with its bearing on women he reiterated:

> On the one hand rank materialism through foreign literature has caused a tremendous stir; on the other through the confounding din of all these discordant sounds she hears in low yet unmistakable accents the heartrending cries of her ancient Gods, cutting her to the quick. There lie before her various strange luxuries ... new manners, new fashions, dressed in which moves about the well educated girl in shameless freedom. All these are arousing ... desires. Again the scene changes and in its place appear, with stern presence Sita, Savitri, austere religious vows, fastings, the forest retreat, the matted locks and the orange garb of the semi-naked Sannyasin, Samadhi and the search for the self. On the one side is the independence of western society, on the other the extreme self sacrifice of the Aryan society. (ibid.: IV, 476)

Vivekananda also extols the mother and associates true motherhood with chastity. What fulfils a woman is motherhood. He then goes on to turn the tables on Western society for its treatment of the Western woman. While men in America can disinherit their wives, in India according to Vivekananda, the 'whole estate of the husband must go to the wife'. In the West, witches were dragged and burnt amid jeering mobs, while in contrast Indian women mounted the pyre of their husbands cheerfully. Significantly, in response to constant criticism about the treatment of Hindu widows, Vivekananda categorically asserted that he had travelled all over India but failed to see 'a single case of ill treatment' (ibid.: III, 506–8). The closing of ranks is now unmistakable; there is no women's question for Vivekananda. Women have always been respected and given their due. The Hindus as a race could not have produced the image of Sita without revering women and that was all that mattered. Vivekananda confidently asserted that 'a race that produced Sita, even if it only dreamt of her, has a reverence for woman that is unmatched on earth' (ibid.: V, 231).

The nation's identity lay in the culture and more specifically in its womanhood. In the changed political and social environment, the image of womanhood was more important than the reality. Historians and laymen would complete the process by ensuring, through continued writings in the twentieth century, that the image also came to be perceived as the reality.

* * *

The process that I have outlined in the preceding sections has attempted to document the 'invention' of a tradition (Hobsbawm 1983: 1) during the nineteenth century. During this phase what took place was the construction of a particular kind of past which was the context for the construction also of a particular kind of womanhood.[17] The past itself was a creation of the compulsions of the present and these compulsions determined which elements were highlighted and which receded from the conscious object of concern in historical and semi-historical writings.

In the context of the women's question, the entire focus of attention in the nineteenth century had been on the high-caste Hindu woman, whether it was to highlight her high status in the past or in reforming her low status in the present. The emphasis on the Shastras in settling the debates of the present ensured that the only issues taken up about women in the past were those that had a bearing on legal and familial questions. Reaction to the attacks by colonial writers ensured that Indian women were almost built up as superwomen: a combination of the spiritual Maitreyi, the learned Gargi, the suffering Sita, the faithful Savitri, and the heroic Lakshmibai. Spiritual power and the sahadharmini model in particular were central to the idea of womanhood because these could be transformed to play other roles in the regeneration of the nation. Nationalism itself came to occupy the same place that religion had before; it was a permitted area for women's participation. In this model of womanhood there was no difference between the perceptions of progressives and of conservatives.

The limited focus, from the days of Rammohun onwards, on a particular section of women which, in turn, led to the consideration of a particular kind of womanhood was an aspect of the nationalist project which excluded various sections from its ambit. The obsession with effeminacy, for example, was confined to the educated elite. The construction of a heroic identity was similarly a contribution of the intelligentsia. While the Marathas were being transformed into champions of nationalism, sections left out from participating in the creation of such myths were still voicing their perception of the Marathas as marauders.[18]

---

[17] Hobsbawm suggests that 'invented' traditions are highly relevant to that 'comparatively recent historical innovation, the nation with its associated phenomena; nationalism, the nation state, national symbols, histories' (1983: 13). We might add womanhood to the list. All these rest, according to them, on social engineering, which is often deliberate and always innovative.

[18] Mothers in Bengal continued to put their babies to sleep with the lullaby.

Chheley ghumolo, para jurolo bargi elo deshey
Bulbulitey ahan kheyechhe, khajina debo kishey

(My child sleeps, the neighbourhood is peaceful, Suddenly the Bargis [Maratha horsemen] come; the birds have destroyed all the crops, with what will we pay the revenue.)

—Bengali folk song translated by Sumanta Banerjee

The focus on the upper sections of society to the total exclusion of all others is evident also from Dayananda's injunctions that Arya mothers should not nurse their babies, but employ wet nurses instead so that they might recover quickly and so be ready to produce strong sons once more. But what of the wet nurse? Who was she? What about her place in the system of procreation? Was she not required to produce strong sons too? Clearly Dayananda's injunctions were meant for one section at the expense of another. Vast sections of women did not exist for the nineteenth century nationalists. No one tried to read the ancient texts to see what rights the Vedic dasi and others like her had in the Vedic golden age. Recognizing her existence would have been an embarrassment to the nationalists. The twentieth century has continued to reproduce, in all essentials, the same kind of womanhood that the nineteenth century has so carefully, and so successfully, constructed as an enduring legacy for us.

REFERENCES

Bader, Clarisse (1925/1867), *Women in Ancient India*. London: Longmans Green.

Bagchi, Jashodhara (1985), 'Positivism and Nationalism: Womanhood and Crisis in Nationalist Fiction, Bankim Chandra's *Anandmath*', in Review of Women Studies, *Economic and Political Weekly*, 20(43): 60–1.

Ballhatchet, K.A. (1956), 'Some Aspects of Historical Writing on India by Christian Missionaries', South Asia Seminar, School of Oriental and African Studies, London, May.

Bankim Racnabali (1968), 5th ed. Calcutta: Sahitya Sangsad.

Borthwick, Meredith (1984), *The Changing Role of Women in Bengal 1849–1905*. Princeton: Princeton University Press.

Chakravarti, Uma (1985), 'Of Dasas and Karmakaras: Servile Labour in Ancient India', in Utsa Patnaik and Manjari Dingwaney (eds), *Chains of Servitude: Bondage and Slavery in India*. Delhi: Orient Longman, pp. 35–75.

—— (1987), *The Social Dimension of Early Buddhism*. New Delhi: Oxford University Press.

Chandra, Sudhir (1987), 'Lake of Palms: An Essay in Understanding Early Indian Nationalism without the Imperialist Discourse', unpublished paper, Seminar on 'Communication and Society', Nehru Memorial Museum and Library, Delhi, 22–5 July.

Chattopadhyaya, Gautam (1965), *Awakening in Bengal: Early Nineteenth Century Selected Documents, I*. Calcutta: Progressive Publishers.

Choudhari, Nirad C. (1974), *Scholar Extraordinary: The Life of Rt. Hon. Frederick Max Muller P.C.* New Delhi: Oxford University Press.

Clark, T.W. (1961), 'The Role of Bankimcandra in the Development of Nationalism', in C.H. Philips (ed.), *Historians of India, Pakistan and Ceylon*. London: Oxford University Press, pp. 429–45.

Cohn, Bernard (1985), 'The Command of Language and the Language of Command', in Ranajit Guha (ed.), *Subaltern Studies IV: Writings on South Asian History and Society*. New Delhi: Oxford University Press, pp. 276–329.

Colebrooke, H.T. (1805), 'On the Vedas, or Sacred Writings of the Hindus', *Asiatic Researches*, 8: 377–498.

—— (1895), 'On the Duties of the Faithful Hindu Widow', *Asiatic Researches*, 4: 205–15.

Cunningham, J.D. (1849/1918), *History of the Sikhs*, reprint. London: Oxford University Press.

Dayananda, Swami (1915), *Satyarth Prakash* (translated by Chiranjiva Bharadvaja). Agra: Arya Pratinidi Sabha.

Duff, Grant (1826), *History of the Marathas*. London: Longmans Green.

Dutt, R.C. (1888/1972), *A History of Civilization in Ancient India*, reprint. Delhi: Vishal.

—— (1947), *Pratap Singh, The Last of the Rajputs*. Allahabad: Kitabistan.

Ghose, J.C. (1885), *The English Works of Raja Rammohun Roy*. Calcutta: Oriental.

Hatalkar, V.G. (1973), 'M.G. Ranade', in S.P. Sen (ed.), *Historians and Historiography in Modem India*. Calcutta: Institute of Historical Studies.

Hobsbawm, Eric (1983), 'Introduction: Inventing Traditions', in Eric Hobsbawm and Terence Ranger (eds), *The Invention of Tradition*. Cambridge: Cambridge University Press, pp. 1–14.

Jones, Kenneth (1976), *Arya Dharma: Hindu Consciousness in 19th Century Punjab*. Delhi: Manohar Publishers and Distributors.

Jones, William (1807), 'On the Chronology of the Hindus', in Lord Teignmouth (ed.), *The Works of William Jones, Vol. IV*. London: John Stockdale, Picadilly, and John Walkes.

Jordens, J.T.F. (1978), *Dayananda Saraswati, His Life and Ideas*. New Delhi: Oxford University Press.

Kaviraj, Sudipto (1987), 'The Myth of Infinity: The Construction of the Figure of Krishna in Krishnacarita', Occasional Papers, Nehru Memorial Museum and Library, Delhi.

Kopf, David (1969), *British Orientalism and the Bengal Renaissance*. Calcutta: Firma K.L. Mukhopadhyaya.

Majumdar, R.C. (1961), 'Nationalist Historians', in C.H. Philips (ed.), *Historians of India, Pakistan and Ceylon*. London: Oxford University Press, pp. 416–28.

Mallik, A.R. (1961), 'Modern Historical Writing in Bengali', in C.H. Philips (ed.), *Historians of India, Pakistan and Ceylon*. London: Oxford University Press, pp. 446–60.

Mani, Lata (1986), 'Production of an Official Discourse on Sati in Early Nineteenth Century Bengal', in Review of Women Studies, *Economic and Political Weekly*, 21(17): WS 32–WS 40.

Max Muller, F. (1859), *A History of Sanskrit Literature*. London: Longmans Green.
—— (1892), *India: What It Can Teach Us*. London: Longmans Green.
Max Muller, Georgina (ed.) (1902), *Life and Letters of F. Max Muller*. London: Longmans Green.
Mill, James (1840), *The History of British India* (with notes by H.H. Wilson), 5th ed. London: James Madden.
Murshid, Ghulam (1983), *Reluctant Debutante*. Rajshahi: Rajshahi University.
Nandy, Ashis (1983), *The Intimate Enemy Loss and Recovery of the Self under Colonialism*. New Delhi: Oxford University Press.
Neufeldt, Ronald W. (1980), *Max Muller and the Rig Veda: A Study of Its Role in His Work and Thought*. Calcutta: Minerva.
Philips, C.H. (1961), 'James Mill, Mountstuart Elphinstone and the History of India', in C.H. Philips (ed.), *Historians of India, Pakistan and Ceylon*. London: Oxford University Press, pp. 217–29.
Poddar, Aravind (1976), *Renaissance in Bengal: Search for Identity*. Simla: Indian Institute of Advanced Study.
Rosselli, John (1980), 'The Self Image of Effeteness: Physical Education and Nationalism in 19th Century Bengal', *Past and Present*, February, 86: 121–48.
Sarkar, Jadunath (1928/1979), *India through the Ages*, reprint. Calcutta: Orient Longman.
Sarkar, S.C. (1958), 'Derozio and Young Bengal', in A.C. Gupta (ed.), *Studies in Bengal Renaissance*. Jadavpur: National Council of Education Bengal.
Sen, Sunil (1961), 'Romesh Chandra Dutt', in C.H. Philips (ed.), *Historians of India, Pakistan and Ceylon*. London: Oxford University Press.
Sinha, Mrinalini (1986), 'Colonial Politics and the Ideal of Masculinity', Indian Association of Women's Studies, The Third National Conference of Women's Studies, Chandigarh, 1–4 October.
Mrs Speier (1856/1973), *Life in Ancient India*, reprinted as *Phases of Indian Civilization*. Delhi: Cosmo.
Stokes, E.T. (1961), 'The Administrators and Historical Writing on India', in C.H. Philips (ed.), *Historians of India, Pakistan and Ceylon*. London: Oxford University Press, pp. 385–403.
Tod, James (1920), *Annals and Antiquities of Rajasthan, 1829–30* (edited by William Crooke). London: Oxford University Press.
Vivekananda, Swami (1958), *Complete Works*. Calcutta: Advaita Ashrama.
Voigt, Johannes H. (1967), *F.M. Max Muller—The Man and His Ideas*. Calcutta: Firma K.L. Mukhopadhyaya.

Chapter 6

A CARTOGRAPHY OF RESISTANCE
The National Federation of Dalit Women*

KALPANA KANNABIRAN**

CASTE HAS BEEN CENTRAL TO DEBATES around entitlements and constitutionalism in India for five decades. This period has also witnessed shifts in policy emphasis, jurisprudence, and politics around the issue of caste. Till the mid-1990s, however, the debate was located within a 'national context' and caste itself constructed in terms of its 'peculiarity' to Indian society. The World Conference against Racism (WCAR) held at Durban in 2001 and the process that led to the WCAR in India witnessed the 'freeing' of caste from the confines of India into a larger international

---

* Originally published in Nira Yuval-Davis, Kalpana Kannabiran, and Ulrike Vieten (eds) (2006), *Situating Contemporary Politics of Belonging*. London: Sage Publications, pp. 54–73.

** My discussions with Ruth Manorama, Convenor of the National Federation of Dalit Women, over the years have shaped my understanding of Dalit feminist politics. I thank her for showing me ways of seeing. I am also grateful to her for generosity with her personal archival resources. My sincere thanks to Nira Yuval-Davis, Ulrike M. Vieten, and Peter Fitzpatrick for pointing me in directions I had left unexplored and for useful discussions on earlier drafts.

arena that held out greater possibilities for public debate, alliance building, and more powerful resistance. The participation of Dalits in large numbers at Durban generated an entire discourse in India on questions of funding, the 'proper' contexts of political resistance, the hierarchies of alliance building in resistance movements, and the theoretical/sociological validity of viewing caste through the prism of racism, among others.

The question of violence is fundamental to any discussion on Dalit politics in India. It is perhaps pertinent, therefore, to begin with questions.

What is violence? How may we understand the playing out of 'transgressive' violence and 'legitimate' violence? In a society where some groups rhetorically and through the use of force (violence) occupy the 'restful domain of reason and pacific order' (the domain of passive dependence), the autonomous expression of belonging is by definition transgressive. Further, where it is generally argued that '[l]aw...must forever chase and mark itself against a transgressive violence' (Foucault 1987: 34; cf. Fitzpatrick 2001: 12), what place do we accord to the marking of resistance against transgressive violence within the domain of the law—the court especially (but also the criminal justice system) being a signpost in that domain? How do communities deal with long-term suffering and exclusion that continues unabated despite protections in public law? At the core, how does suffering shape the politics of belonging?

There is a need to look in different places for new and unexpected expressions of a new politics of belonging. Does this invocation of an alternative register of belonging then make for a 'different' governmentality, by re-mapping the possible field of action for others?

This chapter focuses on the interpretation of caste as race by Dalit groups, and the 'different' politics this process gave birth to.[1] It will be divided into four sections. The first will attempt to set out a theoretical framework with the help of which the Durban process might be best understood; the second will attempt an analysis of caste, untouchability, and resistance; the third will examine the debate on caste and race that was part of the Durban process; the fourth section will look at the specific articulations of caste as race by the National Federation of Dalit Women, that foreground the intersections between racism, sexism, and the politics of becoming/belonging.

---

[1] Minow (1990) provides a rich analysis of difference.

THE POLITICS OF BECOMING/BELONGING

The politics of becoming is immediately relevant to an understanding of the trajectory of Dalit politics in the context of Durban. And yet this politics is praxiologically inseparable from the politics of belonging. In putting in place the signposts for this argument, I am drawing on the work of Connolly (1996) and Minow (1996) on the one hand, and Omi and Winant (2002) on the other. I could perhaps anticipate my argument by saying that the politics of belonging encapsulates within itself the politics of becoming. The politics of becoming occurs, in Connolly's words, 'when a culturally marked constituency, *suffering* under its current social constitution, strives to reconfigure itself by moving the cultural constellation of identity/difference then in place' (1996: 255–6; emphasis added). It is a paradoxical politics by which 'new cultural identities are formed out of old energies, injuries and differences' (ibid.: 261). While it is in motion, placing new identities on the cultural field, the politics of becoming also changes the shape and contour of established identities, thus bringing in its wake disturbance, distress, and disruption, throwing in peril the stability of being through which dominant constituencies seek comfort. The politics of becoming in this moment of definition engages actively and comparatively with a number of different constituencies, shaping a regulative ideal in the process and never actually becoming completely conclusive or exclusive, or even completely synchronized with these other constituencies—the constitutive tension between suffering and cultural possibility opening out the field of public discourse in unimaginable ways (ibid.: 274).

Extending this argument somewhat, Minow (1996) suggests that the idea of the politics of becoming could be more usefully probed through a thematic exploration. Of the three themes she identifies, I find two—the first and the third, that is, the 'we' and the place of 'prior experience'—particularly relevant.

The politics of becoming clearly presupposes a community of belonging, a 'we'. If the 'we' is constituted on the basis of suffering, as Connolly suggests, which suffering *should* be more worthy of response? That caused by the disruption of social order and dominant modes by subaltern groups or that caused by the suppression/subordination of resistance by dominant groups (Minow 1996: 280)? This question is fundamentally flawed, even while it evokes concerns ranging from caricaturing of resistance as 'Oppression Olympics' to 'reverse discrimination' caused by affirmative action—all of which are discussed in the context of the Dalit experience later in this chapter. If it is conceded that domination is the source of pain and the cause of suffering, the uprooting of dominance—the removal of pain and suffering—can scarcely be described in the same terms as its infliction. In other words, there cannot, I would argue, be a theoretical equivalence posited between the uprooting of domination and the quashing of resistance to that domination, or a reinforcement of the status quo. Despite the fact of multiple identities, there is a solidarity of location in the context of social suffering that quite clearly separates the 'we' from the 'not we', so that even while reinventing the 'we', the politics of becoming keeps sight of location, of belonging. In this process, the building of the constituency of belonging shatters hitherto unquestioned foundations of location and puts in place *un-imaginable* ones.

Since people build on what they know, Minow (ibid.: 283) suggests that the crafting of prior experience in a way that enhances the possibility for responsiveness, collective redress, and openness to difference may prove enabling in confronting suffering and transforming society. 'What experiences can be planted,' she asks, 'so that people relate new expressions of suffering to a pattern of responsiveness?' 'Why not cast for a broader we? Why not realize the idea that a society progresses when misfortune becomes viewed as an injustice?' (ibid.: 284). But Minow sees the 'we' and by extension the construction of prior experience as contained within a 'collective, national experience' (ibid.: 285). This does not allow for the possibility that the 'collective' experience could be other than—opposed even to—the 'national', that the national—to the extent that the term evokes sentiments of citizenship—is not necessarily coterminous with territory, and could in its mildest expressions undermine fundamental notions of territoriality, and finally, that the casting of the broadest possible 'we' since it keeps sight of location and is mindful of memory, could shatter every received notion of belonging in a society, in particular national loyalty/patriotism/territorial integrity.

Both Connolly (1996) and Minow (1996) proceed on the fundamental assumption that plurality provides a condition of possibility for the politics of becoming and move towards a position that the politics of becoming necessarily solidifies into another form of being—a better, more ethical, collectively responsive form of being. However, it is often the case, as I hope to demonstrate later in this chapter, that pluralism does not preclude practices that are exclusionary and violently hegemonic. On the other hand, plurality provides the coherence that threads different groups and their diverse experiences into a single coordinated system. Practices of dominance, hegemony, and exclusion are tied to social location within this system and cohere through (and tend to be masked by) the prism of plurality. It is the exclusion and the consequent systemic and systematic violence that provides the condition of *necessity* for the politics of becoming. By definition then, this politics and the assertion of different axes of belonging, of which it is an intrinsic part, are distinct from being. In sharp contrast, being is solid, hegemonic, ascribed, seeming to disintegrate but constantly re-congealing in new forms—scholarship on caste is illustrative, as I hope to demonstrate—without fundamentally new content.

This process of becoming in the Dalit context draws in critical notions of race and racial formation, to demarcate a new field for the politics of becoming and mapping the route from becoming to belonging. Drawing on Omi and Winant's formulation of racial formation as 'the socio-historical process by which racial categories are created, inhabited, transformed, and destroyed' (2002: 124), I argue that the politics of becoming in the present context is a project that attempts also to interpret, represent, and explain racial dynamics, while simultaneously underscoring the need to reorganize and redistribute resources along racial lines (ibid.: 125).

The politics of becoming is a self-conscious movement—a reinvention of the 'we', to echo Minow (1996)—towards a goal of belonging better somewhere else, interrogating the foundations of culture and solidarity, transgressing every notion of territoriality and 'integrity', in order *not to arrive* at a different level of being in the same space at the same time in different yet recognizable ways, *but to cross the black waters* (the ocean, *kaala paani*, crossing which would defile an upper caste Hindu)[2] to a different politics of belonging. What results is a politics of becoming/belonging as resistance to caste, patriarchy, and the state, and through that route, resistance to all forms of descent-based discrimination/exclusion. This transgression of territoriality and integrity is extremely significant because it obstructs and fragments the re-solidification of being.

The politics of becoming/belonging then is an essentially enabling, fundamentally transformative process that forges a larger community of belonging beyond borders; that merges histories of oppression as also those of resistance, creating new measures of solidarity and shared citizenship, and forces on states a public accountability outside of the 'internal' space of the nation, rupturing old comfortable ways of thinking about 'social evils' by renaming the problem: Caste is not merely a social evil. Caste is race. Discrimination based on caste is racial discrimination. This idea is

---

[2] The punishment of transportation under Section 53 of the Indian Penal Code (repealed in 1949), also known colloquially as kaala paani, had its genesis in this taboo.

immediately relevant to an understanding of resistance to social exclusion in societies where 'race' is not a standard measure of difference.

CASTE, UNTOUCHABILITY, AND RESISTANCE

Caste is the defining characteristic of Indian society. Views on caste vary. There are those who see it as a predominantly religious system, others who view it as merely social and economic, and yet others who see in its elaboration the spiritual essence of the Hindu faith and view the aspect of discrimination as a mere aberration; several view it as the centre point of brahminical tyranny; some see it as the Indian equivalent of community. Dirks (2002: 5) suggests that

> caste, as we know it today, is not in fact some unchanged survival of ancient India, not some single system that reflects a core civilizational value, not a basic expression of Indian tradition. Rather...caste is a modern phenomenon, specifically the product of an historical encounter between India and Western colonial rule...[i]t was under the British that 'caste' became a single term capable of expressing, organizing and above all 'systematizing' India's diverse forms of social identity, community, and organization.

To summarize the characteristics of caste (Kannabiran 2002), it is a hierarchical, hegemonic ranking of social groups found predominantly on the Indian subcontinent. A word of Portuguese and Spanish origin, the word 'casta' in the early sixteenth century embraced several meanings, one of which was 'purity of blood'. By the eighteenth century, it was used to designate two levels of groups in the subcontinent: the *jati*s, roughly about 3,000 or more are loosely grouped into four *varna*s, the latter finding systematic elaboration in the brahminical scriptural tradition of the Vedic period.

In the Brahman/upper-caste construction, which is elaborated in the Hindu Dharmasastras, as part of a tradition of universal law, caste has its origin in the varna system, which was constituted by four orders: Brahman (priests), ksatriya (warriors), vaisya (traders), and sudra (artisans, labourers, peasants, and such others). Of these, the first three were the *dvija* (twice born 'clean') castes, the men of which are entitled to initiation into Hinduism. A fifth order, the *panchama* or the untouchables, slaves who performed 'menial chores' (cleansing villages—in general engaged directly in production and connected closely to organic life), was included later.

Dalits, in early sociological and scriptural literature (a telling combination) referred to as panchamas, the 'untouchable' castes, have for centuries been confined in *vada*s (colonies), enslaved to the other four varnas in perpetual bondage.³ The word *asprsya* (literally 'untouchable') was first used in the *Visnusmrti*, which prescribes death for any member of these castes who deliberately touches a member of a higher caste.⁴

The critique of caste has its origin in the work of Jotirao Phule and Savitribai Phule in Maharashtra in the nineteenth century, E.V. Ramaswami Naicker 'Periyar' in Tamil Nadu in the early twentieth century, and B.R. Ambedkar in the twentieth century. Gandhi condemned social exclusion and practices of untouchability but did not extend this to a fundamental critique of Hinduism itself, as these others did. And yet, the critique of untouchability itself hit at the base of the caste system, eroding caste supremacist ideologies.

Phule and his associates founded the Satyashodhak Samaj ('Truth Seeking Society') in 1873. The overarching themes of Phule's addresses at meetings of the Samaj were on the character and unity of the labouring classes, the unequal division of labour between women of different castes, and the vital contribution of peasant women to production. He established the first school in all of India for *sudratisudra* (Dalit today) girls in 1848, following it up with another school for girls of all castes in 1851 (Deshpande 2002: 3). His seminal work, *Gulamgiri* ('Slavery'), juxtaposes the situation of the sudratisudra with the Negro slave in America:

> This system of slavery, to which the Brahmins reduced the lower classes is in no respects inferior to that which obtained a few years ago in America. In the days of rigid Brahmin dominancy ... my Sudra brethren had even greater hardships and oppression practiced upon them than what even the slaves in America had to suffer... This is even true at the present time ... the Sudra ... is so far reconciled to the Brahmin yoke, that like the American slave he would resist any attempt that may be made for his deliverance and fight even against his benefactor. (Phule [1873] 2002: 31–2)

Tarabai Shinde's *Stree Purusha Tulana* ('A Comparison between Women and Men') ([1882] 1994), also part of the Satyashodhak tradition, confronts brahminical patriarchy as well as patriarchy within non-Brahman castes.

In mapping a non-Brahman worldview through the Self Respect Movement launched in 1925, Periyar stood the caste system on its head. The new social order, *samadharma* (equality), could emerge only through

---

³ Dalit is a noun and adjective that can be used equally in the masculine, feminine, and neuter genders. It means burst, split, broken or torn asunder, scattered, crushed, or destroyed.

⁴ Much later in the twentieth century, Dumont (1970: 52) cites the instance of a Candala appearing before two kshatriya girls—the girls had to wash their eyes and the Candala beaten for such indiscreet appearance.

a radical transformation of structures of feeling and material conditions. This immediately freed women and Adi Dravidas (Dalits) from caste-bound traditions, created a moral ground on which women exercised choice and consent, both in matters of marriage and sexuality, and eliminated the priesthood and the chanting of Vedic hymns in marriage solemnities (Geetha and Rajadurai 1998).

Ambedkar, an intrepid advocate of formal rights for the untouchables, belonged to the untouchable Mahar caste. He coined the word 'Dalit' (literally 'downtrodden') to designate untouchables as a political entity and spoke of the caste system as one of graded inequality—a system of hierarchies built on notions of relative superiority and inferiority, with the Dalits occupying the last rung in the system and thus bearing the brunt of a cumulative domination by all the other castes. During the struggle for independence in the early part of the twentieth century, Ambedkar's concerns centred on finding ways in which Independence could bring freedom to the oppressed. As an architect of the Indian constitution, he instituted constitutional safeguards for the depressed classes against exclusion (social boycott) and active discrimination by majority upper-caste Hindus in independent India. Significant among these provisions was the right to substantive equality through reservations in education and employment. In general, the early twentieth century witnessed the consolidation of resistance to the caste system in different parts of British India.

At the time that the resistance to practices of caste was gaining ground, colonial ethnography had reached its peak in the subcontinent. Ideas about the racial dimension of caste derived from European interpretations of Indian society that began with William Jones in the eighteenth century. Bayly, for instance, points out that many pre-independence ethnographers from Britain

> ... portrayed India as a composite social landscape in which only certain peoples, those of superior 'Aryan' blood, had evolved historically in ways which left them 'shackled' by a hierarchical, Brahmanically-defined ideology of 'caste'. At the same time large numbers of other Indians—those identified in varying racial terms as Dravidians, as members of 'servile' classes, aborigines, wild tribes, and those of so-called 'mixed-racial origins—were portrayed as being ethnologically distinct from this so-called Aryan population, and were not all thought to belong to a ranked Brahmanical caste order. (Bayly 1995: 170)

Jaffrelot observes that the British administration gradually propagated these categories in society so that '[g]radually, Non-Brahminism and Dravidianism coincided and the low castes looked at themselves as forming an ethnic category (Jaffrelot 2003: 152).

In contemporary India, the three themes that we find constantly recurring in the field of caste are untouchability,[5] violence,[6] and affirmative action through reservations in education and employment.[7] These are also the points at which the institution of caste comes in direct contact with the state. In 2001, Dalits from the Indian subcontinent stormed into the WCAR at Durban, pushing debates on caste and untouchability out of the narrow confines of 'insider debates' within the subcontinent into an international forum that held possibilities for alliance building and international advocacy in unprecedented terms.[8]

This alliance building had a history. In 1873, Phule had dedicated his work *Slavery* to:

the good people of the United States
as a token of admiration for their
sublime disinterested and
self sacrificing devotion
in the cause of Negro Slavery; and with
an earnest desire, that my countrymen
may take their noble example as their guide
in the emancipation of their Sudra Brethren
from the trammels of Brahmin thralldom. (Phule [1873] 2002: 25)

It was this legacy the Dalits drew upon in tracing their kinship along lines of race in the Durban process. Although this was not a legacy that was stated beyond invoking Phule as a forefather of the anti-caste movement, the influence of Phule's writings on Dalit movements and anti-caste ideologies is so pervasive that this connection is self-evident.

RACIAL FORMATION OF CASTE

Apart from the provisions in favour of non-discrimination in the Universal Declaration of Human Rights, the International Convention on the Elimination of All Forms of Racial Discrimination adopted in 1965 defined racial discrimination as 'any distinction, exclusion, restriction or preference, based on race, colour, descent, national or ethnic which has the

---

[5] Article 17 of the Indian Constitution.
[6] The Protection of Civil Rights Act, 1955, and the Scheduled Castes, Scheduled Tribes (Prevention of Atrocities) Act, 1989.
[7] Article 16 of the Indian Constitution.
[8] The Dalit question had been discussed in the UN's Sub-Commission on Promotion and Protection of Human Rights since 1996. The proceedings were largely closed (Thorat and Umakant 2004: xiii–xxxv).

purpose or effect of nullifying or impairing the recognition, enjoyment or exercise on an equal footing of human rights and fundamental freedoms in the political, economic, social, cultural or any other field of public life'. In 1996, the Committee on the Elimination of Racial Discrimination (CERD) stated that the Convention on the Elimination of Racial Discrimination does not refer only to race, but that 'the situation of the Scheduled Castes and Scheduled Tribes falls within [its] scope', further observing that despite legal safeguards provided to members of these groups, 'the relative impunity of those who abuse them point to the limited effect of these measures' (Thorat and Umakant 2004: vii).

The shift from race alone to descent- and occupation-based discrimination, and the recognition that it was not the physical appearance or race but their membership in 'an endogamous social group that has been isolated socially and occupationally from other groups in the society', led to the CERD General Recommendation:

Reaffirmed that discrimination based on 'descent' includes discrimination against members of communities based on forms of stratification such as caste and analogous systems of inherited status which nullify or impair their equal enjoyment of human rights.

To take measures against any dissemination of ideas of caste superiority and inferiority or which attempt to justify violence, hatred or discrimination against descent-based communities.

To educate the general public on the importance of affirmative action programmes....[9]

The Indian government, however, persisted in its view that descent in the Convention referred specifically to racial descent and responded to the query with respect to untouchability by citing legislations as evidence of justice and non-discrimination on the ground, and has consistently refused the United Nations Special Reporter on Racism and Racial Discrimination permission to 'evaluate the situation in cooperation with the government and the communities concerned'.[10] The official position cited *The New Encyclopaedia Britannica*:

On balance, the evidence that the Indian caste system is racial in origin and that India is or was a racist society is unconvincing. Race and caste are mentioned separately in the Indian Constitution as prohibited grounds for discrimination. They are not considered to be interchangeable or synonymous. The principal architect of the Indian Constitution was

---

[9] R.K.W. Goonasekere, 'Discrimination based on Occupation and Descent', Working Paper of the UN Sub-Commission on the Promotion and Protection of Human Rights, presented at its 53rd session in 2001, cf. Thorat and Umakant (2004: xx).

[10] Report of the Special Rapporteur, E/CN.4/1998/79, Paras 57–59, cf. Divakar and Ajai (2004: 11).

Dr. Ambedkar, a Dalit. He certainly knew the distinction between race and caste. If the concept of caste was included in race, there was no reason to mention them separately. (*The New Encyclopaedia Britannica*, 15th ed., Vol. 15: 361, cited in Sorabjee 2004: 47)

Deliberation on the kinship between caste and race meant not just remapping the field of caste in the new context of race, but also investing other groups in similar social location in that context with the marks of caste, thus creating a multilayered field for deliberation—interest, relation and assertion attaining new and more effective possibilities both within the country and within the international arena of the WCAR (see Fitzpatrick 2001). Take for instance the following statement that represents the stand of the National Campaign for Dalit Human Rights:

... the term Dalits refers to the people of South Asia who were outside the pale of the hierarchical caste system, and, therefore, deemed outcastes. Regarded as the most marginalized of the castes in society, they were and are still considered polluted and assigned the occupations deemed too defiling for other castes to do.... Born into her or his caste, a Dalit could not hope to escape her or his low social status....

Conceived more broadly, the term Dalit could be extended to communities, which suffer discrimination on the basis of descent and occupation. This would include such communities as the Burakumin in Japan, Osu in Nigeria, Roma-Shinti (gypsies) in Europe.... Considered in this broad term, that is, those that suffer discrimination based on descent and occupation, would constitute the single largest discriminated community on the globe today. (Divakar and Ajai 2004)

Apart from theoretical frameworks to understand the modern history of caste, the focus on practices of forced labour akin to slavery—bonded labour—made the navigation on the argument of caste as race easier, but more importantly, this single issue bonded the Dalit experience with the experience of peoples of African descent in slavery. The estimate of 1.25 million people in bonded labour in the state of Tamil Nadu alone in 1995, drawn up by the Commission on Bonded Labour appointed by the Supreme Court, despite the legal prohibition of bonded labour by the Bonded Labour (Abolition) Act, 1976, and the Scheduled Castes and Scheduled Tribes (Prevention of Atrocities) Act 1989, was cited in the Anti Slavery International's submission to the Working Group on Contemporary Forms of Slavery of the United Nations Economic and Social Council Commission on Human Rights in 2000 (Divakar and Ajai 2004).

The contentious terrain of the deliberations around caste and race was not confined to the space of the WCAR alone. Caste in India has been a major sociological concern, straddling colonial and postcolonial academes. Like other realms of subcontinental realities (criminal law, for instance), scholarship on caste in postcolonial India drew on colonial scholarship in deeply problematic ways, informing state policy, pre-empting any rupture that might be caused by the deliberations in the Constituent Assembly or through proactive legislations.

There were, as a result, two separate streams of governmentality on the caste question. The first related to the implementation of anti-untouchability provisions both as law and policy (a stream influenced considerably by the Ambedkarite formulation); the second related to the production of official knowledge regarding reasonable, theoretically tenable, and legitimate articulations of caste (a stream influenced by 'standpoint-free sociology'). The second stream, while discussing in great ethnographic detail the realities of microsystems of caste in different pockets of the country, or in different scriptures, leaves out of the reckoning any theorizing of violence that this ethnography throws up. Dumont (1970: 52) offers us the best example of this:

> The literature [of the dharma or religious law] ... shows the transition from ... occasional or temporary impurity to the permanent impurity of certain human groups. The laws of Manu say, 'When he has touched a Candala, a menstruating woman, an outcaste, a woman who has just given birth, a corpse...he purifies himself by bathing'. Here the occasional impurities are identified with that of the 'outcaste' and Candala, who is none other than the old prototype of the Untouchable. There is another list in the same book.... 'A Candala, a domestic pig, a cock, a dog, a menstruating woman and a eunuch must not look on Brahmans while they are eating' ... the animals mentioned feed on refuse and filth ... the Candala is relegated to the cremation grounds and lives on men's refuse....

For Phule, as we saw earlier, this same reality demonstrated the enslavement of the sudratisudra and women by the Brahmans. For anti-caste activists, this is a violent demonstration of social exclusion and the most vicious expression of apartheid/segregation.

Further, postcolonial ethnographic accounts of caste focused on the microsystems of caste without mapping the microphysics of power that named social exclusion. These accounts also resisted any comparisons with race as being theoretically untenable. The genealogy of this resistance to caste-as-race formulations may be traced to the colonial ethnographic project, which was without doubt deeply problematic on questions of racial classification and enumeration. Béteille, writing in the context of the Durban process, argued that not only was the linking of caste to race 'scientifically nonsensical' (Béteille 2004b: 52), it was also 'bound to give a new lease of life to the *old and discredited notion of race* current a hundred years ago' (ibid.: 51). However, from the debates generated by Dalit groups in the country, it is clear that they were tracing their genealogy not to European scholarship on caste/race but to the legacy of Phule, which stood in stark contrast.

The second part of the resistance to the caste-as-race debate located it within North–South politics, making a clear distinction between 'internal' and international issues. Dipankar Gupta argued that by taking caste to the UN, Indians were merely ceding

> knowledge advantage to the West on one front after another—beginning with the economic, then flowing on to the political and now we need tips on how to handle cultural discrimination as well...How do the enthusiasts who want to go to the Durban conference imagine that international agencies will help fight caste in India? *Have they thought this through?* Will the UN sanction a bombing raid on Delhi? An economic embargo? Or ... provide intellectual and strategic direction, *as if we haven't had enough of that already.* (Gupta 2004a: 53–4; emphasis added)

Gupta then goes on to hold the government responsible for 'washing a whole lot of dirty linen'—poverty, leprosy, AIDS, Kashmir—in front of strangers so that it lost the right to argue that caste was an 'internal' matter. Béteille, on the other hand, has no objection to discussing things in the open, he himself having done so at numerous conferences, '[b]ut the discussion should be in *good faith*' (Béteille 2004a: 65; emphasis added). Radhakrishnan (2004: 60) charged the Dalits with the 'political appropriation of the caste system', arguing that 'their existential problem cannot be isolated from that of the rest of society'.

The crux of the Dalit intervention, which provided a counterpoint, was that social exclusion cannot any more be an 'internal' matter—it had to be settled and accounted for in full view of the world, drawing on the constitutional framework of the absolute non-negotiability of fundamental rights, especially to life and dignity.

The third set of arguments related to affirmative action, reducing the demand for affirmative action to a 'game of numbers and proportionate representation. It does not employ reservations to uproot caste identities in public life, but rather to perpetuate it' (Gupta 2004b: 82). Interestingly, yet again, what gets demonstrated is the kinship of caste and race, in this instance through the prism of reactions against affirmative action, echoing the debates particularly in the US.

Finally, the question of the authentic voice is one that gets foregrounded in this debate. Gupta argues that it can only be victims of untouchability who can speak about it. Yet he also observes that having transcended the oppressions of caste through mobility, 'ex-untouchables' only want to move on, not continue to be identified as untouchables. Who will then speak? Those that espouse the cause of the Dalits—for the most part Dalit intellectuals and activists—do not 'belong' to that experience because they have tasted the fruits of liberalization and economic success. They also do not belong, by this argument, because essential to the fact of belonging for a Dalit is mobility and amnesia—the compulsion to Sanskritization, Srinivas would say. Untouchability, therefore, cannot lead to 'mandalism' (a pejorative allusion to the unequivocal demand for affirmative action)—Dalits who press for proportionate reservation, in laying a claim to affirmative action in education, employment, and politics, fall within the ranks of the 'imposters' (not the *genuine* sufferers) because they persist with caste identities. Claiming representation, this argument goes, entrenches caste rather than uproots it. And after all, caste is about belonging, not just for Dalits, but those above them as well in the social hierarchy.

The circle of the second stream of governmentality is complete. Violent exclusion is argued out of the theoretical scheme of caste through sociological acrobatics, a process that uncovers for us the collusions between the production of knowledge, processes of dominance and hegemony, and the conferment of legitimacy in governance.

The counter-production of knowledge becomes critical, therefore, to this process of destabilizing hegemonic knowledge:

Untouchability produces repulsion in the minds of non-Dalits at the very sight, approach and touch of Dalits. The Dalit touch for them brings impurity and defilement. *There being no biological differences either in terms of the skin colour or the body structure between Dalits and non-Dalits, the knowledge of caste identity becomes a pre-condition of discrimination.* (Anonymous 2003)

Evidence of the violent exclusionary practices could be found in the experience of the Chakkiliyar caste, the members of which could only light a fire in their homes if there was a dead animal in the village. At all other times they had 'to survive, much like slaves, on the crumbs that fell off the table of those who happened to be their masters' (ibid.) The rationalization of these practices—in stark contrast to the 'spiritual' brahminical frameworks—was located in the material conditions of village life—consuming carcasses being the way that dominant castes ensured removal of defilement and environmental pollution.

The other aspect of the Dalit experience is the question of segregation of entire villages consequent on untouchability—'hidden apartheid'.[11]

'Untouchables' may not cross the line dividing their part of the village from that occupied by higher castes. They may not use the same wells, visit the same temples, drink from the same cups in tea stalls, or lay claim to land that is legally theirs. Dalit children are frequently

---

[11] Statement by the International Dalit Solidarity Network to the First Preparatory Committee for the World Conference against Racism, Racial Discrimination, Xenophobia and Related Intolerance, Geneva, 1–5 May 2000, published in *Communalism Combat*, 2000, May, p. 10.

made to sit in the back of classrooms, and communities as a whole are made to perform degrading rituals in the name of caste. (Human Rights Watch 2000: 2)

Caste for Dalit peoples *is* what race is for peoples of African descent in the Americas and South Africa. Becoming is the route to belong where one belongs. Belonging is shaped by radical ideas of the 'we' that are based on historically established and documented 'prior experience' that forges an identity of interest through an identity of location—regardless of territorial citizenship.

CASTE, GENDER, AND RACE: THE NATIONAL FEDERATION OF DALIT WOMEN

To bounce like a ball that has been hit became my deepest desire, and not to curl up and collapse because of the blow. (Bama 2005: vii)

How does gender figure in this entire discourse around caste and race? While gender has been central to the constitution of the caste system, it was theorized only much after the major mainstream formulations were already in place. In the excerpts from Dumont cited earlier, there are very specific ways in which women's experiences and bodies are structured into the caste order, indeed very specific ways in which bodies are gendered reproductive capacities being central to that definition (the menstruating woman, the new mother, and the widow being equally sources of pollution in the brahminical schema, as also the eunuch).

Within this framework, women and slaves figure as subjects, women by nature fickle and unchaste, whose sexuality, bodies, and minds must be reined in by the 'dharma', the Manusmriti epitomizing this view. Evidence from the eighteenth century points to the vulnerability of all women, irrespective of *jati*, to enslavement for infringement of moral codes. In relation to women from the panchama groups (categorized broadly as *asprsya* or untouchable), which were tied in perpetual bondage, the additional implication for women of these castes was sexual slavery. However, this proscription on physical contact did not extend to sexual relations between upper-caste men and Untouchable women, sexual labour being part of the physical labour provided by slave women and appropriated by the upper-caste owner/master (Kannabiran 2004: 273–308).

In modern India, gender within caste society is

defined and structured in such a manner that the 'manhood' of the caste is defined both by the degree of control men exercise over women and the degree of passivity [and complicity] of the women of the caste. By the same argument, demonstrating control by humiliating women of another caste is a certain way of reducing the 'manhood' of those castes. (Kannabiran and Kannabiran 1991: 2131)

Spaces—domestic and public—are similarly structured both along lines of caste and gender. The Scheduled Castes and Scheduled Tribes (Prevention of Atrocities) Act, 1989 recognizes the gendered nature of caste experience, especially for Dalit women. In the definition of atrocity, therefore, it makes explicit mention of the kinds of violence that women may be subjected to—sexual assault, non-consensual contact using the position of dominance, stripping and parading naked are acts that fall within the meaning of atrocity in the law.

A critical part of the effort to re-articulate the issue of caste in the theoretical/political context of anti-racism has been the mobilizing of Dalit feminist resistance by the National Federation of Dalit Women (NFDW) in India, which began its work in 1995. The manifesto of the NFDW sets it apart from autonomous women's movement in India, on the one side, and the 'male dominated secular and progressive movements' including the Dalit movement, on the other side—underscoring the need for critical reflection on caste-based discrimination *and* the violence inflicted on Dalit women (see also Thorat 2001).

> NFDW endeavours to seek and build alliances with all other progressive and democratic movements and forces, in particular the women's movement and the wider Dalit movement at the national level. It thus aspires in a significant way to widen the democratic spaces while at the same time to create and preserve its identity and specificity.
>
> This framework will enable the Dalit women's movement to seek the roots of its oppression, the diversities, the nature of changes, if any, in specific regions and historical contexts and in particular, perceive the varied levels of consciousness that exist within it.[12]

This project, while it got submerged in the larger Dalit mobilization in Durban, is one that must be examined in greater detail, raising as it does questions of the relationship between gender and racism as reflective of questions of intersectionality in feminist struggles, even while examining the specificities of the Dalit woman's question in India. Central to the question of belonging, of course, are questions of identity, diversity, and power. How has feminism in India fashioned a new politics of identity and belonging that resists sexism and casteism–racism in very direct ways?

Within the larger politics of becoming, Dalit women attempted to combat both racism and sexism together, wresting space within the larger Dalit mobilization for a representation of interest and identity as women,

---

[12] *Transforming Pain into Power: The Manifesto of the National Federation of Dalit Women*, n.d. National Federation of Dalit Women (2003).

and occupying space without—in opposition to other socially dominant groups within the country and the Indian state on the one hand, building solidarities with other groups suffering descent-based discrimination in different locales across the world, on the other. The pivotal bridge was with women of African descent. The recognition of diversity and difference was set against the homogenizing practices of majoritarian Hindu nationalism on the one side and the appropriating spaces of showcasing of 'exotic' Dalit–bahujan cultures and their commoditization by the state on the other. The deliberation on the Dalit woman's position therefore was based on notions of dignity of labour, cultural expression, and democratic politics, the notion of belonging for Dalit women situated firmly within an autonomous space that drew its strength from the resistance to appropriation and the building of alliances on equal terms.[13]

In terms of the delineation of issues, the NFDW focused on the specific interpretation of civil and political rights, the recognition of productive contribution to society in terms of equality, dignity, fair wages, and popular perception, the guarantee of security of person and freedom from the threat of sexual and physical assault, right to freedom of religion in a context where conversion for a better life resulted in denial of protections, and the right to leadership—a claim pitted against non-Dalit men, Dalit men, and non-Dalit women. Drawing on the definition of racial discrimination in Article 1 of the CERD, the NFDW asserted in the Durban process that discrimination based on caste is indeed a specific form of racism, intertwined with gender since Dalit women

> face targeted violence from state actors and powerful members of dominant castes and community especially in the case of rape, mutilation and death; they face discrimination in the payment of unequal wages and gender violence at the workplace that includes fields [as agricultural labourers], on the streets [as manual scavengers and garbage pickers], in homes [as domestic workers], and through religious custom.... (National Federation of Dalit Women 2001a, 2001b)

The NFDW argues that it is necessary to look at the intersectionality of gender, race, and caste in order to appreciate Dalit women's location adequately. Dalit women are 'dalit among the dalits' because they are thrice alienated—on the basis of caste, class, and gender. The oppression of Dalit women echoes issues of state violence, denial of land rights, social and legal discrimination, infringement of civil liberties, inferior status, dehumanizing living and working conditions, total impoverishment, malnutrition, poor health conditions, the adverse effect of various contraceptives and new

---

[13] Ibid.

family planning devices, social ostracism, and untouchability.[14] The role of Dalit women, the NFDW argues, is critical to Dalit liberation and Dalit identity—the Dalit woman is by definition feminist, non-patriarchal, non-hierarchical, and positively oriented towards ecology.

The charter of rights of Dalit women, formulated in 1999 and christened the Delhi Declaration, sets out the guiding principles of Dalit women's rights.[15] It declares that Dalits are *one* of the indigenous peoples of India, who as a people are sovereign, with a distinct identity, history, culture, and religion. As the original inhabitants of the land, they have a right to the ownership of the knowledge resources of the country as well as the fruit of their labour. Further, the declaration states that the ancient history, culture, and tradition of Dalit people are those in which there is equality between men and women. In this context, Dalit women build their identities on cultures of resistance against the homogenizing hegemonic cultures of brahminical Hinduism and the caste system, and assert their right to free speech and expression and their right to dignity especially with reference to the 'heinous practice of untouchability'. Significantly, Dalit women in this charter declared 'solidarity in the common cause of women's rights in India and the world at large for the establishment of gender partnership in an egalitarian society'. This charter documents the process of transition from becoming into belonging.

Finally, the charter sets out the measures that central and state governments must take in order to demonstrate due diligence in eliminating violence and discrimination against Dalits in general and Dalit women in particular. The first of these measures is to recognize Dalit women as a distinct social group, rather than masking them under the general category of women. Further, the charter demanded that all statutory commissions take note of the specific experience of Dalit women; that land be distributed by the government to Dalits *and* that this land be registered in the name of Dalit women in each household; that wage revision and gender parity committees be constituted to ensure equal agricultural wages for Dalit women, *alongside* enacting a comprehensive Dalit Agricultural Workers Act; that mechanisms to monitor and check the commission of atrocities against Dalit women be put in place; that a ban be imposed on private armies of dominant caste landlords *and* that the government 'distribute

---

[14] *Transforming Pain into Power*, n.d.
[15] *Marching into the New Millennium: Delhi Declaration (Dalit Women Declare the Charter of Gender Rights and Demands)*, New Delhi (December 1999, unpublished); National Federation of Dalit Women (2001a).

weapons and train dalit women to handle them in self defence against the perpetrators of crimes and atrocities'. The diversity and radicalism of this charter of demands is a demonstration of the fact that '[o]ppressed, ruled, and still being ruled by patriarchy, government, caste, and religion, Dalit women are forced to break all the strictures of society to live' (Bama 2005: vii). In trying to break shackles and propel themselves forward, Bama observes, Dalit women have had to roar their defiance and learn to mock the class that oppressed them, finding through this the courage to revolt (ibid.).

The intersectional articulation of the Dalit woman's political position is most evident when the charter affirms that 'Dalit women have the right to self protection in the face of dominant caste male and female aggression, of Dalit male aggression, and of aggression committed by law enforcing machineries of the State'. Bama presents to us the creative articulation of this political standpoint very powerfully in her novel *Sangati* (2005) where extreme forms of patriarchal violence within the family are matched by the intense vulnerability to sexual assault by the men of dominant castes and the economic oppression of Dalit men and women by dominant caste landowners and factory owners. Dalit feminist resistance in this context is an everyday resistance against everyday casteism and exclusion—minute, persistent, cumulative, intense. The charter crystallizes this resistance into a consolidated critique of state and society, forcing the state to grapple with the new measures for justice that this particular feminist praxis threw up.

From being an oppressed class, thrice oppressed, Dalit women declare sovereignty and occupy a moral high ground demonstrating the possibility of being democratic, egalitarian, and humane on the one hand and reaching out to other movements of women's rights in a spirit of solidarity on the other. This assertion of a distinct identity and simultaneous forging of a collective identity in several struggles at once marks the Dalit women's movement in very specific ways. The mapping of identity is superimposed on the mapping of the violence of the caste system and the specific ways in which that violence is gendered—the violence of denial, of degrading work, of religion, of atrocity, of aggression on the body of the Dalit woman, of language, and abuse.

* * *

This chapter has attempted to explore the traditions of feminist resistance in India through the work of the NFDW. In looking at this particular political formation, what has got immediately foregrounded is the convergence of protective legislations, claims to entitlements, social locations, contestations about that location both by the state and in civil society, and the forging of a larger kinship of belonging as a method of enforcing greater accountability and transparency on local forces that repress with impunity. What we witness is also a convergence between the everyday and political society. The use of international soft law mechanisms and parameters of intersectionality in race theory provide the theoretical framework within which the solidarities between race, caste, and gender are forged at the local, national, and international levels by Dalit women, through resistance and struggle.

The disjuncture between justice and the law in this case is stark, with justice lying ever beyond the pale of law. It is impossible for women to belong any more without deliberation—responsible belongingness necessarily means active engagement in deliberation—the community providing commonality of interests and location but not justice. Women, Dalit women in particular, constantly negotiate space for the insertion of justice into that common ground—marking its separation, difference, and distance from the larger public domain in general and public law in particular, not easily conceded by the community of belonging, not standing on its own either, but seeking to govern in similar ways on different terms. The politics of becoming then shapes the politics of belonging and transforms the idea of the community itself.

The larger questions that are relevant to this debate have to do with the politics of masculinity and misogyny in civil society and women's responses to it; the politics of gender within communities and the resistance to sexism from within; the resistance to sexism and xenophobia in the 'national' space by redefining body politics; the demonstration of 'better' politics of belonging by moving back and forth between the political and the moral, rather from the political to the moral. Another useful way of looking at this question is through the lens of social exclusion, tracing the paths of exclusion and thereby contextualizing the struggles of resistance to exclusion.

These are questions that are immediately relevant to an understanding of the ways in which Dalit women have organized themselves over the past decade in India. Resisting pacific order for Dalit women has been critical to survival, since order has for them specifically been based on foundational violence—within the family, in the larger multi-caste communal space, and in the terrain(s) of citizenship(s). The Dalit feminist standpoint, and more specifically the NFDW, provides in very clear terms a cartography of governance that forces an official reckoning of a new way of seeing.

REFERENCES

Anonymous. (2003), 'Dalit Women in India: A Case of Discrimination by Birth', unpublished note, Readings for the First National Leadership Training Institute for Dalit Women: Enhancing Capacities and Building Leadership, organized by the National Federation of Dalit Women, Bangalore, Personal Archives of Ruth Manorama, 24 November–4 December.

Bama (2005), *Sangati* (translated from Tamil by Lakshmi Holmström). New Delhi: Oxford University Press.

Bayly, Susan (1995), 'Caste and Race in the Colonial Ethnography of India', in P. Robb (ed.), *The Concept of Race in South Asia*. New Delhi: Oxford University Press, pp. 165–218.

Béteille, André (2004a), 'Caste Consciousness: Initiate an Open Discussion in Durban', in Sukhadeo Thorat and Umakant (eds), *Caste, Race and Discrimination: Discourses in International Context*. Jaipur and New Delhi: Rawat Publications, pp. 65–8.

—— (2004b), 'Race and Caste', in Thorat and Umakant (eds), *Caste, Race and Discrimination*, pp. 49–52.

Connolly, William E. (1996), 'Suffering, Justice and the Politics of Becoming', *Culture, Medicine and Psychiatry*, 20: 251–77. Reprinted in William E. Connolly (1999), *Why I Am Not a Secularist*. Minneapolis: University of Minnesota Press, pp. 47–71.

Deshpande, G.P. (2002), 'Of Hope and Melancholy: Reading Jotirao Phule in our Times', in G.P. Deshpande (ed.), *Selected Writings of Jotirao Phule*. New Delhi: Left Word Books, pp. 1–21.

Dirks, Nicholas (2002), *Castes of Mind: Colonialism and the Making of Modern India*. Delhi: Permanent Black.

Divakar, Paul N. and M. Ajai (2004), 'UN Bodies and the Dalits: A Historical Review of Interventions', in Thorat and Umakant (eds), *Caste, Race and Discrimination*, pp. 3–30.

Dumont, Louis (1970), *Homo Hierarchicus: The Caste System and Its Implications*. Delhi: Vikas Publishing House.

Fitzpatrick, Peter (2001), 'Consolations of the Law: Jurisprudence and the Constitution of Deliberative Politics', *Ratio Juris*, IV(3): 281–97.

Foucault, Michel (1987), 'Maurice Blanchot: The Thought from Outside', in Michel Foucault and Maurice Blanchot (eds), *Faucault/Blanchot* (translated by Brian Massumi). New York: Zone Books, pp. 7–60.

Geetha, V. and S.V. Rajadurai (1998), *Towards a Non-Brahmin Millennium: From Iyothee Thass to Periyar*. Calcutta: Samya.

Gupta, Dipankar (2004a), 'Caste is Not Race: But Let's Go to the UN Forum Anyway', in Thorat and Umakant (eds), *Caste, Race and Discrimination*, pp. 53–6.

Gupta, Dipankar (2004b), 'Caste, Race Politics', in Thorat and Umakant (eds), *Caste, Race and Discrimination*, pp. 69–84.

Human Rights Watch (2000), 'Violence against and Exploitation of 'Untouchable' Women in India', report prepared for the Committee on the Elimination of Discrimination against Women, 20 January.

Jaffrelot, Christophe (2003), *India's Silent Revolution: The Rise of the Low Castes in North Indian Politics*. Delhi: Permanent Black.

Kannabiran, Kalpana (2002), 'Caste', in *Routledge International Encyclopedia on Women, Vol. 1*. New York: Routledge, pp. 142–4.

—— (2004), 'Voices of Dissent: Changing Gender Values in Hinduism', in Robin Rinehart (ed.), *Contemporary Hinduism: Ritual, Culture, and Practice*. Santa Barbara: ABC-CLIO, pp. 273–308.

Kannabiran, Kalpana and Vasanth Kannabiran (1991), 'Caste and Gender: Understanding the Dynamic of Power and Violence', *Economic and Political Weekly*, 14 September, 26(37): 2130–3.

Minow, Martha (1990), *Making All the Difference: Inclusion and Exclusion in American Law*. Ithaca: Cornell University Press.

—— (1996), 'Comments on "Suffering, Justice and the Politics of Becoming", by William E. Connolly, presented as the Roger Allan Moore Lecture, 11 May 1995', *Culture, Medicine and Psychiatry*, 20: 279–86.

National Federation of Dalit Women (2001a), reading materials prepared for the National Consultation on Gender and Racial Discrimination, New Delhi, February, unpublished, Personal Archives of Ruth Manorama.

—— (2001b), NGO Declaration on Gender and Racism, Racial Discrimination, Xenophobia and Related Intolerance, World Conference against Racism, Durban, South Africa, Personal Archives of Ruth Manorama, 28 August–7 September.

—— (2003), Reading materials of the First National Leadership Training Institute for Dalit Women, unpublished, Bangalore, November–December.

Omi, Michael and Howard Winant (2002), 'Racial Formation', in Philomena Essed and David Theo Goldberg (eds), *Race Critical Theories: Text and Context*. Oxford: Blackwell Publishers, pp. 123–45.

Phule, Jotirao (2002 [1873]), 'Slavery', in G.P. Deshpande (ed.), *Selected Writings of Jotirao Phule*. New Delhi: LeftWord Books.

Radhakrishnan, P. (2004), 'Dalits and Durban', in Sukhadeo Thorat and Umakant (eds), *Caste, Race and Discrimination*, pp. 57–64.

Shinde, Tarabai (1994 [1882]), *A Comparison between Women and Men* (translated and edited by Rosalind O'Hanlon). New Delhi: Oxford University Press.

Sorabjee, Soli (2004), 'The Official Position', in Thorat and Umakant (eds), *Caste, Race and Discrimination*, pp. 43–7.

Thorat, Sukhadeo and Umakant (2004), 'Introduction', in Sukhadeo Thorat and Umakant (eds), *Caste, Race and Discrimination: Discourses in International Context*. Jaipur and New Delhi: Rawat Publications, pp. xiii–xxxv.

Thorat, Vimal (2001), 'Dalit Women Have Been Left Behind by the Dalit Movement and the Women's Movement', *Communalism Combat*, May: 12.

IV. MASCULINITY

Chapter 7

POTENT PROTESTS

The Age of Consent Controversy, 1891*

MRINALINI SINHA

ON 9 JANUARY 1891, THE LAW MEMBER OF INDIA, Sir Andrew Scoble, introduced a Bill in the Legislative Council, raising the age of consent for sexual intercourse for Indian girls from 10 to 12 years (*Abstract of the Proceedings of the Council of the Governor General of India, Assembled for the Purpose of Making Laws and Regulations 1891* [hereafter *Abstract*]). The Bill proposed to define sexual intercourse with married and unmarried Indian girls below the age of 12 as rape, punishable by 10 years' imprisonment or transportation for life. The Bill did not interfere directly with the institution of child marriage in India, but only with the premature consummation of child marriage. While the upper-caste Hindu practice of child marriage was fairly common among different caste/class and religious groups all over India, there was a general consensus that the problem of premature consummation of child marriage was to be found

---

* Originally published in Mrinalini Sinha (1998), *Colonial Masculinity: The 'Manly' Englishman and the 'Effeminate' Bengali in the Late Nineteenth Century*. New Delhi: Kali Press, pp. 138–80.

mainly in the province of Bengal.¹ Nevertheless, by the time the Viceroy, Lord Lansdowne, signed the Age of Consent Act on 19 March 1891, the entire country was sharply divided over the measure. Shortly following the passage of the Consent Act, therefore, the Viceroy, on the initiative of Charles Elliott, the Lt Governor of Bengal, issued an executive order that made it virtually impossible to bring cases of premature consummation of child marriage for trial under the Consent Act.²

In spite of the passage of the Consent Act, one of the most striking features of the Consent controversy, as many scholars have pointed out, was the massive opposition provoked by the Bill. For not only was the limited nature of the Consent Bill itself a compromise with indigenous upper-caste patriarchal norms and practices, but the colonial authorities were so impressed by the agitation against the Bill that they did not again initiate any major social reform legislation in India until the passage of the Child Marriage Restraint Act in 1929.³ Indeed, as several scholars have argued, the agitation against the Consent Bill injected into the incipient political nationalism in India a militant strand that was hitherto unprecedented in the history of elite Indian politics.⁴ Just as the Anglo-Indian agitation against the Ilbert Bill is credited with consolidating a new mood of aggressiveness in the Anglo-Indian population in India, so also the Indian agitation against the Consent Bill is seen as similarly inaugurating a new phase in the history of elite nationalism in India.

The politics of colonial masculinity, however, serves to recontextualize the impact of the agitation against the Consent Bill on elite nationalist politics in India.⁵ It provides a context in which the contribution to nationalist politics of the defence of orthodox Hindu patriarchy in the agitation against the Consent Bill appears as a more complicated matter. Most recent studies of the Consent controversy have focused on the patriarchal politics of the anti-Consent Bill agitation and its role in

---

¹ For the extremely high incidence of child marriage in Bengal, see Census Report of 1881 quoted in *Selections Home Department*. Also, *Parliamentary Papers*, p. 91. For the belief that premature consummation of child marriage was also common in Bengal, see *Abstracts*, p. 10; also Borthwick (1984: 128).

² The Government of India Circular of March 1891 adopted Elliot's circular on the Bill; *India, Home Department, Judicial, April 1891, Pros. Nos 103–104 A*. Also, *A Collection of the Acts Passed by the Governor General of India in Council in the Year 1891*, 1892.

³ For a history of child marriage reform in India, see Forbes (1979). Also Heimsath (1962, 1964).

⁴ See especially Natarajan (1962).

⁵ For an earlier formulation of this point, see Sinha (1989); and in slightly different form, see Sinha (1987).

radicalizing nationalist politics. Dagmar Engels, for example, has argued that nationalist politics in Bengal was radicalized in the conflict between two opposing views of controlling female sexuality: the Bengali male control of female sexuality was pitted against the regulation of female sexuality in a Victorian British gender ideology (Engels 1983). Padma Anagol–McGinn's study of the Consent controversy in the Bombay Presidency suggests that the nationalist opposition to the Bill also expressed male hostility towards Indian women who organized meetings and public demonstrations in support of the Bill.[6] The question of why the defence of an unreformed indigenous patriarchy served as the medium for revitalizing nationalist politics in late nineteenth-century India has been addressed most directly by Tanika Sarkar. Sarkar situates the Consent controversy in the context of the gradual disillusionment of Indian nationalists with the 'public sphere as an arena for the test of manhood'; this disillusionment made 'Hindu' conjugality and domestic social arrangements an intensely politicized arena in colonial and nationalist conflicts.[7] The more crucial point, however, is that the politics of colonial masculinity substantially qualifies the nature of the contribution of the anti-Consent Bill agitation to nationalist politics. For, notwithstanding the bitterness of the conflict over the Consent Bill, the colonial authorities were sympathetic to the claims of native masculinity: not in the demands for a greater military role, as in the native volunteer agitation; nor for a greater administrative role, as in the native civil service agitation; but only in the defence of orthodox Hindu patriarchy in the Consent controversy.

In Bengal, where opposition to the Consent Bill was perhaps the strongest in all of India, a group of orthodox opponents presented the following argument against the Bill in their impassioned *Appeal to England to Save India from the Wrong and Shame of the 'Age of Consent' Act*:

could the Englishman himself, with all his abhorrence of early marriages, tolerate a penal enactment, which made the husband's sexual intercourse with his wife of 15 years of age (for, as has been already said, 12 in India would correspond to about 15 in England) punishable with transportation for life or imprisonment for 10 years? (*An Appeal to England to Save India from the Wrong and the Shame of the 'Age of Consent Act'* 1891: vi [hereafter *Appeal*])

---

[6] Anagol–McGinn (1992). In Calcutta 'Brahmo ladies' who supported the Bill were subject to considerable ridicule; see *Reis and Reyyet* (Calcutta), 28 March 1891, p. 149.

[7] I am indebted especially to the account of the Age of Consent controversy in Sarkar (1993: 1870); also Sarkar (1992). It is significant for my argument that in a footnote in her 1993 article, Sarkar points out that the camps that articulated the strongest nationalist case against the Age of Consent Bill were in the Swadeshi Movement of 1905–8 'quiescent, even loyal to the authorities'; see Sarkar (1993: 1877, nl).

The strategy of the opponents of the Bill was a deliberate attempt to appeal to the logic of colonial masculinity: on the one hand, it centred the terms of the debate not on the sexual abuse of Indian child-wives, but on the curtailment of the rights of the Indian husband; and, on the other, it represented the defence of orthodox Hindu patriarchy in a more universal patriarchal language of the 'natural' rights of all husbands. The strategy of the Bengali opponents of the Consent Bill—arising in part from the perception of the emasculation of the elite Bengali male under colonial rule—not only refocused the Consent controversy on the claims of native masculinity, but also connected its claim with the perception of a growing 'crisis' in British masculinity arising from, among other things, the feminist challenges of the 1880s.[8] Indeed, the problematic of masculinity in a colonial situation serves to reframe the agitation against the Consent Bill in two crucial ways: it both underscores the shared assumptions in colonial and nationalist responses to the Consent Bill and situates the Indian Consent controversy in relation to the larger imperial social formation. Although the agitation against the Consent Bill has been typically understood in terms of the rejuvenation of nationalist politics in India, its contribution was far more ambiguous: for the defence of orthodox Hindu patriarchy resulted, above all, in bringing the claims of native masculinity into closer alignment with the agenda of late nineteenth-century colonial rule.

The first indication that the agitation against the Bill was more ambiguous—aligning with, rather than challenging, colonial politics—was the paradoxical impact of colonial masculinity on nationalist politics: it simultaneously empowered the opposition against the Bill as nationalist and recuperated the nationalist challenge by bringing it in closer harmony with colonial politics. Indeed, the politics of colonial masculinity obscured the colonial interests served in the nationalist backlash against social reform. For, on the one hand, the colonial authorities had conceded the indigenous domestic realm as an 'autonomous' site for native masculinity; and, on the other, this construction of the domestic realm also fostered nationalist scepticism towards the reform of the domestic realm as a threat to Indian autonomy. The contradictory impact of colonial masculinity on social reforms resulted from the convergence of colonial and nationalist interests in the late nineteenth century: the withdrawal of colonial support for social reform initiatives converged with the increasingly defensive

---

[8] For the perception of a crisis of British masculinity in the late nineteenth century, see Walkowitz (1992). For a historical perspective on such 'crises' in Britain and the US, see Kimmel (1987).

response to social reform legislations from Indian nationalists. In the decades after 1857, for example, the colonial authorities were committed to a policy of ostensible non-interference in the social and religious affairs of the country (see Heimsath 1964). The myth of non-interference was sustained by the demarcation of a supposedly 'uncolonized' space untouched by colonial rule. This 'uncolonized' space, as Sarkar reminds us, was itself a product of the legal framework of colonial rule: it demarcated a separate public sphere of criminal codes, land relations, laws of contract, and so on, that was brought under the regulation of British and colonial law, and an alternative private sphere of family relationships, family property, and religious practices regulated by separate Hindu and Muslim laws (which were themselves unified and codified under the imperatives of colonial rule).[9] Yet, whatever the contradictions haunting the policy of non-interference, the colonial authorities were engaged in a much more self-conscious effort in the late nineteenth century to defer to the authority of indigenous interpretations and of customary practices in all matters designated 'private'. The colonial policy of non-interference, therefore, committed itself in no uncertain terms to the nurturing of orthodox indigenous practices.

In addition, colonial masculinity also forged a connection between the changing imperatives of colonial rule and nationalist politics: it smoothed the transfer of responsibility to Indian men for the indigenous domestic realm. For the gradual reconstitution of the domestic realm as an arena for Indian autonomy also coincided with the imperatives of an emerging 'official' Indian nationalism, which, as Partha Chatterjee has demonstrated, constructed its own unique identity by demarcating a separate domain in which to locate its autonomy.[10] Hence, when the Parsi reformer from Bombay, Behramji Malabari, first published his 'Notes on Infant Marriage and Enforced Widowhood' in 1884, his proposal for a government initiative to reform Indian domestic practices received a mixed response both from nationalist Indians and from the colonial authorities (*Infant Marriage and Enforced Widowhood in India* 1887; also see *Selections Home Department*). The opinions collected by the colonial authorities on Malabari's 'Notes' in

---

[9] Sarkar (1993: 1871). For the 'invention of tradition' and its impact on social reform, see Mani (1987).

[10] Chatterjee (1990). Chatterjee's argument of the identity crisis of 'official' Indian nationalism arising out of its 'derivative' project of modernity is made most forcefully in Chatterjee (1986). In his later work, Chatterjee emphasizes that the 'originality' of Indian nationalism lay in the imaginative task of constructing a community in the 'spiritual' or cultural realm; see Chatterjee (1993).

1885 reflected the strength of orthodox Indian opposition to social reforms as well as the new spirit of caution with which even many Indian social reformers approached the question of government interference in Indian domestic arrangements. The argument that an 'alien government' and an unrepresentative legislature had no right to legislate the 'internal' affairs of the people was so popular with nationalist public opinion that even M.G. Ranade, an influential Hindu reformer from Bombay, justified his support for government legislation on the grounds that there was no harm in seeking government intervention in cases where legislative initiative coincided so directly with the welfare of Indians.[11] Equally significant in the responses to Malabari's 'Notes' was the colonial government's anxiety to clarify the limits of its own responsibility: the 'Legislature should keep within its natural boundaries and should not by overstepping these boundaries place itself in direct antagonism to social opinion' (*Selections Home Department*: 2).

The crucial point about the impact of the politics of colonial masculinity was that even as it produced a complicity between colonial/interests and indigenous orthodoxy, it obscured the colonial role in nurturing the indigenous orthodoxy. The result was that colonial masculinity not only discouraged support for reform, but, even more crucially, it underwrote the very protest against social reform. Colonial politics, moreover, continued to use social reform as a test of native masculinity—a handy stick with which to beat Indian nationalists. This was evident, for example, in the colonial insistence that Indian men should concentrate on social rather than on political reforms and the often insulting attitude adopted by missionaries and colonial officials towards the social problems of India. When Revd W. Milne of the Free Church in Calcutta and Revd K.S. Macdonald, editor of the *Indian Evangelical Review*, wrote Resolution Two of the Calcutta Missionary Conference—which proposed, among other things, that either party in an unconsummated child marriage should be given the right to dissolve the marriage and marry again—their ostensible aim of getting Indian reformers to support the proposal was undercut by the disparaging tone adopted towards Indians (Oddie 1979: 84–5). The proposal not only led to a major split between the European and Indian Christian community in Calcutta and to a spirited defence of Hindu child marriage by the Bengali Christian G.J. Shome, but it also alienated other Bengali reformers who may have otherwise shared the outrage of

---

[11] 12 February 1885, *Selections Home Department*, pp. 92–3. For an account of the consent controversy in Bombay, see Kosambi (1991).

the missionaries at the abuses of child marriage. Bipan Chandra Pal, the author of a series of articles on 'Infant Marriage in Bengal and its Poisonous Effects', and Surendranath Banerjea, a critic of child marriage in his paper the *Bengalee*, were critical of the tone adopted by the Calcutta Missionaries and apprehensive of government interference in the matter:

> What would Englishmen think, if we wrote strong articles and presumed to hold strong opinions regarding their divorce laws? Social reform is a matter which eminently concerns those who are the members of the society that needs to be reformed. Any interference from outside is the officious impertinence of strangers, and it can do no good but may do a great deal of harm. (*Bengalee* 1887: 329)

The result of such debates was deliberately paradoxical; it neither committed colonial authorities to encourage social reforms, nor allayed nationalist scepticism against colonial interference in social reform. Herein lay the paradoxical dynamics of masculinity as the site for colonial conflict: it channelled nationalist energies into a protest against social reform, a stance which in fact brought the nationalist challenge into closer alignment with colonial politics.

The paradoxical role of colonial masculinity does indeed recontextualize the meaning of the revivalist–nationalist opposition to the Consent Bill. In the opposition against the Consent Bill, it was not just domestic reform that was sacrificed at the altar of a more militant nationalist politics: rather, nationalist politics itself was sacrificed to a more thorough recuperation within the limited arena of colonial masculinity. The complicity between the revivalist–nationalist opposition to the Consent Bill and colonial politics thus constitutes an important context for the Consent controversy. Although it was the colonial authorities who introduced the Consent Bill, and then insisted on passing it over the opposition of a sizeable Indian public opinion, it was clear from the outset that they were simultaneously anxious to validate the very ground from which the strongest opposition to the Bill was raised. The government initiative to undertake the Consent Bill itself followed only after the public indignation in India over the much-publicized case of Hari Mohan Maitee, which was committed for trial to the Sessions Court at Calcutta on 6 July 1890. Maitee, a man of about 35, was accused of having caused the death of his child-bride Phulmoni in 1889 through brutal sexual intercourse.[12] Justice Wilson, who presided over the

---

[12] Scoble to Lansdowne, 6 July 1891, *Lansdowne Papers: Correspondence with Persons in India*, July to December 1890, Letter No. 20 (hereafter *Lansdowne India*). The colonial authorities believed that there was sufficient public indignation against 'Hari Maitism' in the 'native press' in the 1890s. See *India Legislative Proceedings, Nos 1–73, Act 10 of 1891 and Connected Papers*, April 1891, Pros. No. 5 (hereafter *Proceedings*).

case, declared that Phulmoni was 11 years old and, therefore, Maitee could not be tried for rape but only for the lesser charge of committing a 'rash and negligent act'; the Exception to the Fifth Clause of Section 375 of the Indian Penal Code, introduced in 1860, declared that 'sexual intercourse by a man with his own wife not being under ten years of age is not rape'.[13] The Phulmoni case brought to light other cases of 'Hari Maitism' in which husbands guilty of causing the death of their child-brides had been either acquitted by the courts or else had been awarded relatively minor sentences for causing 'bodily harm'.[14] Scoble, the Law Member, introduced a proposal that drew upon the recommendations that had been formulated earlier by the Bombay reformer, Dayaram Gidumal, for raising the age of consent from 10 to 12 years in the Fifth Clause and its Exception in Section 375 of the Indian Penal Code.[15]

Yet after having been forced by circumstances into initiating government legislation to protect child-brides, the colonial authorities were anxious to return to the colonial–nationalist agreement on the domestic realm as the arena of Indian autonomy: thus the colonial justification for the Consent Bill was that it did not interfere with indigenous religious principles. In the speeches that introduced the Bill in the Viceroy's Council, colonial officials were eager to commend the Bill for conforming with orthodox religious practices. In his speech to the Legislative Council, Scoble quoted from the orthodox *pundit* (priest) Sesadhur Turkachuramani of Bengal to establish that the proposed Bill did not violate the injunctions of the *Shastra*s (Hindu scriptures).[16] It was an indication of the extent to which the colonial authorities were cut off from Bengali public opinion when, much to Scoble's embarrassment, the Pundit shortly afterwards publicly castigated the Law Member for misrepresenting his opinions, and went on to become one of the leading opponents of the Bill on the grounds of religious interference.[17] It was not until it was fully apparent that the religious opposition to the Bill could not be placated so easily that Scoble eventually appealed to universal principles of humanity and morality to justify the Consent Bill.[18]

[13] Wilson's opinion was cited in Scoble's speech, 9 January 1891, *Abstracts*, pp. 10–11.
[14] For other cases of 'Hari Maitism', see Scoble's speech, 19 March 1891, *Abstracts*, pp. 79–80.
[15] See Gidumal (1889). For Gidumal's contribution, see Narain (1972: 140–1).
[16] Scoble's speech, 9 January 1891, *Abstracts*, p. 10.
[17] The Pundit's letter contradicting Scoble was printed in *The Statesman and Friend of India* (hereafter *The Statesman*), weekly edition, 17 January 1891, p. 1. The gaffe was discussed in *The Statesman*, 4 February 1891, p. 1.
[18] Scoble's speech, 19 March 1891, *Abstracts*, pp. 81–2.

The government, moreover, conceived the nature of its initiative in a manner that compromised with the opponents of reform without in any way encouraging its supporters. Partly out of considerations of political expediency, for example, the government was willing to go beyond merely reiterating the policy of colonial non-interference to accommodate the prejudices of orthodox Hindu patriarchy. The colonial initiative was thus deliberately designed to be extremely limited in scope. Scoble stressed that the proposed Bill did not create any 'new offence', but was limited only to amending a provision already existing in the Indian Penal Code. The Viceroy, in his speech to the Legislative Council, was careful to dissociate the limited nature of the Consent Bill from the more comprehensive proposals that were being proposed by Malabari and his London Committee.[19] Malabari, having failed to persuade the Indian Government to undertake legislation to protect child-brides, had taken his campaign to Britain to exert the pressure of British public opinion on the colonial government. On 14 July 1890, Malabari's London Committee, drawing on the support of prominent ex-India hands like Lord Reay, former Governor of Bombay, and C.P. Ilbert, former Law Member of the Government of India, Orientalist scholars like professor Max Mueller, and British feminists like Millicent Fawcett, had issued a resolution urging the Indian Government to undertake reform legislation. The resolution of the London Committee recommended the raising of the age of consent, the ratification of child marriages by law, the repeal of the restitution of conjugal rights imported to India from ecclesiastical law in England, and the further encouragement of widow remarriage through the proper implementation of the Hindu Widow Remarriage Act of 1856.[20] In private letters to the Viceroy, however, prominent British members of Malabari's London Committee, like Northbrook and Reay, drew the Viceroy's attention to their own heroic efforts in diluting Malabari's 'radical' proposals and urged the Viceroy to show similar caution in undertaking any reforms.[21] Furthermore, the logic of colonial masculinity empowered

[19] Viceroy's speech, 9 January 1891, *Abstracts*, pp. 21–4.

[20] Malabari set up a Standing Committee in London at 37 Wimpole Street at the residence of a Mrs Jeune; see *The Pioneer Mail and Indian Weekly News* (hereafter *The Pioneer*), 17 September 1890, p. 356. For the involvement of Fawcett, see *Bengalee*, 29 November 1891, p. 548. For the contribution of the private meeting at Jeune's residence, see *Proceedings*, No. 10. The Committee's Resolution is quoted in Lord Reay to Lansdowne, 1 August 1890, *Lansdowne Papers: Correspondence with Persons in England* (hereafter *Lansdowne England*), January–December 1890, Letter No. 51.

[21] Reay to Lansdowne, 4 July 1890, Letter No. 43; Reay to Lansdowne, 7 August 1890, Letter No. 51; Northbrook to Lansdowne, 7 August 1890, Letter No. 52; Lansdowne to

the arguments of the revivalist–nationalist opponents at the expense of the reformist–nationalist supporters of the Bill. The major nationalist positions on the Consent Bill—in spite of the differences between the reformist support for and revivalist opposition to the Bill—were framed within the politics of colonial masculinity. Even for the most prominent nationalist supporters of the Bill, the autonomy of the domestic realm as the site for native masculinity necessarily competed with any commitment to social reform as the basis for the Bill; they were thus left justifying their support for the Bill by demonstrating that it was sanctioned within Hindu religious principles and entailed no 'new interference' in indigenous practices. Indeed, the colonial mediation of masculinity had produced an acute self-consciousness about accepting colonial legislative interference, as well as providing greater political momentum to the nationalist arguments against the Bill.

The Consent controversy—unlike previous debates on child marriage, which were concerned primarily with the impact of child marriage on the development of the race or on the progress of female education in India—made available alarming statistics on the sexual abuse of child-wives; but for the majority of Indian nationalists the sexual abuse of child-wives was not in itself sufficient as a justification for the Consent Bill. This was especially true in Bengal, where reformist concern for the child-wife was most mediated by the constraints of a colonial politics of masculinity. Apart from the men and women of the Sadharan Brahmo Samaj, the most radical of the reform organizations in Bengal, and their paper the *Sanjivani*, which publicized cases of brutal rape and sexual assault of child-wives to build support for the Consent Bill, the majority of the reformists–nationalists in Bengal were more equivocal in their support for the Bill.[22] Unlike the approximately 150 women in Calcutta (headed by Kadambini Ganguly, the first Indian 'lady doctor' and wife of Sadharan Brahmo leader Dwarkanath Ganguly) who petitioned the government in no uncertain terms to protect the child-wives of India, the majority of the Bengali supporters of the Bill

---

Northbrook, 6 September 1890, Letter No. 58, *Lansdowne England*, January–December 1890.

[22] The Sadharan Brahmo, Dwarkanath Ganguly, who was also assistant secretary of the Indian Association, volunteered an independent endorsement of the Bill because the official response from the Indian Association expressed some reservations about it. See Appendix V, *Proceedings*, No. 38; and his letter to *The Statesman*, 17 January 1891, p. 1. For the isolation of the Sadharan Brahmos in Bengal during the Consent controversy, see also the memoirs of another Sadharan Brahmo, Bipan Chandra Pal (1951: 114–18); also *The Statesman*, 7 March 1891, p. 1. This is also discussed in Engels (1983: 115–20).

were more ambivalent about endorsing colonial legislative interference.[23] Few, at least, were willing to go as far as the women petitioners of Bengal and of other parts of India who stated clearly that 'our sex is solely dependent on the government for the protection of our rights, the necessity for which has been made more urgent by the opposition with which the Bill has met'.[24] The majority of the reformists–nationalists were indeed eager to demonstrate that the Consent Bill did not represent an interference with the social and religious practices of the Hindus. Even one of the most ardent champions of reforming government legislation, Malabari, could not afford to ignore the implications of colonial interference in Indian social and religious matters. In August 1890 in the pages of *The Times*, Malabari justified his proposals by arguing that the legislative initiatives he proposed constituted no 'new interference' in the social and religious practices of the Indians, but merely aimed at getting the government to 'undo the wrong it has [already] done'.[25] Malabari couched his proposals in terms of the need to undo the low age of consent fixed by the government in 1860, the importation of the law for the restitution of conjugal rights from Britain to India, and the loopholes in the Hindu Widow Remarriage Act. Other reformists–nationalists were similarly anxious to establish religious precedence in the Shastras for the changes proposed in the Consent Bill. The basis for this strategy, as Uma Chakravarti has demonstrated, was already well established in the strand within cultural nationalism which justified the reform of oppressive social practices as a return to a pristine 'Golden Age' in which the upper-caste 'Aryan' woman was supposedly free from the degradations suffered by contemporary women (Chakravarti 1990: 27–87).

The major weakness of basing the justification for the Bill on the reformist interpretation of the Shastras—apart from the fact that its 'script for the past' was exclusively Hindu and elitist—was that it already conceded an important point to the opponents of reform: that the preservation of the domestic realm as an autonomous site for native masculinity was the final arbiter for justifying social reform. It was not surprising, therefore, that the reformist position was the weakest in places like Bengal where the objections to 'religious interference' were the strongest. Commenting on the predominantly Bengali aspect of the religious objections to the

---

[23] See *Papers Relating to Act 10 of 1891*, pp. 677–80, cited in Vatsa (1971: 295).

[24] Quoted in Scoble's speech, *Abstracts*, pp. 79–80. For some of the petitions from women's organizations, see *Proceedings*, Nos 31, 54, 55, and 61.

[25] Letter to *The Times* (London), 30 August 1890, p. 13; for other letters, see 20 August 1890, p. 3, and 4 September 1890, p. 12.

Bill, one Anglo-Indian paper pointed out the irony in the non-Brahmin Bengali member of the Legislative Council R.C. Mitter's quoting from the Shastras to oppose the Bill, while the high-caste Brahmin member from Bombay, K.L. Nulkar, found no objections to the Bill in the Shastras.[26] The Bengali opponents argued that the Bill interfered in the Bengali ceremony of *garbhadhan*, or the 'second marriage' that was performed by the upper castes after the actual betrothal ceremony to mark the period when the child-bride was considered ready for sexual intercourse. Conceding, at least in principle, the significance of the garbhadhan argument, Bengali reformers argued that the better educated classes in Bengal rarely performed the garbhadhan ceremony any more and that the Shastras neither enjoined the garbhadhan at the very first menstruation of the child-bride nor prescribed a severe penalty for delaying the ceremony. The Calcutta Committee in Support of the Consent Bill, which consisted of 54 Hindus and 11 Muslims, published a pamphlet entitled *The 'Garbhadhan Vyavastha': Opinion on the Question in Hindu Religion Arising Out of Consent* to demonstrate that the garbhadhanist argument against the Bill was invalid.[27] Similarly in Bombay and Madras, reformists–nationalists, like K.T. Telang, R.G. Bhandarkar, and Raghunath Rao, engaged in highly publicised debates with the religious orthodoxy to demonstrate that the higher age of consent proposed by the Bill conformed with Hindu religious practices.[28] The reformers were backed by the support of the pundits of Benares, the centre of Hindu religious learning; the pundits, under the leadership of Pundit Ram Misra, issued a categorical statement declaring the Consent Bill to be free from any religious objections.[29] The reformers also cited ancient medical authorities such as Sushruta, Charaka, and Agnibes to show that, unlike the latter day interpreters of the Shastras, ancient medical texts supported a higher age at which Indian girls first

---

[26] *Englishman* (Calcutta), 17 January 1891, p. 2. Also, Lansdowne to Cross, 14 January 1891, *Lansdowne Papers: Correspondence with Secretary of State*, from January 1891, Letter No. 2 (hereafter *Lansdowne Sec. of State*).

[27] The pamphlet by Ramnath Tarkaratna and Nilmani Mukherjee was reprinted from the *Reis and Reyyat*; see *Tracts on Indian Marriage Customs 1887–1891*, No. 12 (hereafter *BM Tracts*).

[28] See the debate between Bhandarkar and Tilak on the Shastras, reprinted from *The Times of India* (Bombay), B.G. Tilak, *Express Texts of the Shastras Against the Age of Consent Bill*, and R.G. Bhandarkar, *A Note on the Age of Marriage and its Consummation According to Hindu Law*, in *India Office Library Tracts*, Vol. 711 (hereafter *IOR Tracts*). Also see K.T.T. (Telang), Notes on Consent, *BM Tracts*, No. 13; and N.G. Chandavarkar, The *British Government and Hindu Religious Customs—A Plea for Consent*, *BM Tracts*, No. 10.

[29] Scoble's speech, *Abstracts*, pp. 82–3. Also, Appendix 17, *Proceedings*, No. 60.

menstruated and hence became ready for sexual intercourse. Even the Laws of Manu, the text with arguably the most severe restrictions against women, was mobilized by the pro-reform lobby to show support for a later age of marriage and for consummation of marriage in the Shastras.[30]

So long as the logic of colonial masculinity framed the terms of the Consent controversy, however, it favoured the nationalist opponents over the nationalist supporters of the Bill. If, from one perspective, the reformist–nationalist interpretation of the Shastras reflected a tactical engagement with the strength of the religious objections against the Bill, then, from another, it also reflected a failure to grasp the arbitrary nature of the religious objections in the service of orthodox patriarchal politics. For the religious objections raised against the Bill were bound by neither the constraints of consistency nor logic. The opponents, for example, dismissed the views of the ancient medical authorities cited by the reformists on the grounds that the experience of the ancient authorities was drawn largely from 'up-country' girls; in the hot and humid climate of Bengal, they argued, girls menstruated at a much earlier age (cited in Sen 1980–1: 171). Those references from the Shastras that did not support the arguments of the orthodoxy in Bengal were similarly dismissed on the authority of the sixteenth-century Pundit Raghunandan Siromani, whose interpretation of the Shastras was considered the most authoritative for Bengalis. Raghunandan, it was argued, had clearly laid down that if the garbhadhan was not performed at the first *ritu* (menstruation), then the womb would become impure and children conceived subsequently would be deprived of the right to offer *pinda*s (literally, rice balls) or ritual offerings at the death of their parents.[31] Summing up the impact of the opponents of the Bill in Bengal, Alfred Croft, the Director of Public Instruction in Bengal, noted, 'the *pundits* as a class' had 'pronounced what may be called an official opinion against the provisions of the Bill'.[32]

Still another example of how the logic of colonial masculinity favoured the opponents rather than the supporters of the Bill was evident in the inconsistency of arguments of 'colonial interference'; for such arguments

---

[30] See Nulkar's speech, *Abstracts*, p. 110. Also Kosambi (1991: 1859–60).

[31] For the defence of Raghunandan's interpretation of the garbhadhan, see Appendix 5, from Babu Bhudeb Mookerjee; and for a challenge to the significance of the ritual, see 'Note from Rash Behary Ghose', *Proceedings*, No. 38. Also the pamphlet by Sarat Chandra Some, *Glory Unto Loyalty—An Open Letter to the Empress Not to Interfere With Religion*, BM Tracts, No. 11.

[32] Appendix A 16, *Proceedings*, No. 59. Croft noted that even the famous Bengali reformer Pundit Ishwar Chandra Vidyasagar was opposed to the Bill.

were once again manipulated freely by the opponents of reform in the interests of indigenous patriarchal social relations. This had become apparent, for example, in the Rukmabai case of 1887. Rukmabai, after several years of court battles, had been found guilty by the Bombay High Court of failing to fulfil her conjugal obligations to her husband Dadaji Bhikaji.[33] Sensitive to the impact of a law for the restitution of conjugal rights in cases of non-consensual child-marriage in India, Indian reformers supported Rukmabai's right to live apart from her husband and appealed to the government to repeal the law by which husbands could force their wives to fulfil their conjugal obligations. Since the law was not based on Indian religious texts but had been imported from Christian ecclesiastical law in England, the reformers did not anticipate much religious objection to the change. Nevertheless, the anti-reformist campaign successfully mobilized religious arguments against the change: they produced evidence to demonstrate that suits for the restitution of conjugal rights had their basis in the Shastras. They argued that the colonial law was only providing legal recognition to precepts that were already sanctioned in religion.[34] The further point, as Engels shows, is that in the Rukmabai case revivalists–nationalists—despite all their arguments of native autonomy in religious and domestic affairs—had no compunction in turning to an imported colonial legislation if it served to shore up orthodox indigenous patriarchy (Engels 1989).

The reformist efforts to demonstrate that the Consent Bill did not constitute any 'new interference' in indigenous practices were no match for the highly exaggerated rhetoric of the opponents: the opponents claimed that the Consent Bill represented an unprecedented interference by the colonial authorities that threatened to rend asunder the entire Indian social fabric. The argument that the Consent Bill was the first real breach of Indian autonomy, as Sarkar has suggested, was the core of the revivalists–nationalist strategy against the Bill; it was based on the dubious claim that previous colonial legislations on *sati* (widow immolation), on widow remarriage, and on female infanticide were of much less significance for the autonomy of the Indian social fabric compared to the present legislation that interfered in marriage practices (Sarkar 1993: 1876). The opponents of

---

[33] For the Rukmabai case, see Chandra (1977, 1992).

[34] V.S. Apte, *The Law for the Restitution of Conjugal Rights, IOR Tracts, Vol. 711*; for a dispute between Hindu pundits on whether Section 260 of the Civil Procedure Code, dealing with the restitution of conjugal rights, accorded with Hindu Shastras, see *The Hindu Marriage Question—Correspondence Between R. Raghunath Rao and Pandit Shyamji Krishnavarma, IOR Tracts, Vol. 711.*

the Bill absolved even the previous age of consent legislation of 1860 from the charge of such interference; since the Hindu Shastras themselves did not sanction pre-puberty consummation of child marriage and no Indian girl achieved puberty before 10, the 1860 legislation was considered a dead letter. The increase in the age of consent to 12, however, was presented as a direct interference because Indian girls allegedly attained puberty between the ages of 10 and 12. In interfering with the consummation of child marriage, therefore, the Consent Bill was portrayed as more odious than any previous colonial legislation. The Consent Bill, it was argued, would destroy the entire social and religious fabric of Indian society and reduce 'Indians to the European levels in matters social and religious' by imposing the 'hateful English marriage system' and importing 'the gross sexual vices of Europe into India' (quoted in *Appeal*: 4). The final flourish in the arguments against colonial interference was provided by the 'Indian Magna Carta' or the Queen's Proclamation of 1858, which had committed the colonial government to a policy of non-interference.

Perhaps the crowning irony of the Consent controversy was the fact that, within the logic of colonial masculinity, the reformist–nationalists became more vulnerable—despite all their efforts to present the Bill as sanctioned by the Shastras and as constituting no 'new interference' with indigenous practices—to charges that they were an elite out of touch with the people. It was, in the first place, the anomaly in the social position of the nationalist political leadership as a whole—reformists and revivalists alike—that framed the Consent controversy in the limited terms of colonial masculinity. Yet, although all of the nationalist political leadership was vulnerable to a 'populist' critique for its elite and upper-caste orientation, the terms of colonial masculinity placed the onus of establishing 'proper' indigenous credentials disproportionately on the reformist–nationalist supporters of the Bill. A new alliance of elite groups in Bengal, therefore, coalesced around opposition to the Consent Bill; the alliance was the product of the specious manoeuvring of different factions within the Bengali elite, all equally cut off from a base of popular support. For, as Rajat Ray points out, it was the powerful and orthodox landed magnates of the British Indian Association who allied with the lower middle class and smaller gentry in rural Bengal—whose views were represented in such papers as the *Amrita Bazar Patrika* and the vernacular newspapers the *Bangabasi* and the *Dainik O Samachar Chandrika*—to challenge the reform party identified with the more 'Westernized' and cosmopolitan gentry of the Congress and the Banerjea-led Indian Association in Calcutta (Ray 1984: 89–95, 125–7). The opposition characterized the reformist–nationalist faction in

Bengal as a deracinated elite. When, at a protest meeting against the Bill, the *Maharanee* Sumomoyee—a powerful female zamindar (landlord) of Cossimbazar and a noted philanthropist and patron of a hostel for female medical students in Calcutta—chose to indict Bengali reformers as an elite out of touch with their countrymen, who had 'been to England and returned to their mother country with new-fangled ideas', her indictment was very telling: it pointed out the limits in the social position of not just the nationalist supporters of the Bill but, equally crucially, of the nationalist opponents who launched such critiques.[35]

It was precisely such limits in the position of the revivalist–nationalist opponents of the Bill that were conveniently elided by the mediation of anti-colonial struggle by the politics of masculinity. In thus invigorating the opponents of the Bill over its supporters, colonial masculinity also obscured the greater complicity of the former with the politics of colonial rule. Nothing, therefore, better demonstrates the impact of colonial masculinity in empowering the revivalist–nationalist opposition than the injection of a supposedly 'populist' element in the defence of orthodox Hindu patriarchy. Whereas in the Rukmabai case the anti-reformers were content to invoke the upper-caste strictures on divorce in the Shastras against the customary recognition of divorce among the carpenter caste to which Rukmabai had belonged, the anti-reformers in the Consent controversy found themselves willing not only to validate the weight of local customs over the prescriptions of the Shastras, but also to sympathize with the difficulties of lower-caste men in following the upper-caste prescriptions of the Shastras.[36] This strategic retreat from the Shastras was enabled in part by the recent division in official colonial policy over the respective weight of, on the one hand, the textualized interpretation of Hindu and Muslim religious practices that the colonial authorities had enshrined in the unitary Hindu and Muslim law recognized by the courts, and, on the other, the varied local customs and practices that were not always at one with the textualized codes (Sarkar 1993: 1873; see also Caroll 1983). The opponents of the Bill were concerned less with validating popular or lower-caste customs—which were typically less restrictive for women than the upper-caste prescriptions in the Shastras—than with

---

[35] The Maharani's telegram was sent to the protest meeting organized by the Sovabazar Rajbari; see *The Statesman*, 24 January 1891, p. 4; for her role, also see Dutt (1935: 74–5). Another female zamindar, the Maharanee Bhivasundari of Dighapatia, also organized protest meetings against the Bill; cited in Sen (1980–1: 173).

[36] For the upper-caste argument of revivalists–nationalists during the Rukhmabai case, see Sarkar (1993: 1873).

validating their own interpretations of such upper-caste customs as the garbhadhan even against any interpretation to the contrary derived from the Shastras.

Although the revivalist–nationalist case against the Consent Bill was embedded in upper-caste practices, it did not stop some opponents of the Bill from invoking the special hardships of lower-caste and labouring men to defend their position. A precedent for such a strategy was once again to be found in colonial policy: in his speech to the Legislative Council on 9 January 1891, Lansdowne explained away his reluctance to repeal the law for the restitution of conjugal rights, recommended by Malabari's London Committee, on the grounds that it was a 'poor man's remedy' and of great benefit to the lower classes in India.[37] Taking a chapter out of Lansdowne's speech, some of the orthodox opponents of the Consent Bill claimed to have the interests of the lower castes at heart in opposing the Bill. Their reasoning was based on the confusion regarding the castes and classes that were most guilty of premature consummation of child marriage. It was widely acknowledged that although child marriage itself was prescribed only for the upper castes, its practice was much more widespread: high and low castes as well as Muslims and other communities practised some form of child marriage. There was less agreement, however, on the question of which castes and class routinely practised premature consummation of child marriage. H.H. Risley, an Anglo-Indian ethnologist, argued that child marriage and premature consummation in Bengal was more or less confined to the Bengali upper castes and that lower-caste Gops and Bagdis were free from such practices.[38] Other officials consulted by the government reported that, unlike child marriage, the practice of 'consummating marriage before girls attain puberty' was 'more prevalent among the lower than the higher castes'.[39] Mitter, in his Note of Dissent to the Report of the Select Committee, to oppose the Bill invoked the special hardship that the Consent Bill imposed on poor and lower-caste men. Quoting from a pamphlet entitled *The Sisters of Phulmani (or the Child Wives of India)* by T.N. Mukharji (1890), Mitter presented the case against the Consent Bill thus:

We must not overlook what would be the hard case of thousands of males, chiefly of the low castes. These poor fellows possessing only one little hovel, have to live alone with their

---

[37] *Abstracts*, pp. 21–4; also Lansdowne to Benjamin Jowett, 3 February 1891, *Lansdowne England*, From January 1891, Letter No. 15. For the use of such suits in litigation, see Masselos (1992).

[38] Quoted in *The Statesman*, 10 January 1891, p. 3.

[39] Cited in *Abstracts*, p. 78.

child wives because under the existing marriage system they have no chance of procuring grown-up girls recognized by law as adults. All in a day the law will not turn them into saints and it might blight their young lives by seven years imprisonment with hard labour for one single instance of momentary weakness under one of the most trying temptations to which flesh is subject.[40]

The impact of colonial masculinity, therefore, added to the potency of the protest against the Bill: it not only empowered the nationalist opponents over the supporters of the Bill, but also, in the process of empowering the opposition, obscured the level of colonial complicity with the opposition against the Bill.

Insofar as the protests against the Consent Bill came to be identified with militant nationalism, therefore, their impact was to recuperate the anti-colonial challenge of the nationalist movement. A nascent elite nationalist leadership, trying to consolidate itself more sharply against colonial rule, could not, because of the contradictions of its own social position, fail to be impressed by the demonstrable proof of public support mobilized by the opponents of the Bill; the price of succumbing to this appeal, however, was not just the consolidation of the nationalist movement around an unreconstructed patriarchal politics, but also the bringing of nationalist politics in closer harmony with a colonial agenda. For the very impressiveness of the protests against the Bill was marked by greater complicity with a certain colonial politics. The protest meetings against the Bill in Bengal invariably drew much larger crowds than the meetings organized in support of the Bill (Natarajan 1962: 84; also see Narain 1970–1). The 'circus-like' atmosphere at the infamous protest meeting in the Calcutta Maidan on 25 February 1891 attracted an unprecedented crowd from Calcutta and the suburbs for any public meeting in Bengal.[41] The protest meetings, as Amiya Sen's account of Hindu revivalism in the Consent controversy demonstrates, were usually organized by local religious bodies that raised the cry of 'religion in danger' to swell the numbers at the meetings; but the meetings typically attracted crowds made up of different religious denominations, including Hindus, Jains, and Buddhists, as well as Muslims from Calcutta and its surrounding suburbs.[42] The predominantly Hindu religious objections against the Bill, therefore, did not preclude

---

[40] R.C. Mitter, Note of Dissent, *Proceedings*, No. 63. Mitter was quoting from Mukharji (1890: 20–1).

[41] *Bangabasi*, 25 February 1891; *Report on the Bengal Native Press* (hereafter *RNBP*), 1891, Vol. 17, No. 2.

[42] I am drawing from Amiya Sen's account of the impressive strength of the Hindu revivalist agitation against the Bill. See Sen (1980–1, esp. pp. 170–5).

sympathy for the opposition from the public opinion of different religious orthodoxies. Despite efforts of many in the Muslim community to demonstrate that the Bill did not have any bearing on Islamic religious prescriptions, the public opinion in the Muslim community was more divided on the Bill. There was some prominent Muslim support for the Bill: the Muslim members of the Viceroy's Legislative Council supported the Consent Bill; the Secretary of the Muhammedan Literary Society in Calcutta published a pamphlet entitled *A Practical View of the Consent Act for the Benefit of the Mahomedan Community in General* to assure the Muslim community that the Bill did not affect Muslim religious practices. But the *Sudhakar*, a Muslim vernacular newspaper in Bengal, as well as the Central National Mahomedan Association in Calcutta, expressed criticism of the Muslim members of the Council and of Muslim organizations that supported the Bill.[43] Another measure of the popularity of the opposition was the large circulation enjoyed by anti-Bill newspapers in Bengal: of the vernacular newspapers, the anti-Bill newspaper the *Bangabasi* had the highest annual subscription at 20,000 compared to the 4,000 subscription of the pro-Bill *Sanjivani*; the English-language weekly the *Amrita Bazar Patrika* was converted from a weekly to a daily to represent the opposition that was not adequately represented in the two prominent native English-language newspapers of Calcutta, the *Bengalee* and the *Indian Mirror*.[44] Such indeed was the paradoxical role of colonial masculinity that at one and the same time it empowered the opposition against the Bill as nationalist and accommodated it to colonial interests.

Another indication that the agitation against the Bill was less than unalloyed nationalism was that its success in fact depended upon the intersection of the nationalist perception of a 'crisis' of Indian/Bengali masculinity with a growing perception in Britain of a 'crisis' of British masculinity. The responses to these crises were different and even contradictory in India and in Britain; but they intersected—albeit in uneven ways—to reframe the Consent controversy as a referendum on native masculinity. For if one context for the response of the colonial authorities to the Consent Bill was dictated by political expediency and the fear of

---

[43] For Abdool Luteef's pamphlet on behalf of the Muhammedan Literary Society, see *BM Tracts*, No. 5. For Muslim opposition to the Bill, see *Sudhakar*, 13 February 1891; *RNBP*, No. 8; and Lansdowne to Reay, 14 January 1891, *Lansdowne England*, From January 1891, Letter No. 7. The Calcutta-based Muslim paper, *Ahmadi*, was also against the Bill. See Narain (1970–1: 14).

[44] Extract from *Amrita Bazar Patrika* (Calcutta), 9 August 1890, *Proceedings*, No. 5. For the tremendous popularity of the *Bangabasi*, see Banerjee (1968).

arousing anti-government feeling from the orthodox Hindu community in India, then another was dictated by the anti-feminist backlash in Britain: both produced greater tolerance for patriarchal institutions in India. There was considerable masculinist anxiety in Britain following the gradual reconstitution of the traditional male public sphere in response to such feminist challenges as the activities of Josephine Butler and the Ladies' National Association for the repeal of the Contagious Diseases Acts in the 1880s and the feminist and purity crusades for the passage of the British Criminal Amendment Act of 1885.[45] This anxiety had its counterpart in the growing admiration for the merits of child marriage in the writings of several late nineteenth-century commentators in Britain. Whereas professor Max Mueller, as a member of Malabari's London Committee, was willing to endorse a limited reform of Indian marriage practices, he also published the same year an essentially celebratory account of child marriage in India.[46] The words of a special correspondent of *The Times*, who wrote a three-part series on 'Child Marriage and Enforced Widowhood' to support Malabari's London campaign, bears quoting at some length:

> For more than a thousand years the supreme need of Hindu women was not independence, but safety. To meet this supreme need the Hindoo marriage system was developed into a powerfully constructed organisation of protection—a system which endeavoured to give the maximum security to Hindoo women as a whole, and which deliberately acted on the principle that their general safety must be insured, even at the cost of hardships to individuals among them. It assured to every woman the protection of a lawful husband and the legal status of wife; and it also assured her of that protection and status as soon as she achieved physical maturity.[47]

For W.W. Hunter, *The Times*' special correspondent, the main objective in reforming Indian marriage practices was clear: 'how to secure for wives and daughters the *old safety of dependence* with a larger measure of the freedom of modern independence' (emphasis added).[48] By conceding merit to the arguments of orthodox Hindus who cited 'statistics of prostitution in Europe' against adult marriages in India, moreover, Hunter was far from sanguine about the value of his cause. Insofar as Hunter was considered one of the more vocal Anglo-Indian friends of social reform in India, his

---

[45] See Walkowitz (1980, 1992). Also see Ryan (1990). For the changes in the construction of 'masculinity', see Hearn (1992).

[46] Mueller (1891). For a discussion of the admiration of Indian patriarchal institutions in Englishwomen's writings on India during this period, see Nair (1990, esp. pp. 18–21).

[47] Part 1, *The Times*, 13 September 1890, p. 8.

[48] See Part 3, *The Times*, 7 October, 1890, p. 8. The identity of the author is mentioned in the *Bengalee*, 11 October 1890, p. 486. Also cited in Kosambi (1991: 1860).

attitude is instructive. The ambivalence towards the Consent Bill in Britain was nicely summed up in the following comment on the Indian Consent controversy: 'England has as much to learn from India [about the control of women?] as she has to teach that country' (quoted in Kosambi 1991: 1864).

Nowhere, however, was the anti-feminist context for the British response to the Indian Consent Bill more apparent than in the stand taken by the *Saint James Gazette* of London. The *Saint James Gazette*, which defended aristocratic male privileges against feminist challenges during the debate on the Criminal Amendment Act or the British Consent Act of 1885, was also an outspoken critic of the Indian Consent Bill.[49] The paper drew a parallel between the discomfort of orthodox Hindus towards the Indian Consent Bill and its own discomfort at the growing political visibility of single and independent women in Britain: 'what will the English friends of the Indian child wife say if some acute Hindoo moves a resolution denouncing London society on account of the superabundance of unmarried ladies in Kensington? We Hindoos manage these things better, he would argue, very much better in Bengal.'[50] The paper went on to justify the Indian opposition to the Consent Act:

> It is perfectly clear that the strongest and best native opinion is against the Age of Consent Bill promoted in London drawing rooms and praised by globe trotting philanthropists.... And it is tolerably certain that the rite of child marriage is, in fact, so rarely abused that our consciences need not be very sorely vexed about enormities which we cannot abolish. The most important and significant point is that the women of India are against a Bill professing to protect them.[51]

This was written after at least one newspaper in Britain, *The Times*, carried information about a petition from approximately 2,000 'women living in India' to Queen Victoria in support of raising the age of consent for Indian women.[52] Members of the Legislative Council in India quoted similar petitions in support of the Bill received by the Government of India from

---

[49] I am grateful to Professor Walkowitz for drawing my attention to this connection. The paper was also an outspoken critic of the Indian National Congress in India. For mention of its role in the Consent controversy in Britain, see Pearson (1972: 156).

[50] *Saint James Gazette* (London), 20 January 1891, p. 4.

[51] Ibid., 2 March 1891, p. 4. The *Dainik O Samachar Chandrika* was pleased to note the *Saint James Gazette*'s support to the opposition, 12 September 1890, *RNBP* 1890.

[52] *The Times*, 13 January 1891, quoted in *English Opinion on India: A Monthly Magazine Containing Select Extracts from English Newspapers on Indian Subjects*, No. 2 of March 1891 (hereafter *English Opinion*). The petition signed by approximately 1,600 'women living in India' was sent in December 1890; see Appendix N, *Proceedings*, No. 31; also *India, Home Department, Judicial, February 1891*, Nos 155–159A.

Indian women in Ahmedabad, Calcutta, Bombay, Lahore, Poona, and Mymensingh.[53]

The highly publicized criticisms in Britain of the Government of India for undertaking the Consent Bill provided valuable support for the Indian opponents of the Bill. Sir George Birdwood, a retired senior Anglo-Indian official, wrote a series of letters to *The Times*, criticizing the government initiative; he concluded that 'Hindu family life was of a very high order' and did not require government interference.[54] For Dr Richard Congreve, the High-Priest of Positivism in England, the Consent legislation raised important questions about Indian cultural autonomy: 'with the usual feeling of superiority,' he wrote, 'instead of mending ourselves we are but too anxious to intrude our crude actions on others as necessary reforms'.[55] The most vigorous champion of Hindu orthodoxy in Britain during the Consent controversy was Frederic Pincott, whose article 'Hindu Marriage Agitation' in the *National Review* bolstered all of the arguments of the orthodox Hindu opponents of the Consent Bill. So sensitive was Pincott about respecting the 'prejudices of [the] people' that he promised his services to Hindu revivalists to continue the agitation against the consent regulations in Britain after the Consent Bill was passed in India.[56]

Colonial politics, however, mediated the crisis of British masculinity very differently in India. Whereas in Britain the sympathy for the orthodox Hindu opposition to the Bill was expressed freely in public, the Anglo-Indians in India were obliged to express greater unanimity for the government-sponsored Bill. Although some Anglo-Indians in India, including senior officials, did convey reservations about the Bill in private communications, the Viceroy strongly discouraged any impression in public that there were doubts about the Bill among senior government officials.[57] The Anglo-Indian paper *The Statesman* attributed the relative unanimity of Anglo-Indian public opinion in India to the recent

---

[53] *Abstracts*, pp. 79–80, 125.

[54] *The Times*, 11 February 1891, p. 4.

[55] Quoted in *Appeal*, p. 40. His support was welcomed by Bengali Positivists in Calcutta; Jogendra Chundra Ghosh, one of the most famous Bengali Positivists, was the author of an anti–Consent Bill pamphlet, *Listen Slowly. Age of Consent, BM Tracts*, No. 14. For the impact of Positivism in Bengal, see Forbes (1975).

[56] Cited in *Amrita Bazar Patrika*, 9 November 1891, p. 3; 1 September 1891, p. 2; 25 August 1891, p. 2.

[57] Lansdowne expressed his displeasure at the prospect of the new Lt Governor of Bengal appearing less than enthusiastic about the Bill; see Lansdowne to Scoble, 21 February 1891, *Lansdowne India*, January–June 1891, Letter No. 144. For dissenting opinions from senior government officials, see Lord Connemara (Governor of Madras) to

changes in the political climate: the ex-India hands in Britain, who were typically members of a pre-Congress generation, felt free to express their reservations about the Bill, but Anglo-Indians in India could not afford to miss the opportunity to embarrass Indian political leaders. In the words of *The Statesman*:

> The advocacy of W. W. Hunter and the English Committee [for the Consent Bill] would have had a dividing effect [on Anglo-India] earlier. Nothing has occurred to modify materially the inner convictions of Anglo-India on such points as these, [but] something has occurred to lead them very generally to subordinate those convictions to considerations of another kind; and that something is the Congress movement. In the opposition to the Bill (embracing as it did some educated Bengalis), [Anglo-Indians in India] saw an unrivalled opportunity to discredit the Congress in the eyes of the public at home. To do this they sink all differences about the Bill among themselves and represent its merits in the strongest possible light, as something which no one with any pretensions to true enlightenment could possibly have any doubt about.[58]

The Anglo-Indian case in India was helped by the position adopted by the Indian National Congress, the most prominent of the Indian political organizations: even though the General Secretary, A.O. Hume, privately assured the Viceroy that at least four-fifths of the Congress members were secretly in favour of the Bill, the Congress refrained from giving an official opinion on the Bill.[59] The fact that prominent Bengali Congressmen, like Banerjea and W.C. Bonnerjee, did not rally behind the government to support the Consent Bill gave Anglo-Indian public opinion further ammunition to attack the political aspirations of Indian politicians. The *Englishman* of Calcutta questioned the 'impossible schemes for the reform of the Indian government' promoted by the educated class in Bengal when these same groups were indifferent to 'the social problems that await solution in their country as they are pleased to call India'.[60] The cynical manipulation of the Consent controversy was openly acknowledged in the pages of the *Daily Chronicle* in London, which pointed out that Indian

---

Lansdowne, 23 October 1890, *Lansdowne India*, July–December 1890, Letter No. 313. Also *Proceedings*, Nos 38, 47, and 51.

[58] *The Statesman*, 21 March 1891, p. 1.

[59] Quoted in *Englishman*, 11 February 1891, p 4. Also, Hume to Lansdowne, 10 February 1891, *Lansdowne India*, January–June 1891, Letter No. 159.

[60] *Englishman*, 21 July 1890, p. 7; 23 February 1891, p. 4. *The Pioneer*, 12 February 1891, p. 199. Rudyard Kipling wrote in the *Contemporary Review* in September 1890 of Indian political leaders: 'they talk about the cow but the protection of women is a new and dangerous idea', quoted in *Bengalee*, 27 September 1891, p. 461. Lansdowne was obviously disappointed not to receive the support of Congress stalwarts like Banerjea and Bonnerjee on the Bill (Lansdowne to Ilbert, 4 February 1891, *Lansdowne England*, from January 1891, Letter No. 16).

opposition to the Bill was 'useful in a way' because it served to discredit thoroughly Indian political aspirations.[61]

It was thus in the context of the political climate of India that Anglo-Indian public opinion turned to the colonial distinction—by now profoundly over-determined—between 'manly' and 'effeminate' natives. They used this distinction to mediate between the imperatives of an embattled British masculinity and support for the Indian Consent Bill. Despite the more unanimous support for the Consent Bill among Anglo-Indians in India, therefore, the distinction made by colonial officials between the practice of child marriage among 'manly' natives and the practice of premature consummation of child marriage among 'effeminate' natives preserved a certain ambivalence towards the reform of orthodox Hindu patriarchy. This distinction both limited the nature of the challenge to orthodox Hindu patriarchy and associated the challenge more narrowly with the 'effeminacy' of the Bengali male. When Lansdowne sent Scoble's proposals for comment to local officials in 1890, the reports of the colonial officials underscored the difference between child marriage as it was practised among the 'manlier' races of India and the premature consummation of child marriage as practised among the 'effeminate' Bengalis. The Lt Governor of Bengal, Steuart Bayly, reported as follows:

It is a general practice for Hindu girls after they are married but before puberty is even indicated, much less established, to be subjected to more or less frequent acts of connection with their husbands. The custom appears to be widespread.... [It] prevails generally over Bengal Proper, especially over Eastern and Central Bengal. It does not extend generally to Behar, nor is it prevalent in Orissa, and the aboriginal tribes are apparently free from it.[62]

It was more widely held among Anglo-Indians that in the Punjab, where 'the work of women in the fields was valuable', a father, 'though marrying his daughters off before puberty, after ancient custom, would keep them from their husbands' house as long as possible'.[63]

The image of native effeminacy did in fact perform an important ideological function in the Consent controversy: the distinction between the results of premature consummation and of child marriage was used to reinforce colonial contempt for the class from which came most of India's nationalist politicians and intellectuals as well as to limit the full implications of the brutal murder of Phulmani. The work of Risley, the

---

[61] *Daily Chronicle* (London), 3 January 1891, quoted in *English Opinion*, No. 2, March 1891.

[62] Bayly's views were collected in August 1890; quoted by Scoble, *Abstracts*, p. 10.

[63] This was to become the dominant Anglo-Indian view on the impact of child marriage in India; see Steel (1929: 161).

well-known amateur ethnologist of the Bengal Civil Service, provided the scientific basis for distinguishing between child marriage and premature consummation of child marriage: 'in different parts of India', he argued, 'infant marriage prevails in two widely different forms, one of which is at least free from physiological objections, while the other deserves, from every point of view the strongest condemnation' (Risley 1908: 185). In an article in *Blackwood's Magazine* in December 1890, Risley commented on the impact that the two systems of child marriage had on the physique of the people of India:

as we leave the great recruiting ground of the Indian Army and travel south eastward along the plains of the Ganges, the healthy sense which bid the warrior races to keep their girls at home until they are fit to bear the burden of maternity, seems to have been cast out by the demon of corrupt ceremonialism ever ready to sacrifice helpless women and children to the traditions of fancied orthodoxy.[64]

Risley's opinions were confirmed by other Anglo-Indian officials with ethnological experience, like Denizel Ibbetson, who argued that, at least in the Punjab, child marriage was free from the harmful effects found in Bengal: 'No one who has seen a Punjabi regiment march past, or has watched the sturdy Jat women lift their heavy water jars at the village well, is likely to have any misgivings as to the effect of the marriage system on the physique of the race' (quoted in Risley 1908: 185). The focus on native effeminacy thus restricted the Consent controversy to a referendum on native masculinity in which the physical and moral deterioration of the race occupied at least as much attention as the sexual abuse of child-wives.

The stereotype of Bengali effeminacy during the Consent controversy, moreover, drew its strength precisely from the varied contexts in which the discourses of masculinity were deployed. One context for Bengali effeminacy was the political climate in India; it suggested connections with the distinctions Anglo-Indian public opinion made between 'loyal' and 'disloyal' natives. *The Pioneer* concluded of the Indian responses to the Consent Bill: the 'agitation which has been set on foot will not command the sympathy of the more manly races which are free from the outrage upon child wives'.[65] The Private Secretary to the Viceroy expressed relief that the public protests against the Consent Bill were confined mainly to the 'effeminate' native races; commenting on a circular advertising a protest meeting to be held in Calcutta, he wrote that 'a less timid race might have been aroused to acts of violence by the exaggerations

[64] Quoted in *The Statesman*, 19 January 1891, p. 3.7.
[65] *The Pioneer*, 29 January 1891, pp. 134–5.

and misrepresentations of this Circular'.⁶⁶ Another context for Bengali effeminacy suggests connections with what Jeffrey Weeks has identified as a new development in scientific and medical discourses in the late nineteenth century: the emergence of the concept of the homosexual (Weeks 1977, 1981, 1991). The tone, however tentative, was set in the link between sexuality and 'unmanliness' suggested by the *Indian Medical Gazette*: early sexual intercourse among Bengalis was linked to 'physical deterioration', 'effeminacy', 'mental imperfection', and 'moral debility'.⁶⁷ A more direct allusion to popular theories of the aetiology of homosexuality was suggested in the discussion of masturbation and its consequences for the effeminacy of the Bengali male.⁶⁸ Hume, who was not unsympathetic to the political aspirations of the educated community in India, found in the prevalence of masturbation among Bengali men the connection between early sexual intercourse and their physical and moral debility. According to Hume, therefore, the 'disgusting habit' of masturbation which was 'one of the reflex consequences of the premature sexuality engendered by the early marriage and consummation system' had become 'universal in Lower Bengal'.⁶⁹ He further stated that the answer to the question why 'diabetes is so prevalent amongst all Bengalis' is to be found not in the Bengali diet of rice but in the Bengali vice of masturbation.

The most telling example of the overdetermined context for 'Bengali effeminacy', however, was the popular colonial accusation that Bengali 'manhood' had succumbed to the undue influence of Bengali women by opposing the Consent Bill. This view was supported by the belief, common among many a 'manly' Anglo-Indian and Indian official alike, that it was the female members of the Indian household who were chiefly responsible for encouraging the 'scandal' of the premature consummation of child marriage. Older female relatives, it was argued, took tremendous delight in encouraging sexual intimacy between a young couple.⁷⁰ The Bengali man's effeminacy, therefore, was attributed to the inability of Bengali

---

⁶⁶ 3 March 1891, *Lansdowne Sec. of State*, from January 1891, Letter No. 26.

⁶⁷ September 1890, *Proceedings*, No. 3. For the links between 'unmanliness' and 'homosexuality' in popular perceptions, see Hilliard (1982).

⁶⁸ For popular attitudes that linked masturbation with homosexuality, see Neuman (1975); Bullough and Voght (1973). For the Anglo-Indian belief that Indian men were particularly prone to masturbation, see Ganga Din, *The Young Man's Guide: Medical Companion*, p. 12, in IOR Tracts, Vol. 735.

⁶⁹ Hume to Lansdowne, 10 February 1891, *Lansdowne India*, January–June 1891, Letter No. 159.

⁷⁰ Bayly to Lansdowne, 5 October 1890, *Lansdowne India*, July–December 1890, Letter 257. Also see letter to *Bengalee*, 31 January 1891, p. 53.

men to stand up to the recalcitrant women of their families. In a letter to *The Statesman*, Hume declared that Indians 'who know or think, that their womankind will not abandon [their role in encouraging premature consummation of child marriage] and who are not *masters of their own houses*' are behind the opposition to the Bill (emphasis added).[71]

It is thus in such an overdetermined context for native effeminacy that the revitalized Indian masculinity in the opposition to the Consent Bill appears in its full ambiguity: much more closely allied to the context of an embattled British masculinity than at first appears. B.G. Tilak, one of the most prominent nationalist opponents of the Bill, responded to Hume's portrait of the Indian opponents as inadequate 'masters of their own houses' by questioning the masculinity of Indian reformers who, because they were unable to 'manage their [own] household affairs', had appealed to the government for help.[72] The *Mahratta*, edited by Tilak, commented that it was the Indian reformers who were 'unmanly' because they had shown themselves to be 'so helpless as not to be able to protect their daughters from their sons-in-law or their daughters-in-law from their own sons'; instead, they 'pray Government to keep a watch in their private rooms'.[73] So long as the colonial legislature was unrepresentative of Indian public opinion, the opponents of the Bill argued, the support that Indian men demonstrated for government legislation was a symbol of effeminacy and not of masculinity. Despite the fact it was based on a fierce opposition to the Consent Bill, the revitalized Indian masculinity did in fact converge quite nicely with colonial apprehensions about challenges to British masculinity.

That the nationalist triumph claimed on behalf of the revitalized Indian masculinity was based on a disregard of the plight of the child-wife is perhaps an obvious point; but the further point is that the revitalized Indian masculinity was scarcely even a nationalist triumph. The apparent resurgence, indeed, was based on its greater affinities with the agenda of colonial rule. For it was the uneven ways in which colonial politics mediated the crises of British and Indian masculinities that allowed revivalists–nationalists to claim their revitalized Indian masculinity as an unambiguous nationalist triumph: a supposed reversal of the colonial emasculation of the Indian male. This was evident, for example, in the apparent victory of the revivalist–nationalist challenge to one of the

---

[71] *The Statesman*, 31 January 1891, p. 1.
[72] *Mahratta*, 12 April 1891, *Report on Bombay Native Press*, 1891.
[73] Ibid.

favourite colonial arguments: the eugenics-based distinction between child marriage and premature consummation for the physical and moral development of the race. The Standing Committee of the Sobhabajar protest meeting in Calcutta published a document with medical evidence from 34 Indian medical practitioners and one Anglo-Indian surgeon, Major J.F.P. McConnell, the Medical Inspector of Emigrants, to refute the connection that the advocates of the Bill made between early sexual intercourse and racial deterioration. Contradicting the dominant Anglo-Indian medical establishment, Dr Juggobandhu Bose of Calcutta University declared that there was no medical proof to establish that early childbirth hindered the development of an organism and so caused a permanent injury to the physical development of either the mother or the offspring.[74] Taking up this logic, Raja Rajendra Lala Mitra, the president of the Asiatic Society of Bengal, informed the Chief Secretary of the Government of India that the link that was being drawn between early sexual intercourse and the physical weakness of the race was at best 'pseudo-scientific':

In the case of racial determination the reporters who have written on the subject are peculiarly unscientific. In a question of biology, or physiology, every thing must depend on statistical information and in this respect we have not a single fact to show that like mortal sin, improper consumption is visited in the race several generations after the first offender.[75]

Nabogopal Mitter, the editor of the *National Paper* and the founder of the National Training Academy for the physical development of Bengali youth, provided further concrete examples of young Bengali married men from his academy who had impressed even Europeans with their physical prowess.[76] Others, while conceding that the Bengali male had become physically enervated, argued that to emphasize only the physiological circumstances for the physical development of the race would be to apply the 'laws of cattle breeding' to human beings. The editor of *Hope*, an anti-reform paper in Bengal, put it thus: 'the forces which lie at the root of racial development are so many and varied, the intellectual and moral ones presumably predominant in the case of man, who is more a spiritual

---

[74] The most detailed medical argument against the Bill was presented by the Standing Committee of the Sobhabajar meeting in Bengal. See *Full Proceedings of a Public Meeting Held on 22 January 1891 to Protest Consent Bill, BM Tracts*, No. 4. Dr Juggobandhu Bose, a distinguished MD of Calcutta University, was the most active in leading the rebuttal against the medical arguments for the Bill; see *Appeal*, pp. 2–3.

[75] Appendix 5, 7 February 1891, *Proceedings*, No. 38. Also see Ray (1975: 283–6).

[76] Cited in *The Statesman*, 14 March 1891, p. 1.

and moral being than an animal for purposes of exhibition'.[77] In any case, as the revivalists–nationalists argued with the impeccable logic of colonial masculinity, a government that still adhered to the Arms Act and persisted in refusing to enrol Bengalis as volunteers could hardly be credited for showing concern about the 'conversion of Indians into a nation of sturdy men'.[78]...

...The best indication of the ambiguous nature of the agitation against the Indian Consent Bill was in the complex and contradictory impact of the British Consent debate on the consent debate in India: the efforts to recuperate the feminist challenges to British masculinity converged with the revivalist–nationalist efforts to reassert Indian masculinity. Each reinforced the other by limiting and narrowing the terms of the Indian Consent debate. Following on the heels of the British Consent debate, the debate over female consent in India became a means of containing any radical potential in the redefinition of female consent. In Britain, the feminist and purity crusaders—who were provoked by sensationalized cases of child prostitution—mobilized women as a group in the British Consent debate of 1885 to define a new public discourse of sexuality. The mobilization of women by the purity movement was undoubtedly limited and contradictory: it paved the way, as various scholars have pointed out, for the involvement of middle-class women in social regulation and class-disciplining in Britain. Yet the moral discourse of purity in the British consent debate, as Frank Mort among others has suggested, was a 'battleground on which conflicting aims and intentions struggled for space': it opened the way, on the one hand, for further coercive regulations of sexuality; on the other hand, it also provided for middle-class women's challenges to male sexual double standards and for a definition, however limited, of their own image of female sexuality (Mort 1987: 126; also see Gorham 1978; Walkowitz 1982).

It was precisely the recuperation of this possible redefinition of female consent and female sexuality in Britain that made allies out of colonial and orthodox indigenous interests in limiting the terms of the Indian Consent debate. When the purity movement confronted directly the context of marital sexual relations in the Indian Consent debate, therefore, its contradictions in reconstituting patriarchal privileges were more thoroughly exposed. For, as we have seen, the British Consent debate not only retained but reinforced the irrelevance of female consent within

---

[77] Quoted in *The Statesman*, 31 January 1891, p. 1.
[78] *Sakti*, 10 February 1891; *RNBP* 1891, No. 8.

marriage for British women. The more crucial point, however, is that the challenge of the British Consent debate was recuperated in the revitalized colonial masculinity of the Indian Consent debate. If an important contribution of the purity crusaders in Britain, as Mort points out, was their intervention in 'speaking out' about sex, the opposite was true in the contributions of the colonial advocates of the Indian Consent Bill. In the dialogue between 'puritanical' reformers and the Hindu orthodoxy, for example, their significant disagreements did not mask their shared investment in the logic of colonial masculinity. According to the Bengali orthodoxy, as Engels points out, moral purity was a matter of ensuring male control of female sexuality. The view was expressed in the pages of the *Bangabasi*, a staunch opponent of the Consent Bill; it predicted a terrible scenario of 'females in groups hurrying from door to door begging males to gratify their lust' if the Bill were passed.[79] More dire consequences were predicted by a pundit of the *Hindu Sabha* who believed that a wife was bound to 'go astray' if she was 'in heat' and her husband did not satisfy her, just as her husband would 'go astray' if his wife 'who has attained her puberty, that is accessible in the provision of nature, cannot cohabit with him'.[80]

Although 'puritanical' opinion in the Indian Consent controversy did counter the male sexual double standard in the orthodox Hindu view, it nevertheless also discouraged 'speaking out' about sexuality, which could pose a challenge, however limited, to male prerogatives. On the one hand, for example, *The Pioneer* lambasted Mitter for criticizing the advocates of the Consent Bill for excessive 'sexual moralism'. The paper pointed out that Mitter's arguments for a more lenient attitude towards sexual intercourse between a young couple was nothing but the 'selfish gratification of voluptuous men'; it countered Mitter's charge of 'puritanism' with the argument that 'male persons are bound to exercise self restraint in this matter [and all] truly civilized persons [could not condone the] self indulgence excused by Mitter'.[81] On the other hand, however, *The Pioneer*, along with other Anglo-Indian papers, was equally critical of any public

---

[79] *Bangabasi*, 7 March 1891; *RNBP* 1891, No. 1.

[80] Appendix M, A. Sankariah, President Founder Hindu Sabha, Trichoor, *Proceedings*, No. 30. Also see reference to the pamphlet *Ain! Ain!!Ain!!! Bhayanak Bipad!! Sarbanaser Katha!!! Kamalkamini o Sureshbhamanir Kathopkathan* (*Oh! Oh!! Oh!!! Terrible Calamity!! Tale of Destruction!!! Dialogue between Kamalkamini and Sureshbhamini*), cited in Borthwick (1984: 127); and also Sircar (1891).

[81] *The Pioneer*, 26 March 1891, p. 396. Also *The Statesman*, 17 January 1891, p. 1. For a more successful deployment of a 'purity' argument for child marriage reforms in the 1920s and 1930s, see Sinha (1995).

discussion of sex. Much of the criticism was directed at 'Hindu women' who supposedly 'delighted' in talking about sexual practices:

> such is the debased atmosphere of the domestic life in which Hindu women move that they are aware of no impropriety in openly discussing subjects, the merest mention of which a more enlightened civilization would lead them to shun. The much talked of 'garbhadan' ceremony is to them a subject of delighted conversation.... The subject of the garbhadan ceremony is too odious for description in a newspaper read in respectable households.[82]

For Lionel Ashburner of the Bengal Civil Service, it was the Indian widows who were the 'chartered libertines' who 'declined to be reformed by philanthropic legislation and thus relinquish the Bohemian freedom of an amateur member of the "Demi Monde"!' (cited in Narain 1970–1: 20, n32).

The surprisingly limited terms of the debate on female sexuality in the Indian Consent controversy are best reflected in the similarity between two opposite responses to the Bill: one by the Bengali *Brahmo* reformer, P.C. Majoomdar, who supported the Bill; and the other by the Bengali Christian Inspector of Girl's Schools in Calcutta, Manhomini Wheeler, who opposed it. Majoomdar favoured the Consent Bill, but was opposed to adult marriages. In fact, he supported the Consent Bill precisely because it did not directly challenge child marriages. The Consent Bill could prevent 'familiarity with sex'—which he believed was responsible for polluting the imagination of Bengali boys in early youth—without risking the sexual immorality attendant with allowing men and women to marry at a later age.[83] In contrast, Wheeler was opposed to the Consent Bill, but favoured a law to prohibit or discourage child marriage. In two separate letters to the Lt Governor of Bengal, she recorded her dissent against the Bill for encouraging sexual immorality among girls. Since 'continence is not in (the) blood' of Bengali girls, she argued, the prohibition against consummation cannot be enforced without first prohibiting child marriage.[84]

The Indian Consent debate reveals much more in common between the Indian opponents of the Bill and its colonial advocates than has been assumed from the bitterness of their conflict. For, together their efforts to offer a revitalized colonial masculinity served to marginalize the public contributions of Indian women as a group. The dominant debate on the Consent Bill, as Anagol–McGinn has demonstrated, ignored the 'gendered critique for the raising of the age of consent' expressed in Indian women's journals and in their support for the Consent Bill in petitions and in separate

---

[82] *The Pioneer*, 26 March 1891, p. 396.

[83] Quoted in *The Pioneer*, 19 March 1891, p. 359.

[84] Wheeler's letters of 2 March and 3 March 1891 are quoted in Elliott to Lansdowne, 6 March 1891, *Lansdowne India*, January–June 1891, Letter No. 232.

public meetings, at least in the Bombay Presidency (Anagol–McGinn 1992: 106). The perspective of Indian women was largely overwhelmed by the claims of colonial masculinity that recuperated the implications of redefining female consent in an imperial social formation. Indian women activists, like Pandita Ramabai and Rakhmabai Modak, organized women in support of the Consent Bill in Poona and Bombay respectively; many prominent male advocates of the Bill even acknowledged the contributions of Indian women in supporting the Bill. Yet the very logic of a revitalized politics of masculinity rested on the erasure of the public contributions of Indian women as a group; as the *Liverpool Post* in Britain wrote, 'no one thinks of assuming that a Hindoo or Mahomeddan woman should be capable of knowing what is best for her own welfare'.[85] The crucial point, however, is not that Indian women's role was erased because their contributions were simply overlooked; but, rather, that the logic of colonial masculinity precluded visibility for certain kinds of contributions from Indian women. For, as in the case of the *Saint James Gazette*, the opponents of the Bill were often pleased to note that some Indian women were opposed to the Consent Bill. The press in Bengal recorded the support to the opposition from ordinary housewives who lined the streets of Calcutta on the occasion of the *Mahapuja* (prayer ceremony) held at the *Kalighat* on 16 March 1891 to protest against the Consent Bill.[86] In similar vein, there was much talk about the contribution of the nameless older female relatives who supposedly encouraged young couples in the practice of premature consummation. It was the public contributions of women representing women as a group that were antithetical to the logic of the assertion of masculinity on colonial terms.

It was in Bengal that the intersection between the colonial recuperation of the redefinition of female consent and the nationalist 'crisis' of Bengali masculinity most effectively marginalized women from the debate over the Consent Bill. While Kadambini Ganguly, together with some 150 Hindu, Christian, Brahmo, Buddhist, and Muslim women, officially endorsed the Consent Bill; and though at least one other meeting of women was held in Calcutta in support of the Bill, there was a relative absence of more public contributions from elite Bengali women to the Consent controversy. It may be plausible, as Anagol–McGinn suggests, that the *bhadramahila*, or middle-class Bengali woman, was less conspicuous in the public debate on

---

[85] *Liverpool Post* (Liverpool), 27 January 1891, in *English Opinion*, No. 2 of March 1891.
[86] See reports of the *puja* in the pro-Bill newspaper, *Reis and Reyyat*, 28 March 1891, p. 149. Also see Sen (1980–1: 173).

the Consent Bill than her counterpart in the Bombay Presidency because upper-caste Bengali women suffered greater orthodox restrictions than women in Bombay; but a more plausible explanation lies perhaps in the constraints of the terms of the Consent debate in Bengal (Anagol–McGinn 1992: 116–17). For although there was a long tradition of women's writings on child marriage and early maternity in Bengal, as in Bombay, the Bengali female periodical literature, as Ghulam Murshid has demonstrated, was curiously silent about the Bill throughout the Consent debate. It was only in 1894 when the *Bamabodhini Patrika*, one of the leading journals for women in Bengal, was celebrating its thirtieth jubilee that Murshid finds a passing reference to the Consent Act. Mankumari Basu, in her article 'Bigata Shata Barshe Bharat Ramaniganer Abastha' ('The Situation of Women in the Last Hundred Years'), listed the Consent Act as one of the legislative initiatives that aimed to benefit the position of women in Bengal (Murshid 1983: 184–5). The terms of the Consent controversy thus not only overwhelmed the recognition of Indian women's actual contributions, but also discouraged their fuller participation in a debate that was strictly limited to revitalizing the claims of masculinity.

Given the limited agenda of the debate, the colonial advocates and nationalist opponents of the Bill marked the differences in their positions by highly exaggerated claims—claims that, nevertheless, expressed a surprising similarity in their attitudes towards women. The definition of female consent, for example, was tied, by almost universal consensus, to the reproductive capacity of women: the age at which women could be considered physically fit to bear healthy children without injury to themselves or to the future of the race. The dominant Anglo-Indian view, as expressed in the report of the Calcutta Medical Society, coincided with the orthodox Hindu view: puberty, as defined by the onset of the first menstruation, declared a woman fit for sexual intercourse.[87] The dissenting voice in the Anglo-Indian medical establishment came mainly from European 'lady doctors' associated with the National Association for Supplying Medical Aid by Women to the Women of India, also known as the Lady Dufferin's Fund.[88] Although Edith Pechey-Phipson, who had

---

[87] The ninth meeting of the Calcutta Medical Society on the 'Nubile Age of Females in India' was held on 10 September 1890; the majority view of Brigade Surgeon K. Macleod that puberty was determined by first menstruation was upheld over the minority view of Major C.H. Jourbet, Professor of Midwifery; see 'Transactions of Medical Societies, October 1890', *Proceedings*, Nos 3 and 4; also see Appendix B, 9 August 1890, From C.H. Jourbet, *Proceedings*, No. 13. This was also the view reiterated by Scoble, see *Abstracts*, p. 10.

[88] *India, Home Department, Judicial, February 1891*, Pros. Nos 155–159A.

served seven years as a 'lady doctor' in Bombay, accepted a physiological criterion for determining female consent, her definition of puberty and physical maturity at least made a case for a much higher age of female consent.[89] Within the dominant terms of the debate, however, the differences between the supporters and opponents of the Bill were reduced simply to a disagreement over the average age of menstruation of girls in India.

Confronted with conflicting evidence on the average age of menstruation, the supporters of the Bill invoked the medical authority of Dr Cheevers, who in his 1856 *Manual of Medical Jurisprudence for Bengal* had argued that Bengali girls were often deliberately 'ripened' for sexual intercourse through the 'artificial stimulation' of their sexual organs and the excitation of their sexual instincts.[90] Accordingly, the colonial advocates of the Bill suggested that few Indian girls menstruated 'naturally' and that 'unaided menstruation' was an especially 'rare event' in Bengal. Furthermore, Anglo-Indian officials laid the blame for this primarily on the 'female members of the bride's family' who adopted 'measures to hasten menstruation'.[91] The opponents of the Bill bitterly contested the consensus in the Anglo-Indian medical establishment on the average age of menstruation for Indian girls; but they too reserved their greatest contempt for women: the European 'lady doctors'. The *Dainik O Samachar Chandrika*, for example, singled out the 'lady doctors' for criticism; it wrote disparagingly of the 'characteristic irrepressibility of their sex', which did not make the 'lady doctors' hesitate in giving their opinion 'on a subject on which even the learned Surgeon-General, Dr Cornish, has not been able to pronounce himself confidently'.[92]

For all their differences, both sides on the debate over the Indian Consent Bill constituted mutually reinforcing rather than oppositional positions in eliding the real implications of the redefinition of female

[89] Quoted in *The Times*, 7 November 1890, p. 6.

[90] Extract from the *Indian Medical Gazette*, December 1890, p. 51, *Proceedings*, Pros. No. 14. For the quote from Dr Cheevers, see Nulkar's speech, *Abstracts*, p. 119.

[91] E.E. Lowis, Commissioner Rajshaye Division, 18 October 1989, *Proceedings*, No. 13. This view of menstruation among Indian women is also given credence in Staley (1908: 66–7).

[92] *Dainik O Samachar Chandrika*, 17 November 1890, *RNBP* 1890, p. 1051. Also see *Amrita Bazar Patrika*, 30 August 1891, p. 2. In addition, opponents of the Bill came up with the recommendation of substituting 'puberty' for the age of 12 in the consent regulations; they argued the present Bill made 'children out of mature girls'; see *Dainik O Samachar Chandrika*, 14 January 1891, *RNBP* 1891, No. 2. Even more 'liberal' papers like the *Bengalee* and the *Sanjivani* supported this change.

consent. The advocates of the Bill made available alarming statistics of the physical injury done to child-wives. Morelle Mansell, an American medical missionary, and 49 other 'lady doctors' publicized cases of the sexual abuse of child-wives in India in their petition to the Viceroy on the Consent Bill.[93] The Calcutta medical establishment further substantiated these statistics with medico-legal returns of the sexual abuse of Indian girls between the ages of seven and 12.[94] Yet the attention on the sexual abuse of child-wives seldom led to an exploration of the broader sexual exploitation of women; instead, as one official in the Viceroy's Legislative Council declared in a telling comment, the information shed light on 'fiendish husbands' whose 'moral depravity' was to be pitied. For their part, revivalists–nationalists converted the information into an affront to national pride. They charged that the statistics about sexual abuse were unrepresentative because the information was collected from the criminal population. In what was perhaps one of the more ingenious arguments adopted by the opponents of the Bill, Dr Juggobandhu Bose, an MD from Calcutta University, alleged that the European system of 'honeymoon' was far more injurious to a virginal girl than the Indian system of child marriage. For, on the authority of Dr Lawson Tait's *Diseases of Women and Abdominal Surgery*, Bose argued that injury during sexual intercourse had to do with the 'disproportionate size of the male organ' provoked by sexual excitement; and it was adult women more than child-wives who produced sexual excitement among males.[95] Bose and other opponents of the Bill tried to dignify opposition to the Bill as a sign of national independence. The real irony was that, notwithstanding professions to the contrary, it was the opposition against the Bill that remained most dependent on colonial masculinity.

---

[93] Memorial of Lady Doctors in India (sent to the Viceroy in September 1890), 27 February 1891, Appendix A 15, *Proceedings*, No. 58. The memorial received wide publicity; see *The Times*, 8 October 1890; 7 November 1890; 29 November 1890, p. 6.

[94] The Report of the Civil Surgeon of Bengal for 1868–9 demonstrated that out of 48 cases of rape, half the victims were under 10 years of age, in two under 5, and in 17 between 6 and 10; the Report for 1870–2 established that out of 372 cases of rape, 51 per cent of the victims were below 10 and 89 per cent below 15. Quoted in *Englishman*, 12 September 1890, p. 6. The most sensational was the alarming interpretation of the disproportion in the ratio of the sexes during the first four years of child marriage in the 1881 census in Mukharji (1890). Mukharji, however, used the statistics to argue against child marriage and not as support for the Consent Bill. For the concern over the disproportion of the sex ratio in the Indian Census returns, see Ifeka (1982).

[95] Bose, *Appeal*, pp. 2–3.

The politics of colonial masculinity in the Consent controversy did not provide a model for a more militant nationalist politics against colonial rule. Rather, it recuperated the energies of the nationalist movement and brought them into closer harmony with colonial rule. The ambiguity of the Consent controversy thus suggests the need for recontextualizing the relationship between nationalism and other emancipatory political projects. For even a militant critique of colonial rule, if it remains oblivious to the intersection of different contexts, may mask a far deeper complicity with a colonial agenda. The paradoxical role of colonial masculinity in the Indian Consent controversy had as much to do with the politics of the imperial social formation as a whole as with colonial–nationalist politics in India. This over-determined context for colonial masculinity is not unique: it suggests that the intersection of the imperial and the national not only frames the politics of race, class, gender, and sexuality, but is also constitutive of their very meaning.

REFERENCES

Abstract of the Proceedings of the Council of the Governor General of India, Assembled for the Purpose of Making Laws and Regulations 1891, Vol. 30, India Office Library and Records (IOLR), London.

Anagol–McGinn, Padma (1992), 'The Age of Consent Act (1891) Reconsidered: Women's Perspectives and Participation in the Child-Marriage Controversy in India', *South Asia Research*, 12(2): 100–18.

An Appeal to England to Save India from the Wrong and the Shame of the 'Age of Consent Act' (1891). Bali Sadharani Sabha.

Banerjee, Shyamananda (1968), *National Awakening and the Bangabasi*. Calcutta: Amitava-Kalyan Publishers.

Borthwick, Meredith (1984), *The Changing Role of Women in Bengal, 1849–1905*. Princeton: Princeton University Press.

Bullough, V.L. and M. Voght (1973), 'Homosexuality and Its Confusion with the "Secret Sin" in Pre-Freudian America', *Journal of the History of Medicine and Applied Sciences*, 28(2): 143–55.

Caroll, Lucy (1983), 'Law, Custom and Statutory Social Reform: The Hindu Widows Remarriage Act of 1856', *Indian Economic and Social History Review*, 20(4): 363–88.

Chakravarti, Uma (1990), 'Whatever Happened to the Vedic *Dasi*? Orientalism, Nationalism and a Script for the Past', in K. Sangari and S. Vaid (eds), *Recasting Women: Essays in Indian Colonial History*. Brunswick, NJ: Rutgers University Press, pp. 27–87.

Chandra, Sudhir (1977), 'The Problem of Social Reform in Modern India: The Study of a Case', in S.C. Malik (ed.), *Dissent, Protest and Reform in Indian Civilization*. Simla: Institute of Advanced Studies.

—— (1992), 'Whose Laws? Notes on a Legitimising Myth of the Colonial Indian State', *Studies in History*, 8(2): 187–211.

Chatterjee, P. (1986), *Nationalist Thought and the Colonial World: A Derivative Discourse*. London: Zed Books.

—— (1990), 'The Nationalist Resolution of the Women's Question', in K. Sangari and S. Vaid (eds), *Recasting Women: Essays in Indian Colonial History*. Brunswick, NJ: Rutgers University Press, pp. 233–53.

—— (1993), *The Nation and Its Fragments: Colonial and Postcolonial Histories*. Princeton: Princeton University Press.

A Collection of the Acts Passed by the Governor General of India in Council in the Year 1891 (1892). Calcutta: Government Printing Press.

Dutt, Paramanda (1935), *Memoirs of Motilal Ghose*. Calcutta: Amrita Bazar Patrika Office.

Engels, Dagmar (1983), 'The Age of Consent Act of 1891: Colonial Ideology in Bengal', *South Asia Research*, 3(2): 107–32.

—— (1989), 'The Limits of Gender Ideology: Bengali Women, the Colonial State and the Private Sphere, 1890–1930', *Women's Studies' International Forum*, 12: 425–37.

English Opinion on India: A Monthly Magazine Containing Select Extracts from English Newspapers on Indian Subjects (1891), No. 2, March (*English Opinion*).

Forbes, Geraldine (1975), *Positivism in Bengal: A Case Study in the Transmission and Assimilation of an Ideology*. Columbia, MO: South Asia Books.

—— (1979), 'Women and Modernity: The Issue of Child Marriage in India', *Women's Studies International Quarterly*, 2(4): 407–19.

Gidumal, Dayaram (1889), *The Status of Woman in India: Or a Handbook for Hindu Social Reformers*. Bombay: Fort Printing Press.

Gorham, Deborah (1978), 'The "Maiden Tribute of Modern Babylon" Re-examined: Child Prostitution and the Idea of Childhood in Late Victorian England', *Victorian Studies*, 21(3): 353–79.

Hearn, Jeff (1992), *Men in the Public Eye: The Construction and Deconstruction of Public Men and Public Patriarchies*. London: Routledge.

Heimsath, Charles (1962), 'The Origin and Enactment of the Indian Age of Consent Bill, 1891', *Journal of Asian Studies*, 21(4): 491–504.

—— (1964), *Indian Nationalism and Hindu Social Reform*. Princeton: Princeton University Press.

Hilliard, David (1982), 'Unenglish and Unmanly: Anglo-Catholicism and Homosexuality', *Victorian Studies*, 25(2): 181–210.

Ifeka, Caroline (1982), '"Spiritual" and "Statistical" Models of the Sexes in British India, 1871–1931', *South Asia*, 5(1): 16–28.

India, Home Department, Judicial, February 1891, Nos 155–159A, National Archives of India (NAI), New Delhi.

India, Home Department, Judicial, April 1891, Pros. Nos 103-104 A, NAI, New Delhi.

India Legislative Proceedings, Nos 1-73, Act 10 of 1891 and Connected Papers, April 1891 (*Proceedings*), India Office Library and Records (IOLR), London.

India Office Library Tracts (*IOR Tracts*), IOLR, London.

Infant Marriage and Enforced Widowhood in India: Being a Collection of Opinions For and Against Received by B.M. Malabari from Representative Hindu Gentlemen and Officials and Other Authorities (1887). Bombay: Voice of India Printing Press.

Kimmel, Michael S. (1987), 'The Contemporary "Crisis" of Masculinity in Historical Perspective', in Harry Brod (ed.), *The Making of Masculinities: The New Men's Studies*. Boston: Allen & Unwin, pp. 121-54.

Kosambi, Meera (1991), 'Girl-Brides and Socio-Legal Change: Age of Consent Bill (1891) Controversy', *Economic and Political Weekly*, 26(31-2): 1857-68.

Lansdowne Papers: Correspondence with Persons in England (*Lansdowne England*), IOLR, London.

Lansdowne Papers: Correspondence with Persons in India (*Lansdowne India*), IOLR, London.

Lansdowne Papers: Correspondence with Secretary of State (*Lansdowne Secretary of State*), from January 1891, IOLR, London.

Mani, Lata (1987), 'Contentious Traditions: The Debate on Sati in Colonial India', *Cultural Critique*, Fall, 7: 119-56.

Masselos, Jim (1992), 'Sexual Property/Sexual Violence: Wives in Nineteenth-Century Bombay', *South Asia Research*, 12(2): 81-99.

Mort, Frank (1987), *Dangerous Sexualities: Medico-Moral Politics in England since 1830*. London: Routledge & Kegan Paul.

Mueller, Max (1891), 'The Story of an Indian Child Wife', *Contemporary Review*, August, 60: 183-7.

Mukharji, T.N. (1890), *The Sisters of Phulmoni (or the Child Wives of India)*. Calcutta: Indian Nation.

Murshid, Ghulam (1983), *Reluctant Debutante: Response of Bengali Women to Modernization 1849-1905*. Rajshahi: Rajshahi University Press.

Nair, Janaki (1990), 'Uncovering the *Zenana*: Visions of Indian Womanhood in Englishwomen's Writings, 1813-1940', *Journal of Women's History*, 2(1): 8-34.

Narain, Prem (1970-1), 'The Age of Consent Bill (1891) and Its Impact on India's Freedom Struggle', *Quarterly Review of Historical Studies*, 10(1): 7-21.

Narain, V.A. (1972), *Social History of Modern India: Nineteenth Century*. Meerut: Meenakshi Prakashan.

Natarajan, S. (1962), *A Century of Social Reform in India*. Bombay: Asia Publishing House.

Neuman, R.P. (1975), 'Masturbation, Madness and the Modern Concepts of Childhood and Innocence', *Journal of Social History*, Spring, 8(3): 1-27.

Oddie, G.A. (1979), *Social Protest in India: British Protestant Missionaries and Social Reforms 1885-1900*. Delhi: Manohar Publishers and Distributors.

Pal, Bipan Chandra (1951), *Memories of My Life and Times*, Vol. 2, 1886–1900. Calcutta: Yugayatri Prakashak Ltd.

Parliamentary Papers: Moral and Material Progress and Condition of India During The Year 1890–91 and the Nine Preceding Years, Vol. 59, Paper No. 43, IOLR, London.

Pearson, Michael (1972), *The Age of Consent: Victorian Prostitution and Its Enemies*. London: Newton Abbot, David & Charles.

Ray, Alok (ed.) (1975), *Counterpoint, Vol. 2*. Calcutta: Riddhi India.

Ray, Rajat Kanta (1984), *Social Conflict and Political Unrest in Bengal, 1875–1927*. New Delhi: Oxford University Press.

Report on the Bengal Native Press (*RNBP*), IOLR, London.

Report on Bombay Native Press, 1891, IOLR, London.

Risley, Sir Herbert (1908), *The People of India*. Calcutta: Thacker, Spink & Co.

Ryan, Mary P. (1990), *Women in Public: Between Banners and Ballots 1825–1880*. Baltimore: Johns Hopkins University Press.

Sarkar, Tanika (1992), 'The Hindu Wife and the Hindu Nation: Domesticity and Nationalism in Nineteenth-century Bengal', *Studies in History*, 8(2): 213–35.

——— (1993), 'Rhetoric against Age of Consent: Resisting Colonial Reason and Death of a Child-Wife', *Economic and Political Weekly*, 28(36): 1869–78.

Selections Home Department—Selections from the Records of the Government of India in the Home Department, No. 223: Home Department Serial No. 3, Papers Relating to Infant Marriage and Enforced Widowhood in India, IOLR, London.

Sen, Amiya (1980–1), 'Hindu Revivalism in Action—The Age of Consent Bill Agitation in Bengal', *The Indian Historical Review*, 7(1–2): 160–84.

Sinha, Mrinalini (1987), 'Gender and Imperialism: Colonial Policy and the Ideology of Moral Imperialism in Late Nineteenth Century Bengal', in Michael Kimmel (ed.), *Changing Men: New Directions in Research on Men and Masculinity*. Berkeley: Sage Publications, pp. 217–31.

——— (1989), 'The Age of Consent Act: The Ideal of Masculinity and Colonial Ideology in Late Nineteenth Century Bengal', in T. K. Stewart (ed.), *Shaping Bengali Worlds: Public and Private*. East Lansing, MI: Asian Studies Center, pp. 99–127.

——— (1995), 'Nationalism and Respectable Sexuality in India', *Genders*, 21: 30–57.

Sircar, N.N. (1891), *A Note on the Age of Consent Bill*. Calcutta, IOLR, London.

Staley, M.E. (1908), *Handbook for Wives and Mothers in India*. Calcutta: Thacker, Spink & Co.

Steel, Flora Annie (1929), *The Garden of Fidelity: Being the Autobiography of F.A. Steele, 1847–1929*. London: Macmillan Publishers Ltd.

Tracts on Indian Marriage Customs 1887–1891 (*BM Tracts*), British Museum (BM), London.

Vatsa, Rajendra Singh (1971), 'The Movement against Infant Marriages in India 1860–1914', *Journal of Indian History*, April/August/December, 49: 280–95.

Walkowitz, Judith R. (1980), *Prostitution and Victorian Society: Women, Class and the State*. Cambridge: Cambridge University Press.

Walkowitz, Judith R. (1982), 'Male Vice and Feminist Virtue: Feminism and the Politics of Prostitution in Nineteenth-Century British History', *History Workshop Journal*, Spring, 13: 77–93.
—— (1992), *City of Dreadful Delight: Narratives of Sexual Danger in Late-Victorian London*. Chicago: University of Chicago Press.
Weeks, Jeffrey (1977), *Coming Out: Homosexual Politics in Britain from the Nineteenth Century to the Present*. London: Quartet.
—— (1981), *Sex, Politics and Society*. London: Routledge & Kegan Paul.
—— (1991), *Against Nature: Essays on History, Sexuality and Identity*. London: Rivers Oram Press.

Chapter 8

STYLE

LAWRENCE COHEN*

PREFACE: ESCAPE

NAUSHAD LEFT VARANASI ('there's nothing here') in 1989 for Bombay (now Mumbai), carrying some clothes, some presents for the cousins in the large slum of Cheetah Camp where he would be staying, and a camera. He acquired the last from an American development researcher, and with it he hoped to make his fortune as a still photographer in the film industry. Like a lot of men in Varanasi going astray at a time when heroin was beginning to pass through the city in large quantities, he had developed a habit of stealing from family, friends, and the foreign students and tourists who were a longstanding source of income for some Banarsis. Naushad's father was an artisan recycling scrap metal, and his brother was an apprentice tailor: for Naushad, these were jobs for a *naukar*, a servant. For some

---

* Thanks to Raka Ray for the provocation to write this chapter; to a University of California Berkeley Faculty Research Grant and an Arcus Foundation Grant for enabling much of the research; and to Deepak Mehta, Sanjay Srivastava, and Ashley Tellis for the wisdom of their own scholarship and generosity of conversation over some years. Though this chapter emerged independently of the rigorous Delhi-based conversations on masculinity and sex in which they and others played a significant part, it is indebted to my (limited) exposure to these conversations. Since I wrote it, I have encountered critically important and relevant new works by a number of scholars, which I hope to incorporate in future expansions of this work. Finally, the varied work of my colleagues and former students William Mazzarella, Jordyn Steig, and Anupama Kapse has been a particular provocation for this chapter.

years, Naushad brought foreign researchers into their household as paying guests, through connections he had developed ever since he had been part of an anthropologist's study of children's games. But the heroin and petty theft had dried up that source of income. His parents and brother, who hinted but never spoke openly to the author that this early contact with the *rehensehen* or lifeways of foreign youth had ruined Naushad, hoped against hope that a steady job in the film industry would change things.

Vijay left the city the same year for Bangalore (now Bengaluru). He was the second of 10 children and the oldest boy. Their mother died while giving birth to the child, and their father, who held a series of mediocre jobs in his capacity as a temple priest after his elder brother forced him out of their shared property, was unable to support them all. Another son told me that their father had become 'cracked' due to the 'tension' of the sequential losses of his home, livelihood, and wife, and was *ekdam bekar*, unemployed and useless. Vijay felt the mantle of nine siblings, including two sisters who needed husbands, descending on him, and quarrelled more and more with Babuji, his father. One day, according to his younger brothers, he just left for far-off Bengaluru in south India for a job in the sari business. A second brother left soon after to find work in Patna in the east, and the third brother and two sisters supported the *bacche log*, the youngest five boys. Pressure was on these five, as they became teenagers, to find a job in the city's *chowk*, the central commercial area, usually in sales and often, like Vijay, in the sari or readymade clothes' business. In 1993, the family's debt increased exponentially: the youngest brother and eldest sister were hospitalized, the latter dying; Babuji passed away; and weeks after Vijay returned from Bengaluru with a wife and child, he was in a scooter accident and, like his father, became 'cracked', unable to speak or leave the house and refusing food. He too died, at home, within the year. The remaining family moved into a much smaller room, down the lane from Naushad's brother.

In 1995, the eldest of the five bacche log, Sanjeev, stole some of his elder siblings' money and left for Delhi with a friend. They had heard of a 'film school' where they would learn to be dancers and actors, and if they were good, would land a job in the Bombay film industry. Of the brothers, Sanjeev fashioned himself the smartest, the most likely possessor of the quality of *style* that could propel a Banarsi boy into other worlds that were, by the mid-1990s, no longer restricted to the lifeways of foreign expatriates, but far more evident in the circulation of national masculinities in current films, magazines, and, increasingly, television. Sanjeev returned several months later, with some new dance moves and stories of near misses as a 'model' but no job in film or television. Within the year he was arrested for his involvement as a carrier in the heroin trade.

THE MASCULINITY OF FASHION

Between the mid-1980s and mid-1990s, the expanding English and Hindi media cyclically reported on an ongoing revolution in Indian masculinity, like femininity, under the label of 'fashion'. As an argument for an epochal transition, fashion pointed to an emerging set of elements: a liberalizing economic order apparently flush with new commodities, a resulting 'new middle class' that could recognize itself in proliferating media scenes of consumption and romance, and the rise of Indian prominence in global circuits of apparel design, bringing with it new jobs in corporations like Benetton, The Gap, and Lacoste. The pre-eminent figure securing this epoch of fashion was the model. Attention in urban media markets over this decade to the model included not only the expansion of advertising but the proliferation of fashion shows as *rites de passage* for middle-class students in schools and colleges in India and among South Asians overseas. The pleasures these contests offered were acutely aspirational: modelling could promise both national and global circulation. The iterated evidence was provided by many Indian women winning the Miss Universe and Miss World beauty titles. Several of these contest winners along with some male models successfully made the transition to stardom in various regional language cinemas. The star system of Hindi film industry, in particular, shifted to accommodate the rise of the model, and advertising revenues in upmarket newspapers and magazines came to depend on significantly expanded celebrity journalism, the so-called 'Page 3' phenomenon. (While 'Page 3' was designated the celebrity and society page, in some Anglophone publications and notably the once sober *The Times of India* many pages were devoted to 'Page 3' coverage.) In most cities and towns beyond the major centres of film production, society and celebrity journalism came to depend on local fashion designers, models, and shows for their source of spectacular charisma.

Masculinity under the sign of fashion was often staged as an elite and Anglophone masculinity. Within the expanding features press, repeated pronouncements staging fashion as a heroic masculine enterprise (such as 'the new Indian man is not afraid to get a facial') might be viewed as corporate experiments both structuring and structured by a consolidating the apparatus of class distinction. Men were now free, readers were informed, to dress up and coif themselves. The new rules were offered in a masculinist idiom no less about competition and warfare than the prefacial masculinity preceding them: Indian men were conquering the world stage, simultaneously masters of the twin pinnacles of an emerging global style—the Western and the ethnic. Stylistic mastery became transcultural mastery of these dual codes of competence.

This *mastery of code* went hand in hand with India's new achievements in other fields of code, most notably information technology. I spent the summer of 2001 doing interviews with a succession of players within the assemblage of fashion design, advertising firms, apparel manufacture, and journalism in five 'metros' (then named Bengaluru, Calcutta [now Kolkata], Chennai, Delhi, and Mumbai) and two smaller cities (Lucknow and Varanasi). For a decade, from the late 1990s to 2008, I wrote letters describing my research to several hundred prospective models. These young men had posted their pictures and bio-data on India-focused Internet sites to which they paid a fee, hoping to be discovered online for a career in Indian or international modelling. I have corresponded with over 50 such prospective models from large cities to small towns across India, increasingly from the Indian 'diaspora', and occasionally from Pakistan and Bangladesh. Both experts and aspirants felt that certain cities provided better conditions for the training of world-class models. Bangalore was often mentioned, at times in relation to its noted designers like Prasad Bidippa. Bidippa was one of the many male designers celebrated in 'Page 3' and features journalism as an archetype for the competitive mastery of global style. Bangalore, several journalists and aspirants told me, produced both the best models and the best software engineers.

Fashion as parallel to information technology emerged as a theme in interviews, as with a business student at Lucknow University who told me business was his third choice, after failed attempts first to get into a first-ranked 'IIT-type' (Indian Institute of Technology) training programme and second to be accepted at one of the National Institutes of Fashion Technology (NIFTs). Designers and male models offered an embodied alternative to an imagined earlier and less globally competitive masculinity. Their feel for the global went beyond sartorial distinction, beyond the ubiquitous modern 'problem of what to wear' (to cite Emma Tarlo's [1996] study of clothing as a critical site of national modernity). To make it in the world of global fashion crucially suggested the ability to exploit the code-based challenges of the new economy.

This signifiably new *model masculinity* of media industry para-ethnography was not inevitably marked in generational terms. The major models were men in their late teens through early thirties, but the designers ranged from their twenties through sixties and beyond. The media pundits saw the new man as willing to take risks that his father might not have, but seldom were these newspaper or magazine features offering binaries of young dandies and wastrels set against either more prudent or more avaricious fathers, as in the struggle between Harpagon and Cléante in Molière's *L'Avare*. Some left journalism notwithstanding, there was not a prominent critique of model masculinity as wasteful or effeminate.

Model masculinity in the 1990s and 2000s offered a global future without the pejoratives attached to it in the popular cultural production of the US and the UK (the male model as stupid as in the 2001 film *Zoolander* or as a narcissist as in the 1991 hit song 'I'm too sexy'). Nonetheless, like European and North American images of model masculinity, Indian framings of male fashion were often linked to a signifiably 'gay' style or biography. What *being gay* entailed in the popularization of fashion celebrity was not always clear: a designer might be described as married with children and as having a gay style in different paragraphs. I want to suggest that what was at stake here was not only or even primarily the epistemology of the closet. I have elsewhere argued that part of what might have been at stake was the emergence of a form labelled 'gay' or far less often 'lesbian' within diverse and often experimental technical practices tied to the liberalization of the consumer market (Cohen 2007).

A truism in various advertising agencies over the late 1980s and 1990s was that the 'Indian consumer' was still 'feudal', dominated by a conservatism reluctant to embrace new object choices. A friend of mine from Kolkata who trained at Jadavpur University as an engineer shifted to the expanding and more promising field of advertising. He worked with a creative team to design settings conveying a 'sense of fun' among young people—heterosexual couples, for example, enjoying themselves in an elegant setting. The challenge he and his colleagues faced was the creation of a form of relatedness within a scene of consumption that they saw as set against the presumptively more fiscally abstemious relations of an older generation. The older 'feudal' or 'freedom fighter' consumer was understood to maintain allegiance to tried and true brands. The modern 'Western' couple form, set against a more crowded and multi-generational family scene, was one of several experiments in eliciting affects differentiated from this older generation that would engender identification with other alternate or emergent brands.

My earlier effort was to make sense of a different form of relatedness, one staged by occasional 'gay'-themed advertisements that circulated from the mid-1980s through the 1990s: linking a youth-oriented product like jeans to a provocatively arrayed same-sex couple (Cohen 2002). Inspired by the feminist literary critic Ruth Vanita, who first focused on the profusion of such ads to argue that they demonstrated emergent practices of marketing to a gay and lesbian public that could not be openly acknowledged (Vanita 2002), I argued something different. Based on interviews with advertising professionals in Delhi, Kolkata, and Mumbai, and drawing from the extensive work of William Mazzarella (2003), I came to see these ads much like the heterosexual couple form staging the possibility of a desire that stood against the so-called feudal or joint family. If the focus of such a desire, according to the ad professionals, was a subject marked as 'not your father', the bodies and relations that exemplified that desire ranged across a series of forms foregrounded by globalizing media.

The recognizably lesbian or gay forms were potentially high-risk experiments. With several political parties attacking the 1996 film *Fire* made by an Indo-Canadian director, centred on an erotic relation between two women in a Hindu extended family, ads featuring two women together in a sexualized relation became less tenable. But 'gay' relations between men seldom caused similar controversy, in part as they were arguably extensions of an often comic tradition of female impersonation with broad roots in the urbanizing 'folk' theatres of India (Banerjee 1989; Hansen 1992; Rege 1996) and formative of modern theatrical and cinematic treatment of gender (Hansen 2004), affect (Kapse 2009), and homoerotic desire. If bodies and relations within not only advertisements but increasingly in television serials and films were marked as gay, 'gay' here was less a (stigmatized) object choice than a complex signifier, promoting affects of the new, the ludic, and the individual within the comfortable frame of the traditional joke. With the widespread transnational emergence of the English-language category 'metrosexual' in the first decade of the new millennium, the ambiguity of the gay could be pared down to a figure that stood for the contemporary dandy without the presumption of particular sexual positionings.

The complexity of the new elite masculinity's relation to 'the gay' lies in part in how middle and upper class and Anglophone urban gay male collective formations utilize the fashion/celebrity circuit and the overlapping space of the metrosexual. On the one hand, these positions ground style and identity within a relatively conservative domain of practices of relationship and of consumption reproducing class distinction (Cohen 1994). On the other, they may trouble norms of gender, kinship, and age and open onto progressive or 'queer' practices of self-formation and collective action. The emergence of scholarly attention to the metrosexual as a site for the critical reframing of urban culture can be in part located as an experimental practice mobilizing queer critique of neo-liberal urbanism (see Verma 2004). Such academic metrosexuality is not simply the celebration of commodity culture under liberalization but an imagined site for the reworking of class-based and nationality-based structures of distinction.

In popular media engagements with new scenes of masculine identification, class may be staged in intriguing ways. Among the most noted of such scenes is the one in which the male friendship between the characters played by actors Shah Rukh Khan and Saif Ali Khan in the 2003 film *Kal Ho Naa Ho* (Tomorrow May Never Come; *KHNH* for short) is misinterpreted by an older female servant as a sexual, 'gay' relationship. The servant's ability to serve the two men tea in the morning is compromised (her hands cannot stop shaking) as each interaction between the two men produces a double entendre confirming her diagnosis.

This interlude is worth reflecting on for several reasons beyond the comic conventions that structure it. The film is set in and around New York City. The two men are rivals for the heroine, and yet they do not fight but remain bound by friendship. Though the hero sacrificing his own love for his friend is far from a new narrative form in Hindi films, here it is framed through a servant's misrecognition within a film, self-consciously representing a metropolitan 'lifestyle'. Her presence allows for a splitting between two orders of masculinity, a traditional order in which rivals fight as opposed to love versus an elite order of friendship not organized around the figure of martial distinction. Again, there is nothing necessarily novel in this treatment of male friendship, habitus, and sacrifice, which have been staples of numerous earlier variants of the *dosti* (friendship) picture. Even the linkage in *KHNH* of joyously sacrificial friendship with elite urban masculinity brings to mind a much earlier film—*Anand* (1971)—in which, as Philip Lutgendorf (n.d.) wittily notes, it is not a female servant but an entire slum that is given the cameo role, similarly staging the relation of masculine generosity and love to a privileged milieu.

And yet *KHNH* repeatedly affirms the emergent quality of this form of male sociality, associating it most obviously with the transnational success and pride of a growing Indian middle class and framing it in relation to a mode of relationship—the *gay*—that calls attention to the contemporaneity of the situation. That the film's writer and co-producer Karan Johar has assiduously developed a form of 'Page 3' celebrity hovering on the infinite border of gayness and modern consumer fun, offered further pleasures for those viewers who encountered the ubiquitous Johar in the cinema or fashion news or on his own talk show 'Koffee with Karan'.

Rachel Dwyer (2000) has argued, with reference to the later romantic films of producer Yash Chopra, that these stage love in a new and different way. Love is no longer what Anthony Giddens (1992) might term *amour passion*, that is, a source of powerful affects inevitably set against family norms and demands as in the pre-eminent genre of the social film, but rather love becomes a site for work on the self through the liberal recasting of relations. The relational work in *KHNH* is as much between men or between women (a warring mother and daughter-in-law in a different section of the plot, or a mother and a daughter) as between woman and man. Beyond the intergenerational ties of family, however, women's extrafamilial friendship is not the privileged site that male friendship remains. Johar's masculine metrosexuality can stand for liberal work on the self and the recasting of relations in a way no female celebrity has yet been able to do. The beauty queen, the closest parallel to the metrosexual male celebrity in 'Page 3' mythology, is inevitably recuperated by becoming a daughter-in-law.[1]

If the servant misreads the stakes in the men's friendship, she is one of several plot elements that stand for an earlier, older, and, in her case, structurally subordinate India—that India is one in which marriages are arranged and 'love marriages' are doomed to tragedy. One reason for doom is masculine honour. Thus, in earlier social films where parental demands are portrayed as self-serving and romantic love stands for the nationalist dream of a purer India, as in the 1985 movie *Ram Teri Ganga Maili*, the rival cannot create a relation with the victor and the only resolution is punishment or death. In the film, an idealistic city boy escapes his corrupt businessman father for the Arcadian hills, where he meets, falls in love, and elopes with a simple mountain girl whose intended husband is furious and begins a fight to the death with the girl's brother. Here, too, and despite the corruption of the city, the urban young man's idealism suggests an order of simultaneously heroic and yet abstemious masculinity (his name is Naren

---

[1] Johar's celebrity arguably was extended to the figure of lesbian relationship in the much-postponed 2008 film *When Kiren Met Karen*, his own first name (Karan) being homonymous with and often spelled the same as the English-language female name in the title. The experiment, if its purpose was to link the figure of lesbian relationship with the self-knowledge of the transnational Indian middle class, was not a success.

and his hero is the nationalist saint Vivekananda) that protects him from the harm to which more poor and rural men doom one another.[2]

Elite masculinity in *Ram Teri Ganga Maili* is split between Naren's nationalist piety and the corruption and libertinage of his father and his father's friend, a politican, eliciting from the masculinized viewer the sense that a choice between worldly politics and a more sublime 'anti-politics' (Hansen 1999) is demanded of him or her. In contrast the choices in *KHNH* are not framed in relation to the anti-politics of the modern nation but involve the 'post-political' dilemmas inherent in cosmopolitan self-formation. In such a world, the life-threatening divide between purifying love and traditional war is legible as the comic distinction between forms of friendship that a globally mobile language positions as straight and gay. That calling the new elite masculinity of fashion 'gay' is an error of a poor old woman both stages the distinction of the new formation of gender and class and allows for Johar—who on 'Koffee with Karan' continually plays with his being or not being gay as part of his celebrity persona—in effect to suggest that any reduction of his own fashionable masculinity to homosexuality would be a similar *déclassé* misreading. The gayness of the transnational middle class evades stigma precisely in its class distinction.

YEH HAI STYLE

I used the terms 'fashion' and 'style' above in a metonymic, as opposed to metaphoric, relation to one another, to use the classic anthropological distinction between elements that can be *combined* into one another (metonym) versus elements that are *substitutable* one for the other

---

[2] Naren's idealism and abstemious masculinity are framed in relation to his regional identity as a Bengali. Though the eponymous hero of the movie *Anand*, discussed earlier, has a Punjabi name, he continually addresses his Bengali friend with the Bengali words '*babu moshai*', a reference to a similar practice by the famed director and actor Raj Kapoor. Bengali-ness here may convey varied conditions of masculinity. Many scholars have examined colonial-era debates over the supposed effeminacy of the Bengali man, in some cases recasting this presentation of gender as an alternate masculinity and a critical resource for anti-colonial and nationalist practice (Chowdhury 1998; Nandy 1983; Sinha 1995). A second referent for how these films stage masculinity or male friendship as Bengali may be tied to the imagined *politesse* of a Bengali presence in an increasingly Punjabi-dominated film industry. Arguably, this regionalization of a masculine register is marginally present in *KHNH*'s Saif Ali Khan, a descendant of the famed Bengali Tagore family, who has several times been assigned roles that play with the *gay* quality of emergent masculinity (see in particular the 1994 movie *Main Khiladi Tu Anari*). But the 'gayness' of relations, unlike their earlier Bengali-ness, stages them as emergent, transnational, and consumption-oriented.

(metaphor). That is, I noted that one of the assembled elements of the contemporary order of fashion is a particular 'stylistic mastery'. In this sense, style is part of the aspirational complex of fashion. Similarly, Sanjeev runs away to Delhi to seek his fortune in a 'film school' because of his conviction, or hope, that his presumptive mastery of 'style' gives him access to the new dreamworld of fashion. But the theme of failure that runs both through these recounted histories and the differentiation in films like *KHNH* between elite fashion and its non-elite misrecognition point us towards a different trope of relation, not metonym but metaphor. In other words, I want to suggest here that fashion and style may at certain points seem to stand not as parts of the same thing but as alternative versions of a thing: one may have fashion, or one may only be able to muster style.

We get a hint of how the relation between style and fashion can become a site around which distinctions of class are produced and reproduced in the language ideologies that structure perceptions of their diglossic usage. Both terms are ubiquitous as loan words from the English language in everyday Hindi usage, and both may be pronounced differently in Hindi. But the transformation of 'style' into 'shtyle' or 'ishtyle' is frequently the subject of comment or joking reference: 'ishtyle' is the poor man's style, reflected in the painful phonemes of fashion's vernacularization. Style, in other words, is the non-elite misrecognition of fashion, whereas fashion—particularly in the narrative of the fashion designer able to craft the best of both 'Western' and 'ethnic' style—can encompass and recognize the best of style as vernacular form. To put the difference in the structuralist language of metaphor and metonym: elite fashion metonymically encompasses vernacular style, whereas vernacular style fails to achieve a metonymic relation to elite fashion and remains a parallel, that is metaphoric, and inferior project of becoming.

Sanjay Srivastava evocatively distinguishes between style and fashion as follows: 'Ishtyle is the art of surfaces, whereas fashion ascribes a "deep" meaning to life: a history, a knowledge, and a trajectory of being that must first "comprehend", "contextualise", and "gloss" the styles that are present for adornment.' Fashion 'arises from the political economy of validated knowledges' while what he terms 'ishtyle' uses 'Maussian "techniques of the body" towards an *excessive* relationship with fashion...a haphazard and unpredictable praise-critique dynamic' (Srivastava 2007: 228). Drawing on careful readings of the Hindi 'sexology' magazine *Sexology Darpan* and its apparel advertisements, Srivastava frames style in relation to the 'threshold subjectivity' of a lower-class urban population that has achieved a 'foothold' on a 'relatively settled' form of life (Srivastava 2007: 231–2). Style suggests 'a lower middle-class fantasy of middle-classness' (ibid.: 225).

But the binary of style and fashion is not only available for the second-order observation of sociologists and anthropologists like Srivastava and myself. There may be a critical limit to my positing such a gap here between fashion and style. Similarly, there may be a limit to the argument that the excess of 'ishtyle' will inevitably misrecognize the habitus of the elite consumer and bring accusation on the lower middle-class. I want here to return to two sites: to the many modelling, fashion, dance, and acting institutes, like the one I mentioned in Sanjeev's story, that capitalize on these aspirations of the lower middle-class, and to the popular film in its staging of this aspiration.

My discussions with numerous urban lower middle-class and small town aspirants to the hopeful future of modelling suggest that not only do invitations to the excess of 'ishtyle' circulate widely but also, if to a much lesser extent, what we might term critical pedagogies of fashion. Many of these modelling or acting institutes only reaffirm the elements of 'ishtyle' that aspirants bring, and to an elite observer convey the sense of pathos I mobilized earlier in narrating Sanjeev's efforts to go to a 'film school'. Their pedagogy demonstrates a similar attention to surface and excess that Srivastava finds in the threshold quality of the lower middle-class sex literature. From the vantage of elite fashion, they appear as the 'fake' modelling institutes that form a staple of news reports investigating the sites of recruitment into sexual trafficking.

And yet the possibility of an effective pedagogy of fashion is evinced by the intense scrutiny of successful models by working- and lower-middle class aspirants to careers in fashion. Critiques of 'ishtyle' were as frequent among would-be lower middle-class models as among more elite observers. Such critiques were not fungible: they did not translate into hoped-for careers. But in the acknowledgement of repeated failure, in these interviews, fashion aspirants were at times explicit that their own failures were not due to an inability to recognize the difference between the body techniques of 'ishtyle' and of fashion.

Films repeatedly stage *both* the failure and the success of style's aspiration to fashion; what is produced through such films is a widely available site for thinking about what both style and fashion do in contemporary India.

Perhaps the most useful film to engage with in this regard is called, not surprisingly, *Style*. Released in 2001, it was the comeback film of N. Chandra, the director, writer, and producer of a series of hits in the 1980s, which, like his 1988 movie *Tezaab* (an adaptation of the 1984 Hollywood film *Streets of Fire*), featured a dystopian world putting men in violent confrontations. Like the 'angry young man' films of the late 1970s and early 1980s, *Tezaab* featured a split masculinity in which there are strong, dutiful men under the law, and violent, triumphant men who stand against the law: the hero fails at the first role, given the corruption of society, and after a wrongful imprisonment returns as an avenging gangster.

Style retains elements of the dystopian film but links these to the possibilities and limits of the masculinity of fashion. Though considered a box-office hit in India (leading to a sequel, *Excuse Me*), the film has not received much critical attention and I will narrate its plot and song sequences at some length. The film opens with a prologue, the scene of a happy and well-off family: the mother and her newly married son are preparing for the festival of Diwali while the father is phoning his daughter Reshma, away at college in Mumbai. Nikki, the new daughter-in-law, is, however, a con artist, and she stages her own immolation by fire, causing her husband to die of a heart attack and her in-laws to be sent to prison. All that remains between her and the family's wealth is Reshma, the daughter in college. Nikki's accomplice and lover—a classic *bhai* or criminal-type—wants to kill the girl. But Nikki thinks that a second violent event coming so quickly would cast too much suspicion on her and counsels her paramour to wait. He does not. Both Reshma and a school friend of hers, Rose, are murdered.

If the prologue features rich, happy families destroyed by the machinations of the greedy seeking 'shortcuts' (a word Nikki will later use to describe her desire), *Style* quickly shifts to two young men in the same Mumbai college—Chantu and Bantu—in unhappy families. Like most of their friends, the two see college as a place for joking with or ragging one another, bunking classes, and tricking the college principal and others in order to evade punishments they accrue. Unlike their friends, however, Chantu and Bantu are not from wealthy families, and they both blame their fathers for being failures who will not provide them with a job upon graduation. In both cases, the mothers side with the boys against their husbands. One father is a government clerk and the other a *ghar jamai*, a man unsuccessful in his own right and dependent on his in-laws' money.

The first one-third of the film demonstrates the boys' ability to out-trick and out-rag any of their classmates or teachers, and to support their love of expensive clothes and food through these ploys. Such a love is necessary, the two along with their college mates sing, because it is 'style', and style is the essence of life:

Yeh hai style, yeh hai style
Life hai kya ek style
Style hai style, sab kuch style
Life hai kya ek style
Chaal mein meri gazab ka style hai
Baalon ka bhi kya ajab sa style hai
Lab pe jo smile hai, yeh mera style hai…

This is style, this is style
What is life? A style
Style is style, everything is a style
What is life? A style
In my walk, there's the passion of my style
My hair also has an extraordinary style
The smile on my lips is my style [author's translation]

The song begins with the two *pretending* to use a mobile and a pager to emulate wealthier friends, and throughout the film style involves the successful copy of the high-status commodity. The camera shifts to a party scene, with Bantu singing, 'This is style', while a gigantic illuminated sign features the transliterated Hindi spelling for 'style' to his side. A later song, 'Style mein rehne ka' (Always keep in style), celebrates youthful opposition to societal and family conventions:

Kanghi ghuma ke, ulta topi tika ke
Goggle laga ke, apna collar chadha ke
Saj dhaj ke ghar se tak-a-tak nikalne ka
Style mein rehne ka…
Istyle mein rahenga to ladki patenga
Nahi to milega jhatke mein thenga
Istyle mein bikta hai baingan bataata
Istyle mein maarti hai ladki bhi chaanta
Nayi jeans khareed ke usko phaad de
Phir ja ke tailor se rafu maar de
Computer pe jaa ke ladki se chatting kare
Chatting me ladki se setting kare
Nahi paas gaadi ho, gaadi ki chaabi ho
Chaabi ghumaane ka
Style mein rehne ka…
Jaldi bulaaya hai deri se jaana
Raaton ko kaam dhaam, din ko ho sona
Shaadi se pehle ho shaadi ki party
Shaadi hui to kunwara bataana
Kaam pe agar tu lag jaaye kahin
Aise rehna jaise worker nahi
Koi jo poochhe kya karta hai tu
Keh dena mai to abhi college mein hoon

Har ek ladki se dil ki saari baatein mobile pe karne ka
Style mein rehne ka...

Run a comb through your hair, wear your cap backwards
Put on goggles [shades] and pull up your collar
Walk out of the house smartly dressed
Always keep in style...
If you'll keep in style, you'll get all the girls
Or you will be shooed away by them
Even potatoes and eggplants are now sold in style
 [the dancers hold out new brands of fancy packaged chips]
Even girls slap you now in style
Buy new clothes, tear them, bring them to the tailor to be resewn
Chat on the computer, and get the girls while chatting
Even if you don't have a car, show off with a key...
When she invites you to come on time, go late
Have your affairs at night and sleep through the day
Throw a marriage party before getting married
If you've gotten married, say you're a bachelor
If you start working, don't act like an employee
If anyone asks you what you do
Say you are still in college
Speak your heart out to a girl over the mobile
Always keep in style [author's translation]

The focus of style—enjoying or, more often, emulating expensive things (cars, cell phones, designer jeans, Western-style fast food) and relating to friends and girls through them—can include being tough and protecting girls from the bhais, the gangster-types. Of the two heroes, Chantu (played by Sahil Khan) is muscle-bound and leads the pair in a reprise of 'This is Style' while they beat up a group of toughs threatening women in their college class:

Marti hain ladkiyaan mere pe pyaar se, hey, hey, hey
Lena na dushmani tu mere yaar se
Yeh meri muscle se dekh side pose se
das kilo ka mukka hai yeh, dekh close se
Ya ya ya, yeah
Yeh hai style, yeh hai style

Girls could die for my love
Do not make enemies with my buddy
Take a side profile of my muscles
It's a ten-kilo punch...here you go.
This is style, this is style [author's translation].

The middle section of the film begins when two girls in their class, the sisters Rani and Sheena, outsmart Bantu and Chantu, who thought they were enjoying a fancy meal and liquor at a five-star hotel at a friend's expense, only to be beaten up and thrown out as good-for-nothings. The boys realize that the only way they can truly enjoy life without 'acting like an employee' or government clerk is to use their style to win the hearts of rich girls. In a song that became the film's biggest hit, 'Excuse Me', the two young men go from woman to woman, trying to find someone both wealthy and 'available'. The pleasures of the song lie in part in its rich lyrics, which draw on particular conventions of representing the language and accent of the *tapori*, the rowdy or street thug of Mumbai. The most eligible wealthy girls turn out to be Rani and Sheena, who know the boys to be smart-alecks and cheaters. So, Bantu and Chantu use the identity cards, which they happen to find, of two other girls and dress in drag to gain access to Rani and Sheena. Through complicated machinations, their ploy works and the girls fall in love with the two men.

The third and final part of the film brings in the police and the villainous Nikki. Reshma and her friend Rose, whom Bantu and Chantu are emulating, turn out to be the two women killed by the villain. The police suspect the two boys. The four young people eventually figure out that the villain must be Nikki, who has taken on a position as a teacher in their college. In the penultimate scene, Nikki is suspended from a lighthouse tower, about to fall to her death. As she is still their teacher, Bantu and Chantu, despite her evil deeds, try to save her. She tells them, in Hindi, 'So learn one final lesson. Don't make the mistake that I made in my own life' (author's translation) and then in English, just before falling to her well-deserved death, 'There is no shortcut. There is no shortcut.'

Nikki and the world of violent greed she represents stand at *the limits to style*. If there are no shortcuts, what hope the Bantus and Chantus of the world have for the Ranis and Sheenas? Still, it is a film. Heroes for saving the day, the boys may have a shot at redemption, and the final song reprised 'Excuse Me', with the girls singing this time as the aggressors to a new commodity beat:

Pizza Hut mein dekha tujhe pehli baar
McDonalds mein hoge tere se pyaar
Bolti hoon main sachchi baat
Dhabawala se pooch lena yaar

I saw you at Pizza Hut for the first time
At McDonald's I fell in love with you
I'm telling you the truth
Asks the guy who runs the canteen, dude [author's translation]

But when the girls tell the boys they will need to get their father's permission, Bantu and Chantu look over in the film's final shot to see with dawning horror that their prospective father-in-law is one of the many men they have tricked: no shortcuts?

The danger of emulating the elite world of fashion by a person from a *mamuli* or ordinary background is a repeated theme in both film and news reportage. In the 2003 film *Oops*, Jahaan is a young man who along with his friends works as a background dancer in Hindi films and hopes for a career as a star. His friends counsel patience, but they are from wealthier families while Jahaan's father is a drunkard and yet another paternal failure. So Jahaan takes a position as a model, which turns out to be a job as a male stripper for socialite women. He disastrously ends up as a gigolo with a demanding older lover, who incestuously turns out to be his best's friend's mother.

In the 2005 film *Bunty aur Babli*, Rani Mukherjee plays a young woman from a small town, who dreams of making it big as a fashion model and beauty queen, only to find out at her first competition that success involves sexual favours to contest organizers. Along with an equally disillusioned small-town boy, played by Abhishek Bachchan, she turns to a life of con artistry among the wealthy, cheating the cheaters, but here too shortcuts have their price. The two are forced back into ordinary life. Babli, Mukhejee's character, sees her future reduced to a doomed life of making pickles. But in a last-minute *deus ex machina*, the pair is allowed to return to glamour as special police officers charged with exposing the shortcuts of others. If con artistry, an offence under Indian Penal Code 420, has a venerable position as a sign of urban elite life in films, in *Bunty aur Babli* it becomes the mimesis of fashion.

And in Sony Entertainment's television serial *Jassi Jaisi Koi Nahin* (There's No One Like Jassi; 2003–5), based on the Columbian telenovela *Yo Soy Betty, La Fea*, a *mamuli ladki* (ordinary girl) survives the cut-throat world of high fashion without losing her values, eventually discovering her 'inner beauty' and then undergoing a total style makeover. The last of these narratives is a global media property, generating over one dozen remakes in countries from Turkey to China, Russia, and Belgium and including the serial *Ugly Betty* in the US. The theme of two orders of life and their hopeful, troubling nexus in the face of globalizing fashion—the ordinary or ugly and the beautiful—extends far beyond Varanasi.

Newspapers and websites throughout India recount 'modelling scams' as a ubiquitous feature of crime reporting in the 2000s. Similar stories appear in European, US, and Australian media, for example, but with far less prominence than in India, given fashion's centrality to the contemporary structure of celebrity.

Websites, both India-based and foreign, proliferate with head and body shots and statistics of would-be male and female models from cities and small towns across South Asia. Stories like the episode from *Bunty aur Babli* are legion, but another common plot line features a would-be young male model or actor being seduced by a powerful older male in the fashion business. Thus, in the 2004 movie *Let's Enjoy*, a young, working-class body-builder in Delhi hopes to make it onto the elite modelling scene by gate-crashing a tony farmhouse party on the city's outskirts, only to be told by a gay fashion designer that sex was the precondition for his help. And in the 2005 film *Page Three*, an indictment of the vapidity and selfishness of the eponymous celebrity culture, the heroine asks her well-connected gay best friend to help her struggling boyfriend find a job in the industry, only to discover them sleeping together as the price of admission. The figure of the predatory gay man, who manipulates the gap between poor men's style and rich men's fashion, extends beyond the movies. I have elsewhere examined the media circus following the 2006 murder of two men in Delhi by two other men they had picked up for sex. One of the two victims, development expert Pushkin Chandra, was posthumously accused not only of being responsible for his own death but of being the criminal mastermind of a modelling scam tricking young men into stripping for pornographic photos (Cohen 2007). The intensity of this media attention to the figure of the predatory designer led to months of enhanced police presence at clubs, parties, and cruising areas, with a chilling effect for many persons in networks and communities of men who have sex with men and in particular for poor and lower middle-class male sex workers. The gayness of the new middle class may have little to do with sex. But the extent to which the limits of fashion as a pedagogy of class mobility get routed through the bogey of the predatory gay designer, this sexualized figure of violent privilege may have very real effects on men who have sex with men.

THE FATHER'S LACK AND STYLE'S REVERSAL

I began with the accounts of Naushad and Sanjeev because they suggest the continuing attraction of the world of films and media for 'small town' men in the face of an apparent impasse in imaginable futures and relations. Additionally, one local interpretation of the failures of these young men is worth pondering over: the responsibility of the father in the son's turn to style.

Another of Sanjeev's brothers once complained, in reference to Sanjeev's drug dealing, 'Our father is useless—what do you expect us to do?' This lament is ubiquitous in the cinema of style: a young man's sense that his father substantively and materially had failed him. Style may evoke the danger of the 'shortcut.' Its excessive cultivation of the immaterial world of code may threaten to be more a simulacrum of, than a pathway to, new possessions and substantive relations. But the turn to self-making as con artistry is justified in terms of the failure of kin relations of descent: specifically, of a father who cannot adequately 'settle' his sons. In the case of Naushad, few, except his close friends, saw in his hardworking father the failure or wastrel of the films, but what was shared was a sense that he could offer his son only the future of being a naukar, the servant or labourer many young men perceive their fathers to be or have been.

The figure of the father's lack and the doom he offers comes out comically in *Style* and tragicomically in *Bunty aur Babli* in the resistance of Bunty, the male hero, to following his father as a petty official (a railway ticket inspector) dependent upon the bribes of the powerful. The film's ending rescues the errant heroes from a return to mamuli life by offering the pleasurable resolution of a new father, the police officer who had ended their life of stylish fraud but who calls them back to take up style once again, but now within the law. That Amitabh Bachchan, the famed actor playing the policeman, is the real-life father of the actor playing Bunty, secures our recognition that style can be redeemed if only we can imagine a new kind of father.

Adoptive fathers abound in the cinema of the 1990s through 2000s. One narrative offers the adopted or illegitimate child's demonstration of true filial devotion set against the modern selfishness of legitimate children. In the 2003 movie *Baghban*, only an adopted orphan son engages his ageing parents with respect while the four biological and legitimate sons and their wives treat them cruelly. In the 2002 movie *Yeh Hai Jalwa*, only an illegitimate son is willing to give his kidney to the dying father who refuses to acknowledge him, while the latter's legitimate children refuse to donate. In both these films, the poor hero (played in each case by actor Salman Khan) masters the codes of elite self-presentation but rather than encounter style's limit, he is revealed as the one authentic child. The poor boy's emulation of a legitimate filial relation is revealed as more real than the fashionable lives of the 'real' children.

In both cases, Salman Khan's characters demonstrate great success at business in corporate India. The pleasure of these films reverses the situation of *Style*: because elite sons can depend on the support of their fathers, they do not have the edge of boys who must rely on their own skills. The latter are revealed as the true harbingers of the nation's corporate future. Style—the poor boy's resource—is imaginatively re-fashioned as the creative potential needed for India to master the world's codes. Far from being a shortcut that brings poor boys into dangerous proximity with villains, style figures the creative demands of a new global economy against the less improvisational world of fashionable daughters and sons. Similarly, in the global formula of *Yo Soy Betty, La Fea* through its transmutation into *Jassi Jaisi Koi Nahin*, the ordinary and ugly Jassi in her constant battle against the 'legitimate' children of wealth and beauty, masters a form of life that allows her, in the end, to achieve a beauty that is more than skin deep.

Such productions are fantasies, of course: a large body of collective experience affirms style in its excess as an ultimately failed project of evading the life of an abject naukar or a pickle-making and painfully ordinary daughter-in-law. But many in the small town colleges and modest city neighbourhoods that these films represent as dead ends continue to imagine a relation to something called fashion as the pre-eminent site not only of hope's limit but also of its persistence. Style is not only a threshold form; it stands as an open question, as the possibility of a *relation to what it is not*. Style is not only misrecognition but one of the more reflexive sites for thinking through the possibilities and limits of human projects in the age of fashion. As such, and as the song says, it may well pack a 10-kilo punch.

REFERENCES

Banerjee, Sumanta (1989), *The Parlour and the Streets: Elite and Popular Culture in Nineteenth-Century Calcutta*. Calcutta: Seagull Books.

Chowdhury, Indira (1998), *The Frail Hero and Virile History: Gender and the Politics of Culture in Colonial Bengal*. New Delhi: Oxford University Press.

Cohen, Lawrence (1994), 'The Pleasures of Castration: The Postoperative Status of Hijras, Jankhas, and Academics', in Paul Abramson and Steven Pinkerton (eds), *Sexual Nature, Sexual Culture*. Chicago: University of Chicago Press, pp. 276–304.

——— (2002), 'What Mrs. Besahara Saw: Reflections on the Gay Goonda', in Ruth Vanita (ed.), *Queering India: Same-Sex Love and Eroticism in Indian Culture and Society*. New York: Routledge, pp. 149–60.

Cohen, Lawrence (2007), 'Song for Pushkin', *Daedalus*, Spring, 136(2): 103–15.
Dwyer, Rachel (2000), *All You Want Is Money, All You Need Is Love: Sex and Romance in Modern India*. London: Cassell.
Giddens, Anthony (1992), *The Transformation of Intimacy: Sexuality, Love, and Eroticism in Modern Societies*. Stanford: Stanford University Press.
Hansen, Kathryn (1992), *Grounds for Play: The Nautanki Theatre of North India*. Berkeley: University of California Press.
—— (2004), 'Theatrical Transvestism in the Parsi, Gujarati and Marathi Theatres (1850–1940)', in Sanjay Srivastava (ed.), *Sexual Sites, Seminal Attitudes*. New Delhi: Sage Publications, pp. 99–122.
Hansen, Thomas (1999), *The Saffron Wave: Democracy and Hindu Nationalism in Modern India*. Princeton: Princeton University Press.
Kapse, Anupama (2009), 'The Moving Image: Melodrama and Early Cinema in India, 1913–1947', PhD dissertation, Department of Rhetoric, University of California, Berkeley.
Lutgendorf, Philip (n.d.), 'Anand', available at http://www.uiowa.edu/~incinema/Anand.html (accessed on 29 July 2009).
Mazzarella, William (2003), *Shoveling Smoke: Advertising and Globalization in Contemporary India*. Durham: Duke University Press.
Nandy, Ashis (1983), *The Intimate Enemy: Loss and Recovery of Self under Colonialism*. New Delhi: Oxford University Press.
Rege, Sharmila (1996), 'The Hegemonic Appropriation of Sexuality: The Case of the *Lavani* Performers of Maharashtra', in Patricia Uberoi (ed.), *Social Reform, Sexuality and the State*. New Delhi: Sage Publications, pp. 23–38.
Sinha, Mrinalini (1995), *Colonial Masculinity: The 'Manly Englishman' and the 'Effeminate Bengali' in the Late Nineteenth Century*. Manchester: Manchester University Press.
Srivastava, Sanjay (2007), *Passionate Modernity: Sexuality, Class, and Consumption in India*. New Delhi: Routledge.
Tarlo, Emma (1996), *Clothing Matters: Dress and Identity in India*. Chicago: University of Chicago Press.
Vanita, Ruth (2002), 'Homophobic Fiction/Homoerotic Advertising: The Pleasures and Perils of Twentieth-Century Indianness', in Vanita (ed.), *Queering India*, pp. 127–48.
Verma, Himanshu (2004), *The Metrosexuals: Exploring the Unexplored*. New Delhi: Red Earth.

V. LABOUR

Chapter 9

FAMILY AND FACTORY

Women in the Bombay Cotton Textile Industry, 1919–39 *

....

RADHA KUMAR

WOMEN CONSTITUTED A HIGH PROPORTION of the workforce in the cotton textile industry between 1919 and 1939, touching 22.9 per cent in 1926. From 1929 onwards there was a steady decline in their number, reaching 14.9 per cent in 1939. Various reasons for this decline have been cited, such as the passing of the Maternity Benefit and the Prohibition of Night Work Acts, and the mechanization of the industry. Further analysis shows, however, that these causes should be treated rather as symptoms; underlying them are attempts to reform the working class family.

Always an important part of any community, the family assumed vital importance for administrators, planners, and employers in the 1920s and 1930s. It was at this time that family budget surveys were sponsored, investigations conducted into infant and maternal welfare, and charitable institutions supported. At the centre of all these activities stood the concept of woman as mother—in particular, the working class woman as mother of the second generation proletarian.

* Originally published in *The Indian Economic and Social History Review*, 1983, 20(1): 81–96.

In fact, this concept has dominated a majority of statements regarding women: not merely those made by capitalists, bureaucrats, and philanthropists, but also those made by Marxists, trade unionists, and labour historians. Their assumptions seem to be that women are, and therefore identify themselves as, sisters, wives, and mothers, as family goddesses and domestic drudges. This is their primary 'role', and, therefore, even when they are workers they lack class consciousness, since wage work is for them only a secondary influence in their lives. Thus, capitalists complain of women's 'lack of commitment' to wage work—the reason being that women are supported by their men, or can be, and therefore wage labour is not essential to their survival.

On the same premise, trade unionists argue that women are 'docile' and exert a restraining influence on the militancy of the labour movement. Underlying both views is the definition of women's wage labour as being 'supplementary' to the man's wage. In fact, this definition is a complex one. Actually, the women employed by the Bombay cotton textile industry were not working to supplement their family wage—almost 40 per cent of them were widows and another 30 per cent supported their husbands and children (Dwarkadas 1962: 98).[1] All the same, it seems to have been accepted that women were to be paid less than men. Rationalizing this, the argument of the capitalists was that women's wage labour *was* supplementary; but why was it that women themselves did not demand equal pay for equal work? Was it because they too saw their wage work as supplementary, even when it was not? My argument is that the issue was so complicated by distinctions of time and piece-work, and by the sexual division of labour, that this question of equal pay for equal work did not really arise. The winding and reeling departments were staffed almost entirely by women; they rarely worked as spinners and never as weavers. In this context, asking why women did not demand wage parity with men is like asking why spinners did not demand the same wage as weavers.

Moreover, the notion that workers had a 'right' to earn a family wage was not a prevalent one. It was introduced only in the late 1920s and early 1930s, and was defined with reference to the male worker alone. As it came hand-in-hand with retrenchment for women, it cannot be argued that women accepted lower wages because they did not expect to support a family. Women accepted lower wages because that was what winders

[1] Dwarkadas's figures refer to one group of mills alone, and there is some doubt as to their accuracy. Even so, one could estimate that in 45–50 per cent of the cases it was the woman's wage which was the major one in supporting the family, if it was not the sole one, as among widows.

and reelers were paid; they did not demand a wage sufficient to support a family on because the concept did not exist—they made do with what they had, and when they could not make do, they borrowed.

Logically, the notion of women's wage labour being supplementary can only follow from the idea that the man's wage ought to be a family wage—that is, that it ought to be the 'primary' wage. If this notion itself was not a widespread one, then women's wage labour could not have been supplementary. My contention is that it became so only at a certain period of time, after the introduction of the concept of the family wage.

If this is the case, then the assumption that a woman's role is primarily that of wife and mother—and all those deductions following it—is also a historically conditioned one. My aim here is to show how these assumptions appeared, and how they determined the wage work of women. My thesis is that attempts to rationalize the industry were linked with attempts to rationalize the working class family and that both were directed towards stabilizing the working class in Bombay.

IN SEARCH OF A FAMILY

Attempts to define the working class family are present in many government reports of the period, from the 1922 *Family Budget Survey* conducted by the Bombay Labour Office onwards. A flexible form till then, the family was transformed by the 1922 report into a 'unit', comprising father, mother, and children. This unit was termed the 'self-contained' family, and held to be representative of working class families of the period. 82.1 per cent of their sampled budgets were of this kind. The average size of a working class family, according to this survey, was 4.2 persons—1.1 men, 1.1 women, and 2 children under 14, 'exclusive of 0.6 dependants living away from it' (*Working Class Family Budget Survey* [FBS] 1921–2: 7). The survey defines 'dependants' as consisting of 'relatives living away from the family and partially or wholly relying for their maintenance on the remittance from Bombay' (ibid.: 6).

In the *Family Budget Survey* of 1932, the 'self-contained unit' was renamed the 'natural family', outlawing in effect the joint family of several centuries. Here, again, the 'natural family' was held to be the form representative of working class families but, strangely enough in the face of this claim, the proportion of natural families to total families surveyed seems to have dwindled from 82 per cent in 1922 to around 66 per cent in 1931–2. The size of the family too had dwindled (from 4.2 in 1922 to 3.7 in 1932), while the 'number of dependants living away from the family' rose marginally to 0.65 (*FBS* 1932–3: 11). This decline in family size is rather puzzling, given that the 1932 survey shows an increase in the number of joint families, from 17.9 per cent in 1922 to 34 per cent in 1932. The compilers of the survey suggest that the apparent decline in family size is due to differences in the sampling method between the 1922 survey and the 1932 survey rather than to actual changes. According to them, the 1922 survey revealed a larger family size because it chose to primarily sample families of 'father, mother, and children', while the 1932 survey showed families 'as they were', that is to say, it included childless couples (ibid.: 8). While it is true that the sampling procedures of the 1922 survey were somewhat selective,[2] they did include figures for childless couples. Moreover, though the fertility rate probably declined between 1921 and 1931, so did the rate of infant mortality, so there were more live infants proportionately in 1931 than in 1921. My estimated fertility rates show that there were 1,020 births per 1,000 mothers in 1921, while there were 791 births per 1,000 mothers in 1931. These are figures for live births only, since still-birth figures for these two years are not available. When we consider that the average rate of still-births per 1,000 mothers from the 'mill-worker class', under the best conditions, was 115 in 1930, then we can estimate by how great a degree these fertility rates are an underestimation.[3] I have given them here only to provide a comparison between 1921 and 1931. However sharp the decline in fertility rates might have been in this decade, it was offset by a decline in infant mortality—while in 1921 there were 348 children aged between 0 and 5 per 1,000 women aged between 15 and 45, in 1931 the comparative figure was 507 (*COI* 1921: 24; *COI*: Vol. IX, Part II, p. 170). If anything, the family size would have increased rather than decreased.

This thesis is corroborated by the 1930 Labour Office Enquiry into the family budgets of cotton mill workers in Bombay city, which gave remarkably divergent figures for the size of the working class family. According to this survey, the average size of the family was 5.46 people,

---

[2] Attempts were made to select, as far as possible, a self-contained family consisting of a husband, wife, and children. It was, however, discovered that families were made up of more than two adults and these were, therefore, included. See *FBS* (1921–2: 4).

[3] These fertility rates have been calculated by dividing the total number of married women aged 15–45 by the total number of live infants aged 0–5, and then adding infant mortality figures for those particular years. Infant mortality figures for 1931 were not available, but I had figures for 1927 and 1936, so I calculated the infant mortality rate for 1931 from these two sets of figures. For the figures of married women aged 15–45 and infants aged 0–5, I used the *Census of India* (*COI*) tables on age, sex, and civil condition, for 1921 and 1931. See *COI* (1921: xi–xiii; 1931: Part II, p. 167).

of which 3.58 lived in Bombay and 1.88 away. This latter number is three times that of the 1932 survey. The fact that the 1930 enquiry referred to cotton mill workers alone is not particularly significant in explaining the difference between family sizes given in it and in 1932, for around 70 per cent of the budgets used for the 1932 survey were also those of cotton mill workers. Equally, the argument that due to disturbed conditions the head of the family may have sent some 'dependants' to the village, while providing a plausible explanation for the swell of out-city dependants, leaves a further problem—if these people properly belonged to the in-city family, then its size would have been 4.76, a number which is considerably higher than that given in the 1932 enquiry (*Labour Gazette* 1931: 476).

In fact, between 1921 and 1931, the proportion of 'dependants' to actual workers rose sharply. In 1921, 39 per cent of the total population of Bombay city were 'dependants' while 61 per cent were actual workers; in 1931, 51 per cent were 'dependants' while only 49 per cent were workers (*COI* 1931: Part I, p. 20). Equally, the proportion of the population under 15 years to the total population showed an increase from 21.1 per cent in 1921, to 24.4 per cent in 1931, to 26.1 per cent in 1941. At the same time, there was a decline in the number of people married.

TABLE 9.1 Percentages of Married, Unmarried, and Widowed to the Total Population, by Sex

Year	Married		Unmarried		Widowed	
	Male	Female	Male	Female	Male	Female
1921	59.83	55.75	37.01	29.67	3.16	14.58
1931	59.70	53.81	38.38	35.05	1.92	11.14
1941	53.19	48.50	43.80	39.75	3.01	11.75

Sources: 'Age, Sex and Civil Condition' tables, *COI* (1921: xi–xii); *COI* (1931: Part II, p. 167); *COI* (1951: 2).

The decline appears to be due in part to an increase in the age of marriage. This was most noticeable in the decade 1931–41 (see Table 9.2).

In the 10–15 age group, this increase in the age of marriage took place mainly between 1921 and 1931; but in the 15–20 and 20–5 age groups, 1931–41 were the decisive years. It would appear from this that there was a continuous rise in the age of marriage—while 31 per cent of the women aged 10–15 were married in 1921, only 14 per cent were married in 1931; while 73 per cent of the women aged 15–20 were married in 1931, only 58 per cent were married in 1941. The equivalent decline for men is from 8 per cent to 5 per cent in the age group 10–15 in 1921, and 33 per cent to 17

TABLE 9.2 Age, Sex, and Civil Condition: Variations in Proportions of Married Population, Bombay City, 1921–41

Age	Men*			Women*		
	1921	1931	1941	1921	1931	1941
0–5	0.7	0.5	1.1	1.0	0.5	0.6
5–10	1.8	1.9	1.5	4.8	3.3	2.4
10–15	8.2	4.7	3.1	31.0	13.8	12.7
15–20	25.3	33.3	16.8	75.4	73.2	58.3
20–5	54.8	53.3	45.5	86.5	85.5	83.6
25–30	75.2	81.9	70.5	86.4	89.9	87.2
30–35	85.8	87.7	85.3	81.0	86.9	84.7
35–40	88.4	91.0	88.3	71.1	72.8	74.8
40–5	88.5	90.6	88.4	64.2	62.3	61.3
45–50	86.6	87.7	86.2	47.0	42.3	43.6
50–5	82.6	85.4	81.8	33.9	35.3	35.8
55–60	80.4	79.2	77.2	33.2	25.4	24.7
60–5	75.9	76.2	71.9	21.1	22.8	18.6
65–70	70.4	72.3	66.7	22.1	21.4	16.7
70+	67.7	70.0	62.8	18.6	20.9	16.3

Sources: 'Age, Sex and Civil Condition' tables, *COI* (1921: xi–xii); *COI* (1931: Part II, p. 167); *COI* (1951: 2).

Note: *These figures are percentages of married men or women within each age group to the total population of men or women within that age group.

per cent in the age group 15–20 between 1931 and 1941. In general, men married much later than women did, and women were widowed younger and in far greater number than men were.

Even though the age of marriage was rising and fewer people were getting married, there was a rise in the number of married men who brought their families to the city. The proportion of this category to the total figures for married men was 48.9 per cent in 1921, 49.9 per cent in 1931, and 53 per cent in 1941.[4]

Taken together, these factors seem to indicate a rise in the number of working class families in Bombay city, and a rise in the size of these families. In other words, there were a larger number of unmarried sons and daughters living with their parents than before, and the number of 'dependants', which includes widowed parents of wage earners, etc., had risen.

---

[4] Percentages compiled from the same *COI* tables which were used to compile Table 9.2.

The decline in the number of people marrying during this period and the rise in the age of marriage was caused partly by the spiralling retrenchment of women which reduced the number of wage-earners per family quite considerably and aided in the growing pauperization of the working classes in Bombay city. The extent of pauperization is shown by an increase in the number of families earning below Rs 40 per month.

When in 1932 the *Family Budget Survey* defined the 'natural family' as consisting of 'members who have a right to be fed, housed, and clothed by the head of the family, that is to say, the wife and unmarried children of an individual' (*FBS* 1932–3: 6), it was like wishful thinking. Women constituted 21.95 per cent of the labour force in the cotton textile industry by then, and in around 30 per cent of the natural families surveyed by the family budgeteers, the woman (wife and mother) worked. All of them were in the Rs 30–50 income group, and most belonged to families whose total income was less than Rs 40. Of the total budget considered by the survey, 27 per cent was in this category, and there was no way in which they could make ends meet had the woman not worked (ibid.: 9–14). Given these conditions, it is difficult to understand the foundations on which this straw man, the patriarch of the modern 'natural family', was built.

Yet the statement was made, and made in the context of the rapid rationalization of the industry and the consequent retrenchment of women. Two significant points emerge from this statement: first, that this definition of the family contravened customary 'law' in India, under which parents had a right to be supported by their sons, brothers acknowledged a responsibility to each other, to widowed sisters and daughters-in-law, and even to distant relatives. This is not a semantic point, since the size of the family and the financial obligations of its 'head' had a distinct bearing on the budget considered adequate to support a family. The smaller the family, the lower the cost of maintaining it, and hence the lower the wage required.

The second point is that this statement makes explicit the notion of a 'family wage', that is, that the wage of the man alone should suffice to support the whole family. Notably, none of the earlier official reports made this point: though the woman's wage appears always to have been a 'supplementary wage' (that is, it was not expected that women would support their families entirely), the man's wage was not earlier considered to be a 'family wage'.

Given the changes in industrial organization which were to follow, this statement of a 'family wage' sounds prophetic. According to the 1932 *Family Budget Survey*, the proportion of workers to dependants was 41.4

per cent to 58.6 per cent;[5] in 1944, this proportion became 34.9 per cent to 65.1 per cent. While women workers constituted 22 per cent of the total workers in the 1932 survey, by 1944 they constituted only 18 per cent. And there was a continuous decline in the number of wage earners per family from 1920 to 1940. While in 1921, 46.5 per cent of the families covered by the survey had two or more wage earners, in 1932 there were 43.8 per cent of such families, and in 1944 there were only 33 per cent.[6] The sharpest decline seems to have been between 1932 and 1944, which corroborates the thesis that rationalization and the one-wage-per-family concept came in simultaneously.

When placed in this context, the 1932 statement on the 'family wage' begins to read like a declaration of intent. After all, if 41.4 per cent of working class families in 1932 lived on the wages brought in by two or more workers, then it is difficult to believe that the wives and children of male workers felt they had a 'right' to be supported by their husbands and fathers. Yet this right was formulated by the 1932 survey, and by 1940 the 'family wage' had come to stay—according to the Textile Labour Enquiry Committee's report, it was not to be expected that the women should work since her domestic duties, which had first priority, would preclude wage work. If at all the woman did engage in wage labour, then it was economic hardship which forced her to do so, and her wage was intended to 'supplement' the family income (*TLECR* 1940: 305).

This point about the woman's wage being a 'supplementary wage' was also made by the 1932 *Family Budget Survey*, in a slightly different context:

The controversy regarding the demand for equal pay for equal work is an old one but even to this day statistical proof is wanting, at least so far as the Indian working class is concerned, as regards the extent to which women workers have to support dependants, especially children under 14 years of age. During the present enquiry information was specially gathered on this point and separately tabulated...only in nine cases had a female worker any children under 14 years of age to support and in no case was the number of dependants more than two (*FBS* 1932–3: 12).

This conclusion is somewhat peculiar, given that a fair proportion of women workers were widows. In a survey of the Sassoon Group of Mills, made between 1937 and 1941, Kanji Dwarkadas found that over one-third of the women employed there were widows.

---

[5] These figures are rather different from those given earlier. A probable explanation for the difference is that while the earlier figures were for all Bombay, these figures represent mainly cotton textile workers' families. The fact that there was a higher proportion of dependants to workers for such families could indicate a larger family size.

[6] For all these figures, see *FBS* (1932–3: 12; 1944–6: 13–15).

TABLE 9.3 Classification of Women according to Age Groups, 1937–41

Age Group	Women with Husbands Living				Widows		
	Total Women Workers	Number	Per Cent to Total in Age Group	Per Cent to Total in Category	Number	Per Cent to Total in Age Group	Per Cent to Total in Category
Below 20	74	71	95.9	2.8	3	4.1	0.2
20–5	781	675	86.4	26.6	106	13.6	6.8
26–35	1,851	1,258	68.0	49.5	593	32.0	38.0
36–45	1,006	439	43.6	17.3	567	56.4	36.3
46–55	359	93	25.9	3.6	266	74.1	17.1
Over 56	30	5	16.7	0.2	25	83.3	1.6
Total	4,101	2,541	62.0	100.0	1,560	38.0	100

Source: Dwarkadas (1962).

Note: Dwarkadas does not give figures for unmarried women workers here, but in another series of tables he puts the total number of women workers at 4,302. This means that there were 201 unmarried women working in the E.D. Sassoon Group of Mills, which is where he conducted this survey.

As can be seen from Table 9.3, a significant proportion (38 per cent) of widows were between 26 and 35 years old, and within the 36–45 age group widows outnumbered women with husbands living. Moreover, 55 per cent of these widows had children and 25 per cent of them had more than two children (see Table 9.4).

Certainly most women with more than two children would have at least two 'dependants under 14 years of age'. Equally, even if those within the 36–45 age group had children who were wage labourers and contributing to the family income, surely few in the 25–35 age group would. And finally, would these children not, according to the methods of categorization used by the survey, be 'supplementing' their mother's income? Would she not, as

TABLE 9.4 Children of Widowed Women Workers, 1941

Age of Women	Number of Women with				
	1 Child	2 Children	3 Children	4 and more than 4 Children	Total
Below 20	–	–	1	–	1
20–5	24	13	7	2	46
26–35	150	95	45	26	316
36–45	149	95	51	42	337
46–55	74	39	24	17	154
Over 55	6	3	1	2	12
Total	403	245	129	89	866
Per cent in each category to total	46.5	28.3	14.9	10.3	100.0

Source: Dwarkadas (1962: 104).

'head of the family', be the 'principal breadwinner'? And, according to the principle of the 'family wage' enunciated in 1932, would this not entitle her to a wage which, if not equal to the male wage, at least suffices to support her family?

Kanji Dwarkadas, in the same survey, shows that of the women with husbands living, 25.9 per cent of these men had wives who were between 20 and 35 years old (Dwarkadas 1962: 100). Commenting on this figure, Kanji Dwarkadas notes 'with regret that the husbands of 659 women were unemployed and the principal breadwinners of the family were the women themselves' (ibid.: 99).

Clearly he was a man to call a spade a spade unlike the Labour Office budget-makers. Not that this directness was of much help to women workers, to whose wage work the label 'supplementary', which was affixed in 1932, continues to adhere even today.

THE SLOUGH OF LABOUR

Should any allowance be made for the possible earnings of a wife? It has been argued that, under a proper interpretation of the term 'living wage standard', a wife should be spared for the duties of the household and for looking after the children. She cannot be and should not be expected to supplement the earnings by extra paid work.

To this an important consideration has to be added, in our case, an argument of another type. An allowance for the earnings of the wife can only be made if it is always or at least ordinarily possible for the wife to obtain suitable gainful employment. On this point, the evidence of the family budget studies is overwhelmingly clear. They show that in a vast majority of cases the wife was not, in actual fact, in any employment (*TLECR* 1940: 305).[7]

So far I have shown how the attitude of the state, of capitalists, and of reformers towards the working class family all tended to reinforce the notion that women's wage labour was 'supplementary' to the family income, which was earned by the male labourer. We have also seen how this attitude revealed itself more strongly as the years advanced (as did capitalism), culminating in the statement quoted earlier. I have also

---

[7] Interestingly, male workers did not demand in Bombay, as they did in Britain in the mid-nineteenth century, that women be retrenched and a family wage paid. See Hartmann (1979).

tried to show that when statements of this nature were first made, they reflected intent rather than fact, since women's wage labour was anything but supplementary, being in the majority of cases the sole family income. Further, I have suggested that the intent underlying these statements was not to turn women's wage labour into supplementary labour but to assert that the 'primary role' of women was to reproduce labour power. It follows from this that to put women in this position it was required that they be gradually withdrawn from wage labour. In fact, from the late 1920s onwards, there was a steady fall in the number of women employed.

In 1919, women constituted 20.3 per cent of the labour force. In 1930, this proportion rose to 22.9 per cent, but from 1930 onwards there was a consistent decline in their numbers—from 18.9 per cent in 1934 to 14.9 per cent in 1939 (Morris 1965: 66). In absolute numbers, the peak year for the employment of women was 1926.

While the highest number of women workers in the industry was in 1926, the proportion of women workers to the total cotton textile labour force was highest in 1930 (Morris 1965: 66, 217–18). Between 1926 and 1930, the fall in the number of women employed was over 20 per cent—in fact, there was a corresponding fall in the number of men employed. The years of the great strike, 1928–9, saw a decline of almost 30,000 in the total cotton textile labour force as compared to 1926. It is not surprising, therefore, that 1930 should show a sharp rise both in the total number of workers in the cotton textile industry and in the number of women employed. What is intriguing is that this was the year in which the proportion of women workers to all workers in the cotton textile industry was highest, higher even than in 1926. In fact, between 1929 and 1930, the rise in the number of women employed was about 7 per cent greater than the increase in the total cotton textile labour force. Why was this? Does it show that women were quicker to rejoin work than men, and if so, why?

One possible explanation, supported by the evidence of Balfour and Talpode (1931: 362–3), is that fewer women in proportion to their total number went back to their villages during the strike than men did. The women employed by the cotton textile industry were, after all, either married and living with their families in Bombay, or widows who had been forced to leave their villages by the reversion of property, pauperization, or ill-treatment by their families. In any case they had weaker links with their villages than many of the men who had come to Bombay mainly in search of a living, leaving their families behind. Unfortunately, figures are not available to prove this hypothesis for all workers, but Kanji Dwarkadas's survey of women workers in the Sassoon Group of Mills shows that roughly

30 per cent of them were married to men working either in the same mill or in the cotton textile industry; that slightly over 30 per cent were married to men employed by other enterprises; and that almost 40 per cent of them were widows (Dwarkadas 1962: 98).

Several questions are raised by these statistics. It is, after all, fairly unusual to find that such a large proportion of women workers were widows. In contrast, relatively few women workers in either the Ahmedabad or Sholapur textile industry were widows. Why was Bombay different? Where did these widows come from? What castes were they and under what circumstances did they migrate from their native villages and come to Bombay in search of work?

When we look at birthplace statistics for women mill workers, we find that over 60 per cent of them came from Ratnagiri, and over 90 per cent from Bombay Presidency. The 1921 Census shows that 60.8 per cent of the women working in the Bombay cotton textile industry came from Ratnagiri; according to the Mill Owners' Association (MOA) Survey of 1940, 76.8 per cent of women mill workers came from the Konkan. (An increase in women's immigration from Ratnagiri can, however, be discounted, as the 'Konkan' included, besides Ratnagiri, Bombay Suburban, Poona, and Thana.) On the other hand, we cannot assume a fall in immigration either, since the Konkan, excluding Ratnagiri, supplied a fairly small proportion of immigrant mill workers (approximately 9 per cent in 1921) (*COI* 1921: xiv). Furthermore, Kanji Dwarkadas's survey of the India United Group of Mills shows that 65.7 per cent of the women workers came from Ratnagiri (Dwarkadas 1962: 98).

These figures become more significant when we see that in 1921, 35.5 per cent of the total workforce in the Bombay cotton textile industry were immigrants from Ratnagiri (*COI* 1921: xiv), and around the same in 1940 (Gokhale 1958: 17).[8] These figures would tend to indicate that a fairly high proportion of mill hands from Ratnagiri were women—which is substantiated by the MOA's proportionate district-wise break down of figures by departments. According to this break down, 23.2 per cent of the total immigrant workers from the Konkan were in the winding and reeling departments—that is, were women. Moreover, a high proportion of the women immigrants from Ratnagiri worked—25.7 per cent of them in 1921

---

[8] The figure for total immigrants from the Konkan is given as 45 per cent of all mill-hands. Of this, the proportion coming from Ratnagiri would probably be slightly over 35 per cent but it seems dangerous to hazard too precise a guess.

were workers and at least 76.6 per cent of this figure were employed by the cotton textile industry.[9]

Given these figures, one would tend to assume that the ratio of women to men would also be amongst the highest for the immigrants from Ratnagiri. However, in 1921, the sex ratio of Ratnagiri immigrants ranked fairly low in E, F, and G wards (the three working class wards in Bombay).

TABLE 9.5 Sex Ratio in Three Wards, 1921–31 (Women per 1,000 Men)

	E Ward		F Ward		G Ward	
Birthplace	1921	1931	1921	1931	1921	1931
Nasik	842	633	868	795	700	660
Ahmednagar	830	792	856	781	746	734
Bombay City	814	787	841	813	804	791
Poona	766	755	803	713	646	568
Kolaba	633	703	669	597	693	727
Hyderabad (Deccan)	589	307	755	655	446	582
Thana	586	653	614	782	710	758
Ratnagiri	581	614	619	585	613	687
Kattuawar	573	525	604	606	5!2	719
Satara	555	634	563	573	564	614
Ahmedabad	528	533	516	488	328	657
Madras	490	607	395	550	370	466
Surat	474	61	429	622	590	723
Cutch	404	592	447	586	421	279
United Provinces	253	308	149	136	93	105

Source: COI (1921: ix–xi; 1931: Part II, pp. 165–6).

As we can see from Table 9.5, Ratnagiri ranked eighth in E ward in 1921 and seventh in F and G wards. Immigrants from Nasik, Ahmednagar, Bombay city, Poona, Kolaba, and Thana showed a higher sex ratio in all three wards, the difference approaching 200 between Ratnagiri and Nasik, Ahmedabad, or Bombay city. By 1931, a slight evening out in sex ratios can be seen. However, Ratnagiri did not move up in position—in E ward

[9] The *COI* of 1921 gives a break down of women mill workers by birthplace. They are divided into two categories—(a) mill operatives; (b) insufficiently described occupation. Both categories are put down as mill workers, but the totals thus arrived at outnumber the figures given for 'average daily attendance'; so I have taken the numbers in category (a) to give the percentage 76.6 and the two categories together for the percentage 25.7. I obtained the numbers for total women immigrants from Ratnagiri from birthplace statistics.

it retained the eighth position with Satara replacing Hyderabad; in F ward it was downgraded to eleventh position; while in G it remained seventh.

How then do we explain the high proportion of women workers from Ratnagiri in comparison with the relatively low sex ratio of its migrants to Bombay? First, the number of immigrants from Ratnagiri was far larger than the number of immigrants from any other part of the Presidency—particularly, women immigrants. Even so, as has been shown, a higher proportion of Ratnagiri-born immigrant women worked than from any other area, so this is by no means a complete explanation. According to one trade union activist, the reason for the large number of women workers from Ratnagiri was that the Muslims had virtually no influence in the Konkan and, therefore, the ideology governing customs such as purdah, sexual segregation, and other such customs, had little impact on the women.[10] This too can be at best only a partial explanation, for the Konkan includes Poona, Thana, and the Bombay Suburban district. Seen in conjunction with Burnett-Hurst's (1925: 10) statement that over-population drove large numbers to emigrate from Ratnagiri, we have a partial explanation for the huge number of women workers from Ratnagiri. A few details give substance to this explanation.

The large majority of women workers from Ratnagiri were Marathas or Kunbis. This caste constituted the greater proportion of women workers (*COI* 1931: Part II, p. 169); others were the Dhed, Mahar, and Chamar sub-castes of the Dalit community. Amongst the Muslims, the two main groups were the Bohras and the Sheikhs. Much has been said about the caste–class nexus, some asserting that caste undercuts class consciousness and class unity; others stating, on the contrary, that class weakens caste alliances. As can be expected, the problem was a more complex one. That workers defined themselves through caste groupings has been amply shown by Newman's study of the jobbers; equally, we know that relations of caste helped to provide jobs, housing, and support during times of need (Newman 1979).

Recent labour history in Europe and America has shown that the earlier, static view of community ties acting in opposition to class solidarity was a false one. As Ira Katznelson (1981: 13–14) says:

Under some circumstances, ethnic and racial ties may actually stimulate collective class activity.... Herbert Gutman has found that the process of industrialising native and immigrant rural and artisanal cultures in the United States, which has regularly recurred, has repeatedly provoked the kind of class-forming collisions that E.P. Thompson found

---

[10] Interview with D.S. Kulkarni of the Shramik Sangathana and formerly of the Lal Bavta Union, 16 June 1980.

to be the core elements in the making of the English working class.... Different though their particularistic pasts may be, most American workers share a heritage of material and cultural traumas, as well as common experiences in their present labours, which provide the *potential* for collaboration. Indeed, as Gutman shows, the highly differentiated community lives of ethnic workers often served as separate but reinforcing sources of refuge and energy for rebellion.

It is probably more difficult to show the same for Bombay, but it is clear that women workers saw themselves as identified by caste, and that caste could often provide a source of opposition to the managers. We can see how deep caste affiliations went through the following incident:

While I was working at the India United Mills, a group of Konkani Kunbi women winders came to me and said they had come to know that all women workers of their caste were going to be dismissed. I told them they had been told a lie, but it shows how deep their fears go.... (Dwarkadas 1962: 122)

In the latter case we have the example of a strike in the Jacob Sassoon Mill. The women workers of the winding department went on strike on 9 February 1935, demanding an increase in their wages for January and asking for the dismissal of the winding master, who they said was harassing them. The strike lasted two days, after which the women 'resumed work unconditionally'. A week later, the same women were on strike again, this time against the introduction of a 9-hour day starting at 7.30 AM. The other 'cause' for this strike was that the European manager of the mill had touched the food basket of one of the women and, therefore, polluted it. We know that food pollution was a serious grievance:

Food that has to be prepared in the early morning makes a big demand on the woman worker, and her anxiety is not at an end when the meal has been prepared. It must be kept from contamination of every kind till it is actually eaten. The fear of having it touched or even shadowed is one cause of the difficulties that sometimes prevent mills from employing members of the depressed classes in the same room with caste women. Curious bundles, wrapped in cloths that have seen much use, are poised high on machinery or hung from a nail on the wall and it is strange to think that if the covering of one were but touched the contents would be flung away, no matter how hungry the owner might be. (Kelman 1923: 76)

On the surface this might be construed as supporting the view that caste obedience undermined possibilities of class solidarity, but in conjunction with the history of the strike it can be seen as demonstrating quite the contrary. After all, it seems likely that the caste regulation on food pollution was used deliberately to humiliate the mill manager, since even under the best conditions it would have been difficult to extract an apology from him. In conjunction with their defeat in the earlier strike, under which the women may have been chafing, this gesture of accusing the manager of being a 'pollutant' displayed, at the very least, a finely attuned sense of malice.

There was always, as I have tried to show, a fairly ambivalent attitude towards women's wage labour. While from the early 1920s onwards (as the number of women workers decreased steadily), there were attempts to deny recognition of women as 'workers'—or rather, to deny that they were a substantial enough category of workers to merit recognition—it was only from the 1930s onwards that women began to be actually de-registered from the ranks of the 'productive classes'.

The official elucidation of the reasons for women's retrenchment focused on the Maternity Benefit Act and the Act restricting women from working at night.

> The percentages for both women and children employed are the smallest since 1920. This may be due to the enforcement of the Maternity Benefit Act as well as to the fact that male labour can be got very cheaply. Another factor that would affect the percentage of women employed to men is that, owing to the provisions of the Factories Act, women can't be employed at night. The number of mills working night shift has materially increased....
> (*Labour Gazette* 1935: 965)

Debates on the payment of maternity benefits in fact began almost a decade before the Act was passed, soon after the Washington Conference of 1919 which recommended that legislation on this issue be enacted by all governments. Though one mill owner in Ahmedabad and one in Sholapur were already paying benefits, no mill in Bombay did so before 1921.[11] Between January 1921 and March 1922, nine mills in Bombay introduced maternity benefit schemes, that is, a little over 10 per cent of the mills in Bombay paid such benefits. In fact, of the nine that did, two (the David Mills Nos 1 and 2) discontinued the scheme after three years, at the end of 1923. According to the information given by them, 65 women applied for and were paid the benefit of two months' wages in 1923 alone, which gives us an idea of the popularity of the scheme. No reasons were given for discontinuing it; perhaps the management decided that the scheme was expensive, and since few other mills paid benefits there was no reason why they should continue to do so. These were the only mills in the Sassoon Group to pay benefits before the Maternity Benefit Act of 1929.

---

[11] The two mills were the Ahmedabad New Textile Mills and the Sholapur Spinning and Weaving Company. For information on mills paying maternity benefits, see *Royal Commission of Labour in India*, p. 35.

In 1922, Kanji Dwarkadas tried to move a resolution in the Bombay Legislative Council demanding legislation for maternity benefits but was refused permission by Sir George Lloyd, on the grounds that such a legislation could be handled only by the central government. Sir Ibrahim Rahimtoola, one of the Rahimtoola family of mill owners, added that the government felt that legislation on the lines of the Washington Conference recommendations was 'unnecessary at present' (Dwarkadas 1962: 35).

The matter rested there for two years. Then, in July 1924, S.K. Bole moved a resolution in the Bombay Legislative Council urging the central government to introduce legislation for the provision of maternity benefits 'in all organised industries of India'. The Bombay Government decided that such a legislation would be premature, but conceded that the matter required some investigation (*Royal Commission of Labour in India*, p. 37).

In August 1924, N.M. Joshi introduced a Bill in the Bombay Legislative Council, which proposed the following measures for the provision of maternity benefits:

1. It prohibited women's employment for six weeks after confinement and allowed her the right to stop working six weeks before confinement, on the production of a medical certificate. Under the Bill, pregnant women were entitled to a maternity allowance which would be paid by the local government out of a fund called the Maternity Benefit Fund.
2. If a woman died during confinement, the benefit would be paid to whoever undertook to look after the child.
3. All employers were prohibited from dismissing women who were absent from work either six weeks before or six weeks after confinement. Any employer breaking the provisions of the Bill would be liable to a fine of up to Rs 500 (*Labour Gazette* 1924: 31).

This Bill was overruled in 1926. After another two-year gap, R.S. Asavle introduced a Bill in the Legislative Council for the provision of maternity benefits. This Bill, proposed in July 1928, two months after the general strike had started, was along the lines of N.M. Joshi's Bill, with one important difference—it placed the responsibility for paying benefits on the mill owners and not the government. Even so, the government's attitude towards maternity benefits remained unchanged.

Government opposed Mr Asavle's Maternity Benefits Bill, to grant such benefits to factory women, on the grounds of impracticality, cost, etc. However, Government was defeated, and the Bill has been sent up to a Select Committee, who have been given carte blanche, even in regard to the main principles, to redraft the Bill, if necessary, and to examine the best way of distributing and meeting the cost. (*Fortnightly Reports*, No. S.D. 882)

The Bill produced by the Select Committee, which was finally passed as an Act on 15 March 1929, had the following provisions:

1. It entitled women workers in Bombay factories, and in certain other cities in the Presidency, to maternity leave and benefit for seven weeks; three weeks before, and four after, confinement. A flat rate of 8 annas per day was to be paid to each woman, and the entire cost was to be borne by the employers.
2. The benefit was to be paid only on production of the birth registration certificate, that is, after childbirth.
3. The Act required women to work up to the first week of the ninth month of pregnancy.
4. Six months of continuous service entitled a woman to claim the benefit (*Royal Commission of Labour in India*, p. 367).

The problems created by these provisions were enormous. As shown by Balfour and Talpode, it was before childbirth that the woman needed rest most—and yet under provision 1, she was given only three weeks' leave before confinement. If she were to take more time off, she would lose her claim to the benefit. Second, the payment of the benefit only after childbirth meant that the woman could not use it to buy better food for herself. Finally, the requirement of six months of 'continuous' service permitted the same misuse by employers as the Tata regulation of 1921 had done.[12] The Textile Labour Enquiry Committee Report of 1940, in fact, quotes cases in which this regulation had been misused and also lists the various ingenuous ways by which this regulation allowed capitalists to evade payment of maternity benefit. The guiding principle in all these evasions was a strict interpretation of the terms of 'service'. That is, any break in service meant that the qualifying period for claiming the benefit would have to be re-worked. Thus, if a woman was discharged and then re-employed, the qualifying period would not include her previous months of wage work, but would start from her re-engagement. The same

---

[12] According to this regulation, a woman had to put in 11 months' 'continuous' service before she was eligible for the maternity benefit. This meant that any time taken off for sickness, marriage, or childcare, as well as participation in strikes, annulled a woman's claim to maternity benefits. For details on the Tata regulations governing the payment of maternity benefits, see *Indian Textile Journal* (1925: 47).

interpretation applied to strikes and closures (*TLECR* 1940: Vol. I, pp. 307–8).

The Act was amended in December 1933. While one of its amendments extended the qualifying period from six to nine months, making it even more difficult for women to claim benefits, another added a new complication. Under the 1929 Act, a woman who was discharged from work when a factory was closed was held to have been dismissed. Dismissal entitled her to claim the benefit if she had completed the qualifying period of work. The amendment read: 'A women entitled to maternity benefit shall not be deemed dismissed within the provisions of section 8, if she is discharged on account of the closing of the factory in which she is employed' (*Labour Gazette* 1933c: 264–5).

Between August 1932 and August 1933, there were 12 strikes by women workers alone in the cotton textile industry. The major causes of these strikes were the reduction in wages and retrenchment. Several mills had closed down owing to the depression, and many were cutting down on the number of workers they employed, especially in the 'unskilled' departments of winding and reeling. Framed in this context, the amendment withdrew one of the few rights of women workers, paving the way for capitalists to close down their mills with minimum liability.

Yet another amendment raised the period for payment of maternity benefit from seven to eight weeks but, in a period of soaring prices and growing unemployment, retained the flat rate of 8 annas per day. The sole improvement in these amendments was that one of them divided the period of payment into pre- and post-maternity, and allowed half the benefit to be paid before confinement, so that it was possible for the woman worker to use one month's pay to buy nourishing food (*Labour Gazette* 1935: 960–7).

The conditions regulating the payment of maternity benefits seem to improve with a decrease in the number of women employed. In fact, the Act itself seems to have been passed only as a palliative to the introduction of rationalization schemes from 1928 onwards, which retrenched workers in all occupations, but particularly in the unskilled departments of winding and reeling. The great strike of 1928 was against the introduction of rationalization schemes and retrenchment. The strikers did not achieve their demands but were presented with the Maternity Benefit Act instead. Though there is no direct evidence to support this thesis, it appears plausible to interpret the speedy enactment of Asavle's Bill (after six years of procrastination) as a sop to make rationalization slightly more tolerable.

Unfortunately, the depression created conditions in which even the payment of maternity benefits became a cost which the mill owners wished to avoid. In fact, the depression was, in this context, convenient for the mill owners since, in the face of mass closures, rationalization appeared as a side effect instead of a goal. After a last attempt to oppose rationalization—in the general strike of 1934, when the workers once again failed to press their demands—it was accepted as a *fait accompli* resulting from the depression.

It was, therefore, in 1936, after the industry had taken a turn for the better, that some action on implementing the Act was taken. With women now constituting less than 16 per cent of the labour force in cotton textiles, mill owners could afford a few additional allowances to women. 'The usual period of maternity benefit leave is two months, but having regard to the exceptional nature of this type of absence, a woman should be allowed to retain a lien on her job for a period of three months when the absence is due to maternity' (MOA 1936a).

Given that this statement was merely a recommendation issued by the MOA to all its affiliates, it was no more than a gesture. The Association did not have powers of ratification. The two other actions on maternity benefit which followed this were similar. In December 1936, the Municipality offered to issue birth certificates 'free of charge' on condition that the applicant produced a certificate from her mill manager saying that the birth certificate was required in order to settle maternity allowances (MOA 1936b). In March 1937, the MOA formulated a 'standard form of notice to be given by women operatives going on maternity leave'. The notice included a statement from the mill manager, addressed to the Municipality, requesting a birth certificate, and copies of the form were circulated to all mills affiliated to the Association. It was suggested that these forms 'should be made available free of charge to women operatives who wish to go on maternity leave' (MOA 1937). However, the forms were printed in English and were not translated, so they would have been incomprehensible even to women who could read.

Records kept by the government on the working of the Maternity Benefit Act in Bombay Presidency indicate that the rate of claimants for maternity benefits was consistently lower in Bombay city than in Ahmedabad or Sholapur, even though the number of women employed by the Bombay cotton textile industry was far greater than those employed in Ahmedabad and Sholapur (see Table 9.7). It seems likely that the reason for this was the high proportion of widows employed by the Bombay mill owners. The women employed by the Ahmedabad and Sholapur cotton textile industry were drawn from the immediate vicinity of the two cities, and tended to be married to workers in Ahmedabad or Sholapur, or to be their relatives. By contrast, a large number of women workers in the Bombay mills were

TABLE 9.6 Working of the Bombay Maternity Benefit Act, 1929, in Bombay City, Ahmedabad, and Sholapur, 1933–9

Year	Average No. of Women Employed Daily	Average No. of Women Claiming Maternity Benefit, Section 6	No. of Women Paid Maternity Benefits for Actual	No. of Other Persons Paid Maternity Benefits, Section 7	Total Maternity Benefits Paid	Claims Paid per 100 Women Employed
Bombay City					Rs as. p.	
1933	21,744	961	771	9	18,208 8 0	3.5
1934	22,155	1,362	1,248	10	28,780 5 0	5.7
1935	26,350	1,589	1,405	18	36,420 5 3	5.4
1936	23,977	1,924	1,846	22	48,428 13 0	7.8
1937	26,689	1,705	1,510	15	40,911 6 0	5.7
1938	28,882	1,841	1,677	20	44,599 15 9	5.9
1939	24,837	1,970	1,767	22	47,769 10 0	7.2
Ahmedabad						
1933	11,175	1,349	1,270	8	30,411 4 0	11.3
1934	11,150	1,830	1,756	7	43,131 8 0	15.8
1935	10,386	1,426	1,339	8	33,873 0 0	12.9
1936	9,528	1,294	1,179	5	31,068 0 0	12.4
1937	10,168	1,105	968	4	26,625 5 0	9.6
1938	10,624	1,210	1,035	3	27,643 6 6	9.8
1939	9,502	1,397	1,247	5	33,708 2 6	13.2
Sholapur						
1933	4,352	412	311	4	7,595 8 0	7.2
1934	4,080	535	473	35	11,286 9 9	12.4
1935	4,236	620	567	1	11,350 14 3	13.4
1936	3,879	514	477	—	9,876 6 0	12.3
1937	4,229	486	438	1	8,874 15 3	10.4
1938	4 998	584	522	—	10,893 10 0	10.4
1939	5,266	692	624	1	14,216 11 9	11.9

Source: *Annual Factory Reports* (1933–9), published by the Commissioner of Labour, Bombay.

migrants from the Konkan; many of them widows who had been pushed by circumstances into leaving their villages.[13]

The Bombay mill owners did not pay fewer claims in proportion to claimants than the Ahmedabad and Sholapur mill owners did. Though the proportion of women who claimed maternity benefits to the total employed daily were much lower in Bombay than in Ahmedabad or Sholapur, the proportion of claims accepted to total claims were much the same in all

---

[13] For details, see *FBS* (1927).

three centres, with a few qualifications. Of these, the most striking is that in 1933 Ahmedabad mill owners were by far the readiest payers of maternity benefits, while the Sholapur mill owners were clearly the most reluctant to honour their obligation. As the years passed, however, all three centres stabilized at an even 90 per cent payment of claims (see Table 9.7).

TABLE 9.7 Proportion of Women Workers Claiming Maternity Benefits and Proportions of Claims Paid, 1933–9

Year	Proportion of Women Claiming Maternity Benefit to Total Women Employed Daily (per cent)			Proportion of Claims Paid to Total Claims Made		
	Bombay	Ahmedabad	Sholapur	Bombay	Ahmedabad	Sholapur
1933	4.4	12.1	9.5	80.2	94.1	75.5
1934	6.2	16.4	13.1	91.6	96.0	88.4
1935	6.0	13.7	14.6	88.4	93.4	91.5
1936	8.0	13.6	13.3	95.9	91.1	92.8
1937	6.4	10.9	11.5	88.6	87.6	90.1
1938	6.4	11.4	11.7	91.1	85.5	89.4
1939	7.9	14.7	13.1	89.7	89.3	90.2

Sources: COI (1921: ix–xi; 1931: Part II, pp. 165–6).

After the 1933 amendments, the amount of the benefit, at the rate of 8 annas per day for the eight-week period, should have been Rs 28. At no point was this full amount paid in any of the three centres, though over the years the amount paid gradually increased in Bombay and Ahmedabad (see Table 9.8). For some reason it actually decreased in Sholapur, which always paid substantially less than the other two centres.

TABLE 9.8 Average Amount Paid per Claim, 1933–9

Year	Amount		
	Bombay	Ahmedabad	Sholapur
1933	23.3	23.8	24.1
1934	22.5	24.5	22.2
1935	25.6	25.2	19.9
1936	25.9	26.2	20.7
1937	26.8	27.4	20.2
1938	26.3	26.6	20.9
1939	26.7	26.9	22.8

Sources: COI (1921: ix–xi; 1931: Part II, pp. 165–6).

MECHANIZATION, RATIONALIZATION, AND RETRENCHMENT

The prohibition of night work for women is also cited by M.D. Morris as a reason for the decline in the number of women employed by the cotton textile industry, but this does not seem a strong enough reason since the Act was passed in 1911 and women began to be retrenched only at the end of the 1920s. Moreover, between 1911 and 1926, women's employment in the cotton textile industry increased steadily, so it seems fair to conclude that this Act had little to do with the retrenchment of women. Finally, if we look at changes in the labour process which occurred around the time that women began to be retrenched, it becomes clear that mechanization was the most important factor in the decline in the number of women workers.

The prohibition of night work for women was suggested by the Washington Conference on Labour. Notably, Indian mill owners in Bombay ratified this recommendation before it was actually enacted by the government (*Report of the Indian Textile Tariff Board* [ITB] 1927: Vol. II, 352–4). It is significant that the prohibition became a grievance only when competition from Japanese mills was depressing the market for Indian cotton textiles (ibid.) but it is questionable how serious a grievance this really was, since mill owners did not demand the lifting of the prohibition, and it was already clear that they saw increasing mechanization as the solution to their problems.

The cheese-winding machine was introduced in the Bombay cotton mills in 1925, changing the winding process from one entailing hand labour to one using machines. In March 1926, women colour winders in the Rachel Sassoon Mill went on strike against being made to use cheese-winding machines and remained on strike for five days. At one point during the strike, the management called the police to take the strikers off 'the mill premises for throwing bobbins around' (*Labour Gazette* 1926: ii). Despite protests, work was resumed unconditionally after five days. Mill owners felt that strikes of this kind were not caused by 'serious' grievances but by the desire for a holiday from the daily grind of labour. If this was the case, then here is clear evidence of how women workers resisted the alienation capitalism brought in tow.

Soon after this, more dramatic changes were heralded by the use of the Universal winding machines. Fundamentally, the introduction of these machines simplified the winding and reeling processes, compressing them into one. As these machines wound straight on to the cheese or the beam, which could be dyed, reeling yarn into banks for dyeing became unnecessary. Pirn winding too was introduced at the same time, speeding up the winding process.

Even while these changes were being introduced, mill owners denied their efficacy:

Mr Majumdar: You have given us 4 pies per lb as the cost of winding on the pirn-winding machine. What is the increase of production on the loom due to the use of that?

Answer (Mr Wadia): You are talking of Northrop looms. I am talking of the use of pirn wound bobbins on the ordinary loom against the usual weaving on ring bobbins. We found absolutely no increase in the loom production and we find that it costs us more...

Question: We were told at some places that there is an increase of production of about 5 per cent by the use of Universal winders.

Answer: I should say that 5 per cent is the highest figure. But consider this point: if you use the winders you must put in rather more twist on your weft than you would if you spin direct onto the weft cop. Moreover these winders are very wasteful. For instance, our waste comes to 5 or 6 per cent from re-winding.

Question: That is because you are re-winding mule cops. Supposing you are re-winding from the ring bobbins?

Answer: Our experience shows that there is no benefit from re-winding from ring bobbins. If ring bobbins are properly made and properly shaped, you cannot get more than 33 per cent more weft onto the re-wound pirn, and for the sake of this 33 per cent more it does not pay us to incur an additional expenditure of 4 pies to re-wind the stuff. (ITB 1927: 354–6)

Yet we know that mill owners, instead of ceasing to use these 'wasteful' machines, which Mr Wadia dismissed so contemptuously, actually steadily increased investment in them. According to the 1934 Indian Textile Tariff Board (ITB):

...economies have also been effected in the matter of numbers employed in the departments preparatory to weaving by the adoption of high speed warping and winding, improved types of cheese and beam dyeing plants which facilitate yarn being dyed in the cheese or in the beam, thereby saving the cost of winding it into banks before dyeing and re-winding again on beams for weaving. A large number of mills had also installed Universal winding machines which enabled a larger quantity of weft to be carried by the shuttle, thus reducing stoppages for weft replenishment at the loom. (ITB 1934: 48)

The use of these machines was recommended by the ITB of 1927, whose schemes for rationalization the mill owners put into effect almost immediately. The great general strike of 1928 was against the implementation of these recommendations, and was prefigured by a strike of women winders in the Jacob Sassoon Mill. On 2 January 1928, 250 women winders of this mill refused to work in protest against the notice posted by the management saying that from 1 February rates would be 'reduced by 1 to 4 pies for 10 lbs of yarn produced in respect of certain counts of yarn in order to bring them down to standard rates' (*Labour Gazette* 1928: 16).

In the afternoon of 2 January, 350 spinners joined the winders. The next morning all the workers in the mill joined the strike. The management threatened a closure, whereupon the strikers went to Apollo, Rachel, E.D. Sassoon, and Alexandra mills and brought the workers out. By 5 January, workers of the entire Sassoon Group of Mills were on strike. Commenting on the situation, the *Labour Gazette* remarked:

> The dispute was primarily due to the proposed reduction in rates of wages in the winding department but the real cause of its extension to the other mills was the proposed introduction of new systems of work in accordance with the recommendations of the Indian Textile Tariff Board. (ibid.: 15)

This statement implies that wage reductions were in no way linked to the recommendations of the ITB. In the case of women workers, however, the standardization of wage rates (recommended by the Board) actually led to a fall in absolute wages (see Table 9.9).

TABLE 9.9 Average Earnings in Winding and Reeling Departments, 1921–37 (in Rs)

Occupation	Average Daily Earnings				Percentage Increase			
	1921	1926	1934	1937	1921–6	1926–34	1934–7	1921–37
Winding Dept								
Naikins	2.31							
Drum-winders	0.76							
Cheese-winders	0.88	0.77						
Pirn-					−12.5			
winders	0.69	0.85	0.72	0.68	+23.2	−15.3	−4.6	−1.5
Grey-winders		0.73	0.62	0.62		−15.1	0	−15.1
Colour-winders		0.93	0.84	0.79		−9.7	−6.0	−15.1
Reeling Dept								
Naikins	1.27	1.85	2.10		+45.7	+13.5		
Reelers	0.84	0.68	0.64	0.56	−19.1	−5.9	−12.5	−66.7

Sources: Various surveys of the Bombay Labour Office, such as *Wages and Hours of Labour* (1921); *Wages and Hours of Labour* (1926); *General Wage Census* (1934); and *TLECR* (1940).

The official argument in favour of wage standardization was that it would, by imposing a minimum wage rate on mill owners, infinitely better the position of most workers, even if it cut the wages of the higher paid (ITB 1927: Vol. I, pp. 204–6). But statistics compiled by them would, in fact, show the contrary (see Table 9.10).

Several points are clarified by Table 9.10. In the first place, in both the winding and reeling departments mean wages fell between 1926 and 1931—in the winding department they fell from Rs 24.5 to Rs 22.5, and in the reeling department they fell from Rs 23.2 to Rs 17.6. Moreover, between 1926 and 1931 the median wage rate fell—that is, where there were 80.4 per cent winders earning below Rs 25 in 1926, this percentage went up to 97 in 1931. Similarly, in the reeling department, 47 per cent earned below Rs 15 in 1926, while in 1931, 66 per cent did. In other words, not only did wages fall but an increasing number of women were in lower paid income groups.

Second, we find that for both years reelers earned less than winders. In 1926, when 73.4 per cent of women reelers earned below Rs 20, only 55.6 per cent of winders did. In 1931, when 99.1 per cent of women reelers earned below Rs 20, 80 per cent of winders did. Finally, we see that in both periods there was a huge variation in wages paid by different mills for presumably the same work, but that in 1931 the limits within which this variation took place were narrower than in 1926. This can be seen both in the decrease in the number of people earning below Rs 10 in 1931 and in the more marked decrease in the numbers of those earning above Rs 20.[14]

In all fairness, these are not arguments against wage standardization per se. What emerges is that wages were not actually standardized over the period; instead the range of their variation was narrowed, leading to the pauperization of women workers. In this context, arguments for standardization, in effect, provided a rationale for lowering women's wages.

As we have seen, the effects of rationalization were felt most drastically by women. Reelers were made redundant by developments in industrial technology; the huge fall in the number of women workers which we see in this period was partly caused by the shutting down of the reeling departments in some mills. It is unfortunately not possible to give break downs of increases or decreases by departments for the period under survey, since the wage censuses did not always cover the whole industry,

---

[14] A note of caution regarding official surveys of wages was sounded by Burnett-Hurst. His own, more limited, survey of mill-hands living in Parel showed that in 1917–18, 80 per cent of women workers earned below Rs 10 and another 15.6 per cent earned between Rs 10 and Rs 15. Only 4.4 per cent earned above Rs 15. While quoting the 1921–2 *FBS* figures, which gave the average wages of women workers as Rs 10.0.10 in 1914 and Rs 17.6.6 in 1921, he states that his own average monthly wage for women workers in Parel in 1917–18 was Rs 8.8.6, and comments, 'It would appear that either the cotton mill industry is badly paid compared to other occupations (which is not the case), or that the budgets selected were taken from "better class households" and are not typical' (1925: 130–1).

TABLE 9.10 Frequency of Monthly Earnings, 1926 and 1931

Limits of Monthly Wage	Proportion of Operatives Earning Monthly Wages within the Limits of Monthly Wage Department			
	Winding		Reeling	
	1926	1931	1926	1931
Below Rs 10	12.4	7.4	16.8	10.1
Rs 10 to 15	17.0	33.3	30.2	55.9
Rs 15 to 20	26.2	39.3	26.4	33.1
Rs 20 to 25	24.8	17.0	19.3	1.9
Rs 25 to 30	12.0	3.0	4.9	
Rs 30 to 35	4.7		0.7	
Above Rs 35	2.9		1.7	
Mean Wage	24.5	22.5	23.2	17.6

Sources: *Wages and Hours of Labour* (1926: 98); *FBS* (1922–33: 37).

but gave 'representative figures'.[15] However, even a cursory reading of these censuses shows that several occupations in which women were employed ceased either to employ women or ceased to exist as occupations. After 1926, for example, we find no women waste pickers (this task was taken over by machines); no women doffers in the frame department; no women cheese-winders (cheese-winding was rationalized out of existence); no women creelers in the warping department; and no women washers in the bleaching department. After 1934, there were no women employed in the carding room—neither as machine tenters, nor lap carriers, nor fly collectors. Nor were there any women hand-folders left in the folding department.[16]

We cannot assume that women were not aware of the potential consequences of rationalization—the 1928 strike is evidence of their knowledge. The years to follow not only substantiate this evidence, but they also show the development of unionization amongst women. Between late 1930 and 1932, unions intervened in almost all strikes by women, the most active union being the Girni Kamgar Union, followed by the Bombay Textile Labour Union. Their activism is best reflected in the Sassoon Alliance Silk Mill strikes of 1932. On 4 August, 84 women winders went

---

[15] The Report on *Wages and Hours of Labour* (1926), for example, surveyed 19 representative mills.

[16] See the 1921 survey of *Wages and Hours of Labour*; the 1926 survey of *Wages and Hours of Labour*; *General Wage Census* (1934); and *TLECR* (1940).

on strike demanding a raise of 5 paise per lb of silk. On 5 August, they were joined by 300 weavers also demanding a raise in wages. The management responded by giving notice of closure; within two days the strike was over and 'work was resumed unconditionally'. The next month, the winders went on strike again in the same mill. This time the number of strikers increased from 84 to 185. Their purpose was to protest against a reduction in working days, from 24 to 15. The strike lasted for five months, resulting in the management closing down the mill and dismissing 639 people. S.V. Parulekar of the Bharat Textile Labour Union (BTLU) intervened in the strike and a group of 'volunteers' set up a strike fund in September. Very little was collected since the workers were by now unemployed. At the same time, a strike committee was set up with 15 workers on it and 5 BTLU leaders. Through October, November, and December the Committee distributed rations—one *patti* of rice and one *seer* of dal—to 550 people. The strike fund ran out towards the end of December. Anticipating this, around 50 women workers went to the mill at 11 AM on 16 December and asked for an interview with the manager, who asked them to send a deputation instead. The women, however, refused to move away from the mill gates until their demand for an interview was granted. At 11.30 AM, the police were called in to 'disperse' them. The women gathered together at a distance and held a meeting at which they 'condemned' the management's refusal to see them and the calling in of the police.

This information was reported in the *Labour Gazette* (1933a: 14). In February, the *Gazette* carried a brief note to the effect that during January 'rations' were distributed four times to 400 people. Because the management said they did not intend to re-open the mill for some time, they added, the strike was 'presumed concluded with an inconclusive result' (*Labour Gazette* 1933b: 12).

Several points can be made about this strike. First, women were not only militant, but could be unionized. Second, they were aware of circumstances which affected them, such as rationalization. Third, they clearly wished to keep their jobs, that is, were interested in wage labour.

This latter point was emphasized by official reports in quite a different context:

>...the variations from month to month of work available for a department led to variations in the numbers of workers required and hence to the maintainence of a labour force somewhat in excess of average requirements. Secondly, it is said that through the course of time the excess number has been suffered to grow and that it has been found difficult to reduce it as the workers themselves are willing to share work and are opposed to a reduction. While realising fully the difficulties in the way of reducing this excess of workers, we are of the

opinion that a large permanent excess is in the interest neither of workers nor of employers and that steps should be taken immediately to reduce it. We realise that action cannot be very rapid, but we also feel that no effective action may be taken if some continuous pressure from without is not exercised. (*TLECR* 1940: Vol. I, p. 139)

This statement was made at a time when the decrease in the number of women employed was acute. It is intriguing that statements about the overstaffing of departments employing women (the one quoted earlier referred to the winding and reeling departments) grew in length and emphasis at around the same time that women were being retrenched. For instance, the 1934 Wage Census said much the same as was said in the Report of 1940, quoted earlier—with the important exception that they do not suggest that overstaffing was desired by women, or that solidarity led many to give up the possibility of more work and increased wages in favour of more jobs.

As regards operatives in reeling, they are usually women, and, as is well known, till very recently in most mills in Bombay city a larger number of women were employed than were required, with the result that the women, although they might work for all the days in the month, had not sufficient work every day for part of the time and also their hours of work were shorter than of other operatives. Recently, however, some of the mills have increased the hours of work in departments where women are employed and there is, moreover, a tendency not to employ more women than are actually employed. It would appear that these factors must have operated in showing that the wages of reelers in 1933 were the same as in 1926 in spite of the cuts effected by several cotton mills in Bombay city. (*General Wage Census* 1934: 92)

The effect of women's retrenchment can, in fact, be seen in the increase in the number of 'dependants' in working class families from 1921 to 1932; and even more strikingly from 1932 to 1944. The 1931 Census shows that between 1921 and 1931 there was a 12 per cent decrease in the number of workers in each family with a corresponding increase in the number of 'dependants' (*COI* 1931: Part II, p. 163); the family budget surveys of 1932 and 1944 show that in 1932 the ratio of workers to dependants within the family was 41:59 (*FBS* 1932–3: 16), while in 1944 this ratio fell to 39:61 (see Table 9.11).

Several points can be made on the basis of this evidence. First, though the ratio of dependants to workers appears to have risen by only 3 per cent, this is offset by a fall in the ratio of female to male workers of 6.5 per cent—more than twice the increase of the number of dependants. As we know, from 1934 onwards the male labour force expanded while the female labour force dwindled. Hence, the full extent of women's retrenchment does not show up proportionately to an increase in the number of dependants in

TABLE 9.11 Earners in Working Class Families, 1932–44

Income Group	Percentage of Women to Total Earners		Percentage of Earners in Family	
	1932	1944	1932	1944
Below Rs 30	19.9		34.9	33.3
Rs 30 to 40	23.4	45.7	42.8	37.1
Rs 40 to 50	27.7	20.4	47.2	33.0
Rs 50 to 60	23.6	10.2	42.6	33.3
Rs 60 to 70	19.1	10.4	37.2	33.0
Rs 70 to 80	20.4	10.4	43.7	33.6
Rs 80 to 90	21.1	21.6	46.1	40.2
Rs 90 and over	12.1	—	42.8	—

Sources: FBS (1932–3:16; 1944: 12).

the working class family, even though it clearly affects the ratio of workers to dependants.[17]

* * *

The basic argument of this chapter has been that the period 1919–39 saw a shift in the development of capitalism which led to a new focus on the conditions under which labour power and the labour force were reproduced. At the same time, as attempts to 'rationalize' the labour process took place, there were also attempts to 'rationalize' the process of reproduction of the labour force—attempts which over time led to the complete withdrawal of women from wage work, pushing them back into the home.

When women's wage labour was first described as supplementary, the description reflected intent rather than fact, since at that point most women workers supported their families. In fact, a chronology of the events of that period would suggest that underlying these statements was an assertion that women's 'primary role' was as reproducer. For, while ideologues talked of women's lack of commitment to wage work, labelling it supplementary, and philanthropists glorified 'motherhood', the industry retrenched women in large numbers.

From analyses of strikes of the period we can see that responses to the threat of rationalization were immediate and often spearheaded by women. The major issues of protest were cutbacks in the working day, cuts in

---

[17] See Bhattacharya (1981) for an analysis of the rise in number of dependants in the working class family and its connections with rationalization and the retrenchment of women.

wages, and cuts in the number of workers employed. Cornelius Castoriadis (1976–7) said that these can be seen as centring on attempts to define the work day—from the side of capitalists to shorten and concentrate it; and from the side of the workers to retain some part of its flexibility. Women were particularly affected by this, since they snatched moments of rest at intervals in the work day, during which they also suckled their babies and visited the creche. Examples such as the 1928 and 1933 strikes show the extent to which women attempted to define what they saw as their 'right'; and the 1933 strike shows how cuts in wages and the concentration of work—in terms of hours—were inextricably linked. A cut in working hours meant a cut in wages—but as the cut in working hours effectively meant the abolition of all intervals for rest, lower wages meant less money for the same amount of work.

Originally, retrenchment too meant an increase in work load, with a smaller number of women having to do the work of those retrenched. But as greater numbers were retrenched, the threat was more clearly seen, though perhaps not located in the context of 'motherhood' (that is, the need to organize reproduction more efficiently). That there was a struggle against this is clear from statements that women were prepared 'even' to work shorter hours and accept lower wages so that more of them could retain employment. Unfortunately, as trade unions did not take up these suggestions, there are very few records to show how women analysed a situation in which they were being retrenched while the male work force was being expanded.

REFERENCES

Annual Factory Reports (1933–9). Bombay: Commissioner of Labour.
Balfour, Margaret and Shakuntala Talpode (1931), 'The Maternity Conditions of Women Mill Workers', *Royal Commission of Labour in India*, Vol. I, Part I.
Bhattacharya, S. (1981), 'Capital and Labour in Bombay City 1928–29', *Economic and Political Weekly*, XVI(42–3): PE 36–PE 46.
Burnett-Hurst, A.R. (1928), *Labour and Housing in Bombay: A Study in the Economic Conditions of the Wage Earning Classes in Bombay*. London: P.S. King & Son Ltd.
Castoriadis, Cornelius (1976–7), 'On the History of Workers' Movements', *Telos*, 30: 3–42.
Census of India (COI) (1921), Vol. IX, Part II.
——— (1931), Vol. IX, 'Cities of Bombay Presidency'.
——— (1951), Paper No. 10, 'Area Tables B on Y Sample'.

Dwarkadas, Kanji (1962), *Forty-five Years with Labour*. Bombay: Asia Publishing House.
Fortnightly Reports (1928), Home Department, Political, Knight to Haig, No. S.D. 882, 8 August.
General Wage Census (1934), Bombay Labour Office, Government Central Press, Bombay.
Gokhale, R.G. (1958), *The Bombay Cotton Mill Worker*. Bombay: Mill Owners' Association.
Hartmann, Heidi (1979), 'Capitalism, Patriarchy and Job Segregation by Sex', in Zillah R. Eisenstein (ed.), *Capitalist Patriarchy and the Case for Socialist Feminism*. New York: Monthly Review Press, pp. 206–47.
Indian Textile Journal (1925), January.
Katznelson, Ira (1981), *City Trenches: Urban Politics and the Patterning of Class in the United States*. New York: Pantheon Books.
Kelman, Janet Harvey (1923), *Labour in India*. London: George Allen and Unwin.
Labour Gazette (1924), 'Mr Joshi's Proposed Bill on Maternity Benefits', report, August.
—— (1926), April.
—— (1928), February.
—— (1931), An Enquiry into the Family Budgets of Cotton Mill Workers, Bombay Labour Office, January 1930, pp. 473–89.
—— (1933a), January.
—— (1933b), February.
—— (1933c), December.
—— (1935), Annual Factories Report, August 1934.
Mill Owners' Association (MOA) (1936a), Circular No. 561/45 A, 6 March.
—— (1936b), Circular No. 5379/3, 22 December.
—— (1937), Circular No. 1285/37, 25 March.
Morris, M.D. (1965), *The Emergence of an Industrial Labour Force in India: A Study of the Bombay Cotton Mills*. Bombay: Oxford University Press.
Newman, R.K. (1979), 'Social Factors in the Recruitment of the Bombay Millhands,' in K.N. Chaudhuri and D.K. Dewey (eds), *Economy and Society*. New Delhi: Oxford University Press, pp. 277–98.
Report of the Indian Textile Tariff Board (ITB) (1927), Government Central Press, Bombay, 1928.
—— (1934), *Vol. I*, Government Central Press, Bombay.
Royal Commission of Labour in India (1931), *Vol. I*, Part I.
Textile Labour Enquiry Commission Report (*TLECR*) (1940), Bombay Labour Office, Government Central Press, Bombay.
Wages and Hours of Labour (1921), Survey by Bombay Labour Office, Government Central Press, Bombay.
—— (1926), Survey by Bombay Labour Office, Government Central Press, Bombay.
Working Class Family Budget Survey (*FBS*) (1921–2), Bombay Labour Office, Government Central Press, Bombay, 1923.

Working Class Family Budget Survey (*FBS*) (1927), Ahmedabad.
—— (1932–3), Bombay Labour Office, Government Central Press, Bombay.
—— (1922–33), Bombay Labour Office, Government Central Press, Bombay.
—— (1944–6), Bombay Labour Office, Government Central Press, Bombay.

Chapter 10

WOMEN WORKERS, LIBERALIZATION, AND SOCIAL CITIZENSHIP IN INDIA

AMRITA CHHACHHI

THIS CHAPTER DRAWS ON A GENDERED political economy and social citizenship framework, integrating issues of redistribution and recognition (Fraser 1997), to highlight the implications of contemporary processes of globalization and liberalization for women industrial workers in India. It recasts the discussion on gender, labour, and liberalization/globalization from a narrow focus on the workplace and examines women workers' experience of the broader process of economic and industrial restructuring, labour control, and entitlements to social citizenship. It explores the interconnections between the domains of the workplace and the household and elaborates the concept of 'citizenship in practice' as a bridging link to understand the processes and consequences of contemporary trends of global restructuring and flexible employment. Social and economic citizenship rights develop 'through a process of struggle' (Cook 2000), that is, through the exercise of individual and collective agency at the workplace and the assertions of autonomy within the household and community.[1] These struggles occur in and through different collectivities reflecting the multilayered construction of citizenship, particularly in developing countries (Yuval-Davis 1999). Given the limited nature of state provision of citizenship-based entitlements in India, and the secondary status accorded to women in most religious personal laws regulating the private domain, regular employment remains an important route for women to access independent rights to social citizenship entitlements. These provide the enabling conditions for individual and collective agency at the workplace and within the household, thereby creating the basis for democratic citizenship.

In demonstrating the significance of the practice of citizenship, this chapter seeks to address the victimology that continues to pervade some Indian studies of women industrial workers. Whether it is women in the unorganized sectors or in the modern garments and electronics export-oriented factories, the stories that emerge depict women as the poorest of the poor, discriminated against at all levels, unorganized, unorganizable, and helpless victims. This view is not incorrect, but it is partial.[2] It does not take into account women's agency, and the covert/overt methods women deploy either to maintain or to better their work and life situations. Labour markets, patriarchal household structures, and gender ideologies are not homogenous, stagnant, or inert. Assumptions about appropriate gender roles vary across class/caste/ethnic/religious axes. In fact, Indian feminists have put forward the notion of 'multiple and overlapping patriarchies' that are both legally as well as sociologically diverse, which undermine the assumption of a singular monolithic 'Indian patriarchy' (Sangari 1995). The existence of a patriarchal household is not in itself a barrier to women's employment.[3] The victim approach tends to be static and slides over the existence in India of a number of innovative organizations

---

[1] 'Negotiating autonomy' is used to refer to the processes that allow for an expansion of choices rather than a set of attributes which can be measured. This allows for a more grounded analysis rather than an open concept of 'female agency' per se and the more ambiguous and loaded concept of 'empowerment'. The term 'empowerment' is too heavy to describe the non-linear, often reversible, constantly negotiated dynamics of gender relations in the workplace and the household.

[2] Such an approach constructs and reinforces—be it inadvertent—the notion of the passive 'Third World woman (worker)' (Mohanty 1988).

[3] A notable characteristic of the formation of a neophyte female labour force in contemporary industrialization in other Asian countries has in fact been the conjunction of capitalism and patriarchy, often the active intervention of traditional patriarchies, sometimes even in direct collusion with religious leaders.

(such as Self Employed Women's Association [SEWA] and the National Campaign Committee for Unorganized Sector Workers) which show that even informal economy women workers, given the opportunity, do organize despite debilitating conditions of work and existence.

Contemporary processes of liberalization/globalization are leading to an erosion of such enabling conditions for the assertions of 'citizenship in practice', and a new model of 'market-oriented citizenship' is being ushered in. This is illustrated through a case study of women workers from the electronics industry in India over the last two decades,[4] a period when, with a major policy shift, a process was initiated to dismantle the structures of state intervention and openly embrace liberalization and integration into the world economy. This micro-level analysis of gendered labour regimes, domestic regimes, and instances of 'citizenship in practice', brings in women workers' experiences and voices and relates them to the ongoing broader debates on distributive justice and social citizenship entitlements.

In the 1990s, there was a major shift in Indian economic policy with the onset of economic reforms and liberalization, resulting in changes in the overall structure of employment. Glaring contradictions emerged as the rising curve of economic growth (9 per cent in 2007) was accompanied by a considerable decline in employment. Although 60 per cent of an estimated working population of 400 million are still employed in agriculture, this, too, is declining, and in some states there is a festering 'agrarian crisis'; only 16.8 per cent are employed in manufacturing and 22.8 per cent employed are in the service sector (Government of India, Tenth Five Year Plan 2002–7, quoted in Venkata Ratnam 2006: 4). There is a consensus that there has been a sharp deterioration in the quality of employment through intensification of the growth of the informal sector (93 per cent) as well as decline of formal sector employment (7.1 per cent) due to labour market flexibility. This reflects a major shift from an earlier welfare orientation and tripartite compact between state, industry, and labour to an 'eyes closed' attitude to labour rights violations. Legislative changes have been on the anvil but remain stalled so far. At the same time there is an increase in judicial actions by the state to curtail and suspend implementation and monitoring of workers' rights presenting threats for

---

[4] The main database for this study is research, undertaken in 1994–6, of 20 enterprises manufacturing televisions in the industrial areas around Delhi. A follow-up survey of 100 workers' households was conducted in 2000 (see Chhachhi 2004).

trade unions. Overall there is a decline in workers' bargaining power and the onset of aggressive managerial strategies for industrial restructuring.

Where do women workers fit in this changing landscape? Mirroring international debates on 'feminization of the labour force', the discussion in India on recent trends in women's employment has one position arguing convergence with global trends (Desphande and Desphande 1999) and another arguing Indian exceptionalism (Banerjee 1999a, 1999b).[5] Arguments about a general trend towards feminization or de-feminization have been based on nation-wide (large-scale) survey data such as the Census and National Sample Survey (NSS).

Data from the National Sample Survey Organisation (NSSO) 61st Round shows that work participation rates of women workers have *increased* in 2004–5, particularly in comparison with the last decade, reversing the fall in work participation rates documented in 1999–2000 (GoI 2006). The increase is sharper in urban areas (3 per cent for both men and women) but also seen in rural areas (2 per cent for men and 3 per cent for women). The decline in rural employment continues with the proportion of men engaged in agricultural activities declining from 81 per cent in 1977–8 to 67 per cent in 2004–5, and a lower rate noted for women workers—from 88 per cent in 1977–8 to 83 per cent in 2004–5. Another significant feature was the entry of younger women in the labour force—the peak work participation rate for urban women had shifted from the 40–4 years age group in 1993–4 to the 35–9 years age group in 2004–5. The NSS data also records continuing change in employment status distribution, with an increase in *regular* employment for urban women (more than 42 per cent) and a decline in casual employment.

Does this then revive the 'feminization thesis' in India? Chandrashekar and Ghosh (2007) are cautious and note that in examining specific sectors, activities, and trends in wages, the picture that emerges is more complex. Very few manufacturing sectors account for employment of women workers—some indeed are in the export industries, notably textiles, garments, and leather goods, and there has also been a significant increase in women's employment in the service sector (women are 36 per cent of the total usually employed). However, the greatest increase has been in domestic service while the much talked about information technology (IT) and finance sectors only account for 0.3 per cent and 1.4 per cent,

---

[5] Other economists such as Kundu (1999) and Ghosh (1999) also interpreted national-level data published in the early 1990s as indicating a process of feminization, though they focused more on the broader process of casualization.

respectively, of urban women workers. For all women workers—casual and regular—real wages have fallen between 1999-2000 and 2004-5. Overall as well, there remained a clear gender differential in the worker population ratio (WPR): 55 per cent for men and 33 per cent for women in the rural areas; 55 per cent for men and 17 per cent for women in the urban areas (Chandrashekhar and Ghosh 2007).

The latest NSS data can be interpreted in different ways and there are clearly limits to analysis based on such a broad sweep of statistical data. Data collection methods continue to be gender-biased, ignoring large areas of the informal economy that predominate in the use of women's labour.[6] While such a level of analysis is useful to map broad trends in relation to the overall changes in employment, it is necessary to complement and supplement these observations with more fine-grained analysis through micro-level studies at industry, factory, and household levels. Evidence from micro studies is far more contradictory. On the one hand, there is confirmation of the continued marginalization of women and masculinization of the labour force as firms restructure to meet the demands of competition unleashed by liberalization (Gothoskar 1997; Soni-Sinha 2001). On the other hand, studies of women workers in different industries conducted during the 1980s had pointed out that women workers in export industries such as garments, electronics, and food processing were mainly young, unmarried, and relatively better educated than the profile of the average woman worker. A study of a synthetic gem-cutting industry in rural Tamil Nadu shows how a traditional single-caste, semi-bonded labour force was replaced in the 1990s by a young, unmarried female labour force from lower middle-class households in urban areas—an unusual case of urban to rural migration (Kapadia 1999).[7]

To understand the dynamics of liberalization and employment of women workers we need to go beyond two contemporary images of gender and labour in India; one focuses on the seamless prevalence

---

[6] The NSS continues to be restrictive in its definition of economic activity although it does take into account some household enterprises, artisan production, and transacted service provisions. It does not include the complete list of economic activities defined in the United Nations System of National Accounts. This implies an underestimation of economic activity and work participation rates of women, and it becomes difficult to accept generalizations regarding women's 'declining participation' as a result of overall economic trends (Ghosh 2000; Unni 2001).

[7] Other studies on the footwear industry have documented a growth in home-based female employment as a result of shifts in export and domestic markets (Knorringa 1999). In the fast-growing IT sector, home-based teleworkers, predominantly women, are increasing in cities such as Mumbai (Gothoskar 2000; Mitter 2000).

of the 'informal sector as the main location of women's labour market participation' and the second on 'India shining with high technology/ call centres' providing new work opportunities for young women. While these are certainly the main sites for women's employment today, at the same time, women have also been employed in other sectors of industrial manufacturing in different phases of industrialization.

After independence, India's industrialization strategy resulted in a three-tiered structure: the public sector controlling the 'commanding heights of the economy'; the private corporate sector operating as monopolies in certain fields; and a mass of small-scale enterprises. Till today industrial output relies on the co-existence of different structures of production, industrial organization, and concomitantly different types of employment ranging from household and cottage industries to large modern factories, consisting of multilayered categories of capital and labour (Kannan and Rutten 2003).

Despite idealizing and striving towards Fordism, cheap, unprotected labour remained contiguous to a Fordist core which was restricted primarily to the public sector and the large-scale private sector where unionization was strong. Similar to the experience in other countries, the dominant basis of entitlements has been employment in the organized manufacturing sector, which has been essentially male, reinforcing 'male industrial citizenship'. In the first phase of Indian industrialization, though women formed a critical segment of the industrial labour force, they were relatively excluded from modern production. In the early 1920s, they were around 20–5 per cent of the labour force in textile mills and 35–40 per cent in the coal mines and plantations (Nair 1996; Sen 2003). The progressive decline of women in all these industries started in the 1930s, and the extension of labour regulations and the emergence of an organized sector ran in tandem with the masculinization of industrial employment. The explicit and implicit assumptions about gender relations and the family in labour regulations forged a male-breadwinner gender contract which underpinned the subsequent marginalization of women, confirming Guy Standing's assessment of the twentieth century as 'the century of the labouring man' (2003).

Labour regulations in the post-independence period have reinforced the segmentation of labour. The inclusions and exclusions parallel the organised/unorganized sector division, which is also a gender division. The initiation of economic reforms in 1991 led to a major shift in state discourse from a surface commitment to social protection to explicit talk of 'rigidities' in the Indian labour market and the need for flexibility through labour market reforms. Although overall drastic changes have not yet been made in labour laws—though they were recommended by the Second National Commission on Labour in 2003—in many industries there has been implicit deregulation since the 1980s onwards. Existing legal regulations have been made less effective or have been bypassed.

The undermining of labour rights has serious consequences. In India, as in most developing countries, the near absence of citizenship-based entitlements to social protection has meant an extreme dependence on selling one's labour power as the only means for survival and security. Although the Indian Constitution professes a commitment to a welfare state, and there are constitutional provisions for the right to work and education, support for old age, sickness and disability, and social assistance for disadvantaged groups, these are rarely implemented. Overall, there has been a focus on 'promotive' forms of social security through anti-poverty and targeted development schemes, employment guarantee programmes, and food security through a public distribution system rather than strengthening protective measures (Harriss–White and Subramanian 1999). These limited measures have been patchily implemented, and employment in the organized sector regulated by labour legislation remains the main basis for social citizenship entitlements such as pensions and health insurance. It was estimated that in the early 1990s only 10 per cent of workers (out of a labour force of 375 million) were covered by social security schemes in the organized sector (Harriss-White and Gooptu 2000; Van Ginneken 1998). The Second National Commission on Labour notes that only about 7 per cent to 8 per cent of the workforce in the organized sector is protected (GoI 2003: 26). The bulk of women's employment (96 per cent) is concentrated in the unorganized sector. Unlike welfare regimes in the north or erstwhile socialist countries where the 'reproductive bargain' between the state and corporate sector provided for a range of non-wage benefits and other measures of social protection, access to such entitlements for Indian workers were limited to a small section.

WOMEN WORKERS IN THE ELECTRONICS INDUSTRY

The electronics industry in Delhi represents a good example to assess changes, since it includes enterprises from a pre-liberalization policy regime as well as those established in the post-liberalization period, employs women in large numbers, and spans a wide range of enterprises in the unorganized and organized sectors. The growth, structure, and deve-lopment of this industry reflect three different policy regimes: self-reliance with regulation (1960–80); self-reliance and partial liberalization (1980–90); and liberalization and globalization (1991 onwards). From the 1980s there was a process of 'creeping liberalization' leading to changes in the structure of the industry. By the 1990s, with the entry of multinational giants, electronics production in India was subject to the forces of global competition through a variety of indirect and direct subcontracting relations and systems of governance, but it was primarily oriented towards the *local* market. Hence, this case study on television manufacturing departs from the overwhelming focus on and contemporary debates about women's employment in export-oriented manufacturing (Razavi and Pearson 2004). In addition, it analyses *gendered labour regimes* as 'negotiated orders that emerge through the interplay of state intervention via labour regulations and industrial policy, the social organisation of the labour market, market competition, managerial strategies of labour control and workers' responses' in interaction with '*domestic regimes*' (Chhachhi 2011). This enables capturing the multidimensionality of conditions of employment rather than a simple focus on the presence or absence of labour regulations. Such a perspective identifies the degree of workers' dependence on the enterprise or the state for social protection and examines the enabling and constraining conditions for asserting entitlements in the workplace as well as the household.

LABOUR REGIMES IN THE ELECTRONICS INDUSTRY IN DELHI

In the television industry in Delhi, there were four co-existent gendered labour regimes (differentiated on the basis of domestic or foreign capital, age of enterprise, and labour process), which reveal variations in recruitment strategies, gendered forms of labour control, construction of gendered work identities, and resistance and struggle over employment-based entitlements. The liberalization of the Indian economy, particularly in the electronics sector, has affected its workers in different ways depending on the nature of the labour regime.

The Pre-liberalization Era

Highlighting the inclusion/exclusion dynamic inherent in labour regulations and the multistructural character of Indian manufacturing, there were two characteristic labour regimes of the pre-liberalization era in the industry. The first was a classical example of the unorganized sector consisting of tiny enterprises employing less than 10 workers with minimal labour regulation. Manufacturing television components such as printed circuit boards, they were the lowest link in a subcontracting chain extending down from large electronics enterprises. A company's survival depended on extreme flexibility and was contingent on a quick shift in product items. The overall nature of this regime was characterized by market despotism as suspicion and fear, internally and externally, dominated interactions and relationships. Owners were in constant fear of raids from tax departments and government inspectors. Internally, this was reflected in the recruitment and control over workers who were employed only on the basis of personal recommendations, with very few women—the ratio of women to men rarely exceeding 1:3. The women came primarily from Delhi-based poor households and typified the 'distress entry' worker, that is, they were main earners, a large proportion was divorced or deserted and had minimal education. Coming from extremely vulnerable households, with no other support systems, they were completely dependent on wage work. There was therefore an in-built element of labour control given their socio-economic backgrounds.

Work discipline was directly supervised by the owner, relations were personalized, and management control ranged from moderate to extreme despotism. There was flexibility in the sexual division of labour, which was a simple, manual assembly of components with no clear wage discrimination between men and women. The main reason for the presence of women was a conscious strategy to control men workers because of the former's 'calming influence', their 'natural' docility, and, most importantly, their 'trustworthiness' rather than the standard assumption of 'nimble fingers'. Aware of their limited options, owners constantly used the phrase *bechari* (poor thing) and implied they were doing them a favour by employing them. Women workers colluded in and were themselves controlled through this mutual construction of victimhood and vulnerability. Socialized into bodily self-regulation (they never went to the toilet at all during their working hours), combined with restrictions on associating with strange men, plus domestic responsibilities, which limited their time and mobility in public spaces, these women were constituted as an ideal docile and reliable workforce.

Although all the workers were equally vulnerable, men, at least intermittently, challenged this and looked for other options. Women, however, were tied into total dependence and colluded with the construction of themselves as becharis.[8] Rather than confront the owner on wage cuts, they often used their victim status as widows, main earners, or mothers with small children to get leave and exemption from too large deductions. Financial assistance locked the workers and owners further into a relationship of loyalty and trust. However, this was not totally hegemonic. In spite of stressing that they had no choice but to accept the low wages, the bad working conditions, and the despotic disciplinary regime, even to be grateful for them, a number of women also expressed their frustration and awareness of exploitation, but felt trapped by the absence of labour regulations and difficulties of unionization.

The second type of labour regime based on a different stage of the labour process and a different structure of the workforce was characteristic of enterprises established in the mid-1960s, all indigenously owned with some technical collaboration agreements with foreign companies. These small- and medium-scale companies employed between 100 and 200 workers and all statutory labour regulations were applicable. A crucial mediating factor was the unionization of workers since the 1980s, which freed them from absolute dependence. Both job security and housing security were significant in changing the despotic nature of the regime to one of moderate control that resulted in a social compact between labour and capital illustrative of the pre-liberalization era.

The workers came from different segments of the labour market: hinterland migrants, Delhi-based industrial worker households, and middle/lower-middle class and poor households. Recruited mainly through informal channels, their educational background ranged from functional literacy to graduates, with some who also had technical diplomas. The semi-automatic labour process and distinct gender division of labour were subject to classic Taylorist principles of control and discipline. There were wide variations in wages across as well as within particular occupations with a clear gendered job hierarchy. There were very few women assistant technicians or junior engineers, and none in the senior categories such as engineer, technician, and foreman. Overtime, which

---

[8] See Hossfeld (1990), who describes a similar strategy deployed by immigrant workers in Silicon Valley to gain some respite from work discipline.

was often compulsory, led to further gender differentials in take-home pay. Non-wage benefits varied across the factories, except for the provision of provident fund and Employees' State Insurance (ESI) scheme benefits (which included maternity benefits) for all workers. Some factories also provided conveyance allowance, washing allowance, and uniforms, but none had a crèche or subsidized canteen.

Labour control combined hierarchical and technical methods. Line speeds pushed production quotas up constantly, and piece-rate wage systems were introduced. The imposition of daily discipline was both crude and gendered. During periods of pressured production, women were not allowed to go to the toilet. If they did, the foreman would stand outside 'making eyes', described by them as *badtamizi* and *nazar theek nahi* (lewd behaviour). The foreman's behaviour often extended to actual physical harassment and assault.[9] Punishment was more often given for links with the union rather than production issues. Women who spoke up were sent off to sit in the men's section, or vice versa. This form of humiliation used gendered cultural attributes, making women feel insecure and stigmatized amongst strange men, and the men 'unmanly' if they were sent to sit among the women.

Control and discipline needed to be asserted and reasserted almost on a daily basis, since all the workers were aware of and used their legal entitlements. Women, for instance, would take leave immediately if they were sick or wanted to avoid a conflict or had domestic pressures. In this environment, women were able to assert their woman worker identity as reflected in their demands and their use of legal entitlements. Worker resistance, despite the swift and severe forms of punishment, came from three crucial factors: long labour histories in the same company; a union which would defend them; and security of housing. The mere existence of labour legislation and mediating institutions of the state in regulating industrial relations was not enough. Labour rights were not just given by the management—they were demanded and struggled for by the workers. The process of unionization led to a more moderate despotic regime and simultaneously made workers aware of their rights. Subsidized housing provided by the state also involved a process of struggle and gave the workers an important fallback position, illustrating the significance of the

---

[9] A common general punishment for defying the foreman, or for any act of 'indiscipline', consisted of sending workers out to sit at the gate in the blazing summer sun until they apologized and begged to be allowed to return to work.

linkage between citizenship-based and employment-based entitlements (see Chhachhi 2011).

This small but significant generation of women workers has been eliminated. Enterprises of this era have closed down, retrenching all workers and relocating to low-wage, non-unionized industrial areas in neighbouring states.

The Post-liberalization Period

A different picture emerges in the enterprises established or expanded in the era of liberalization with closer ties with multinational capital where the labour process and the labour market were more significant factors. A far more conscious managerial strategy to recruit a particular kind of mixed workforce was deployed. Differences of region and class played an important role through the recruitment of single women migrants from Kerala in south India and young unmarried women from Delhi and neighbouring areas. There was also a more specific demand for young unmarried men and women with secondary school education.

These enterprises approximate most closely the stereotype that emerged from the early literature on women workers in world market factories. Characterized by a more automated production process, clear job designations, and an occupational hierarchy in each production line and department, the sexual division of labour was sharpest at the two ends of the production process: only women did insertion of components and only men did servicing of the final product. All of them had permanent job status and written contracts, though within a gendered job hierarchy that was reflected in the higher maximum wage available for men.

Labour control in these 'new' enterprises was based on a more sophisticated combination of technological/bureaucratic controls, gender and ethnic divisions, and institutional structures and ideologies outside the factory—crucially, the family and the neighbourhood. Continuous process production required an evolved system of work discipline, and a formalized procedure of reward and punishment was instituted. Gender and ethnic differences in the workforce were consciously used to create divisions, and the tension was expressed in the shifting meanings of masculinity and femininity. As men tried to carve out and preserve an 'essentially masculine, heavy machine' area of work, management stressed women's natural qualities and women workers asserted simultaneously their special dexterity as well as capability to handle all jobs. Ethnic differences between the Delhi-based north Indians and the migrants from

Kerala were accentuated and played out around perceptions of productivity and capacity to work. The managerial construction of the migrant women workers as more 'productive, clever, and educated' functioned as a mechanism of pace setting and regulating productivity. The north Indian women saw the migrants as 'clever, liars, and promiscuous' and just as men were threatened with replacement by women, they felt threatened by the migrants. In the subtle power play by management, the north Indian women were threatened but also treated paternalistically as daughters/insiders, and migrant women were held up as models but still treated as 'outsiders'. Here extra-factory institutional structures and ideologies played a role: the migrants lived in rented rooms, and as single young women were constantly subjected to high levels of harassment by landlords and local goons. Residential space contained a constant threat of violence, and the factory provided safety and security. The lack of neighbourhood and housing security played a key role in their acquiescent attitude and non-involvement in collective action.

Until 1995, the situation in these factories was one of a complex form of despotism and conflict directed laterally rather than vertically, presenting a typical picture of hegemonic despotism. However, this was ruptured by an outbreak of spontaneous militancy. Beginning with assertion against a supervisor's harassment and struggle to abolish the 'toilet register', which represented demands to be treated with dignity and respect, young women workers moved on to challenge the management's attempts to abolish job designations and bypass payment of statutory minimum wages. They formed a union and carried their struggle into the public space of the labour office and courtrooms. As factory daughters turned disobedient, management tried to reimpose control through appealing to parental authority, the ideology of the factory as a family, and direct threat and coercion.

Contrary to the paradigmatic image of the 'docile third world woman worker', these women did not succumb to these pressures. Once this ideological hegemony was ruptured, they challenged and confronted managerial control, organized, and engaged in a classical industrial dispute. A broader awareness of workers' rights and organizational strategies developed as the dynamics of organizing collectively led to a 'leap in consciousness' from which there was no turning back, and they were transformed from dutiful daughters to 'disobedient daughters' and then into industrial worker citizens.

The fourth type of enterprises, symptomatic of the liberalization process, were large units with foreign collaboration, established from 1993 onwards, and located in low-wage industrial estates and export processing zones. The production process was modern and highly automated with a rigid gender division of labour and a gendered hierarchy of control and supervision. A polarization was created between employees from middle-class families with technical degrees who were granted all statutory rights and given further training; and the mass of production workers who were maintained as a non-permanent 'apprentice' workforce and denied job security. Voice representation, in particular, was crushed through gendered methods of labour control.

Managers gave the classic reasons of 'nimble fingers' and docility for employing girls but an additional criterion was that these girls were 'freshers', which implied not just that they were unmarried and straight out of school but also that their minds were fresh for indoctrination. Training involved a transfer of key 'home practices' associated with the general features of total quality management emphasized by all Japanese companies introducing a new work ethic and corporate culture. The gendered nature of labour control lay in the reconstitution of high school girls and electronic engineering graduates into 'industrial housekeepers' committed to the company ideology through inculcation of the five principles of Japanese housekeeping (5Ss).[10] This carefully planned training started with the recitation of the morning prayer and continued through the day. Boards with the 5Ss were placed strategically all around, daily discipline was very strict, and workers were dismissed for the smallest errors. They were frisked whenever they left the production hall, departments were kept segregated, the company provided transport, and all contact with other workers was controlled. Based on sophisticated methods of surveillance and labour control, the training in 'industrial housekeeping' combined the skills of domesticity with industrial efficiency to create a new kind of gendered workforce. Till this research ended, women in these factories had not challenged management except in one instance over the required uniforms of trousers and shirt, which was resisted as being against 'Indian culture'.

---

[10] The term 5Ss is based on five Japanese ideograms whose meaning starts with 'S': *Seiri* (Sorting), *Seiton* (Systematizing), *Seisou* (Sweeping), *Seiketsu* (Sanitizing), and *Shitsuke* (Self-disciplining).

Resistance, Collective Action, and the Struggle for Entitlements

Involvement of women workers in collective action and the emergence of women union leaders mark the second and third labour regimes. Because over 96 per cent of women work in the unorganized sector, their level of unionization is extremely low. While there are difficulties in organizing in the informal economy, this is less due to lack of the legal right to representation and more due to trade union focus on large-scale factories. In addition, the male-biased culture, structure, procedures, and violence associated with trade unions prevent women's involvement, whose demands are often focused on non-wage benefits and their struggle more non-confrontational (Chhachhi and Pittin 1996). In all four labour regimes, women workers resisted managerial controls through individualized actions of 'using managerial logic against them', controlling speed-ups, negotiating leave, and the like. These forms of resistance were most characteristic of the first and fourth labour regimes where possibilities for collective action were limited.

In the second and third regimes, women workers were able to demand the implementation of employment-based entitlements through 'citizenship in practice', that is, collective action by workers to force management to implement statutory labour rights where they were applicable. This process forged a 'woman worker identity' which encapsulated consciousness and solidarity around issues and entitlements related to being workers as well as women. In the course of various struggles the younger women workers challenged gender norms such as 'good' behaviour, required for marriage and the acceptance of male leadership. Interestingly, their families supported them in these struggles. In many cases, the challenge to managerial authority was paralleled with a demand within the family to reciprocate the financial support that the young women had provided to the family. As a 23-year-old worker stated:

We have no fear of pressure from the family. I tell my family that all these years I gave you my entire salary. Now you better feed and maintain me these few months. They have no choice!

Even if these struggles could not be sustained in the long run, the learning process itself and the ways it had changed women unionists' self-perception remain significant.[11] As Elson (1996: 50) points out, even if workers lose

---

[11] This change in consciousness is important since women union leaders continued to

their jobs, they would have acquired something permanent: 'more self confidence, more organisational and advocacy skills, more knowledge of how their society works'. These transformations were only one aspect of the changes women workers in unionized enterprises have undergone. A more subtle process of change also occurred within domestic regimes, involving women from both unionized and non-unionized enterprises.

Negotiating Autonomy in Domestic Regimes

While in many cases there was a link between industrial militancy and domestic autonomy, the process of negotiating autonomy varied, depending upon their employment in either pre-liberalization or post-liberalization labour regimes, with significant differences in kinds of domestic regimes[12] as well as the woman's life cycle status, that is, whether she was a daughter, mother, or wife. In general, older women as well as single women were employed in pre-liberalization labour regimes while younger women were employed in post-liberalization labour regimes. There were significant differences in the structures and forms of domestic regimes in terms of internal patriarchal control, and of power and entitlements based on whether the household was complex, nuclear, or sub-nuclear.

Women workers were making substantial contributions to total household income: 46 per cent of the workers contributed from 50 per cent to 100 per cent, and 38 per cent contributed from 25 per cent to 50 per cent, of total household income, with only 16 per cent contributing less than 25 per cent.[13] The translation of these substantial and visible earnings into 'perception' or into greater autonomy was not automatic.[14] Gendered cultural norms, rules, and practices conferred different degrees of power

---

face gendered constraints. Freedom from domestic responsibilities and reliance on male support, with constant proof of moral respectability, being important elements that enabled their involvement.

[12] Drawing on feminist extensions of A. Sen's 'bargaining model' of the household as a site of cooperative conflict (Agarwal 1997; Sen 1990), domestic regimes are conceptualized as a 'locus of competing interests, rights, obligations and resources, where household members are often involved in bargaining, negotiation, and possibly even conflict. Socially and historically specific views about the rights, responsibilities, and needs of particular individuals, which draw on normative understandings and practices linked to accepted power differences and ideologies, determine the dynamics of relations within the household' (adapted from Moore 1994: 91).

[13] Data based on fieldwork conducted in 1996 in Delhi.

[14] The Engelian assumption that waged work is a sufficient condition for improving women's status has been qualified further with Sen's (1990) notion of 'perceived income contribution'.

and entitlements, with a sharp distinction between the ways in which the incomes of daughters and wives are perceived. In complex and nuclear households, wives tended to avoid confrontations around control over income, but mainly through covert strategies, were able to claim and use parts of their income autonomously. These 'reclaimed wages' provided a sense of self-worth and independence even though the retrieved portion was often disbursed in household expenses. It was only in situations of open marital conflict that wives overtly used their earning capacity to bargain. Independent access to an income did notionally strengthen a woman's fallback position, but this did not necessarily mean that they used the 'exit option' in every case. The social opprobrium attached to divorced women, which limited the possibility of remarriage, plus the continued need for male protection, made 'exit' an option only in extreme cases.

Amongst single women, widows spoke with pride about not being dependent on relatives and the companionship offered at work. Single mothers had to subordinate their needs to accommodate natal family members but had some bargaining power. Older single women who had virtually given up the possibility of marriage since taking on the role of main 'male provider' of the family were able to exercise a great deal of autonomy. They were proud of and respected for taking on the role of fathers.

Daughters' income earning was more complicated—their actual contribution to the household was euphemized as earning for a dowry or just passing time before getting married, leading to a non-recognition/non-perception of these earnings. This lack of overt recognition did not mean that there was no change in their status. They could and did use their 'non-recognized' contribution to household income to bargain and assert choices when it was necessary, particularly in decisions about further education, delaying marriage, and choosing their own marriage partner without 'verbalizing' their contributions.

Gender roles showed rigidity as well as some flexibility. Overall, freedom from a specific aspect of reproductive work, childcare, was important for women's entry into waged work, and the primary responsibility for this remained with women through a redistribution of domestic tasks between women in the family. Though men's contribution to domestic labour was limited, many men did do external jobs such as shopping and paying bills (confirming the private/public divide). In some nuclear households, men also cooked, looked after children, and repaired things in the house. While no young man (brother/son) contributed to care work, fathers and husbands in many cases did do so. Despite the small number, it is important to note that there was a change in the traditional division of domestic responsibilities. Partly due to work demands such as overtime but also in many cases due to a conscious articulation of sharing household tasks, a process of democratization was occurring in some households.[15]

Finally, in discussion with young women workers, quite radical views emerged on marriage, work, and typical gender roles. For instance, the polarized ideal qualities of husband and wife symbolized by the legendary Ram and his devoted wife Sita were seen as good and correct, but at the same time almost all the women stated that this ideal was unrealistic and could not be emulated, with one young woman worker declaring, 'If today a man is not like Ram, then why should we be like Sita?'[16]

These young women expressed a more pragmatic and less romanticized view of marriage and men, a point noted by Kabeer (2000: 171) in her study of Bangladeshi garment workers. While marriage remained a necessary objective, it was not seen as taking predominance over work and study.[17] Despite the 'non-recognition' of daughters' contribution to the family economy, it did strengthen their fallback position and expand the horizon of choices available to them, without an open acknowledgement of the source of that strength. The fact that daughters have taken over the traditional responsibilities of fathers and brothers to provide for their dowries heralds a major shift in the material structure of patriarchal authority, even if at an ideological level there has been no overt, direct challenge to elder male authority.

The complexities of internal power dynamics and cultural norms within the household make it difficult to identify the transformational potential of waged work. As Kabeer (2000) points out, formal control over income was not as important as the expansion of choice and options due to wage work. The resort to covert strategies, particularly by young wives, the 'games' played by wives in nuclear households, and the non-recognition of daughters' earnings in this study all confirm Kabeer's major finding that male protection remains socially significant, even though male provisioning has been undermined in many cases. It is important to note that waged work here is regular, visible, and undertaken in a collective context—an important qualification to Sen's (1990) blanket endorsement

---

[15] A similar observation was made in a study of women workers employed in the industrial area of NOIDA near Delhi (Soni-Sinha 2001).

[16] Focus Group Discussion, Delhi 1996.

[17] 'In computer terms, marriage and associated domesticity are the "default setting", the norm, the ever-present point at which one arrives, or to which one returns, although other possibilities may (temporarily) intervene' (Chhachhi and Pittin 1996: 110).

of waged work per se and the promotion of any kind of income earning as good for women.

Younger women workers are aware of rights at their workplace and in relation to the family. Their views on male protection are far more cynical and overt acceptance more pragmatic. They are aware that getting a good dowry for a good stable marriage no longer holds. Dowry demands continue and refusal to meet them often leads to murder. Public exposure of this by the women's movement and the media has had an effect, and these women express disillusionment with the idea that marriage means lifetime security. So, while the discourse of earning one's dowry may still be used to explain their entry into waged work, many see employment as a more reliable and long-term basis for security.

However, as a result of industrial and economic restructuring in India, two processes have undermined the enabling conditions that facilitated the practice of citizenship: informalization of labour at the workplace and increasing vulnerability of the household.

EROSION OF EMPLOYMENT-BASED ENTITLEMENTS THROUGH INFORMALIZATION OF LABOUR

All four gendered labour regimes analysed earlier underwent major restructuring due to market competition in the first phase of liberalization, leading to informalization and increasing vulnerability of labour. The Vulnerability/Security Index (Figure 10.1) shows changes in the status of women workers in the total sample between 1993 and 1999.[18] The index resulted in the classification of women workers into three broad categories which, in 1993, were: unprotected (17 per cent), marginally protected (40

---

[18] This is a composite of data on work status, nature of contract, legally entitled benefits, minimum wages, and trade union organization. Based on the presence/absence of legally specified entitlements, the index highlights three dimensions of protection and security: employment security, income security, and labour representation security. Employment security depends on the job being permanent or temporary, and if there is a written or verbal contract. Income security refers to the implementation of minimum wage regulations and legally entitled benefits for health, pension, and so on. Labour representation security refers to the presence or absence of a trade union. The index is a modification of the labour status approach developed by Harriss et al. (1990). Here the focus is on different dimensions of protection and security, many included in the Decent Work Index developed by the International Labour Organization (ILO).

per cent), and protected (42 per cent). In six years, the number of workers in the unprotected and insecure category increased from 17 per cent to 60 per cent (including those who were retrenched), and this shift has been primarily from the protected, secure category.

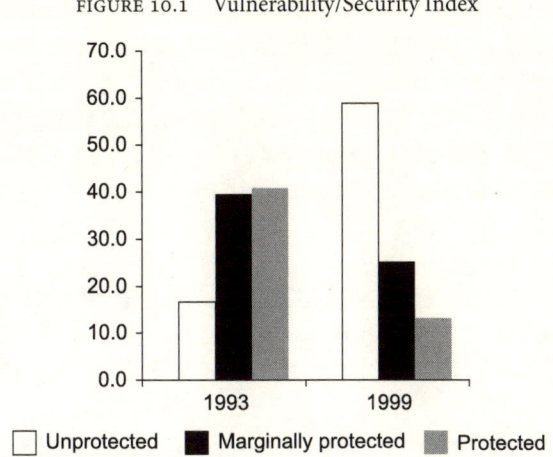

FIGURE 10.1 Vulnerability/Security Index

Source: Fieldwork conducted in Delhi in 1996.
Note: N = 162.

This major change clearly demonstrated the resort to labour market flexibility in the Delhi electronics industry. Changes due to market competition and restructuring led to: (a) the dismantling of the organized sector and mass retrenchment of workers with long service records. That generation of unionized workers has been eliminated. There was a reversal of regularization and implementation of statutory rights and a ban on new recruitment in locally owned enterprises with closer ties to multinationals, and an overall shift from a permanent to non-permanent workforce; (b) a shrinking of the lowest end of the unorganized sector as tiny and small enterprises, which always employed a casual workforce, were faced with extinction due to the flood of cheap electronics imports from China; (c) an increase in income insecurity—in 1994, 42 per cent of the workers interviewed were getting wages below the minimum wage and in 1995 this category increased to 57 per cent; (d) new employment in multinational enterprises based on a hierarchy between a mass of non-permanent women workers with minimum benefits and a layer of women workers from middle-class backgrounds who receive specialized training, full statutory benefits, and permanent status; and (e) increase in representation insecurity with unions in a defensive position. The increased harassment of militant union leaders, demoralization, spatial distancing labour courts from industrial areas, and the reduction in the scope of the mandatory requirement of labour inspection have made unionization difficult.

The managerial strategy of 'defensive flexibility' was not new—what was new was that this strategy of informalization was implicitly sanctioned by the state now. In the pre-liberalization era, similar attempts to 'dis-organize the organized sector' could be, and often were, successfully challenged and checked. But, now this 'organized informalization' appears to have state sanction, as the state withdraws its commitment to the provision or implementation of statutory labour regulations.

EROSION OF CITIZENSHIP-BASED ENTITLEMENTS AND INCREASING VULNERABILITY OF THE HOUSEHOLD

The process of undermining the enabling conditions at the workplace has been accompanied by increasing vulnerability at the household level. The phenomenal increase in prices of basic necessities since 1991 has forced workers to make major household budgetary adjustments in levels and quality of consumption, health, and education, leading to changes in everyday life and tensions in gender relations. While earlier the majority of worker households used the Public Distribution System (PDS) for some part of their consumption requirements, now many had to buy only from the open market while others became completely dependent on subsidized food. Changes in consumption took gender-differentiated forms, with further differences between married and unmarried women. The hidden costs were borne primarily by married women workers, particularly mothers in nuclear families, who experienced an increase in care-work labour time and reduction in food intake. There was an increase in the intangible aspects of care-work. In 50 per cent of the households surveyed, the responsibility for household provisioning rested predominantly on female earners. There was a shift from women making a contribution to household income to women taking on the primary responsibility (due to increasing male unemployment or low male wages and precarious irregular jobs), a transfer of even the few tasks that men undertook in domestic labour (shopping) and the help provided by daughters or domestic servants to mothers who now had complete responsibility for domestic labour. This meant an increase in 'time poverty' for these women. The stress and strain of a situation where pre-existing gender roles, rights, and responsibilities could no longer be relied upon had in some cases led to an increase in domestic conflict and violence.

There did not appear to be a reduction of food for children, although there was a shift to bad quality and junk food that will have long-term health implications. Despite a rise in costs of schooling, children were not withdrawn, and primary education was prioritized through taking loans and cutting other areas of consumption. Gender differences occurred in higher education as young men undertook vocational training while young women took up jobs. Unlike studies in Latin America and Africa which point to drastic reductions in consumption in times of inflation and crisis, the worker households in this study had managed to cope, partly through the 'cushioning' of the effects of price rise through women's labour and ingenuity, and partly through the deployment of labour.

Dependence on the labour market was critical for survival and security. Research on workers who lost their jobs particularly from the second labour regime of the pre-liberalization era showed that a large section remained unemployed and only a few got irregular jobs in the unorganized sector. Contrary to earlier patterns, hinterland male migrant workers did not return to their villages. The village did not constitute a refuge, and rural links only acted as a short-term buffer. Women's earnings became crucial for the survival of these households. No woman worker could enter into the higher end of work in the unorganized sector, that is, self-employment. Instead, they were pushed into the lowest paid work as domestic servants or at best, home-based garment workers. Income reduction in the space of two years was drastic. Cuts in household budgets, the changes in everyday life, food reduction, an increase in ill health, and the negative effects on education of children—all had immediate and intergenerational consequences. Gender relations within these households were under great stress. Men hid the fact that women were sustaining the household. Women felt their autonomy was being restricted, and there were increased controls on their mobility. There was a loss of dignity and identity as workers slipped from a self-identity of being organized, unionized workers with a highly developed consciousness and pride in their skills and contribution to the industry, to extreme vulnerability, insecurity, and in some cases, destitution (Chhachhi 2011).

These processes foreground the linkage between changes in the workplace and the household. The undermining of enabling conditions in both locales reversed the possibility for women to assert 'citizenship in practice' in both arenas. The absence of a strong asset base and strong and extensive citizenship entitlements from the state sector implies that

> It is over-optimistic to expect the domestic sector to absorb all the risks. When people have to live from hand to mouth, human energies and morale are weakened. 'Contingent labour' is conducive to 'contingent households' which fragment and disintegrate with costs for the people from these households and for the wider society. (Elson 2002: 94)

Both men and women workers paid these costs, but with a greater burden on women who continued to provide a buffer to prevent a descent into more extreme conditions of distress, insecurity, and vulnerability—a real threat as the experience of job loss workers discussed earlier illustrates. Apart from the limits to the 'elasticity' of women's labour, noted by feminist economists, the emotional pressures can also reverse the processes which were leading to a democratization of gender relations.

A disturbing development is an emerging 'crisis of masculinity' as male unemployment increases and a key gender marker for men—a permanent job—becomes rare. In reaction to the changes and stresses on gender roles, a number of men who lost their jobs in the electronics industry committed suicide, disappeared, or were depressed. In contrast, all the women, though extremely pressured, continued to juggle limited household resources and searched for means of livelihood, saying they were too busy to be depressed (Chhachhi 2011). Studies of job loss amongst public sector workers in Bangladesh highlighted a distinction between household masculinity, which was upheld, and public masculinity, which was being undermined (Haque and Kusakbe 2005). The reverse process occurred amongst men in the case study discussed earlier where retrenched men continued to maintain hegemonic masculinity in the public sphere and denied the undermining of male authority within the household. The crisis of masculinity reflects a crisis of the working class, and the consequences are detrimental to both men and women, since attempts at reconstituting and reasserting hegemonic masculinity can take violent forms at an individual level (Chowdhury 2005). At a collective level, forces of religious fundamentalism (Hindutva in India, for instance) provide glorified notions of masculinity, a convenient 'other', as well as constructed collectivities for this reconstitution. Informalization and flexibilization of the labour market along with the reversal in the process of democratization at the workplace and within the household noted earlier, therefore, have wider implications.

The processes mapped earlier are not just specific to the electronics industry. The pace of informalization has accelerated. The National Commission for Enterprises in the Unorganised Sector (NCEUS 2009) estimated that of the total employment of 458 million in 2004–5, 14 per cent were in the organized sector and 86 per cent were in the unorganized sector. Informal employment has grown overall, constituting 46.6 per cent of workers in the organized sector. Accordingly, almost 92.4 per cent of employment in India is informal. The NCEUS also noted that the net increase in employment between 1999–2000 and 2004–5 has been of informal workers.

Post-liberalization, the informal economy has also been affected. Women workers in the informal economy had lost jobs in the silk spinning, gum collecting, and *bidi* rolling industries due to changes in technology and Chinese imports (Jhabvala and Sinha 2002). Liberalization had also created some areas of new employment in the unorganized sector such as crafts, with women entering into hitherto male areas of stone cutting and metal and wood work. However, the financial crisis has affected many of these enterprises, particularly those integrated into the global economy and producing for export, such as diamonds, gems, jewellery, textiles, garments, engineering goods chemicals, leather, and handicrafts, hitting primarily the small-scale unorganized sector. Overall, it is estimated that over one million jobs have been lost with cultivators, migrants, and home-based workers affected the most (see Ghosh 2009; Kumar 2009). The loss of livelihoods has put great pressure on organizations in the informal economy, which had evolved many local innovative schemes using state and non-state resources to meet some the needs of informal economy workers (Lund and Srinivas 2000). Today, these organizations are struggling to defend those gains.

* * *

In each phase of capital accumulation in India, women's labour has been incorporated in specific ways with a continuing dynamic of exclusion and inclusion occurring in multiple sites along with individual acts of resistance and instances of collective action. If the nineteenth and early twentieth centuries were characterized by the masculinization of the organized labour force, the main trend in the contemporary period is the feminization of the conditions of work—that is, work that is informalized, irregular, insecure, often low paid for most workers, male or female. As India liberalizes its economy further and de-regulates its labour market linking production with global and local commodity chains which extend right down to informal economy and into home-based production at one end and the high technology service economy at the other end along with the setting up of special economic zones (SEZs) across the country, what does the future hold for women workers? There remain debates about whether the new economy generated by the proliferation of call centres is creating a cybertariat or a new middle class. However, the conditions of work in these call centres parallel the processes of flexibilization and informalization in the manufacturing sector with both 'electronic panoptican' forms of control and surveillance combined with more 'classical' direct forms of control, despite the high income earned by workers employed particularly in the IT-enabled services (ITES) sector. New forms of work are emerging that are de-territorialized and disembodied, creating 'virtual identities', which disable traditional forms of collective organizing (Upadhaya and Vasavi 2008).

A new landscape of labour is being created, and it remains gendered as well as classed and casteist. State policy is geared towards a trade-off between employment-based entitlements and the provision of minimal social security. The Sengupta Commission (NCEUS 2009) had raised hopes for a new model for social security, and its reports have provided evidence and rationale for a rights-based and broad-based inclusive approach for informal economy workers. The Unorganized Sector Workers' Social Security Act, 2008, is an important step towards providing a minimum level of social security to about 300 million informal economy workers. The initial proposals recommended by the NCEUS (2005) were fairly comprehensive and significant in stressing that the Unorganized Sector Social Security Act would be a legally enforceable entitlement like the National Rural Employment Guarantee Act (NREGA). However, as with the NREGA, the current Act has many flaws and is being opposed by workers' organizations: the package is minimal, covering only contingencies (health, maternity, old age), and basically provides only for 'a national floor level social security for all the informal workers' (Kannan and Pillai, 2007); there is no mandatory provision on the minimum level, nor a clearly defined funding obligation and a time frame.

It is not formulated as a right, and the funds allocation is discretionary, ignoring the recommendation for establishment of a social security fund. Coverage is not universal—a major section left out is unpaid family workers, a majority of whom are women (Neetha 2006). There is a great danger of further levelling down—not just in the loss of possibilities to access benefits possible in the formal sector, but also the reversal of gains made for informal economy workers at local levels.

Most significantly, the links between three measures for National Minimum Social Security, Minimum Conditions of Work, and National Minimum Wage as constituting a 'social floor' proposed by the NCEUS have been effectively severed. Since the latter two measures have not been accepted, once again there has been a trade off between labour market flexibility and a minimalist social security.

What is being promoted is a market-based entrepreneurial model through the fostering of competitive individualism and consumerism. This is a conscious managerial strategy in call centres (Upadhaya and Vasavi 2008) which creates new subjectivities but is also part of the policy fostering micro-credit as a panacea for reducing poverty (see Chhachhi 2008). These policies avoid the key issue of employment generation and provision of social security, which create the enabling conditions for 'democratic citizenship'. The struggles of women workers in India have shown the importance of state responsibility for social provisioning and the need to integrate both employment and citizenship entitlements. In assessing the continuities and discontinuities in the new forms in which women's labour provides a source of local and global capital accumulation in the present conjuncture (apart from their centuries old invisible contribution to the care economy), we need to apply a longitudinal perspective. This needs to be combined with more nuanced and ethnographic analysis that challenges the dichotomies of global/local and workplace/household and explores the creation of women workers subjectivities in the fierce new world of globalized neo-liberal capitalism.

REFERENCES

Agarwal, B. (1997), 'Bargaining and Gender Relations: Within and Beyond the Household', *Feminist Economics*, 3(1): 1–51.

Banerjee, N. (1999a), 'Can Markets Alter Gender Relations?', *Gender Technology and Development*, 3(1): 103–22.

——— (1999b), 'How Real is the Bogey of Feminization?' in T.S. Papola and A.N. Sharma (eds), *Gender and Employment in India*. New Delhi: Indian Society of Labour Economics, Institute of Economic Growth in association with Vikas Publishing House, pp. 299–317.

Chandrashekar and Ghosh (2007), 'Women Workers in Urban India', MACROSCAN, New Delhi, available at http://www.macroscan.com/fet/feb07/fet060207Women_Workers.htm.

Chhachhi, A. (2004), 'Eroding Citizenship: Gender and Labour in Contemporary India', PhD thesis, University of Amsterdam.

——— (2008), 'Ensuring Democratic Citizenship: A Gender Perspective on Contending Pathways for Socio-economic Security in South Asia', *Indian Journal of Human Development*, 2(1): 134–64.

Chhachhi, A. (2011), *Gender and Labour in Contemporary India: Eroding Citizenship*. UK: Routledge.

Chhachhi, A. and R. Pittin (1996), 'Multiple Identities, Multiple Strategies', in Amrita Chhachhi and Renée Pittin (eds), *Confronting State, Capital and Patriarchy: Women Organising in the Process of Industrialisation*. London: Macmillan Publishers Ltd, pp. 93–130.

Chowdhury, P. (2005), 'Crisis of Masculinity in Haryana: The Unmarried, the Unemployed and the Aged', *Economic and Political Weekly*, 3 December, pp. 5189–98.

Cook, J. (2000), 'Flexible Employment—Implications for a Gendered Political Economy of Citizenship', in J. Cook, J. Roberts, and G. Waylen (eds), *Towards a Gendered Political Economy*. New York: St. Martin's Press, and London: Macmillan Publishers Ltd., in association with the Political Economy Research Centre, University of Sheffield, pp. 145–64.

Deshpande, S. and L.K. Deshpande (1999), 'Gender-based Discrimination in the Urban Labour Market', in Papola and Sharma (eds), *Gender and Employment in India*, pp. 223–48.

Elson, D. (1996), 'Appraising Recent Developments in the World Market for Nimble Fingers', in Chhachhi and Pittin (eds), *Confronting State, Capital and Patriarchy*, pp. 35–55.

——— (2002), 'Gender Justice, Human Rights, and Neo-Liberal Economic Policies', in Maxine Molyneux and Shahra Razavi (eds), *Gender Justice, Development, and Rights*. Oxford: Oxford University Press, pp. 78–114.

Fraser, N. (1997), *Justice Interruptus: Critical Reflections on the 'Post-Socialist' Condition*. New York/London: Routledge.

Ghosh, J. (1999), 'Macro-economic Trends and Female Employment: India in the Asian Context', in Papola and Sharma (eds), *Gender and Employment in India*, pp. 318–50.

——— (2000), 'Globalization, Export-Oriented Employment for Women and Social Policy: A Case Study of India', paper presented at 'Conference on Globalization, Export-Oriented Employment for Women and Social Policy', UNRISD, Bangkok, October.

——— (2009), *Global Crisis and the Indian Economy in Global Financial Crisis: Impact on India's Poor: Some Initial Perspectives*. New Delhi: UNDP.

Gothoskar, S. (ed.) (1992), *Struggles of Women at Work*. New Delhi: Vikas Publishing House.

——— (1997), 'Women, Work and Health: An Interconnected Web: Case of Drugs and Cosmetics Industries', *Economic and Political Weekly*, 32(43): 45–52.

Government of India (GoI) (2003), *Report of Second National Commission on Labour*. New Delhi: Ministry of Labour, GoI.

——— (2006), *Employment and Employment Situation in India, 2004–2005*. New Delhi: National Sample Survey, Union Ministry of Statistics and Programme Implementation.

Haque, Md. Mozammel and K. Kusakbe (2005), 'Retrenched Men Workers in Bangladesh: A Crisis of Masculinities?', *Gender, Technology and Development*, 9(2): 185–208.

Harriss, J., K.P. Kannan, and G. Rodgers (1990), *Urban Labour Market Structure and Job Access in India: A Study of Coimbatore*. Geneva: International Institute for Labour Studies.

Harriss-White, B. and N. Gooptu (2000), 'Mapping India's World of Unorganized Labour', *Socialist Register 2001*. London: The Merlin Press, pp. 89–118.

Harriss-White, B. and S. Subramanian (eds) (1999), *Illfare in India: Essay on India's Social Sector in Honour of S. Guhan*. New Delhi: Sage Publications.

Hossfeld, K. (1990), '"Using Their Logic against Them": Contradictions in Sex, Race, and Class in Silicon Valley', in K. Ward (ed.), *Women Workers and Global Restructuring*. Cornell International Industrial and Labor Relations Report Series, No. 17. Ithaca: ILR Press, pp. 149–78.

Jhabvala, R. and R. Subramanya (eds) (2000), *The Unorganised Sector: Work Security and Social Protection*. New Delhi: Sage Publications.

Jhabvala, R. and S. Sinha (2002), 'Liberalisation and the Woman Worker', *Economic and Political Weekly*, 25 May, 37(21): 2037–44.

Kabeer, N. (2000), *The Power to Choose: Bangladeshi Women and Labour Market Decisions in London and Dhaka*. London: Verso.

——— (2001), 'Conflicts over Credit: Re-evaluating the Empowerment Potential of Loans to Women in Rural Bangladesh', *World Development*, 29(1): 63–84.

Kannan, K.P. and M. Rutten (2003), 'Labour and Capital in Asia's Transformation: On Dichotomies, Continuities and Linkages', in A. Das and M. van der Linden (eds), *Work and Social Change in Asia: Essays in Honour of Jan Breman*. Delhi: Manohar Publishers and Distributors, pp. 111–30.

Kannan, K.P. and V. Pillai N. (2007), 'Conceptualizing Social Security in a Human Development and Rights Perspective', *Indian Journal of Human Development*, January, 1(1): 31–51.

Kapadia, K. (1999), 'Gender Ideologies and the Formation of Rural Industrial Classes in South India Today', in J. Parry, J. Breman, and K. Kapadia (eds), *The Worlds of Indian Industrial Labour*. New Delhi: Sage Publications, pp. 329–52.

——— (2002), 'Introduction: The Politics of Identity, Social Inequalities and Economic Growth', in K. Kapadia (ed.), *The Violence of Development: The Politics of Identity, Gender and Social Inequalities in India*. New Delhi: Kali for Women, pp. 1–42.

Knorringa, P. (1999), 'Artisan Labour in the Agra Footwear Industry: Continued Informality and Changing Threats', in Parry, Breman, and Kapadia (eds), *The Worlds of Indian Industrial Labour*, pp. 303–28.

Kumar, R. (2009), 'Global Financial Crisis and Economic Crisis: Impact on India and Policy Response', *Global Financial Crisis: Impact on India's Poor: Some Initial Perspectives*. New Delhi: UNDP.

Kundu, A. (1999), 'Trends and Pattern of Female Employment: A Case of Organised Informalisation', in Papola and Sharma (eds), *Gender and Employment in India*, pp. 52–70.

Lund, F. and S. Srinivas (2000), *Learning from Experience: A Gendered Approach to Social Protection for Workers in the Informal Economy*. Geneva: STEP/ILO and WIEGO.

Mohanty, C. (1988), 'Under Western Eyes: Feminist Scholarship and Colonial Discourse', *Feminist Review*, 30: 61–88.

Molyneux, M. (2000), 'Comparative Perspectives on Gender and Citizenship: Latin America and the Former Socialist States', in J. Cook, J. Roberts, and G. Waylen (eds), *Towards a Gendered Political Economy*. New York: St. Martin's Press, and London: Macmillan Publishers Ltd., in association with the Political Economy Research Centre, University of Sheffield, pp. 121–44.

Moore, H.L. (1994), *A Passion for Difference*. Cambridge: Polity Press.

Nair, Janaki (1996), *Women and Law in Colonial India*. New Delhi: Kali for Women.

National Commission for Enterprises in the Unorganised Sector (NCEUS) (2005), *Unorganised Sector Workers' Social Security Bill*. New Delhi: NCEUS.

—— (2009), *The Challenge of Employment in India: An Informal Economy Perspective*. New Delhi: NCEUS.

Neetha, N. (2006), '"Invisibility" Continues? Social Security and Unpaid Women Workers', *Economic and Political Weekly*, XLI(32): 3497–9.

Ong, A. (1991), 'The Gender and Labour Politics of Postmodernity', *Annual Review of Anthropology*, 20: 279–309.

Pearson, R. (1998), '"Nimble Fingers" Revisited: Reflections on Women and Third World Industrialization in the Late Twentieth Century', in C. Jackson and R. Pearson (eds), *Feminist Visions of Development: Gender Analysis and Policy*. London and New York: Routledge, pp. 171–88.

Razavi, S. (1999), 'Export-oriented Employment, Poverty and Gender: Contesting Accounts', *Development and Change*, 30(3): 653–82.

Razavi, S. and R. Pearson (2004), 'Globalisation, Export-oriented Employment and Social Policy: Gendered Connections', in S. Razavi, R. Pearson, and C. Danloy (eds), *Globalization, Export-oriented Employment and Social Policy: Gendered Connections*. Basingstokes, UK: Palgrave Macmillan.

Sangari, K. (1995), 'Politics of Diversity: Religious Communities and Multiple Patriarchies', *Economic and Political Weekly*, December, 30(51 and 52): 3287–310 and 3381–9.

Sen, A. (1990), 'Gender and Cooperative Conflicts', in I. Tinker (ed.), *Persistent Inequalities: Women and World Development*. New York: Oxford University Press, pp. 123–45.

Sen, S. (2003), 'Politics of Gender and Class: Women in Indian Industries', in M. Pernau, I. Ahmad, and H. Reifield (eds), *Family and Gender: Changing Values in Germany and India*. New Delhi: Sage Publications, pp. 296–321.

Soni-Sinha, U. (2001), 'Income Control and Household Work-Sharing', in R.M. Kelly, J.H. Bayes, M.E. Hawkesworth, and B. Young (eds), *Gender, Globalization and Democratisation*. Lanham, Boulder, New York, and Oxford: Rowman & Littlefield Publishers, Inc., pp. 121–36

Standing, G. (1989), 'Global Feminization through Flexible Labor', *World Development*, 17(7): 1077–95.

——— (2003), 'Human Security and Social Protection', in J. Ghosh and C.P. Chandrasekhar (eds), *Work and Well-being in the Age of Finance*. New Delhi: Tulika Books, pp. 579–602.

Unni, J. (2001), 'Gender and Informality in Labour Market in South Asia', *Economic and Political Weekly*, 36(26): 2366–77.

Upadhaya, C. and Vasavi, A.R. (2008), *In an Outpost of the Global Economy: Work and Workers in India's Information Technology Industry*. New Delhi: Routledge.

Van Ginneken, Wouter (ed.) (1998), *Social Security for All Indians*. New Delhi: Oxford University Press.

Venkata Ratnam, C.S. (2006), *Industrial Relations*. New Delhi: Oxford University Press.

Wolf, D. (1992), *Factory Daughters: Gender, Household Dynamics and Rural Industrialisation in Java*. Berkeley: University of California Press.

Yuval-Davis, N. (1999), 'The "Multi-Layered Citizen": Citizenship in the Age of "Glocalization"', *International Feminist Journal of Politics*, 1(1): 119–36.

VI. RELIGION

Chapter 11

HEROIC WOMEN, MOTHER GODDESSES

Family and Organization in Hindutva Politics *

TANIKA SARKAR

I

THE EMERGENCE OF A WOMEN'S MOVEMENT within the Hindu right may lead us to reassess certain assumptions about women's relationship with violence, religion, politics, and the contemporary urban middle class culture. In moments of mass violence, the only women who have engaged our attention so far have been the victims from the vulnerable community who need to pick up the pieces of a shattered community life and laboriously, painfully, begin a healing process. Within religion, women are usually regarded as quietist devotees who use its mythical and ritual resources to create an autonomous cultural space that wrests from patriarchy some relief and even power. They are vested with a more intimate and deeper relationship with and a custodianship of authentic religious traditions of the community. As far as politics goes, the thrust of

---

* Originally published in Tanika Sarkar and Urvashi Butalia (eds), 1995, *Women and the Hindu Right*. New Delhi: Kali for Women, pp. 181–215.

research has been towards debating their location within mass nationalism with only occasional glances at women of the left. The cultural aspects of upper-caste urban middle class life, especially the tenor of change from the 1980s have not yet drawn much systematic attention, and we operate with nebulous impressions of a new kind of market formation that is dominated increasingly by commodities and images flooding in from the West.

The study of the women of the Hindutva brigade is not to invalidate these assumptions but to add to them very different experiences of contemporary Indian life that may open up other trajectories. I wanted to place the women of the right at the intersection of all these processes—politics, violence, the new middle class, and religion. At the same time, while it is important to see the formation as overdetermined by these multiple experiences, in the ultimate analysis I recognize the fundamentally political nature of the agenda, however much it may project itself as religious or cultural. In fact, the women's movement of the right reveals the political possibilities and resources of the new culture and religion of the middle class.

The need to precisely assess the gender politics of the right is linked up with a larger compulsion to understand the specificities of right-wing politics in India. Despite the continued existence of a 70-year-old, self-multiplying, innovative, and uniquely experimental semi-fascist formation in our country, we tend to veer away from any focused encounter with it. The right is constantly dissolved into either an economic conjuncture that may or may not be conducive to fascism[1] or it is written about as a hard form of nationalism, born out of a Westernist modernity. The accent then inevitably shifts to the history of mainstream nationalism which totally ignores the specific mediations of the Sangh family[2] or mentions the Sangh as a communal discursive pattern whose ideology is not seen to be anchored in socio-economic conjunctures and political contingencies.

After the Ramjanmabhoomi movement reached a climax around 1990, Sangh politics at last became a matter of overwhelming concern. The focus, however, was on one member of the family—the Bharatiya Janata

---

[1] Left political observers seem to be reluctant to focus on aspects which do not relate to the material and class base of political formation. It is a curious reluctance since Marx, in his historical writings, analysed the practice and character of decisive political actors with great care and insight.

[2] A telling example will be Gyan Pandey. His focus on a rather undifferentiated and monolithic colonial discourse and its nationalist derivatives completely ignores the Indian right as a participant in the making of communalism.

Party (BJP)—and its machinations for the takeover of state power.[3] This, to my mind, is a fragmentary and seriously incomplete and limited way of looking at the right. The right aims at nothing short of transforming the upper-caste/middle-caste leaders of Hindu society individually and collectively. It is this larger and ultimately far more crucial ambition which opens up a space for the political importance of the women of the Sangh family.

II

The Rashtriya Swayamsevak Sangh (RSS), the most effective organizer and bearer of the politics of the Hindu right, and the founder and teacher of a whole range of mass and electoral wings tied to its training programme and general guidance, was founded in 1925, at a time when Indian nationalists had already been able to organize one of the largest mass movements in history. It was set up as an alternative to the politics of mass anti-colonial struggles since it neither joined nor initiated any anti-British movement up to independence, and its only activism was expressed in anti-Muslim violence. Its ideological guru, Savarkar, had turned away from participation in the politics of revolutionary terrorism before he evolved an agenda for the Hindu right. The Rashtrasevika Samiti, its women's wing, was set up in 1936 (Basu *et al.* 1993).

The Gandhian struggle had, from the early 1920s, gradually involved women from urban middle class, as well as from peasant and tribal backgrounds in open, mass movements. From the late 1920s a vibrant left-wing tradition of working class politics also emerged, pitted against the colonial state and its allies—a predominantly European class of industrial capitalists. Women were prominent occasionally as union organizers and as working class militants (see Kumar 1993). In the early 1930s, the revolutionary terrorists of Bengal began to invite women cadres into their ranks as full-scale comrades in arms, rather than as mere providers of logistic support. The women of the Hindu right, therefore, had a wide array of political alternatives, of models of activism to choose from. The decision to stick to the politics of the right was, therefore, not exercised in a vacuum but it was an informed choice. It is important to recuperate this counterpoint, since any choice made by women is often assumed

[3] From the early 1990s Indian journalism produced an impressive corpus on the BJP.

to be made out of helplessness and an absence of alternatives towards empowerment.

Lakshmibai Kelkar, the mother of a Maharashtrian RSS veteran, persuaded the RSS *Sarsanghchalak* Hegdewar in 1936 to help her set up a separate women's wing. Up to this time, the RSS had been confined to an uncompromisingly upper-caste highly educated middle class base, largely from the deeply privileged Maharashtrian Brahmin group. The women came from identical backgrounds, from nearly identical families. This was the first front that the RSS founded, after a gap of 11 years of its own foundation. It was also after a fairly long period of persuasion from Kelkar, who had initially wanted the all-male Sangh to open itself up to women members, and eventually got Hegdewar's help in setting up a women's wing as a compromise gesture. The foundation of the Samiti was, then, a departure and a new turn in RSS strategy. What lay behind this decision?

The 1930s were a time of rapid left advance in Indian politics, of consolidation of peasant and trade union fronts, of unity among socialistic elements both inside and outside the Congress. The United Front tactic of the Communist International, which advised communist parties of colonized countries to join mass anti-colonial movements even under a nationalist bourgeois leadership, had helped Indian communists significantly to establish themselves as a national presence and to enlarge the political possibilities of their working class and peasant fronts (Sarkar 1983). A more telling challenge came from the rapid organizational initiative of low-caste politics that threatened not only to challenge upper-caste authority, but to break away from the Hindu political constituency altogether. The crisis coincided with an enlargement of the scope of electoral politics. Under the circumstances, the decision of untouchables to form a separate political constituency would permanently affect the definition of the Hindu community and would fatally circumscribe the scope of established upper-caste authority.

There was, then, a crisis in the politics of social base and of mobilization. The RSS tackled it in its own way. It did not develop other thrust areas immediately, socially or even geographically. It only accepted the demand of the women of its own families for a public political space and for a non-domestic existence and organization. The Samiti could form daily centres for physical, martial, and ideological training. But no other forms of politics were made available to it. The women stayed out of anti-colonial mass struggles as well as out of women's organizations that had been debating and agitating over issues of gender justice and rights in autonomous, middle-class organizations. Ideological instruction consisted of a violent creed of patriotism where the Motherland and the community were seen to be threatened not by the British but by the Muslim.

Yet the departure did not lead to a significant broadening of the RSS gender ideology as a whole. We must note that while the name Rashtriya Swayamsevak Sangh means 'Nationalist Volunteers', the term Rashtrasevika denotes women who serve the nation. The difference in the names is significant in several ways. It not only relegates women's work within the Samiti organization to a domestic role, but also consigns their domestic labour firmly to the sphere of humble service. The sense of autonomy and self-choice that are associated with the word 'volunteer' are notably missing. In the formative period of the Samiti, neither Hegdewar nor his successor, M.S. Golwalkar, the super ideologue of the RSS, attached much importance to women's formal organizational work, and the Samiti led a low-priority, non-innovative, routine-bound existence. In Golwalkar's corpus of writings, women are predominantly mothers who could help the Sangh cause most by rearing their children within the RSS framework of *samskaras*—a combination of family ritual and unquestioning deference towards family elders and RSS leaders (Golwalkar 1980). The crisis, therefore, led to an intensive self-mobilization on a broader basis that encompassed its own women. This response is fairly typical of RSS strategy. After the Emergency had been imposed, for instance, it went in for large-scale primary school formation, to train the children of the urban upper-caste trader-service sectors, its standard class base. This mode of progress does not expose the women of the Hindutva brigade to polluting lower-class/caste milieus or take them away from familial environs. It does not confront them with the larger problems of their socially exploited sister, so that the Hindutva women are never forced to choose between gender and their own class/caste privileges. It keeps them tied to family interests and ideology while spicing their lives with the excitement of a limited but important public identity. The Samiti seeks to deepen the conformist character of its constituency by diverting their attention away from concern about victims of social oppression and their own class/caste complicity with existing orders of power relations to an alleged non-concretized notion of Muslim oppression of Hindu women through the ages. From Savarkar's formative writings on Muslim rule in India, the stereotype of an eternally lustful Muslim male with evil designs on Hindu women has been reiterated and made a part of a historical common sense (see Agarwal 1995). The stereotype helps to restrict the concern of women within the desired framework. From certain affirmative actions undertaken during the V.P. Singh government, the women of the RSS combine (the RSS, BJP,

Vishwa Hindu Parishad [VHP], and affiliated groups) have reason to fear an imminent breach of their upper-caste movements. Their caste and class position therefore ensures that they lend their commitment exclusively to a highly militant yet socially conservative movement.

It is interesting that on their daily training grounds an identical schedule has always been followed by both the RSS and the Samiti. There are regular physical training programmes for women, with a special focus on the martial arts, including practice in shooting. RSS-run schools, similarly, teach exactly the same course to their boys and girls. When the Samiti was first established, it was certainly most unusual, if not a transgression, for respectable women to go through such exercises. The only parallel in those times would have been with the terrorist women of Bengal. Those women, however, were prepared to leave home while the Samiti originally had no plan of direct political action.

Lakshmibai Kelkar, the founder of the Samiti, was keen that her girls must have strong, trained bodies. The aspiration seems curious, given the fact that it was put to no active or public use for a long time to come. We shall see later that the cult of the strong physique came to include an extra meaning for women, over and above that inscribed within the organization by the founders. At the same time, body-centred practices for women have old and varied meanings and values within different currents of Hindu patriarchy. A variety of physical rites and rituals meant to preserve her virtue and family welfare are taken to constitute nearly the entirety of prescribed religious activity for the pious Hindu woman. Late-nineteenth-century Hindu revivalist-nationalists, from whom the RSS drew much inspiration, added another meaning to such practices. The Hindu woman's body, hemmed in with scriptural ritual, was imagined as a pure space that escaped the transformative effects of colonization, whereas the Hindu man, seduced by the operations of Western power and knowledge, had surrendered himself and had lost his autonomy. The woman's body, having passed through the grid of Hindu ritual exercises, therefore alone remained, for these Hindus, the site of an existent freedom as well as the future nation (Sarkar 1993).

The Samiti has preserved the accumulated meanings but transformed the essential rituals. The symbolic function of ritual has been interpreted literally with the mystical notion of female virtue and power materialistically translated as sheer physical strength. Possibly the influence of contemporary eugenics was at work; a healthy feminine body would bear strong children. From the turn of the century, many high-born militant Hindus have been anxiously preoccupied with the supposedly higher fertility rate of Muslims and low-caste Hindus that seemed to doom the leadership of upper-caste Hindus in Indian society (Datta 1993). The incarcerated and leisure-softened bodies of upper-caste women would also be regarded as inadequate vessels to bear the soldiers of the imagined Hindu nation. Since all fascist movements cast their men as able soldiers and killers, their women are invariably asked to ensure exceptionally healthy bodies that would guarantee the production of the most efficient combatants (see Koonz [1977], 'Mothers in Fatherland').

III

The RSS response to the political crisis of the 1930s might seem inappropriate, given the limited base that they could command. Surely, women of their milieu, of their families, did not require immediate attention and organizational investment formally, since their consent to RSS politics was more secure than that of any other category? The investment would seem blatantly uneconomic unless we have a precise and careful understanding of its broader strategy and political vision.

It is an inch by inch, person by person mode of advance which brings to mind the Gramscian model of molecular hegemony. It places more importance on a totalitarian conquest of the existing base than on a thinly spread out numerical expansion. An active mobilization of women was also a priority as even among socially privileged castes and classes, women have a relatively insecure and tenuous location.

Even after the Samiti had been founded, M.S. Golwalkar, second Sarsanghchalak and supreme ideologue of the RSS, restricted his observations on Hindu women to a 'Call to Motherhood'. The women of upper-caste and middle-class families had to manage the home front and to keep it free of individualistic aspirations, of libertarian tendencies, of democratic relationships within the family. 'Let our mothers make the children wake up early in the morning, make them salute their elders, and offer worship to the family deity.' They should teach girls to avoid European dress and not to 'expose their bodies more and more' and their children to resist 'a blind aping of the West'. They should keep alive the observance of sacred occasions and ceremonies and take children on regular visits to temples. They must also teach them literacy, but the teaching of 'noble *samskaras*' or a pious disposition was far more useful than formal learning. Samskaras would include deference to family elders, Hindu historical heroes and deities, and to RSS great men. They would thus at once encompass the family, the Sangh, and the nation into one single whole which the mother's mediation renders an intimate reality (Golwalkar 1980).

In Golwalkar's authoritative pronouncements on the woman's role, there is a strong accent on learning the value of deference within the family. The mother mediates the process of the complete submersion of the child within such a family. The child learns obedience to the Sangh, which appears to him as an extension of the familial space, demanding, initially, the same ideological teaching and personal bearing. On all important Samiti occasions, mothers bring their children over, as do non-Samiti wives of RSS members. The Samiti, I was told, was second home to the small children. At a Delhi Samiti, office-bearers told me that even though the Samiti encourages girls to go in for higher education and professions, they also insist that they teach them unquestioning obedience to family decisions even when families decide against education and career. Their success was ensured by their supplementary role in maintaining and deepening family discipline.[4]

In the Samiti literature, motherhood is remarkably emptied of its customary emotional and affective load and is vested with a notion of heroic political instrumentality. The Hindu heroes, we are told, reared their children to teach them to die for the Motherland. In recent times, the VHP woman ascetic leader Sadhvi Rithambara reiterated the same message in her audio cassette which was the most potent VHP instrument for whipping up anti-Muslim violence. The nationalist martyr Bhagat Singh's mother, she narrates in her apocryphal story, wept after the son's execution, not because her son was dead, but because she had no other son who could die a similar death. The accent was on her lack of motherly grief, her eagerness to re-experience the loss. A transgressive departure from the model of natural or ideal motherhood, but stripped of all libertarian or larger human possibilities. The point is that the Samiti makes departures in norms and conventions, it expands the horizons of domesticity, and adds serious, politicized dimensions to femininity. At the same time, the thrust of the transformation is to obliterate the notion of selfhood, to erase concern with social and gender justice, and to situate the public, political, extra-domestic identity on authoritarian community commands and a totalitarian model of individual existence, every particle of which is derived from an all-male organization which not only teaches her about politics but also about religion, human relationships, and child rearing.

---

[4] For my interviews with office-bearers, see Sarkar (1991).

The mother is pivotal to the RSS scheme of mobilizing its own family. Golwalkar also advised her to make 'useful contacts among the women folk within the neighbourhood and carry out programmes which would inculcate our cherished ideas among them and their children' (Golwalkar 1980). Mothers, then, are political creatures and agents, and we will not grasp the deeply political import of this agenda unless we are clear about the directly political and not merely ideological significance of everyday relations, personal disposition, and habits, of domestic ritual and practice within the RSS scheme for hegemony, and the full significance of the much used and key term 'samskaras' in the Sangh vocabulary. The mother is to instil habits of deference, of obedience, of respect for the RSS version of patriotism. She should scramble the child's earliest notions of history, mythology, and patriotism through moral lessons about 'faith in Dharma and pride in our history', and instructions about '*tirtha*s and temples'. The importance of learning them in earliest infancy when critical faculties are not aroused, of learning them through stories whose format demands a suspension of questioning and passive listening is enormous. As to how important the lessons in Dharma and history, pilgrimages and temples lumped together are, should be evident in the success of the Ramjanmabhoomi campaign which pitted a Muslim king against the sacred figure of Ram, and insisted that the destruction of the Babri Mosque was not only a religious but also a patriotic duty. One cannot learn these lessons too young.

IV

In a bitterly ironic inversion of women's former invisibility in the domain of public violence, large numbers of women have been extremely active and visible, not only in the rallies and campaigns but even in the actual episodes of violent attacks against Muslims. The complicity has also involved an informed assent to such brutalities against Muslim women as gang rapes and the tearing open of pregnant wombs in Bhopal and Surat in December 1992 and January 1993—informed, because these episodes had been widely reported and publicized and there was no way that these women could have escaped knowledge of them. We will explore the factors in their social experiences that have enabled their politicization on precisely these issues and agendas, and reflect on the large meanings and implication of women establishing themselves as political subjects through an agenda of hatred and brutality against a besieged minority.

I shall argue that the new communal phase enables the women's self-constitution as an active political subject in dangerously unprecedented ways.

Kar sevikas have been mobilized from what are traditionally some of the most conservative backgrounds—upper, middle-ranking service sector, and trading families. The very limits of the movement may then be taken as signs of strength within a different kind of reading. Nor can we draw false comfort from any illusion that these women are not speaking their own minds, their own words. Pradip Kumar Datta who visited Ayodhya in January 1991, speaking to a bunch of male satyagrahis was, for some time, faced with an array of archaeological-cum-historical arguments as well as the standard RSS definition of Bharat as *pitribhumi, matribhumi,* and *karmabhumi*. Then Chandravati, a woman from Aligarh, excitedly broke into the conversation and introduced a very different note: '*Yahan aye hain khoon barsane ke liye ... mandir ka arth hai mulla ko phansi lag jai ... Mulayam aur VP ko phansi lag jai ...*' ('We have come here to shed blood ... the meaning of temple building is that mullahs should be hanged, Mulayam and VP should be hanged'). The whole discussion subsequently shifted to a markedly more violent plane.

Each of the kar sevikas interviewed—those affiliated with VHP as well as those not so affiliated—played a distinctive individual variation on the themes of Ramjanmabhoomi and Hindutva. For Vijay Dube, a would-be *sanyasin* from Ghaziabad, Hindutva implied a sweeping, millenarian vision of collectivity (*samiti*). '*Yeh [Hindustan] samudra jaisa gambhir hai, akash jaisa vyapak hai ... Hindu hi adi ant hai*' ('This country is as deep as the ocean, as endless as the sky ... the Hindu is the beginning and the end'). Unlike other religions, Hinduism is not time-bound but eternal. It is not an individual but a collective experience. It finds its centre of gravity in Ramjanmabhoomi which then becomes: '*Hamara servaswa dharam ki bat nahin hai, sarvasaarvaswa hai*' ('It is everything to us, it is not just a matter of religion: it is all, it is our everything'). With the liberation of Ayodhya, '*poora vishwa badal jayega ek nayee shrishti ka nirman hoga*' ('The whole world will change, a new creation will come into being').

For Mithilesh Vashisht, a VHP worker from Modinagar, on the other hand, the value of the Ramjanmabhoomi movement lay in the assertion of strength and self-respect against oppression: '*Atyachar, anyachar, anyaya nahin sahenge, har cheez ki seema hoti hai*' ('We will not tolerate oppression and injustice, everything has limits'). Another (unidentified) woman intervened with a more poetic-mythical version of the necessity: '*Yeh hamara ang hai, hamara abhushan hai ... Krishna bhagawan ka chakra hai*'

('This is a limb [of our body], our ornament ... it is the "chakra" of Lord Krishna'). All kar sevikas were bursting with speech—with arguments and descriptions—each had an accent very distinctively her own. Within a hitherto limited social and geographical scope then, the Ramjanmabhoomi movement seems to have enabled major breakthroughs in women's political self-activization, unwitnessed in earlier communal upsurges.[5]

In a curious way the present movement inverts the usual pattern of symbolization within national and earlier communal movements. So far, in both, the fetishized sacred or love object to be recuperated had been a feminine figure—the cow, the abducted Hindu woman, the motherland. When we interviewed B.L. Sharma, secretary of the VHP Indraprastha unit, in April 1990, he had woven an entire anti-Muslim tirade around the figure of the repeatedly raped or threatened Hindu woman. The Sanatan Dharmi and Arya Samajist office-bearers extended the image into that of a perpetually exposed and endangered motherland (Datta *et al.* 1990). Here, however, the occupied 'janmabhoomi' belongs specially to a male deity, and women are being pressed into action to liberate and restore it to him, to bring back honour to Ram. Ram's army of monkeys and squirrels has now acquired a new combatant and Sita's sex is coming to the rescue of Ram—an inversion of the epic narrative pattern where Ram and his army had to rescue Sita. The reversal of roles equips the communal woman with a new and empowering self-image. The woman has stepped out of a purely iconic status to take up an active position as a militant.

In this context, the very careful and significant handling of the Ram *lalla* (infant Ram) image acquires a new meaning. Stalls in Ayodhya sell a large number of stickers and posters depicting a chubby infant baring his pink gums in a toothless smile. Local legend has it that in 1949, just before the deity miraculously reinstalled itself within the mosque, a police constable had found a dark and lovely child playing by himself in that corner: the homeless baby had come back home to claim his patrimony. The VHP video-cassette produced by Dr J.K. Jain, *Bhaye Prakat Kripala*, reproduces the event over a long time, with the child within the mosque displaying himself in a variety of 'cute' poses and eventually stringing a bow. We must remember that the Ramayana and the Ramkathas resonate with the many losses of Ram: he loses his kingdom, his father, he is a figure bathed in tears, a reason, perhaps, why the common man and woman can identify more with him than with other mythical heroes. The entire series of deprivations has now been collapsed into the shape of that irresistible

---

[5] I am indebted to P.K. Datta for the taped interviews.

human idol—the deprived male infant. On top of that, within the mosque and next to the main deity, is an icon of the crawling Ram lalla—a posture traditionally associated with the baby Krishna—and linked in a long chain of associations with emotional and aesthetic structures. While the appeal of the homeless baby would be a general one, it would be especially poignant for women. Readings of recent events that insist on a monolithic militarization of Hinduism by present iconic trends, therefore, miss out on the versatility which is perhaps their most remarkable feature. While the Ram lalla appeals to the mother in a woman, the warrior Ram probably simultaneously arouses a response to an aggressive male sexuality.

All this, as I have said earlier, is a relatively new development. Up to the middle of 1990, well after the *shilanyas* (ceremonial laying of the foundation stone) ceremonies with their attendant riots, there was practically no literature by women that VHP or RSS offices sold regularly. VHP news sheets that covered *shilapujan* (ceremonial worship and consecration of bricks) and shilanyas ceremonies gave no space to women's writings. Even Rithambhara's cassette addresses exclusively men in its invocations to rise and fight: '*Vir bhaiyon, jago*' ('Brave brothers, awake'). Her speech obviously targets women listeners as well. There are intimate references to domestic politics among mothers, sisters, and daughters-in-law, to women's work within the home. Yet, each time the call for action is issued, it is addressed to brothers: 'You have to make yourselves into a clenched fist, my brothers.' 'You have to make yourselves into motherhood: remember how Bhagat Singh's mother was found crying after his death, not because she had lost her son, but because she had no other son to be martyred.' Even Rani Jhansi is invoked as the mother of a brave patriot.

It is true that the *Bhaye Prakat Kripala* cassette inserts the warrior figure of a queen as an adversary of Babar, and, within the current movement, Sadhvi Rithambhara, Uma Bharati, and Vijayaraje Scindia are endowed with an exalted position. They remain exceptional, rare figures, however. Up to this point, then, women are still the productive womb, mothers of heroes. Their presence was minimal on the crucial days of 30 October and 2 November 1990.

V

The Rashtrasevika Samiti has kept a remarkably low public profile through the six decades of its existence. Even though it is one of the oldest women's organizations in the country, its total membership is about a lakh now and is largely restricted to traditional RSS and BJP bases—Maharashtra, Karnataka, and Andhra Pradesh. The Delhi wing was formed in 1960 and now includes about 2,000 members. *Shakha*s (a local branch in the RSS, where members and recruits meet for education and training) are located almost entirely in middle-class areas: Karolbagh, Patel Nagar, Janakpuri, Naraina Vihar, R.K. Puram, Lajpat Nagar, and Kamla Nagar. Volunteers come from enterprising trading families or from middle-ranking government service backgrounds. The VHP Mahila Mandal, which started operating in Delhi from the 1980s, has about 500 members. The two mass fronts of the VHP—the Bajrang Dal and the Durga Vahini—are strictly segregated.[6]

The growth in spatial, numerical, and social terms has been quite low compared to the Delhi-based radical women's organizations which have come up much later, or mass women's organizations under left political parties. The All India Democratic Women's Association, linked to the Communist Party of India (Marxist) [CPI(M)], was founded in 1981 and now has a membership of about 29 lakh, overwhelmingly rural in composition. The Janwadi Mahila Samiti, its Delhi branch, has about 15,000 members, with large bases in labouring areas. The comparison is relevant since the VHP Mahila Mandal and the Rashtrasevikas also work (unlike other voluntary women's organizations) in close collaboration with an electoral party and a number of affiliated mass organizations.[7]

What does the apparent contrast between the austere reserve of these organizations and the recent flamboyant wave of a militant reclaiming of the public spaces by Hindu women denote? Is it a break, a radical departure, or the culmination of a long drawn-out strategy? Or is it a consciously planned extension in activity and concerns that stretches out old boundaries?

VI

It seems that we can usefully approach this problem through an extended reference to the very well-known cassette of Sadhvi Rithambhara. One remembers that voice only too well: high-pitched, shrill, breathless, delivering a non-stop harangue with no modulation. The voice seems

---

[6] Interview with office-bearers of Rashtrasevika Samiti in December 1991 and January 1992.

[7] Interviews with office-bearers of Janwadi Mahila Samiti in December 1990.

always almost about to crack under the sheer weight of passion. The overwhelming and constant impression is one of immediacy, urgency, passion, spontaneity. For over 60 minutes, extreme stress is continuously conveyed and the speech seems to be improvised as if on a battlefield—an inspired voice speaking recklessly from the gut. The later ban heightened the earlier impression of impending martyrdom, while legends about the 'martyrs' of 30 October and 2 November subsequently fed back into the effects of the cassette. The cassette, then, is not a finished product but one that grows with events.

New technology opens up unprecedented audio–visual possibilities for political messages and stretches boundaries of morality. The startling impact of the original *maidan* speech becomes simultaneously preserved and fixed and can duplicate its own efforts endlessly, to ever-growing audiences, in changed political conditions. By preserving and replaying the human voice and the spoken word, a different kind of impact is attained from the one that results from re-reading a written text. The latter also grows and acquires new meanings over time but it remains an individual exercise that involves the text and the reader in a private relationship. The speech, on the other hand, is based on a public relationship of a speaker addressing an entire congregation and proceeds through a continual interchange of passion between the speaker and the listeners. New technology is able to recapture that exchange *ad infinitum* for freshly or differently constituted congregations, and, at the same time, allows the first message to fatten on new meanings and associations gathered from the movement unleashed by itself, growing from its own self-fulfilling prophecies. Rithambara's words on martyrdom would have much enlarged and transformed meanings for people listening to them after 30 October 1990.

Technology naturalizes the intended effect to such an extent, and covers its own traces so completely, that we forget that what we are listening to is recorded speech, and not a live recording of an actual speech either. That sustained high pitch and that non-stop delivery would be impossible to improvise without breaks or modulation. It is a studio composition, an artefact which, with meticulous deliberation and coordination, pieces together, over long stretches, a carefully rehearsed address. The greatest success of technology lies neither in preservation nor in duplication but in its naturalizing abilities, in its self-effacement.

Such an understanding of this speech may illuminate the complex organizational structure within which the Samiti is located. Without drawing an exact and mechanical parallel, and without reducing the Hindutva movement to a mere contrived effect, we can still relate the impression of spontaneous militancy to an elaborate and finely tuned institutional structure and a shared ideological stockpile that tie together a wide range of party organs, mass fronts, and movementalist bodies to the apex body—the RSS. Each individual organization—the BJP, the VHP, and their various fronts—has developed its own distinctive thrust area and all have internally circulating members. A senior VHP Mahila Mandal leader, in 1991, went over to help out with BJP Mahila Mandal work. Rashtrasevikas claim to have trained the Durga Vahini for the *kar seva*, even though the Durga Vahini is affiliated to the VHP.[8] Almost all BJP women members of Parliament (MPs) are members of the Rashtrasevika Samiti. Coordination, in fact, stretches beyond the core institutional cluster. Rashtrasevikas are offered hospitality for their training camps by Sanatan Dharma mandirs and Arya Samajist Dayanand Anglo Vedic (DAV) schools. The Samiti is closely associated with a chain of nursery schools run by the Saraswati Shishu Mandir, which is an RSS outfit. The VHP headquarters at Ramakrishna Puram in Delhi houses one of those schools. The school at Naraina Vihar (Delhi) has a very distinctive visual plan and layout. Instead of the usual pictures of flora and fauna or of nursery tales that decorate conventional nursery schools, walls on one side display frescoes of historical Hindu heroes locked in battle against Muslims. On the other side are portraits of 'Hindu' freedom fighters protesting against the British with appropriate messages inscribed below. The central building has the map of *Akhand Bharat* (undivided India) draped around the figure of Bharatmata with the entire *Bande Mataram* hymn inscribed below it. The DAV school on Aurobindo Marg follows an almost identical visual display.

An intricate and delicately balanced system of interlocking personnel functions and interests is ultimately monitored by the apex parent organization, the RSS. The Sangh calls itself a family, not a political organization. As proof of this it claims that all its members are equal and uniform in dress, disposition, and functions. This stems from a peculiar notion of what a family is, since there cannot be a family without women in it and there cannot be a family that is ever undifferentiated in functions and habits. Only by developing a women's wing, then, does the family metaphor partly realize itself. The Rashtrasevika Samiti was, after all, the first affiliate that the RSS helped to foster, although a good 11 years after its own foundation. The family model is, in some ways, more than just a metaphor. All the Samiti members that I talked to had male relatives in the

[8] Interviews with Samiti and VHP Mahila Mandal office-bearers in January 1991.

RSS. In fact, the striking ease and self-confidence that animate the very vocal participation of even junior office-bearers in a discussion with their elders may partly be explained by the status of their male relatives within the Sangh. This might carry greater importance than the order of ranking within the Samiti itself.

The organizational principles of the Sangh provide the pattern for the Samiti. The Samiti does not have internal elections and the *pramukh sanchalika* (chief organizer) nominates her successor. Office-bearers are selected by senior members. The Samiti *pracharika*s (propagandists) are unmarried women, advocating celibacy that characterizes RSS Sarsanghchalaks (chief leaders), all of whom so far have been bachelors. Much of the RSS ritual is also replicated within the Samiti. The strict and detailed code of regulations for setting up and disbanding the daily shakha, a physical and martial arts training (the Samiti provides for lessons in yoga, sword and lathi play, judo, and stengun fighting), regular *boudhik* or ideological discussion, and the discipline and protocol within shakha programmes are common to both. Whereas the RSS observes six annual festivals—five of which are connected with traditional religious events and the sixth, the Shivaji Utsav, is a Hindu nationalist celebration—the Samiti observes five and omits the non-traditional festival. The major hymns are also more or less the same and are recited individually as well as collectively in exactly the same order. At the same time, a fine tension exists between vociferous claims to complete autonomy and pride in sharing the RSS heritage. Vidushi, a young office-bearer, told me rather defiantly that the two bodies are totally distinct as two railway lines are: which run parallel, and yet are always separated. The analogy, however, comes straight from M.S. Golwalkar (Sarkar 1991). In a different sense, too, as we shall see later, the Samiti supplements certain kinds of Sangh work, thereby reiterating, in a way, the conventional place of the Hindu *dharma patni* (wife by sacred ritual) within the household—a related yet subordinate sphere.

In the boudhik sessions within the Samiti, I came across the same finished structures of thought, the same basic themes on which variations are played by Rashtrasevikas, the BJP, the VHP, individual *kar sevak*s and sevikas and loose fragments of which have come to constitute parts of popular common sense among non-affiliated informal support groups for Hindu *rashtra* (Hindu nation). The RSS occasionally plugs into a whole range of otherwise radical issues—ecology, world peace, interrelated critiques of Western materialistic and rationalistic and monolithic notions of truth that lead to imperialist suppression of non-Western identities.

I shall summarize here a single theme which I heard being expounded at a Samiti training camp and which I read up in Samiti and RSS literature. This was the symbolism of the *bhagwatdhwaj*, or the saffron flag, which is ritually worshipped at the beginning and end of each shakha. The discourse starts with the unique philosophical concept of tolerance within Hinduism—*Sarva dharma samabhava*—which celebrates pluralism and the many equally valid ways of reaching god. This very pluralism and tolerance, however, is taken to characterize a single national ethos which is essentially Hindu, and to which all immigrant religions into India have adapted themselves. The notion of an essentially Hindu national ethos came under attack when 'fanatic' Muslim rulers ruled the land and tried to destroy it with 'brute strength'. The British, however, 'planned to subvert the Hindu mind itself'. This was achieved through a seemingly superior and successful mode of Western knowledge which induced self-forgetting and which substituted alien categories of thought for self-knowledge. The perception of a single national ethos was broken up and Indian history was restructured to prove that the nation means simply a geographical space inhabited by different but equal communities, each with its separate ethos. This false and alien notion of secularism destroyed the single shared culture and fractured the sense of wholeness, led to communalism and violence, and eventually culminated in the partition of the country. The Sangh aspires to recuperate that essential wholeness through its struggle for a Hindu rashtra. An RSS pamphlet, *Vishal Hindu Bharatiya Samaj Bhavi Swayam Sevak*, puts it: 'Sangh samaj me sanghathan nahin, samaj ka sangathan hai' ('The Sangh is not an organization within society, it is organization of society').

Our true history today (so the discourse ran) is folded back into certain symbols that have resisted Western distortion. The saffron flag, used in the past by Maharana Pratap and Shivaji, is one of them. At the National Flag Committee deliberations even Maulana Abul Kalam Azad had apparently accepted it as our national flag, but Jawaharlal Nehru, the alienated, 'wrong-headed' secularist that he was, refused to do so. Yet another symbol is the hymn *Bande Mataram* which captures the essential entirety of Bharatmata and for that reason must be recited in its entirety—akhand recitation being the equivalent of akhand Bharat. This was apparently substituted by *Jana gana mana* as our national anthem which Rabindranath Tagore had actually composed to welcome George V. The story is of course a complete fabrication, but was reiterated by a whole range of Samiti members with complete assurance (Sarkar 1991).

VII

Somewhat like the Sangh, but much more emphatically so, the Samiti leaves alone charity or social welfare work and has no interest in union activities. Numerical expansion or extensive mobilization has not, then, so far been the primary concern which explains their low growth rate. It is an intensive physical and ideological training-centre out of which a small group of hand-picked cadres is regularly selected and sent out to circulate among the affiliated organizations and movements.

This kind of intensive mobilization works best during its initial, formative phase within a 'same class' situation where recruits and teachers do not constantly need to break down boundaries within their own disposition and habits to communicate and interact with one another. Mobilization is then horizontal unlike the vertical spread of radical women's organizations which reach out to less privileged sisters as soon as they form themselves. The breadth of the latter's concerns and connection is undoubtedly their greatest initial ease in interaction among all its members. A VHP worker described the Sangh–Samiti combine as engaged in class work rather than in mass work. Class here refers to a classroom situation where all participants usually share the same social milieu. The description is quite precise since the training is pedagogical in a very total sense. Not just the arguments but an entire mode of arguing, a particular disposition is slowly nurtured with the person, leaving a distinct mark. On the more engaged activists—a calm, quiet confidence, an unhurried, patient, and seemingly reasonable exposition which proceeds by agreeing with the other person as much as possible and then gently suggesting and building up its own basic themes.

For the Samiti, the daily shakha is not the sole or even the most major form of activity. The family concept is extended to cover the members' families in a number of ways. The Samiti's guardianship role in the case of unmarried girls is carefully meshed in with an acknowledgement of the primary rights of the family. If the family obstructs a girl's desire for further studies, a particular profession, or a late marriage, the Samiti at first tries persuasion. If this fails completely, the family's decision stands. The same policy is followed over problems of the girl's boyfriend or self-choice in marriage. Rekha Raje, a pracharika, hastened to assure me that the Samiti tries to fill up their time with 'health' pursuits and such 'problems', therefore, rarely arise. If they do, the Samiti first inspects the boyfriend. If he is found to be suitable, it then tries to persuade the family. Again it is the family which must ultimately decide and on no account should the girl be encouraged to disobey.

Prospects of persuasion are enhanced and problems of divided loyalties averted by regular visits to the girl's home and the systematic cultivation of warm personal connections. A young Samiti member told me that they make a point of visiting each other's homes and dropping in for tea whenever they happen to pass that way, so that the entire family is included within the circle of the Samiti solidarity. *Adhyapikas* (women teachers) from the shakha go over regularly to discuss a member's behaviour and prospects with her relatives. The Samiti is then carried right into the heart of the domestic space and ceases to be an institution within the public sphere. Even if the girl's own connections with her shakha snap for some reason, durable contacts have been made with the parental family and the zone of influence permanently expanded. For small towns, where individual Samiti workers find it difficult to keep a shakha going, the Samiti sends instructions every three months, keeping the member posted on Samiti developments, rituals to be observed within this period and on how to attain a base among women of her acquaintance on a non-formal basis (Sarkar 1991). At Khurja in western Uttar Pradesh, Prabha Aggarwal, coming from a staunch RSS family, managed to set up a shakha which acquired 50 members.[9] A scandal involving a local BJP pracharak, however, made parents withdraw their daughters from the shakha. Prabha now follows the 'correspondence course' of posted instructions, and spreads Samiti festivals and rituals on a home-based format. The local Saraswati Shishu Mandirs do the rest of the propaganda work, on school premises.

Solidarity and warm supportiveness are more actively expressed when Samiti members take turns with cooking and nursing whenever there are major illnesses in a member's house. The shakhas have a strictly local character and these gestures enable them to strike deep roots in the entire neighbourhood. When a girl marries into a non-RSS family and her new domestic situation prevents active shakha work, senior shakha members regularly visit her in-laws and strike up a close relationship with them. The married girl then acts as a pivot within a new domestic set-up, a new neighbourhood. The Samiti, in fact, encourages her to drop shakha work for the first few years after marriage, until her status in her new home is firmly established and her Samiti friends are accepted by the entire family. If, however, the in-laws still discourage a connection with the old shakha,

---

[9] Interview with her family members at Khurja, March 1991.

she is again not advised to assert her choice. Her old Samiti members, of the local branch, keep in close touch with her and her family. She is given a few easy exercises that may be done even within a fairly crowded home, and she is told to teach them to women relatives in the new family. She is also advised to establish herself as an ideal counsellor and arbiter to enable her to informally discuss the ideas she received during her shakha days or which her Samiti members have kept her attuned to. One can see how useful such a loose and informal network would be in inculcating notions of 'Hindutva' and Hindu rashtra over a long period of time, and then swiftly linking them up with a particular agitation which would find a ready support base without any direct and immediately organizational investment.

Gradually, the woman's reputation as a dependable adviser and friend in need will spread to the women in the neighbourhood and enlarge and stabilize a circle of dependents and listeners. For the women within the kinship network and the immediate neighbourhood, the presence of such a woman ensures an informal forum for the discussion of general topics. In this way she fills up a crucial gap and appeases a very real hunger for serious intellectual discussion among women, a need which traditionally only religious topics used to meet. Women's religiosity is usually explained in terms of certain emotional, cultural, or social needs. One vital function of religion is rarely taken into account, that it alone gives her access to a world of meanings enclosed in epics, allegories, or other forms of religious texts that she can interpret and dwell on, and thereby transcend her own immediate and closed world of limited experience. The Samiti partly continues these themes and partly weaves them into a different and larger political fabric. A Haryana housewife-turned-activist told me that for her the highest value of the Samiti lay in exposing her to the world of thinking beyond household, or personal matters. Golwalkar had seen a lot of possibilities in such household-cum-neighbourhood circles for women working for the Sangh and these possibilities have been much extended since his time.

Informal training for unaffiliated wives of RSS activists is yet another important field for Samiti work. At a Samiti training camp, a whole session was reserved for them, followed by a joint lunch and a group discussion on their problems and possible activities. I found that the wives were as familiar with Samiti activists and activities as any formal member. I met a schoolteacher, wife of an RSS activist, who had been married for five years, before which she had had no contact with that organization. Although not a member of the Samiti herself, she managed single-handedly to persuade her entire body of colleagues to join a day-long protest fast at Ajmal Khan Park, Delhi, after the 30 October deaths. Her accounts of the Samiti and the Sangh were as detailed and as confident as those of any activist's. Her work, she told me, was manifold. She has to coach her two tiny children thoroughly in the daily Sangh mantra recitations and cultivate proper *samskaras* (traditions) in them. Along with wives of other RSS activists, she makes it a point to take her children to Samiti ceremonies from an early age so that it becomes a second home to them. Another function was to help out with needy RSS families in her locality. Her husband, for instance, would tell her if one of them was getting a daughter married. In that case, all the wives of RSS activists would divide up parts of the dowry to be collected among themselves. They would also get together to help out if an ailing RSS member or someone in his family suddenly needed blood. RSS members are required to donate blood and keep their certificates precisely for this purpose—to have access to the blood bank in emergencies. Apart from being a far-sighted and practical form of support, this probably fosters the notion of a blood brotherhood. In her place of work the wife is expected to gather influence and respect for her ideas and attitudes. Much of the Samiti's activity is then informal, but no less effective for that reason (Sarkar 1991).

Is the Samiti then merely filling up a space marked out for it by the Sangh for its own purpose? And, if so, does not this conclusion contradict a statement that I had made earlier—that the strength of the movement lies in the exhilarating possibilities it creates for certain sections of deeply conservative women, in its being an expression partly of their own creativity?

I think that the original parameters worked out by Sarsanghchalaks have proved to be flexible and accommodating. The major body of Golwalkar's instructions had carved out a sort of '*Lakshmangandi*' of faithful motherhood, within which the properly instructed mother carefully guards her children from corrupting Western influences and instils in them the right samskaras—filial piety, and knowledge of patriotic heroes and of religious texts. Rashtrasevikas have travelled a long way since then without overtly resisting the original instructions. The gap between the original impulse and the new self-definition may or may not open up fissures within the movement, depending upon the versatility and suppleness of the Sangh ideology (Sarkar 1991).

Somewhat different forces seem to be working within the Samiti itself, although it would be false and crude to posit a clear dichotomy between the two: to see one as potentially feminist and the other as overly fundamentalist. At the Delhi office of the Samiti in 1991, I was told quite frankly that the decision to train kar sevikas was the result of an internal debate that was eventually won by younger Samiti members. The charges against Uma Bharati, by sections of the party leadership, inspired a group of BJP women MPs to come out in criticism of the leaders. It was a remarkable instance of an inner party dispute on a gender issue (Sarkar 1991).

The differences of emphasis between men's and women's accounts of the Samiti's history are interesting. In the first place, there are somewhat different origin-myths of the organization. Neither the authorized history of the Samiti, nor the account of a senior pracharika had mentioned that Hegdewar was approached to admit women to the Sangh. They are equally silent about the fact that he had refused and had asked Lakshmibai Kelkar to set up a parallel organization. An RSS publication, however, wrote about it and claimed that he had convinced Kelkar about the problems of a common organization. Samiti narratives, then, seem to push the fact of the refusal out of sight. Official Samiti history has a somewhat different explanation for the event that had led to its establishment. It says: '*Hindutva jagaran ka pramukh dheyya lekar is swatantra sangathan ka shubharambha hua* ('This independent organization made its auspicious beginning with the primary aim of awakening Hindus'). On the other hand, Rekha Raje, a pracharika, recounted how, on a train journey, Kelkar had witnessed the rape of young girl by goondas. She clarified 'in response to my question' that the rapists were not Muslims. The girl's husband had been present there, but he proved helpless. Kelkar realized that since Hindu husbands could not help their wives, women had to protect themselves. Whereas the edge in this story is turned against Hindu failures (the Hindu male's lust and the Hindu male's cowardice), the official text overlays that version by the more amorphous aim of 'Hindutva jagaran'.

The self-definitions of the Samiti place primary emphasis on physical courage, on a trained, hardened female body. The Sangh agrees with its supreme importance and then goes on to list 'intellectual grasp of the values of Hindu culture and devotional attachment to the ideals of Hindu woman-hood'. A Samiti publication puts it even more strongly: *Swasangrakshanksham nari ki samaj me adhik pratishtha hoti hai* ('A woman who is able to defend herself gets a higher status in society'). The specific deity that embodies their aspirations is the eight-armed Durga, a militant icon who subsumes Saraswati, Lakshmi, and Kali. Sevikas see themselves as full-fledged soldiers in an impending apocalyptic war. Their pre-prandial mantra translates as follows: 'Our limbs have been nourished by our Motherland and we must give them back to her in her service.' Asha

Sharma, in charge of the Delhi organization, explained that the mantra tied the theme of patriotic sacrifice with that of active combat. She agreed that when war is mentioned, they see a civil war as a possibility. The patriotic war in whose aid the female body is being trained, then, seems to be a war against the Muslims. The large place that the myth of 'Muslim lust' occupies within the general mythology of Hindu communalism would also explain the need for self-strengthening (Sarkar 1991).

Yet we must remember the oral version of the origin-myth—Hindu goondas raping a girl in the presence of her Hindu husband—and also the reference to the larger status of the 'Swasangrakshanksham nari' within her own social milieu. Defence against attackers, and respect within her own environment, is then the implicit sub-text which might, in everyday calculations, become a more powerful motive force and a more real compulsion than the ultimate political intention of 'Hindutva jagaran'.

The force of the compulsion becomes clearer when we consider the milieu from which the Samiti mobilizes its cadres. As we have seen earlier, sevikas come from upwardly mobile, trading or middle-ranking service sectors, which are fertile breeding grounds for dowry murders. Women's organizations deal with huge numbers of divorce or maintenance suits at this social level. They are familiar with the violence and oppression that flourish against women here. In the large northern cities, if not in the small towns so far, education and professional opportunities for women have come late but they have come in big way. Nor are families opposed to women's employment, since they are a valuable source of extra income. Thrust into public and mixed spaces for the first time, women encounter all the time, new forms of overt or covert sexual discrimination and violence. Small wonder, then, that the physical training programmes of shakhas have proved to be extremely attractive, with their promise of a powerful body and the self-confidence that it generates. The empowered body would be a shield against gender oppression within domestic as well as within public spaces.

We may, then, assume that despite the overarching aim of Hindu power, the woman needs to utilize Samiti facilities against her own hostile environment as well. The problems of the newly mobile professional woman are often discussed in the Samiti journal, *Jagriti*. An article narrated how the author withstood the offensive behaviour of a police officer to whom she had gone to report a street accident. Several others take up similar problems. With suggestions and examples, they try to project the image of a responsible and confident woman-citizen who would know how to exercise her civic rights even in this chauvinistic world.

Authoritative statements on the women's location in Hindu society tend to make entirely positive assessments. The pramukh sanchalika's speech at the 1990 annual Samiti conference proclaimed, rather grandly, that 'the women of India have always been free'. A lead article in *Jagriti* ('Rashtra ka Adhar Nari') elaborated the assertion, tracing a history of her power with highly selective examples from Manu to the present Ram movement. At the same time, other assessments also jostle for space. 'Nari Jagaran', an article in *Jagriti*, postulates that oppression of women is a deep-rooted social condition, and that only an organized women's movement can resist and change it. It does not equate the women's movement in India with the Hindu movement. Whereas the earlier article I have referred to was highly critical of the international women's movement as allegedly being shaped by a corrupt, Westernized modernity, the latter legitimizes them. Yet another article, 'Parivartit Parivesh Me Bharatiya Nari', is extremely critical of Indian men for obstructing the entry of women into politics. Entering politics is described as a condition of protecting women's rights. A basic conflict of gender interests is seen to underlie social divisions of other kinds, and communal identities are not believed to interfere at this point.

It is interesting to find that whereas writing by leaders—Golwalkar, official RSS statements, Samiti leaders' pronouncements—applauds the new Hindu woman for apparently resisting the trap of Westernized modernity, women's own articles in Samiti publications, when dealing with everyday problems, are scarcely concerned with the so-called danger of surrendering traditional virtues to modernity. In fact, the new Hindu woman is often cast in a mould that comes close to the pattern of bourgeois feminism. As an article in *Jagriti* put it:

In order to attain the comprehensive development of women, it is extremely important for them to be economically independent. Therefore, in order to ensure economic independence, they need reservation in employment, and they need women judges to conduct all cases related to such issues.

The Hindu woman is, therefore, to be a person with professional and economic opportunities, secure property-ownership, legal rights to enforce them, and some degree of political power to ensure her rights.

How would the new Hindu woman relate to Hindu tradition? I feel that tradition exists as a cherished but remote icon, requiring ritual worship but seldom brought out for daily use or inspection. Very often the question of religious faith is displaced on to the realm of patriotic faith. The greatest triumph of the present communal movement has been to blend two potent sources of emotional involvement—*desh bhakti* and Ram bhakti (devotion to the country and devotion to Ram)—into a homogeneous whole. Adherents now use them interchangeably. When Pradip Kumar Datta asked kar sevika Vijay Dube how Ram came to mean so much to her, she immediately traced back its source to her childhood experience of the China war and the passions it had aroused in her. Patriotic faith, in her case, was the original impulse that had fuelled religious passion, and she herself was not aware of any distinction between the two.

Verdicts on specific gender questions within present Hindu society seemed, on the whole, modernistic. A young activist protested that there could be no such thing as voluntary sati. 'It isn't possible. Why should a woman wish to burn?' She conceded that it could be done out of 'depression and frustration'—that is, as a mark of weakness and not as a mark of moral strength. Neighbours and relatives, however, must shore up her will to live. The Samiti, theoretically, does not ban inter-caste or even inter-communal marriage provided, of course, the family agrees. The cover page of *Jagriti* depicts two women crouching in a helpless posture against a dark background. A young, rather grim-looking woman steps out of that frame on to the radiant half of the page with an uplifted head. There are no Hindu marks on her body—no veil, no *sindur*, no *bindi*. She wears sandals, her sari is draped tightly around, her whole stance is free, even aggressive. Of course, she does wear the Samiti uniform—a purple-bordered white sari. The magazine is almost uncompromisingly non-'feminine' in nature, making no concessions to conventional women's topics. There are no hints on beauty aids, no cookery or embroidery section, no advice on child rearing. Stories are scrupulously bare of the individual romantic element. They deal, instead, with the romance of Hindu civilization or that of modern patriotism (Sarkar 1991).

Women's power is a theme that is celebrated, occasionally, in grotesque circumstances. At the Ayodhya kar seva, at a peak point in a violently communal agitation, women were chanting the beautiful feminist slogan: '*Hum Bharat ki nari hain, phul nahi chingari hain*' ('We are the women of India. We are sparks, we are not flowers'). When Pradip Kumar Datta asked some of them why Sita was absent in their invocations to Ram, the men fell silent, but women had their answers ready. One said that this was Ram's birthplace and not Sita's and this accounts for her absence. But Vijay Dube had a more effective answer: Shri actually means Sita; hence in the chant 'Shri Ram', Sita is placed before Ram. Datta asked: 'You mean that Sita is contained in Ram?' 'No,' said Dubey, 'Sita comes before Ram.' In a VHP children's publication, *Hanuman ki Kabaddi*, Hanuman says he is neither Ram's *bhakt* (devotee) nor Sita's, but he is the bhakt of Sitaram.[10]

I do not want to convey the impression that a sort of women's liberation is going on happily within a somewhat unfortunate Hindutva framework. The limited public identity that has become available to these women is made conditional on their submission to a new form of patriarchy. When I asked Asha Sharma where the Samiti differs from other women's organizations, she replied: 'We do not believe that in marital disputes the husband is necessarily to blame. When we arbitrate, we do not take the woman's side, we are neutral. We will tell the woman that she must do everything to preserve her home life. We are not wreckers of homes.' They do not offer legal counselling to women, nor is divorce at all encouraged. Dowry is called an evil, but its practice is obviously not banned among Sangh or Samiti members. Samiti members, in fact, collect dowry for poorer sisters. When kar sevikas at Ayodhya were asked if their status would improve in Hindu rashtra, one of them said yes, because Muslims would not be allowed to have four wives. That alone would ensure greater respect for women. She could not, on the spur of the moment, conceive of any other possibility for herself.

The same silence surrounds the question of caste. It is formally denounced and there is community dining to ensure the absence of distinctions. Yet the caste system is never made a theme for discussions or criticism in their study sessions. Class struggles are yet another field of resounding silence and non-involvement.

* * *

One important way of looking at women's relationship to the right—and it is a way that the RSS itself prefers to project—has been to obliterate the political movement from the frame of references and to fill up the space exclusively with religious compulsion. The political movement, since it is in Ram's name, presumably then ceases to be political, and only then becomes a movement women can identify themselves with. The visibility of women coincides, we must remember, with the simultaneous visibility of ascetics in the movement. Both are there to make the same point. It would seem that people who have been traditionally aloof from the realm of power politics are now 'spontaneously' coming forward to assert the Hindu faith, and that professional politicians of the BJP are humbly and faithfully following the commands of the whole people.

---

[10] P.K. Datta's interview with kar sevikas at Ayodhya.

There are three sets of underlying assumptions behind this opinion. First of all, women are depicted as a homogenous mass and are identified with the common folk or the whole people. Women's presence in the movement is then used as a sign of the movement's ubiquity, its universality. The social base of the women of the Hindu right, however, is easily identified as overwhelmingly upper-caste, middle class, and urban. A Delhi office-holder has, for example, frankly admitted the middle-class character of the movement.

The second and third unstated assumptions are interrelated. There is a notion that faith is timeless and above historical change and political manipulation. It further assumes that any demand made in the name of a religious issue always harks back to this timeless faith and not to any modern variant that can be open to political appropriation. There is also a conviction that women are custodians of this eternal faith, and that they can respond to a call that comes from the heart of age-old Hindu beliefs.

Here we need to remind ourselves that prior to the Ram Janmabhoomi movement, no traditional text, ritual, or myth ever made a statement that Ram's birthplace had been made into a mosque, or that it was a matter of religious duty to build a temple on the site of the Babri Mosque. The most sacred vernacular version of the Ramayana that is in use in northern India and is revered by the VHP was written after the presumed destruction of the alleged temple, and yet there is no mention of that event in the text, nor is any injunction laid on Hindus to build the temple. Women are, therefore, not responding to a call of eternal Hindu feelings, but to certain contemporary transformations that are grafted onto a crucial cluster of Hindu institutions—temples, big religious foundations, and monastic establishments that are now acting as auxiliaries of political parties and organizations. They are not acting according to time-honoured ritual or texts or devotional traditions; instead they are accepting versions of faith that have been created by high-tech modern media—video films, audio, cassettes, the televised version of the epic. Recognition of this puts a very different complexion on both the presumed immutability of faith and tradition and women's relationship to them.

Finally, there remains the vexing question of whether this movement, despite women's growing commitment to it, authentically expresses the empowerment of women or reflects a manipulated, constructed 'false' consent and intentionality. Two separate questions and problems are tied to this—the question of 'real' interests, and the question of power. No feminist can possibly argue that the movement can contribute anything to the broad rights of women. We have explored its uncompromising orthodox compulsions as well as the positively fundamentalist tendencies. Yet among women of a specific conservative milieu it certainly has bestowed a degree of empowerment and a sense of confidence and larger solidarities. It has brought them into activist, public roles, and has thereby probably increased their bargaining power within their homes, as political activism invariably does to some extent. It has allowed them to go beyond a purely domestic or feminine identity. At the same time, this limited yet real empowerment leads them to a complicity with fascist intolerance and violence, towards the creation of an authoritarian, anti-democratic social and political order. Eventually, it is going to lead these women, in the name of the feigned authenticity of indigenism, to resisting notions of justice, even for their own sex. In Iran, masses of women have supported compulsory incarceration of women, and in Nazi Germany women agreed to give up their right to vote.

This brings us to the question of manipulation. Gender, like class, does not have an emancipatory potential that is 'natural' or innate. Gender power grows from a sense of solidarity to being a force for itself only through intervention, contestation, and an exercise of and struggle over choices. Certainly, a feminist consciousness does not nestle within a woman, ready to attain progressive self-realization within a congenial environment, but is acquired through bitter conflicts and problems of choices—within herself, most of all. The point about the women of the Hindutva brigade is not that they are simply being conned into belief, for the same applies to men. Our interviews with women demonstrators at Ayodhya convinced us that their affirmation of the Ramjanmabhoomi issue was no mindless gesture but a highly informed conviction. The point is to assess the nature of the issues they assent to.

Self-assertion through violent communalism is probably accompanied by a certain growth in self-confidence that the Samiti has generated over several generations. We cannot write off the gender ideology of the Hindu right as unproblematically fundamentalist despite its overarching conservative patriarchalism which we have noted. For a certain section of affluent, middle-class women of north Indian cities and towns, where women's education and professional opportunities have come rather late, the Samitis do offer a limited but real empowerment. These upwardly mobile trading or service sector families are breeding grounds for dowry violence and murder. Women are also being thrust into mixed public spaces and jobs for the first time and face new forms of sexual discrimination and violence. Physical training programmes, with their assurance of tough, hardened bodies and the attendant self-confidence, help them to negotiate the newly founded extra-domestic identities.

The limits of equality should be noted. The RSS continues to plan and lead every step of the movement and the RSS remains an all-male body. This means that women are necessarily excluded from the highest decision-making bodies. In a sense, the dazzling presence of the spectacular triad—Sadhvi Rithambhara, Uma Bharati, Vijayaraje Scindia—is meant to blind us to the crucial absence of women at the heart of effective action.

Equality in the political role and violence develops within an overall context where the women of the Hindutva brigade stay out of contemporary women's agitations for enlargement of gender rights and justice, which have been one of the most potent forms of radical politics in the country today. In recent months, there has been an open turn towards unabashed fundamentalism. The VHP leader Bamdev has asked for a restoration of male polygamy and the abolition of divorce among Hindus, and BJP women leaders like Vijayaraje Scindia and Mridula Sinha have defended widow immolation. The VHP woman leader Krishna Sharma has demanded that women should return to their homes unless they are impelled by dire economic necessity. She has also defended dowry and polygamy as traditional resources and signs of cultural automomy that alienated pseudo-secularists have made into a bogey (Anitha *et al.* 1995). The earlier pride in a reformed Hindu family law, which the BJP had used as the sign of Hindu superiority over the backward conservative Muslims, seems to have become a somewhat outmoded rhetoric.[11] It seems that Hindu patriarchy, uncontaminated by Western influence, has once again emerged as the embodiment of preferred values. And once again, women must forget about gender rights to ensure community supremacy.

Perhaps, a subsidiary reason would be that the Hindu right always tends first to stereotype the Muslim and then proceeds to appropriate the features of that stereotype for itself, out of a profound yet unstated conviction in the superior political strength of the Muslim community. The Muslims are fanatical about Islam—and Hindus are asked to put the community and religion above every other consideration. The Muslim breaks temples—and so the Hindu must wreck a mosque. Muslim polygamy has always been seen as a ploy for overpopulating the country with Muslims and a sign of irrepressible virility. It is also a right, a privilege that the Muslim male has in excess over that of the Hindu male.

---

[11] I am indebted to Zoya Hasan for this observation.

The main reason, however, would relate directly to the contradictory pulls within the movement which makes it imperative to foreground women and, simultaneously, to limit and contain the consequences of their prominence and the enlarged bargaining power that their politicization could fetch within the family. The recent growth of urban consumerism, so much of which targets the woman, expands their claim to a larger share of the family budget. It is also the site of an individualism, not based on a notion of rights but on consumerist preoccupations and demands, on a new self-image, fashioned by the ad culture. This puts new strains on relating to women as older forms of control begin to slip. While professional women have access to unprecedented self-reliance, even housewives, faced with the ad culture and the shopping arcades, seek out things that are specially meant for themselves. Older ways of feminine domesticity and patriarchal control face new strains—the more so, since the new consumerism is largely the basis of the new middle-class prosperity and self-advancement. And the Sangh *parivar* is, above all, based on this middle class.

At this moment it becomes imperative to recover and articulate explicitly the submerged patriarchal norms. The televised version of the Ramayana epic which was made to coincide with the building up of the Ramjanmabhoomi movement, restated the older codes of patriarchal command through the irresistible, erotic appeal of the self-abnegating figure of Sita. Also, now that the movement has transcended the boundaries of carefully trained Samitis and RSS families, and encompasses much of the urban middle class which, despite its support, is insufficiently indoctrinated in the broader RSS samskaras, controls need to be spelt out precisely. More of its women are joining white-collar jobs and that has the threat that they may succumb to the more militant varieties of trade union politics. A broader normative disciplining is a safeguard against that.

The language in which the Hindu right restates its patriarchal purposes points to a larger imperative. The assertion of the greater dignity, even sacrality of the chaste and good Hindu woman covertly substitutes for, and ultimately displaces, a demand for equal rights. The Hindu right depends on a seemingly radical contestation of 'modern secularism', a critique of modernity that opposes the liberal theories of rights that it considers an alien and alienating colonizing influence. In their place it tries to claim the existence of 'traditional' notions of community obligations and mutuality. The claim can establish itself through a suppression of the historical realities of caste and gender asymmetries. The non-historicized claim of a sustaining, nurturant Hindu community and tradition is then used to undercut radical attacks on Hindu gender and social hierarchies, of demands for equal rights and affirmative action. However, it does not frontally oppose these demands since that will demystify the notion of a nurturant Hindu community. It will also reduce eventually the potential mass base of the right which cannot hope to ride a 'Ram wave' for ever. It therefore concentrates attack on the notion of equal rights on different grounds. It denounces its pseudo-secular nature since it suffers from contaminated historical origins, having reached this country through the colonial connection and Western education. An indigenist reasoning is used to oppose the notion of civil liberties, democratic rights, social equality, and gender justice. At the same time, it manages to conceal its socially inegalitarian face and wear a spuriously radical demeanour since it is apparently contesting colonial residues.

REFERENCES

Agarwal, Purushottam (1995), 'Surat, Savarkar and Draupadi: Legitimising Rape as a Political Weapon', in Tanikar Sarkar and Urvashi Butalia (eds), *Women and the Hindu Right*. New Delhi: Kali for Women, pp. 29–57.

Anitha, S., Manisha, and Vasudha Kavitha (1995), 'Interviews with Women', in Tanika Sarkar and Urvashi Butalia (eds), *Women and the Hindu Right*. New Delhi: Kali for Women.

Basu, Tapan and Tanika Sarkar (eds) (1993), *Khaki Shorts and Saffron Flags: A Critique of the Hindu Right*. Delhi: Disha Books.

Datta, P.K. (1993), 'Dying Hindus: Production of Hindu Communal Commonsense in Early 20th Century Bengal', *Economic and Political Weekly*, 19 June, 28(25).

Datta, P.K., Biswamoy Pati, Sumit Sarkar, Tanika Sarkar, and Sambuddha Sen (1990), 'Understanding Communal Violence: Nizamuddin Riots', *Economic and Political Weekly*, 10 November.

Golwalkar, M.S. (1980), *Bunch of Thoughts*. Bangalore: Vikrama Prakashan.

Koonz, Claudia (1977), 'Mothers in Fatherland: Women in Nazi Germany', in Bridenthal and Koonz (eds), *Becoming Visible: Women in European History*. Boston: Houghton Mifflin, pp. 445–73.

Kumar, Radha (1993), *The History of Doing: An Illustrated Account of the Women's Movement and Feminism in India*. New Delhi: Kali for Women.

Sarkar, Sumit (1983), *Modern India: 1885–1947*. Delhi: Macmillan Publishers Ltd.

Sarkar, Tanika (1991), 'The Woman as Communal Subject: Rashtra Sevika Samiti and Ramjanmabhoomi Movement', *Economic and Political Weekly*, 31 August, 26(35): 2057–65.

—— (1993), 'Rhetoric against the Age of Consent: Resisting Colonial Reason and the Death of a Child Wife', *Economic and Political Weekly*, 4 September, 28(36): 2265–9.

Chapter 12

FEMINIST THEORY, AGENCY, AND THE LIBERATORY SUBJECT

Some Reflections on the Islamic Revival in Egypt

SABA MAHMOOD*

IN THE LAST TWO DECADES, one of the key questions that has occupied many feminist theorists is how issues of historical and cultural specificity should inform both the analytics and politics of any feminist project. While this questioning has resulted in serious attempts at integrating issues of sexual, racial, class, and national difference within feminist theory, questions of religious difference have remained relatively unexplored. The vexed· relationship between feminism and religious traditions is perhaps most manifest in discussions of Islam. This is partly because of the historically contentious relationship that Islamic societies have had with what has come to be called 'the West', and partly because of the challenges contemporary Islamic movements pose to secular–liberal politics of which feminism has been an integral (if critical) part. The

* I would like to thank Princeton University Press for allowing me to reprint this excerpt from my book *Politics of Piety: The Islamic Revival and the Feminist Subject*, 2005.

suspicion with which many feminists tended to view Islamist movements only intensified in the aftermath of 11 September 2001 attacks on the US, especially the immense groundswell of anti-Islamic sentiment that has followed since. If supporters of the Islamist movement were disliked before for their social conservatism and their rejection of liberal values (key among them 'women's freedom'), their association with terrorism—now almost taken for granted—has served to further reaffirm their status as agents of a dangerous irrationality.[1]

In this chapter, I will probe some of the conceptual challenges that women's participation in the Islamist movement poses to feminist theorists and gender analysts through an ethnographic account of an urban women's mosque movement that is part of the Islamic Revival in Cairo, Egypt.[2] 'Islamic Revival' is a term that refers not only to the activities of state-oriented political groups but more broadly to a religious ethos or sensibility that has developed within Muslim societies more generally, particularly in Egypt, since the 1970s.[3] I conducted two years of fieldwork with a grassroots women's piety movement based in the mosques of Cairo. This movement is composed of women from a variety of socio-economic backgrounds, who gather in mosques to teach each other about Islamic scriptures, social practices, and forms of bodily comportment considered germane to the cultivation of the ideal virtuous self.[4] Even though

---

[1] This dilemma seems to be further compounded by the fact that women's participation in the Islamic movement in a number of countries (such as Iran, Egypt, Indonesia, and Malaysia) is not limited to the poor and working classes (classes often considered to have a 'natural affinity' for religion), but also from the upper- and middle-income strata.

[2] There are three important strands that constitute the Islamic Revival: state-oriented political groups and parties, militant Islamists (whose presence has declined since the 1980s), and a network of socio-religious non-profit organizations that provide charitable services to the poor and perform the work of proselytization. The women's mosque movement is an important subset of this network of socio-religious organizations and draws upon the same discourse of piety (referred to as 'da'wa'). For an analysis of the historical and institutional relationship between the non-profit organizations and the women's mosque movement, see Mahmood (2005: 40–78).

[3] This sensibility has a palpable public presence in Egypt, manifest in the vast proliferation of neighbourhood mosques and other institutions of Islamic learning and social welfare, in a dramatic increase in attendance at mosques by both women and men, and in marked displays of religious sociability. Examples of the latter include the adoption of the veil (*hijab*), a brisk consumption and production of religious media and literature, and a growing circle of intellectuals who write and comment upon contemporary affairs in the popular press from a self-described Islamic point of view. Neighbourhood mosques have come to serve as the organizational centre for many of these activities.

[4] My research is based on two years of fieldwork (1995–7) conducted in five different mosques that attracted attendees from a range of socio-economic backgrounds. I also

Egyptian Muslim women have always had some measure of informal training in Islam, the mosque movement represents an unprecedented engagement with scholarly materials and theological reasoning that had to date been the purview of learned men. Movements such as this, if they do not provoke a yawning boredom among secular intellectuals, certainly conjure up a whole host of uneasy associations such as fundamentalism, the subjugation of women, social conservatism, reactionary atavism, and cultural backwardness. My aim in this chapter is not to analyse the reductionism of an enormously complex phenomenon that these associations entail; nor am I interested in recovering a redeemable element within the Islamist movement by recuperating its liberatory potentials. Instead, I want to focus quite squarely on the conceptions of self, moral agency, and embodiment that undergird the practices of this non-liberal movement so as to come to an understanding of the ethical projects that animate it.

I want to begin by exploring how a particular notion of human agency in feminist scholarship—one that seeks to locate the political and moral autonomy of the subject in the face of power—is brought to bear upon the study of women involved in patriarchal religious traditions such as Islam. I will argue that despite the important insights it has provided, this model of agency sharply limits our ability to understand and interrogate the lives of women whose sense of self, aspirations, and projects have been shaped by non-liberal traditions. In order to analyse the participation of women in religious movements such as the Egyptian mosque movement I describe, I want to suggest we think of agency not as a synonym for resistance to relations of domination but as a capacity for action that historically specific relations of subordination enable and create. This relatively open-ended understanding of agency draws upon poststructuralist theory of subject formation but also departs from it in that I explore those modalities of agency whose meaning and effect are not captured within the logic of subversion and resignification of hegemonic norms. As I will argue, it is only once the concept of agency is detached from the trope of resistance that a series of analytical questions open up that are crucial to understanding non-liberal projects, subjects, and desires whose logic exceeds the entelechy of liberatory politics. In conclusion, I will discuss the political effects of such a modality of analysis.

---

carried out participant observation among the leaders and members of the mosque movement in the context of their daily lives. This was supplemented with a year-long study with a sheikh from the Islamic University of al-Azhar on issues of Islamic jurisprudence and religious practice.

TOPOGRAPHY OF THE MOSQUE MOVEMENT

The women's mosque movement occupies a somewhat paradoxical place in relationship to feminist politics. It represents the first time in Egyptian history that such a large number of women have mobilized to hold lessons in Islamic doctrine in mosques, thereby altering the historically male-centred character of mosques as well as Islamic pedagogy.[5] This trend has, of course, been facilitated by the mobility and sense of entitlement engendered by women's greater access to education and employment outside of the home in post-colonial Egypt. In the last 40 years, women have entered new social domains and acquired new public roles from which they were previously excluded. A paradoxical effect of these developments is the proliferation of forms of piety that seem incongruous with the trajectory of the transformations that enabled them in the first place.[6] Notably, even though this movement has empowered women to enter the field of Islamic pedagogy in the institutional setting of mosques, their participation is critically structured by, and seeks to uphold, the limits of a discursive tradition that regards subordination to a transcendent will (and, thus, in many instances, to male authority) as its coveted goal.[7]

According to the organizers, the women's mosque movement emerged in response to the perception that religious knowledge, as a means to organizing daily life, has become increasingly marginalized under modern structures of secular governance. The participants of this movement often criticize what they consider to be an increasingly prevalent form of religiosity in Egypt that accords Islam the status of an abstract system of beliefs that has no direct bearing on the way one lives and structures one's daily life. This trend, usually referred to as secularization (*'almana*) or

---

[5] Mosques have played a critical role in the Islamic Revival in Egypt: since the 1970s there has been an unprecedented increase in the establishment of mosques by local neighbourhoods and non-governmental organizations, many of which provide a range of social services to the Cairene, especially the poor, such as medical, welfare, and educational services. Given the programme of economic liberalization that the Egyptian government has been pursuing since the 1970s and the concomitant decline in state-provided social services, these mosques fill a critical lacuna for many Egyptians.

[6] Currently there are hardly any neighbourhoods in this city of 11 million inhabitants where women do not offer religious lessons to each other. The attendance at these gatherings varies between 10 and 500 women, depending on the popularity of the teacher. The movement continues to be informally organized by women, and has no organizational centre that oversees its coordination.

[7] This is in contrast, for example, to a movement among women in the Islamic republic of Iran aimed at the reinterpretation of sacred texts so as to derive a more equitable model of relations between Muslim women and men; see Afshar (1998) and Najmabadi (1998).

Westernization (*taghrib*) of Egyptian society, is understood to have reduced Islamic knowledge (both as a mode of conduct and as a set of principles) to the status of 'custom and folklore' (*ada wa fukloriyya*). The women's mosque movement, therefore, seeks to educate lay Muslims in those virtues, ethical capacities, and forms of reasoning that the participants perceive to have become either unavailable or irrelevant to the lives of ordinary Muslims.

In Egypt today, Islam has come to be embodied in a variety of practices, movements, and ideas.[8] Thus, some Egyptians view Islam as constitutive of the cultural terrain upon which the Egyptian nation has acquired its unique historical character, some understand Islam as a doctrinal system with strong political and juridical implications for the organization of state and society, and others, such as the women I worked with, see Islam first and foremost as individual and collective practices of pious living. This does not mean, however, that the women's mosque movement is apolitical in the wider sense of the term, or that it represents a withdrawal from socio-political issues. On the contrary, the form of piety it seeks to realize is predicated upon, and transformative of, many aspects of social life.[9] The women's mosque movement has affected changes in a range of social behaviours among contemporary Egyptians, including how one dresses and speaks, what is deemed proper entertainment for adults and children, where one invests one's money, how one takes care of the poor, and what are the terms by which public debate is conducted.

While at times the mosque movement has been seen as a quietist alternative to the more militant forms of Islamic activism, in many ways this movement sits uncomfortably with certain aspects of the secular liberal project promoted by the state.[10] These tensions owe in part to the

---

[8] For recent studies of the Islamic movement in Egypt, see Hirschkind (2001, 2006), Salvatore (1997), and Starrett (1998).

[9] Piety here refers more to one's practical (and thus 'secular') conduct than to inward spiritual states as the term connotes in the English Puritan tradition. For an analysis of the politics that the piety movement (and the mosque movement) has enabled, see Mahmood (2005).

[10] Secularism is commonly thought of as the domain of real life emancipated from the ideological restrictions of religion. As Talal Asad has argued, however, it was precisely the positing of the opposition between a secular domain and a religious one (in which the former comes to be seen as the ground from which the latter emerges) that provided the basis for a modern normative conception not only of religion but politics as well. See Asad (2003). This juxtaposition of secular and religious domains has been facilitated through the displacement of religious authority to the state and its institutions of law. To say that a society is secular does not mean that religion is banished from its politics, law, and forms of association. Rather, religion is admitted into these domains on the condition that it takes a particular form; when it departs from these forms it confronts a set of regulatory barriers.

specific forms of will, desire, reason, and practice this movement seeks to cultivate, and the ways it reorganizes public life and debate in accordance with orthodox standards of Islamic piety. It is, therefore, not surprising that the Egyptian government has recently sought to regulate and sanction this movement, recognizing that the proliferation of this kind of Islamic sociability makes the task of securing a secular–liberal society difficult, if not impossible.[11]

AGENCY, RESISTANCE, FREEDOM

The pious subjects of the women's mosque movement occupy an uncomfortable place in feminist scholarship: they pursue practices and ideals embedded within a tradition that has historically accorded women a subordinate status, and they seek to cultivate virtues that are associated with feminine passivity and submissiveness (for example, shyness, modesty, perseverance, and humility—some of which I discuss later). In other words, the very idioms that women use to assert their presence in previously male-defined spheres are also those that secure their subordination. While it would not have been unusual in the 1960s to account for women's participation in such movements in terms of false consciousness, or the internalization of patriarchal norms through socialization, there has been an increasing discomfort with explanations of this kind. Drawing on work in the humanities and the social sciences since the 1970s that has focused on the operation of human agency within structures of subordination, feminists have sought to understand the ways women resist the dominant male order by subverting the hegemonic meanings of cultural practices and redeploying them for their own interests and agendas. A central question explored within this scholarship has been: How do women contribute to reproducing their own domination, and how do they resist or subvert it? Scholars working in this vein have thus tended to explore religious traditions in terms of the conceptual and practical resources

---

The banning of the veil as a proper form of attire for girls and women in Turkey and France is a case in point.

[11] In 1996, the Egyptian parliament passed a law that aimed to nationalize the vast majority of neighbourhood mosques, and the Ministry of Religious Affairs now requires all women and men who want to preach in mosques to enrol in a two-year state-run programme regardless of their prior training in religious affairs. See *al-Hayat* (1997). In addition, women's mosque lessons are regularly recorded and monitored by state employees. The government continues to suspend lessons delivered by women mosque teachers for making remarks critical of the state.

they offer which women may usefully redirect and recode to secure their 'own interests and agendas', a recoding that stands as the site of women's agency.[12]

It should be acknowledged that the focus on locating women's agency, when it first emerged, played a critical role in complicating and expanding debates about gender in non-Western societies beyond the simplistic registers of submission and patriarchy. In particular, the focus on women's agency provided a crucial corrective to scholarship on the Middle East that had portrayed Arab and Muslim women for decades as passive and submissive beings, shackled by structures of male authority.[13] This scholarship performed the worthy task of restoring the absent voice of women to analyses of Middle Eastern societies, showing women as active agents who live an existence far more complex and richer than past narratives had suggested.

While such an approach has been enormously productive in complicating the oppressor/oppressed model of gender relations, I would submit such a framework remains not only encumbered by the binary terms of resistance and subordination, but is also insufficiently attentive to motivations, desires, and goals that are not necessarily captured by these terms. Notably, the female agent in this analysis seems to stand in for a sometimes repressed, sometimes active feminist consciousness, articulated against the hegemonic male cultural norms of Arab Muslim societies. Even in instances when an explicit *feminist* agency is difficult to locate, there is a tendency to look for expressions and moments of resistance that may suggest a challenge to male domination. When women's actions seem to reinscribe what appear to be 'instruments of their own oppression', the social analyst can point to moments of disruption of, and articulation of points of opposition to, male authority that are located either in the interstices of a woman's consciousness (often read as a nascent feminist consciousness) or in the objective effects of the women's actions, however unintended they may be.[14] Agency, in this form of analysis, is understood

---

[12] In the Muslim context, see, for example, Boddy (1989), Hegland (1998), MacLeod (1991), and Torab (1996). For a similar argument made in the context of Christian evangelical movements, see Brusco (1995) and Stacey (1991).

[13] For a review of this scholarship on the Middle East, see Abu-Lughod (1990).

[14] Consider, for example, Janice Boddy's rich ethnographic work on women's *zar* cult in northern Sudan, which uses Islamic idioms and spirit mediums. In analysing the practices of these women, Boddy argued that the women she studied 'use perhaps unconsciously, perhaps strategically, what we in the West might prefer to consider *instruments of their oppression* as means to assert their value both collectively, through the ceremonies they organize and stage, and individually, in the context of their marriages, so insisting on their

as the capacity to realize one's own interests against the weight of custom, tradition, transcendental will, or other obstacles (whether individual or collective). Thus, the humanist desire for autonomy and expression of one's self-worth constitute the substrate, the slumbering ember that can spark to flame in the form of an act of resistance when conditions permit.[15]

What is seldom problematized in such an analysis is the universality of the desire to be free from relations of subordination and, for women, from structures of male domination, a desire that is central for liberal and progressive thought, and presupposed by the concept of resistance it authorizes. This positing of women's agency as consubstantial with resistance to relations of domination, and its concomitant naturalization of freedom as a social ideal, I would argue, is a product of feminism's dual character as both an *analytical* and a *politically prescriptive* project. Despite the many strands and differences within feminism, what accords this tradition an analytical and political coherence is the premise that where society is structured to serve male interests, the result will be either the neglect or a direct suppression of women's concerns.[16] Feminism, therefore, offers both a *diagnosis* of women's status across cultures as well as a *prescription* for changing the situation of women who are understood to be marginal/subordinate/oppressed (Strathern 1988: 26–8). Thus, the articulation of conditions of relative freedom that enable women both to formulate and enact self-determined goals and interests remains the object of feminist politics and theorizing. As in the case of liberalism, freedom is normative to feminism: critical scrutiny is applied to those who want to limit women's freedom rather than those who want to extend it.[17]

---

dynamic complementarity with men. *This in itself is a means of resisting and setting limits to domination*' (Boddy 1989: 345; emphasis added).

[15] Aspects of this argument may also be found in a number of anthropological works on women in the Arab world, such as Davis (1983), Dwyer (1978), Early (1993), and MacLeod(1991).

[16] Despite the debates within feminism, this is a premise that is shared across various feminist political positions including radical, socialist, liberal, and psycho-analytical, and marks the domain of feminist discourse. Even in the case of Marxist and socialist feminists who argue that women's subordination is determined by social relations of economic production, there is at least an acknowledgment of the inherent tension between women's interests and those of the larger society dominated and shaped by men. See Harstock (1983) and MacKinnon (1989). For an anthropological argument about the universal character of gender inequality, see Yanagisako and Collier (1987).

[17] John Stuart Mill, a central figure in the liberal and feminist tradition, for example, argued, 'The burden of proof is supposed to be with those who are against liberty; who contend for any restriction or prohibition.... The *a priori* assumption is in favor of freedom' (1991: 472).

A number of feminist scholars over the years have offered trenchant critiques of the liberal notion of autonomy from a variety of perspectives.[18] For example, while earlier critics drew attention to the masculinist assumptions underpinning the ideal of autonomy, later scholars faulted this ideal for its emphasis on the atomistic, individualized, and bounded characteristics of the self at the expense of its relational qualities formed through social interactions within forms of human community.[19] Consequently, there have been various attempts to redefine autonomy so as to capture the emotional, embodied, and socially embedded character of people, particularly of women (Friedman 2003; Joseph 1999; Nedelsky 1989). A more radical strain of poststructuralist theory has situated its critique of autonomy within a larger challenge posed to the *illusory* character of the rationalist, self-authorizing, transcendental subject presupposed by Enlightenment thought in general, and the liberal tradition in particular. Rational thought, these critics argue, secures its universal scope and authority by performing a necessary exclusion of all that is bodily, feminine, emotional, non-rational, and inter-subjective (Butler 1993; Gatens 1996; Grosz 1994). This exclusion cannot be substantively or conceptually recuperated through recourse to an unproblematic feminine experience, body, or imaginary (*pace* Beauvoir and Irigaray), but must be thought through the very terms of the discourse of metaphysical transcendence that enacts these exclusions.[20]

In what follows, I would like to push further in the direction opened by these poststructuralist debates. In particular, my argument for separating the notion of self-realization from that of the autonomous will is indebted to poststructuralist critiques of the transcendental subject, voluntarism, and repressive models of power. Yet, as will become clear, my analysis also departs from these frameworks insomuch as I question the overwhelming tendency of poststructuralist feminist scholarship to conceptualize agency in terms of subversion or resignification of social norms, to locate agency within those operations that resist the dominating and subjectivating modes of power. In other words, the normative political subject of poststructuralist feminist theory often remains a liberatory

---

[18] For an interesting discussion of the contradictions generated by the privileged position accorded to the concept of autonomy in feminist theory, see Adams and Minson (1978).

[19] In the first group, see Chodorow (1978) and Gilligan (1982); in the second, see Benhabib (1992) and Young (1990).

[20] For an excellent discussion of this point in the scholarship on feminist ethics, see Colebrook (1997).

one whose agency is conceptualized on a binary model of subordination and subversion. This scholarship thus elides dimensions of human action whose ethical and political status does not map onto the logic of repression and resistance. In order to grasp these modes of action that are indebted to other reasons and histories, I want to argue that it is crucial to detach the notion of agency from the goals of progressive politics.

The ideas of freedom and liberty as *the* political ideals are relatively new in modern history. Many societies, including Western ones, have flourished with aspirations other than these. Nor, for that matter, does the narrative of individual and collective liberty exhaust the desires of people in liberal societies. If we recognize that the desire for freedom from, or subversion of, norms is not an innate desire that motivates all beings at all times, but is also profoundly mediated by cultural and historical conditions, then a question arises: How do we analyse operations of power that construct different kinds of bodies, knowledges, and subjectivities whose trajectories do not follow the entelechy of liberatory politics?

If the ability to effect change in the world and in oneself is historically and culturally specific (both in terms of what constitutes 'change' and the means by which it is effected), then the meaning and sense of agency cannot be fixed in advance, but must emerge through an analysis of the particular concepts that enable specific modes of being, responsibility, and effectivity. Viewed in this way, what may appear to be a case of deplorable passivity and docility from a progressivist point of view may actually be a form of agency—but one that can be understood only from within the discourses and structures of subordination that create the conditions of its enactment. In this sense, the capacity for agency is entailed not only in acts that resist norms but also in the multiple ways in which one inhabits norms.

It may be argued in response that this kind of challenge to the natural status accorded to the desire for freedom in analyses of gender runs the risk of Orientalizing Arab and Muslim women all over again—repeating the errors of pre-1970s Orientalist scholarship that defined Middle Eastern women as passive submissive Others, bereft of the enlightened consciousness of their 'Western sisters', and hence doomed to lives of servile submission to men. I would contend, however, that to examine the discursive and practical conditions through which women come to cultivate various forms of desire and capacities of ethical action is a radically different project than an Orientalizing one that locates the desire for submission in an innate ahistorical cultural essence. Indeed, if we accept the notion that all forms of desire are discursively organized (as much of recent feminist scholarship has argued), then it is important to interrogate the practical and conceptual conditions under which different forms of desire emerge, including desire for submission to recognized authority. We cannot treat as natural and imitable only those desires that ensure the emergence of feminist politics.

Consider, for example, the women from the mosque movement that I worked with. The task of realizing piety placed these women in conflict with several structures of authority. Some of these structures were grounded in instituted standards of Islamic orthodoxy, others in norms of liberal discourse; some were grounded in the authority of parents and male kin, and others in state institutions. Yet the *rationale* behind these conflicts was not predicated upon, and therefore cannot be understood only by reference to, arguments for gender equality or resistance to male authority. Nor can these women's practices be read as a reinscription of traditional roles, since the women's mosque movement has significantly reconfigured the gendered practice of Islamic pedagogy and the social institution of mosques. One could, of course, argue in response that, the intent of these women notwithstanding, the actual effects of their practices may be analysed in terms of their role in reinforcing or undermining structures of male domination. While conceding that such an analysis is feasible and has been useful at times, I would nevertheless argue that it remains encumbered by the binary terms of resistance and subordination, and ignores projects, discourses, and desires that are not captured by these terms, such as those expressed by the women I worked with.[21]

---

[21] Studies on the resurgent popularity of the veil in urban Egypt since the 1980s provide excellent examples of these problems. The proliferation of studies on the veil reflects scholars' surprise that, contrary to their expectations, so many 'modern Egyptian women' have returned to wearing the veil. Some of these studies offer functionalist explanations, citing a variety of reasons why women take on the veil voluntarily (for example, the veil makes it easy for women to avoid sexual harassment on public transportation, lowers the cost of attire for working women, and so on). Other studies identify the veil as a symbol of resistance to the commodification of women's bodies in imported Western media, and more generally to the hegemony of Western values. See, for example, El Guindi (1981), Hoffman-Ladd (1987), Macleod (1991), Radwan (1982), and Zuhur (1992). While these studies have made important contributions, it is surprising that their authors have paid little attention to Islamic virtues of female modesty or piety, especially given that many of the women who have taken up the veil frame their decision precisely in these terms. Instead, analysts often explain the motivations of veiled women in terms of standard models of sociological causality (such as social protest, economic necessity, anomie, or utilitarian strategy), while terms like morality, divinity, and virtue are accorded the status of the phantom imaginings of the hegemonized.

My argument should be familiar to anthropologists who have long acknowledged that the terms people use to organize their lives are not simply a gloss for universally shared assumptions about the world and one's place in it, but are actually constitutive of different forms of personhood, knowledge, and experience.[22] For this reason I have found it necessary, in what follows, to attend carefully to the specific logic of the discourse of piety: a logic that inheres not in the intentionality of the actors, but in the relationships that are articulated between words, concepts, and practices that constitute a particular discursive tradition.[23] I would insist that an appeal to understanding the coherence of a discursive tradition is neither to justify that tradition nor to argue for some irreducible essentialism or cultural relativism. It is, instead, to take a necessary step towards explaining the force that a discourse commands.

DOCILITY AND AGENCY

In order to elaborate my theoretical approach, let me begin by examining the arguments of Judith Butler, who remains, for many, the pre-eminent theorist of poststructuralist feminist thought, and whose arguments have been essential to my own work. Drawing on Foucault's insights, Butler asks a key question: 'if power works not merely to dominate or oppress existing subjects, but also forms subjects, what is this formation?' (Butler 1997: 18). By questioning the prediscursive status of the concept of subject, and inquiring instead into the relations of power that produce it, she breaks with those feminist analysts who have formulated the issue of personhood in terms of the relative autonomy of the individual from the social. Thus, the issue for Butler is not how the social enacts the individual (as it was for generations of feminists), but what the discursive conditions are that sustain the entire metaphysical edifice of contemporary individuality.

I find Butler's critique of humanist conceptions of agency and subject very compelling and, indeed, my arguments are manifestly informed by it. I have, however, found it productive to argue with certain tensions that characterize Butler's work in order to expand her analytics to a somewhat different, if related, set of problematics. One key tension in Butler's work owes to the fact that while she emphasizes the ineluctable relationship between the consolidation and destabilization of norms, her discussion

---

[22] See, for example, Keane (1997) and Rosaldo (1982).
[23] The concept 'discursive tradition' is from Asad (1986).

of agency tends to focus on those operations of power that resignify and subvert norms. In other words, the concept of agency in Butler's work is developed primarily in contexts where norms are thrown into question or are subject to resignification. An important consequence of these aspects of Butler's work is that her analysis of the power of norms remains grounded in an agonistic framework, one in which norms suppress and/or are subverted, are reiterated and/or resignified—so that one gets little sense of the work norms perform beyond this register of suppression and subversion within the constitution of the subject. Butler's exploration of agency therefore remains subservient, on the one hand, to her overall interest in tracking the possibilities of resistance to the regulating power of normativity,[24] and, on the other hand, to her model of performativity, which is primarily conceptualized in terms of a dualistic structure of consolidation/resignification, doing/undoing of norms.

THE SUBJECT OF NORMS

I would like to push the question of norms further in a direction that I think allows us to deepen the analysis of subject formation and also address the problem of reading agency primarily in terms of resistance to the regulating power of structures of normativity. In particular, I would like to expand Butler's insight that norms are not simply a social imposition on the subject but constitute the very substance of her intimate, valorized interiority. But in doing so, I want to move away from an agonistic and dualistic framework—one in which norms are conceptualized on the model of doing and undoing, consolidation and subversion—and instead to think about the variety of ways in which norms are lived and inhabited, aspired to, reached for, and consummated. As I will argue, this in turn requires that we explore the relationship between the immanent form a normative act takes, the model of subjectivity it presupposes (specific articulations of volition, emotion, reason, and bodily expression), and

---

[24] Butler argues, for example, that Foucault's notion of subjectivation can be productively supplemented with certain reformulations of psychoanalytic theory. For Butler, the force of this supplementation seems to reside, however, in its ability to address the 'problem of locating or accounting for resistance: Where does resistance to or in disciplinary subject formation take place? Does [Foucault's] reduction of the psychoanalytically rich notion of the psyche to that of the imprisoning soul [in *Discipline and Punish*] eliminate the possibility of resistance to normalization and to subject formation, a resistance that emerges precisely from the incommensurability between psyche and subject?' (Butler 1997: 87).

the kinds of authority upon which such an act relies. Let me elaborate by discussing the problems a dualistic conception of norms poses when analysing the practices of the mosque movement.

Consider, for example, the Islamic virtue of female modesty (*al-ihtisham, al-haya'*) that many Egyptian Muslims uphold and value. Despite a consensus about its importance, there is considerable debate about how this virtue should be lived, and particularly about whether its realization requires the donning of the veil. A majority of the participants in the mosque movement (and the larger piety movement of which the mosque movement is an integral part) argue that the veil is a necessary component of the virtue of modesty because the veil both expresses 'true modesty' and is the means through which modesty is acquired (see Tantawi 1994). They posit, therefore, an ineluctable relationship between the norm (modesty) and the bodily form it takes (the veil) such that the veiled body becomes the necessary means through which the virtue of modesty is both created *and* expressed. In contrast to this understanding, a position associated with prominent secularist writers argues that the virtue of modesty is no different than any other human attribute, such as moderation or humility: it is a facet of character but does not commit one to any particular expressive repertoire such as donning the veil (Ashmawi 1994b).[25] Notably, these authors oppose the veil but not the virtue of modesty which they continue to regard as necessary to appropriate feminine conduct. The veil, in their view, has been invested with an importance that is unwarranted when it comes to judgements about female modesty.

The debate about the veil is only one part of a much larger discussion in Egyptian society wherein political differences between Islamists and secularists, and even among Islamists of various persuasions, are expressed through arguments about ritual performative behaviour. The most interesting features of this debate lie not so much in whether the norm of modesty is subverted or enacted, but in the radically different ways in which the norm is supposed to be lived and inhabited. Notably, each view posits a very different conceptualization of the relationship between embodied behaviour and the virtue or norm of modesty: for the pietists, bodily behaviour is at the core of the proper realization of the norm, and for their opponents, it is a contingent and unnecessary element in modesty's enactment.

---

[25] For an argument between these two groups about the veil and the virtue of modesty, see the exchange between the then-mufti of Egypt, Sayyid Tantawi and the prominent intellectual, Muhammed Said Ashmawi who has been a leading voice for 'Islamic liberalism' in the Arab world. See Ashmawi (1994a) and Tantawi (1994).

In what follows I will elaborate upon these points by analysing two ethnographic examples drawn from my fieldwork with the Egyptian women's mosque movement. The ethnographic here stands less as a signature for the 'real', and more as a substantiation of my earlier call to tend to the specific workings of disciplinary power that enable particular forms of investment and agency.

CULTIVATING SHYNESS

Through my fieldwork, I came to know four lower-middle class working women, in their mid to late thirties, who were well tutored and experienced in the art of Islamic piety. Indeed, one may call them virtuosos of piety. In addition to attending mosque lessons, they met as a group to read and discuss issues of Islamic doctrine and Quranic exegesis. Notably, none of these women came from a devout family, and in fact some of them had had to wage a struggle against their kin in order to become devout. They told me about their struggles, not only with their families, but also, and more importantly, with themselves in cultivating the desire for greater religious exactitude.

Not unlike other devout women I worked with from the mosques, these women also sought to excel in piety in their day-to-day lives—something they described as the condition of being close to God (variously rendered as *taqarrab allah* and/or *taqwa*). While piety was achievable through practices that were both devotional as well as worldly in character, it required more than the simple performance of acts: piety also entailed the inculcation of entire dispositions through a simultaneous training of the body, emotions, and reason until the religious virtues acquired the status of embodied habits.

Among the religious virtues that are considered to be important to acquire for pious Muslims in general, and women in particular, is modesty or shyness (al-haya'), a common topic of discussion among the mosque participants. To practice al-haya' means to be diffident, modest, and able to feel and enact shyness. While all of the Islamic virtues are gendered (insofar as their measure and standards vary when applied to men and women), this is particularly true of shyness and modesty (al-haya'). The struggle involved in cultivating this virtue was brought home to me when in the course of a discussion about the exegesis of a chapter in the Quran, called 'The Story' (*Surat al-Qasas*), one of the women, Amal, drew our attention to verse twenty-five. This verse is about a woman walking shyly—with al-haya'—towards Moses to ask him to approach her father for her hand in marriage. Unlike the other women in the group, Amal was particularly outspoken and confident, and would seldom hesitate to assert herself in social situations with men or women. Normally I would not have described her as shy, because I considered shyness to be contradictory to qualities of candidness and self-confidence in a person. Yet as I was to learn, Amal had learned to be outspoken in a way that was in keeping with Islamic standards of reserve, restraint, and modesty required of pious Muslim women. Here is how the conversation proceeded:

Contemplating the word *istihya'*, which is form ten of the substantive *haya'*,[26] Amal said 'I used to think that even though shyness (*al-haya'*) was required of us by God, if I acted shyly it would be hypocritical (*nifaq*) because I didn't actually feel it inside of me. Then one day, in reading verse (*aya*) twenty-five in *Surat al-Qasas* ('The Story') I realized that *al-haya'* was among the good deeds and given my natural lack of shyness (*al-haya'*), I had to make or create it first. I realized that making (*sana'*) it in yourself is not hypocrisy (*nifaq*), and that eventually your inside learns to have *al-haya'* too.' Here she looked at me and explained the meaning of the word *istihya'*: 'It means making oneself shy, even if it means creating it (*Ya'ni ya Saba, ya'mil nafsuhu yitkisif hatta lau san'ati*).' She continued with her point, 'And finally I understood that once you do this, the sense of shyness (*al-haya'*) eventually imprints itself on your inside (*al-sha'ur yitba' 'ala juwwaki*).' Another friend, Nama, a single woman in her early thirties, who had been sitting and listening, added: 'It's just like the veil (*hijab*). In the beginning when you wear it, you're embarrassed (*maksufa*), and don't want to wear it because people say that you look older and unattractive, that you won't get married, and will never find a husband. But you *must* wear the veil, first because it is God's command (*hukm allah*), and then, with time, your inside learns to feel shy without the veil, and if you were to take it off your entire being feels uncomfortable (*mish radi*) about it.'

To many readers this conversation may exemplify an obsequious deference to social norms that both reflects and reproduces women's subordination. Indeed, Amal's struggle with herself to become shy may appear to be no more than an instance of the internalization of standards of effeminate behaviour, one that contributes little to our understanding of agency. Yet if we think of 'agency' not simply as a synonym for resistance to social norms but as a modality of action, then this conversation raises some interesting questions about the relationship established between the subject and the norm, between performative behaviour and inward disposition. To begin with, what is striking here is that instead of innate human desires eliciting outward forms of conduct, one's practices and actions determine one's desires and emotions. In other words, action does not issue forth from natural feelings but *creates* them. Furthermore, it is through repeated

---

[26] Most Arabic verbs are based on a tri-consonantal root from which ten verbal forms (and sometimes fifteen) are derived.

bodily acts that one trains one's memory, desire, and intellect to behave according to established standards of conduct. Notably, Amal *does not* regard simulating shyness in her initial self-cultivation to be hypocritical, as it would be in certain liberal conceptions of the self, according to which a dissonance between internal feelings and external expressions is a form of dishonesty or self-betrayal (as captured in the phrase: 'How can I do something sincerely when my heart is not in it?'). Instead, taking the absence of shyness as a marker of an incomplete learning process, Amal further develops the quality of shyness by synchronizing her outward behaviour with her inward motives until the discrepancy between the two dissolves. This is an example of a mutually constitutive relationship between body learning and body sense—as Nama says, your body literally comes to feel uncomfortable if you do *not* veil.

What is also significant in this programme of self-cultivation is that bodily acts—like wearing the veil or conducting oneself modestly in social interactions (especially men)—do not serve as manipulable masks detachable from an essential interiorized self in a game of public presentation. Rather they are the *critical markers* of piety as well as the *ineluctable means* by which one trains oneself to be pious. While wearing the veil serves at first as a means to tutor oneself in the attribute of shyness, it is simultaneously integral to the practice of shyness: one cannot simply discard the veil once a modest deportment has been acquired, because the veil itself partly defines that deportment.[27] This is a crucial aspect of the disciplinary programme pursued by the participants of the mosque movement, the significance of which is elided when the veil is understood solely in terms of its symbolic value as a marker of women's subordination or Islamic identity.

The complicated relationship among learning, memory, experience, and the self undergirding the model of pedagogy followed by the mosque participants has at times been discussed by scholars through the Latin

---

[27] This concept can perhaps be illuminated by analogy to two different models of dieting: an older model in which the practice of dieting is understood to be a temporary and instrumental solution to the problem of weight gain; and a more contemporary model in which dieting is understood to be synonymous with a healthy and nutritious lifestyle. The second model presupposes an ethical relationship between oneself and the rest of the world and in this sense is similar to what Foucault called 'practices of the care of the self'. The differences between the two models point to the fact that it does not mean much to simply note that that systems of power mark their truth on human bodies through disciplines of self-formation. In order to understand the force these disciplines command, one needs to explicate the conceptual relationship articulated between different aspects of the body and the particular notion of the self that animates distinct disciplinary regimes.

term *habitus*, meaning an acquired faculty in which the body, mind, and emotions are simultaneously trained to achieve competence at something (such as meditation, dancing, or playing a musical instrument). While the term habitus has become best known in the social sciences through the work of Pierre Bourdieu (1997), my own work draws upon a longer and richer history of this term, one that addresses the centrality of gestural capacities in certain traditions of moral cultivation.[28] Aristotelian in origin and adopted by the three monotheistic traditions, this older meaning of habitus refers to a specific pedagogical process by which moral virtues are acquired through a coordination of outward behaviour (for example, bodily acts, social demeanour) with inward dispositions (for example, emotional states, thoughts, intentions).[29] Thus, habitus in this usage refers to a conscious effort at reorienting desires, brought about by the concordance of inward motives, outward actions, inclinations, and emotional states through the repeated practice of virtuous deeds.

This Aristotelian understanding of moral formation influenced a number of Islamic thinkers, foremost among them the eleventh-century theologian Abu Hamid al-Ghazali (d. 1111), but also al-Miskawayh (d. 1030), Ibn Rushd (d. 1198), and Ibn Khaldun (d. 1406). Historian Ira Lapidus draws attention to this genealogy in his analysis of Ibn Khaldun's use of the Arabic term *malaka*.[30] Lapidus argues that although Ibn Khaldun's use of the term malaka has often been translated as 'habit', its sense is best captured in the Latin term habitus, which Lapidus describes as 'that inner quality developed as a result of outer practice which makes practice a perfect ability of the soul of the actor'.[31] In terms of faith, malaka, according to Lapidus,

---

[28] As a pedagogical technique necessary for the development of moral virtues, habitus in this sense is not a universal term applicable to all types of knowledges, and neither does it necessarily serve as a conceptual bridge between the objective world of social structures and subjective consciousness as it does in Bourdieu's formulation.

[29] In *Nicomachean Ethics*, Aristotle argues,

For the things we have to learn before we can do them, we learn by doing them, for example, men become builders by building and lyre players by playing the lyre; so too we become just by doing just acts, temperate by doing temperate acts, brave by doing brave acts.... By doing the acts we do in our transactions with other men we become just or unjust, and by doing the acts that we do in the presence of danger, and being habituated to feel fear or confidence, we become brave or cowardly. (McKeon 1941: 592-3)

[30] See Leaman (1999) for a discussion of the term malaka in the Islamic tradition.

[31] Lapidus (1984: 54). Consider, for example, Ibn Khaldun's remarks in *The Muqadimmah*, which bear remarkable similarity to Aristotle's discussion: 'A habit[us] is a firmly rooted quality acquired by doing a certain action and repeating it time after time,

is the acquisition, from the belief of the heart and the resulting actions, of a quality that has complete control over the heart so that it commands the action of the limbs and makes every activity take place in submissiveness to it to the point that all actions, eventually, become subservient to this affirmation of faith. This is the highest degree of faith. It is perfect faith. (Lapidus 1984: 55–6)

This Aristotelian legacy continues to live within the practices of the contemporary piety movement in Egypt. It is evident in the frequent invocation of Abu Hamid al-Ghazali's spiritual exercises and techniques of moral cultivation, found in popular instruction booklets on how to become pious, and often referred to among the participants of the Islamic Revival.[32]

TO ENDURE IS TO ENACT?

In this section I would like to return to the exploration of different modalities of agency whose operations escape the logic of resistance and subversion of norms. In what follows I will investigate how suffering and survival—two modalities of existence that are often considered to be the antithesis of agency—came to be articulated within the lives of women who lived under the pressures of a patriarchal system that required them to conform to the rigid demands of heterosexual monogamy. Given that these conditions of gender inequality uniformly affect Egyptian women, regardless of their religious persuasion, I was particularly interested in understanding how a life lived in accordance with Islamic virtues affected a woman's ability to inhabit the structure of patriarchal norms. What resources and capacities did a pious lifestyle make available to women of the mosque movement, and how did their mode of inhabiting those structures differ from women for whom the resources of survival lay elsewhere? In particular, I want to understand the practical and conceptual implications of a religious imaginary in which humans are considered to be only partially responsible for their own actions, versus an imaginary in which humans are regarded as the sole authors of their actions. It is not so much the epistemological repercussions of these different accounts of

---

until the form of that action is firmly fixed [in one's disposition]. A habit[us] corresponds to the original action after which it was formed.' See Khaldun (1958: 346).

[32] See, for example, Farid (1990) and Hawwa (1995). On A.H. al-Ghazali's reworking of Aristotle's theory of virtue, see Sherif (1975) and the introduction by T.J. Winter in al-Ghazali (1995: xv–xcii). For A.H. al-Ghazali's seminal work on practices of moral self-cultivation, see al-Ghazali (1992).

human action that interest me (cf. Chakrabarty 2000; Hollywood 2004), but how these two accounts affect women's ability to survive within a system of inequality and to flourish despite its constraints.

In what follows, I will juxtapose an example drawn from the life of a woman who was part of the mosque movement with another taken from the life of a woman who considered herself to be a 'secular Muslim', and who was often critical of the virtues that the mosque participants considered necessary to the realization of their ability to live as Muslims. I want to highlight the strikingly different ways in which these two women dealt with the pressures of being single in a society where heterosexual marriage is regarded as a compulsory norm. Even though it would be customary to consider one of these strategies to be 'more agentival' than the other, I wish to show that such a reading is in fact reductive of the efforts entailed in the learning and practising of virtues—virtues that might not be palatable to humanist sensibilities but are nonetheless constitutive of agency in important ways.

The full extent to which single women in Egypt are subjected to the pressure to get married was revealed to me in a conversation with Nadia, a woman I had come to know through her work in the mosques. Nadia was in her mid-thirties and had been married for a couple of years, but did not have any children; she and her husband lived in a small apartment in a lower-middle-income neighbourhood of Cairo. She taught in a primary school close to her home, and twice a week after work she taught Quranic recitation to young children in the Nafisa mosque as part of what she considered to be her contribution to the ongoing work of da'wa. Afterwards, she would often stay to attend the lesson at the mosque, delivered by one of the better-known da'iyat. Sometimes, after the lesson, I would catch a bus back with her and her friends. The ride was long and we would often have a chance to chat.

During one of these rides, I observed a conversation between Nadia and her long-time friend Iman, who was in her late twenties and who also volunteered at the mosque. Iman seemed agitated that day, and upon getting on the bus immediately spoke to Nadia about her dilemma. A male colleague who was married to another woman had apparently approached her to ask her hand in marriage.[33] By Egyptian standards, Iman was well over the marriageable age. Iman was agitated because although the man was very well respected at her place of work and she had always held him in high regard, he already had a first wife. She was confused about what she

---

[33] Islamic jurisprudence permits men to have up to four wives.

should do, and was asking Nadia for advice. Much to my surprise, Nadia advised Iman to tell this man to approach her parents formally to ask for her hand in marriage, and to allow her parents to investigate the man's background in order to ascertain whether he was a suitable match for her.

I was taken aback by this response because I had expected Nadia to tell Iman not to think about this issue any further, since not only had the man broken the rules for proper conduct by approaching Iman directly instead of her parents, but he was also already married. I had come to respect Nadia's ability to uphold rigorous standards of pious behaviour: on numerous occasions I had seen her give up opportunities that would have accrued her material and social advantages for the sake of her principles. So a week later, when I was alone with Nadia, I asked her the question that had been bothering me: why did she not tell Iman to cut off any connection with this man?

Nadia seemed a little puzzled and asked me why I thought this was proper advice. When I explained, she said, 'But there is nothing wrong in a man approaching a woman for her hand in marriage directly as long as his intent is serious and he is not playing with her. This occurred many times even at the time of the Prophet.'

I interrupted her and said, 'But what about the fact that he is already married?' Nadia looked at me and asked, 'You think that she shouldn't consider marriage to an already married man?' I nodded yes. Nadia gave me a long and contemplative look, and said, 'I don't know how it is in the United States, but this issue is not that simple here in Egypt [*il-mas'ila di mish sahla fi masr*]. Marriage is a very big problem here. A woman who is not married is rejected by the entire society as if she has some disease [*il-maraa'*], as if she is a thief [*harami*]. It is an issue that is very painful indeed [*hadhahi mas'ila mu'allima jiddan, jiddan*].'

I asked Nadia what she meant by this. She replied: 'If you are unmarried after the age of say late teens or early twenties—as is the case with Iman—everyone around you treats you like you have a defect [*al-naqs*]. Wherever you go, you are asked, "Why didn't you get married [*matjawwaztish ley*]?" Everyone knows that you can't offer to marry a man, that you have to wait until a man approaches you. Yet they act as if the decision is in your hands! You know I did not get married until I was thirty-four years old: I stopped visiting my relatives, which is socially improper ['*aib*], because every time I would go I would encounter the same questions. What is even worse is that your [immediate] family starts to think that you have some failing in you because no man has approached you for marriage. They treat you as if you have a disease.'

Nadia paused reflectively for a moment and then continued: 'It's not as if those who are married necessarily have a happy life. For marriage is a blessing [na'ma], but it can also be a trial/problem [fitna]. For there are husbands who are cruel [qasi]: they beat their wives, bring other wives into the same house, and don't give each an equal share. But these people who make fun of you for not being married don't think about this aspect of marriage, and only stress marriage as a blessing [na'ma]. Even if a woman has a horrible husband, and has a hard married life, she will still make an effort to make you feel bad for not being married.'

I was surprised at Nadia's clarity about the injustice of this situation towards women and the perils of marriage. I asked Nadia if single men were treated in the same way. Nadia replied resoundingly, 'Of course not! For the assumption is that a man, if he wanted to, could have proposed to any woman: if he is not married it's because he *didn't want* to, or there was no woman who deserved him. But for the woman it is assumed that no one wanted *her* because it's not up to her to make the first move.' Nadia shook her head again, and went on, 'No, this situation is very hard and a killer, O Saba. You have to have a very strong personality [shakhsiyya qawiyya] for all of this not to affect you because eventually you also start thinking that there is something deeply wrong with you that explains why you are not married.'

I asked her what she meant by being strong. Nadia said in response, 'You must be patient in the face of difficulty [lazim tiku'ni sabira], trust in God [tawwakali 'ala allah], and accept the fact that this is what He has willed as your fate [qada']; if you complain about it all the time, then you are denying that it is only God who has the wisdom to know why we live in the conditions we do and not humans.' I asked Nadia if she had been able to achieve such a state of mind, given that she was married quite late. Nadia answered in an unexpected manner. She said,

> O Saba, you don't learn to become patient [sabira] or trust in God [mutawakkila] only when you face difficulties. There are many people who face difficulties, and may not even complain, but they are not *sabirin* [patient, enduring]. You practice the virtue of patience [sabr] because it is a good deed [al-'amal al-salih], regardless of your situation: whether your life is difficult or happy. In fact, practicing patience in the face of happiness is even more difficult.

Noting my look of surprise, Nadia said: 'Yes, because think of how often people turn to God only when they have difficult times, and often forget Him in times of comfort. To practice patience in moments of your life when you are happy, is to be mindful of His rights [úaqqahu] upon you at all times.' I asked Nadia, 'But I thought you said that one needs to have patience so as to be able to deal with one's difficulties?' Nadia responded by saying, 'It is a secondary consequence [al-natija al-thanawiyya] of your doing good deeds, among them the virtue of patience. God is merciful and He rewards you by giving you the capacity to be courageous in moments of difficulty. But you should practice sabr [patience] because this is the right thing to do in the path of God [fi sabil lillah].'

I came back from my conversation with Nadia quite struck by the clarity with which she outlined the predicament of women in Egyptian society: a situation created and regulated by social norms for which women were in turn blamed. Nadia was also clear that women did not deserve the treatment they received, and that many of those she loved (including her kin) were equally responsible for the pain that had been inflicted on her when she was single. While polygamy is allowed in Islam, Nadia and other participants of the mosque movement would often point out that, according to the Quran, marriage to more than one woman is conditional upon the ability of a man to treat all his wives equally (emotionally and materially), a condition almost impossible to fulfil.[34] For this reason, polygamous marriages are understood to create difficult situations for women, and the mosque participants generally advise against it.[35] Nadia's advice to Iman that she consider marriage to a married man, however, was based on a recognition of the extreme difficulty entailed in living as a single woman in Egypt.

While Nadia's response about having to make such choices resonated with other, secular, Egyptian friends of mine, her advocacy of the cultivation of the virtue of sabr (roughly meaning 'to persevere in the face of difficulty without complaint') was problematic for them.[36] Sabr invokes in the minds of many the passivity women are often encouraged to cultivate in the face of injustice. My friend Sana, for example, concurred with Nadia's description of how difficult life could be for a single woman in Egypt, but strongly disagreed with her advice regarding sabr.

---

[34] Both the Hanbali and Maliki schools of Islamic jurisprudence permit a woman to stipulate in her marriage contract that if the husband takes a second wife, she has the right to seek divorce. What is quite clear is that none of the schools give the woman the legal right to prevent her husband from taking a second wife. For recent debates on polygamy among contemporary religious scholars in Egypt, see Skovgaard-Petersen (1997: 169–170, 232–3).

[35] This is further augmented by the liberal ideal of nuclear family and companionate marriage, which, as Abu-Lughod (1998) points out, has increasingly become the norm among Islamists as well as secular-liberal Egyptians.

[36] I have retained the use of sabr in this discussion rather than its common English translation, 'patience' because sabr communicates a sense not quite captured by the latter: one of perseverance, endurance of hardship without complaint, and steadfastness.

Sana was a single professional woman in her mid-thirties who came from an upper-middle-class family—a self-professed 'secular Muslim' whom I had come to know through a group of friends at the American University at Cairo. In response to my recounting of the conversation with Nadia, Sana said, 'sabr is an important Islamic principle, but these religious types [*mutadayyinin*] think it's a solution to everything. It's such a passive way of dealing with this situation.' While Sana, too, believed that a woman needed to have a 'strong personality' (*shakhsiyya qawiyya*) in order to be able to deal with such a circumstance, for her this meant acquiring self-esteem or self-confidence (*thiqa fil-nafs wal-dhat*). As she explained, 'Self-esteem makes you independent of what other people think of you. You begin to think of your worth not in terms of marriage and men, but in terms of who you *really are*, and in my case, I draw pride from my work and that I am good at it. Where does sabr get you? Instead of helping you to improve your situation, it just leads you to accept it as fate—passively.'

While Nadia and Sana shared their recognition of the painful situation single women face, they differed markedly in their respective engagements with this suffering, each enacting a different modality of agency in the face of it. For Sana, the ability to survive the situation she faced lay in seeking self-empowerment through the cultivation of self-esteem, a psychological capacity that, in her view, enabled one to pursue self-directed choices and actions unhindered by other people's opinions. In this view, self-esteem is useful precisely because it is a means to achieving self-directed goals.[37] For Sana, one of the important arenas for acquiring this self-esteem was her professional career and achievements. Nadia also worked, but clearly did not regard her professional work in the same manner.

Importantly, in Nadia's view, the practice of sabr does not necessarily make one immune to being hurt by others' opinions: one undertakes the practice of sabr first and foremost because it is an essential attribute of a pious character, an attribute to be cultivated regardless of the situation one faces. Rather than alleviating suffering, sabr allows one to bear and live hardship *correctly* as prescribed by one tradition of Islamic self-cultivation.[38] As Nadia says, if the practice of sabr fortifies one's ability to deal with social suffering, this is a secondary, not essential, consequence. Justification for the exercise of sabr, in other words, resides neither in its ability to reduce

---

[37] In the language of positive freedom, Sana may be understood to be a 'free agent' because she appears to formulate her projects in accord with her own desires, values, and goals, and not those of others.

[38] For contemporary discussions of sabr among leaders of the Islamic Revival, see al-Ghazali (1990) and Qaradawi (1989).

suffering nor in its ability to help one realize one's self-directed choices and/or goals. When I pressed Nadia for further explanation, she gave me the example of Ayyub, who is known in Islam for his exemplary patience in the face of extreme physical and social hardship (Ayyub is the equivalent of Job in the Christian tradition). Nadia noted that Ayyub is famous *not* for his ability to rise above the pain, but precisely for the manner in which he *lived* his pain. Ayyub's perseverance did not decrease his suffering: it ended only when God had deemed it time for it to end. In this view, it is not only the lack of complaint in the face of hardship, but the way in which sabr infuses one's life and mode of being, that makes one a *sabira* (one who exercises sabr). As Nadia notes in the conversation reported earlier, while sabr is realized through practical tasks, its consummation does not lie in practice alone.

Just as the practice of self-esteem structured the possibilities of action that were open to Sana, so did the realization of sabr for Nadia, enabling certain ways of being and foreclosing others. It is clear that certain virtues (such as humility, modesty, and shyness) have lost their value in the liberal imagination, and are considered emblematic of passivity and inaction, especially if they do not uphold the autonomy of the individual: sabr may, in this view, mark an inadequacy of action, a failure to act under the inertia of tradition. But sabr in the sense described by Nadia and others does not mark a reluctance to act. Rather, it is integral to a constructive project: it is a site of considerable investment, struggle, and achievement. What Nadia's and Sana's discussions reveal are two different modes of engaging with social injustices, one grounded in a tradition that we have come to value, and another in a non-liberal tradition that is being resuscitated by the movement I worked with.

Note that even though Nadia regarded herself as only partially responsible for the actions she undertook (the divine being at least equally responsible for her situation), this should not lead us to think that she was therefore less likely to work at changing the social conditions under which she lived. Neither she nor Sana, for a variety of reasons, could pursue the project of reforming the oppressive situation they were forced to inhabit. The exercise of sabr did not hinder Nadia from embarking on a project of social reform any more than the practice of self-esteem enabled Sana to do so. One should not, therefore, draw unwarranted correlations between a secular orientation and the ability to transform conditions of social injustice. Further, it is important to point out that to analyse people's actions in terms of realized or frustrated attempts at social transformation is necessarily to reduce the heterogeneity of life to the rather flat narrative of succumbing to or resisting relations of domination. Just as our own lives do not fit neatly into such a paradigm, neither should we apply such a reduction to the lives of women like Nadia and Sana, or to movements of moral reform such as the one discussed here.

RECUPERATING THE FEMININE SUBJECT?

A significant body of literature in feminist theory argues that patriarchal ideologies—whether nationalist, religious, medical, or aesthetic in character—work by objectifying women's bodies and subjecting them to masculinist systems of representation, thereby negating and distorting women's own experience of their corporeality and subjectivity (Bordo 1995; Göle 1996; Mani 1998; Martin 1987). In this view, the virtue of al-haya' can be understood as yet another example of the subjection of women's bodies to masculinist or patriarchal valuations, images, and representational logic. A feminist strategy aimed at unsettling such a circumscription would try to expose al-haya' for its negative valuation of women, simultaneously bringing to the fore alternative representations and experiences of the feminine body that are denied, submerged, or repressed by its masculinist logic.

The analysis I have presented of the practice of al-haya' (and the practice of veiling) departs from this perspective. It is important to note that even though the concept of al-haya' embeds a masculinist understanding of gendered bodies, far more is at stake in the practice of al-haya' than this framework allows, as is evident from the conversation between Amal and her friend Nama. Crucial to their understanding of al-haya' as an embodied practice is an entire conceptualization of the role the body plays in the making of the self, one in which the outward behaviour of the body constitutes both the potentiality and the means through which interiority is realized. A feminist strategy that seeks to unsettle such a conceptualization cannot simply intervene in the system of representation that devalues the feminine body, but must also engage the very armature of attachments between outward behavioural forms and the sedimented subjectivity that al-haya' enacts. Representation is only one issue among many in the ethical relationship of the body to the self and others, and it does not by any means determine the form this relationship takes.

Finally, since much of the analytical labour of this article is directed at the specificity of terms internal to the practices of the mosque movement, I want to clarify that the force of these terms derives not from the motivations and intentions of the actors but from their inextricable entanglement within conflicting and overlapping historical formations. My project is therefore based on a double disavowal of the humanist subject. The first disavowal is evident in my exploration of certain notions of agency that cannot be reconciled with the project of recuperating the lost voices of those who are written out of 'hegemonic feminist narratives' to bring their humanism and strivings to light—precisely because to do so would be to underwrite all over again the narrative of the sovereign subject as the author of her voice and her story.

My project's second disavowal of the humanist subject is manifest in my refusal to recuperate the members of the mosque movement either as 'subaltern feminists' or as the 'fundamentalist Others' of feminism's progressive agenda. To do so, in my opinion, would be to reinscribe a familiar way of being human that a particular narrative of personhood and politics has made available to us, forcing the aporetic multiplicity of desires and aspirations to fit into this exhausted narrative mould. Instead, my ruminations on the practices of the women's mosque movement are aimed at unsettling key assumptions at the centre of liberal thought through which movements of this kind are often judged. Such judgements do not always simply entail the ipso facto rejection of these movements as antithetical to feminist agendas; they also at times seek to embrace such movements as forms of feminism, thus enfolding them into a liberal imaginary.[39]

* * *

In conclusion, I would like to clarify the implications of this analytical framework for how we think about politics, especially in the light of some of the questions posed to me when I have presented this chapter in public. In pushing at the limits of the analytical project of feminism, I am often asked: have I lost sight of its politically prescriptive project? Does attention to the ways in which moral agency and norms function within a particular imaginary entail the suspension of critique? What, I am asked, are the 'implicit politics' of this chapter?

I have argued that the liberatory goals of feminism should be rethought in light of the fact that the desire for freedom and liberation is historically situated and its motivational force cannot be assumed *a priori*, but needs to be reconsidered in light of other desires, historical projects, and capacities that inhere in a discursively and historically located subject. What follows from this, I would contend, is that in analysing the question

---

[39] On the former, see Moghissi (1999). On the latter, see Fernea (1998).

of politics we must begin with a set of fundamental questions about the conceptual relationship between the body, self, and moral agency as constituted within different ethical–moral traditions, and not hold any one model to be axiomatic as progressive-feminist scholarship often does. This is particularly germane to the movement I am discussing here insofar as it is organized around self-fashioning and ethical conduct (rather than the transformation of juridical and state institutions), an adequate understanding of which must necessarily address what in other contexts has been called the politics of the body—namely, the constitution of the body within structures of power.

For a scholar of Islam, none of these issues can be adequately addressed without encountering the essential tropes through which knowledge about the Muslim world has been organized, especially the trope of patriarchal violence and Islam's (mis)treatment of women. The veil, more than any other Islamic practice, has become the symbol and evidence of the violence Islam has inflicted on women. I have seldom presented my arguments in an academic setting, particularly my argument about the veil as a disciplinary practice that constitutes pious subjectivities, without facing a barrage of questions from people demanding to know why I have failed to condemn the patriarchal assumptions behind this practice and the suffering it engenders. I am often struck by my audience's lack of curiosity about what else the veil might perform in the world beyond its violation of women. These exhortations to condemnation are only one indication of how the veil and the commitments it embodies, not to mention other kinds of Islamic practices, have come to be understood through the prism of women's freedom and subjugation such that to ask a different set of questions about the practice is to lay oneself open to the charge of indifference to women's oppression. The force this coupling of the veil and women's freedom commands is equally manifest in those arguments that endorse or defend the veil on the grounds that it is a product of women's 'free choice' and evidence of their 'liberation' from the hegemony of Western cultural codes.

It was in the course of the encounter between my own objections to the form-of-life the piety movement embodies, and the textures of the lives of the women I worked with, that the political and the ethical converged for me again in a personal sense. As I conducted fieldwork with this movement, I came to recognize that a politically responsible scholarship entails not simply being faithful to the desires and aspirations of 'my informants' and urging my audience to 'understand and respect' the diversity of desires that characterizes our world today. Nor is it enough to reveal the assumptions of my own or my fellow scholars' biases and (in)tolerances. As someone who has come to believe, along with a number of other feminists, that the political project of feminism is not predetermined but needs to be continually negotiated within specific contexts, I have come to confront a number of questions: What do we mean when we as feminists say that gender equality is the central principle of our analysis and politics? How does my being enmeshed within the thick texture of my informants' lives affect my openness to this question? Are we willing to countenance the sometimes violent task of remaking sensibilities, life worlds, and attachments so that women like those I worked with may be taught to value the principle of freedom? Furthermore, does a commitment to the ideal of equality in our own lives endow us with the capacity to know that this ideal captures what is or should be fulfilling for everyone else? If it does not, as is surely the case, then I think we need to rethink, with far more humility than we are accustomed to, what feminist politics really means. (Here I want to be clear that my comments are not directed at 'Western feminists' alone, but also address 'Third World' feminists and all those who are located somewhere within this polarized terrain, since these questions implicate all of us given the liberatory impetus of the feminist tradition.)

As for whether my framework calls for the suspension of critique in regard to the patriarchal character of the mosque movement, my response is that I urge no such stance. But I do urge an expansion of a normative understanding of critique, one that is quite prevalent among many progressives and feminists (among whom I have often included myself). Criticism, in this view, is about successfully demolishing your opponent's position and exposing her argument's implausibility and its logical inconsistencies. This, I would submit, is a very limited and weak understanding of the notion of critique. Critique, I believe, is most powerful when it leaves open the possibility that we might also be remade in the process of engaging another's worldview, that we might come to learn things which we did not already know before we undertook the engagement. This requires that we occasionally turn the critical gaze upon ourselves, to leave open the possibility that we may be remade through an encounter.

The aforementioned questions I have posed about politics should not be seen as a call for the abandonment of struggle against what we consider to be unjust practices in the situated context of our own lives, or as advocating the pious lifestyles of the women I worked with. To do so would be only to mirror the teleological certainty that characterizes some of the versions of progressive-liberalism that I criticized earlier. Rather, I suggest that we leave open the possibility that our political and analytical certainties might be transformed in the process of exploring non-liberal movements of the kind I studied, that the lives of the women with whom I worked might have something to teach us beyond what we can learn from the circumscribed social scientific exercise of 'understanding and translating'. If there is a normative political position that underlies this chapter, it is to urge that we—my readers and I—must embark upon an inquiry in which we do not assume that the political positions we uphold will necessarily be vindicated or provide the ground for our theoretical analysis, but instead hold open the possibility that we may come to ask of politics a whole series of questions that seemed settled when we first embarked upon the inquiry in the first place.

REFERENCES

Abu-Lughod, Lila (1990), 'The Boundaries of Theory on the Arab World', in Hisham Sharabi (ed.), *Theory, Politics, and the Arab World: Critical Responses*. New York: Routledge, pp. 81–131.

—— (1998), 'The Marriage of Feminism and Islamism in Egypt: Selective Repudiation as a Dynamic of Postcolonial Cultural Politics', in L. Abu-Lughod (ed.), *Remaking Women: Feminism and Modernity in the Middle East*. Princeton: Princeton University Press, pp. 243–69.

Adams, Parveen and Jeff Minson (1978), 'The "Subject" of Feminism', *m/f*, 2: 43–61.

Afshar, Haleh (1998), *Islam and Feminisms: An Iranian Case-Study*. New York: St. Martin's Press.

Asad, Talal (1986), *The Idea of an Anthropology of Islam*. Washington, DC: Center for Contemporary Arab Studies, Georgetown University, Occasional Paper Series.

—— (2003), *Formation of the Secular: Christianity, Islam, Modernity*. Stanford, CA: Stanford University Press.

Ashmawi, Said Muhammed (1994a), 'al-Hijab laisa farida', *Ruz al-Yusuf*, 13 and 22 June.

—— (1994b), 'Fatwa al hijab ghair shar'iyya', *Ruz al-Yusuf*, 8 and 28 August.

Benhabib, Seyla (1992), *Situating the Self: Gender, Community, and Postmodernism in Contemporary Ethics*. New York: Routledge.

Boddy, Janice (1989), *Wombs and Alien Spirits: Women, Men, and the Zar Cult in Northern Sudan*. Madison: University of Wisconsin Press.

Bordo, Susan (1995), *Unbearable Weight: Feminism, Western Culture and the Body*. Berkeley: University of California Press.

Bourdieu, Pierre (1997), *Outline of a Theory of Practice* (translated by R. Nice). Cambridge: Cambridge University Press.

Brusco, Elizabeth (1995), *The Reformation of Machismo: Evangelical Conversion and Gender in Colombia*. Austin: University of Texas Press.

Butler, Judith (1993), *Bodies that Matter: On the Discursive Limits of 'Sex'*. New York: Routledge.

——(1997), *The Psychic Life of Power: Theories in Subjection*. Stanford, California: Stanford University Press.

Chakrabarty, Dipesh (2000), *Provincializing Europe: Postcolonial Thought and Historical Difference*. Princeton: Princeton University Press.

Chodorow, Nancy (1978), *The Reproduction of Mothering: Psychoanalysis and the Sociology of Gender*. Berkeley and Los Angeles: University of California Press.

Colebrook, Claire (1997), 'Feminism and Autonomy: The Crisis of the Self-Authoring Subject', *Body and Society*, 3(2): 21–41.

Davis, Susan (1983), *Patience and Power: Women's Lives in a Moroccan Village*. Cambridge: Schenkman.

Dwyer, Daisy (1978), *Images and Self Images: Male and Female in Morocco*. New York: Columbia University Press.

Early, Evelyn (1993), *Baladi Women of Cairo: Playing with an Egg and a Stone*. Boulder, CO: Lynn Rienner.

El Guindi, Fadwa (1981), 'Veiling Infitah with Muslim Ethic: Egypt's Contemporary Islamic Movement', *Social Problems*, 28(4): 465–85.

Farid, Ahmed (1990), *al-Bahr al-raiq*. Alexandria: Dér al-imdén.

Fernea, Elizabeth Warnock (1998), *In Search of Islamic Feminism: One Woman's Global Journey*. New York: Doubleday.

Friedman, Marilyn (2003), 'Autonomy and Social Relationships: Rethinking the Feminist Critique', in D.T. Meyers (ed.), *Feminists Rethink the Self*. Boulder, CO: Westview Press, pp. 40–61.

Gatens, Moira (1996), *Imaginary Bodies: Ethics, Power, and Corporeality*. London: Routledge.

al-Ghazali, Muhammed (1990), *Al-Janib al-Atifi min al-Islam*. Alexandria: Dar al-Dawa.

—— (1992), *Inner Dimensions of Islamic Worship* (translated by M. Holland). Leicester, UK: Islamic Foundation.

—— (1995), *On Disciplining the Soul and Breaking the Two Desires: The Revival of the Religious Sciences* (Ihya 'Ulum al-din), Books XXII and XXIII (translated by T.J. Winter). Cambridge, UK: Islamic Foundation.

al-Hayat (1997), 'Wazir al-auqaf al-masri lil-Hayat: muassasat al-Azhar tu'ayyid tanzim al khataba fi-al-masajid', 25 and 27 January.

Gilligan, Carol (1982), *In a Different Voice: Psychological Theory and Women's Development*. Cambridge, MA: Harvard University Press.

Göle, Nilüfer (1996), *The Forbidden Modern: Civilization and Veiling*. Ann Arbor: University of Michigan Press.

Grosz, Elizabeth (1994), *Volatile Bodies: Toward a Corporeal Feminism*. Bloomington: Indiana University Press.

Harstock, Nancy (1983), *Money, Sex, Power: Toward a Feminist Historical Materialism*. New York: Longman Press.

Hawwa, Said (1995), *al-Mustakhlas fi tazkiyyat al-anfus*. Cairo: Dar al-salam.

Hegland, Marty (1998), 'Flagellation and Fundamentalism: (Trans)forming Meaning, Identity, and Gender through Pakistani Women's Rituals of Mourning', *American Ethnologist*, 25(2): 240–66.

Hirschkind, Charles (2001), 'Civic Virtue and Religious Reason: An Islamic Counterrepublic', *Cultural Anthropology*, 16(1): 3–34.

—— (2006), *The Ethical Soundscape: Cassette Sermons and Islamic Counterpublics*. New York: Columbia University Press.

Hoffman-Ladd, Valerie (1987), 'Polemics on the Modesty and Segregation of Women in Contemporary Egypt', *International Journal of Middle East Studies*, 19: 23–50.

Hollywood, Amy (2004), 'Gender, Agency and the Divine in Religious Historiography', *The Journal of Religion*, 84(4): 514–28.

Joseph, Suad (ed.), (1999), *Intimate Selving in Arab Families: Gender, Self, and Identity*. Syracuse: Syracuse University Press.

Keane, Webb (1997), 'From Fetishism to Sincerity: On Agency, the Speaking Subject, and Their Historicity in the Context of Religious Conversion', *Comparative Studies in Society and History*, 39(4): 674–93.

Khaldun, Ibn (1958), *The Muqaddimah: An Introduction to History* (translated by F. Rosenthal). New York: Pantheon Books.

Lapidus, Ira (1984), 'Knowledge, Virtue, and Action: The Classical Muslim Conception of *Adab* and the Nature of Religious Fulfillment in Islam', in B.D. Metcalf (ed.), *Moral Conduct and Authority: The Place of Adab in South Asian Islam*. Berkeley and Los Angeles: University of California Press, pp. 38–61.

Leaman, O.N. (1999), *The Encyclopedia of Islam*, CD-ROM, version 1.0. Leiden: Brill.

MacKinnon, Catharine (1989), *Toward a Feminist Theory of the State*. Cambridge, MA: Harvard University Press.

MacLeod, Arlene Elowe (1991), *Accommodating Protest: Working Women, the New Veiling, and Change in Cairo*. New York: Columbia University Press.

Mahmood, Saba (2005), *The Politics of Piety: The Islamic Revival and the Feminist Subject*. Princeton, NJ: Princeton University Press.

Mani, Lata (1998), *Contentious Traditions: The Debate on Sati in Colonial India*. New Delhi: Oxford University Press.

Martin, Emily (1987), *The Woman in the Body: A Cultural Analysis of Reproduction*. Boston: Beacon Press.

McKeon, Richard (ed.) (1941), *The Basic Works of Aristotle*. New York: Random House.

Mill, John Stuart (1991), *On Liberty and Other Essays* (editd by J. Gray). New York: Oxford University Press.

Moghissi, Haideh (1999), *Feminism and Islamic Fundamentalism: The Limits of Postmodern Analysis*. London and New York: Zed Books.

Najmabadi, Afsaneh (1998), 'Feminism in an Islamic Republic: "Years of Hardship, Years of Growth"', in Y. Haddad and J. Esposito (eds), *Islam, Gender, and Social Change*. New York: Oxford University Press, pp. 59–84.

Nedelsky, Jennifer (1989), 'Reconceiving Autonomy: Sources, Thoughts and Possibilities', *Yale Journal of Law and Feminism*, 1(1): 7–36.

Qaradawi, Yusuf (1989), *Al-Sabr fil al-Quran*. Cairo: Maktabat Wahba.

Radwan, Zeinab Abdel (1982), *Zahirat al-hijab baina al-jami'at*. Cairo: al-Markaz al-qaumi lil-buhuth al-ijtima'iyya wa al-jinaiyya.

Rosaldo, Michelle (1982), 'The Things We Do with Words: Ilongot Speech Acts and Speech Act Theory in Philosophy', *Language in Society*, 11(2): 203–37.

Salvatore, Armando (1997), *Islam and the Political Discourse of Modernity*. UK: Ithaca Press.

Skovgaard-Peterson, Jakob (1997), *Defining Islam for the Egyptian State Muftis and Fatwas of the Dar al-Ifta*. Leiden: Brill.

Sherif, Mohammed Ahmed (1975), *Ghazali's Theory of Virtue*. Albany: State University of New York.

Stacey, Judith (1991), *Brave New Families: Stories of Domestic Upheaval in Late Twentieth Century America*. New York: Basic Books.

Starrett, Gregory (1998), *Putting Islam to Work: Education, Politics, and Religious Transformation in Egypt*. Berkeley: University of California Press.

Strathern, Marilyn (1988), *The Gender of the Gift: Problems with Women and Problems with Society in Melanesia*. Berkeley: University of California Press.

Tantawi, Muhammed Sayyid (1994), 'Bal al-hijab farida islamiyya', *Ruz al-Yusuf*, 27 June, p. 68.

Torab, Azam (1996), 'Piety as Gendered Agency: A Study of *Jalaseh* Ritual Discourse in an Urban Neighborhood in Iran', *Journal of the Royal Anthropological Institute*, 2(2): 253–2.

Wikan, Unni (1991), *Behind the Veil in Arabia: Women in Oman*. Chicago: University of Chicago Press.

Yanagisako, Sylvia and Jane Collier (eds) (1987), *Gender and Kinship: Essays Toward a Unified Analysis*. Stanford: Stanford University Press.

Young, Iris (1990), *Justice and the Politics of Difference*. Princeton, NJ: Princeton University Press.

Zuhur, Sherifa (1992), *Revealing Revealing: Islamist Gender Ideology in Contemporary Egypt*. Albany: State University of New York Press.

VII. MEDIA

Chapter 13

DHARMA AND DESIRE, FREEDOM AND DESTINY

Rescripting the Man–Woman Relationship in Popular Hindi Cinema*

PATRICIA UBEROI

PROLOGUE: ON A PERSONAL NOTE

THE BACKSTALLS OF SHIMLA'S old Regal cinema, nestled against the slope of Jakko Peak; the rhythmic roar of roller-skates on the wooden floor of the adjacent skating rink; cacophonous background music of no recognizable genealogy or vintage.

---

* This chapter originated in a presentation made under the title 'Phantasms of Desire' in the 'Indian Screen Event' held at the Australian Film, Television and Radio School, Sydney, 21–4 October 1994, accompanying the screening of Guru Dutt's *Sahib, Bibi aur Ghulam*. I am grateful to Kari Hanet, Maree Delofski, and Safina Uberoi, organizers of that event; to Uma Chakravarti and Urvashi Butalia who encouraged me to take up the challenge; to Laleen Jayamanne, Ravi Vasudevan, and Meenakshi Thapan who have commented on the chapter in its several versions; and to Aradhya Bhardwaj for her assistance throughout. Subsequently, it was published in Meenakshi Thapan (ed.), 1997, *Embodiment: Essays in Gender and Identity*. New Delhi: Oxford University Press, pp. 145–71.

Sahib, Bibi aur Ghulam (1962, producer Guru Dutt, director Abrar Alvi)[1] was one of the first 'real' Indian films I had ever seen. Of course, in my student days in Australia I had joined other *aficionados* of avant-garde and foreign cinema to watch Satyajit Ray's *Pather Panchali* (1955) and Merchant–Ivory's *The Householder* (1963). And, like my companions, I was under the impression that these were 'Indian' movies—that is, until I saw first *Sahib, Bibi aur Ghulam* and then *Brahmachari* (1968, director Bhappi Sonie) at the Regal. Where *Pather Panchali* had seemed exotic but somehow aesthetically familiar, the latter films (good examples of what would now be classed as 'middle' and 'popular commercial' cinema, respectively) were a completely new cinematic experience—cognitively and aesthetically.

There was one particular scene in *Sahib, Bibi aur Ghulam* that left a very deep impression on me—at the time, and in subsequent recall. It is the innocence and authenticity of that moment that I attempt to recapture in this chapter, against the grain of conventional anthropological good sense: 'Never trust first impressions.' The advice would seem particularly pertinent, considering how very little I had understood of the dialogue, sporadically translated, and how unprepared I was for the whole experience. 'Rather "Russian"', I remember remarking to my companions, in lieu of any more profound opinion.

Contemporary reception theories, however, have recently sought to revalorize the remembered fragments of viewers' experiences, suggesting that these condensed moments may disclose resistant readings of cinematic texts whose narrative structures tell quite different stories. Not unexpectedly, such studies are often the work of feminist critics who, rejecting both the misogynist concept of feminine masochism and the patronizing idea of 'false consciousness', seek to identify the sources of female viewers' pleasure within manifestly androcentric texts (for example, Mash 1995; Mazumdar *et al.* 1996).[2]

---

[1] After the failure of *Kaagaz ke Phool* (1959), Guru Dutt never again signed a film as director. Direction of *Sahib, Bibi aur Ghulam* was credited to his close friend and long-term lyricist and dialogue writer, Abrar Alvi, for whom it won the 1962 *Filmfare* award for direction. (*Sahib, Bibi aur Ghulam* also won the awards for best film, best actress [Meena Kumari], and best photography [V.K. Murthy]). Understandably, there has been some controversy over who is to be considered the 'real' director of the film, Guru Dutt or Abrar Alvi, especially considering Guru Dutt's depressed state of mind during the making of *Sahib, Bibi aur Ghulam*. See Kabir (1996: 120); also see Rajadhyaksha and Willemen (1995: 348).

[2] Cf. Kazmi's (1994) discussion of the problematics of the role of the female protagonist in Muslim 'socials'.

Though I can claim no such elevated rationale for my own selective recall of *Sahib, Bibi aur Ghulam*, I do believe that there is a purpose to be served in affirming the authenticity of that moment when I found myself confronted by a truly exotic aesthetic, and a completely unfamiliar body language. This moment (which I will revert to later on in this chapter) was the meeting of the film's chief female and male protagonists—Chhoti Bahu (Meena Kumari) and 'Bhoothnath'[3] (Guru Dutt). It was clearly a moment of *mystery*, for the film narrative unfolds in flashback from the memory of that scene: the echo of a woman's voice saying, ever so gently, 'Come, come here.' It was a moment of heightened eroticism, artfully anticipated in the preceding scenes. And it was a moment of transgression, as Bhoothnath enters the private space of the grand *haveli*, becomes party to its secrets and sorrows, and transgresses on the relationship of another man, of an 'other' class, with his wife. That this double transgression is the focus of attention and the site of desire is signalled by the film's polysemous title—*King, Queen, Knave/Jack*; *King, Queen, Slave*; or *Master, Mistress, Servant* (Rajadhyaksha and Willemen 1995: 348)—which privileges this particular love triangle over the two other three-cornered relationships that the film narrative also explores: (a) that of the husband, the wife, and the 'other woman', who is a courtesan; and (b) that of the man, the woman he is destined to marry, and the woman who is the object of his fascination. Indeed, when the film was first released, this transgression proved unacceptably explicit, and Guru Dutt felt obliged to replace the final scene, showing Chhoti Bahu resting her head on Bhoothnath's lap as they journey out of the haveli together, with an alternative sequence, less offensive to conservative audience sensibilities, and less morally and narratively open-ended (see Kabir 1996: 113–14).

Now, follow Bhoothnath's gaze as he hesitatingly enters Chhoti Bahu's chamber—the room which, as we have come to know, her husband never deigns to visit:

Black and white tiled floor.
A small mat is placed for him to sit on.
Across a floral carpet, the sight of a woman's painted and ornamented feet.
Three slow steps across the carpet, and the feet come to rest.
Her face, in close-up.

---

[3] 'Bhoothnath' (Bhutnath), an epithet of Shiva, the pet-name given by the child's aunt for the reason that he had been born on the night of the festival of Shivratri. I follow here the transliteration system of the Allied Chambers' *Transliterated Hindi: Hindi–English Dictionary* (1993), excepting those names and terms already familiar in different spellings in discourse on popular Indian cinema.

Her eyes and forehead.
Her lips, smiling.
Her seated figure, beautiful, bejewelled.[4]
Her seated figure in the wider setting of the bed-chamber.
Again, the seated figure.
She leans forward, as though to confide.

That the spectacle of a woman's feet should focus this intensity of mystery, of desire, and of transgression was the beginning of my awareness of the cultural 'otherness' of the body language of desire in *Sahib, Bibi aur Ghulam*. No doubt it was my own cultural otherness that had inscribed this podoerotic scene so unforgettably, but a reviewing of the film some 30 years later only affirms and re-inscribes that first intense impression. It suggests, moreover, that the podoerotic rendering of this encounter was merely an aspect of a more complex podosemiotics, an almost obsessive focus throughout this film on feet as the most condensed of corporeal signifiers. Here (a) as already remarked, women's feet (or feet and hands together) are presented as the erotic objects of the camera's/the male gaze, a look then returned with eyes of extraordinary expressiveness;[5] (b) male as well as female feet serve as the diacritical markers of different social roles, statuses, relationships, and professions; and (c) feet function as the highly condensed visual foci of dramatic moments in the unfolding of the cinematic narrative. Specifically, in the matrix of man–woman relationships that *Sahib, Bibi aur Ghulam* explores, feet present the very first objects of gaze, in one way or another: women's feet as objects of male desire, or male feet to index the man's social status and role-relationship vis-à-vis the woman observer, and the tensions and ambiguities inherent within their relationship. This podosemiotic rendering of first encounters throughout the film is surprisingly, almost inexplicably, consistent, and assumes special significance in the light of Guru Dutt's reputed concern,

---

[4] This is the same image that Bhoothnath's imagination superimposes on the skeletal remains of the body exhumed from the ruined haveli. The lastingly iconic quality of this image is affirmed by its evocation in a recent jewellery exhibition advertisement (Art Karat Gallery), featuring the former filmstar Rakhee (who, coincidentally, like Meena Kumari, also reportedly had an alcohol problem. *The Times of India* [1994]). By contrast, Chhoti Bahu's image of Bhoothnath, interspersed in the same sequence, is of a shy, artless, and endearingly childish young man.

[5] Looking is conceived very much as a two-way process in India, epitomized in the devotee's visual interaction with the deity (see Babb 1981 and Eck 1981: 5). As a filmmaker, Guru Dutt was extremely conscious of the communicative power of eyes in close-up shots; as an actor he was always worried that his own eyes lacked adequate expressive power (see Kabir 1996: 45, 71, 73).

as director, with the initial images of all dramatically important scenes and songs.[6]

The foregoing account of the impact of my first viewing of *Sahib, Bibi aur Ghulam*, of my sense of wonder that an erotic encounter should be rendered so powerfully in the concentration of a man's gaze on a woman's feet, suggests the contours of a distinctively South Asian corporeal aesthetic. It illustrates Marcel Mauss's (1934) observation that the human body, though universal, is very differently understood and deployed in different cultural settings. On the other hand, it might also be possible—though this would require a closer investigation of body language throughout Guru Dutt's corpus of films—to construe the podoerotic and podosemiotic focus of *Sahib, Bibi aur Ghulam* as an 'idiolect', expressing the filmmaker's personal vision/obsession.[7] Alternatively, one might point to the role of local and contextual factors—notably the notorious censorship policies of the Indian government and the self-censorship code of post-independence Indian film directors which, puritanically suppressing display of the kiss and scenes of explicit love-making, deflect the expression of sensuality into other modalities (Rangoonwalla 1979: 100–5).

But beyond the contingent, the personal, and the culturally particular, one may also acknowledge the several insights of Frazerian anthropologists, clinical psychologists, Freudian psychoanalysts, scholars of comparative religion and symbolism, sexologists, and self-confessed foot fetishists[8] who, in their different ways and from different vantages, have pointed to some universals of foot imagery. Such studies have demonstrated the consistency with which, across human cultures, (i) women's feet serve as the signifiers of the female genitals in particular, and female sexuality in general; (ii) the big toe serves as the signifier of the phallus (in fact, much better than that organ itself, for the toe is never flaccid) (Rossi 1977: 4); (iii) the kissing and caressing of feet is simultaneously an act of homage and of sexual pleasure;[9] (iv) styles of footwear convey psychosexual messages, as of sexual availability or repulsion; and (v) shoes and boots disclose,

---

[6] Comment on BBC Channel 4 programme, 'In Search of Guru Dutt' (1989).

[7] Available analyses of these films (as Kabir 1996 or Rajadhyaksha and Willemen 1995) do not indicate such an obsession, but on the other hand these critics have also not remarked on the podoerotic and podosemiotic focus of *Sahib, Bibi aur Ghulam*.

[8] See, for instance, the sources cited in Rossi (1977). I am grateful to Veena Das for reminding me of the Freudian reading of the big toe.

[9] Rossi (1977: 11) quotes Dr G. Aigremont, a German psychologist and author of *Foot and Shoe Symbolism and Eroticism* (1909) as follows: 'In India, in the art of love, there exists a toe kiss, which serves as an exceptionally strong and successful erotic arousal. The woman kisses the big toe of the man in order to arouse him to love.' This is one of the few references

apparently with great economy, various social roles and statuses.[10] The fact that podoeroticism is often categorized as 'abnormal' sexual response—the most common form of sexual 'fetishism' in a continuum from normal to abnormal sexuality—need not detain us further here.

THE BODY LANGUAGE OF POPULAR CINEMA

Though a number of critics and Guru Dutt's former colleagues have testified to the importance Guru Dutt attached to the expressive qualities of eyes (for example, Kabir 1996: 45, 71, 73), the podoerotics and podosemiotics of *Sahib, Bibi aur Ghulam* have not, so far as I know, been the subject of critical notice or comment. Thus, Kabir, for instance, identifies the scene in which Chhoti Bahu and Bhoothnath first meet as a pivotal one in the film narrative, but construes Bhoothnath's gaze at Chhoti Bahu's feet—as she herself does—as merely an indication of his extreme shyness in the presence of a woman: 'this is as high as Bhoothnath's eyes dare venture', she concludes (ibid.: 112), completely discounting the complex erotic overtones of the encounter.[11]

But whatever the interpretation of the camera's gaze in films such as *Sahib, Bibi aur Ghulam*, on one matter there is very widespread public agreement—that is, that the body language of popular Indian cinema has undergone enormous change over the last generation, particularly through the last few years. For the most part, this change is deplored, and attributed to the crude tastes of the lowest common denominator of the viewing public, to the concupiscence of unscrupulous directors and producers, and lately to the seditious influence of an alien 'cultural invasion'. Countless

---

to Indian podoculture in Rossi's book in which, not unexpectedly, his chapter on 'oriental podoerotomania' is dominated by Chinese examples.

[10] Rossi (1977: 69–70) refers to a number of psychological studies whereby respondents, shown only pictures of faces and shoes, succeeded with a high degree of accuracy in identifying the persons' occupations and personalities. Rossi concludes from this that: 'The shoe appears to be a particularly expressive item in the identification of roles and statuses.'

[11] Kabir's description of this scene is worth quoting in full:

The entire sequence of Chhoti Bahu's introduction is seen from Bhoothnath's perspective and because he is terrified of meeting her, his eyes are lowered: the camera takes Bhoothnath's angle of view and follows the patterns of a rich carpet on which he walks to enter the room. We hear Chhoti Bahu, still off screen, telling him to be seated. Then we see a pair of feet adorned by *alta* vermillion colour walk across the room; this is as high as Bhoothnath's eyes dare venture. He sits humbly on the floor and is asked his name. Finally when he does look up, the camera tracks in dramatically and holds on a close-up of Chhoti Bahu. Her intense and tragic aura startles Bhoothnath, and from that first look, he becomes her slave—her '*ghulam*' as referred to in the film's title (1996: 112–13).

articles and public statements condemn the body language of the song–dance items in popular cinema, particularly the simulated coitus that has now substituted the erstwhile innocence of 'running around trees', near-miss kisses, and ever-ruptured embraces. But even more than the display of aggressive masculinity, the explicit display of female sexuality, collapsing the long-established cinematic opposition of 'good girl'/vamp, wife/whore, has become the subject of widespread public outcry and indignation.[12] Of course, guardians of public morality have always warned of the corrupting influence of popular cinema—on women, on youth, and on the uneducated masses—but from today's vantage films like *Sahib, Bibi aur Ghulam* have now come to be viewed, with great nostalgia, as representing both superior histrionics and—linked to this—more controlled, less 'vulgar', body language. As some recent articles in the Indian 'men's' magazine, *Debonair*, opined, where Waheeda Rehman (the film's other female lead) could express great depths of passion simply through 'her large soft eyes', and where Meena Kumari 'could evoke deep personal grief merely by raising her eyebrows' (Khubchandani 1993: 44),[13] the heroines of today tend to express themselves almost entirely through 'their assets'; 'the bigger the better' (Gangadhar 1993: 22).[14]

There is no denying a major discontinuity between the idiom of smouldering eyes and that of heaving bosoms and gyrating bellies, between heroines counterposed against vamps and heroines who act (dance) like vamps. But before making facile judgements about the changing values of popular cinema, it might be as well to attend first to the underlying problematics that popular cinema addresses, albeit with the materials

---

[12] Swimming against the tide of popular and feminist indignation, a number of feminists have sought to reinterpret the role and character of the vamp, and to revalorize—positively rather than negatively—the recent collapsing of heroine and vamp roles (see, for example, Mazumdar *et al.* 1996).

[13] The burden of the article quoted here, a piece entitled 'Some Women are Forever', was that the most 'ethereal' Indian screen beauties, and the most memorable screen performances, have always been by 'women in love', typically, with 'the directors who created them'. Waheeda Rehman's outstanding performance in *Sahib, Bibi aur Ghulam* was seen as animated by her reputed affair with Guru Dutt. Meena Kumari's emergence as a 'tragedienne *par excellence*' through her performance in the same film was similarly seen as coloured by 'the pathos in her life' (presumably referring to the breakdown of her relationship with her husband, Kamal Amrohi, which dated from that time). Public reactions to this film, at the time of its release and in retrospect, illustrate the typical elision of on-screen and off-screen personas and events (see Vasudevan 1995: 103–6).

[14] This article was a spoof on the notorious song–dance item, 'Choli ke peechey kya hain?' from Subhash Ghai's *Khalnayak* (1993). Though ultimately banned in response to public outcry, this piece has been immensely popular nonetheless.

at hand and in the idiom and body language of the day. In this sense, recognizing the podosemiotic idiom of *Sahib, Bibi aur Ghulam* is not an end in itself, but merely an entry-point to interpretation of the film's message, a set of signposts to the quality of significant relationships and to critical moments in the unfolding of the film narrative.

THE PROBLEMATICS OF ROMANCE

What is the problematic that *Sahib, Bibi aur Ghulam* addresses? What is the film all about?

One answer to this question, very commonly suggested, is that *Sahib, Bibi aur Ghulam* is a story about the demise of a decadent feudal society which is subverted not only by its own inner corruption but by the emerging consciousness of the exploited classes, by the relocation of political power in the hands of the British colonial rulers, by the rising fortunes of the ruthless new commercial class that prospered under colonial patronage, and by movements of nationalist self-reform such as the Brahmo Samaj.[15] The set of male protagonists present these various alternatives. The zamindar and his younger brother (Rehman) represent the dissolution of the old feudal society; the rival zamindars, the equally corrupt and rapacious new moneyed class; the Brahmo factory owner, the idea of non-violent social reform towards the goal of national liberation; the nationalist revolutionary, violent opposition to foreign rule; the hero, the new India of the professional classes.[16]

The decline of feudalism is indeed the explicit backdrop of the film, whose story is told in flashback through the eyes of an engineer supervising the demolition of a ruined mansion. As an innocent and rustic young man, the engineer—Bhoothnath—had once been witness to the extravagant lifestyle of its owners, the Chowdhury family, and to the corruption that

---

[15] This is especially the interpretation of those familiar with Bimal Mitra's Bengali novel, *Sahib, Bibi, Golam* (1952), on which the film and its earlier Bengali stage and screen versions were based. (The novel was also, apparently, available in Hindi translation.) The film's scriptwriter and 'official' director, Abrar Alvi, has recently made the same comment on the BBC Channel 4 Movie Mahal programme, 'In Search of Guru Dutt' (1989). See also Rajadhyaksha and Willemen (1995: 348) and Kabir (1996: 115) for the comparison of *Sahib, Bibi aur Ghulam* with Satyajit Ray's *Jalsaghar* (1958).

[16] Similarly, Rajadhyaksha and Willemen (1995: 348) see the contrast of the past and the future exemplified in the contradictory attitudes of the two female figures: in Meena Kumari's impassioned plea to her husband not to leave her (that is, as in the song 'Na jao saiyan'), counter-pointed against Waheeda Rehman's 'robust and girlish presence'.

underlay its magnificent facade. The estate owners whiled away their time in the characteristically decadent pursuits of men of their class—in drinking and dalliance with courtesans, in celebrating with pomp and ceremony the wedding of a pet cat, and in competitive pigeon-flying[17]—equally oblivious of the sufferings of the peasantry they mercilessly exploited and their own growing indebtedness to moneylenders.

Confined within the zenana quarters, their womenfolk were unhappy and unfulfilled. The senior woman of the household, the zamindar brothers' pathetically deranged mother, was incessantly immersed in superstitious and purificatory rituals, while the elder brother's mean-mouthed wife (Bari Bahu) was preoccupied with the petty vanities that became her husband's status as the master of a great house. Forever disconsolate, the younger brother's beautiful and neglected wife, Chhoti Bahu, yearned for her husband's attention, and for someone to call her 'Mother'. But the young zamindar's desire lay elsewhere, with one of the city's most famous and beautiful courtesans. All actors in this drama of barren decadence seemed unaware that time was running out for them and for their self-destructive way of life, though the reminder was ever-present in the symbolic figure of a madman, obsessed with clockwork, who inhabited the liminal space between the public and the private quarters of the mansion. The process of self-destruction was ultimately completed with the brutal elimination of Chhoti Bahu by the elder zamindar's henchmen in their final act of loyal service to their master.

A second opinion has it that *Sahib, Bibi aur Ghulam* was a revolutionary film in so far as it allowed for the frank expression of a 'good' woman's sexual desire.[18] (Conventionally, in Hindi cinema, only the bad woman, the seductive 'vamp' figure, could openly and unashamedly call attention to her sexual needs.) The reference is to Chhoti Bahu's (ultimately unsuccessful) attempt to seduce her husband into staying away from the *kotha* (courtesans' house) by herself playing out the part of the courtesan. This observation comes somewhat closer to the line I will be pursuing here but, in valorizing Chhoti Bahu's transparent expression of sexual desire, it misses the crucial fact that her acknowledgment of desire was not emancipatory,

---

[17] Pigeon-flying was a favourite pastime of the Muslim nobility, as recalled with considerable nostalgia in both cinema and fiction (for instance, Ahmed Ali's *Twilight in Delhi*). In *Sahib, Bibi aur Ghulam*, the motif of pigeon-flying has rather the same function as an index of feudal indulgence as does chess-playing in Satyajit Ray's film, *Shatranj ke Khiladi* (1977). See also Kesavan (1994: especially pp. 251–3).

[18] For instance, comments by Shabana Azmi on Movie Mahal, BBC Channel 4 (1989); also Kabir (1996: 113).

but actually personally humiliating and deeply trans-gressive; conceivable only when she was intoxicated and rewarded, ultimately, with death. Thus, the good wife's display of desire is merely a voyeur's delight. In the end, deviance finds its just reward and the viewer is returned, through fantasized transgression, to endorsement of the normative moral order.

Both the interpretations cited earlier affirm the politically and socially 'progressive' features of *Sahib, Bibi aur Ghulam* against a more general theory of the development (or maldevelopement?) of commercial Indian cinema in counterpoint to Western cinema on the one hand, and to the emerging Indian art cinema on the other (see Vasudevan 1993). By the same token, however, they are perhaps more assessments of political correctness than insights into the problems that the film seeks to address, and to which it provides some fictionalized resolutions. To my mind, the story of the decline of the old feudal order in *Sahib, Bibi aur Ghulam* merely constitutes the backdrop for an elaboration through the cinematic narrative of the dynamics of the man–woman relationship and the limits of feminine desire for modern times and for the new nation (cf. Vasudevan 1995).[19] In other words, I see *Sahib, Bibi aur Ghulam* not so much as a treatise on feudalism but as a treatise on 'love'—love within marriage, love outside marriage, love as duty, love as passion, unconsummated love—set against the background of an emerging new society. The acknowledgment of feminine desire and the plotting of its limits is one aspect of this exploration—and undoubtedly a most important one (cf. Orsini n.d.: 1–2; Vasudevan 1995). But it is not the whole of it.

There are altogether four man–woman relationships explored in *Sahib, Bibi aur Ghulam*: (i) that of the Brahmo reformer's daughter, Jabba (Waheeda Rehman), and Bhoothnath (Guru Dutt), the chief male protagonist, from whose perspective the story unfolds; (ii) that of the younger zamindar, Chhote Sarkar (Rehman) and a courtesan; (iii) that of Chhoti Bahu (Meena Kumari) and her Chhote Sarkar; and (iv) that of Bhoothnath and Chhoti Bahu. Taken together, I will seek to demonstrate here, this matrix

---

[19] A similar case is argued by Orsini in her paper on the 'social romance' type of popular fiction of the 1920s and 1930s. She noted that in these social novels, 'the element of romance often came to overshadow the original aim [that is, of social critique for social reform]. Social critique became part of the plot, a voice, the cause of further *frisson* and of dramatic, extreme situations, while feelings of love and the vicissitudes of desire emerged as the crux of the narration' (1995: 34). Referring in particular to J.P. Srivastava's novel, *Dil ki ag urf diljale ki ah*, she comments that in this novel 'only a brief mention of [a social] issue is enough to recall the whole argument about it. The thrust of the novel is the multiple romance, the *mise en scene* of desire—meeting, romance, separation (penance) and fulfilment—hindered by family, class and social propriety, or by chance and destiny' (ibid.: 17).

of relationships presents the problematics of the man–woman relationship in terms of two dominant conceptual oppositions—of dharma (duty) and desire; and of freedom and destiny—transposed onto the world of the imaginary (cf. Jayamanne 1992: 150). And while the expressive idiom may have been transformed over the years since 1962, from feet and hands and eyes to bosoms and bellies and 'pelvic thrusts' (so-called), the problem of reconciling duty and desire, and freedom and destiny in the context of love and marriage remains a constant preoccupation of the romantic genre of popular Hindi cinema, as well as of other genres of popular (and possibly elite) culture (see, for example, Orsini 1995: especially pp. 11, 19; Singh and Uberoi 1994; Uberoi 1995a, 1995b).[20]

Before looking in greater detail at the four relationships presented and explored in the cinematic narrative of *Sahib, Bibi aur Ghulam*, it might be as well to try and identify, howsoever crudely at this point, the *sociological* referents of the conceptual oppositions that I have posited here as defining the problematics and dynamics of the man–woman relationship in popular cinema.

Dharma and Desire

The classical or normative Hindu understanding of conjugality enumerates the goals of marriage as: dharma ([*dharm*], duty), *praja* (progeny), and *rati* (pleasure)—in that order of importance.[21] Obviously, progeny are the outcome of sexual union, but carnality is not meant to be an independent

---

[20] Of course, such a sweeping characterization of the romantic mode across time and genre needs further substantiation, especially since 'romance' is not usually recognized as an independent genre of popular cinema. *Sahib, Bibi aur Ghulam* is conventionally identified as a 'melodrama', a genre in which Guru Dutt is said to have specialized, and/ or as a 'social' film. (See entries under these titles in Rajadhyaksha and Willemen 1995.) In view of its horrific and tragic elements, the film might even be classed as 'gothic', to use a category that is not conventionally deployed in the classification of types of popular Indian cinema. Writing on a similar problem in reference to genres of twentieth-century popular fiction, Orsini has coined the term 'social romance' to emphasize the consistent melding of social (reformist) and romantic themes in these novels which, as she notes, 'bear strong resemblances to the "social" of commercial Indian cinema' (1995: 1). Interestingly, and conversely, the romantic element is characteristically downplayed in 'serious fiction' (ibid.: 17–18).

[21] See Kapadia (1966: 167ff). These three goals equate roughly with three of the four Hindu aims of life—dharma, artha, and kama—these goals being opposed to the highest goal of spiritual liberation (*moksha*). Liberation implies withdrawal from productive and reproductive roles, and the elimination of desire. For a thought-provoking analysis of the conceptualization of women that each of these goals entails, see Allen (1982).

end in itself (except, possibly, in the Tantric tradition); nor is sexual passion considered a proper and lasting basis for marriage. On the contrary, it is felt that the conjugal relation should be governed by the notion of duty: the duty of a husband to provide adequately for his wife according to his means, and to impregnate her in her proper 'season'; and of a woman to make her body available for this purpose, and to serve her husband as her 'god' with loyalty and unquestioning devotion. That is, in this conceptual scheme, the 'love' of husband and wife is ideally conceived as one of affection and respect, protection and service, but not—essentially—of sexual passion.[22]

Though this is an ideal, enshrined in rules of etiquette that require husband and wife to avoid all public displays of intimacy, and in the overall cultural valorization of sexual continence (*brahmacarya*), it is widely recognized that sexuality is a very strong bonding force which has a logic and potentially threatening dynamics of its own (cf. Das 1976; Trawick 1990). Thus, while a wife's *fertility* is highly valued (and indeed necessary to establish her position in her husband's home and to consolidate her marriage), her *sexuality* is regarded as a dangerously bewitching force: a man over-infatuated with his wife is likely to forget his primary loyalty to his parents and siblings and, if provoked, to demand the division of the joint family. As sociologist M.S. Gore has put it in the typically dry language of his discipline, 'minimising the significance of the conjugal bond' is 'a functional requirement of the joint family, as a system' (1968: 34–5).

Anthropologists, too, have consistently recorded the duality and alternation of themes of auspiciousness and danger, as well as purity and impurity, in South Asian puberty and marriage rituals (as a well-known instance, see Yalman 1963), and related this to the ambiguousness of the feminine principle as expressed in the structure of the Hindu pantheon. That is, in the role structure of the pantheon, goddesses may be benign and auspicious, when paired with and controlled by a male deity (the 'spouse' goddesses); or independent and powerful, either protective or destructive as the situation may require, or downright malevolent unless properly appeased.

Psychologists have their own explanations for the salience of this split-feminine phenomenon in South Asian cultures: they identify it as the fantasized projection of the Indian male child's intense relation with his powerfully protective punishing mother (for example, Kakar 1978:

---

[22] This is a theme that I have explored at greater length in another paper (see Uberoi 1995b; also Singh and Uberoi 1994).

chapter 3; Nandy 1980). This in turn is construed as the outcome of the mother's unfulfilled longing for an emotionally satisfying relationship with her husband, beyond the constraints imposed by the joint family structure.

Be that as it may, the conceptual separation of functions of procreativity and sexuality found an institutionalized form in some of the traditional lifestyles of the aristocratic and wealthier classes of Indian society—for instance, in the leisure culture of the nobility of Awadh (see, for example, Oldenburg 1991; Rao 1996), or in the system referred to as temple dedication (for example, Marglin 1990; Srinivasan 1988). In either case, the 'other' women were independent professionals and property owners, highly cultivated in music and the arts. They were not only considered permanently auspicious, since technically they could not be widowed, but they conferred social prestige on the powerful men who successfully won and maintained them. As Bari Bahu reminded her younger sister-in-law in *Sahib, Bibi aur Ghulam*, she ought to have been proud, and not resentful, of the fact that her husband had both the material means and the potent masculinity to attract and retain the affections of the most sought-after of the city's courtesans.

As is well-known, the conceptual and institutionalized separation of roles of wife and courtesan came under challenge in the colonial period, when efforts were made to reform or refashion the ideal of Indian marriage after the Victorian model of monogamous companionability. This created a legitimate and widened space for the expression of romance and sexuality within—rather than outside of—the marital relation. However, since the joint family remained (or now was consciously advocated as) a cultural ideal, an immense tension was created between the ideal of conjugal intimacy and the renunciation of that intimacy in the wider interests of the solidarity of the joint family.

In the Hindi cinema, as often observed, the opposed dimensions of wifehood—procreativity and sexuality, love as duty and love as sexual passion—have typically been separated into distinct social roles and assigned to different social spaces.[23] The wife is loyal, dutiful, and fulfilled through motherhood, while the 'other' woman—the bad girl, 'vamp', prostitute, courtesan—is the repository of sterile sexuality. She must be narratively kept in her separate place lest she endanger the family and the social order. The wife belongs to the home; the other woman to space

---

[23] See Uberoi (1990: WS45) for a discussion of this opposition in the genre of calendar art, a genre historically closely linked with popular cinema.

outside the home—the street, the kotha, the nightclub floor (Kazmi 1994: especially pp. 237–8; Kesavan 1994: 253–5).

Though ideally the categorical opposition of wife and other woman should not be blurred, popular cinema constantly plays with the challenge of bringing about a seamless fusion of wifeliness and sexuality, dharma and desire. Needless to say, this is a very dangerous game, ever-pregnant with the possibility of disaster. Dharma may negate desire, or desire overwhelm dharma, leaving nothing but the 'vulgarity' that contemporary public discourse on the deportment of screen heroines so deplores. Indeed, it normally requires an extraordinary happenstance to make the inconceivable conceivable and to engineer the reconciliation of opposed social roles and their attendant moral values. This is surely the function of many of the convoluted plots of Hindi commercial cinema, that is, to mediate the tension between social duty and individual desire.[24]

Freedom and Destiny

As problematic as the reconciliation of dharma and desire is the resolution of the opposition of freedom and destiny in the process of mate-selection. Despite a century or more of the introduction of Western liberal values and the valorisation of modern individualism in other aspects of social life, marriages in India are still usually parentally arranged. Indeed, this is widely believed to be the safest and most appropriate method of mate-selection. Sexual experimentation before marriage is for the most part deeply disapproved (though differentially for boys and girls), while 'romance' is conceived not so much as a legitimate prelude to marriage as an aspect of the successful consolidation of the conjugal relation, that is, *after* the marriage has already taken place (see Singh and Uberoi 1994). So-called 'love' (that is, self-arranged) marriages are viewed with considerable suspicion,[25] no doubt justifiably so in the sense that (by definition) they undermine parental authority, threaten the basis of the social order of a caste society, rupture the chains of reciprocity that unite affines in relations of material/marital exchange and, in some understandings, also defy the forces of destiny that are believed to link two individuals uniquely through several successive lifetimes of partnership.

---

[24] Hansen (1992: 163, 169–70) has made a similar observation regarding the popular Nautanki theatre of north India.

[25] There is some evidence to suggest that self-arranged marriages are increasingly tolerated, so long as they are reasonably caste/class isogamous. In self-arranged marriages, dowry is usually not required.

However, if romance has only a dubious and limited role in the man–woman relationship in India before, or even after, marriage, it is fulsomely celebrated in myth and fantasy—for instance, in representation of the playful passion of Radha and Krishna (Kakar 1986), in the popular theatrical traditions (see, for example, Hansen 1992: especially chapters 6 and 7), and latterly in the mass media, especially stories, novels, popular music, and films. Nonetheless, even in the contemporary media there exists a marked tension between the value of free individual choice and social or cosmological necessity. Obviously, the best resolution—in celluloid as in real life—is that one should freely choose as a partner the sort of person whom elders, or a procedure of horoscopic matching, would have chosen for one: this is the subcontinental meaning of the phrase 'made for each other'. The plots of many popular films do exactly that, albeit with many devious twists and turns, and one cannot imagine a happier ending to a romantic quest. Alternatively, the aspect of sexual attraction that underlies romantic love and invests it with danger should be domesticated and transformed in the course of the film narrative into the idiom of dharma: of protection and self-sacrificing service. The exercise of unalloyed free choice, without these other mediations, is usually a prescription for doom—cognitive and commercial.

A PARADIGM OF DESIRE

As might be expected, the dynamics and problematics of the four man–woman relationships explored in the cinematic narrative of *Sahib, Bibi aur Ghulam* are made evident in the very first encounter of the respective protagonists. We take up each of these encounters, in turn here, focusing as a point of entry on the corporeal imagery of feet.

Jabba and Bhoothnath

Bhoothnath is the pet-name of a simple but educated young Brahmin man whose brother-in-law, the tutor in a great house, finds him a job as a clerk in a workshop owned by a wealthy and cultivated Brahmo social reformer, Suvinay Babu. The workshop produces a very special *sindur* (vermillion)[26] according to an old family formula, which claims for it the power to inspire

---

[26] The red powder used by married Hindu women to mark the hair parting, a symbol of the married state.

passion: conjugal passion, that is. Bhoothnath's first worry, on learning that his future employer is a Brahmo, is that he might incur impurity in eating the food his employer provides as part of his contract, but he is reassured that a Brahmin cook will prepare his meals specially for him.

Bhoothnath's initial encounter with his employer and his employer's sophisticated daughter, Jabba (played by Waheeda Rehman), is a disconcertingly embarrassing occasion, for his entrance is presaged by the loud squeaking of his brand new leather shoes[27] (the same squeaking also precedes his first meeting—alone—with Jabba). Jabba laughingly mocks him for his comic pet-name and his rustic awkwardness; and the scene ends with Bhoothnath standing apologetically and tongue-tied in front of her, clutching the offending shoes to his breast. Despite her mocking tones, however, it is clear that Jabba is instinctively, almost inexplicably, attracted to this gauche young man. He, for his part, is completely disconcerted by her unwomanly forwardness.

Gradually, to Bhoothnath's perplexity and embarrassment, Jabba begins to take over some of the personal functions that family members perform for each other: as he later complains in confidence to Chhoti Bahu (in the course of their very first meeting), Jabba treats him as though they have some sort of 'relationship' (*sambandh*) with each other. The corrupt Brahmin cook who had been purloining his rations is sacked, and Jabba herself begins to cook for him. (His high-caste scruples are apparently overcome now by either hunger or gratitude.) When he is accidentally injured in police firing in the bazaar following a bomb-throwing incident, she takes it on herself to nurse him. Significantly, too, she reveals herself as rather unreasonably suspicious and jealous of his undisguised adoration for Chhoti Bahu.

There are, however, some seemingly insurmountable obstacles to the recognition and declaration of their feelings for each other. The first is Bhoothnath's 'innocence'—his unwillingness to recognize and acknowledge the stirring of physical attraction when, in two memorable scenes, the two come into very close physical proximity to each other,[28]

---

[27] Bhoothnath, who has arrived at the great house barefoot, and in rustic attire, is now dressed out in the garb of a *babu*—*dhoti* and jacket, socks and garters, and shiny leather shoes. He is not only uncomfortable in this new attire, but in the Westernized ambience of a tea-party.

[28] Significantly, (a) in the domesticated space of the kitchen; and (b) by the sick-bed. It is actually Jabba, not Bhoothnath, who first acknowledges erotic arousal, in flashback, as she watches Bhoothnath leave to take up a new job after the closing of the Mohini Sindoor Factory.

and his failure to understand the many hints that Jabba drops, in prose and in verse. This tongue-tied innocence is complemented by Jabba's own transformation from a forward, 'modern'-type girl, to a demure woman who shyly hides her growing love and waits patiently for its recognition and consummation.[29]

The second is the considerable religious and class differences that make the rustic and orthodox Bhoothnath a misfit in the sophisticated and Westernized society of the Brahmo social reformers. The squeaking shoes index this social incompatibility with remarkable economy. As it turns out, however, the incompatibility is more apparent than real, for the two were actually already husband and wife, married in their childhood before Suvinay Babu's conversion to Brahmoism.[30] Thus, their mutual attraction was not transgressive under the circumstances, but an affirmation of their destiny with each other. They did, indeed, already have a 'relationship'.

Chhote Sarkar and the Courtesan

We first see the courtesan in the kotha as the reclining and intoxicated zamindar himself sees her—as a pair of peremptory but alluring feet, teasingly offered for his eager grasp as she sings of her intoxication with him. Dalliance with courtesans, as we are told in the course of the film, is both a recognized aspect of the lifestyle of men of Chhote Sarkar's class and a natural outlet for the 'hot-blooded' masculinity that a wife could not be expected to satisfy. But his infatuation with the dancing girl is, clearly, quite excessive and his neglect of his wife too complete, for he provides

---

[29] This change is signalled in the song that the formerly bold Jabba sings as Bhoothnath departs to take up his new job (see Note 28):

Meri bat rahi mere man men
Kuch kah na saki uljhan men

(What I wanted to say remained in my heart
In my confusion, I could not utter a word) (Kabir 1996: 118–19).

[30] In contemporary films also—for instance, *Hum Aapke Hain Kaun...!* or *Dilwale Dulhaniya Le Jayenge*—a romantic commitment marks the end of youthful playfulness and boisterousness, and the beginning of a new restraint, responsibility, and seriousness (see Uberoi 1995a).

In the film narrative, the opposition initially set up between the enlightened and modernizing Brahmo, Suvinay Babu, and the ritualistic and traditional Bhoothnath is also dissolved: Suvinay Babu's factory actually turns out a product—the love-inducing sindur—whose efficacy is shown to be illusory. Bhoothnath, on the other hand, in time becomes a professional engineer, Westernized in manner and lifestyle, and dressed in the costume appropriate to his profession—'safari suit', boots, and solar topi, blueprints in hand. This is how we see him in both the first and the closing scenes of the film.

her neither sexual satisfaction nor the satisfaction of motherhood. It is this double excess that indexes the moral corruption of this declining way of life: the system is no longer stable. Expectedly, despite her bold declaration of undying passion, the courtesan quickly switches her affections to a rival zamindar when Chhote Sarkar is persuaded to indulge himself at home with his wife. In the fight that ensues when the zamindar returns to the kotha, he is seriously injured. Bedridden and paralysed, he is ultimately potent neither for his wife nor for his mistress.

The zamindar's relationship with the courtesan is an elective one, based on both mutual sexual attraction and cultural compatibility. But it is asymmetrical, for the zamindar's excessive passion is not genuinely reciprocated. More to the point, it is neither endorsed by destiny nor transformed into a quasi-conjugal relation by appropriate acts of protection, devotion, and self-sacrifice. Under the circumstances, it could only have a tragic outcome.

Chhoti Bahu and Chhote Sarkar

Chhoti Bahu's relationship with her husband is expressed in two contradictory registers that merge dangerously as the narrative proceeds. The first is that of the dutiful and self-sacrificing Hindu wife, who worships her husband as god and seeks to please him in every possible way. The second, as already suggested, is that of a woman who so actively desires her husband's presence and love that she dangerously exceeds the proper limits of wifely devotion and seeks instead to become the sole object of her husband's sexual desire. Blinded by her frustration, she becomes involved in a socially transgressive (if sexually innocent) relationship with the young Bhoothnath.

Two scenes in particular give expression to the ideal image of wifely devotion. In the first of these, Chhoti Bahu is represented by a proxy, the loyal and sympathetic manservant, Bansi, who goes on her behalf to the zamindar's private chamber to dip his big toe into a cup of water. Without first ritually consuming this water, the young wife refuses to eat. In fact, for this reason she has remained hungry since the previous day as her husband, unmindful, was whiling away his time as usual at the kotha. Bansi tries first to achieve his goal by stealth, and then by pleading, and finally succeeds in distracting the still half-intoxicated zamindar with a glass of wine, awakening his recollections of the pleasures of the previous night. Chhote Sarkar is revealed as callously indifferent to this conventional gesture of wifely devotion.

The second scene is a climactic one. Rejected and taunted by her infuriated husband, angry that she had called him back from the kotha on a false excuse, Chhoti Bahu recklessly accepts his malicious challenge to provide him the sort of services (*seva*) that the courtesan provides—to drink with him and entertain him. Though their relationship is thus consummated, to the eerie echo of Chhoti Bahu's delirious and drunken laughter, Chhote Sarkar in due course feels suffocated by his wife's cloying devotion, dishonoured by her unwifely deportment, and unmanned by his new domestication. He decides to resume his old life and renew his old passion. Desperately, Chhoti Bahu tries to detain him with a song—the famous 'Na jao saiyan'—in which wifely devotion and sexual passion merge seductively:

Beloved, do not leave
the gentle embrace of my arms.
My eyes fill with tears.
I long for your embrace.
If you will not stay
What will become of me?
...
This cascade of hair
These *kohl*-darkened eyes
This glittering veil
The desire of my heart—
All this is for you alone.
Today I will not let you go.
I am devoted to you
I thirst for you
You are my love,
the light of my eyes.
I shall take the dust from beneath your feet
And powder my brow with it.
You who elude me
I implore you to heed me
I am all yours
I am at your feet.
Here I shall live, and
here I shall die.[31]

---

[31] Translation, BBC Channel 4, Movie Mahal, 1987. This is arguably the most famous scene in the film, both summarizing the tragically asymmetrical relationship of Chhoti Bahu and her husband, and demonstrating the considerable histrionic talents of the actress Meena Kumari. In fact, all the songs and song–dance sequences in this film are regarded in nostalgic recall as classics of their type. Guru Dutt was reputed to take unusual pains over the songs in his films, insisting that the songs advance the dramatic narrative (see Kabir 1996: 25–6; 54–5, 57), rather than being opportunistically inserted for mere entertainment

Predictably, she falls at his feet, but he is unrelenting. In the bitter exchange that follows, she defends her alcoholism as the great 'sacrifice' (*balidan*) that she has had to make for her husband's sake, but her protestations of innocence are subverted by the excess of desire that had motivated her and betrayed her wifely dharma. Resolutely, Chhote Sarkar slips on his shoes and walks out of the room, heading back to the kotha, where his erstwhile mistress has meanwhile found herself a new admirer.

Though Chhote Sarkar had initially found the idea of wifely sensuality transgressively exciting, he ultimately seeks to re-establish the proper separation of the wife/courtesan roles; too late, perhaps, for Chhoti Bahu (like the real-life Meena Kumari) has become an alcoholic. Finally, from his sick bed, he asks Chhoti Bahu to give up drinking. 'I began drinking for your sake; now I will give it up for you,' she answers, with rather unconvincing bravado.

Bhoothnath and Chhoti Bahu

The relationship of Bhoothnath and Chhoti Bahu, the last to be presented to the viewers, is one of intuitive understanding and barely sublimated eroticism.

Somewhat to his consternation, Bhoothnath is told by the manservant Bansi that Chhoti Bahu wishes to see him in her room, alone, at night. This is a most improper suggestion, but the innocent Bhoothnath—though nonplussed—does not read it as a sexual invitation, for he has already formed a poignant image of Chhoti Bahu as a sad and pining wife, forever awaiting her husband's return from the pleasures of the kotha. At the outset of their first encounter, like Lakshman in the presence of Sita, Bhoothnath's gaze is first focused on her feet. With trepidation he looks up—at her face, her eyes, her soft lips, her seated figure. This vision is iconic of the cinematic image of Meena Kumari, whose beautiful aspect both conceals and discloses a life of personal sorrow and tragedy.

Unlike the haughty Jabba, Chhoti Bahu speaks kindly to Bhoothnath. She does not mock his name: 'It's one of the many names of God,' she says. Instinctively, he feels that she understands him, and he blurts out to her his embarrassment over Jabba's familiar behaviour with him. The feeling of closeness is clearly reciprocated as Chhoti Bahu reveals to him the reason why she had called him and, despite herself, discloses something

---

value (the charge against most contemporary directors). 'Na jao saiyan' was one of the top 10 film songs of 1962.

of her sorrow and frustration. She asks Bhoothnath to bring her, very discreetly, a pot of the special love-inducing sindur that is manufactured in the Brahmo's factory where he works. Bhoothnath willingly does so, and is deeply dismayed when he later hears that it has failed to enchant the neglectful zamindar.

Chhoti Bahu next sends for Bhoothnath for a very different sort of errand, to procure wine for her so that she can be her husband's drinking companion/lover: 'If my husband asks me to drink, I must drink,' she says defiantly, overruling Bhoothnath's reluctance. In this scene, she is no longer sitting, adorned, smiling, in the light, but standing in the dark, face averted with shame.[32]

The physical effect of Chhoti Bahu's attempt to play the courtesan for her errant husband is apparent when Bhoothnath next visits to ask her to keep some money for him in safe-keeping. She is now reclining, draped carelessly over her bed. The words she had first used to him, kindly, are now uttered in slurred and seductive tones: 'Come, come here.' 'Are you afraid of me?' she asks, as he hesitates. Protesting her drunkenness, Bhoothnath momentarily takes on the disciplinary role of the proper husband: 'You can't drink in front of me,' he says angrily, forgetful of his station and his relationship to her. 'You can drink in front of your husband if you like.' Snatching the bottle away from her, he grabs hold of her arm. 'What, you laid hands on me,' she shouts in fury and collapses, as Bhoothnath retreats in dismay from her room.

It is only when her husband, from his sick-bed, finally requests her to stop drinking that Chhoti Bahu determines to make the effort.[33] Chhoti Bahu asks Bhoothnath to escort her to meet a famous *sadhu*—to pray for her husband's health, or perhaps for the strength to renounce liquor. Touching her head to her husband's feet in parting, Chhoti Bahu leaves the haveli in the company of Bhoothnath. This is yet another act of impropriety on her part, observed by the elder zamindar, who orders her execution. In the carriage, alone with Bhoothnath, she seems to have a premonition of her impending doom and asks him to see that, when she dies, her corpse

---

[32] This scene is almost repeated when he brings the wine flask to her: her face is invisible as her trembling hand takes delivery of the substance of her self-destruction. The scene of the delivery of the wine flask contrasts sharply with the scene earlier when she receives the pot of love-inducing sindur—with the reverence with which one receives *prasad*, or a sacred blessing.

[33] Reportedly, in the film as first released, Chhoti Bahu begs her husband to let her take one last sip of liquor. Guru Dutt deleted this scene in response to public disapproval, and instead had the paralysed zamindar repent of his ways, finally showing Chhoti Bahu the sort of respect and affection she had so desperately craved (Kabir 1996: 114).

is dressed in bridal attire and sindur put on her forehead so that everyone will know her for a virtuous wife. That her corpse is ultimately buried, secretly and ignominiously in the crumbling haveli suggests, perhaps, that her virtue was indeed in doubt, that she had suffered the punishment that was her due.

Chhoti Bahu and her husband were linked by destiny in sacramental marriage, and Chhoti Bahu protests the sanctity and eternity of this relation to the end. But her love was not reciprocated. On the other hand, between Chhoti Bahu and Bhoothnath there existed an instinctive and reciprocal understanding: 'You're the only one who understands me,' are her last words to him. They are in so many senses kindred spirits, instinctively attracted. But their circumstances do not allow the self-recognition of the transgressive and adulterous passion that the film's title iconicized and that ultimately provokes Chhoti Bahu's assassination. The problem was that both Bhoothnath and Chhoti Bahu were linked by destiny elsewhere.

HAPPY AND UNHAPPY ENDINGS

Across several genres of popular culture, 'endings'—happy or tragic—index right and wrong, true and false. Only one of the four man–woman relationships of *Sahib, Bibi aur Ghulam* ends happily, and this, surely, carries an important lesson for the viewer.

The attempt to reconcile the roles of wife and seductress, husband and lover, as articulated in the tragedy of Chhoti Bahu and her husband, Chhote Sarkar, is unsuccessful. Excess of passion in a relationship *outside* marriage, with the 'other' woman, and excess of passion, asymmetrically, *within* marriage, led equally to tragedy; to paralysis, death, and murder. When not endorsed by social sanction and cosmological destiny, relations of instinctive companionability and sexual attraction could lead nowhere, whether they were sexually fulfilled, as in that of the zamindar and the courtesan, or continent, as between Chhoti Bahu and Bhoothnath.

The only relationship that ended happily from the protagonists' point of view—that of Jabba and Bhoothnath—was one where the end was pre-empted in the beginning. They were already married, and their rediscovery of each other, despite the Brahmos' repudiation of the custom of child marriage, was almost foreordained. This was also a relation in which the slow growth of sexual attraction was firmly subordinated within the compass of normative conjugal proprieties. This is no doubt a near solution, but it is ultimately an unsatisfactory one. Almost a sad ending to a happy-ever-after story.[34] The reason is, quite clearly, that the romance of destiny has almost eclipsed the romance of individual freedom and desire, such as Bhoothnath did indeed have with his soulmate, Chhoti Bahu. For the more satisfactory resolution of this tension, one needs to look elsewhere—for instance, to the story of *Pakeezah* (1971, director Kamal Amrohi)[35]—which plays dangerously with the same elements—dharma and desire, freedom and destiny, and arrives at a less ambivalent resolution.

Perhaps Guru Dutt was too much a realist, or too sad a person, to have indulged such a fantasy. His marriage to Geeta Dutt (the playback singer, Geeta Roy) having broken up, his affair with Waheeda Rehman ended, depressed and drinking heavily, he committed suicide not long afterwards without completing another film.

REFERENCES

Allen, Michael (1982), 'The Hindu View of Women', in Michael Allen and S.N. Mukherjee (eds), *Women in India and Nepal*. Canberra: Australian National University, pp. 1–20.
Babb, Lawrence A. (1981), 'Glancing: Visual Interaction in Hinduism', *Journal of Anthropological Research*, 37(4): 47–64.
Das, Veena (1976), 'Masks and Faces: An Essay on Punjabi Kinship', *Contributions to Indian Sociology*, n.s., 10(1): 1–30.
Eck, Diana L. (1981), *Seeing the Divine Image in India*. Chambersburg, PA: Anima Books.
Gangadhar, V. (1993), 'The "Choli ke neeche" Syndrome', *Debonair*, September, 22–3.
Gore, M.S. (1968), *Urbanisation and Social Change*. Bombay: Popular Prakashan.
Hansen, Kathryn (1992), *Grounds for Play: The Nautanki Theatre of North India*. Delhi: Manohar Publishers and Distributors.
Jayamanne, Laleen (1992), 'Sri Lankan Family Melodrama: A Cinema of Primitive Attractions', *Screen*, 33(2): 145–53.
Kabir, Nasreen Munni (1996), *Guru Dutt: A Life in Cinema*. New Delhi: Oxford University Press.
Kakar, Sudhir (1978), *The Inner World: A Psycho-Analytic Study of Childhood and Society in India*. New Delhi: Oxford University Press.

---

[34] Possibly this ambiguity was the reason for the film's commercial lack of success, despite its starring both the leading female stars of the day, and despite Guru Dutt's formidable reputation as director following the commercial success of *Chaudhvin ka Chand* (1960).

[35] I hope to take this up in another paper. *Pakeezah*, which also stars Meena Kumari (it was released posthumously), is incidentally also a podoerotic/podosemiotic—indeed, if one might coin another such phrase, *podosadomasochistic*—text.

Kakar, Sudhir (1986), 'Erotic Fantasy: The Secret Passion of Radha and Krishna', in Veena Das (ed.), *The Word and the World*. New Delhi: Sage Publications, pp. 75–94.

Kapadia, K.M. (1966), *Marriage and Family in India*. Bombay: Oxford University Press.

Kazmi, Fareed (1994), 'Muslim Socials and the Female Protagonist: Seeing a Dominant Discourse at Work', in Zoya Hasan (ed.), *Forging Identities: Gender, Communities and the State*. New Delhi: Kali for Women, pp. 226–43.

Kesavan, Mukul (1994), 'Urdu, Awadh and the Tawaif: The Islamicate Roots of Hindi Cinema', in Zoya Hasan (ed.), *Forging Identities: Gender, Communities and the State*. New Delhi: Kali for Women, pp. 244–57.

Khubchandani, Lata (1993), 'Some Women are Forever', *Debonair*, September, pp. 43–4.

Marglin, F. Apffel (1990), 'Refining the Body: Transformative Emotions in Ritual Dance', in Owen M. Lynch (ed.), *Divine Passions: The Social Construction of Emotion in India*. New Delhi: Oxford University Press, pp. 213–36.

Mash, Melinda (1995), 'The Audience and the Public: Text, Context and Pretext in a Feminist Project', paper presented at the seminar on 'Images of Women in Media', International Institute for Asian Studies, Leiden, 6–8 November.

Mauss, Marcel (1979 [1934]), 'Body Techniques', in *Sociology and Psychology: Essays by Marcel Mauss* (translated by Ben Brewster). London: Routledge & Kegan Paul, pp. 95–123.

Mazumdar, Ranjani, Shikha Jhingan, and Shohini Ghosh (1996), 'Pleasurable Engagements: Bombay Cinema and the Female Spectator', paper and video screening at the Centre for the Study of Developing Societies, Delhi, 2 February.

Nandy, Ashis (1980), 'Woman versus Womanliness in India: An Essay in Cultural and Political Psychology', *At the Edge of Psychology: Essays in Politics and Culture*. New Delhi: Oxford University Press, pp. 32–46.

Oldenburg, Veena (1991), 'Lifestyle as Resistance: The Case of the Courtesans of Lucknow', in Douglas Haynes and Gyan Prakash (eds), *Contesting Power: Resistance and Everyday Social Relations in South Asia*. New Delhi: Oxford University Press.

Orsini, Francesca (1995), 'From Social Critique to Romance: The "Social" in Popular Hindi Fiction', paper presented at the seminar on 'The Consumption of Popular Culture in South Asia', School of Oriental and African Studies, London, 19–21 June.

Rajadhyaksha, Ashish and Paul Willemen (eds) (1995), *Encyclopaedia of Indian Cinema*. New Delhi: Oxford University Press.

Rangoonwalla, Firoze (1979), *A Pictorial History of Indian Cinema*. London: Hamlyn.

Rao, Vidya (1996), 'Wives, Tawaifs and Nayikas: Transcending the Boundaries of Identity', *The Indian Journal of Social Work*, 57(1): 39–67.

Rossi, William A. (1977), *The Sex Life of the Foot and Shoe*. London: Routledge & Kegan Paul.

Singh, Amita Tyagi and Patricia Uberoi (1994), 'Learning to "Adjust": Conjugal Relations in Indian Popular Fiction', *Indian Journal of Gender Studies*, 1(1): 93–120.

Srinivasan, Amrit (1988), 'Reform or Conformity: Temple Prostitution and the Community in the Madras Presidency', in Bina Agarwal (ed.), *Structures of Patriarchy*. New Delhi: Kali for Women, pp. 175–98.

The Times of India (1994), 'Rakhee with Other Gems', 20 December.

Trawick, Margaret (1990), The Ideology of Love in a Tamil Family', in Owen M. Lynch (ed.), *Divine Passions: The Social Construction of Emotion in India*. New Delhi: Oxford University Press, pp. 37–63.

Uberoi, Patricia (1990), 'Feminine Identity and National Ethos in Indian Calendar Art', *Economic and Political Weekly*, 25(17): WS 41–8.

―― (1995a), 'Imagining the Family: An Ethnography of Viewing "Hum Aapke Hain Kaun…!"', paper presented at the seminar on the consumption of popular culture in India, School of Oriental and African Studies, London, 19–21 June.

―― (1995b), 'A Suitable Romance? Trajectories of Courtship in Indian Popular Fiction', paper presented at the seminar on 'Images of Women in Media', International Institute for Asian Studies, Leiden, 6–8 November.

Vasudevan, Ravi (1993), 'Shifting Codes, Dissolving Identities: The Hindi Social Film of the 1950s as Popular Culture', *Journal of Arts and Ideas*, 22(3): 51–84.

―― (1995), '"You Cannot Live in Society—and Ignore It": Nationhood and Female Modernity in *Andaz*', *Contributions to Indian Sociology*, n.s., 29(1–2): 83–108.

Yalman, Nur (1963), 'On the Purity and Sexuality of Women in the Castes of Ceylon and Malabar', *Journal of the Royal Anthropological Institute*, 93(1): 25–58.

Chapter 14

FORBIDDEN LOVE AND PASSIONATE DENIALS
A Dialogue on Domesticities and Queer Intimacy

SHOHINI GHOSH

THIS CHAPTER EXPLORES ARTICULATIONS of queer intimacy and domesticities in the narratives of film and television at the turn of the twentieth century. At a historical moment when, in popular narratives, the family emerges as a site of cultural stability and commodity display, other articulations around social organization, sexual contact, and community lay claim to a different set of entitlements. In the decades contoured by transnational flows of global capital, commodities, and material and psychic desires, queer dissidence emerges to haunt the interstitial spaces between heteronormative institutions and sexual practices. The focus of the study is Bengali filmmaker Kaushik Ganguly's television film *Ushno Taar Jonno* (2002), which can be translated as both 'For the Sake of Warmth' and 'Warm for Her'. Locating the film within the larger discursive universe around debates on sexuality, the chapter traces the emergence of queer representations through a series of meditations on self-reflexive intertextuality and spectatorial (re)readings of earlier cinematic texts. It discusses emergent notions of intimacy, friendship, and 'family' through the first Bengali film to explicitly address same-sex love and desires.

THE CHANGING MEDIASCAPE AT THE TURN OF THE CENTURY

Film and television narratives of the late twentieth and early twenty-first centuries sit embedded within violent contradictions propelled by sharp inequalities of caste, class, communal tensions, and the simultaneous presence of global wealth and local poverty. The neo-liberal urban middle class is witness to increasing crime, corruption, and terror on the one hand, while on the other, enthralled by the myriad possibilities of desire and consumption. The most commonly accessed and visible navigation of these competing discourses happens in the popular visual media that are situated at the heart of India's spectacular culture industry.

The national developments at the start of the 1990s had far-reaching implications for media and communications in India. In 1991, the Government of India initiated a widespread restructuring of the economy with globalization as its main imperative. This was accompanied by an open-sky policy, thereby initiating and accelerating the growth of satellite television in India. The entry and popularity of satellite television facilitated a simultaneous and paradoxical response by audiences and policymakers. Enthusiastic and interactive dialogue ran concurrently with anxieties around the intrusion of Western values and the erosion of 'Indian Culture'. Due to its visibility and psychological presence, the anxieties around larger cultural transitions began to be articulated through media-centred debates. These two developments ran concurrently with the darkest phenomenon of the 1990s—the rise of the Hindu Right.

The Hindu Right intervened significantly in these debates by raising the nightmarish spectre of moral decay and the erosion of 'Indian cultural values'. After the release of Deepa Mehta's lesbian love story *Fire* (1999), Bharatiya Janata Party (BJP) ideologue K.R. Malkani wrote that the film was a threat to the 'very foundations of the institutions of marriage' and cautioned Indians against the 'death wish that has gripped millions of Americans' and 'all societies that go American' where 'non-marriages, teenage mothers and single parent "families" have become common.'[1]

As globalization initiatives swept the Indian mediascape, film and television narratives saw the emergence of the space of the family as a crucial site where the aspirations and apprehensions unleashed by the forces of globalization were negotiated.

---

[1] Article published in *The Times of India*, 22 November 1988, p. 15.

THE FAMILY RETURNS IN THE AGE OF GLOBALIZATION

The defining moment for family-centred narratives in the 1990s was Sooraj Barjatya's blockbuster film *Hum Aapke Hain Kaun...!* ('Who Am I of Yours?' 1994; hereafter *HAHK*). *HAHK* inaugurated the visual pleasures of elaborate spectacles even as they stood on virtually non-existent plots.[2] Replete with iconography popularized by the Hindu Right, *HAHK* evokes a conservative and renascent Hindu ambience and presents a dream family that negotiates its way through numerous social and religious rituals. The film was released in the violent aftermath precipitated by the demolition of the Babri Mosque. Released at the peak of moral panics around 'obscenity and vulgarity', *HAHK* was applauded as clean and wholesome entertainment. Although some reviewers initially dismissed it as nothing but a long 'wedding video', the film, described by its maker as 'a tribute to the Indian joint family', created box-office history in India.

HAHK is best described as a family carnivalesque. The origins of this film can be traced to an earlier film made by the same director, titled *Maine Pyar Kiya* ('I Have Fallen in Love', 1989), where the hero persuades the heroine to say 'I love you' through a medley of songs from popular films. This sequence becomes an embodiment of carnivalesque egalitarianism with hierarchies of social classes collapsing as cooks, domestic help, and other employees of the household participate in the revelry. *HAHK* is an extended version of this sequence. In the fragmented and dystopian early 1990s, *HAHK* proffered the utopic dream of a happy and supportive community.[3]

In the post–Babri Masjid moment of strife and turmoil accompanied by the rise of the Hindu Right, *HAHK* searches for 'communality' and solidarity within the recesses of the home and the family. Cinematically, the idea is reinforced by having the film shot indoors with very few outdoor locations. The happy and extended family of *HAHK* embraces even non-biological members like domestic workers, family friends (including a Muslim couple), and the pet dog. The portrait is completed by family gods who, when invoked, respond with suitable favours. Predictably, the hero's car sports the slogan: 'I love my family'.

---

[2] The British stage version effectively summed up the plot in its title, 'Two Weddings, Fourteen Songs and a Funeral'.

[3] For a fuller discussion, see 'Hum Aapke Hain Kaun...! Pluralizing Pleasures of Viewership', *Social Scientist*, March–April 2000, 28(3).

The success of *HAHK* was followed by box-office hits whose narratives revolved around the family. These included films like *Dilwale Dulhaniya Le Jayenge* ('The One with the Heart Wins the Bride', 1995; hereafter *DDLJ*), *Dil To Pagal Hai* ('The Heart is Crazy', 1997), *Kuch Kuch Hota Hai* (1998), *Dil Se* ('From the Heart', 1997), *Pardes* ('Foreign Land', 1997), and *Hum Dil De Chuke Sanam* ('Beloved, I've Given My Heart Away', 1999).

The films of urban romance make one significant departure from the past. The pre-1990s films valorized rebel lovers who resisted family opposition to either live or die together. The defining love story of the 1960s was the epic *Mughal-E-Azam* ('The Mughal Emperor', 1960), a story where Prince Salim goes to war against his father Akbar because the latter disapproves of his relationship with the palace dancer Anarkali. In the 1970s, *Bobby* (1973) created box-office history when two teenage lovers protested against parental opposition by running away and attempting to kill themselves, only to be rescued by their repentant fathers. The super hits of the 1980s were *Ek Duje Ke Liye* ('Made for Each Other', 1981), where the lovers killed themselves in protest against familial opposition, and *Love Story* (1981), where the rebel lovers run away to set up a dream house and, after battling parental authority, end up living happily. The defining love stories of the late 1980s, *Qayamat Se Qayamat Tak* ('Journeying through Eternity', 1988) and *Maine Pyar Kiya*, follow a similar trajectory. In the former, the lovers die fighting family authoritarianism, while in the latter they survive after rebelling against the family. In the 1990s, however, the idea of privileging romantic love over family duty and authority was transformed. Personal desires could no longer be extricated from the interests of the family. As Anupama Chopra (2004: 103) writes, 'In DDLJ, Raj's dissent is unique. He rebels by refusing to do so.'

In *DDLJ*'s significant predecessor *HAHK*, Nisha (Madhuri Dixit) agrees to marry her brother-in-law Rajesh (Mohnish Behl) when actually she is in love with his brother Prem (Salman Khan). Nisha is required to take her sister's place when the latter dies leaving behind a husband and baby. Nisha initially consents to the wedding by misunderstanding the situation to think that she is being married not to Rajesh but Prem. It is only the day before the wedding is to take place that she realizes that she is being married off to her sister's widowed husband. At this revelation, she faints in shock. On recovering, she contemplates clarifying the matter but proceeds no further after she watches Rajesh playing with his 'motherless' son. She then decides to sacrifice her love for the sake of the family. When she calls Prem on the phone, she is holding the baby. Unable to speak, they sing a song in which they valorize duty above love. At the end of the film, the dog (with the help from the family gods) pulls a trick whereby it is revealed that Prem and Nisha love each other. Rajesh selflessly hands Nisha over and all ends well as the two lovers are reunited.

The compulsory reconciliation of family approval and romantic love is also the theme of Aditya Chopra's blockbuster *DDLJ*. Despite the exhortations of Simran and his mother, Raj refuses to elope. He tells them that there is a 'right way' and a 'wrong way' of doing things and that running away together against her father's wishes would be the 'wrong path to take'. With the collapse of past certitudes around notions of loyalty, fidelity, and women's chastity, the 'arranged "love" marriage' becomes a way of accommodating both romantic love and familial responsibility. In *Kuch Kuch Hota Hai*, the widowed Shah Rukh Khan's romantic attraction to Kajol and second marriage could well cause audience anxieties around his devotion to his eight-year-old daughter and first wife. This anxiety is allayed by having the dead wife and little daughter, through elaborate plot twists, 'arrange' the second marriage. Similarly, in Sooraj Barjatya's film *Vivah* ('Marriage', 2007), a young couple, brought together by their families for an arranged marriage, discovers how seamlessly love, sexual attraction, and monogamous devotion can be reconciled through conventional marriage alliances.

At the turn of the twentieth century, the family emerges as a central protagonist in television soap operas. Market surveys, their unreliability notwithstanding, continue to indicate that the urban family serials rank among the most successful shows on television. Soaps like *Kasauti Zindagi Kay* ('The Challenges of Life', Star Plus), *Kyunki Saas Bhi Kabhi Bahu Thi* ('Because, Mother-in-Law was Once a Bride', Star Plus), *Kahani Ghar Ghar Ki* ('The Story of Every Home', Star Plus), *Mehendi Tere Naam Ki* ('Henna for Your Sake', Zee TV), *Ghar Ek Mandir* ('The Temple That Is Home', Sony Entertainment), *Ek Mahal Ho Sapnon Ka* ('A Palace of Dreams', Sony Entertainment), and *Kora Kagaz* ('Blank Paper', Star Plus) have enjoyed huge popular success.

At first glance, the family soaps would seem to gesture towards a certain cultural nostalgia for the undivided Hindu joint family and a fantasmatic communitarian universe. But as the loyal viewer soon discovers, the family space on television is less than utopic. On the contrary, and in contrast to the utopic denouements of its celluloid counterpart, television represents the space of the family and conjugality as deeply conflicted. Moving away from the thin screenplays of the family films, television serials ground their narratives on thick plots and complicated narratives. By representing the family and home as fraught with marital discord, multiple marriages, treachery, betrayal, domestic violence, sibling rivalry, property disputes, and oppressive hierarchies, television soaps present a dystopic universe where the imagined notion of 'Indian family values' lies defeated. In the deeply conflicted family space of the television narratives, romantic love, sexual attraction, and monogamous devotion can rarely be reconciled.

But what accounts for this return to the family? Why does it become important, for the fictional narratives at this historical juncture, to reaffirm the space of the family and conjugality? The staging of visual spectacles and the creation of dynamic spaces for mega-consumption are two unprecedented features of the post-liberalization decades. The occasion of the Hindu wedding with its attendant cultural practices allows for both a staging of the spectacular and the creation of a space for unembarrassed consumption and display of commodities.[4] While the worlds of lived experience and of representation do not 'reflect' each other in any simple way, it bears contemplation that the globalization decades also witnessed the emergence of a 50,000-crore wedding industry accompanied by a proliferation of unique and specialized service providers. As Mazumdar observes, 'Cinema mobilizes the fantasy of a lifestyle unblemished by chaos and poverty' (2007).

Jigna Desai has argued that, in the diasporic context, the Bollywood film wedding sutures the diaspora and the nation in a way that is both nostalgic and evocative of the idealized relationship between 'diaspora and the homeland nation-state' that is inevitably 'mapped onto heteronormativity' (Desai 2004: 217). Similarly, one could suggest that the spectacular Hindu wedding of Mumbai films is a site where contesting notions of local/global and tradition/modernity get negotiated. The wedding also allows for a construction of a temporary portmanteau landscape against which the spectacle of the Hindu joint family is staged. While shooting for her series on family photographs, photographer Dayanita Singh noted that the family photograph was a utopic fantasy because it was so hard to get the members in one place for that one photo session. The wedding spectacle could, therefore, be seen as a fantasmatic 'installation' that provides an occasion to stage and enact the idealized undivided family that otherwise is rapidly disintegrating into nuclear units. In a world riven by individual

---

[4] The mise-en-scene of the family soaps closely resembles Ranjani Mazumdar's description of *HAHK*'s 'panoramic interior' where 'hybrid architectural designs and techniques of an earlier era of films and the new aesthetics of global consumption coexist in peculiar harmony' (Mazumdar 2007: 123).

desires and personal gratification, the great wedding fantasy is a nostalgic evocation of a vanished way of life.

In an age of transnational capital flows, the global citizen's sense of belonging must be founded on material and emotional anchors. If the family is an emotional anchor, then global capital is another. The relationship between marriage, monogamy, and private property is too well known to bear repetition. The neo-liberal family is the individual's access to and inheritance of global capital. In the late twentieth century, where lifestyle, consumptive practices, and romantic love are inseparable, family wealth is the individual's access to wealth and social mobility.

THE QUEER HAUNTING AND NEW DOMESTICITIES

Globalization, with its attendant promise of travel, lifestyle, and magnificence, also sets in motion fears and uncertainties. Zygmunt Bauman suggests that while fear is arguably the most sinister of the many demons that haunt the open societies of our times, it is 'the insecurity of the present and uncertainty of the future that hatch and breed the most awesome and least bearable of our fears'. He writes, 'We seem no longer to be in control, whether singly, severally or collectively, of the affairs of our communities just as we are not in control of the affairs of the planet' (Bauman 2006: 128).

Patricia Uberoi (2006) has noted that despite changing lifestyles, the idea of romantic love and courtship continues to provide a great deal of public anxiety since women's sexual lives are no longer governed by family and matrimony. The public debates around issues of sex, sexuality, sex work, and sexual preferences, including litigations and public campaigns for the decriminalization of sex work and homosexuality, have assaulted conventional notions of heteronormative social arrangements. Television and (to a lesser extent) film narratives have dislocated sexual and erotic desire from the conventional locations of monogamy, marriage, and the family. I would like to suggest that one of the greatest anxieties of contemporary times is the fear of the queer triggered by the many assaults on heteronormativity. Take, for instance, television narratives at the turn of the century. Despite dislocating sexuality and erotic desire from the conventional locations of monogamy, marriage, and the family, the fraught relationships on television soaps have been determinedly heteronormative. The emergent queer space of television soaps and sitcoms of the mid-1990s was never developed fully in the following decade. So, while political assertions around queer sexuality are common in non-fiction programming (such as news, documentaries, talk shows, and interviews), queer desires in the realm of fiction seem to have met with premature closure.

In the mid-1990s television soaps and sitcoms had characters and situations whose cultural legibility as 'queer' could be indexed through allusion, inference, and connotation. For instance, one of the five protagonists of the hugely popular Zee TV serial *Hum Paanch* ('Five of Us') is the masculinized Kajal, who wears only men's clothing and passes as a boy. A local rowdy with underworld contacts, she is called Kajal*bhai* by her four sisters and the rest of the neighbourhood.[5] Kajal disdains all feminine preoccupations, including marriage, and dreams of running a mafia empire. In one futuristic episode, Kajalbhai's father dreams of celebrating his fiftieth wedding anniversary with his five daughters. While the rest of his daughters are married, Kajalbhai is single and a powerful underworld don. In another episode, a feminine male dance instructor falls in love with Kajalbhai. In another popular sitcom *Shriman Shrimati* ('Mr and Mrs'), Dilruba (Rakesh Bedi) is the excessively feminine house-husband of a popular actress. His marital status and failed attempts to woo the neighbour's wife notwithstanding, Dilruba carries all the subcultural markers of a feminine gay man.

Similarly, several soaps have located same-sex bonding in the slippery zone between friendship and eroticism. Serials such as *Adhikar* ('Rights'), *Mujhe Chand Chahiye* ('I Want the Moon'), *Kabhi Kabhi* ('Once in A While'), and *Hasratein* ('Desires') depicted female friendships of varying intensity. In *Mujhe Chand Chahiye*, a young girl falls in love with a woman teacher.[6] One of the longest running and most critically acclaimed serials, *Adhikar* revolves around the relationship between Shama, a Muslim woman, and Amita, a Hindu woman. Their male partners notwithstanding, the relationship between the two women remains pivotal. In one episode, a crisis is precipitated when Amita's boyfriend, Narendra, jealously accuses her of loving Shama more than she loves him. In another episode, an anguished Amita tells her father that she and Shama are one and inseparable. The women are not oblivious to their mutual attraction, as is evident from a sequence in the twenty-third episode. This sequence is located in Shama's marital home after Amita has provided eloquent

---

[5] The affix 'bhai' literally means brother and also refers to members of the underworld.
[6] The serial was based on a Hindi novel by the same name written by Surinder Verma and published by Radhakrishna Publishers in 1993.

testimony in a rape trial. Amita and Shama are seated on the bed gazing into each other's eyes. Amita raises her mouth and blows a kiss towards Shama who laughs in delight. The conversation is as follows:

Shama: You are unmatched. Only you could have said what you did in that crowded courtroom. When I look at you, I wonder—what am I? I am probably beautiful, my complexion is fair—what else do I have? But look at you—I so feel like kissing you.

Amita: Don't! You'll spoil me. Narendra has already kissed me.

Shama: What? You shameless woman...

Amita: Why shameless? If he doesn't kiss me on such an occasion...

Shama: What nonsense you can speak...

Amita: Even when I speak nonsense, I speak the truth. Really—if I were a man, I swear, I would have married you.

Shama [laughing]: Earlier, I only suspected it but now it's confirmed.

Amita: What?

Shama: That you are not a woman. There is nothing woman-like in you. There is a man inside you.

Amita [delighted]: Wah! How well you have spoken. That's precisely the point, my friend. You have described me absolutely right. Now, what prize should I give you? Should I kiss you?

[Leans over and kisses her on her lips]

Amita: I've kissed you.

Shama [delighted and laughing]: You've polluted me.

Amita: Pollution is part of our religion—not yours. You people drink from the same cup.

Shama: I don't want to drink from everyone's cup.

Amita: Not everyone—just two! [Holds up two fingers.]

Shama [amused]: Two?

Amita: Yes. First it was only me. [Your husband] arrived much later.

Shama [Amused, looks towards the door of the room to see if anyone has heard]: Idiot! You don't care about your reputation. At least, worry about mine. [She gets up and shuts the door. Returns and sits in front of Amita.] What if someone had heard?

Radical ideas have more frequently emerged first in the realm of independent films before making their way into mainstream cinema. Therefore, it was Riyad Wadia's experimental film *BomGay* (1996) that inaugurated queer-identified films in India. Starring the now-popular star Rahul Bose, *BomGay*, a highly stylized avant-garde film structured around six poems by R. Raj Rao, circulated widely in queer circles and international film festivals. Wadia's next film, *A Mermaid Called Aida* (1996), was a portrait of the well-known transsexual Aida Banaji.

The debate on queer sexuality exploded into public life with the release of Deepa Mehta's *Fire*, starring actresses Shabana Azmi and Nandita Das. *Fire* is about the relationship between two sisters-in-law in a middle class Delhi neighborhood who fall in love. The widely exhibited posters of the film allowed the two women to occupy the same visual space that had conventionally belonged to heterosexual lovers. Predictably, a furious public debate raged, with the Hindu Right and other moral police condemning homosexuality while others defending the human rights of queer people and the Freedom of speech and expression.

Fire is a significant film because it places queer sexuality at the centre of the narrative. Moreover, it allows a new interpretive strategy to come into play by explicitly crossing the line between female bonding and female homosexuality. Mundane homosocial activities like cooking together, hanging clothes to dry, oiling each other's hair, or a foot massage become invested with sexual and erotic energy. It can now no longer be assumed that things are what they *appear* to be.[7]

Today, public opinion around homosexuality is deeply fraught and the public is split between those who support the move to decrimininalize and those who do not. Contemporary popular film expresses this conflicted ambivalence. Apart from rare affirmative films like *My Brother Nikhil* (2005), *Rules: Pyar Ka Superhit Formula* ('Rules: The Superhit Formula for Love', 2003), and *Chameli* (2003), there is an inability to express the homoerotic without acknowledging the homophobic. *Kal Ho Na Ho* ('If Tomorrow Never Comes', 2003), for example, plays self-consciously on the overlaps of friendship and eroticism but maintains ambivalence on the issue by incorporating homophobia (albeit humorously) through a disapproving character called Kantaben. *Masti* ('Fun', 2004) deploys a similar strategy whereby two men camp it up for a homophobic sexologist. The ambivalence about whether the audiences are being invited to laugh at homophobia or homosexuality remains unresolved.

Conversely, homophobia becomes a vehicle for eroticism. In *Masti* one of the men ends up dating a beautiful woman who turns out be transsexual. The horrified hero jumps out of the building and escapes. In the next instant he's shown cleaning out his mouth with all manner of things, including a plumbing device. But the moment of discovery is preceded

---

[7] For a detailed discussion regarding the controversy on *Fire*, see Ghosh (2010).

by a prolonged romantic sequence between the couple, thereby making homophobia an alibi for queer desires. *Girlfriend* (2004) also frames its narrative with a simultaneous address to the phobic and the erotic. One of the protracted love-making sequences between the two women appears as the jealous boyfriend's phobic imagining. Predictably, the film managed to enrage both the Hindu Right and the queer community. *Dostana* ('Friendship', 2008) marks a significant shift by building the gag of 'misreading' into an integral plot element while decentering the key role played by the homophobe. It is no longer the on-screen homophobe who misreads (or reads) but the on-screen queers! The earlier preoccupation with simultaneously invoking the phobic and the erotic is displaced when the homophobic mother, who fails to exorcise the ghost of 'gayness' from her son, ends up accepting his imagined (or real) sexuality. The rapturous climax features the first kiss between male protagonists in any Bombay film. At the end of the film, it is likely that the spectators (like the on-screen protagonists) will be 'haunted' by the spectre of the kiss and a sneaking suspicion that things may well be what we fear they might be!

The emergence of new sexualities and a diversity of desires in cinema are clearly a response to many years of feminist and queer rights movements. As I have discussed earlier, mainstream films register an acknowledgement of queer sexualities while simultaneously expressing anxieties that attend that awareness. The horror and fascination with which queer sexualities are being regarded in contemporary culture allow for both radical ruptures and reactionary closures. The ambivalent discourses of popular films establish a tolerance for queer desires while eventually reaffirming the inevitability of heterosexuality. Consequently, it is hard to determine whether the texts could be read as phobic or erotic, reactionary or progressive. If these films establish anything with certainty it is a struggle to grapple with new gender identities and redefinitions in codes of gender.

Queer Intimacy and New Domesticities

Since Mumbai cinema is exposed to a vast public both within India and around the world, its representational world tends to have a larger, more visible, presence. Despite film and television narratives' occasional, but persistent, acknowledgement of queer desires and an attendant challenge to naturalized heterosexuality, the fear of the queer resolutely remains. To this, the Bengali regional television film *Ushno Taar Jonno* is a significant text. It makes visible queer desires and challenges heteronormativity through the remaking of notions of marriage, family, domesticity, and intimacy. The telecast of this film as part of a larger series titled 'Stories of Domesticity' is an indication of the magnitude of transformations unleashed by queer activism and the processes of globalization that have allowed for new articulations of desire and intimacy.

Directed by Bengali filmmaker Kaushik Ganguly and telecast on the regional television channel ETV Bangla, *Ushno Taar Jonno* (2002) has a running time of an hour-and-a-half. The title, with a subtle shift, reconciles two meanings. The title first appears as two words, *Ushnotar Jonno*, which literally means 'For the Sake of Warmth'. Then the first word splits into two words and now the three-word title reads *Ushno Taar Jonno*, which means 'Warm for Her' or less literally 'desirous of her'.[8] The twin reading has significant implications as the first meaning elevates desire before the person (the object of desire) while the second meaning puts the person before desire. The second meaning is reinforced at the end of the film. The film is structured around two parallel stories. The first story revolves around the relationship between documentary filmmaker Shumona (Rupa Ganguly) and her banker housemate and intimate friend, Brinda (Choorni Ganguly). The second story is one that Shumona is directing about a veteran female impersonator and plays out in the narrative as a film within a film.

Shumona and Brinda live in happy domesticity, sharing a house and a life together. When Shumona routinely works late into the night, Brinda's evenings are long and lonely. Their peaceful domesticity is ruptured when Shumona announces her decision to shoot her new film *Notir Kotha* ('The Tale of the Actress/the Words of the Actress') based on the life of Sharoda Ranjan Babu (Chapal Bhaduri), a retired female impersonator of the *Jatra*. The shooting involves long outdoor stints and, therefore, long separations for the women. Brinda, having used up all her leave nursing Shumona during an ailment, is unable to accompany the crew during shooting. Worse, Brinda dislikes Sanju, the camera person. In addition to being presumptuous and over-familiar, Brinda thinks he is a flirt who has a sexual interest in Shumona.

As the shooting draws near, the tensions between the women escalate. Brinda spends sleepless nights crying in bed while Shumona, affectionately but impatiently, asks her to stop fussing. One day, the women have a furious argument when Brinda asks Shumona to sack Sanju from the project. Shumona refuses and takes offence at Brinda's suggestion that

---

[8] In Bengali, the gender neutrality of the third person singular heightens the ambiguity around whether the object of desire is a man or a woman.

her relationship with Sanju is anything but professional. The argument escalates and ends with Brinda telling Shumona, 'It's over.' When Shumona leaves for location, the couple have already separated (chronologically this is revealed much later in the film).

The parallel story is *Notir Kotha*, the biographical film on the life of Sharoda Ranjan that Shumona is in the process of making. As the shooting begins, the life of Sharoda Ranjan starts unfolding in front of the camera. Sharoda had joined a Jatra troupe as an adolescent boy and assigned to play the roles of women. Master, the director of the play, falls in love with Sharoda, and initiates him into this new career. Despite protests from his manager Adhikari, the besotted Master insists that Sharoda play the role of the lead actress. Master renames her Sharoda *Shundari* (Sharoda, the beautiful) and proceeds to 'awaken the woman' in her through their love-making.[9]

The gradual unravelling of Sharoda's biographical narrative confronts Shumona with enormous questions about herself as she struggles with her sexual indeterminacy. She fondly recalls her childhood days as a tomboy. 'When I was young,' Shumona says, 'my cousin used to greet me with "hello, young man" and I really used to enjoy it.' Shumona talks about playing football with the boys and being scornful of hyper-feminized women. Ironically, it is Sanju, the object of Brinda's suspicion, who catalyses Shumona's self-realization. 'If you like only tomboyish women,' he asks on one occasion, 'why do you live with someone like Brinda who does not fit the description at all?' As the shooting comes to an end, Sanju, Shumona, and Sharoda sit and watch a group of Santhal women dance sensuously around the fire. Sanju remarks that while Shumona was gazing at the women, he was gazing at her when he saw her 'take her by her own hand and walk Shumon away from Shumona.' At this, Shumona breaks down and confesses that she never loved anyone as much as Brinda. 'I am drowning,' she says, 'the more I try to save Shumona, the more I drag out Shumon. The wretched Shumon.'

When the shooting ends, Shumona returns to Kolkata but not to Brinda. The epilogue of the film is structured through a series of alternating monologues between Brinda and Shumona. In a direct address to the audience, Brinda says she continued to stay in that house waiting for Shumona to return. After waiting for many long months, with nothing but Shumona's traces and memories for company, the loneliness becomes

---

[9] Here I deliberately switch to referring to Sharoda as 'she' because from this point on, Sharoda self-identifies as a woman.

unbearable. As she loses hope of Shumona ever returning, she accepts her friend Rahul's proposal of marriage. Shumona remains single and lives alone but is unable to bring herself to return to Brinda. At the end of the film, the two women remain within normative living arrangements, seemingly contented but deeply sad.

Ushno Taar Jonno displaces a linear story-telling structure by moving back and forth on temporal and chronological registers. The parallel stories unfold through sequences identified through different colour casts. The ongoing present is shot in colour while Brinda and Shumona's flashbacks unfold in black and white. Sharoda's flashbacks carry a sepiatone cast and are performed with a heightened degree of theatricality reminiscent of stage performances.

The Many Journeys of Desires

Ushno Taar Jonno is a story of many journeys. Perhaps for this reason, the sound of a moving train accompanies the appearance of the opening credits. All the protagonists undertake complex journeys into the labyrinthine world of erotic desires.

The idea of a new domesticity is inaugurated in the very first sequence of the film which opens at daybreak with a Tagore song playing over the soundtrack. Brinda, still in her nightdress, is preparing tea while humming the song that has now stopped playing over the track. She walks down to the bedroom and places the teapot on a tray that already has two cups. Someone is still sleeping on the bed with a pillow hiding the face. Brinda affectionately teases the person awake. The familiarity of this morning ritual, common to so many heteronormative narratives, is ruptured when the sleeping person wakes up in mock annoyance and playfully wrestles Brinda back to bed. A brief musical flourish accompanies the revelation of the 'partner' as a woman while acknowledging, possibly, actress Rupa Ganguly's star status. The playful discussion around the sharing of household responsibilities that follows is accompanied by a physical intimacy that is located precariously on the slippery slope of friendship and eroticism. The two women not only share a house but also share a bed.

Having established the intimacy of the couple, the opening sequence also hints at an impending crisis and the subsequent sequences develop the erotic tensions further. Brinda accuses Shumona of forgetting their 'anniversary', marking the day that they had first moved into the house, promising to celebrate its annual return. As the tensions aggravate over the shooting of *Notir Kotha*, it becomes clear that at the heart of the crisis lies Shumona's unspoken near-homophobic denial of the relationship. Her refusal to acknowledge the nature of their relationship prevents Brinda from speaking its name. During the argument that finally leads to the break up, Brinda exclaims: 'You are ... [stops abruptly and stares into Shumona's eyes, then rephrasing her sentence] ... you mean a lot to me.' Shumona understands the full implications of Brinda's declaration but can only respond with, 'I am not denying that...'

To this end, Shumona's journey is most significant. When, as a filmmaker, she bears witness to Sharoda Ranjan's testimonies, she begins to confront her own dreaded desires and anxieties. It is ironic that the extroverted and self-confidently masculine Shumona should struggle to accept her sexual attraction to another woman, while the introverted and feminine Brinda is fully reconciled to the relationship and its various implications. Early in the film, in a direct address to the audience (and perhaps to Shumona) Brinda says, 'I can't call you Shumona. I'll call you Shumon. Shumon?' This self-conscious transfer to a more masculine address ('Shumon' being the masculine counterpart to 'Shumona') recalls Sharoda's transformation from 'Ranjan' to 'Sundari'. In both stories that run parallel, masculinity and femininity are extricated from biological male and female bodies. This is shored up in an early sequence where Sanju, after meeting Brinda for the first time, asks flirtatiously whether she would like to act in films. Understandably put off by his presumption, Brinda ignores the question and asks him to send 'Shumon' into the kitchen. 'You mean Shumona,' says Sanju, a bit taken aback. Relishing his bafflement, Brinda replies, 'Shumona for you and Shumon for me.' Through this exchange, Brinda dismisses Sanju's heterosexist assumptions while invoking a heterosexual figuration alluding to a slippage between friendship and eroticism to someone who seems oblivious to the intimate homoerotics of the domestic space he has entered.

Ushno Taar Jonno is the first Bengali film to explicitly and affirmatively represent queer desires. To this end, it recalls perhaps its only significant predecessor, Purnendu Patrea's *Streer Patra* ('Letter from A Wife', 1976). Based on Tagore's short story by the same name, the film is about a married woman's resistance to the dictates of conventional society that culminates in her walking out of the marriage in search of a world bigger than her family. Mrinalini, the central protagonist and author of the wife's letter, is driven to confront the oppressive condition of her married life when Bindu, a younger woman, takes shelter in her house. Mrinalini mentors and nurtures this young woman who is treated with utmost cruelty by the rest of the household. At the end of the story, when Bindu is driven to suicide, Mrinalini decides never to return to her husband's home. In her last letter to her husband she writes:

> When Bindu lost her fear of me, she tied herself in yet another knot. She developed so a great a love for me that it made me afraid. I have never seen such an image of love in my household. I have read of such love in books but that was love between men and women. For a long time there had been no occasion for me to recall that I was beautiful. Now, after so many years, this ugly girl became obsessed with my beauty. It was as if her eyes could never have enough of gazing on my face. …On days that I braided my hair myself, she would be hurt and offended. She loved to handle the weight of my hair. I did not need to dress up unless we were invited out but Bindu would plague me to dress up everyday. The girl was infatuated with me (Tagore 2000).

In Patrea's film, homoeroticism is represented through a strategy of indirection and inscription that seems to rely on the audience's familiarity with the written text to infer suggestions of lesbian desire. In one sequence from the film, Mrinalini nurses an ailing Bindu as they lie in bed together. The moment is specially charged because Mrinalini has walked out of her husband's bedroom to join Bindu who has been banished by the family to sleep in a far corner of the house. After blowing out the night lamp, Mrinalini asks Bindu to turn and face her, inviting her to come into her arms as it were. As Bindu turns to face Mrinalini, the sequence fades to black. In an architecturally similar composition, *Ushno Taar Jonno* re-enacts this moment, as Brinda attends to an ailing Shumona at night, but provides a different closure. Here the embrace, as they lie in bed, is complete as Brinda kisses an ailing Shumona.

CROSSING GENDERS/CROSSING GENRES

The most significant trope in *Ushno Taar Jonno* lies in the casting of Chapal Bhaduri in the role of Sharoda Ranjan Babu. Chapal Bhaduri is a veteran female impersonator who spent a lifetime playing the roles of women and goddesses in Bengali folk theatre known as Jatra ('Journey'). It is said that Chapal Bhaduri (whose stage name was Chapal Rani) was so compelling as a female impersonator that even the Bengali matinee idol Uttam Kumar insisted on meeting this beautiful and talented woman after a particular performance. Later, he was taken aback when he realized that Chapal Bhaduri was a man. This incident could well be exaggerated or even imagined but nevertheless points to the kind of reputation that Chapal Rani enjoyed as a performer on the Jatra stage.

Chapal Bhaduri was introduced to a more contemporary audience through the circulation of the documentary titled *Performing the Goddess* by Naveen Kishore. Kishore's documentary is primarily a long interview with Chapal Bhaduri. In this documentary the filmmaker is almost entirely absent. The mise-en-scene is largely empty and Chapal Bhaduri addresses the camera directly. The opening sequence is a stylized montage of the female impersonator doing his make-up as he transforms himself into a stage goddess. The only visual interludes are more *verite* shots of Jatra performances or enactment by Chapal Bhaduri. An intermittent visual leitmotif is the ritual of wearing the make-up where Chapal Bhaduri transforms into Chapal Rani and subsequently the character that he portrays.

The notion is that the documentary by virtue of its form privileges 'reality' and 'authenticity' over fictional forms has been persuasively displaced by film and cultural studies. In his celebrated statement against the truth-telling claims of cinema verite, documentary filmmaker Errol Morris had said, 'Truth is not guaranteed by style or expression. It is not guaranteed by anything' (*Cineaste* 1989: 17). Similarly, Michael Renov points out that while the documentary may or may not take recourse to fiction, it is *fictive* in that it uses all the cinematic and rhetorical tropes and devices of the fiction film. Both fiction and non-fiction are concerned with semiotics, narrativity, and questions of performance, and therefore share key conceptual characteristics. But what is it that fundamentally distinguishes the documentary from a work of fiction? While the answer is no longer simple, I will invoke for the purposes of this chapter Renov's idea that what distinguishes the documentary form from its fictional counterpart is 'the differing historical status of the referent' (1993: 2). Therefore, it is the actual presence of Chapal Bhaduri in *Performing the Goddess* that constitutes valuable visible evidence. A documentary bears witness and is able to construct a testimony. Through the ostensible effacing of fictive tropes, *Performing the Goddess* becomes even more of an act of bearing witness and recording testimony. The intertextual dialogue, therefore, between *Performing the Goddess* and *Ushno Taar Jonno* invests the latter with an additional register of meaning.

Ushno Taar Jonno greatly complicates the connections between performance and gender. Where precisely is gender being performed? Is Shumona playing Shumon? Or Shumon playing Shumona? Conversely, is Sharoda Ranjan performing Sharoda Shundori, or is it the converse? The film delivers no easy answers but presents an endless relay of possibilities. Sharoda and Shumona have a crucial exchange. 'Do you know why Master called me Sharoda Shundori?', asks Sharoda and then explains, 'Because he wanted to awaken the woman in me.' 'So what happens to the person who was born as a man?', asks Shumona. 'Whatever happened, happened only to him,' says Sharoda and using the metaphor of the flower and the leaf, he says that the two cannot be separated.

In one flashback sequence, Sharoda's distressed young wife asks, 'Tell me what are you? What kind of a man are you?' Sharoda says that the woman and man in him are inseparable. 'What about Master? Is he also like you?', she asks. Sharoda tells her that Master is different from him. He explains that the Master who visits women is also a man while the Master who comes to Sharoda is also a man. 'Then you two are the same...', exclaims the wife. 'No, we are not,' says Shaorda absentmindedly, 'you won't understand these things.' During the shoot, Sharoda tells Shumona, 'If you have been called a woman all your life and then suddenly one day you are addressed as a man, how can you respond?' 'Did he never tire of playing women characters,' asks Shumona. 'How could I?', asks Sharoda, 'I became a woman...playing the roles of *Behula*, *Chintamani*, and *Draupadi*...'

In *Ushno Taar Jonno* Sharoda describes his 'becoming' a woman as being sculpted through his sexual relationship with Master and his performances of femininity until gradually the lines blur red. Referring to his childhood, Sharoda describes himself as an extroverted boy who joined the Jatra Company. However, the 'boy' who appears visually in the flashback sequences bears no resemblance to his self-description. The flute-playing young boy is feminine and gentle—almost childlike—and speaks with feminized inflections. The disjuncture between Sharoda's verbal self-description and the visual representation of that description, through its dissonance, tells a complex story. An intertextual reference to *Performing the Goddess* could further complicate our reading. In the documentary, Chapal Bhaduri talks of taking a lover, who partners him for 30 years, at the age of 18, much before he joined the Jatra. Later, in his conversations with women, he discovers that the pleasures of sexual intercourse that he felt were identical to those felt by women. Moreover, he says, his body experienced the changes brought on by the onset of menstruation in women. Every month he felt indisposed for sometime followed by period of restlessness and heightened sexual arousal.

Ushno Taar Jonno successfully extricates maleness and femaleness from male and female bodies. But does it suggest that maleness and femalenesses are the only two ways to be? The labyrinthine journey of desire, performance, and identity that the various characters—Sharoda, Master, Adhikari, Shumona, Brinda, and even Sanju—inhabit in the film would suggest otherwise. If Sharoda desires only to be a woman, Master desires to be a man and also desires a man. If Shumona loses Brinda to a heteronormative man, then the latter makes it clear that she only chose one because the woman she loved refused to recognize their love. The revelation through the course of the story that Sharoda's long-time partner is actually Adhikari (manager of Master's Jatra troupe and father of the woman who Sharoda had married) further complicates the many registers of sexual desires. The film's acknowledgement of the complexities of the many journeys of desires is articulated during a light-hearted exchange between Sanju and Sharoda:

Sanju [to Sharoda]: Can I ask you a very personal question? It has nothing to do with the film.

Sharoda: Yes…

Sanju: When you wear false breasts…they are artificial…cosmetic…I mean actually you don't have anything there…does it disturb you?

Sharoda: Rascal! [pauses]…not you…but God. He's very bad. He could give me everything but not the body? [Then in a more flippant mood] …but you have both long hair and beard. Now you should decide to sport either one or the other. You can't go around wearing both.'

Sanju [laughing heartily]: Rabindranath Tagore would have been very angry with what you just said.

The film's creation of a polyvalency of desire assaults the simple binaries of hetero and homo, thereby queering the terrain of desires. Butler has observed that the term 'queer' gained currency precisely to address such moments of productive undecidability (Butler 1993).

* * *

The narrative of *Ushno Taar Jonno* is significantly complicated by the deployment of fictive tropes that recall the documentary film's ability to bear witness while at the same time recreating and visibilizing what had remained invisible in *Performing the Goddess*. The film within the film recalls *Performing the Goddess* while, at the same time, transforming it. In *Notir Katha*, the story of Sharoda unravels through interviews and reconstructed flashbacks, thereby deploying the narrative tropes of both documentary and fiction. How closely Sharoda's story approximates Chapal Bhaduri's biographical details may never be resolved but the reconstructed flashbacks invite at least two interpretations. First, the reconstructions could be seen as Shumona's visualizing of Sharoda's life. Second, one could suggest that *Ushno Taar Jonno* reads into the silences of *Performing the Goddess*. It is not my intention here to argue in favour of 'authorial intention' but to suggest that intertextual reading possibilities, along with cinematic speculation, may help uncover the deep stories of subaltern sexualities. In which case, *Ushno Taar Jonno* is not only in dialogue with *Performing the Goddess* but a reworking of it. If *Performing the Goddess* presents Chapal Bhaduri, the 'differing historical status of the referent' in Renov's words (1993: 2), then *Ushno Taar Jonno* animates the possible absences in his testimony through the deployment of fantasmatic 'confabulation'. Vivian Sobchack's observations about the writing of history hold true for the making of biographies. She writes, 'History has lost its stability as the grounded site upon which knowledge of the past is accumulated, coherently ordered, legitimated; rather it has become an unstable site in which fragments of past representations do not necessarily add up or cohere but, are instead subject to "undisciplined" (and often "undisciplining") contestation and use' (Sobchack 2000: 301). Therefore, the historian, biographer, and filmmaker are left with fragments not of an authentic past, but with an already represented, irrecoverable past. Sobchack suggests that in such a situation we need to mobilize new hermeneutic strategies with which to fabricate and confabulate the stories and meanings of 'historical ruins'. (Here, Sobchack draws our attention to the psychological definition of the word 'confabulate' as precisely the invention of imaginary experiences to fill gaps in our memory.) In such an exercise, it is not the story that is told that is subject to greater complication but the telling itself.

The story of Chapal Bhaduri has found another layering with the 'remake' of *Ushno Taar Jonno* as *Arekti Premer Golpo* ('Just Another Love Story', 2011). The story once again revolves around a documentary being made on the life of Chapal Bhaduri but this time, the two lovers are men. Abhiroop (Rituparno Ghosh) is the gender non-normative director of the film while Basu (Indraneel), the cameraperson, is his lover. Both men also play the role of the younger Chapal Bhaduri and his male lover. Abhiroop's non-normative clothing and appearance cause much confusion as the unit members do not know whether to address him as 'madam' or 'sir'. The film makes several significant departures from *Ushno Taar Jonno*. It moves homophobia from residing within protagonists into the larger social world. The moral dilemma of the lovers is not about their sexual preference but about issues of non-monogamy and social recognition. The film also assaults directly the homophobia of the Bengali middle class. The casting of the openly queer filmmaker Rituparno Ghosh allows the film to enter a more contemporary register of meaning as the talented filmmaker is an object of both public admiration and homophobic insinuations. The film sparked a major public debate in West Bengal while it ran to packed houses. The spectacular success of *Arekti Premer Golpo* (which deserves an essay of its own) is likely to turn *Ushno Taar Jonno* into a lesser known subaltern text.

It is my suggestion, therefore, that the thicker accounts of subaltern sexual desires are likely to emerge not through definitive versions, but through the exploration of interstitial spaces between multiple texts, many readings, and a diversity of narrative tropes. At the very end, I would like to return to the question of *Ushno Taar Jonno*'s politics of representation around new domesticities. Despite articulating the promise of new domesticity and queer intimacy, the story of Brinda and Shumona does not end happily. Many self-identified queer and straight members of the film's audience continue to voice the disappointment that the filmmaker did not take the brave step forward of ending the film with the happy union of the two women. Instead, he chose to keep them separate and unhappy while one of them finally opted for a heterosexual marriage. So here is the conundrum. Does the film perpetuate the commonplace idea that domesticities based on non-normative sexualities are doomed to fail? Or does it merely illustrate the difficulties creating queer family spaces in a heteronormative society? If the urban romance films offer utopian optimism around sustaining versions of intimacy, however aspirational, by reconciling marriage and romantic love, then does *Ushno Taar Jonno*'s failure to manoeuvre such a meld lead to a dystopian denouement? Before, addressing the questions I have raised, I would like to recall Ellis Hansen's observation that 'every film with a queer theme, no matter what the sexuality of the director or the origin of its funding, is still embattled in a highly moralistic debate over the correctness of its politics, as though art were to be valued as only sexual propaganda'. Taking Hansen's cue, I will suggest that *Ushno Taar Jonno*'s complex sexual politics are embedded within a larger discussion of romantic practices, fantasies, institutions, and ideologies, which cannot be reduced to the political stance that the exigencies of the plots would suggest.

"'I didn't think it would turn out this way" is the secret epitaph of intimacy,' writes Lauren Berlant (2000: 1). The film ends with an epilogue that addresses the 'unhappy ending' through a return to the documentary convention of direct address, recalling the narrative strategy of *Performing the Goddess*. Shumona and Brinda's alternating testimony, delivered in direct address to the audience, brings a closure to their love story. Explaining her decision to marry her friend Rahul, Brinda says, 'It was Shumon who got me unused to being alone...why did she have to tie us down to convention? I never wanted it.' Brinda draws attention to what Butler has called 'the significant suffering and disenfranchisement 'that are the psychic, cultural and material consequences of 'living without norms of recognition'. Reflecting, as it were, on Shumona's description of her as 'happily married', Brinda says it is not important whether or not one is happy but 'what is important is how, why and with whom one desired to be happy'. It may be useful here to recall Judith Butler's meditations on fantasy as the 'articulation of the possible' and its ability to move us beyond the realm of what is actual and present into a 'realm of possibility' (2004: 28–9). She writes, 'The critical promise of fantasy, when and where it exists, is to challenge the contingent limits of what will and will not be called reality. Fantasy is what allows us to imagine ourselves and others otherwise; it establishes the possible of the excess of the real; it points elsewhere, and when it is embodied it brings the elsewhere home.' Here it is not the lesbian woman or the lesbian couple that queers the normative discourse around sexual desire and fulfilment but the seemingly heteronormative, 'happily married' woman. At the end of *Ushno Taar Jonno*, heterormative spaces and bodies become haunted by the spectre of lesbian desire.

Yet, the film also does deliver its promise of articulating 'happy endings' around new domesticities. About a third into the film, it is revealed that Sharoda's long-time live-in companion is Adhikari, his former father-in-law. When the shooting crew leaves for Kolkata, the elderly couple returns to the business of everyday living at the end of the film. Two generations of queer intimates pose a constant dare to public norms of living and the social organization of friendship, social contacts, and community.

REFERENCES

Bauman, Zygmunt (2006), 'Terrors of the Global', in *Liquid Fear*. Cambridge and Malden: Polity Press.

Berlant, Lauren (ed.) (2000), *Introduction to Intimacy*. Chicago and London: The University of Chicago Press.

Butler, Judith (1993), 'Critically Queer', *Bodies That Matter: On the Discursive Limits of Sex*. New York: Routledge, pp. 223–42.

—— (2004), *Undoing Gender*. New York and London: Routledge.

Cineaste (1989), '"Truth not Guaranteed": An Interview with Errol Morris', Issue No. 17, p. 17.

Chopra, Anupama (2004), *Dilwale Dulhaniya Le Jayenge: The Making of a Blockbuster*. New Delhi: Harper Collins/India Today Group.

Desai, Jigna (2004), 'Migrant Brides, Feminist Films and Transnational Desires', *Beyond Bollywood: The Cultural Politics of South Asian Diasporic Film*. New York and London: Routledge.

Ghosh, Shohini (2010), *Fire: A Queer Film Classic*. Vancouver: Arsenal Pulp Press.

Mazumdar, Ranjani (2007), *Bombay Cinema: An Archive of the City*. Ranikhet: Permanent Black.

Renov, Michael (1993), *Theorizing Documentary*. London and New York: Routledge.

Sobchack, Vivian (2000), 'What Is Film History? Or the Riddle of the Sphinxes', in Christine Gledhill and Linda Williams (eds), *Reinventing Film Studies*. London: Arnold, pp. 300–15.

Tagore, Rabindranath (2000), 'The Wife's Letter', in Sukanta Chaudhuri (ed.), *Selected Short Stories*. New Delhi: Oxford University Press, pp. 205–18.

Uberoi, Patricia (2006), 'Imagining the Family', *Freedom and Destiny: Gender, Family and Popular Culture in India*. New Delhi: Oxford University Press.

VIII. ENVIRONMENT

Chapter 15

THE GENDER AND ENVIRONMENT DEBATE
Lessons from India*

BINA AGARWAL**

WHAT IS WOMEN'S RELATIONSHIP with the environment? Is it distinct from that of men's? The growing literature on ecofeminism in the West, and especially in the US, conceptualizes the link between gender and the environment primarily in ideological terms. An intensifying struggle

---

* This is a substantially revised and abridged version of a paper presented at a conference on 'The Environment and Emerging Development Issues' at the World Institute of Development Economics Research, Helsinki, 3–7 September 1990. A longer version is also available as Discussion Paper No. 8, 'Engendering the Environment Debate: Lessons from the Indian Subcontinent', CASID Distinguished Speaker Series, Michigan State University, 1991. Subsequently published in *Feminist Studies*, Spring 1992, 18(1): 119–58.

** I am grateful to several people for comments on the earlier versions: Janet Seiz, Gillian Hart, Nancy Folbre, Jean Dreze, Lourdes Beneria, Gail Hershatter, Pauline Peters, Tariq Banuri, Myra Buvinic, and *Feminist Studies*' editors and anonymous reviewers. I also gained from some lively discussions following seminar presentations of the paper at the Center for Population and Development Studies, Harvard University, February 1991; the Center for Advanced Study in International Development, Michigan State University, April 1990; the Hubert Humphrey Institute of Public Affairs, University of Minnesota, April 1990; and the departments of City and Regional Planning and Rural Sociology, Cornell University, May 1990.

for survival in the developing world, however, highlights the material basis for this link and sets the background for an alternative formulation to ecofeminism, which I term 'feminist environmentalism'.

In this chapter, I will argue that women, especially those in poor rural households in India, on the one hand, are victims of environmental degradation in quite gender-specific ways. On the other hand, they have been active agents in movements of environmental protection and regeneration, often bringing to them a gender-specific perspective and one which needs to inform our view of alternatives. To contextualize the discussion, and to examine the opposing dimensions of women as victims and women as actors in concrete terms, this chapter will focus on India, although the issues are clearly relevant to other parts of the Third World as well. The discussion is divided into five sections. The first section outlines the ecofeminist debate in the US and one prominent Indian variant of it, and suggests an alternative conceptualization. The next three sections, respectively trace the nature and causes of environmental degradation in rural India, its class and gender implications, and the responses to it by the state and grass-roots groups. The concluding section argues for an alternative transformative approach to development.

SOME CONCEPTUAL ISSUES

Ecofeminism

Ecofeminism embodies within it several different strands of discourse, most of which have yet to be spelled out fully, and which reflect, among other things, different positions within the Western feminist movement (radical, liberal, socialist). As a body of thought, ecofeminism is as yet underdeveloped and still evolving, but carries a growing advocacy. My purpose is not to critique ecofeminist discourse in detail, but rather to focus on some of its major elements, especially in order to examine whether and how it might feed into the formulation of a Third World perspective on gender and the environment. Disentangling the various threads in the debate, and focusing on those more clearly articulated, provides us with the following picture of the ecofeminist argument(s):[1] (a) there are

---

[1] See especially King (1981, 1989, 1990), Salleh (1984), Merchant (1980), and Griffin (1978). Also see discussions and critiques by Zimmerman (1987), Warren (1987), Cheney (1987), and Longino's (1981) review of Merchant.

important connections between the domination and oppression of women and the domination and exploitation of nature; (b) in patriarchal thought, women are identified as being closer to nature and men as being closer to culture. Nature is seen as inferior to culture; hence, women are seen as inferior to men; (c) because the domination of women and the domination of nature have occurred together, women have a particular stake in ending the domination of nature, 'in healing the alienated human and non-human nature' (King 1989: 18); and (d) the feminist movement and the environmental movement both stand for egalitarian, non-hierarchical systems. They thus have a good deal in common and need to work together to evolve a common perspective, theory, and practice.

In the ecofeminist argument, therefore, the connection between the domination of women and that of nature is basically seen as *ideological*, as rooted in a system of ideas and representations, values, and beliefs, which places women and the non-human world hierarchically below men. And it calls upon women and men to reconceptualize themselves, and their relationships to one another and to the non-human world, in non-hierarchical ways.

We might then ask: In what is this connection between nature and women seen to be rooted? The idea that women are seen as closer to nature than men was initially introduced into contemporary feminist discourse by Sherry Ortner who argued that 'woman is being identified with—or, if you will, seems to be a symbol of—something that every culture devalues, defines as being of a lower order of existence than itself.... [That something] is "nature" in the most generalized sense.... [Women are everywhere] being symbolically associated with nature, as opposed to men, who are identified with culture' (Ortner 1974: 72–3). In her initial formulation, the connection between women and nature was clearly rooted in the biological processes of reproduction although, even then, Ortner did recognize that women, like men, also *mediate* between nature and culture.

Ortner has since modified her position, which was also criticized by others (particularly social anthropologists) on several counts, especially because the nature–culture divide is not universal across all cultures, nor is there uniformity in the meaning attributed to 'nature', 'culture', 'male', and 'female'.[2] Still, some ecofeminists accept the emphasis on biology uncritically and in different ways reiterate it. An extreme form of this position is that taken by Ariel Kay Salleh who grounds even women's consciousness in biology and in nature. She argues: 'Women's monthly

---

[2] See the case studies, and especially MacCormack's (1980: 13). Also see Moore (1989).

fertility cycle, the tiring symbiosis of pregnancy, the wrench of childbirth and the pleasure of suckling an infant, these things already ground women's consciousness in the knowledge of being coterminous with nature. However tacit or unconscious this identity may be for many women ... it is nevertheless "a fact of life"' (Salleh 1984: 340). Others such as Ynestra King and Carolyn Merchant argue that the nature–culture dichotomy is a false one, a patriarchal ideological construct which is then used to maintain gender hierarchy. At the same time they accept the view that women are ideologically constructed as closer to nature because of their biology (see Merchant 1980: 144).

Merchant, however, in an illuminating historical analysis, shows that in pre-modern Europe the conceptual connection between women and nature rested on two divergent images, co-existing simultaneously, one which constrained the destruction of nature and the other which sanctioned it. Both identified nature with the female sex. The first image, which was the dominant one, identified nature, especially the earth, with the nurturing mother, and culturally restricted 'the types of socially and morally sanctioned human actions allowable with respect to the earth. One does not readily slay a mother, dig into her entrails for gold, or mutilate her body...' (ibid.: 2–3). The opposing image was of nature as wild and uncontrollable which could render violence, storms, droughts, and general chaos. This image culturally sanctioned mastery and human dominance over nature.

Between the sixteenth and seventeenth centuries, Merchant suggests, the Scientific Revolution and the growth of a market-oriented culture in Europe undermined the image of an organic cosmos with a living female earth at its centre. This image gave way to a mechanistic worldview in which nature was reconceived as something to be mastered and controlled by humans. The twin ideas of mechanism and of dominance over nature supported both the denudation of nature and male dominance over women. Merchant observes:

> The ancient identity of nature as a nurturing mother links women's history with the history of the environment and ecological change.... In investigating the roots of our current environmental dilemma and its connections to science, technology, and the economy, we must re-examine the formation of a worldview and a science that, by reconceptualizing reality as a machine rather than a living organism, sanctioned the domination of both nature and women.

Today, Merchant proposes, juxtaposing the egalitarian goals of the women's movement and the environmental movement can suggest 'new values and social structures, based not on the domination of women and nature as resources but on the full expression of both male and female talent and on the maintenance of environmental integrity'.[3]

Ecofeminist discourse, therefore, highlights (a) some of the important conceptual links between the *symbolic* construction of women and nature and the ways of *acting* upon them (although Merchant alone goes beyond the level of assertion to trace these links in concrete terms, historically); (b) the underlying commonality between the premises and goals of the women's movement and the environmental movement; and (c) an alternative vision of a more egalitarian and harmonious future society.

At the same time the ecofeminist argument as constructed is problematic on several counts. First, it posits 'woman' as a unitary category and fails to differentiate among women by class, race, ethnicity, and so on. It thus ignores forms of domination other than gender which also impinge critically on women's position.[4] Second, it locates the domination of women and of nature almost solely in ideology, neglecting the (interrelated) material sources of this dominance (based on economic advantage and political power). Third, even in the realm of ideological constructs, it says little (with the exception of Merchant's analysis) about the social, economic, and political structures within which these constructs are produced and transformed. Nor does it address the central issue of the means by which certain dominant groups (predicated on gender, class, and so on) are able to bring about ideological shifts in their own favour and how such shifts get entrenched. Fourth, the ecofeminist argument does not take into account women's lived material relationship with nature, as opposed to what others or they themselves might conceive that relationship to be. Fifth, those strands of ecofeminism that trace the connection between women and nature to biology may be seen as adhering to a form of essentialism (some notion of a female 'essence' which is unchangeable and irreducible).[5] Such a formulation flies in the face of wide-ranging evidence that concepts of nature, culture, gender, and so on, are historically and socially constructed and vary across and within cultures and time periods.[6]

---

[3] For this and the previous quote, see Merchant (1980: xix, xx–xxi).

[4] King (1981) (unlike in her earlier work) does mention the necessity of such a differentiation but does not discuss how a recognition of this difference would affect her basic analysis.

[5] For an illuminating discussion of the debate on essentialism and constructionism within feminist theory, see Fuss (1989).

[6] See case studies in MacCormack and Strathern (1980).

In other words, the debate highlights the significant effect of ideological constructs in shaping relations of gender dominance and forms of acting on the non-human world, but if these constructs are to be challenged it is necessary to go further. We need a theoretical understanding of what could be termed 'the political economy of ideological construction', that is, of the interplay between conflicting discourses, the groups promoting particular discourses, and the means used to entrench views embodied in those discourses. Equally, it is critical to examine the underlying basis of women's relationship with the non-human world at levels other than ideology (such as through the work women and men do and the gender division of property and power) and to address how the material realities in which women of different classes (castes/races) are rooted might affect their responses to environmental degradation. Women in the West, for instance, have responded in specific ways to the threat of environmental destruction, such as by organizing the Greenham Commons resistance to nuclear missiles in England and by participating in the Green movement across Europe and the US. A variety of actions have similarly been taken by women in the Third World, as discussed later. The question then is: Are there *gendered* aspects to these responses? If so, in what are these responses rooted?

Vandana Shiva's work on India takes us a step forward. Like the ecofeminists, she sees violence against nature and against women as built into the very mode of perceiving both. Like Merchant, she argues that violence against nature is intrinsic to the dominant industrial/developmental model, which she characterizes as a colonial imposition. Associated with the adoption of this developmental model, Shiva argues, was a radical conceptual shift away from the traditional Indian cosmological view of (animate and inanimate) nature as Prakriti, as 'activity *and* diversity' and as 'an expression of Shakti, the feminine and creative principle of the cosmos' which 'in conjunction with the masculine principle (Purusha) ... creates the world'. In this shift, the living, nurturing relationship between man and nature as earth mother was replaced by the notion of man as separate from and dominating over inert and passive nature. 'Viewed from the perspective of nature, or women embedded in nature', the shift was repressive and violent. 'For women ... the death of Prakriti is simultaneously a beginning of their marginalisation, devaluation, displacement, and ultimate dispensability. The ecological crisis is, at its root, the death of the feminine principle...' (Shiva 1988: 39, 42).

At the same time, Shiva notes that violence against women and against nature are linked not just ideologically but also materially. For instance,

Third World women are dependent on nature 'for drawing sustenance for themselves, their families, their societies'. The destruction of nature thus becomes the destruction of women's sources for 'staying alive'. Drawing upon her experience of working with women activists in the Chipko movement—the environmental movement for forest protection and regeneration in the Garhwal hills of northwest India—Shiva argues that 'Third World women' have both a special dependence on nature and a special knowledge of nature. This knowledge has been systematically marginalized under the impact of modern science: 'Modern reductionist science, like development, turns out to be a patriarchal project, which has excluded women as experts, and has simultaneously excluded ecology and holistic ways of knowing which understand and respect nature's processes and interconnectedness as *science*' (ibid.: 14–15).

Shiva takes us further than the Western ecofeminists in exploring the links between ways of thinking about development, the processes of developmental change, and the impact of these on the environment and on the people dependent upon it for their livelihood. These links are of critical significance. Nevertheless, her argument has three principal analytical problems. First, her examples relate to rural women primarily from northwest India, but her generalizations conflate all Third World women into one category. Although she distinguishes Third World women from the rest, like the ecofeminists she does not differentiate between women of different classes, castes, races, ecological zones, and so on. Hence, implicitly, a form of essentialism could be read into her work, in that all Third World women, whom she sees as 'embedded in nature', *qua women* have a special relationship with the natural environment. This still begs the question: What is the basis of this relationship and how do women acquire this special understanding?

Second, she does not indicate by what concrete processes and institutions ideological constructions of gender and nature have changed in India, nor does she recognize the co-existence of several ideological strands, given India's ethnic and religious diversity. For instance, her emphasis on the feminine principle as the guiding idea in Indian philosophic discourse, in fact, relates to the Hindu discourse alone and cannot be seen as applicable for Indians of all religious persuasions.[7] Indeed, Hinduism itself is

---

[7] Also see the discussion by Dietrich (1989: 353–4). Apart from the religion-specificity of the discourse on the feminine principle, an interesting example of the relationship between different religious traditions and the environment is that of sacred groves. These groves, dedicated to local deities and sometimes spread over 100 acres, were traditionally preserved by local Hindu and tribal communities and could be found in several parts of

pluralistic, fluid, and contains several co-existing discourses with varying gender implications.[8] But perhaps most importantly, it is not clear how and in which historical period(s) the concept of the feminine principle *in practice* affected gender relations or relations between people and nature.

Third, Shiva attributes existing forms of destruction of nature and the oppression of women (in both symbolic and real terms) principally to the Third World's history of colonialism and to the imposition of Western science and a Western model of development. Undeniably, the colonial experience and the forms that modern development has taken in Third World countries have been destructive and distorting economically, institutionally, and culturally. However, it cannot be ignored that this process impinged on pre-existing bases of economic and social (including gender) inequalities.

Here it is important to distinguish between the particular model of modernization that clearly has been imported/adopted from the West by many Third World countries (with or without a history of colonization) and the socio-economic base on which this model was imposed. Pre-British India, especially during the Mughal period, was considerably

---

the country. Entry into them was severely restricted and tree cutting usually forbidden (see Gadgil and Vartak 1975). These groves are now disappearing. Among the Khasi tribe of northeast India, elderly non-Christian Khasis I spoke to identify the main cause of this destruction to be the large-scale conversion of Khasis to Christianity which undermined traditional beliefs in deities and so removed the main obstacle to the exploitation of these groves for personal gain.

[8] For instance, the *Rig Veda*, the collection of sacred Sanskrit hymns preserved orally for over 3,000 years, which constitutes the roots of Brahmanic Hinduism, is said to have been traditionally inaccessible to women and untouchable castes, both of whom were forbidden to recite the hymns on the ground that they would defile the magic power of the words (for elaboration, see Flaherty 1990). In contrast, the *Bhakti* movement, which began around the sixth century, sought to establish a direct relationship between God and the individual (without the mediation of Brahmin priests) irrespective of sex or caste and gave rise to numerous devotional songs and poems in the vernacular languages. Many women are associated with the movement, one of the best-known being the sixteenth-century poet-saint, Mirabai. Today the Bhakti tradition co-exists with the more ritualistic and rigid Brahmanic tradition. In fact, a significant dimension of the growing Hindu fundamentalism in India in recent years is precisely the attempt by some to give prominence to one interpretation of Hinduism over others—a visible, contemporary struggle over meanings.

Similarly, several versions of the great epic Ramayana have existed historically, including versions where the central female character, Sita, displays none of the subservience to her husband that is emphasized in the popular version (treated as sacred text) and which has moulded the image of the ideal Indian woman in the modern mass media. Feminist resistance to such gender constructions has taken various forms, including challenging popular interpretations of female characters in the epics and drawing attention to alternative interpretations. See for instance, Chakravarty (1983) and Agarwal (1985).

class/caste stratified, although varyingly across regions.[9] This would have affected the patterns of access to and use of natural resources by different classes and social groups.

Although much more research is needed on the political economy of natural resource use in the pre-colonial period, the evidence of differentiated peasant communities at that time cautions against sweeping historical generalizations about the effects of colonial rule.

By locating the 'problem' almost entirely in the Third World's experience of the West, Shiva misses out on the very real local forces of power, privilege, and property relations that pre-date colonialism. What exists today is a complex legacy of colonial and pre-colonial interactions that defines the constraints and parameters within which and from which present thinking and action on development, resource use, and social change have to proceed. In particular, a strategy for change requires an explicit analysis of the structural causes of environmental degradation, its effects, and responses to it. The outline for an alternative framework, which I term feminist environmentalism, is suggested below.

Feminist Environmentalism

I would like to suggest here that women's and men's relationship with nature needs to be understood as rooted in their material reality, in their specific forms of interaction with the environment. Hence, insofar as there is a gender and class-/caste-/race-based division of labour and distribution of property and power, gender and class/caste/race structure people's interactions with nature and so structure the effects of environmental change on people and their responses to it. And where knowledge about nature is experiential in its basis, the divisions of labour, property, and power which shape experience also shape the knowledge based on that experience.

For instance, poor peasant and tribal women have typically been responsible for fetching fuel and fodder, and in hill and tribal communities have also often been the main cultivators. They are thus likely to be affected adversely in quite specific ways by environmental degradation. At the same time, in the course of their everyday interactions with nature, they acquire a special knowledge of species' varieties and the processes of natural regeneration. (This would include knowledge passed on to them by, for example, their mothers.) They could thus be seen as both victims of

---

[9] See Habib (1984) and his essay in Ray Chaudhuri and Habib (1982).

the destruction of nature and as repositories of knowledge about nature, in ways distinct from the men of their class. The former aspect would provide the gendered impulse for their resistance and response to environmental destruction. The latter would condition their perceptions and choices of what should be done. Indeed, on the basis of their experiential understanding and knowledge, they could provide a special perspective on the processes of environmental regeneration, one that needs to inform our view of alternative approaches to development. (By extension, women who are no longer actively using this knowledge for their daily sustenance, and are no longer in contact with the natural environment in the same way, are likely to lose this knowledge over time and with it the possibility of its transmission to others.)

In this conceptualization, therefore, the link between women and the environment can be seen as structured by a given gender and class/caste/race organization of production, reproduction, and distribution. Ideological constructions such as of gender, of nature, and of the relationship between the two, may be seen as (interactively) a part of this structuring but not the whole of it. This perspective I term 'feminist environmentalism'.

In terms of action, such a perspective would call for struggles over *both* resources and meanings. It would imply grappling with the dominant groups who have the property, power, and privilege to control resources, and these or other groups who control ways of thinking about them, via educational, media, religious, and legal institutions. On the feminist front there would be a need to challenge and transform both *notions* about gender and the *actual* division of work and resources between the genders. On the environmental front there would be a need to challenge and transform not only notions about the relationship between people and nature but also the actual methods of appropriation of nature's resources by a few. Feminist environmentalism underlines the necessity of addressing these dimensions from both fronts.

To concretize the discussion, consider India's experience in the sections that follow. The focus throughout is on the rural environment.

ENVIRONMENTAL DEGRADATION AND FORMS OF APPROPRIATION

In India (as in much of Asia and Africa) a wide variety of essential items are gathered by rural households from the village commons and forests for everyday personal use and sale, such as food, fuel, fodder, fibre, small timber, manure, bamboo, medicinal herbs, oils, materials for house-building and handicrafts, resin, gum, honey, and spices (see especially Kerala Forestry Research Institute 1980: 235). Although all rural households use the village commons in some degree, for the poor they are of critical significance given the skewedness of privatized land distribution in the subcontinent.[10] Data for the early 1980s from 12 semi-arid districts in seven Indian states indicate that for poor rural households (the landless and those with less than two hectares dry land equivalent) village commons account for at least 9 per cent of total income, and in most cases 20 per cent or more, but contribute only 1 per cent to 4 per cent of the incomes of the non-poor (Table 15.1). The dependence of the poor is especially high for fuel and fodder: village commons supply more than 91 per cent of firewood and more than 69 per cent of their grazing needs, compared with the relative self-sufficiency of the larger landed households. Access to village commons reduces income inequalities in the village between poor and non-poor households. Also, there is a close link between the viability of small farmers' private property resources and their access to the commons for grazing draft as well as milch animals (see Blaikie 1985; Jodha 1986).

Similarly, forests have always been significant sources of livelihood, especially for tribal populations, and have provided the basis of swidden cultivation, hunting, and the gathering of non-timber forest produce. In India, an estimated 30 million or more people depend wholly or substantially on such forest produce for a livelihood (Kulkarni 1983). These sources are especially critical during lean agricultural seasons and during drought and famine (see Agarwal 1990; Pingle 1975).

The health of forests, in turn, has an impact on the health of soils (especially in the hills) and the availability of ground and surface water for irrigation and drinking. For a large percentage of rural households, the water for irrigation, drinking, and various domestic uses comes directly from rivers and streams in the hills and plains. Again there are class differences in the nature of their dependency and access. The richer households are better able to tap the (relatively cleaner) groundwater for drinking and irrigation by sinking more and deeper wells and tubewells, but the poor are mainly dependent on surface sources.

---

[10] It is estimated that in 1981–2, 66.6 per cent of landowning households in rural India owned 1 hectare or less and accounted for only 12.2 per cent of all land owned by rural households (National Sample Survey Organisation 1987). The distribution of operational holdings is almost as skewed.

TABLE 15.1 Average Annual Income from Village Commons in Select Districts of India, 1982–5

State[1] and Districts	Per Household Annual Average Income from Village Commons			
	Poor Households[2]		Other Households[3]	
	Value (Rs)	Per cent of total household income	Value (Rs)	Per cent of total household income
Andhra Pradesh				
Mahbubnagar	534	17	171	1
Gujarat				
Mehsana	730	16	162	1
Sabarkantha	818	21	208	1
Karnataka				
Mysore	649	20	170	3
Madhya Pradesh				
Mandsaur	685	18	303	1
Raisen	780	26	468	4
Maharashtra				
Akola	447	9	134	1
Aurangabad	584	13	163	1
Sholapur	641	20	235	2
Rajasthan				
Jalore	709	21	387	2
Nagaur	831	23	438	3
Tamil Nadu				
Dharmapuri	738	22	164	2

Source: Jodha (1986: 1176).
Notes: [1] 'State' here refers to administrative divisions within India and is not used in the political economy sense of the word as used in the text.
[2] Landless households and those owning <2 hectares (ha) dry land equivalent.
[3] Those owning >2 ha dry land equivalent. 1 ha = 2.47 acres.

However, the availability of the country's natural resources to the poor is being severely eroded by two parallel and interrelated trends—first, their growing degradation both in quantity and quality; second, their increasing statization (appropriation by the state) and privatization (appropriation by a minority of individuals), with an associated decline in what was earlier communal. These two trends, both independently and interactively, underlie many of the differential class-gender effects of environmental degradation outlined later. Independently, the former trend is reducing overall availability, and the latter is increasing inequalities in the distribution of what is available. Interactively, an altered distribution in favour of the state and some individuals and away from community control can contribute to environmental degradation insofar as community resource management systems may be more effective in environmental protection and regeneration than are the state or individuals. These two trends I call the primary factors underlying the class-gender effects of environmental change. Several intermediary factors impinge on these primary ones, the most important of which, in my view, are the following: the erosion of community resource management systems resulting from the shift in 'control rights' over natural resources away from community hands,[11] population growth, and technological choices in agriculture and their associated effect on local knowledge systems. These also need to be seen in interactive terms. Consider each in turn.

Forms of Environmental Degradation

Although there is as yet an inadequate data base to indicate the exact extent of environmental degradation in India and its cross-regional variations, available macro-information provides sufficient pointers to warrant considerable concern and possibly alarm. Degradation in India's natural resource base is manifest in disappearing forests, deteriorating soil conditions, and depleting water resources. Satellite data from India reveal that in 1985–7, 19.5 per cent of the country's geoarea was forested and declining at an estimated rate of 1.3 million hectares a year (Government of India 1990). Again, by official estimates, in 1980, 56.6 per cent of India's land was suffering from environmental problems, especially water and wind erosion. Unofficial estimates are even higher. In some canal projects, one-half the area that could have been irrigated and cultivated has been lost due to waterlogging (Joshi and Agnihotri 1984), creating what the local people aptly call 'wet deserts'. The area under periodic floods doubled between 1971 and 1981, and soil fertility is declining due to the excessive use of chemical fertilizers. Similarly, the availability of both ground and surface water is falling. Groundwater levels have fallen permanently in several regions, including in northern India with its high water tables, due to the indiscriminate sinking of tubewells—the leading input in the Green Revolution technology (see, for instance, Bandyopadhyay 1986; Dhawan 1982). As a result, many drinking water wells have dried up or otherwise been rendered unusable. In addition, fertilizer and pesticide runoffs into natural water sources have destroyed fish life and polluted water for human use in several areas (Centre for Science and Environment 1986).

[11] I prefer to use the term 'control rights' here, rather than the commonly used term 'property rights', because what appears critical in this context is less who owns the resources than who has control over them. Hence, for instance, the control of state-owned resources could effectively rest with the village community.

The Process of Statization

In India, both under colonial rule and continuing in the postcolonial period, state control over forests and village commons has grown, with selective access being granted to a favoured few. To begin with, several aspects of British colonial policy have had long-lasting effects (see especially Guha 1983). First, the British established state monopoly over forests, reserving large tracts for timber extraction. Second, associated with this was a severe curtailment in the customary rights of local populations to these resources, rights of access being granted only under highly restricted conditions, with a total prohibition on the barter or sale of forest produce by such right-holders. At the same time, the forest settlement officer could give considerable concessions to those he chose to so privilege. Third, the colonial state promoted the notion of 'scientific' forest management which essentially cloaked the practice of encouraging commercially profitable species, often at the cost of species used by the local population. Fourth, there was virtually indiscriminate forest exploitation by European and Indian private contractors, especially for building railways, ships, and bridges. Tree clearing was also encouraged for establishing tea and coffee plantations and expanding the area under agriculture to increase the government's land revenue base. In effect these policies (a) severely eroded local systems of forest management; (b) legally cut off an important source of sustenance for people, even though illegal entries continued; (c) created a continuing source of tension between the forestry officials and the local people; and (d) oriented forest management to commercial needs.

Post-independence policies show little shift from the colonial view of forests as primarily a source of commercial use and gain. State monopoly over forests has persisted, with all the attendant tensions, as has the practice of scientific forestry in the interests of commercial profit. Restrictions on local people's access to non-timber forest produce have actually increased, and the harassment and exploitation of forest dwellers by the government's forest guards are widespread (see Chand and Bezboruah 1980; Swaminathan 1982).

The Process of Privatization

A growing privatization of community resources in individual (essentially male) hands has paralleled the process of statization. Customarily, large parts of village common lands, especially in northwest India, were what could be termed 'community–private', that is, they were private insofar as user rights to them were usually limited to members of the community and therefore exclusionary; at the same time they were communal in that such rights were often administered by a group rather than by an individual.[12] Table 15.2 reveals a decline in village commons ranging between 26 and 63 percentage points across different regions, between 1950 and 1984. This is attributable mainly to state policy acting to benefit selected groups over others, including illegal encroachments by farmers, made legal over time; the auctioning of parts of commons by the government to private contractors for commercial exploitation; and government distribution of common land to individuals under various schemes which were, in theory, initiated for benefiting the poor but in practice benefited the well-off farmers.[13] For 16 of the 19 districts covered, the share of the poor was less than that of the non-poor (Table 15.2). Hence, the poor lost out collectively while gaining little individually.

Similarly, in the tapping of groundwater through tubewells, there are dramatic inequalities in the distribution of what is effectively an underground commons. Tubewells are concentrated in the hands of the rich, and the noted associated fall in water tables has, in many areas, dried up many shallow irrigation and drinking water wells used by the poor. In some regions, they have also depleted soil moisture from land used by poor households (Bandyopadhyay 1986).

Now consider the intermediary factors mentioned earlier: the erosion of community management systems, population growth, and choice of agricultural technology and local knowledge systems.

The Erosion of Community Resource Management Systems

The statization and privatization of communal resources have, in turn, systematically undermined traditional institutional arrangements of resource use and management. The documentation on this is growing, but even existing work reveals systems of water management, methods of gathering firewood and fodder, and practices of shifting agriculture which were typically not destructive of nature.[14] Some traditional religious

---

[12] However, the degree to which the village community acted as a cohesive group and the extent of control it exercised over communal lands varied across undivided India: it was much greater in the northwest than elsewhere (see Baden-Powell 1957).

[13] For a detailed discussion on these causes, see Jodha (1986).

[14] On traditional systems of community water management, see Sengupta (1985), Leach (1967), and Seklar (1981). On communal management of forests and village commons, see Guha (1985), Gadgil (1985), and Moench (1988). On firewood gathering practices, see

TABLE 15.2 Distribution of Privatized Village Commons in Select Districts of India

State and Districts	VCs as Per Cent of Village Area, 1982–4	Per Cent Decline in VC Area, 1950–84	Per Cent of Land to		Per Cent of recipients among		Per Household Area Owned (ha)			
			Poor	Others	Poor	Others	Poor		Others	
							Before[1]	After[2]	Before	After
Andhra Pradesh										
Mahbubnagar	9	43	50	50	76	24	0.3	0.9	3.0	5.1
Medak	11	45	51	49	59	41	1.0	2.2	3.1	4.6
Gujarat										
Banaskantha	9	49	18	82	38	62	0.8	2.0	5.4	8.8
Mehsana	11	37	20	80	36	64	1.0	1.7	8.0	9.8
Sabarkantha	12	46	28	72	55	45	0.5	1.1	7.0	9.8
Karnataka										
Bidar	12	41	39	61	64	36	1.0	2.0	6.4	9.2
Gulbarga	9	43	43	57	60	40	0.8	2.4	4.5	7.7
Mysore	18	32	44	56	67	33	0.9	1.9	4.1	11.6
Madhya Pradesh										
Mandsaur	22	34	45	55	75	25	1.2	2.5	7.7	12.4
Raisen	23	47	42	58	68	32	1.3	2.2	6.2	9.0
Vidisha	28	32	38	62	48	52	1.3	2.5	4.9	6.8
Maharashtra										
Akola	11	42	39	61	58	42	1.0	1.6	3.1	4.6
Aurangabad	15	30	30	70	42	58	1.1	2.2	6.4	6.3
Sholapur	19	26	42	58	53	47	0.7	2.2	3.4	5.6
Rajasthan										
Jalore	18	37	14	86	37	63	0.3	1.7	7.2	12.5
Jodhpur	16	58	24	76	35	65	0.4	1.3	2.3	3.8
Nagaur	15	63	21	79	41	59	1.3	2.5	2.4	5.2
Tamil Nadu										
Coimbatore	9	47	50	50	75	25	0.8	2.5	3.8	5.8
Dharmapuri	12	52	49	51	55	45	1.0	1.9	4.6	7.5

Source: Jodha (1986: 1177–8).
Notes: [1] Before the distribution of VC land.
[2] After the distribution of VC land.

and folk beliefs also (as noted) contributed to the preservation of nature, especially trees or orchards deemed sacred.[15]

Of course, much more empirical documentation is needed on how regionally widespread these traditional systems of management were and the contexts in which they were successful in ensuring community cooperation. However, the basic point is that where traditional community management existed, as it did in many areas, *responsibility for resource management was linked to resource use* via local community institutions. Where control over these resources passed from the hands of the community to those of the state or of individuals, this link was effectively broken.

In turn, the shift from community control and management of common property, to state or individual ownership and control, has increased environmental degradation.[16] As Daniel W. Bromley and Michael M. Cernea (1989: 25) note, 'the *appearance* of environmental management created through the establishment of government agencies, and the aura of coherent policy by issuance of decrees prohibiting entry to—and harvesting from—State property, has led to continued degradation of resources under the tolerant eye of government agencies'.

Property rights vested in individuals are also no guarantee for environmental regeneration. Indeed, as will be discussed at greater length later, individual farmers attempting tree planting for short-term profits have tended to plant quick-growing commercial trees such as eucalyptus, which can prove environmentally costly.

Population Growth

Excessive population growth has often been identified as the primary culprit of environmental degradation. And undoubtedly, a rapidly growing population impinging over time on a limited land/water/forest base is likely to degrade the environment. However, political economy dimensions clearly underlie the *pace* at which this process occurs and *how the costs of it are distributed*. The continuing (legal and illegal) exploitation of forests, and the increasing appropriation of village commons and groundwater

---

Agarwal (1987). Firewood for domestic use in rural households was customarily collected in the form of twigs and fallen branches, which did not destroy the trees. Even today, 75 per cent of firewood used as domestic fuel in northern India (and 100 per cent in some other areas) is in this form.

[15] The preservation of sacred groves described in Note 7 is one such example.

[16] Also see discussion in Dasgupta and Maler (1990).

resources by a few, leave the vast majority to subsist on a shrinking natural resource base. Added to this is the noted erosion of community resource management systems which had enforced limitations on what people could and did take from communal resources, and which could perhaps have ensured their protection, despite population pressure (ibid.).

Population growth can thus be seen as exacerbating a given situation but not necessarily as its primary cause. It is questionable that interventions to control population growth can, in themselves, stem environmental degradation, although clearly, as Paul Shaw argues, they can 'buy crucial time until we figure out how to dismantle more ultimate causes' (1989: 7).

What adds complexity to even this possibility is that in the link between environmental degradation and population growth, the causality can also run in the opposite direction. For instance, poverty associated with environmental degradation could induce a range of fertility-increasing responses—reduced education for young girls as they devote more time to collecting fuel, fodder, and so on, leading to higher fertility in the long term, given the negative correlation between female education and fertility; higher infant mortality rates inducing higher fertility to ensure a given completed family size; and people having more children to enable the family to diversify incomes as a risk-reducing mechanism in environmentally high-risk areas (Rosenzweig and Wolpin 1985). These links are another reminder that it is critical to focus on women's status when formulating policies for environmental protection.

Choice of Agricultural Technology and Erosion of Local Knowledge Systems

Many of the noted forms of environmental degradation are associated with the Green Revolution technology adopted to increase crop output. Although dramatically successful in the latter objective in the short run, it has had high environmental costs, such as falling water tables due to tubewells, waterlogged and saline soils from most large irrigation schemes, declining soil fertility with excessive chemical fertilizer use, and water pollution with pesticides. Moreover, the long-term sustainability of the output increases achieved so far, itself appears doubtful. Deteriorating soil and water conditions are already being reflected in declining crop yields.[17] Genetic variety has also shrunk, and many of the indigenously

---

[17] Under some large-scale irrigation works, crop yields are *lower* than in the period immediately prior to the project (Joshi and Agnihotri 1984).

developed crop varieties (long-tested and adapted to local conditions) have been replaced by improved seeds which are more susceptible to pest attacks. The long-term annual growth rate of agricultural production in India over 1968–85 was 2.6 per cent, that is, slightly *lower* than the pre-Green Revolution, 1950–65, rate of 3.08 per cent. Crop yields are also more unstable (Hanumantha Rao *et al.* 1988). All this raises questions about the long-term sustainability of agricultural growth, and more generally of rural production systems, under present forms of technology and resource management in India, and indeed in South Asia.

The choice of agricultural technology and production systems cannot be separated from the dominant view of what constitutes scientific agriculture. The Green Revolution embodies a technological mix which gives primacy to laboratory-based research and manufactured inputs and treats agriculture as an isolated production system. Indeed, indiscriminate agricultural expansion, with little attempt to maintain a balance between forests, fields, and grazing lands, assumes that the relationship between agriculture, forests, and village commons is an antagonistic, rather than a complementary, one. By contrast, organic farming systems (now rapidly being eclipsed) are dependent on maintaining just such a balance. More generally, over the years, there has been a systematic devaluation and marginalization of indigenous knowledge about species varieties, nature's processes (how forests, soils, and water are formed and sustained interrelatedly), and sustainable forms of interaction between people and nature. These trends are not confined to countries operating within the capitalist mode. Similar problems of deforestation, desertification, salination, recurrent secondary pest attacks on crops, and pesticide contamination are emerging in China (Glaeser 1987).

What is at issue here is not modern science in itself but the process by which what is regarded as 'scientific knowledge' is generated and applied and how the fruits of that application are distributed. Within the hierarchy of knowledge, that acquired via traditional forms of interacting with nature tends to be deemed less valuable (also see Marglin 1988). And the people who use this knowledge in their daily lives—farmers and forest dwellers and especially women of these communities—tend to be excluded from the institutions which create what is seen as scientific knowledge. These boundaries are not inevitable. In Meiji Japan, the farmer's knowledge and innovative skills were incorporated in the broader body of scientific knowledge by a systematized interaction between the farmer, the village extension worker, and the scientist. This enabled a two-way flow of information from the farmer to the scientist and vice-versa: 'Intimate knowledge of the best of traditional farming methods was thus the starting point for agricultural research and extension activities' (see Johnston 1969: 61).

Such attempts contrast sharply with the more typical top–down flow of information from those deemed experts (the scientists/professionals) to those deemed ignorant (the village users). The problem here is only partly one of class differences. Underlying the divide between the scientists/professionals (usually urban-based) and the rural users of innovations (including user-innovators), whose knowledge comes more from field experience than from formal education, are also usually the divides between intellectual and physical labour, between city and countryside, and between women and men.

CLASS–GENDER EFFECTS

We come then to the class–gender effects of the processes of degradation, statization, and privatization of nature's resources, and the erosion of traditional systems of knowledge and resource management. These processes have had particularly adverse effects on poor households because of the noted greater dependency of such households on communal resources. However, focusing on the class significance of communal resources provides only a partial picture—there is also a critical gender dimension, for women and female children are the ones most adversely affected by environmental degradation. The reasons for this are primarily threefold. First, there is a pre-existing gender division of labour. It is women in poor peasant and tribal households who do much of the gathering and fetching from the forests, village commons, rivers, and wells. In addition, women of such households are burdened with a significant responsibility for family subsistence and they are often the primary, and in many female-headed households the sole, economic providers.

Second, there are systematic gender differences in the distribution of subsistence resources (including food and health care) within rural households, as revealed by a range of indicators: anthropometric indices, morbidity and mortality rates, hospital admissions data, and the sex ratio (which is 93 females per 100 males for all-India).[18] These differences,

---

[18] For a review of issues and literature on this question, see Agarwal (1986a).

especially in health care, are widespread in India (and indeed in South Asia).[19]

Third, there are significant inequalities in women's and men's access to the most critical productive resource in rural economies, agricultural land, and associated production technology.[20] Women also have a systematically disadvantaged position in the labour market. They have fewer employment opportunities, less occupational mobility, lower levels of training, and lower payments for same or similar work.[21] Due to the greater task specificity of their work, they also face much greater seasonal fluctuations in employment and earnings than do men, with sharper peaks and longer slack periods in many regions and less chance of finding employment in the slack seasons (see Agarwal 1984; Ryan and Ghodake 1980).

Given their limited rights in private property resources such as agricultural land, rights to communal resources such as the village commons have always provided rural women and children (especially those of tribal, landless, or marginal peasant households) a source of subsistence, *unmediated by dependency relationships* on adult males. For instance, access to village commons is usually linked to membership in the village community and therefore women are not excluded in the way they may be in a system of individualized private land rights. This acquires additional importance in regions with strong norms of female seclusion (as in northwest India) where women's access to the cash economy, to markets, and to the marketplace itself is constrained and dependent on the mediation of male relatives (see Agarwal 1989; Sharma 1980).

It is against this analytical backdrop that we need to examine what I term the 'class–gender effects' (the gender effects mediated by class) of the processes of environmental degradation, statization, and privatization. These effects relate to at least six critical aspects: time, income, nutrition, health, social survival networks, and indigenous knowledge. Each of these effects is important across rural India. However, their intensity and interlinkages would differ cross-regionally, with variations in ecology, agricultural technology, land distribution, and social structures, associated with which are variations in the gender division of labour, social relations,

[19] These sex ratios are particularly female-adverse in the agriculturally prosperous northwestern regions of Punjab and Haryana where these figures are, respectively, 88 and 87 females per 100 males. For a discussion on the causes of this regional variation, see Agarwal (1986a) and Miller (1981).

[20] Women in India rarely own land, and in most areas also have limited access to personal assets such as cash and jewellery. See Agarwal (1988).

[21] See discussions in Agarwal (1984, 1986a) and Bardhan (1977).

livelihood possibilities, and kinship systems.[22] Although a systematic regional decomposition of effects is not attempted in the following, all the illustrative examples are regionally contextualized.

On Time

Because women are the main gatherers of fuel, fodder, and water, it is primarily their working day (already averaging 10–12 hours) that is lengthened with the depletion of and reduced access to forests, waters, and soils. Firewood, for instance, is the single most important source of domestic energy in India (providing more than 65 per cent of domestic energy in the hills and deserts of the north). Much of this is gathered and not purchased, especially by the poor. In recent years, there has been a several fold increase in firewood collection time (see Table 15.3). In some villages of Gujarat, in western India, even a four-to-five-hour search yields little apart from shrubs, weeds, and tree roots which do not provide adequate heat.

Similarly, fodder collection takes longer with a decline in the village commons. As a woman in the hills of Uttar Pradesh (northwest India) puts it:

When we were young, we used to go to the forest early in the morning without eating anything. There we would eat plenty of berries and wild fruits ... drink the cold sweet [water] of the *Banj* [oak] roots.... In a short while we would gather all the fodder and firewood we needed, rest under the shade of some huge tree and then go home. Now, with the going of the trees, everything else has gone too. (Quoted in Bahuguna 1984: 132)

The shortage of drinking water has exacerbated the burden of time and energy on women and young girls. Where low-caste women often have access to only one well, its drying up could mean an endless wait for their vessels to be filled by upper-caste women, as was noted to have happened in Orissa.[23] A similar problem arises when drinking water wells go saline near irrigation works (Agarwal 1981).

In Uttar Pradesh, according to a woman grassroots' activist, the growing hardship of young women's lives with ecological degradation has led to an increased number of suicides among them in recent years. Their inability to obtain adequate quantities of water, fodder, and fuel causes tensions with their mothers-in-law (in whose youth forests were plentiful), and

---

[22] For a detailed cross-regional mapping of some of these variables in the context of women's land rights in South Asia, see Agarwal (1994).

[23] Personal communication, Chitra Sundaram, Danish International Development Agency (DANIDA), Delhi, 1981.

TABLE 15.3 Time Taken and Distance Travelled for Firewood Collection

Country/Region	Year of Data	Firewood Collection*		Data Source
		Time taken	Distance travelled	
India				
Chamoli (hills)				
(a) Dwing	1982	5 hr/day@	over 5 km	Swaminathan (1984)
(b) Pakhi	1982	4 hr/day		
Gujarat (plains)				
(a) Forested		once every 4 days	n.a.	
(b) Depleted	1980	once every 2 days	4–5 km	Nagbrahman & Sambrani (1983)
(c) Severely depleted		4–5 hr/day	n.a.	
Madhya Pradesh (plains)	1980	1–2 times/week	5 km	Chand & Bezboruah (1980)
Kumaon (hills)	1982	3 days/week	5–7 km	Folger & Dewan (1983)
Karnataka (plains)	n.a.	1 hr/day	5.4 km/trip	Batliwala (1983)
Garhwal (hills)	n.a.	5 hr/day	10 km	Agarwal (1983)
Bihar (plains)	c. 1972	n.a.	1–2 km/day	Bhaduri & Surin (1980)
	1980	n.a.	8–10 km/day	
Rajasthan (plains)	1988	5 hr/day (winter)	4 km	Personal observation
Nepal				
Tinan (hills)	1978	3 hr/day	n.a.	Stone (1982)
Pangua (hills)	late 1970s	4–5 hr/bundle	n.a.	Bajracharya (1983)
WDA (lowlands)**				
(a) low deforestation	1982–3	1.5 hr/day	n.a.	Kumar & Hotchkiss (1988)
(b) high deforestation	1982–3	3 hr/day	n.a.	

Sources: Swaminathan (1984); Nagbrahman and Sambrani (1983); Chand and Bezboruah (1980); Folger and Dewan (1983); Batliwala (1983); Agarwal (1983); Bhadhuri and Surin (1980); Stone (1982); Bajracharya (1983); Kumar and Hotchkiss (1988).

Notes: * Firewood collected mainly by women and children.
@ Average computed from information given in the study.
n.a. Information not available.
** Western Development Area.

soil erosion has compounded the difficulty of producing enough grain for subsistence in a region of high male out-migration (Bahuguna 1984).

On Income

The decline in gathered items from forests and village commons has reduced incomes directly. In addition, the extra time needed for gathering reduces time available to women for crop production and can adversely affect crop incomes, especially in hill communities where women are the primary cultivators due to high male out-migration. For instance, a recent study in Nepal found that the substantial increase in firewood collection time due to deforestation has significantly reduced women's crop cultivation time, leading to an associated fall in the production of maize, wheat, and mustard which are primarily dependent on female labour in the region. These are all crops grown in the dry season when there is increased need for collecting fuel and other items (Kumar and Hotchkiss 1988). The same is likely to be happening in the hills of India.

Similar implications for women's income arise with the decline in common grazing land and associated fodder shortage. Many landless widows I spoke to in Rajasthan (northwest India) in 1988 said they could not venture to apply for a loan to purchase a buffalo under the government's anti-poverty programme as they had nowhere to graze the animal and no cash to buy fodder.

As other sources of livelihood are eroded, selling firewood is becoming increasingly common, especially in eastern and central India. Most 'head loaders', as they are called, are women, earning a meagre Rs 5.50 a day for 20 kg of wood (see Bhaduri and Surin 1980). Deforestation directly impinges on this source of livelihood as well.

On Nutrition

As the area and productivity of village commons and forests fall, so does the contribution of gathered food in the diets of poor households. The declining availability of fuel wood has additional nutritional effects. Efforts to economize induce people to shift to less nutritious foods which need less fuel to cook or which can be eaten raw, or force them to eat partially cooked food which could be toxic, or eat leftovers that could rot in a tropical climate, or to miss meals altogether. Although as yet there are no systematic studies on India, some studies on rural Bangladesh are strongly indicative and show that the total number of meals eaten daily as well as the number of cooked meals eaten in poor households is already declining (Howes and Jabbar 1986). The fact that malnutrition can be caused as much by shortages of fuel as of food has long been part of the conventional wisdom of rural women who observe: 'It's not what's in the pot that worries you, but what's under it.' A trade-off between the time spent in fuel gathering versus cooking can also adversely affect the meal's nutritional quality.

Although these adverse nutritional effects impinge on the whole household, women and female children bear an additional burden because of the noted gender biases in intra-family distribution of food and health care. There is also little likelihood of poor women being able to afford the extra calories for the additional energy expended in fuel collection.

On Health

Apart from the health consequences of nutritional inadequacies, poor rural women are also more directly exposed than are men to waterborne diseases and to the pollution of rivers and ponds with fertilizer and pesticide runoffs, because of the nature of the tasks they perform, such as fetching water for various domestic uses and animal care, and washing clothes near ponds, canals, and streams (Agarwal 1981). The burden of family ill-health associated with water pollution also falls largely on women who take care of the sick. An additional source of vulnerability is the agricultural tasks women perform. For instance, rice transplanting, which is usually a woman's task in most parts of Asia, is associated with a range of diseases, including arthritis and gynaecological ailments (Mencher and Saradamoni 1982; United Nations Development Program 1979). Cotton-picking and other tasks done mainly by women in cotton cultivation expose them to pesticides which are widely used for this crop. In China, several times the acceptable levels of DDT and BHC residues have been found in the milk of nursing mothers, among women agricultural workers (Wagner 1987). In India, pesticides are associated with limb and visual disabilities (Mohan 1987).

On Social Support Networks

The considerable displacement of people that results from the submersion of villages in the building of major irrigation and hydroelectric works, or from large-scale deforestation in itself, has another (little recognized) class and gender implication—the disruption of social support networks. Social relationships with kin, and with villagers outside the kin network, provide economic and social support that is important to all rural households but especially to poor households and to the women.[24] This includes reciprocal labour-sharing arrangements during peak agricultural seasons; loans taken in cash or kind during severe crises such as droughts; and the borrowing of small amounts of foodstuffs, fuel, fodder, and so on, even in normal times. Women typically depend a great deal on such informal support networks, which they also help to build through daily social interaction, marriage

[24] These are apart from the widely documented patron–client types of relationships.

alliances that they are frequently instrumental in arranging, and complex gift exchanges (see Sharma 1980; Vatuk 1981). Also, the social and economic support this represents for women in terms of strengthening their bargaining power within families needs to be recognized, even if it is not easy to quantify.[25] These networks, spread over a range of nearby villages, cannot be reconstituted easily, an aspect ignored by rehabilitation planners.

Moreover, for forest dwellers, the relationship with forests is not just functional or economic but also symbolic, suffused with cultural meanings and nuances, and woven into their songs and legends of origin. Large-scale deforestation, whether or not due to irrigation schemes, has eroded a whole way of living and thinking. Two close observers of life among the tribal people of Orissa in eastern India note that 'the earlier sense of sharing has disappeared.... Earlier women would rely on their neighbors in times of need. Today this has been replaced with a sense of alienation and helplessness ... the trend is to leave each family to its own fate' (Fernandes and Menon 1987: 115). Widows and the aged are the most neglected.

On Women's Indigenous Knowledge

The gathering of food alone demands an elaborate knowledge of the nutritional and medicinal properties of plants, roots, and trees, including a wide reserve knowledge of edible plants not normally used but critical for coping with prolonged shortages during climatic disasters. An examination of household coping mechanisms during drought and famine reveals a significant dependence on famine foods gathered mainly by women and children for survival. Also among hill communities it is usually women who do the seed selection work and have the most detailed knowledge about crop varieties.[26] This knowledge about nature and agriculture, acquired by poor rural women in the process of their everyday contact with and dependence on nature's resources, has a class and gender specificity and is linked to the class specificity and gendering of the division of labour.

---

[25] See Sen (1990) for a discussion on the bargaining approach to conceptualizing intra-household gender relations; and Agarwal (1990) for a discussion on the factors that affect intra-household bargaining power.

[26] Among the Garo tribals of northeast India in the early 1960s, Burling found that the men always deferred on this count to the women, who knew of approximately 300 indigenously cultivated rice varieties. See Burling (1963). In Nepal, even today it is women who do the seed selection work among virtually all communities. See Acharya and Bennett (1981).

The impact of existing forms of development on this knowledge has been two-fold. First, the process of devaluation and marginalization of indigenous knowledge and skills, discussed earlier, impinges especially on the knowledge that poor peasant and tribal women usually possess. Existing development strategies have made little attempt to tap or enhance this knowledge and understanding. At the same time, women have been excluded from the institutions through which modern scientific knowledge is created and transmitted. Second, the degradation of natural resources and their appropriation by a minority results in the destruction of the material basis on which women's knowledge of natural resources and processes is founded and kept alive, leading to its gradual eclipse.

RESPONSES: STATE AND GRASSROOTS

Both the state and the people most immediately affected by environmental degradation have responded to these processes, but in different ways. The state's recognition that environmental degradation may be acquiring crisis proportions is recent and as yet partial; and, as we have seen, state developmental policies are themselves a significant cause of the crisis. Not surprisingly, therefore, the state's response has been piecemeal rather than comprehensive. For instance, the problem of deforestation and fuel wood shortage has been addressed mainly by initiating tree-planting schemes either directly or by encouraging village communities and individual farmers to do so.

However, most state ventures[27] in the form of direct planting have had high failure rates in terms of both tree planting and survival, attributable to several causes—a preoccupation with mono-cultural plantations principally for commercial use, which at times have even replaced mixed forests; the takeover of land used for various other purposes by the local population; and top-down implementation. Hence, in many cases, far from benefiting the poor, these schemes have taken away even existing rights and resources, leading to widespread local resistance. Also, women either do not feature at all in such schemes or, at best, tend to be allotted the role of caretakers in tree nurseries, with little say in the choice of species or in any other aspect of the project. Community forestry schemes, on the other hand, are often obstructed by economic inequalities in the village

---

[27] For a detailed discussion on these schemes and their shortcomings, see Agarwal (1986b).

community and the associated mistrust among the poor of a system that cannot ensure equitable access to the products of the trees planted.

Ironically, the real 'success' stories, with plantings far exceeding targets, relate to the better-off farmers who, in many regions, have sought to reap quick profits by allotting fertile cropland to commercial trees. As a result, employment, crop output, and crop residues for fuel have declined, often dramatically, and the trees planted, such as eucalyptus, provide no fodder and poor fuel (Chandrashekar *et al.* 1987; Shiva 1988). The recent government policy in West Bengal (eastern India) of leasing sections of degraded forest land to local communities for collectively planting, managing, and monitoring tree plantations for local use, holds promise. But in several other parts of the country large tracts of such land have also been given to paper manufacturers for planting commercial species.

As some environmentalists have rightly argued, this predominantly commercial approach to forestry, promoted as 'scientific forestry', is reductionist—it is nature seen as individual parts rather than as an interconnected system of vegetation, soil, and water; the forest is reduced to trees, the trees to biomass. For instance, Shiva notes that in the reductionist worldview only those properties of a resource system are taken into account which generate profits, whereas those that stabilize ecological processes but are commercially non-exploitable, are ignored and eventually destroyed (Shiva 1987).

Indeed, the noted effects of development policies on the environment—be they policies relating to agriculture or more directly to forests and water use—point to a strategy which has been extractive/destructive of nature rather than conserving/regenerative. The strategy does not explicitly take account of the long-term complementarity between agriculture and natural resource preservation, and therefore raises serious questions about the ability of the system both to sustain long-term increases in agricultural productivity and to provide sustenance for the people.

But should we see people in general and women in particular solely as victims of environmental degradation and of ill-conceived top–down state policies? The emergence of grassroots' ecology movements across the subcontinent (and especially India) suggests otherwise. These movements indicate that although poor peasant and tribal communities in general, and women among them in particular, are being severely affected by environmental degradation and appropriation, they are today also critical agents of change. Further, embodied in their traditional interaction with the environment are practices and perspectives which can prove important for defining alternatives.

The past decade, in particular, has seen an increasing resistance to ecological destruction in India, whether caused by direct deforestation (which is being resisted through non-violent movements such as Chipko in the Himalayan foothills and Appiko in Karnataka) or by large irrigation and hydroelectric works, such as the Narmada Valley Project covering three regions in central India, the Koel-Karo in Bihar, the Silent Valley Project in Kerala (which was shelved through central government intervention and local protests in 1983), the Inchampalli and Bhopalpatnam dams in Andhra Pradesh (against which 5,000 tribal people, with women in the vanguard, protested in 1984), and the controversial Tehri dam in Garwal. Women have been active participants in most of these protests.

Although fuelled by differing ideological streams, which Ramachandra Guha identifies as Crusading Gandhian, Appropriate Technology, and Ecological Marxism, these resistance movements suggest that those affected can also be critical agents of change. Common to these streams is the recognition that the present model of development has not succeeded either in providing sustenance or in ensuring sustainability. However, the points from which the differing ideologies initiate this critique are widely dispersed. In particular, they differ in their attitudes to modern science and to socio-economic inequalities. As Guha puts it, under the Crusading Gandhian approach, 'modern science is seen as responsible for industrial society's worst excesses' (1988), and socio-economic inequalities within village communities tend to get glossed over. Ecological Marxism sees modern science and the 'scientific temper' as indispensable for constructing a new social order, and there is a clear recognition of and attack on class and caste inequalities (although the position on gender is ambiguous). Appropriate Technology thinking, which falls within these two strands, is not as well-worked-out a philosophic and theoretical position as Gandhism and Marxism. It is pragmatic in its approach to modern science and emphasizes the need to synthesize traditional and modern technological traditions. Although problems relating to socio-economic hierarchies are recognized, there is no clear programme for tackling them. Over the past decade there has been some cross-fertilization of thinking across these different ideological streams.

However, it is important to distinguish here between the perspectives revealed by an examination of *practice* within the environmental movement and the explicit *theoretical* formulation of an environmental perspective. Although dialectically interlinked, the two do not entirely overlap. The three ideological streams, as identified by Guha, relate to different ways in which groups adhering to pre-existing ideological and philosophic positions (Marxist, Gandhian) have incorporated environmental concerns in their practice. In a sense environment has been added on to their other concerns by these groups. This does not as yet represent the formulation of a new theoretical perspective (that an environmental approach to development needs) by any of these groups.

In terms of practice within the movement, women have been a visible part of most rural grassroots ecological initiatives (as they have of peasant movements in general). This visibility is most apparent in the Chipko movement described later. However, women's participation in a movement does not *in itself* represent an explicit incorporation of a gender perspective, in either theory or practice, within that movement. Yet such a formulation is clearly needed. Feminist environmentalism as spelled out earlier in this chapter is an attempt in this direction.

To restate in this context, in feminist environmentalism I have sought to provide a theoretical perspective that locates both the symbolic and material links between people and the environment in their specific forms of interaction with it, and traces gender and class differentiation in these links to a given gender and class division of labour, property, and power. Unlike Gandhism and Marxism, feminist environmentalism is not a perspective that is consciously subscribed to by an identifiable set of individuals or groups. However, insofar as tribal and poor peasant women's special concern with environmental degradation is rooted in this material reality, their responses to it, which have been articulated both in complementary and oppositional terms to the other ideological streams, could be seen as consistent with the feminist environmentalist framework.

The Chipko movement is an interesting example in this respect. Although it emerged from the Gandhian tradition, in the course of its growth it has brought to light some of the limitations of an approach that does not explicitly take account of class and gender concerns. More generally too it is a movement of considerable historical significance whose importance goes beyond locational specificity, and is a noteworthy expression of hill women's specific understanding of forest protection and environmental regeneration.[28]

The movement was sparked off in 1972–3 when the people of Chamoli district in northwest India protested the auctioning of 300 ash trees to a sports good manufacturer, while the local labour cooperative was refused permission by the government to cut even a few trees to make agricultural

---

[28] Among the many writings on the Chipko movement, see especially Bandyopadhyay and Shiva (1987), Shiva (1988), Jain (1984), and Dogra (1984).

implements for the community. Since then the movement has spread not only within the region but its methods and message have also reached other parts of the country (Appiko in Karnataka is an offshoot).[29] Further, the context of local resistance has widened. Tree felling is being resisted also to prevent disasters such as landslides, and there has been protest against limestone mining in the hills for which the villagers had to face violence from contractors and their hired thugs.

Women's active involvement in the Chipko movement has several noteworthy features that need highlighting here. First, their protest against the commercial exploitation of the Himalayan forests has been not only jointly with the men of their community when they were confronting non-local contractors but also, in several subsequent instances, even in opposition to village men due to differences in priorities about resource use. Time and again, women have clear-sightedly opted for saving forests and the environment over the short-term gains of development projects with high environmental costs. In one instance, a potato-seed farm was to be established by cutting down a tract of oak forest in Dongri Paintoli village. The men supported the scheme because it would bring in cash income. The women protested because it would take away their only local source of fuel and fodder and add 5 km to their fuel-collecting journeys, but cash in the men's hands would not necessarily benefit them or their children.[30] The protest was successful.

Second, women have been active and frequently successful in protecting the trees, stopping tree auctions, and keeping a vigil against illegal felling. In Gopeshwar town, a local women's group has appointed watchwomen who receive a wage in kind to guard the surrounding forest, and to regulate the extraction of forest produce by villagers. Twigs can be collected freely, but any harm to the trees is liable to punishment.

Third, replanting is a significant component of the movement.

But in their choice of trees the priorities of women and men don't always coincide—women typically prefer trees that provide fuel, fodder, and daily needs; the men prefer commercially profitable ones.[31] Once again this

---

[29] I understand there have also been cases of people hugging trees to protect them from loggers in the US, although they appear to have no apparent link with Chipko.

[30] There is a growing literature indicating significant gender differences in cash-spending patterns, with a considerable percentage (at times up to 40 per cent) of what men earn in poor rural households often going towards the purchase of items they alone consume, such as liquor, tobacco, and clothes, and much of what the women earn going towards the family's basic needs. See especially Mencher (1988).

[31] This gender divergence has also been noted elsewhere. See Brara (1987).

points to the association between gendered responsibility for providing a family's subsistence needs and gendered responses to threats against the resources that fulfil those needs.

Fourth, Chipko today is more than an ecology movement and has the potential for becoming a wider movement against gender-related inequalities. For instance, there has been large-scale mobilization against male alcoholism and associated domestic violence and wasteful expenditure. There is also a shift in self-perception. I have seen women stand up in public meetings of the movement and forcefully address the gathering. Many of them are also asking: Why are we not members of the village councils?

Fifth, implicit in the movement is a holistic understanding of the environment in general and forests in particular. The women, for instance, have constructed a poetic dialogue illustrating the difference between their own perspective and that of the foresters (quoted in Shiva 1988).

Foresters: What do the forests bear?
Profits, resin and timber.
Women (Chorus): What do the forests bear?
Soil, water and pure air.
Soil, water and pure air,
Sustain the earth and all she bears.

In other words, the women recognize that forests cannot be reduced merely to trees, and the trees to wood for commercial use, that vegetation, soil, and water form part of a complex and interrelated ecosystem. This recognition of the interrelatedness and interdependence between the various material components of nature, and between nature and human sustenance, is critical for evolving a strategy of sustainable environmental protection and regeneration.

Although the movement draws upon, indeed is rooted in, the region's Gandhian tradition which pre-dates Chipko, women's responses go beyond the framework of that tradition and come close to feminist environmentalism in their perspective. This is suggested by their beginning to confront gender and class issues in a number of small but significant ways. For instance, gender relations are called into question in their taking oppositional stands to the village men on several occasions, in asking to be members of village councils, and in resisting male alcoholism and domestic violence. Similarly, there is clearly a class confrontation involved in their resistance (together with the men of their community) to the contractors holding licences for mining and felling in the area.

At the same time, ecology movements such as Chipko need to be contextualized. Although localized resistance to the processes of natural resource appropriation and degradation in India has taken many different forms, and arisen in diverse regional contexts, resistances in which entire communities and villages have participated to constitute a movement (such as Chipko, Appiko, and Jharkhand) have emerged primarily in hill or tribal communities. This may be attributable particularly to two factors: the immediacy of the threat from these processes to people's survival, and these communities being marked by relatively low levels of the class and social differentiation that usually splinter village communities in South Asia. They therefore have a greater potential for wider community participation than is possible in more economically and socially stratified contexts. Further, in these communities, women's role in agricultural production has always been visibly substantial and often primary, an aspect more conducive to their public participation than in many other communities of northern India practising female seclusion.

In emphasizing the role of poor peasant and tribal women in ecology movements, I am not arguing, as do some feminist scholars, that women possess a specifically feminine sensibility or cognitive temperament, or that women *qua women* have certain traits that predispose them to attend to particulars, to be interactive rather than individualist, and to understand the true character of complex natural processes in holistic terms.[32] Rather, I locate the perspectives and responses of poor peasant and tribal women (perspectives which are indeed often interactive and holistic) in their material reality—in their dependence on and actual use of natural resources for survival, the knowledge of nature gained in that process, and the broader cultural parameters which define people's activities and modes of thinking in these communities. By this count, the perspectives and responses of men belonging to hill or tribal communities would also be more conducive to environmental protection and regeneration than those of men elsewhere, but not more than those of the women of such communities. This is because hill and tribal women, perhaps more than any other group, still maintain a reciprocal link with nature's resources—a link that stems from a given organization of production, reproduction, and distribution, including a given gender division of labour.

At the same time, the positive aspects of this link should not serve as an argument for the continued entrenchment of women within a given

---

[32] For a critique of these lines of argument, see Longino (1987).

division of labour. Rather, they should serve as an argument for creating the conditions that would help universalize this link with nature, for instance, by *declassing* and *degendering* the ways in which productive and reproductive activities are organized (within and outside the home) and how property, resources, knowledge, and power are distributed.

* * *

The Indian experience offers several insights and lessons. First, the processes of environmental degradation and appropriation of natural resources by a few have specific class-gender as well as locational implications—it is women of poor, rural households who are most adversely affected and who have participated actively in ecology movements. 'Women' therefore cannot be posited (as the ecofeminist discourse has typically done) as a unitary category, even within a country, let alone across the Third World or globally. Second, the adverse class-gender effects of these processes are manifest in the erosion of both the livelihood systems and the knowledge systems on which poor rural women depend. Third, the nature and impact of these processes are rooted interactively, on the one hand, in ideology (in notions about development, scientific knowledge, the appropriate gender division of labour, and so on) and, on the other hand, in the economic advantage and political power predicated especially, but by no means only, on property differentials between households and between women and men. Fourth, there is a spreading grassroots' resistance to such inequality and environmental destruction—to the processes, products, people, property, power, and profit-orientation that underlie them. Although the voices of this resistance are yet scattered and localized, their message is a vital one, even from a purely growth and productivity concern and more so if our concern is with people's sustenance and survival.

In particular, the experiences of women's initiatives within the environmental movements suggest that women's militancy is much more closely linked to family survival issues than is men's. Implicit in these struggles is the attempt to carve out a space for an alternative existence that is based on equality, not dominance over people, and on cooperation with and not dominance over nature.

Indeed what is (implicitly or explicitly) being called into question in various ways by the movements is the existing development paradigm—with its particular product and technological mix, its forms of exploitation of natural and human resources, and its conceptualization of relationships among people and between people and nature. However, a mere recognition that there are deep inequalities and destructiveness inherent in present processes of development is not enough. There is a need for policy to shift away from its present relief-oriented approach towards nature's ills and people's welfare in which the solution to nutrient-depleted soils is seen to lie entirely in externally added chemical nutrients, to depleting forests in monoculture plantations, to drought starvation in food-for-work programmes, to gender inequalities in ad hoc income-generating schemes for women, and so on. These solutions reflect an aspirin approach to development—they are neither curative nor preventive, they merely suppress the symptoms for a while.

The realistic posing of an alternative (quite apart from its implementation) is of course not easy, nor is it the purpose of this chapter to provide a blueprint. What is clear so far are the broad contours. An alternative approach, suggested by feminist environmentalism, needs to be *transformational* rather than welfarist—where development, redistribution, and ecology link in mutually regenerative ways. This would necessitate complex and interrelated changes such as in the *composition* of what is produced, the *technologies* used to produce it, the *processes* by which decisions on products and technologies are arrived at, the *knowledge systems* on which such choices are based, and the class and gender *distribution* of products and tasks.

For instance, in the context of forestry programmes, a different composition of the product may imply a shift from the currently favoured monocultural and commercial tree species to mixed species critical for local subsistence. An alternative agricultural technology may entail shifting from mainly chemical-based farming to more organic methods, from monocultural high-yielding variety seeds to mixed cropping with indigenously produced varieties, from the emphasis on large irrigation schemes to a plurality of water-provisioning systems, and from a preoccupation with irrigated crops to a greater focus on dry land crops. A change in decision-making processes would imply a shift from the present top–down approach to one that ensures the broad-based democratic participation of disadvantaged groups. Indeed, insofar as the success stories of reforestation today relate to localized communities taking charge of their environmental base, a viable solution would need decentralized planning and control and institutional arrangements that ensure the involvement of the rural poor, and especially women, in decisions about what trees are planted and how the associated benefits are shared. Similarly, to encourage the continued use and growth of local knowledge about plants and species in the process of environmental regeneration, we would require new forms of interaction between local people and trained scientists and a widening of the definition of 'scientific' to include plural sources of knowledge and innovations, rather than merely those generated in universities and laboratories. This last is not without precedent, as is apparent from the earlier discussion on Meiji Japan's interactive teams which allowed a flow of information not only from the agricultural scientist to the farmer but also the reverse. The most complex, difficult, and necessary to transform is of course the class and gender division of labour and resources and the associated social relations. Here it is the emergence of new social movements in India around issues of gender, environment, and democratic rights, and especially the formation of joint fronts between these movements on a number of recent occasions, that point the direction for change and provide the points of hope.

Indeed, environmental and gender concerns taken together open up both the need for re-examining and the possibility of throwing new light on many long-standing issues relating to development, redistribution, and institutional change. That these concerns preclude easy policy solutions underlines the deep entrenchment (both ideological and material) of interests in existing structures and models of development. It also underlines the critical importance of grassroots political organization of the poor and of women as a necessary condition for their voices to be heeded and for the entrenched interests to be undermined. Most of all it stresses the need for a shared alternative vision that can channel dispersed rivulets of resistance into a creative, tumultuous flow.

In short, an alternative, transformational approach to development would involve both ways of *thinking* about things and ways of *acting* on them. In the present context, it would concern both how gender relations and relations between people and the non-human world are conceptualized, and how they are concretized in terms of the distribution of property, power, and knowledge, and in the formulation of development policies and programmes.

It is in its failure to explicitly confront these political economy issues that the ecofeminist analysis remains a critique without threat to the established order.

REFERENCES

Acharya, Meena and Lynn Bennett (1981), 'Women and the Subsistence Sector in Nepal', World Bank Staff Working Paper No. 526, The World Bank, Washington, DC.

Agarwal, Anil (1983), 'The Cooking Energy Systems—Problems and Opportunities', Centre for Science and Environment, Delhi.
Agarwal, Bina (1981), 'Women and Water Resource Development', photocopy, Institute of Economic Growth, Delhi.
—— (1984), 'Rural Women and the High Yielding Variety Rice Technology in India', *Economic and Political Weekly*, 31 March, pp. A39–A52.
—— (1985), 'Sita Speak', *Indian Express*, 17 November.
—— (1986a), 'Women, Poverty, and Agricultural Growth in India', *Journal of Peasant Studies*, July, 13: 165–220.
—— (1986b), *Cold Hearths and Barren Slopes: The Woodfuel Crisis in the Third World*. London: Zed Books.
—— (1987), 'Under the Cooking Pot: The Political Economy of the Domestic Fuel Crisis in Rural South Asia', *IDS Bulletin*, 18(1): 11–22.
—— (1988), 'Who Sows? Who Reaps? Women and Land Rights in India', *Journal of Peasant Studies*, July, 15: 531–81.
—— (1989), 'Women, Land, and Ideology in India', in Haleh Afshar and Bina Agarwal (eds), *Women, Poverty, and Ideology: Contradictory Pressures, Uneasy Resolutions*. London: Macmillan Publishers Ltd.
—— (1990), 'Social Security and the Family: Coping with Seasonality and Calamity in Rural India', *Journal of Peasant Studies*, April, 17: 341–412.
—— (1994), *A Field of One's Own: Gender and Land Rights in South Asia*. Cambridge: Cambridge University Press.
Baden-Powell, B.H. (1957), *The Indian Village Community*. New Haven, CT: HRAF Press.
Bahuguna, Sundarlal (1984), 'Women's Non-violent Power in the Chipko Movement', in Madhu Kishwar and Ruth Vanita (eds), *In Search of Answers: Indian Women's Voices in 'Manushi'*. London: Zed Books.
Bajracharya, Deepak (1983), 'Deforestation in the Food/Fuel Context: Historical and Political Perspectives from Nepal', *Mountain Research and Development*, 3(3).
Bandyopadhyay, Jayanta (1986), 'A Case Study of Environmental Degradation in Karnataka', paper presented at a workshop on 'Drought and Desertification', India International Centre, New Delhi, 17–18 May.
Bandyopadhyay, Jayanta and Vandana Shiva (1987), 'Chipko', *Seminar*, February, 330.
Bardhan, Kalpana (1977), 'Rural Employment, Welfare, and Status: Forces of Tradition and Change in India', *Economic and Political Weekly*, 25 June, pp. A34–A48; 2 July, pp. 1062–74; and 9 July, pp. 1101–18.
Batliwala, Srilata (1983), 'Women and Cooking Energy', *Economic and Political Weekly*, 24–31 December.
Bhaduri, T. and V. Surin (1980), 'Community Forestry and Women Headloaders', *Community Forestry and People's Participation Seminar Report*. Ranchi Consortium for Community Forestry, 20–2 November.
Blaikie, Piers (1985), *The Political Economy of Soil Erosion in Developing Countries*. London and New York: Longman.

Brara, Rita (1987), 'Commons Policy as Process: The Case of Rajasthan, 1955–85', *Economic and Political Weekly*, 7 October, pp. 2247–54.
Bromley, Daniel W. and Michael M. Cernea (1989), 'The Management of Common Property Natural Resources', World Bank Discussion Paper No. 57, The World Bank, Washington, DC.
Burling, Robbins (1963), *Rensanggri: Family and Kinship in a Garo Village*. Philadelphia: Pennsylvania University Press.
Centre for Science and Environment (1986), *The State of India's Environment: A Citizen's Report, 1985–86*. Delhi: Centre for Science and Environment.
Chakravarty, Uma (1983), 'The Sita Myth', *Samya Shakti*, July, 1.
Chand, Malini and Rita Bezboruah (1980), 'Employment Opportunities for Women in Forestry', *Community Forestry and People's Participation*.
Chandrashekar, D.M., B.V. Krishna Murti, and S.R. Ramaswamy (1987), 'Social Forestry in Karnataka: An Impact Analysis', *Economic and Political Weekly*, 13 June, pp. 935–41.
Cheney, Jim (1987), 'Ecofeminism and Deep Ecology', *Environmental Ethics*, Summer, 9: 115–45.
Dasgupta, Partha and Karl-Goran Maler (1990), 'The Environment and Emerging Development Issues', paper presented at a conference on 'Environment and Development', Wider, Helsinki, September.
Dhawan, B.D. (1982), *Development of Tubewell Irrigation in India*. Delhi: Agricole Publishing Academy.
Dietrich, Gabrielle (1989), 'Plea for Survival: Book Review', *Economic and Political Weekly*, 18 February, pp. 353–4.
Dogra, Bharat (1984), *Forests and People*. Delhi: Published by the author.
Fernandes, Walter and Geeta Menon (1987), *Tribal Women and Forest Economy: Deforestation, Exploitation, and Status Change*. Delhi: Indian Social Institute.
Flaherty, Wendy O. (1990), *Other People's Myths*. New York and London: Macmillan Publishers Ltd.
Folger, Bonnie and Meera Dewan (1983), 'Kumaon Hills Reclamation: End of Year Site Visit', Delhi: OXFAM America.
Fuss, Diane (1989), *Essentially Speaking*. New York: Routledge.
Gadgil, Madhav (1985), 'Towards an Ecological History of India', *Economic and Political Weekly*, November, Special Number: 1909–38.
Gadgil, Madhav and V.D. Vartak (1975), 'Sacred Groves of India: A Plea for Continued Conservation', *Journal of the Bombay Natural History Society*, 72(2).
Glaeser, Bernhard (ed.) (1987), *Learning From China? Development and Environment in Third World Countries*. London: Allen & Unwin.
Government of India (1990), *Forest Survey of India*. New Delhi: Ministry of Environment and Forests, Government of India.
Griffin, Susan (1978), *Women and Nature: The Roaring within Her*. New York: Harper & Row.
Guha, Ramachandra (1983), 'Forestry in British and Post-British India: A Historical Analysis', *Economic and Political Weekly*, 29 October, pp. 1882–96.

Guha, Ramachandra (1985), 'Scientific Forestry and Social Change in Uttarakhand', *Economic and Political Weekly*, November, Special Number: 1939–52.

—— (1988), 'Ideological Trends in Indian Environmentalism', *Economic and Political Weekly*, 3 December, pp. 2578–81.

Habib, Irfan (1984), 'Peasant and Artisan Resistance in Mughal India', *McGill Studies in International Development*, No. 34. McGill University, Centre for Developing-Area Studies.

Hanumantha Rao, C.H., S.K. Ray, and K. Subbarao (1988), *Unstable Agriculture and Drought*. Delhi: Vikas Publishing House.

Howes, Michael and M.A. Jabbar (1986), 'Rural Fuel Shortages in Bangladesh: The Evidence from Four Villages', Discussion Paper 213. Institute of Development Studies, Sussex, England.

Jain, Shobhita (1984), 'Women and People's Ecological Movement: A Case Study of Women's Role in the Chipko Movement in Uttar Pradesh', *Economic and Political Weekly*, 13 October, pp. 1788–94.

Jodha, N.S. (1986), 'Common Property Resources and Rural Poor', *Economic and Political Weekly*, 5 July, pp. 1169–81.

Johnston, Bruce F. (1969), 'The Japanese Model of Agricultural Development: Its Relevance to Developing Nations', in Kazushi Ohkawa, Bruce F. Johnston, and Hiromitsu Kaneda (eds), *Agriculture and Economic Growth—Japan's Experience*. Princeton: Princeton University Press.

Joshi, P.K. and A.K. Agnihotri (1984), 'An Assessment of the Adverse Effects of Canal Irrigation in India', *Indian Journal of Agricultural Economics*, July–September, 39: 528–36.

Kerala Forestry Research Institute (1980), *Studies in the Changing Patterns of Man–Forest Interaction and Its Implications for Ecology and Management*. Trivandrum: Kerala Forestry Research Institute.

King, Ynestra (1981), 'Feminism and the Revolt', *Heresies*, Special Issue on Feminism and Ecology, 13: 12–16.

—— (1989), 'The Ecology of Feminism and the Feminism of Ecology', in Judith Plant (ed.), *Healing the Wounds: The Promise of Ecofeminism*. Philadelphia: New Society Publishers, pp. 18–28.

—— (1990), 'Healing the Wounds: Feminism, Ecology, and the Nature/Culture Dualism', in Irene Diamond and Gloria Orenstein (eds), *Reweaving the World: The Emergence of Ecofeminism*. San Francisco: Sierra Club Books, pp. 98–112.

Kulkarni, Sharad (1983), 'Towards a Social Forestry Policy', *Economic and Political Weekly*, 5 February, pp. 191–6.

Kumar, Shubh and David Hotchkiss (1988), 'Consequences of Deforestation for Women's Time Allocation, Agricultural Production, and Nutrition in Hill Areas of Nepal', *Research Report* 69. Washington, DC: International Food Policy Research Institute.

Leach, Edmund R. (1967), *Pul Eliya—A Village in Ceylon: A Study of Land Tenure and Kinship*. Cambridge: Cambridge University Press.

Longino, Helen E. (1981), Review of *The Death of Nature: Women, Ecology, and the Scientific Revolution* by Carolyn Merchant. *Environmental Ethics*, Winter, 3: 365–9.

—— (1987), 'Can There Be a Feminist Science?' *Hypatia*, Fall, 2: 51–64.

MacCormack, Carol P. (1980), 'Nature, Culture and Gender: A Critique', in Carol P. MacCormack and Marilyn Strathern (eds), *Nature, Culture, and Gender*. Cambridge: Cambridge University Press.

MacCormack, Carol P. and Marilyn Strathern (eds) (1980), *Nature, Culture, and Gender*. Cambridge: Cambridge University Press.

Marglin, Stephen A. (1988), 'Losing Touch: The Cultural Conditions of Worker Accommodation and Resistance', in Frederique A. Marglin and Stephen A. Marglin (eds), *Knowledge and Power*. Oxford: Oxford University Press.

Mencher, Joan (1988), 'Women's Work and Poverty: Women's Contribution to Household Maintenance in Two Regions of South India', in Daisy Dwyer and Judith Bruce (eds), *A Home Divided: Women and Income in the Third World*. Stanford: Stanford University Press.

Mencher, Joan P. and K. Saradamoni (1982), 'Muddy Feet and Dirty Hands: Rice Production and Female Agricultural Labour', *Economic and Political Weekly*, 25 December, pp. A149–A167.

Merchant, Carolyn (1980), *The Death of Nature: Women, Ecology, and the Scientific Revolution*. San Francisco: Harper & Row.

Miller, Barbara (1981), *The Endangered Sex: Neglect of Female Children in North-West India*. Ithaca: Cornell University Press.

Moench, M. (1988), 'Turf and Forest Management in a Garhwal Hill Village', in Louise Fortmann and John W. Bruce (eds), *Whose Trees? Proprietary Dimensions of Forestry*. Boulder, CO: Westview Press.

Mohan, Dinesh (1987), 'Food vs Limbs: Pesticides and Physical Disability in India', *Economic and Political Weekly*, 28 March, pp. A23–A29.

Moore, Henrietta L. (1989), *Feminism and Anthropology*. Minneapolis: University of Minnesota Press.

Nagbrahman, D. and S. Sambrani (1983), 'Women's Drudgery in Firewood Collection', *Economic and Political Weekly*, 1–8 January.

National Sample Survey Organisation (1987), *Thirty-seventh Round Report on Land Holdings—I, Some Aspects of Household Ownership Holdings*. New Delhi: Department of Statistics, Government of India.

Ortner, Sherry (1974), 'Is Male to Female as Nature is to Culture?' in Michelle Z. Rosaldo and Louise Lamphere (eds), *Women, Culture, and Society*. Stanford: Stanford University Press.

Pingle, V. (1975), 'Some Studies of Two Tribal Groups of Central India, pt. 2: The Importance of Food Consumed in Two Different Seasons', *Plant Food for Man*, 1.

Ray Chaudhuri, Tapan and Irfan Habib (eds) (1982), *Cambridge Economic History of India*. Cambridge: Cambridge University Press.

Rosenzweig, Mark and Kenneth I. Wolpin (1985), 'Specific Experience, Household Structure, and Intergenerational Transfers: Farm Family Land and Labor

Arrangements in Developing Countries', *Quarterly Journal of Economics*, 100 (supp.): 961–87.
Ryan, James G. and R.D. Ghodake (1980), 'Labour Market Behaviour in Rural Villages in South India: Effects of Season, Sex, and Socio-Economic Status', progress report, Economic Programme 14, International Crop Research Institute for Semi-Arid Tropics (ICRISAT), Hyderabad.
Salleh, Ariel Kay (1984), 'Deeper Than Deep Ecology: The Eco-Feminist Connection', *Environmental Ethics*, Winter, 16: 339–45.
Seklar, David (1981), 'The New Era of Irrigation Management in India', photocopy, Ford Foundation, Delhi.
Sen, Amartya (1990), 'Gender and Cooperative-Conflict', in Irene Tinker (ed.), *Persistent Inequalities: Women and World Development*. New York: Oxford University Press, pp. 123–45.
Sengupta, Nirmal (1985), 'Irrigation: Traditional vs. Modern', *Economic and Political Weekly*, November, Special Number: 1919–38.
Sharma, Ursula (1980), *Women, Work, and Property in North West India*. London: Tavistock.
Shaw, Paul (1989), 'Population, Environment, and Women: An Analytical Framework', paper prepared for the United Nations Fund for Population Activities (UNFPA), Inter-Agency Consultative Meeting, New York, 6 March.
Shiva, Vandana (1987), 'Ecology Movements in India', *Alternatives*, 11: 255–73.
—— (1988), *Staying Alive: Women, Ecology, and Survival*. London: Zed Books.
Stone, Linda (1982), 'Women and Natural Resources: Perspectives from Nepal', in Molly Stock, Jo Ellen Force, and Dixie Ehrenreich (eds), *Women in Natural Resources: An International Perspective*. Moscow: University of Idaho Press.
Swaminathan, Madhura (1984), 'Eight Hours a Day for Fuel Collection', *Manushi*, March–April.
Swaminathan, Srilata (1982), 'Environment: Tree versus Man', *India International Center Quarterly*, 9(3 and 4).
United Nations Development Program (1979), 'Rural Women's Participation in Development', *Evaluation Study*, No. 3. New York: UNDP, June.
Vatuk, Sylvia (1981), 'Sharing, Giving, and Exchanging of Foods in South Asian Societies', mimeo, University of Illinois at Chicago Circle, Chicago, October.
Wagner, Rudolf G. (1987), 'Agriculture and Environmental Protection in China', in Bernhard Glaeser (ed.), *Learning From China? Development and Environment in Third World Countries*. London: Allen & Unwin.
Warren, Karen J. (1987), 'Feminism and Ecology: Making Connections', *Environmental Ethics*, Spring, 9: 3–20.
Zimmerman, Michael E. (1987), 'Feminism, Deep Ecology, and Environmental Ethics', *Environmental Ethics*, Spring, 9: 21–44.

Chapter 16

GENDERSCAPES
Deepening Our Understanding of Gender–Environment Linkages

SUMI KRISHNA*

EVEN AS OUR UNDERSTANDING of the world is moulded by our lived experience, our experience itself is 're-cognized' through deeply embedded mental pictures. The imageries through which we learn to envisage the world serve to sustain hierarchies between nation-states and within them, as also the relations of power that operate in institutions and among people in communities and households. My attempt here is to conjoin diverse strands of discourse (drawing upon a range of disciplinary sources) to explore more creative ways of enhancing our understanding of women's agency and our conceptualizations of the linkages between gender and environment.

I start with a brief discussion of the politics of imaging and visualizing the world, which resonate with the different approaches to women in the environment–development discourse, delineated in the second section. I

* I thank Raka Ray for the invitation to contribute to this volume and for pertinent comments. This chapter draws upon a longer work, *Genderscapes: Revisioning Natural Resource Management* (2009). Some sections were first presented at the International Conference, 'A World in Transition: New Challenges for Gender Justice', New Delhi, 13–15 December 2006, and Centre for Women's Development Studies and the Gender and Development Network (Sweden).

argue that both conventional and celebratory approaches share a similar ideological space premised on the sexual division of labour: they treat all women simplistically as victims of environmental degradation or valorize them as 'natural' environmental managers. Gendered approaches counter the conventional and celebratory by challenging the power relations that determine this division but are yet to have a significant impact on natural resource management. In the third section, I examine aspects of gender and biodiversity and suggest that the complexity of local situations requires methods that go beyond the kind of gender analysis being practised by environmental conservation/development agencies. Finally, building upon the progressive concepts of landscapes and of gendered spaces, I elaborate the concept of 'genderscapes' to better comprehend the multidimensional locations that make up women's life-worlds. I argue that genderscapes encompass inter-penetrating complexities of gender, age, place, ethnicity, religion, caste, and class. A nuanced understanding is particularly relevant to comprehend and counter the gendered impact of rapid global flows of information, capital, and power.

IMAGES OF THE WORLD: FLAT MAPS, A SPHERICAL EARTH, AND UNSEEN 'FLOWS'

Until the mid-twentieth century, every school girl's idea of the world was shaped by the familiar mosaic of the world's nations in the flat maps of the classroom atlas. The 'rectangular projections' of the planet's continents, designed in the sixteenth century by Belgian cartographer Gerardus Mercator, aided circumnavigation of the earth but strongly distorted the shapes and sizes of land masses, inflating Europe and North America.[1] Extensive reproductions of the Mercator map have altered our image of the relative territorial space of continents and nation-states. Another kind of rectangular projection, devised in the late nineteenth century by James Gall and reinvented in the early 1970s by activist historian Arno Peters, was propagated as being non-racist and more egalitarian. Although it does not depict the polar regions accurately, the 'equal area' Peters (or Gall–Peters) map was accepted by the United Nations Educational, Scientific

---

[1] This is because areas further away from the equator appear much larger than they are. For example, the Danish island of Greenland appears to be about the same size as Africa although the latter is actually 13 times larger.

and Cultural Organization (UNESCO) in 1974. However, most geographers and cartographers in the North resisted the new map.

The debate raged through the late 1980s, when leading geographers in North America rejected all flat world maps as being erroneous images of the spherical earth (*American Cartographer* 1989; Robinson 1990). By then, space travel and television had provided an alternative image of the earth: a blue watery planet of oceans, land masses, and swirling weather systems. Rectangular two-dimensional projections are no longer required for navigation, and map-makers too have other ways of re-presenting the world.

It is ironic that the now familiar pictures of the spherical earth, which seem to render national boundaries immaterial, were the result of the military-space race of the Cold War years. In the 1970s, the image and concept of 'One Earth' provided a powerful impetus for the environmental movement (Ward and Dubos 1972). It was expected that, in a spirit of multilateralism and mutual dependence, all nations would together shape what the Bruntland Report had called *Our Common Future* (WCED 1987).[2] The Report advanced the concept of sustainable development, defined as that which meets the needs of the present without compromising the ability of future generations to meet their own needs. It recognized the need to conserve ecological systems and resources, maintain the sustainability of economic growth, and ensure the equitable sharing of benefits. The two decades between the 1972 Stockholm Conference on the Human Environment and the adoption of the International Convention on Biological Diversity at the 1992 Rio de Janeiro 'Earth Summit' were years of environmental hope.[3] Yet, as the last decade of the twentieth century unfolded, the ideal of sustainable development was far from being achieved. It was business (and more business) as usual in a world where multilateralism was being overshadowed by US hegemony even as the resource rights of the poorest were being profoundly undermined (see Krishna 1996a, 1996b, 2004d).

---

[2] *Only One Earth: The Care and Maintenance of a Small Planet* by Barbara Ward and René Dubos was based on the findings of the United Nation's 1972 Stockholm Conference. Its concerns were taken forward in *Our Common Future*, the Report of the World Commission on Environment and Development, chaired by former Norwegian prime minister Gro Harlem Bruntland.

[3] The UN Convention on Biological Diversity was signed by 150 nations at the 1992 UN Conference on Environment and Development (UNCED), also known as the 'Earth Summit'. It affirms national sovereignty over biodiversity, recognizes the traditional knowledge of local communities in managing natural resources, and provides for a global financial mechanism to support conservation.

The complex technological and political forces of globalization saw the emergence of yet another model of the world, neither flat nor spherical but enmeshed in an ever-growing global network of business and communications, dominated by transnational corporations and the World Wide Web. Global and local processes of homogenization and differentiation pose difficult challenges and inspire novel responses. The Internet, which has made possible instantaneous financial transactions and the transfer of de-stabilizing 'hot' money across continental distances, has also facilitated the networking of new social movements across the world. Arjun Appadurai (1990, 1996) uses the suffix 'scape' to convey the dynamism of global flows across hitherto impassable boundaries: *ethnoscapes*, the mass movements of peoples; *technoscapes*, the speedy transboundary transfer of technologies; *financescapes*, the speculative flow of global capital; *mediascapes*, the dissemination of information, images, and narratives; and *ideoscapes*, the transmission of political cultures of nation-states, ideologies, and counter-ideologies. Viewing the tension between sameness and difference as the core of global cultural processes, he says that the state plays an increasing role in absorbing various homogenizing 'instruments' into local political and cultural economies.

The four-colour mosaics of the flat map, the rounded depictions of planet earth, the unseen flows of information and technology—these are all deeply embedded in our minds, and the force of such images also streams through our institutional structures and practices, to which I now turn.

APPROACHES TO WOMEN AND THE ENVIRONMENT

Internationally, approaches to women and development have evolved through different phases, from Women in/and Development (WID/WAD) to Gender and Development (GAD). The approach categorized as Women and Environment (WED), which is similar to the liberal WID, has been countered both by various strands of ecofeminism and by GAD.[4] The WED approach, adopted by international agencies in the 1980s, emphasizes women's knowledge and skills but tends to treat women's

---

[4] Ecofeminism is generally understood to represent feminist radicalism (Plumwood 1986; Mies and Shiva 1993; Warren 1994). WED is a liberal approach akin to WID, which has been countered by the socialist/Marxist GAD (for various theoretical formulations, see Agarwal 1992; Braidotti *et al.* 1994; Kabeer 1994; Tinker 1990).

labour and time instrumentally as the means to increase the effectiveness of resource management. The more radical ecofeminist approaches highlight women's 'inherent' nurturing qualities and their sustaining roles in resource management. In contrast to both WED and ecofeminisms, the more progressive GAD approaches are centred on the social construction of gender. In my view, in the Indian context, the approach and terminology of WID/WAD/ecofeminism/GAD do not translate easily as concepts and terms of discourse. Perhaps this is because of the political fuzziness of Indian environmentalism (Krishna 1996a, 1996b). Hence, I have suggested a different typology of conventional, celebratory, and gendered (summarized in Table 16.1) as more suitable to encompass the kind of approaches that are encountered in the field of natural resource conservation and development.[5]

TABLE 16.1 Approaches to Women and the Environment

Aspects	Conventional	Celebratory	Gendered
Focus	On people, women are assumed to be included	Concentrate on women	On women and men
Women's role in Natural Resource Management (NRM)	Uncommitted; seek more research	View as naturally determined (or sometimes as biologically determined)	View as socially constructed
Use of Gender Analysis (GA)	No GA, but the term 'gender' is used	No GA, the term 'gender' is rarely used	GA is used; gender is seen as one of many social determinants
Place of women's concerns in projects	Tag women on to projects	Valorize women's subsistence skills and lifestyles	Has difficulties in converting GA into practice
Implication for women in relation to NRM	Use women in instrumental ways, ask what women can do for NRM; address 'women's needs'	Essentialize and treat women alike as skilled nurturers and resource managers; address women's needs	Attempt to address gender relations, and ask what NRM can do for women in the long term
Gender labels/stereotypes	Reinforce existing hierarchical dichotomies	Reverse existing hierarchical dichotomies	Challenge existing hierarchical dichotomies

Source: Krishna 2007 (adapted from Krishna 1997, 2001, 2004a).

[5] I first suggested the typology of conventional, celebratory, and gendered approaches to women and the environment in a presentation at the M.S. Swaminathan Research Foundation, Chennai, in 1997 and elaborated it in subsequent work (Krishna 2001). This broadly corresponds to the three environmental approaches—managerial, popular, and progressive—sketched in my earlier work on environmentalism (Krishna 1996a, 1996b).

Conventional and Celebratory Approaches

Conventional approaches (like WED) recognize gender bias in development and resource management but focus on women's *lack* of skills and opportunities, which is sought to be remedied through training and programme interventions. This generally results in enlisting/appropriating poor women's labour for tasks that can be carried out in or near the home, and which fall within stereotypes of women's work. For instance, livelihood interventions for women tend to be overwhelmingly related to food processing (the 'pickles-and-*papad*' syndrome) or confined to wage labour for activities such as planting and tending seedlings in nurseries. There is an implicit bias that reinforces middle class masculinist norms and hierarchies, subtly devaluing women's productive capabilities, strength, and intelligence. Conventional approaches to women typically characterize the outlook of government development agencies, technocrats, and natural resource managers, but may be shared even by those in the non-government sector and activists who oppose conventional development.

Celebratory approaches include some traditional (indigenous) approaches and South Asian variations of Western ecofeminisms that idealize traditional female roles and view poor, disadvantaged women's productive, resource-related work as biologically or naturally determined. Celebratory approaches resonate with popular environmentalism and the holistic rhetoric of deep ecology. They valorize women's procreative, emotional, and intuitive capacities and presumed closeness to nature. A 'feminine principle' in nature is recognized and contrasted to modern science and technology, which are viewed as masculine projects to subjugate women. In linking the so-called 'feminine principle' in nature to women's subsistence production and lifestyles (Shiva 1988; Mies and Shiva 1993), such approaches tend to a de-contextualized view of women, unmindful of local diversities and historical specificities of ethnicity, caste, and class. This approach has been critiqued by Kelkar and Nathan (1991), Agarwal (1992), Krishna (1995, 1996b), Rangan (1993, 2000), and Williams and Mawdsley (2006), among others.

Both conventional and celebratory approaches have opened up certain spaces for women. The difficulty, however, is that they rest on claims that grow out of the sexual division of roles, labour, and responsibilities, seen as natural and universal (Krishna 2004a). When context-specific differences and inequities of access to resources within communities and households are ignored, traditionally demarcated occupational roles come to be seen as natural and essential to resource conservation. Thus, the sexual division of labour that perpetuates the 'housewifing' of women's 'natural' resource knowledge, skills, and practice is reinforced. Such an understanding leads to exaggerating women's natural resource knowledge and eliding men's responsibilities for resource conservation and food provisioning (see Jewitt 2000). Customary practices that are specific to region, religion, caste, or ethnic group, and which restrict women's autonomy, mobility, and capacity to participate in resource management are also overlooked.

In terms of the visual images of the world, discussed earlier, I suggest that the conventional approaches envision the world in 'flat' technocratic and managerial terms. Like Mercator's rectangular maps that once aided maritime navigation, such an approach serves a limited developmental purpose, but its distorted perspective perpetuates deep social and political biases. Celebratory approaches (reflected in popular Gandhian thought, deep ecology, and certain constituents of ecofeminism) have confronted and exposed the technocratic bias of the conventional–managerial approach but the inspiring and idealistic vision (as of 'One Earth') elides historically contested terrains of class and caste.

Gendered Approaches

Gendered approaches, which I share, neither see women as a homogenous category nor rest on claims that grow out of the sexual division of labour, but they seek to challenge the power relations that determine such division. Deconstructing conventional notions of the natural resource roles and responsibilities of women and men, gendered approaches are also dismissive of celebratory projections of deep, intrinsic linkages between women and nature. In this progressive perspective, gender is central to power relations and the demarcation of physical spaces and mental capacities in specific contexts. Importantly, gendered approaches recognize that women's exclusion from certain domains of knowledge characterizes *both* traditional and modern knowledge systems and that such exclusion impacts upon belief systems and the production of knowledges. This is visible in a range of traditional resource-related taboos that specifically discriminate by gender and caste and also apparent in the modern natural resource disciplines, which carry gender and class 'markings' in their vocabulary, metaphors, and concepts (see Krishna 2009).

Gendered approaches (like GAD) are concerned with the social construction of masculinity and femininity, which may be viewed from a materialist and/or social relations perspective. Material analyses of gender have emphasized asymmetries between women and men in access to and control of resources and power, while cultural approaches have concentrated on the bodily and cultural practices by which women are socialized into femininity. Analyses that overcome the polarity of the material and the cultural have focused attention on political ecology and the gendered social relations that mark the conditions of everyday life, social practices, and institutions (see Joekes *et al.* 1995; Rocheleau *et al.* 1996). In GAD discourse, Gender Analysis (GA) frameworks and tools have been used effectively to differentiate gender roles, responsibilities, and patterns of resource usage (for example, Moser 1993; see also March *et al.* 1999). Yet, the attempts to apply the 'practical instruments' of GA methods and tools in the field have rarely uncovered the deep structures of gender relations and entrenched perceptions about women and nature/environment. The value of GA frameworks in critically unpacking the world do not seem to be taking us any closer to envisioning alternatives that have the practical uses of the flat world of Mercator's map and the spiritual inspiration of the spherical 'One Earth'. I suggest that this may be partly because GA, as it is now practised by many international and national environment-development agencies in South Asia, is reduced to surveys and checklists that can be ticked off without a textured and nuanced understanding of the diversity of women's locations, the edges and interstices of the subterranean structures that shape women's life-worlds, and their own cognition of their role and place in nature and society.

GENDER AND BIODIVERSITY MANAGEMENT

Human beings are part of the earth's biological diversity, holding vital keys to the conservation of the complex web that connects living systems on the earth. The linkages between processes of knowledge production and the shaping of the earth's natural resource base have been variously understood by modern development interventions. For instance, in the mid-1970s, UNESCO's 'Man and Biosphere' programme recognized the association of human beings and the earth but the nomenclature itself reflects that at that time neither gender issues nor biological diversity were specifically in focus. The term 'biodiversity' (abbreviated from 'biological diversity') is itself a creation of recent times, the outcome of attempts to overcome sectoral approaches to the spectrum of living resources. In the 1990s, biodiversity became a principal organizing concept in the conservation movement, overtaking other terms such as environment, ecology, and nature. As defined by the UN Convention (UNEP 1992: Article 2), biological diversity refers to 'the variability among living organisms from all sources', including 'terrestrial, marine and other aquatic ecosystems and the ecological complexes of which they are a part; this includes diversity within species, between species and of ecosystems'. Biological resources include genetic resources, organisms or their parts, populations, and any other biotic components of ecosystems 'of actual or potential use, or value, for humanity'.

The bio-geographic region of India has an enormous diversity of physio-geographic and climatic zones, hundreds of different ecosystems, a variety of floristic and faunal regions, harbouring several thousand species of plants, animals, and micro-organisms. This is considered one of the world's 12 mega-biodiversity areas, comprising over 6.5 per cent of the world's known wildlife (Rani and Swaminathan 1998: 5). For the peoples who have lived and worked in these varied ecosystems, their indigenous methods of managing biodiversity have been primarily intended to secure and sustain food sources. Biodiversity and food are human concerns that are of particular interest to women because of the historical processes that have determined the gendered division of societies in this region, and the socio-political institutions that have shaped male and female roles, responsibilities, needs, and aspirations in particular contexts of class/caste/ethnicity.

Biodiversity has rarely been viewed through a gendered lens, although in most of South Asia, rural women have a primary role in household provisioning and in conserving and managing the living resources of forests, fields, and farms. Even in the relatively egalitarian tribal communities of northeastern India, women's subordinate status is reflected and reinforced by the sexual division of work in the collection of fuel and fodder, the care of animals and poultry, and the cultivation of fields and home gardens (Krishna 1998b, 1998c, 2004b, 2005). Poor adivasi/tribal[6] and other forest-dwelling women have a vast repository of knowledge of lesser-known wild foods that they forage from forests, wetlands, fields and plantations, along streams, and even wayside paths (see Narayanan *et al.* 2005). Wild food sources include leafy greens, fruits, seeds, tubers, mushrooms, honey, crabs, and fish, and several have multiple uses as both food and medicine.

---

[6] The term 'tribe' is used in the Constitution of India. In the Hindi translation of the Constitution, this is *adimjati* (primitive race). Because of the negative connotations of 'tribe' in colonial anthropology, the preferred term in much of India today is adivasi. In northeastern India, however, the preferred term is 'indigenous people' and 'adivasi' is used only for immigrant plantation labourers from northern/central India. Many activist groups now use 'adivasi/indigenous people'.

For the poorest peoples, wild foods provide a reliable buffer in lean seasons and enhance the nutrient quality of the diet.

Even when resource management programmes do have a gendered orientation, the GA methods used do not capture the context specificity and complexity that biodiversity entails (see Krishna 1998a, 1999, 2009). Studies of gender roles in biodiversity in South Asia (Krishna 1998a) have underlined the primacy of women's responsibility for seed exchange, the conservation of varieties and land races, and medicinal plant collection and use. These responsibilities are very variable, often limited to particular crops or locations. Concepts of the sacredness of seed, especially grain seeds, and the fear of their pollution by menstruating women are also widespread. A 'brahminized' tribe of Wayanad, in northern Kerala, believes that women's touch pollutes paddy seeds but not vegetable seeds; so paddy sowing is a male task but vegetables are sown by women (Vedavalli and Kumar 1998). Similar taboos exist on women's entry into sacred groves, especially when the care of the deities has passed from adivasi or Dalit communities to dominant castes. As I have argued elsewhere, the conservation ethic attached to sacred groves loses its sheen when viewed through a gender–caste lens (Krishna 1996b, 1998a, 2009).

Older beliefs and practices, reinforced by modern political and economic developments, shape the age/location/caste-specific norms that govern women's personal autonomy, decision-making power, and control over critical assets: knowledge systems, land, bio-resources, and their own labour. Unlike conventional and celebratory approaches, gendered approaches recognize that class, caste, ethnicity, and gender are significant factors in traditional knowledge systems and community institutions (see, for example, Choudhury 2001, 2004; Krishna 2004; Locke 1999). Some non-governmental organizations (NGOs) have sought to address this in resource management interventions. Rural women are mainly responsible for tending livestock but the specialized traditional knowledge of animal health and healing is generally passed by fathers only to their sons. ANTHRA, an NGO concerned with livestock and biodiversity issues, has worked with pastoral and rural communities in Andhra Pradesh and Maharashtra to facilitate a change in the process of knowledge transfer so that men have begun teaching their daughters about animal health care (Ramdas et al. 2004). Similarly, field staff of the Centre for Women's Development Studies had to find ways to convince local adivasi groups in Bankura district, West Bengal, that women's touch would not pollute the tasar silk cocoon, so women could rear cocoons to improve the family income (Banerjee 2004).

Today, both globally and in South Asia, the policy climate for conservation and sustainable development favours 'involving' women, usually treated as one homogenous constituency. The official biodiversity management system, however, continues to be deeply patriarchal in its understanding of issues. Education, policy planning, programme development, extension, and implementation are all dominated by men.[7] In a synthesis of case studies on the linkages between biodiversity and gender in Bhutan, Nepal, India, Maldives, and Sri Lanka (Krishna 1999), I found that the conventional approach still prevailed; instrumentalist strategies simply made use of poor rural and tribal women's knowledge, skills, and labour to increase the efficiency of programmes. The celebratory rhetoric about women's biological attributes, their nurturing roles, and their participation in biodiversity management obscures the varied experiences of different social groups and classes of women over time. In the short term, many official interventions do benefit some women by easing their labour but these do little for women's subordinate status in the long term because the more wrenching political questions of gender–power relations are ignored. Similarly, after reviewing a wide spectrum of community biodiversity initiatives in India (by both international agencies and national organizations), I found that the projects might be located in rural areas or particular villages and targeted at the village community, but these were designed *for* the people, rarely *by* them (Krishna 1998a: 44–9). Considerable scientific effort goes into project design and monitoring, but local people, especially subordinated groups and women, are involved only in implementation.

New programmes for medicinal plant propagation, raising seed and plant nurseries, and the like, use women's ecological knowledge of biodiversity, plants, animals, and farming systems but do not address

---

[7] Information on the ratio of women in professions related to biological diversity is scattered. Data that I collected a decade ago remain broadly valid today (Krishna 1998a). In 1997–8, the percentages of women in the major official biodiversity-related agencies, other agencies, and NGOs were minuscule, especially in field positions. Women comprised 8.5 per cent of life members in the Indian Society for Seed Technology. Of the 225 persons elected fellows of the National Academy of Agricultural Sciences since its inception, seven were women (under 3 per cent), mainly social scientists and nutritionists. The Indian Forest Service was opened to women in 1980, but 15 years later there were just 72 women forest officers in a cadre of 2,576, that is, 2.8 per cent. The ratio of women rangers and foresters was under 1 per cent. A critical threshold of women in an organization/institution does influence its direction. (It should be noted, however, that there are many gender-sensitive men and that not all women have a gendered approach.)

the sexual division of labour that arises from inequitable relations in the household and community, which are mediated by gender, age, place, ethnicity, religion, caste, and class. Natural resource interventions that either valorize or leave traditional management systems untouched are actually reinforcing gender biases by side-stepping the political questions of women's autonomy and decision-making power in particular households and communities (Krishna 1995). This limits the effectiveness of development interventions (see, for example, Kodoth 2004; Krishna 2007; Raju 2005) and may indeed be contributing to the contemporary advancement of various forms of patriarchy (Krishna 2004c). Therefore, in order to interrogate the linkages of gender with class and caste/tribe, we should locate women's resource needs in a variety of specific contexts and 'open up' the structure of different community institutions, distinguishing between resource management and resource rights. Women's rights in biodiversity must be seen as empowering *human* rights, a moral claim that is not premised on the sexual division of labour.

Gendered approaches that have drawn upon powerful feminist materialist and social relations theories would appear to be well placed to face the new global challenges to resource management, but the methodology of GA (as discussed earlier) has tended to become a desk exercise carried out without imagination, empathy, and political commitment to feminist goals. Perhaps we need a fresh conceptualization of gendered spaces to re-vision traditional and modern resource management practices in specific contexts and against larger structures and processes.

GENDERSCAPES

Since the 1990s, the focus of conservation biology has shifted from the loss of particular species to concerns about the diversity of ecosystems across wider expanses, 'landscapes', and regions. An endangered and protected species, for example, would not be viewed in isolation but as part of a larger landscape that includes protected and unprotected areas. The ecological processes within landscapes are influenced by large-scale processes, such as climatic patterns and the hydrological balance, and by small-scale heterogeneity and biotic interactions. Changes in 'keystone' ecosystems may have significant impacts, such as on water storage over a larger scale (see UNEP 1995: 304–10). Both traditional and modern systems of managing living resources depend on comprehending the various components, processes, and relationships that characterize different ecological landscapes and on understanding how such landscapes are constructed over time.

Landscapes are also intertwined with historical and socio-political notions of land and nature, culture, and heritage. As I have written elsewhere (Krishna 1996b: 262), a 'picturesque landscape of self-contained village communities' has been a central and powerful image in popular Indian environmentalism and some strands of global environmentalism: 'This is an imagined landscape shaped by many different influences—by foreign anthropologists and Indian nationalists. It is above all a visual image of village communities, living close to the land, in harmony with one another and with nature.' Such an idealized visual conception of a landscape strips it of its contextual specificity. This has several developmental implications. In nature, as in art, land is shaped by culture into landscapes (see Mitchell 2002); abstract conceptions of space may negate locally embedded notions of place in a landscape. Judy Whitehead (2003) suggests that a narrowly utilitarian approach that 'measures and surveys the landscape in terms of its commercially viable features' characterizes neo-liberal capitalism and scientific–managerial attempts to reorder landscapes. She argues that developers in the Narmada valley have used the concept of abstract space 'to maintain a highly objectified and external relation to the landscape, which becomes emptied of people, history, entitlements, myth and magic', and is 'replaced by a quantifiable area consisting of commodifiable resources, in this case, water and electricity'. She views the dynamics as 'immense waves' of spatial change (following Lefebvre 1990: 87), colliding rather than intersecting.

Indeed, a landscape is a world produced by the people who dwell and work in/on it, what Tim Ingold (1993: 167) has called a 'taskscape made visible'. Ingold (ibid.: 152) says that landscapes are 'constituted' by the activities of people, and are 'an enduring record of—and testimony to—the lives and works of past generations who have dwelt within it, and in so doing, have left there something of themselves'. When viewed in this way, the paths that criss-cross a landscape can be 'read' not as routes between particular locations but as the social imprint of generations. A landscape is, thus, constructed by a taskscape that shapes its character and invests it with temporality, patterns from the past, and projections into the future. Such a progressive vision of a taskscape resonates with gendered readings of place, space, and landscapes, what I have called 'genderscapes'.

As globalization gathered pace through the 1990s, concepts of space and place illuminated neglected aspects of social relations under patriarchy (for example, Busby 2000; Kapadia 1996; Massey 1994; Niranjana

2001). Spaces are not gendered in simple binary terms of inside/outside, private/public, but in complex ways that reflect the social organization of differences between women and men in the family and the community (Krishna 2003). Gendered space cannot be mechanically measured and mapped, because it is marked by people's perceptions and not by physical boundaries. Such spaces are 'particular locales that cultures invest with gendered meanings, sites in which sex-differentiated practices occur, or settings that are used strategically to inform identity and produce and reproduce asymmetrical gender relations of power and authority' (Low and Lawrence-Zuniga 2003: 7). Thus, 'outside' spaces are those places where women feel, or are made to feel, uncomfortable, unsafe, and unwanted, and those locations and activities that are deemed to be beyond women's domain.

I have suggested that the concept of genderscapes enables us to understand and depict the complex turbulence of gender–power relations, the multiple inequities, conflicts, resistances, and negotiations that mark households, social groups, and wider communities.[8] The seeming ecological 'complementarity' of a landscape, its harmony and balance, mask the particular gendered discourse that has moulded the terrain. Viewed from within, from the inside out as it were, the intricately evolved (and evolving) gender-differentiated pattern of work zones comes into focus. Anoja Wickramasinghe (2004) has shown how the ecological zonation of a landscape in a dry region of Sri Lanka embodies the gender-differentiated work that has shaped it. Consider also the small Apatani valley in Arunachal Pradesh in northeastern India; it is world-famous for its unique high-altitude (at about 2,000 metres) irrigated wet-rice and fish cultivation. Men manage the forests that encircle the valley and the mountain streams that are channelled to the fields; the women manage the paddy fields. The valley's ecological zonation has been shaped by human activities over generations and is intimately linked to the tribal gender ideology that determines the unequal division of knowledge and responsibilities between Apatani women and men. The patriarchal subordination of Apatani women is hidden by the picturesque landscape within which it is ensconced (Krishna 1998b, 2005).

Gendered 'scapes' are not only about gender; women's identities are embedded in their varied languages and cultures, their life-worlds shaped

---

[8] I first delineated the idea of genderscapes in the introductions to a special issue of the *Indian Journal of Gender Studies* (2000) and to *Livelihood and Gender* (2004a); and later elaborated the concept in Krishna 2009.

by multiple locations, their particular histories, and wider processes of social formation. Male domination operates differently from tribe to tribe (Kelkar and Nathan 1991), across tribes and castes (Thamizoli 1997), and within and across different caste groups (Chakravarti 2003). Community codes of conduct, marriage, sexuality, and mobility are intertwined with the selective appropriation of women's labour. Women seem to have a greater political and management role among foraging tribes than among pastoral and settled agriculturist tribes who are nearer to the patriarchal ways of life of caste society. The adivasi/tribal woman's loss of control over land and forest resources is paralleled by the erosion of her ritual, jural, social, and economic positions. Violence against Dalit or adivasi women occurs both within their communities and across them. Yet, most contemporary social movements and action-researchers have found it difficult to focus on overlapping forms of exploitation. Feminist studies that have eroded the rigid boundaries of the social science disciplines are also yet to establish methodologies that can deal with a diversity of locations. The struggle to weave many threads into the fabric of analyses and action is, however, foregrounded in Dalit women's own narratives. For example, Dalit women's autobiographies or 'socio-biographies' reveal a closely knit triple critique of the feminist, Dalit, and left movements, which have all marginalized Dalit women (Pandit 2007). Perhaps sensitive genderscapes could enable us to leaven the GA matrix with creative ethnography and innovative techniques (visual, dramatic, narrative, and so on) that reflect what Foucault (1984) called the 'micropolitics of power', the complex dynamics that lie beneath the surface of a taskscape–landscape.

An example of a study that comes close to my conceptualization of a genderscape is Piya Chatterjee's (2003) *A Time for Tea*, which focuses on a 'dot' on the map, a small tea estate that is just a few hours by road from Naxalbari, the revolutionary centre of 1960s' left politics in India. British tea companies had appropriated the frontier wildernesses of northeastern India (using the arbitrary Wasteland Rules of 1838) and turned them into manicured landscapes, euphemistically called 'tea gardens'. The plantation fiefdoms were created and maintained by indentured adivasi labour brought in from Chhotanagpur (Jharkhand) and elsewhere because the local Assamese and Bengali were more resistant to wage work. Women carried out the most intensive labour of plucking tea, and the gendered stereotype of 'women's nimble fingers' emerged. Chatterjee's study reverberates with the politics of empire and of gender across continents and centuries, tellingly reflected in the contrasting images of upper-class feminine leisure and gentility (the lady in her parlour pouring tea) and in the hands of the women tea-pluckers, which are hardened, cut, and stained black: '*Hath dekho ... Yeh kam ... yeh natak nahi he, didi*' (Look at our hands ... This work ... this is no drama, sister). The company's profits, and the planter's power and efficiency in managing the estate, rest on the disciplining and surveillance of labour. Much of this is achieved through ideologies of sexuality, grafted feudal norms of gender roles and behaviour, bodily controls, and individual coercion. In the tea business, the political economy of the field is a sexual economy (ibid.: 221). At every level of power, men wield the planter's *hukum*, a regime which gives working men the 'right' to rule over women who labour. Yet, in village households there is also a 'displacement' of power with customary masculine authority and honour being eroded because women are the primary wage-earners, and high male unemployment has led to alcoholism and violence. The women know that their wage-earning is one of the reasons they are beaten: 'Violence is the modality of both power and its lack' (ibid.: 284). Today, the politics of 'alliances' between union leaders and plantation managers has replaced the 'indirect' rule of the colonial *sirdars*, recruiters, and overseers. Women are pushed into the frontlines of union action, in demonstrations and gheraos, because notions of women's bodily *izzat* (honour) are expected to make the male police hesitate before laying hands on them. But, within the unions the women continue to be marginalized by innuendoes of immorality and a potent sexual politics. The women express the need for their own collective mobilization, but there is also an abiding endurance ('we are only women'). They are constrained 'by a pan-community lexicon of honor' (ibid.: 322–3). The adivasi women's polyphonic narratives enable us to see how their bodies are the 'bridges' between labour and product, how bodily acts constitute the culture of consumption. Thus, the gendered story of the production, consumption, and distribution of tea is interwoven with the historical and contemporary forces of global capital, information, and power as these collide and sometimes mesh with the local politics of patronage, patriarchy, and coercion. This is a genderscape, its very specificity giving it a wider universality.

I see genderscapes as ranging further than GA frameworks and dwelling deeper, drawing out the material and ideological dimensions of gender-power relations from the standpoint of an engaged and interested 'outsider-within' (Collins 1986, 1990; Harding 1991, 2001).[9] Genderscapes

---

[9] Feminist-scientist Sandra Harding questioned the supposedly objective scientific 'voice from nowhere' arguing that every researcher occupies a specific lived location and speaks from it. But this does not mean that there is a multiplicity of subjective views

would encompass critical reflection of concepts and terms of discourse (*wordscapes*); ethnography of women's life-worlds (*workscapes*); and analysis of research, policy, and programme interventions (*actionscapes*) that elucidate or have an impact upon women's natural resource–based livelihoods (Krishna 2009). Starting with the family and the household, genderscapes would trace the complex and multiple linkages between the sexual division of labour and resource management in the home and the division of labour in the wider community, uncovering patterns of women's subordination, whether through economic vulnerability or through coercive/forceful confinement in domestic arenas by 'ideologies of mothering, caring and nurturing' (Moore 1988). A textured, nuanced genderscape would seek to deepen our observations and analyses, revealing multiple and simultaneous dimensions in the pathways and social imprints of a landscape to provide more meaningful insights into the gendered character of traditional and modern resource management practices.[10]

Furthermore, genderscapes would go beyond GA by blurring the boundaries between researchers and the 'researched'. This requires exploring alternative methods and tools, including oral history and narrative techniques, poetry, song, drama, even folk crafts, as means to recover and represent the complexities and particularities of everyday gendered practice, gendered resistances, and patterns of resource management. Some researcher-practitioners have attempted to break rigid donor/journal-governed research and writing formats. A few have also struggled to incorporate their own experiences and responses, the messy interfaces between life, action, and research, into the research framework. In Chatterjee's (2003) study, the ethnography produces different dialogical registers and the main narrative is also interspersed throughout with

---

because knowledge production is a collective process. So, if we start from the perspectives of women's lives, not women in the abstract but particular groups of women in specific social locations and bio-physical contexts, marginalization itself becomes strength, generating what Harding calls 'strong objectivity' (see Harding 1993).

[10] Reflecting upon the complex intersections of the temporal and the spatial in a world in which economic and cultural boundaries are swiftly crossed, John Berger has remarked that every point is a 'star of lines' (1974: 40). Collins (2003: 16–17) uses the metaphor to track the structuring of apparel production through multiple interactions: the economics of the global garment industry and the social and gender relations that operate at specific locations in the commodity chain, 'enacted by employers and workers within their disparate and shared frameworks of meaning and power'. In my view, a 'star of lines' captures some of the complexity that feminists seek to understand but does not convey the 'immense waves' of spatial change delineated by Whitehead (2003), of dynamic flows colliding rather than neatly intersecting.

excerpts from a fictional play that echoes and repeats the theme, even as it disrupts the narrative sequence. Neera M. Singh (2006), in her ongoing work on the emergence of community forestry networks and women's activism in Orissa, has imaginatively used auto-ethnography and poetry to interrogate the blurred boundaries and shared life-spaces that slip through normal methods of social and participatory action research. I have used a personal narrative to bring the family into the development discourse and to explore the process of change as a semi-nomadic group of adivasi foragers come together to form a village settlement and conserve their environment (Krishna 2003). Despite the more formal structure required of a PhD thesis, Meghana Kelkar's (2008) study of gender and local knowledge of soil management in Maharashtra uses an open and flexible ethnography to reveal how something as material as the soil is constructed by struggles over practices and meanings; she also acknowledges the tensions that such an approach entails for the scientific researcher.

At a time when global forces pose many different kinds of threats to people's biodiversity-based livelihoods, we urgently need to find ways to deepen our understanding both of the local contexts and the broader forces of change. Linking this to the foregoing discussion on images of the world—flat maps, the spherical earth, and unseen flows—we could say that re-visioning the world as dynamic 'scapes' may be a more effective response to contemporary challenges. The concept of genderscapes is relevant to the management of biodiversity and other natural resources, because gender ideologies are meshed into bio-physical environments and seep through a range of traditional and modern institutions, diffusing into life-worlds via belief systems and socio-political structures that in turn shape the environment and resource management. Table 16.2 summarizes the argument.

TABLE 16.2 Summation

Visualizations of the World	Dimensions	Approach to Women–Environment	Implication for Biodiversity-based Livelihoods
Flat maps	Two-dimensional	Conventional–Managerial	Practical for limited purposes
'One Earth'	Three-dimensional	Celebratory–Popular	Inspiring as a call to action
Dynamic 'scapes'	Multiple and simultaneous dimensions	Gendered–Progressive	Better able to respond to global challenges?

Since the early 1990s, landscapes and bio-resources have been rapidly transformed by economic globalization, international trade and agreements (including those related to biodiversity), and by national environmental and natural resource policies and programmes. Local resource-use conflicts and the displacement–relocation of human settlements pose difficult challenges to people's livelihoods, especially those of the poor. In these demanding circumstances, we need varied strategies to keep issues of gender justice in focus in the wider struggles over resource management and the debates over globalization and people's livelihood options. Nations and communities cannot manage their natural resources in a sustainable manner without re-visioning the linkages between gender and environment and incorporating principles of gender justice into policies and practice.

REFERENCES

Agarwal, Bina (1992), 'The Gender and Environment Debate: Lessons from India', *Feminist Studies*, 18(2): 119–53.

American Cartographer, 'Resolution by Seven North American Geographical Groups' (1989), *American Cartographer*, 16(3): 222–3.

Appadurai, Arjun (1990), 'Disjuncture and Difference in the Global Political Economy', *Public Culture*, 2(2): 1–24.

────── (1996), *Modernity at Large: Cultural Dimensions of Globalization* (Public Worlds Vol. 1). Minneapolis: University of Minnesota Press.

Banerjee, Narayan K. (2004), 'Organising Women through Wasteland Development: Bankura District, West Bengal', in Sumi Krishna (ed.), *Livelihood and Gender: Equity in Community Resource Management*. New Delhi: Sage Publications, pp. 109–24.

Berger, John (1974), *The Look of Things*. New York: Viking Press.

Braidotti, Rosi, Ewa Charkiewiwcz, Sabie Hausler, and Saskia Wieringa (1994), *Women, the Environment and Sustainable Development. Towards a Theoretical Synthesis*. London: Zed Books.

Busby, Cecilia (2000), *The Performance of Gender: An Anthropology of Everyday Life in a South Indian Fishing Village*. London and New Brunswick, NJ: The Athlone Press.

Chakravarti, Uma (2003), *Gendering Caste: Through a Feminist Lens*. Kolkata: Stree.

Chatterjee, Piya (2003), *A Time for Tea: Women, Labor and Post-Colonial Politics on an Indian Plantation*. New Delhi: Zubaan (first published in 2001 by Duke University Press).

Choudhury, Arundhuti Roy (2001), *Common Property, Resource Management: Gender, Equity and Participation—A Case Study of the Fish Workers of Kerala*. New Delhi: Indian Social Institute.

────── (2004), 'Community Institutions and Gender: Fishworkers in Kasargode, Kozhikode and Thiruvanthapuram Districts, Kerala', in Krishna (ed.), *Livelihood and Gender*, pp. 375–94.

Collins, Patricia Hill (1986), 'Learning from the Outsider within: The Sociological Significance of Black Feminist Thought', *Social Problems*, 33(6): 14–32.
―― (1990), *Black Feminist Thought*. Cambridge, UK: Cambridge University Press.
Collins, Jane L. (2003), *Threads: Gender, Labour and Power in the Global Apparel Industry*. Chicago: University of Chicago Press.
Foucault, Michel (1984), *History of Sexuality*. London: Penguin Books.
'Gender Relations and Environmental Change', *IDS Bulletin*, Joekes, Susan, Mellissa Leach, and Cathy Green (eds), (1995), 26(1). Sussex: Institute for Development Studies.
Harding, Sandra (1991), *Whose Science, Whose Knowledge? Thinking from Women's Lives*. Ithaca, NY: Cornell University Press.
―― (1993), 'Rethinking Standpoint Epistemology: "What Is Strong Objectivity"?', in Linda Alcoff and Elizabeth Potter (eds), *Feminist Epistemologies*. London: Routledge, pp. 49–82.
―― (2001), 'Just Add Women and Stir?' in Gender Working Group, UN Commission on Science and Technology for Development (ed.), *Missing Links: Gender Equity in Science and Technology for Development*. Ottawa: International Development Research Centre (IDRC); London: IT Publications; and New York: United Nations Development Fund for Women (UNIFEM), pp. 295–307.
Ingold, T. (1993), 'The Temporality of the Landscape', *World Archaeology*, 25(2): 152–74.
Jewitt, Sarah (2000), 'Unequal Knowledges in Jharkhand, India: De-Romanticizing Women's Agroecological Expertise', *Development and Change*, 31: 961–85.
Kabeer, Naila (1994), *Reversed Realities: Gender Hierarchies in Development Thought*. New Delhi: Kali for Women.
Kapadia, Karin (1996), *Siva and Her Sisters: Gender, Caste and Class in Rural South India*. New Delhi: Oxford University Press.
Kelkar, Govind and Dev Nathan (1991), *Women, Land and Forests in Jharkhand*. New Delhi: Kali for Women.
Kelkar, Meghana (2008), 'Gender and Local Knowledge: The Case of Soil Management in Satara District', unpublished PhD thesis, Tata Institute of Social Sciences, Mumbai.
Kodoth, Praveena (2004), 'Gender Aspects of Family Property and Land Rights: Regulation and Reform in Kerala', in Krishna (ed.), *Livelihood and Gender*, pp. 373–94.
Krishna, Sumi (1995), 'It's Time to Clear the Cobwebs! The Gender Impact of Environmentalism', *The Administrator*, XI(3): 94–104.
―― (1996a), 'Environmentalism in India: New Directions in Development', in T.V. Sathymurthi (ed.), *Class Formation and Political Transformation in Post-Colonial India* (Vol. 4 of the series on *Social Change and Political Discourse in India: Structures of Power, Movements of Resistance*). New Delhi: Oxford University Press, pp. 410–36.
―― (1996b), *Environmental Politics: People's Lives and Development Choices*. New Delhi: Sage Publications.

Krishna, Sumi (1997), 'Integrating a Gender Perspective into Environmental Projects', paper presented at a panel discussion, 'Gender and Development: The Research-Action Interface', Uttara Devi Resource Centre for Gender and Development, M.S. Swaminathan Research Foundation, Chennai, 22 September.

―――― (1998a), 'Gender and Biodiversity Management', in M.S. Swaminathan (ed.), *Gender Dimensions in Biodiversity Management*. New Delhi: Konark, pp. 23–61.

―――― (1998b), 'Arunachal Pradesh', in Swaminathan (ed.), *Gender Dimensions*, pp. 148–81.

―――― (1998c), 'Mizoram', in Swaminathan (ed.), *Gender Dimensions*, pp. 182–210.

―――― (1999), 'Involving Women, Ignoring Gender', Paper presented at 'Gender Dimensions in Biodiversity Management and Food Security', FAO Technical Consultation, M.S. Swaminathan Research Foundation, Chennai, 2–5 November.

―――― (2000), 'The Impact of the Structural Adjustment Programme on Gender and Environment in India', in Centre for Women's Development Studies (CWDS), *Shifting Sands: Women's Lives and Globalization*. Kolkata: Stree, pp. 173–234.

―――― (2001), 'Introduction: Towards a "Genderscape" of Community Rights in Natural Resource Management', *Indian Journal of Gender Studies*, 8(2): 151–74.

―――― (2003), 'The Light Shines through Gossamer Threads', *Economic and Political Weekly*, Review of Women's Studies: Democracy in the Family, XXXVIII(17): 1691–6.

―――― (2004a), 'A "Genderscape" of Community Rights in Natural Resource Management: Overview', in Krishna (ed.), *Livelihood and Gender*, pp. 17–63. [Earlier version published in 2002, 'Introduction: Towards a "Genderscape" of Community Rights in Natural Resource Management', *Indian Journal of Gender Studies*, 8(2): 151–74.]

―――― (2004b), 'Gender, Tribe and Political Participation: Control of Natural Resources in North-Eastern India', in Krishna (ed.), *Livelihood and Gender*, pp. 375–94.

―――― (2004c), 'Knowledge Systems, Equity and Rights: A Dialogue with Vina Mazumdar', in Krishna (ed.), *Livelihood and Gender*, pp. 425–31.

―――― (2004d), *Globalisation and People's Development Choices*. Bangalore: Hivos.

―――― (2005), 'Gendered Price of Rice in North-Eastern India', *Economic and Political Weekly*, Special issue on 'Gender and Food Security', XL(25): 2555–62.

―――― (2007), 'Recasting Citizenship for Women's Livelihood and Development', in Sumi Krishna (ed.), *Women's Livelihood Rights: Recasting Citizenship for Development*. New Delhi: Sage Publications, pp. 1–38.

―――― (2009), *Genderscapes: Revisioning Natural Resource Management*. New Delhi: Zubaan.

―――― (ed.) (2004), *Livelihood and Gender*.

Lefebvre, H. (1990 [1974]), *The Production of Space* (translation). Oxford: Blackwell.

Locke, Catherine (1999), 'Women's Representation and Roles in "Gender" Policy in Joint Forest Management', in Roger Jeffrey and Nalini Sundar (eds), *A New Moral Economy for India's Forests*. New Delhi: Sage Publications, pp. 235-53.

Low, Setha and Denise Lawrence-Zuniga (eds) (2003), *The Anthropology of Space and Place: Locating Culture*. Oxford: Blackwell Publishing.

March, Candida, Ines Smyth, and Maitreyee Mukhopadhyay (1999), *A Guide to Gender Analysis Frameworks*. Oxford: Oxfam, GB.

Massey, Doreen B. (1994), *Space, Place, and Gender*. Minneapolis: University of Minnesota Press.

Mies, Maria and Vandana Shiva (1993), *Ecofeminism*. New Delhi: Kali for Women.

Mitchell, W.J.T. (ed.) (2002), *Landscape and Power*, 2nd edition. Chicago: University of Chicago Press.

Moore, Henrietta L. (1988), *Feminism and Anthropology*. Cambridge: Polity Press.

Moser, Caroline (1993), *Gender Planning and Development: Theory, Practice and Training*. London and New York: Routledge.

Narayanan, M.K. Ratheesh, M.P. Swapna, and N. Anil Kumar (2005), *Gender Dimensions of Wild Food Management in Wyanad, Kerala*. Kalpetta, Wyanad: M.S. Swaminathan Research Foundation—Community Agrobiodiversity Centre.

Niranjana, Seemanthani (2001), *Gender and Space: Femininity, Sexualization and the Female Body*. New Delhi, Thousand Oaks, and London: Sage Publications.

Pandit, Maya (2007), 'Dalit Women's Autobiographies and Integrating Difference', Paper presented at the Indian Association for Women's Studies (IAWS) Southern Regional Workshop, 'Feminist Perspectives and the Struggle to Transform the Disciplines', Bangalore, 2-3 February.

Plumwood, Val (1986), 'Ecofeminism: An Overview and Discussion of Positions', *Australian Journal of Philosophy*, 64: 120-38.

—— (1993), *Feminism and the Mastery of Nature*. London and New York: Routledge.

Rangan, Haripriya (1993), 'Romancing the Environment: Popular Environmental Action in the Garhwal Himalayas', in J. Friedmann and H. Rangan (eds), *In Defense of Livelihoods: Comparative Studies in Environmental Action*. Hartford, CT: Kumarian Press, pp. 155-81.

—— (2000), *Of Myths and Movements: Rewriting Chipko into Himalayan History*. London: Verso Press.

Raju, Saraswati (2005), 'Limited Options—Rethinking Women's Empowerment "Projects" in Development Discourses: A Case from Rural India', *Gender, Technology and Development*, 9(2): 253-71.

Ramdas, Sagari R., Nitya S. Ghogte, Ashalatha, Nandini Mathur, M.L. Sanyasi Rao, N. Madhusudan, S. Seethalakhsmi, N. Pandu Dora, N. Kantham, E. Venkatesh, and J. Savithri (2004), 'Overcoming Gender Barriers: Local Knowledge Systems and Animal Health Healing in Andhra Pradesh and Maharashtra', in Sumi Krishna (ed.), *Livelihood and Gender*, pp. 67-91.

Rani, Geetha and M.S. Swaminathan (1998), 'Biodiversity in India: Heritage and Management', in Swaminathan (ed.), *Gender Dimensions*, pp. 4-22.

Rocheleau, Diane, Esther Wangari, and Barbara Thomas-Slayeter (eds) (1996), *Feminist Political Ecology: Global Issues and Local Experiences*. London: Routledge.

Robinson, Arthur (1990), 'Rectangular World Maps—No!' *Professional Geographer*, 42(1): 101–4.

Singh, Neera M. (2006), 'Blurred Boundaries: Action, Research and Shared Life-Spaces', unpublished paper.

Shiva, Vandana (1988), *Staying Alive in India: Women, Ecology and Survival in India*. London: Kali for Women.

Thamizoli, P. (1997), 'Gender Inequality, Tribal and Caste Women: Past and Present: A Case Study of the Nilgiris, Tamil Nadu', *Man in India*, 77(1): 51–62.

United Nations Environment Programme (UNEP) (1992), Convention on Biological Diversity 1992, United Nations Conference on Environment and Development, 'Earth Summit', Rio de Janeiro, Brazil, United Nations Environment Programme.

——— (1995), *Global Biodiversity Assessment* (executive editor V.H. Heywood). Cambridge: UNEP and Cambridge University Press.

Vedavalli, L. and Arun Kumar (1998), 'Wayanad, Kerala', in M.S. Swaminathan (ed.), *Gender Dimensions in Biodiversity Management*, pp. 96–106. New Delhi: Konark.

Ward, Barbara and Rene Dubos (1972), *Only One Earth: The Care and Maintenance of a Small Planet*. An unofficial report commissioned by the Secretary-General of the United Nations Conference on the Human Environment. New York: W.W. Norton & Co.

Warren, Karen J. (ed.) (1994), *Ecological Feminism*. London: Routledge.

World Commission on Environment and Development (WCED) (1987), *Our Common Future*. World Commission on Environment and Development. New Delhi: Oxford University Press.

Whitehead, Judy (2003), 'Space, Place and Primitive Accumulation in the Narmada Valley and Beyond', *Economic and Political Weekly*, XXXVII(40): 4224–30.

Wickramasinghe, Anoja (2004), 'Gender and Ecological Sustainability: The Traditions and Wisdom of the Local Communities in a Dry Zone, Sri Lanka', in Krishna (ed.), *Livelihood and Gender*, pp. 171–92.

Williams, Glyn and Emma Mawdsley (2006), 'Postcolonial Environmental Justice: Government and Governance in India', *Geoforum*, 37: 660–70.

IX. WOMEN'S MOVEMENT

Chapter 17

WOMEN'S POLITICS IN INDIA*

ILINA SEN

THIS CHAPTER MAKES AN ATTEMPT to understand certain aspects of the women's movement and the nature of women's involvement in politics in India. A historical overview is followed by an identification of some major debates facing the movement today. The most important of these debates are taken up for discussion in the concluding section.

Looking at the panorama of conscious political action by women in India today, one is aware of great vitality as well as an enormous variety of positions, strategies, ideologies, and mass bases. One is compelled to conclude that what goes by the name of the women's movement in India is, in reality, made up of a variety of different strands. What one means, when one refers to the women's movement in India, thus depends very much on one's own perspective, ideological position, and the actual political situation. This gives rise to a certain confusion about the nature and scope of the women's movement in India. The confusion prevails at various levels.

From the outside, there are the various (unsuccessful) attempts to locate the nerve centre of the women's movement in India. Does this lie in the mainly urban, so-called 'autonomous' women's groups in many Indian

---

* Originally published in T.V. Sathyamurthy (ed.), *Region, Religion, Caste, Gender and Culture in Contemporary India*, Vol. 3. New Delhi: Oxford University Press, 1996, pp. 441–61.

cities—groups that have organized around specifically women's issues and that have consistently drawn attention to various aspects of women's oppression during the past several years? If so, what is one to make of its narrow support base? Or, should one look for this nerve centre in the very large women's contingents of the various political parties in the country, or even in the large women's contingents in the various Left parties? What about women in the many mass movements around ecological issues, issues of group self-determination, and demands of unorganized workers that have gained prominence during the past several years? And, while these movements have drawn many women to their ranks, to what extent have they, or have they not, raised issues specifically relating to women, and, as a corollary, to what extent do they qualify for definition as women's movements?

These debates rage on the fringes of women's movements and outside them; meanwhile, within women's organizations and groups themselves, a separate set of debates—the meaning and utility of terms such as patriarchy, feminism, and autonomy in the Indian context, the legitimacy or otherwise of a women's movement, the relationship of women's organizations and class organizations or other broader platforms for change—contribute to the unclear picture of the Indian women's movement that emerges.

Such debates have taken place in other countries and at other periods too; what makes the Indian experience unique are several peculiarities of the Indian situation. We have here an extremely populous country and a large proportion of the world's womenfolk, extreme polarities of social and economic situations, a wide range of political organizations representing a range of ideological positions, and a history of political action and struggle that continues well into the present day. In this situation, with the country as a whole still in the process of (so far incomplete) social change, the struggles for change of the people as a whole and of women in particular are inextricably linked. We can begin to unravel the mesh thus created by examining the various foci of women's action in India today, in order to understand whether there is one nerve centre or many in the movement of Indian women.

A HISTORICAL OVERVIEW

Women's participation in the political life of present day India dates back to the early twentieth century, when organizations such as the Women's India Association (WIA), the National Council of Indian Women (NCIW), and the All India Women's Conference (AIWC) were formed in 1917, 1926, and 1927, respectively. All these organizations concerned themselves with eradicating the social problems of women and educating them. At the same time, a strong nationalist trend ran through them, and this sometimes led to contradictions and conflicts within the organizations. For example, the WIA had an interest in home rule and women's suffrage, yet they were not ready to support the civil disobedience movement, for this would have compromised their relationship with the government and interfered with their attempts to seek improvement in women's status through legislation (Chaudhuri *et al.* 1985: 6).The AIWC similarly began working initially from an educational and social perspective, but later adopted a strong nationalistic perspective, as it felt that women needed

... equal rights ... to play their full and legitimate role in the national affairs, otherwise all other rights might become illusory. (Chattopadhyay 1983: 98)

Thus, we can see that the linkage and the debate on the relationship of women's organizations to overt political action is an old one. It is also one that is yet to be resolved.

The largest involvement of women in the national struggle did not, however, come from the WIA or the AIWC, both of which remained confined to the intelligentsia. Women from all walks of life flocked to the national struggle in response to Gandhi's call, in civil disobedience actions and in symbolic gestures of protest such as the Salt Satyagraha. Gandhi used several ideological prongs to mobilize women. These included a commitment to women's equal rights, and as a corollary, equal social responsibility for the national struggle. They also included liberal use of Hindu religious concepts and terminology. Gandhi's methods have drawn varied responses from critics, but the kind of mobilization he activized (for example, in the Salt Satyagraha) was responsible for converting a section of the Congress leadership already committed to progressive liberal ideology to women's equality. This led also to the adoption at the Karachi Congress session (1931) of the Fundamental Rights Resolution (Chaudhuri *et al.* 1985: 19).

Under this resolution, the principle of complete equality between men and women was accepted, even though its implications were not fully worked out. These promises of equality were carried over into the Constitution. The basic principle of equality between the sexes was established in constitutional law, although not all the anomalies and discrimination were eliminated in practice, and women in independent India continued to be victims of several forms of discrimination in and out of the home.

If the Gandhian path of mass civil disobedience and open, legal transfer of power was one part of the pre-independence heritage, there was another, equally powerful heritage that defined the norms for political action by men and women in the decades to follow. The Communist Party of India (CPI), during the late 1930s and 1940s, mobilized men and women based on a class analysis of society and a theory of forcible capture of state power. The industrial workforce was small, and while significant industrial action was organized in centres such as Kanpur, Bombay, Calcutta, and Sholapur, sharecroppers and small and marginal peasants were organized by the CPI through the Kisan Sabhas.

The Kisan Sabha took the lead in two significant attempts to change the oppressive conditions under which the mass of rural people lived. The Tebhaga movement in Bengal and north Bihar began in 1946 and did not subside until it was disowned by the CPI in 1950. Although it was basically a movement for sharecroppers' rights, it achieved in many places the character of an armed guerrilla uprising. It bore the full brunt of state repression, and women were important historical participants at all levels of the struggle.

They were organized on a separate platform—the Nari Bahini—and ran shelters and maintained lines of communication throughout the affected areas (Chakravarty 1980: 70–9; Sen 1982: 161–9). Party women were joined by rural women during the Tebhaga Andolan to raise a host of issues regarding class oppression in general and caste oppression specific to women—such as necessary legal changes in the status of Hindu women, and women's rights to finance and property (Custers 1987: 173–5). Through the village-level Mahila Atma Raksha Sarnitis, they also attacked practical manifestations of patriarchy such as wife-beating. However, on the eve of independence, the struggle was withdrawn by the party leadership under the constraints imposed by Communist 'internationalism'.

Specifically, the CPI was railroaded into accepting the 'nationalist' Congress government as the heir to the colonial government by the Communist Party of the Soviet Union (CPSU) and the government of the Soviet Union, and into withdrawing all peasants' or workers' struggles that might jeopardize the stability of the new government. Although the movement and its demands specific to women were withdrawn, Tebhaga remained an important legacy for toiling women, which they would reclaim in the future.

The Telangana movement in the Nizam of Hyderabad's dominion dates from the same period as 'Tebhaga'. Both the insurrectionary movements shared similar characteristics, in the sense that they were directed against the feudal oppression of rural landlords. However, the Telangana insurrection was specifically directed to the struggle against the Nizam's rule and thus had a nationalistic flavour, although it was very different in spirit from the national struggle led by Gandhi.

In the Telangana movement, men and women throughout the Nizam's kingdom were organized through nationalistic bodies such as the Andhra Maha Sabha as well as through the CPI-led Kisan Sabhas. As in Tebhaga, women were valiant partners in the guerrilla warfare and in facing the fierce repression of those years (Sundarayya 1972: 328–53). However, women's problems were not articulated in the same way, and years later when the Stree Shakti Sangathana members documented the history of women in the Telangana movement, women expressed their sense of disillusionment on this count. Women also resented the patronizing attitude of party cadres towards their special problems (Stree Shakti Sangathana 1989: 25).

Such struggles as well as the struggles of adivasi men and women, for example, in the Thana district of Maharashtra (Parulekar 1975), and industrial workers (Singh 1983) abated temporarily after 1950. Independent India began its career with constitutional promises of equal opportunity and by adopting directive principles promising, among other rights, the right to work. With the national movement at an end, the obvious reasons for mobilizing women disappeared. Many organizations such as the AIWC reoriented themselves as primarily social organizations, running schools and hostels, and providing limited work opportunity. Many political parties maintained token women's fronts, such as the Mahila Congress which primarily concerned itself with mobilizing women for party rallies and vote-catching. Communist women broke away from the AIWC in order to form the National Federation of Indian Women (NFIW) in 1954, which remained a platform for women within the party and in party-led trade unions but was not particularly active in any kind of struggle-oriented activity.

THE CONTEMPORARY WOMEN'S MOVEMENT

This situation of relative calm lasted only 15 years. By the mid-1960s, deep restlessness had gripped the country. By this time, it was fairly apparent that parliamentary government in India had failed to deliver. Poverty, urban and rural, was as rampant, if not more so, than before independence. Land reform had been tardy. Land- and caste-based tensions had assumed gigantic proportions in certain areas such as trans-Gangetic Bihar. Planned development, heavy industrialization, capital-intensive agriculture, and commercial forestry had given rise to a host of new contradictions as they benefited the few at the expense of large sections of the people.

In the face of widespread unemployment, ecological degradation, and rampant poverty, the parliamentary opposition stood exposed as a totally ineffective political force. In this situation, a new ferment of political action began in the country. People organized in order to protest against the situation under many banners, around many issues. There was a new wave of nationwide unrest, and its rumblings could be heard in many parts of the country. It heralded a new chapter in the area of political action, and once again women were among its important protagonists.

The new upsurge of political action brought a breath of fresh air to the stagnancy that had enveloped Indian politics. In some cases, the struggles were launched from party fronts or from joint fronts of coalitions of parties. An example of the latter kind of action is provided by the Anti Price Rise Movement of Bombay and Gujarat in the late 1960s. This was launched by a coalition of the Communist parties and the two socialist parties. In other cases, parties split ranks, the more radical sections launching new parties. This is, indeed, what happened to the CPI. The unified communist party had already split in 1964 into the CPI and the more radical CPI (Marxist) on the international question of the Soviet Union and China (which had of course deeper national implications for India). During the mid-1960s, the CPI(M) split further, with those advocating immediate armed revolution in India on the Chinese model separating to form the CPI(M-L). The fact that no universal strategy for pursuing the common aims could be formed led subsequently to the splintering of this party into several factions and party fronts. Many issue-based mass organizations came into existence in various areas, as did independent trade unions not affiliated to any central organization.

Women entered the political arena through all of these channels, but an important difference that characterized political action by women during this period in the earlier phase was that, as in many other fields, their role was subject to much introspection. It was no longer of importance only to mobilize women; it was at least as important to weave an analysis of the fundamental causes of women's oppression into their political involvements.

During the early 1970s, in crisis-ridden Bihar, a massive upsurge of students enthusiastically supported Jayaprakash Narayan's call for a 'Total Revolution'. It reflected a complete disenchantment with the view that power politics were the only tools available to improve the lives of people. 'Total Revolution' was aimed at a radical transformation of society and its entire fabric. A large number of questions about power structures were raised, which included many about women—questions about family, work distribution, and family violence, unequal access to resources enjoyed by men and women, issues of male–female relationship, and women's sexuality. From the Bihar movement a powerful critique of patriarchy emerged. Its spokespersons were young men and women of the Chhatra Yuva Sangharsh Vahini (CYSV), Jayaprakash Narayan's vanguard of the 'Total Revolution'.

The CYSV cadres went out to the rural areas to organize the masses for the 'Total Revolution'. One of their major areas of involvement became the Bodhgaya Math struggle, where the CYSV organized poor peasants from those villages in which the Bodhgaya Math exercised feudal and religious control. Poor peasants demanded legal rights to the lands they and their families had cultivated for generations, and an important part of the demand was that women be given land rights individually, in their own names. This demand represented the culmination of an extensive process of debate on the question of patriarchy and social power structures that had taken place within the organization. Through this process, rural women participants in the Bodhgaya struggle developed a new level of understanding and provided a powerful model for many future struggles (Kelkar and Galla 1990).

The 1970s constituted a watershed in the history of the women's movement in India. The analysis of women's oppression giving rise to new forms of demand and/or action noticeable in the Bodhgaya movement was utilized by many other mass movements of this period (Sen 1990a: 1–18). These mass movements were a product of the political unrest referred to earlier, and engulfed entire areas and people despite the Indian state's imposition of the internal Emergency in 1975. At the same time, the analysis was taken up by many educated women and students in cities and campuses. The in-depth analysis of the oppression of women, and their possible liberation that these groups struggled for, crystallized eventually into what came to be known as the 'autonomous women's movement'.

The decade of the 1970s also brought women into mass movements in large numbers, although the specific issues and analysis of women's oppression differed from case to case. The Chipko movement in the Garhwal Himalaya dates from the same period as the Bihar movement. The name Chipko is derived from the Hindi word for hugging trees, which is what Garhwal women did *en masse* in order to prevent indiscriminate forest felling by commercial interests. The issue of environmental degradation was linked in this movement to women's increasing toil for fuel and fodder in the face of such degradation, and from this was generated the idea that women, by virtue of their own nature-related activities, have an especially nurturing attitude towards nature. The position was not strictly one arguing for equality, but it did take a woman's perspective into account.

A very important women's organization to emerge from this period was the Self Employed Women's Association (SEWA). Originally established in Ahmedabad as a wing of the Textile Labour Association (TLA), SEWA developed women's cooperatives and credit banks aimed at 'social regeneration and economic uplift among rural women'. In a very short time, its membership grew to 14,000 in Ahmedabad alone, and spread to Indore, Bhopal, Delhi, and other places. Working among women in the unorganized sector, SEWA became an important factor in their empowerment. Problems of emphasis and style and, ultimately, of the equal or subordinate position of SEWA vis-à-vis TLA, however, ultimately forced a parting of the ways between the two.

It is important to bear in mind the fact that many of the movements of this period challenged the fundamental tenets of the developmental policy being followed by the state. The Chipko movement, for example, challenged commercial forestry and forest-based industrialization on environmental grounds. At the same time, a women-specific perspective was developed by the movement as women emerged as the principal activists.

In a way these two aspects were closely interrelated, for it was an alternative vision that opened up the possibilities for incorporating women's points of view. This dual character—strong statement of alternatives to existing state policy, and its definition/orientation attuned to its women cadres and supporters—characterized many mass movements during this period. Thus, the Shramik Sangathana of Dhulia challenged the entire model of capital-intensive agricultural development and skewed asset ownership that was emerging in an adivasi area at the same time that it questioned the relevance of traditional tribal personal laws for women in a just society (Sathe 1990).

The Chhattisgarh Mines Shramik Sangh (CMSS) emerged in 1977 as a militant trade union in the adivasi belt of Madhya Pradesh. Its activities were directed against the public sector giant's (the Bhilai Steel Plant) attempts to mechanize its operations and retrench its contractual workers, especially women. It fought for the rights of marginalized manual miners while at the same time challenging the policy of blind mechanization in industry, and upheld women's equal rights to wage labour (Sen 1990b).

A number of mass movements from this period contributed to an ongoing discussion on the question of women's subordination. By and large, it was generally the case that, in practice, separate women's cells developed within the larger organization. A dialectical process of interaction between these cells and the larger organization developed in which the theory and practice of the women's question were articulated. The process can be observed in Dhulia, in Chhattisgarh, where the Stree Mukti Sangathana (SMS) and the Mahila Mukti Morcha (MMM) developed as separate platforms even though they worked in close conjunction with the larger organizations.

The most recent example of this phenomenon is the emergence of the Samagra Mahila Aghadi (SMA) in the context of the Maharashtra farmers' agitation for remunerative prices (Omvedt 1990). The Aghadi has taken a strong position on the brutalization of present-day politics which affects women more than any other section of society, and has sought to carve out a separate space for itself in Maharashtra's larger politics by committing itself to supporting all-women panels for the zilla parishad elections. It is too early to assess the impact of this work.

The 1970s also witnessed the emergence of the 'autonomous' women's movement. During the mid-1970s, many educated women took to radical, active politics, and simultaneously promoted an analysis of women's issues. Groups of women came together in many cities. Among the incidents that played catalytic roles in crystallizing these meetings into organizational efforts were the Mathura rape case (1978) and the Maya Tyagi rape case (1980). Both were cases of custodial rape by the police, and led to nationwide protest movements by women (primarily from the intelligentsia). The Forum against Rape came into existence in Bombay—a loose, non-hierarchical group that, nevertheless, had the strength to survive and grow into the Forum against Oppression of Women.

The Bombay Forum was officially launched in 1981 and has taken up issues of rape, sex determination, *in vitro* and female foeticide (on this question, a new forum against Sex Determination has existed since 1987), and has organized two national conferences for discussing perspectives on the women's liberation movement (Patel 1985: 22-3). The principal activities of the Forum have been highly visible protest actions, signature campaigns, and other such activities. The Forum has also provided support to organizations of toiling women such as the Shramik Stree Mukti Sangathana (SSMS) in Dhulia.

In 1977, a group of women in Delhi started a journal, *Manushi*, in English and Hindi, about women and society. Although the group was subsequently fragmented and the Hindi edition had to close down for financial reasons, *Manushi* (in English) has survived and become a living documentary of various aspects of the women's movement in India. Subsequently, a group of women formed Saheli, a centre for women's resource, documentation, and legal aid.

During the late 1970s and 1980s, many similar urban groups emerged in Calcutta, Bangalore, Pune, and elsewhere. A number of magazines and journals devoted to promoting women's equality came into being, many of them in regional languages. These included *Feminist Network* (English: Bombay); *Baiza* (Marathi: Pune); *Ahalya, Sabala Sachetana* and *Pratibadi Chetana* (Bengali: Calcutta), *Women's Voice* (English: Bangalore), and *Stree Sangharsh* (Hindi: Patna). The city-based groups also played an important role in mobilizing public opinion and press coverage during the movement against sati, following the Deorala incident in the mid-1980s when Roop Kanwar, a 17-year-old Rajput woman, was immolated at her husband's cremation to the accompaniment of a cheering Rajput community.

Similarly, autonomous groups spearheaded the agitation for reform in rape law and were successful in paving the way for the passage of an amendment which placed the onus of proof of innocence on the accused rapist.[1] Autonomous groups and independent activists also led the campaign and the public interest litigation against Neten, or the proposal to introduce an injectable contraceptive for women which, it was feared, would be used on women without their consent or knowledge in a bid to force policies of population control on them. Autonomous groups have been in the forefront of the campaign for a uniform civil code (UCC) for all Indians as, at present, different people are governed by their own religious personal laws which, in different ways, are discriminatory against women.

In the 1980s, a test case was taken up by the Supreme Court relating to Shah Bano, a Muslim divorcee, who sought maintenance from her husband under a secular interpretation of the law of marriage and divorce. Her case received wide support from the press, but the then government bowed to the weight of counter-opinion originating in orthodox Muslim circles against this interference in their personal affairs and religion. It enacted the Muslim Personal Law Bill under which Muslims in India would continue to be governed by the personal laws of their religion as laid down in the Sharia.

---

[1] Earlier the reverse had been true, the onus of proof being on the woman bringing a case of rape.

Women's autonomous groups continue to play a watchdog role vis-à-vis other issues also, such as the commercialized portrayal of women's bodies in the media and advertising. Some city-based groups have made special efforts to link up with poor urban or rural women's issues and lives. The work of *Pennurimai Iyakkam* in Tamil Nadu (Madras and Madurai) is an example of such groups forging a close relationship with the struggle of women in slums for housing and drinking water.

In Hyderabad, the Progressive Women's Organization (PWO) emerged on the Osmania University campus in the early 1970s. This group related closely to the radical student and peasant movement in Andhra Pradesh and felt that women's liberation struggles needed a strong base in the struggles of the toiling masses. The PWO took up issues of price rise, dowry, 'eve teasing', sexism in advertisements, and so on, and mobilized women students to organize themselves for their own protection and development. As in Delhi and Bombay, the experience of the PWO led to many an offshoot, despite its members facing state repression during the Emergency. In the late 1980s, it gave rise to the Stree Shakti Sangathana (SSS), and to Anveshi, a platform devoted to theoretical studies of questions relating to women.

With the inflow of funds and with international cognizance being given to women's issues by United Nations (UN) fora, the field of women's activities in India witnessed somewhat unusual growth. The period 1975–85 was officially declared as the UN decade for women, and a large amount of money was channelled into women's activities through various groups and voluntary agencies. These groups undertook a programme of conscientization of and/or organized economic activities for women.

At the same time, the state also adopted in the early 1980s—if indeed it did not appropriate—much of the rhetoric of the women's movement, for example, 'Women will never get their due share unless they organize'; 'Women must fight for their own rights'. Under state patronage, the National Perspective Plan (NPP) for women was evolved (Centre for Women's Development Studies 1988; Government of India 1988), and systematic plans were formulated for promoting women's education, health status, and political participation. On the eve of the 1989 elections, the Panchayati Raj Bill introduced reservation for women 'Panches' at the village level in a bid to empower women.

Women and child development activities were channelled through state-established directorates. Through job opportunities thus created, professional social workers gained status as activists in the cause of women, diluting both the concepts of 'activism' and 'organization'. However, state-supported action programmes such as the Mahila Mandals sponsored by Development of Women and Children in Rural Areas (DWCRA) are often the only fora available to poor women to organize and express themselves.

The ferment of the 1970s and 1980s did not leave the political parties untouched. In the work of political parties, too, a new phase began in response to this ferment. The Congress party (until 1989, the ruling party) formalized its own women's front, namely the Mahila Congress. Its principal activities, however, continued to be mobilizing women's votes and publicizing the government's policies on women. During the later 1970s, the socialists, through the various permutations and combinations of factors that led to the formation of the Janata Party, launched the Mahila Dakshata Samiti (MDS). The MDS led and participated in many actions against rape, dowry, and price rise, and provided legal support to many women in distress.

Women's groups and women's fronts belonging to many parties also took a strong stand against communal tendencies and communal violence. For example, after the 1984 Delhi riots, many women's groups came forward to provide support to the victims and to lobby against communal violence. Issue-based cooperation and dialogue spread among many women's groups and women from a number of parties. The earliest example of this kind of cooperation can be seen in the Bombay-based Anti Price Rise Movement between 1972 and 1975.

Women leaders of the two major Communist parties and the Socialist party joined together in building a novel protest movement against soaring prices, in which women marched to the seats of power in *lathi morcha*s, until it came to an abrupt end in 1975 with the proclamation of the Emergency. Once again, in 1988, most groups outside the ruling party attacked the NPP for women on the ground that it offered superficial remedies only, without touching the fundamental causes of women's oppression.

A group of organizations that included the All India Democratic Women's Association (AIDWA), All India Coordination Committee of Working Women (AICCWW), Centre for Women's Development Studies (CWDS), Joint Women's Programme (JWP), MDS, National Federation of Working Women (NFWW), and the Young Women's Christian Association (YWCA) of India issued a document in 1988 criticizing the NPP. In it they argued that the NPP's efforts to change the status of women through government directive were doomed to failure (Centre for Women's Development Studies 1988). The rapid communalization of Indian politics during the last five years, and the participation by large numbers of women in fundamentalist actions such as the call to rebuild the Ayodhya temple have cut against these trends, but it is too early for us to be able to analyse this phenomenon competently.

DISCUSSION

This brief review reveals that a vigorous, if uneven, women's movement has been in existence in India for well over a decade. Leaving aside state-sponsored women's organizations, two major strands in the movement are clearly identifiable:

1. the women's movement acting in conjunction with mass organizations or political parties and
2. the 'autonomous women's' movement.

Some aspects of these can be taken up for comment.

To take the autonomous women's movement first, it is worth noting that the urban women's groups of which it consists and comprising primarily the urban intelligentsia have, despite their greater theoretical development, remained cut off from the mass of the Indian women. The latter—if they have been organized at all—have been organized under more traditional political structures or within mass movements. This is in a way a reflection of the extent to which the Indian intelligentsia is cut off from the lives and concerns of the majority of people. However, as far as the women's movement itself is concerned, there have been several practical consequences. One of these relates to these urban groups sometimes finding greater kinship in 'feminist' groups in the West rather than with the mass of women in India. In structural terms, the relatively open and unstructured way of working that these groups, at their best, have adopted and their vocabulary in describing this aspect of their work have brought them closer to the feminist groups of the West.

For their own part, however, the most vigorously uncompromising of these groups have felt that political parties and mass organizations are not committed enough to the woman question, while enjoying a large base among them. They have thus accused these larger organizations of 'subsuming' the woman question under general questions, and have made a virtue of 'autonomy' in which only women are involved in decision-making. This has exposed them to charges of an excessive obsession with personal issues; of inflating the importance of small experiences in order to hog media attention, and interpreting autonomy to mean autonomy from class, caste, or other organizations.

Another major problem with many of these groups was that as they expanded their sphere of activities, either to individual supportive work for women in distress or to research and documentation, they became dependent on external funds either from the government or from one or other of the many foreign donor agencies operating in the country. In turn, the donor agencies' priorities for possible courses of action for these groups sometimes dictated the way in which they worked.

We have already seen that many mass organizations, which had their origin during the 1970s and 1980s, have been noticeable for the way in which they have introduced women's perspectives in the totality of the movements. However, on this point, one further observation is necessary. The cases cited earlier show that the women's platforms emerging in the context of mass movements do not necessarily provide women with a significant representation in the leadership of the overall movements. In this respect, the situation does not appear to have changed much from the pre-independence mobilization of women for a national cause, although it is an achievement of no mean proportion that women are forcing leaders of various movements to take cognizance of special issues relating to their gender.

This is, however, not always achieved without a struggle. In the Kerala fishworkers' movement against mechanized trawling, women had to struggle for union membership at a fairly advanced stage of the movement. Although women within the traditional fishing communities do not fish themselves, they take the responsibility, exclusively, to market the catch in Kerala; and as it was the shrinking market of the traditional fisherfolk that heralded the entire agitation, women also had to struggle for a separate platform, namely the Coastal Women's Front (Nayak 1988). In some cases, the struggle is sufficiently intense to lead to a complete parting of ways (as in the case of SEWA).

The more common pattern is for the women's group or women's voice involved to accept the dominance of the general line of a struggle, as has happened, for example, in the union of the Chhattisgarh miners. An illustration of a more straightforward situation is provided by the Bhopal Gas Peedit Mahila Udyog Sangathan (BGPMUS), an organization of gas victims of the Bhopal disaster. The women of the BGPMUS have led militant struggles of great intensity demanding justice for the victims of Bhopal. Yet its leader continues to be a man who plans the movement's strategy. The Chhattisgarh example is more complex and is considered in somewhat greater detail in the following.

The 4,000 strong women of Dalli Rajhara make up about half of the membership of the CMSS, an independent trade union of contractual miners. The union has, since 1977, fought for the abolition of the contract system and for the regularization of contractual workers. At the same time, it has vigorously opposed the programme of mechanization of the mine by the management, and the women membership of the CMSS has taken special care to study the relationship between skill, mechanization, and women's representation in the workforce. The women in the CMSS are well aware that, historically, women's jobs have been the first to disappear in any programme of mechanization. This is because women often lack the necessary skill to handle sophisticated machinery.

The strong statement by the CMSS women emphasizing women's equal right to work has added a new dimension to the working of the entire union. However, the union has quite consciously discouraged its women members from straying into discussions of patriarchy, ideology, or theoretical discussions of the theme of women's subordination in the family and society. While this has understandably displeased a number of women in leadership positions, it seems to have been accepted by the women membership as a whole, for whom the experience of unionization itself represents a far greater democratic experience than perhaps anything in their previous experience of other organizational settings.

The situation exemplified by the CMSS has its roots in the organizational history of the Left; for, although the CMSS is not affiliated to any of the Communist parties, its leadership drew its ideological inspiration from the strands of contemporary Indian politics represented by the CPI(M-L). In turn, this particular ideological tendency, despite its diverse ramifications, is firmly anchored to the general theoretical orientation of the mainstream Communist parties. This example throws light on the dialectical nature of the relationship between mass organizations and the women's contingents within them. This aspect of women's participation becomes clearer when we consider the way in which the Communist parties themselves have analysed women's organizations and related to them.

The communist parties' position on the woman question and the history of its evolution is forked. On the one hand, the basic Marxist theoretical position on the question (as revealed in the writings of Marx, Engels, and Bebel) focused on women's oppression as parallel to and rooted in class oppression (Bebel 1971; Engels 1980). Early socialists, such as Bebel, Marx, Engels, and Sylvia Pankhurst, were as ardent fighters in the cause of the working class as they were in the cause of women. However, with the success of the Russian revolution and with the democratic revolution there being (supposedly) complete under proletarian leadership (or rather the leadership of the CPSU, the party of the proletariat), some problems arose in accommodating the woman question.

Lenin was extremely wary of introducing feminist issues (such as sexuality and the male–female dynamic) to working women. By and large, this reluctance on his part reflected the attitude of the CPSU as a whole, with notable exceptions (such as Kollontai) for whom personal liberation as a woman and transformation of the family were as vitally important as socialist liberation itself (for example, Kollontai 1972: 15–51, 52–63).

Lenin's famous interview with Clara Zetkin reveals his distrust of separate organization(s) of women, at the same time recognizing the need for them. For, Lenin referred in this interview to women 'growing worn out in petty monotonous household work, their strength and time dissipated and wasted, their minds growing narrow and stale...'. He also took the then prevailing male assumption of the apolitical, unsocial, backward psychology of women as facts. After recognizing the need for 'separate bodies to work among women', Lenin declared in the same interview that 'No special organization for women' should be countenanced. 'A woman communist is a member of the party just as a man communist' (New Book Centre 1978: 105–24).

Over the years these attitudes hardened in the communist parties and continued to dominate the thinking of the CPI. This was despite the fact that the communist parties contained the largest mass base of poor peasant working women in trade unions and Mahila Sabhas. But the communist parties were also affected by the general climate of the late 1970s. The AIDWA was formed in 1981 from the women's base of the CPI(M). It consisted of units from 15 states and comprised a primary membership of over 1 million. Some of the state units had of course an organizational history in the Mahila Sabhas dating back to the pre-independence agrarian struggles. The Delhi unit of the AIDWA (the Janwadi Mahila Samiti [JMS]) was a particularly active unit. It combined work in the resettlement colonies of Delhi with study, research, and legal aid, and acted as a pressure group on women's issues at the national level.

However, old attitudes continued to dominate much of the thinking of the communist parties. Vimal Ranadive, an ideologue of AIDWA in 1987 (1987: 1–34), attacked the 'self styled Indian feminists' on the ground that their activities served primarily to disrupt the working class movements. She also ridiculed the efforts of the feminists to attribute value to unpaid labour in the household. In a similar vein, she poured scorn on the demands of the feminists for setting up 'autonomous' women's organizations, and accused them of denying the educative and liberating effects of public production.

Much of this criticism, which I have discussed at length elsewhere, borders on hysteria (Sen 1989). For example, Ranadive takes the feminist attribution of women's exploitation to patriarchy to mean that unless women fight men they will not achieve emancipation. Actually, much of the discomfort felt by the communist parties and other class-based organizations with women's issues stems from the bra-burning, man-hating image of Western feminists and the value loading that the word 'feminist' has acquired in the course of its journey from the West. A document similar in spirit to Ranadive's AIDWA statement was issued by a group of women with CPI(M-L) leanings (Mhatre-Purohit et al. 1987: 1–16) and has been discussed by Jayawardena and Kelkar (1989).

In the relationship between women's organizations and the larger politics for overall change, the parameters are by no means unambiguously defined. Ambiguity exists also on the nature and scope of small independent groups of women. Perhaps one reason why there is so much variety in organizational response and its interpretation is that, in India, we are dealing with a complex social reality that is characterized by great variety in the objective conditions of women. All women's organizations in India, whatever may be their form and affiliation, are faced with the problem of achieving a fine balance between preserving certain aspects of tradition, throwing out certain others, and adhering at the same time to a secular notion of equality.

This package is by no means as simple as it sounds. For, the secular notion of equality is ultimately a product of the liberal Western democratic tradition. Through political exposure and receptivity to the West, this notion has become enshrined in the Indian Constitution and in Indian political theory. Traditional mores do not subscribe to the same framework, and even in a situation (for example, that of an upper-caste Hindu widow in Uttar Pradesh) where there is very little that is pro-woman and as such worth preserving or fighting for, there is the social security that tradition offers, to be considered.

In an adivasi society such as Jharkhand or Chhattisgarh, the abject poverty and traditions of witchcraft in which women are often castigated for casting evil spells are issues to fight against. Yet, the same society gives women a place in public production and relatively liberal sexual and marital norms. What then should, in a given situation, be discarded, what should be retained, developed, and perhaps built upon? Women's organizations in India have shown sensitivity to these questions. Thus, for example, the women of the Shramik Sangathana from Dhulia have analysed traditional adivasi law, studied and rejected Hindu law, and articulated a demand for changes and reform within the adivasi legal framework itself, to make it more amenable to women's interests (Sathe 1990). From particular positions such as this, the question of linkages with other women and with the general or national mainstream Indian women's movement becomes an important and as yet unanswered query.

In the women's movement in India, many theoretical and ideological questions are yet to be sorted out. The questions of autonomous women's organization, of the relationship between the women's movement and a larger class-based or other movement continue to cause intense debate. But a live debate and dialogue is a sign of vibrancy and not of disconnectedness. The important factor outweighing the debate and the controversy is the positive achievement since independence of an active articulation of women's issues at all levels and from all kinds of organizational fora. With openness and commitment we can get to the root of the thorny questions to which we still do not have clear answers. From its present position, the Indian women's movement has a strong enough basis on which to build for the future.

POSTSCRIPT (JUNE 1994)

Several important developments have taken place since 1991. First, we have witnessed a rising tide of fundamentalist and communal forces which have taken a grip of the country to an extent unthinkable even a decade ago. This tendency must be viewed in a global context of communalization of politics.

However, the most alarming aspect of this communalization has been the active role which women have tended to play in communal organizations. Whilst it is true that, by and large, women have been victims and not the protagonists of the 1992 communal riots in Ayodhya, the vision of women *kar sevaks* joining hands with their male opposites to demolish the Babri Masjid and the sound of Sadhvi Ritambara's hysterical outbursts will be etched on our collective memory for a long time.

The last three years have also witnessed an inflow of funds into women's groups and women's action programmes on a hitherto unprecedented scale. The internationalization of women's issues has also meant a professionalization of activism and the resulting loss of sharpness of women's vision. The Indian state too has co-opted much of the vocabulary and conceptual apparatus of gender, and today in many parts of the country, large state-funded and bureaucratic women's action programmes are active. While it cannot be denied that these do reach out to many poor and marginalized women, and perhaps even act for them as tools of empowerment that they are meant to be, they also open up a whole range of new questions and problematics. Do they, in the final analysis, serve to uphold the coercive and anti-women state policies such as directives in respect of population control? Do they actually legitimize dissent (that is, feminist critique of society) in order to contain it?

These developments make it all the more important for us to study the participation of women in movements for wider social change.

For, it is by now abundantly clear that mere mobilization of women will not bring about social change conducive to a betterment of the lives of the majority of people. It may uphold the status quo or even promote change in a reactionary direction. However, when movements for women's equality, for equal partnership with men in struggle are combined with a vision of a more just society, the revolutionary potential of woman power may well be rekindled.

REFERENCES

Abeyesekara, S., S. Bastian, and R. Siriwardena (1980), 'The Women's Question', *Asian Exchange*, 485: 85–195.
Bebel, A. (1971), *Women under Socialism*. New York: Schocken Books.
Bhasin, K. and N.S. Khan (1986), *Some Questions on Feminism and Its Relevance in South Asia*. New Delhi: Kali for Women.
Centre for Women's Development Studies (1988), *National Perspective Plan for Women: 1988-2000—A Perspective from the Women's Movement*. New Delhi: Centre for Women's Development Studies.
Chakravarty, R. (1980), *Bharatiya Nari Andolan Communist Meyera 1940-1950* (in Bengali). Calcutta: Manisha.
Chattopadhyay, K. (1983), *Indian Women's Battle for Freedom*. New Delhi: Abhinav
Chaudhuri, M., Z. Hasan, and V. Mazumdar (1985), *Women's Participation in Political Life in India*. New Delhi: Centre for Women's Development Studies.
Custers, P. (1987), *Women in the Tebhaga Uprising*. Calcutta: Naya Prokash.
Engels, F. (1980), *Origin of the Family, Private Property and the State*. Moscow: Progress.
Government of India (1988), *National Perspective Plan for Women 1988-2000*. New Delhi: Women and Children Development Department, Ministry of Human Resource Development, Government of India.

Jayawardena, V.K. (1988), 'Some Comments on Feminism and the Left in South Asia', *South Asia Bulletin*, Spring/Fall, 8(1 and 2): 88–91.

Jayawardena, V.K. and G. Kelkar (1989), 'The Left and Feminism', *Economic and Political Weekly*, 23 September, 24(38): 2123–6.

Kelkar, G. and C. Galla (1990), 'The Bodhgaya Land Struggles', in I. Sen (ed.), *A Space within the Struggle*. New Delhi: Kali for Women, pp. 82–110.

Kishwar, M. (1988), 'The Nature of Women's Mobilization in Rural India: An Exploratory Essay', *Economic and Political Weekly*, 24–31 December, 23(52 and 53): 2754–63.

Kollontai, A. (1972), *Love of Worker Bees*. Bombay: Feminist Resource Centre, Institute of Social Research and Education (ISRE).

Kumar, R. (1989), 'Contemporary Indian Feminism', *Feminist Review*, Autumn, 33: 20–9.

Mhatre-Purohit, S., R. Desai, and S. Brahme (1987), *The Material Basis for Women's Liberation*. Bombay: Research Unit for Political Economy.

Nayak, N. (1988), *The Struggle within the Struggle*. Trivandrum: Programme for Community Organization Centre.

New Book Centre (1978), 'Women and Communism' [being] *Selections from the Works of Karl Marx, Friederich Engels, V.I. Lenin, Joseph Stalin, Mao Tse Tung*. Calcutta: New Book Centre, pp. 105–24.

Omvedt, G. (1981), 'The Women's Movement: Some Ideological Debates', *Lokayan Bulletin* (Special Issue on the Women's Movement), 4(6): 35–43.

—— (1990), 'The Farmers' Movement in Maharashtra', in Sen (ed.), *A Space within the Struggle*, pp. 229–70.

Parulekar, G. (1975), *Adivasis Revolt*. Calcutta: National Book Agency.

Patel, V. (1985), *Reaching for Half the Sky: A Reader in the Women's Movement*. Vadodara: Antar Rashtriya Prakashan.

Ranadive, V. (1987), *Feminists and the Women's Movement*. New Delhi: All India Democratic Women's Association.

Sathe, N. (1990), 'The Adivasi Struggle in Dhulia', in Sen (ed.), *A Space within the Struggle*, pp. 125–40.

Sen, I. (1989), 'Feminists, Women's Movements and the Working Class', *Economic and Political Weekly*, 22 July, 24(29): 1639–41.

—— (ed.) (1990a), *A Space within the Struggle*.

—— (1990b), 'Workers' Struggles in Chhattisgarh', in Sen (ed.), *A Space within the Struggle*, pp. 194–212.

Sen, M. (1982), *Shediner Katha* (in Bengali). Calcutta: Navapatra.

Singh, A. (1983), *Bharat Ka Mazdoor Andolan* (in Hindi). Calcutta: Rekha Prakashan.

Stree Shakti Sangathana (1989), *We Were Making History...Life Stories of Women in the Telangana Peoples' Struggle*. New Delhi: Kali for Women.

Sundarayya, P. (1972), *Telangana Peoples' Struggle and Its Lessons*. Calcutta: Communist Party of India (Marxist).

Chapter 18

FEMINISM, POVERTY, AND THE EMERGENT SOCIAL ORDER*

MARY E. JOHN**

I

IT IS A SIGN OF OUR TIMES THAT when it comes to giving a face to poverty in contemporary India, that face will, more likely than not, be female. Whether it be the endangered girl child or the destitute widow, the images are compelling. Concepts such as the feminization of poverty emanate from everywhere—whether from the state, non-governmental organizations (NGOs), or women's groups, not to speak of international organizations. Much of this visibility is arguably a mark of success, the result of sustained feminist initiatives. The women's movement in India can count itself among the lucky ones—an 'old' social movement that has played a substantial role in contemporary struggles, ebbing, flowing,

* Originally published in Raka Ray and Mary Katzenstein (eds), 2006, *Social Movements in India: Poverty, Power and Politics*. New Delhi: Oxford University Press, pp. 106–34. Different parts of this chapter have been presented in Berkeley, Delhi, and Bangalore. An earlier version has been published in *Feminisms in Asia*, Special Issue of *Inter-Asia Cultural Studies*, 3(2) (2002): 351–67.

** I am particularly grateful to Mary Katzenstein and Raka Ray for their thoughtful and detailed comments on earlier drafts, which helped considerably in revising my arguments. Of course, I remain solely responsible for the views expressed here.

and reinventing itself in myriad ways. Indeed, when compared to other social movements, the impact of 'women' on contemporary institutions, ideologies, and practices may well be unique. And yet, for reasons that I hope will become clearer in the course of this chapter, thinking about issues of women and poverty today seems to throw up more questions than answers, and the future has never been more uncertain. In other words, we are not in the fortunate position of being able to build on cumulated wisdoms, and even less in a situation of consensus over the issues at stake. There is perceptible fatigue in some quarters as the movement ages, with old problems persisting even as the world is being so rapidly transformed. Not everyone believes that the multiple strands and differences that have come to characterize the Indian women's movement should be counted among its strengths.

Precisely because of the experience of being overtaken by enormous changes, by events few would have predicted at the time but which are bound to cast a long shadow into the years ahead, it may be useful to step back from the immediacy of the present to gain a perspective on the historicity of a movement such as the women's movement. More specifically, how and in what ways has poverty figured in this history?

While it is common to go back as far as the mid-nineteenth century to plot the beginnings of public debates over women's rights in the context of social reform movements, especially in the regions of Bengal and Maharashtra, it is only from the turn of the twentieth century that women's organizations were formed in order to stake their own claims, and that women's voices gained a hearing in more numerous locations within the subcontinent. Especially from the 1920s onwards, a multi-stranded movement was clearly in evidence. We are beginning to rediscover and appreciate women's involvements in a range of social movements during the turbulent decades of the early twentieth century, and not only as the force behind more mainstream organizations such as the Women's Indian Association (WIA) or the All India Women's Conference (AIWC). Women were active in the anti-caste movements in southern and western India, in tribal and peasant struggles, in the overseas anti-indenture campaigns, in nationalist, Gandhian, and communist-led movements. Unfortunately, the historical record remains quite sparse where many of these agitations are concerned, so that the nationalist and Gandhian streams continue to leave the strongest legacy.[1]

---

[1] It might be of interest to readers to know that the social reform movements of the nineteenth century have attracted more in-depth historical analysis to date, at least among

Interestingly enough, even though the poverty of India was a major plank in the nationalist attack against colonial rule, this is not central in the more culturally oriented 'status of women' debates of the time. Upper class and caste biases are clearly in evidence in many of the well-known women's struggles of the early twentieth century—such as over the franchise and reservations of seats in political bodies, the publication of Katherine Mayo's book *Mother India*, the introduction of birth control, and the campaign for passing the Sarda Act to raise the age of marriage.[2] According to Geraldine Forbes, if the first generation of women involved in the major women's organizations justified their demands in terms of 'the ideology of social feminism, ... ty[ing] their arguments about women's rights to women's obligation to perform traditional roles and serve the needs of the family' (1996: 7), certainly by the 1940s this ideology was also found wanting. More radical ideas, often drawn from socialism and communism, became influential.

A distinct shift in outlook is visible, for instance, in the deliberations of Nehru's sub-committee on Women's Role in a Planned Economy, initially set up in 1938, which resulted in the first policy document on women as workers and citizens of the new nation-in-the-making. This radical modernist text conceived of women as 'individuals', with economic rights occupying pride of place (in employment, as property inheritors, in marriage and divorce), while questions of 'culture' and 'tradition', clearly still on the horizon, were accommodated somewhat uneasily. An extraordinary document in many ways, one which sought to 'plan' a new future for all working women (in plantations, factories, and a wide range of mainly urban occupations, but without forgetting housewives, domestic servants, even prostitutes), it is significant that in spite of its central emphasis on women's lack of economic rights, this did *not* require addressing poverty as such. When at all, poverty came up rather tangentially and fleetingly. One such instance was the brief discussion of birth control: 'Where population is increasing by leaps and bounds, and where poverty increases in the same proportion, control of population is

---

feminist scholars located in India, than the early twentieth century period when women's organizations first became established. Significant texts on women in the colonial period include Nanda (1976), Krishnamurthy (1989), Sangari and Vaid (1989), Tharu and Lalita (1991, 1993), Kumar (1993), Ray (1995), and Forbes (1996).

[2] In the words of the feminist historian Mrinalini Sinha (2000: 626), during the 1920s and 1930s, 'liberal Indian feminism played a pivotal role in fashioning a bourgeois liberal Indian modernity'.

absolutely necessary' (Report of the Sub-committee 1947: 175); another was the practice of prostitution.³

No active attempts were made to implement the recommendations of the sub-committee on women in the years following independence. This in itself is not particularly surprising. But what has yet to be adequately explained is the complete absence of any references to the document itself once the new state and development planning were institutionalized.⁴ Be that as it may, it is with the era of development that our story really begins. Development has been the epochal ideology that enabled a Third World nation such as India after independence to make a break with the colonial past and will itself a fully modern future.⁵ Sustaining the nation in its initial decades before entering a crisis during the 1970s and 1980s, it is this ideology, moreover, that has been in a state of decline since the 1990s, so much so that we are today at a new conjuncture represented by the rise to dominance of transnationally powerful regimes of economic liberalization and globalization, however confused our understanding of these successor ideologies might be.

The era of development is critical for understanding the post-independence rebirth of the women's movement, and for a number of reasons. First of all, it is not accidental that the heydays of the development decades—the 1950s and 1960s—have, until very recently, been referred to as the 'silent period' of the women's movement in India. Though assessments may differ, feminist scholars have investigated the 'accommodation and acquiescence' if not 'euphoria' of a pre-independence generation of women leaders who placed their hope and trust in the new nation-state and its constitutional claims of gender equality, and so withdrew as a pressure group (see Banerjee 1998; Desai 1986). The repressive capabilities of this state in crushing struggles such as the Telengana people's struggle

---

³ As the authors of the report put it, 'the foundation of prostitution is hunger'. While professing to hold no moral or sexual attitudes against this occupation, they believed that its eradication would be feasible only in 'a planned society where economic conditions will change, education will predominate and the dual standard of morality be replaced by a common but higher and healthier standard of life between man and woman' (Report of the Sub-committee 1947: 186, 192).

⁴ Instead, the 1950s and 1960s saw the re-emergence of 'women' in the community development programmes (financed by the Ford Foundation) whose projects were geared to enable village women to become, in the words of the director of the Women's Programme in 1959, 'a good wife, a wise mother, a competent housewife, and a responsible member of the village community' (cited in Mehra 1983: xx). Women's work and labour are not alluded to anywhere.

⁵ For a fuller discussion, see Deshpande (1997).

(1946–52) (Stree Shakti Sanghatana 1989) and the insurrections in Tebhaga did little to mar the hegemonic articulation of state, nation, and the economy through a secular-universalistic language of inclusiveness, through proclamations of 'unity in diversity' in the forward march to achieve growth through development.

It was only in the late 1960s and 1970s that signs of crisis in the Nehruvian model of state-led development planning became palpable, leading to the first loss of legitimacy for the Congress government and the rise of a range of new social movements, all of which culminated in the imposition of a state of Emergency in 1975. And yet, as I have argued elsewhere, it was precisely at this time of crisis that 'the coding of the Indian nation as socialist, guided by aims of national self-determination still shaped political discourse to such a degree that these were also formative for a number of oppositional struggles' (John 1996: 3072). The emergence of a new phase of the women's movement from the 1970s onwards therefore took shape in a context where the primary institution to address was the Indian state. This could and did emanate from very different positions—by extreme left groups such as the Progressive Organisation of Women (POW) who wished to expose the state's vested interests, by left-liberal women who sought to rewrite state policy to include women, and by 'autonomous' groups who campaigned against the custodial rapes of Mathura and Rameezabee, and who made legal reform a major plank of their activism.[6] For those women who had taken the claims of Nehruvianism and the constitutional guarantees of equality seriously, the biggest shock of the 1970s was the realization of the invisibility of women in the overall developmental process. This was manifested in the form of startling evidence pointing to processes of impoverishment and deteriorating circumstances for the majority, especially rural women, during the very decades devoted to the welfare and progress of all its citizens.[7]

Middle-class in its leadership, a freshly charged women's movement therefore drew on all the cultural and social capital available to it, raiding

---

[6] General overviews of the women's movement are to be found in Omvedt (1980), Kishwar and Vanita (1987), Gandhi and Shah (1992), Kumar (1993), Agnihotri and Mazumdar (1995), Menon (1999), among others.

[7] The 'founding text' here is the *Towards Equality Report*, produced by the Government of India's Department of Social Welfare through setting up the Committee on the Status of Women in India. Unbeknownst to its team of authors, this report was meant to be the country study for India at the first International Year for Women in 1975 organized by the United Nations.

the social sciences in order to better grapple with as yet poorly understood relations between women and poverty. The key discipline here was economics, and the biggest advances of the 1970s and early 1980s were made in the spheres of women's work, its measurement, problems of undervaluation, declining work participation rates, grass-roots organizing, and so on. Other areas grew in tandem with these developments such as an awareness of the significance of women's health, and the first discoveries by demographers such as Pravin Visaria and Asok Mitra of a secular declining trend in the female–male sex ratio since the turn of the twentieth century (which until then had simply been put down to the undercounting of women in the Indian census).[8]

Within the limited space of this chapter it is not possible to provide a fuller account of the multiple beginnings of the women's movement during the 1970s, nor of its further evolution in the 1980s (including the establishment of women's studies as an inter- and anti-disciplinary field), as fresh challenges were encountered, and new areas of concern opened up. But some clarifications may be necessary before moving on, in order to guard against possible misreading of this period. First of all, I do not wish to imply that questions of women and development—synonymous with the problems of poor women—were the most significant or novel issues to have been addressed at this time. Indeed, in the minds of many, it was the agitations against violence—against rape and dowry-deaths—that led to the first major nationwide campaigns for legal reform and resulted in widespread media publicity, thus fuelling the belief that a new phase of the women's movement was genuinely in evidence. Nor do I wish to suggest that there were few differences during these years. The battles over 'autonomy' by newly formed women's groups in relation to political parties and their women's wings, especially those from the left, were but one of many sources of division. The main point really is this: A unique synergy was achieved in relation to critiques of development that was larger than the disparate actors who contributed to it. Local struggles over work, land, and livelihoods, militant feminists with a far-left orientation, 'nationalist' women close to the state apparatus, academics in research centres and universities, and international agencies, often quite critical of each other, created a new cause—poor women at the 'grassroots', whose disenfranchisement none could dispute.

[8] The first discussion of the declining sex ratio was introduced by Visaria (1969). The equally significant essay by Mitra, 'Implications of Declining Sex Ratio in India', first published in 1979, was reprinted with a number of new articles in Mazumdar and Krishnaji (2001).

If pressed further, one might say that in the formative period of the post-independence phase of the women's movement in India—namely the 1970s and early 1980s—the first efforts to conceptualize and campaign around women's issues co-existed at different and complex levels, making it impossible to typify them in textbook fashion into, say, 'liberal', 'socialist', and 'radical' versions of feminist politics. Some organizations undoubtedly espoused the universalist language of 'women's oppression', and drew on individual legal casework to create awareness among a larger public about the widespread structures of violence against women. Others prioritized mass-based mobilization, especially among peasants, agricultural labourers, or in relation to trade union demands. However, even in the case of an avowedly Marxist-feminist group such as the POW in Hyderabad—and with all their emphases on the 'toiling masses'—it is worth noticing that their very first activity in 1974 was a campaign against 'the dowry system which is prevalent mostly in the middle and upper classes', which was followed by a similar campaign against 'eve-teasing' (as the harassment and humiliation of women on city streets and buses has been called) (Lalita 1988: 60–1). In her study of women's organizations in the cities of Bombay (now Mumbai) and Calcutta (now Kolkata), Raka Ray has argued that it is within regionally shaped 'political fields' that women's movements evolved their agendas and self-understanding, so much so that a simple distinction between 'autonomous' and left-identified groups cannot do justice to the actual ideologies, programmes, and constraints of a particular women's organization (Ray 1999).

The task of analysing the political frameworks of different strands within the women's movement becomes even more complex after the 1980s, when issues of communalism, a growing anti-Muslim upsurge, and a reconfigured nationalism speaking the language of Hindutva also became issues that feminists had to confront. Struggles of a more directly economic nature undoubtedly benefited from existing critiques of development. Early trenchant critiques (such as those that were later published in Jain and Banerjee 1985) were deepened by analyses such as Bina Agarwal's review essay of the relationships among women, poverty, and agricultural growth in India. Agarwal's discussion drew on a wide variety of studies to highlight the negative effects of the new agricultural technologies on women's labour, the special vulnerabilities and increasing numbers of 'female headed households', and growing evidence of a systematic bias against girls and women in the intra-household distribution of food and health care. It is telling that her essay ends with the following claim: 'Existing state policies and programmes (even those aimed at alleviating poverty) offer little scope for optimism.... The point of hope, however, lies in the growth of consciousness among rural women in recent years of the need to organise and unite for fighting against oppression, both outside the home and within it' (Agarwal 1986: 213). These and other criticisms of the state notwithstanding, no one was prepared for just how the state itself responded in the decade that followed.

II

With the 1990s, the quieter liberalization measures begun in the mid-1980s led to India's first serious balance of payments crisis of 1991. This in turn resulted in the announcement of a New Economic Policy involving a comprehensive program of economic reform aiming towards structural adjustment in all sectors, thus fundamentally revising, if not undoing, more than four decades of development planning. First publicly initiated when the Congress returned to power in 1991, these policies were subsequently taken forward under the coalition government headed by the Bharatiya Janata Party (BJP) which took control in 1996. 'Economic facts' should not, however, blind us to the transformed larger ideological climate by virtue of which a country like India, as a relative latecomer to the processes of stabilization, structural adjustment, and liberalization, has entered the contested terrain of globalization.

As successor, ideologies, liberalization, and globalization appear as deeply contradictory, indeed, even as negative paradigms. Their economic rhetoric consists of a retreat from the productive and welfarist dimensions of the state in favour of market- and export-led growth, and the creation of a culture built around consumption. The fact that other Third World nations have referred to their time of economic restructuring during the 1980s as 'the lost decade', and that our new models—the Asian tigers—witnessed major crises during the very years when India began to globalize, has accentuated two things—the extraordinarily intense modes of ideological reconstruction of the new Indian global citizen being deployed today (acutely visible in the heightened place occupied by the media in everyday life), and the severe erosion and loss of authority of alternate paradigms, especially with the collapse of the socialist bloc. Promoters of liberalization persist in referring to the opening of the economy as an 'irreversible' process, as not happening quickly enough.

What does all this mean for a social movement such as the women's movement and for contemporary approaches to issues of poverty? In the face of the deeply negative climate of the 1990s (in contrast to the more buoyant and idealistic years of the women's movement's rebirth in the 1970s), and precisely because of the apparent absence of options, one must approach such a question from a range of vantage points. Such an approach is all the more necessary today because the impact of the women's movement is both widespread and uneven. At this stage in its development, the movement has increasingly become more institutionalized, and the future of earlier modes of mobilization is particularly uncertain. Feminists who played an initiating role in the 1970s and 1980s are today 'spokespersons' on a number of issues. As I mentioned at the beginning of this chapter, the multiple forms of visibility of women's issues (including their co-optation and annexation in unintended ways) could well be a unique feature of contemporary Indian social and political life. Whether it be the legacy of local struggles, the shifting concerns of the state, or the very relationship between globalization and poverty, 'women' constitute a significant presence. The rest of this chapter will therefore make different inroads into the broad and heterogeneous thematic of women and poverty in the contemporary context, sometimes with the help of detailed examples, sometimes more briefly. In the process, I also hope to illustrate the difficulties involved in gaining an adequate perspective on what 'globalization' represents, quite apart from possessing the right language to challenge it.

My first approach for thinking about the changes wrought under the sign of liberalization and globalization will be through a discussion of the trajectories of two recent local movements spawned in the name of 'women'. The key to the life of the women's movement in India so far is that it is not simply composed of more or less high-profile leaders—whether activists, writers, or from political parties, the administration, and the academy. Most accounts of major campaigns of the women's movement, as well as of specific struggles and organizations, have dwelt on their formative period, and there is little on the changes wrought since the 1990s (see Basu 1993; Ray 1999; Sen 1990; Sharma 1989). During the 1990s, two women's struggles in particular achieved considerable attention, and in ways that spilled beyond their regional confines. Quite different in their origins and organizational structures, each of them tells a distinct story about the kinds of problems women's movements are facing, especially in relation to the Indian state. My examples are the Women's Development Programme (WDP) in Rajasthan and the anti-arrack (distilled country liquor) agitation in Andhra Pradesh.

The WDP was launched in 1984 (with initial funding provided by United Nations Children's Fund [UNICEF]) as a unique programme of empowerment of rural grassroots women in several districts of Rajasthan in northwest India, a region castigated for its 'feudal'—that is, socioeconomic and cultural—backwardness. What set the WDP apart from other state-led schemes was its emphasis on communication of information, education, and awareness-raising (rather than employment generation), based on an interactive network linking government officials and NGO staff. The most important figures within this organizational structure have been the village-level workers or *sathin*s (literally, female companions), who were entrusted with the task of building women's groups within their villages. These groups were able to generate sensitivity towards each other's problems, build an environment in which women could begin a process of collective questioning, and so support women in their struggle to resolve issues together (Srivastava and Jaya Sharma 1991). Towards this end, a great deal of emphasis was placed on the training of the sathins in the WDP, a process that was intensive, innovative, and deeply committed. Commentators who toured districts where the WDP was active noticed marked differences among the women they met. In the space of a few years it was clear that the WDP had made a significant impact, with women's groups monitoring drought relief works, participating in health education programmes, taking up small savings schemes, contributing to the monthly newsletter, and organizing against specific practices such as mass child marriages to older men (Das 1991).

Of course, this is not to say that the WDP did not encounter plenty of challenges, difficulties, and criticisms from different quarters. Sathins did not find it easy to build groups and hold meetings, whether due to domestic duties, opposition from men, or heavy work schedules especially during the harvest season and religious festivals. Lower caste sathins encountered further obstacles to their leadership. More importantly, from the perspective of the organizational structure of the WDP, after the initial years of flexibility and innovation, the district administration and panchayats wished to take advantage of the sathins' village-level rapport and activism to draw them into government schemes such as family planning, child immunization drives, and poverty alleviation programmes. The family planning programmes in particular became the focus of agitation by the sathins after they obtained evidence of several forced sterilizations and of the linking of famine relief with family planning targets. Sathins were soon criticized for becoming too independent and for participating in alternative women's organizations. Five sathins were fired when they attended the National Conference of the Women's Movement held in Calicut (Kerala) in 1990. (These national meetings, first begun in 1980 in the city of Bombay, have been held every two to three years in different cities, and bring together thousands of participants from all over India. Since then there have been gatherings in Tirupati in 1993 and Ranchi in 1996.)

In the early 1990s, the sathins decided to form their own union (the Sathin Karamchari Sangh) to press for their demands, which included an increase in their honorarium (set at Rs 200 per month to cover incidental expenses) and proper recognition of their status as government rather than 'voluntary' workers. It probably goes without saying that such a demand flew in the face of the liberalization policies set in motion during these very years, when the last thing the government was prepared to contemplate was the induction of poor, predominantly illiterate rural women into the state apparatus. Instead, efforts to dismantle the programme have been initiated on a number of fronts—by leaving vacant posts unfilled, by attempting to 'integrate' sathins into service delivery schemes such as the World Bank–funded Integrated Child Development Scheme (ICDS), and by announcing that the sathin model for women's empowerment would be replaced by a new model—the *sangam* or *samooh* (group) model—that no longer required the special skills of leaders such as the sathins.

The sathins have continued with their struggle, sometimes appearing to gain marginally from outside support such as was provided by the National Commission of Women (1996) or by political changes in the Rajasthan government from the BJP to the Congress in 1999 (Sathin Karamchari Sangh n.d.). In February 2001, the five sathins who were fired in 1990 won a decade-long legal battle for their reinstatement. In March 2002, the contradictions besetting this state-sponsored women's programme reached a flash point, when the government of Rajasthan issued a notification ordering the closure of the entire programme on grounds of its financial unviability. However, the state appears to have been ill-prepared for the mobilization that followed—a broad platform of women's groups was set up in Rajasthan to oppose the government directive, and sathin union activists lobbied intensively in the capital city of Delhi. All the protests did appear to bear fruit—the order for closure was revoked and the status quo maintained. Indeed, the state government has even made appointments of new sathins in districts where there were none before. It remains profoundly unclear, however, whether this can be termed a victory. In the intervening years the programme has been effectively hollowed out and turned into something else: Sathins are no longer provided with any kind of training or collective network, and the single important activity appears to be creating self-help groups (SHGs) among village women.

The second example I wish to discuss here is the anti-arrack agitation that arose in parts of Andhra Pradesh in 1992, especially in the eastern district of Nellore. Perhaps the only common thread with the WDP is that the primary initiators of the anti-arrack movement were also poor rural women with no prior experience in politics as it is conventionally understood. Sporadic struggles against government-backed sales of arrack had been taking place in many districts of the state since the 1980s, and gathered unprecedented momentum in 1992 in Nellore when peasant women, working only in their villages, enforced the closure of local arrack shops and targeted the excise department officials and excise police. In so doing, they were able to effectively confront the state and destabilize its economy, one that had become quite dependent on the massive excise revenues from increasingly aggressive arrack sales.[9]

Arrack became a focal point in the women's struggle, enabling them to comprehend many of their daily problems related to work, the family economy, health, education, and their personal lives. For instance, women felt the acute injustice of a situation where water had to be brought from long distances in villages without schools or hospitals, but which were being regularly supplied with arrack. Some women had no difficulties in tackling their husbands directly over the issue. Others found it easier to confront men by taking them on collectively in a public space like the arrack shop, thus bringing about major changes in gender relations at the village level. The movement had many origins, the most catalytic of which was the government-initiated programme to eradicate illiteracy, taken up in each district by voluntary organizations. Women and girls formed the backbone of the literacy drives, and some of the stories written in the neo-literacy primers about problems related to arrack inspired those attending the classes. Women stopped the arrack carts from entering their villages, forcibly closed arrack shops, resisted pressure tactics and attacks by contractors and excise personnel. It was only much later that an anti-arrack coordinating committee was formed and that women's organizations and political parties began to realize the full extent of what was going on.

As the result of the dispersed and localized nature of the anti-arrack agitation—led by Dalit, backward caste, and Muslim women—the state

---

[9] For details of the anti-arrack agitation, see Anveshi (1993).

was unable to isolate its leaders and simply repress the movement. Women did not take on the state directly but managed to destabilize its power by severing the nexus of the government and the liquor contractors at those points where it functioned most effectively—the arrack shops, stock points, and auctions. What is remarkable is both how the movement spread to neighbouring villages and the extent to which a variety of interest groups, including ultimately the state government itself, felt compelled to support it. The state government first announced a ban on arrack in the district of Nellore in April 1993, followed by a similar ban throughout the state six months later. Everyone sought to appropriate the anti-arrack women, and political parties—both those in power and those in opposition—imaged the women as social reformers and modern Durgas (avenging goddesses) who were cleansing the nation of the evil of arrack. They thus 'predicated onto the woman in the anti-arrack agitation an assortment of complex narratives of which she was the sole heroine' (Tharu and Niranjana 1996: 254). In January 1995, soon after the Telugu Desam Party defeated the Congress and returned to power, Chief Minister N.T. Rama Rao introduced total prohibition as a populist ploy, and the focus shifted from arrack to liquor in general, from the struggle of poor rural women to one of the urban middle classes (Maheswari 1999). But by March 1997, the dry laws were lifted since they were seen to have opened the door to bootlegging, apart from being blamed for severely jeopardizing business interests in the globalizing city of Hyderabad.

The state, in the meanwhile, inaugurated thrift and savings schemes in the very villages where the women had been so active. Awards were instituted to those women who were the most successful microentrepreneurs. The government gave such a strong push to these credit schemes that even the Ninth Five Year Plan (1997–2002) document of the Planning Commission introduced a special box item on 'Podupulakshmi—Pride of Nellore Women—a success story' in their chapter on poverty alleviation schemes.[10] Co-opted in this way, it is perhaps needless to add that the struggle in and around Nellore, which not so long ago had been able to achieve a measure of empowerment among women by calling to account the most oppressive structures controlling their lives, was

---

[10] The box item explains that 'podupu' means saving, Lakshmi being the goddess of wealth. The *podupulakshmi* 'movement' ('the sequel to the total literacy campaign and the anti-arrack movement'), it is said, is going beyond conventional thrift schemes and carrying out a wide variety of women-centred activities, with the aid of local government functionaries such as the public health worker (ANM), school teacher, fair price shop dealer, and *anganwadi* (child care) worker (Planning Commission 1999b: 17).

betrayed. Women's efforts were largely directed towards micro-economic activity. Quite apart from the disputed positive potential of such schemes, they are hardly a substitute for the basic demands raised in the wake of these women's effective exposure of the state's regressive and exploitative policies towards its rural working populations.

Each of these struggles—around the WDP in Rajasthan and the anti-arrack agitation in Andhra—has clearly been shaped by their respective regional contexts. In a drought-prone backward region with strong norms of female seclusion, the sathins emerged as local leaders and mobilizers, thanks to the initiative provided by the state and NGOs (including international funding). Their main demand has been for stronger institutional support, to the point of inclusion within the local state apparatus but without compromising on their unique non-service-oriented modes of functioning. Nellore, on the other hand, is part of Andhra's relatively prosperous coastal rice-growing belt. Here, rural women were agitating against the deprivation and violence they were experiencing due to the drain of men's earnings into arrack. Both these local movements only subsequently gained the attention and support of women's organizations. And in both cases, it is the state that has been in a position to deflect these rural women's protests in similar ways, by refusing to be accountable and by inserting models of 'self-help' and economic entrepreneurship among poor rural women instead.

Indeed, the most disorienting aspect of the emerging social order has to do with the changeling and dissimulative discourse and practice of the state. The 'social mobilization' of women (and other so-called weaker sections) is a catch-phrase frequently deployed by government agencies and spokespersons and can be found in numerous documents. From 'welfare to development to empowerment' is yet another contemporary slogan meant to demonstrate the state's steady advancement in addressing women's issues over the last half century. It certainly cannot be said that poverty has disappeared from the state's agenda. (This is what many had initially feared would be the direct effect of the new rhetoric advocating the retreat of the state from economic development, especially with the entry of the BJP-led coalition government in 1996.) One has to look beyond official texts to gain a sense of how the dominant order is attempting to shift its priorities and strategies. This brings me to my second point of entry into the current conjuncture. The greatest challenge facing a movement such as the women's movement in these rapidly changing times could well be the new consensus that has emerged around the question of population control.

A closer look will reveal just why the population question has turned out to be such a major stumbling block. To begin with, ever since its post-independence rebirth in the 1970s and 1980s, the women's movement has been fundamentally opposed to agendas of population control, a position that has been shared by 'autonomous groups' as much as by left-identified organizations.[11] Moreover, such opposition appeared to have been only too well-founded in the wake of the Emergency years of 1975–7. In the sterilization camps organized by the then Youth Congress leader Sanjay Gandhi, young single men were among those forcibly sterilized, official deaths alone numbered over two thousand, and these widely condemned crimes were among the most shocking violations of the period. The ineffectiveness of the Family Planning Programme, as it was then called, stood starkly exposed. Others believed that these excesses did not represent the dominant agenda of the state, and took comfort from the international propagation of the slogan 'development is the best contraceptive' by Indira Gandhi's cabinet minister Karan Singh at the World Conference on Population in Bucharest in 1974. Feminist critiques of India's initial health policy during the first post-independence decades have been more concerned to highlight its strong urban bias and the fundamental inability of the system of Primacy Health Centres to serve vast rural populations. Moreover, the state paid no attention to maternal health in this period (the 1950s–1970s), concentrating solely on trying to improve child survival in the hope that such a strategy would bring down fertility rates (see Das Gupta *et al.* 1995; Qadeer 1998a).

The latter years of the 1970s and especially the 1980s brought about dramatic changes, and in ways no one could have anticipated. After the Emergency, the Family Planning Programme—still under a cloud—was rebaptized as Family Welfare and integrated within the existing system of general health services. However, far from inaugurating a more genuinely comprehensive approach to the health care needs of poor families, family welfare has been progressively usurping outlays meant for overall public health, especially for the control of communicable diseases: Claiming 15 per cent of the total health budget in the Sixth Plan (1982–7), family

---

[11] This unequivocal stance against population control is itself a mark of the distinctiveness of the women's movement in the post-independence era. In the pre-independence period of the 1920s and 1930s, when the question of birth control was first publicly debated and was a highly controversial subject indeed, it was not uncommon to find advocates of birth control among women's organizations who also viewed it as a means to contain poverty, as we saw in the deliberations of Nehru's Sub-Committee on Women.

planning jumped to consuming as much as 35 per cent of the Eighth Plan budget a decade later, and this rising trend continues.

Even more disorienting for the women's movement has been the scrambling of the discourses and practices of population control with those of women's empowerment: Every potentially emancipatory aspect of a poor woman's life—her education, her employment, her decision to marry, her control over resources, indeed, her very autonomy, is today open to annexation—or so many in the women's movement in India believe—by forces whose primary concern is to reduce population growth. Hesitant attempts by the state to increase female sterilization and contraception, which began in the late 1960s, received a major boost post-Emergency, when the programme was restructured, leading to the official abandonment of target-based approaches, and a decisive shift from focusing on men to concentrating on women. But in 1994, women's organizations—again across a wide spectrum—were shocked and even betrayed by the proposals of the Expert Group on the Population Policy set up by the Indian state: For the first time in post-independence history, a government document—the Draft National Population Policy—announced that population growth was playing a causative role not only in spreading poverty, but also in exacerbating environmental degradation (Government of India 1994). It even went so far as to suggest a range of legislative steps against those with more than two children. It is therefore particularly telling just what aspects of the critiques of India's population policies—levelled by women's organizations and health groups since the 1980s—were subsequently redeployed by the Indian government to produce an updated, target free, voluntary, pro-woman national population policy for the new millennium (Government of India 2000).

Today, there exists a population policy couched in the language of empowering women for improved health and nutrition, through the ostensible convergence of health issues, free and compulsory education up to the age of fourteen, raising the age of marriage, focusing especially on 'under-served' populations. However, feminists and health activists have shown that, as it turns out, current policy is largely concerned with inducting long-acting, provider-controlled, and women-centred hormonal contraceptives in the name of women's 'unmet needs', leaving precisely all the major issues of macro-economic policy unaddressed. Indeed, India seems to be aiming for the historically unprecedented goal of achieving demographic transition and population stabilization without parallel changes in the economy. There is a further twist here: One of the facets of the post-liberalization period has been the growing political autonomy of the different states within the Indian federal system, in spite of being in greater financial crisis. While the overt language of policy at the national level may well be voluntaristic and democratic in tone, this is not the case at the state levels. There are now regional population policies in states such as Madhya Pradesh, Maharashtra, Rajasthan, and Andhra Pradesh, where strong incentives and disincentives have been promoted; where fresh targets have been set; and where a two-child norm is being used to penalize women—preventing anyone with more than two children from standing for election in the panchayats and municipalities,[12] or from receiving government aid, including food rations in the public distribution system. Local women's groups and others in these states are therefore doing what they can to campaign against their respective state governments, while those at the 'centre' in Delhi are discovering the limits of lobbying for change in the national capital (*Healthwatch Update* 2000; Rao 2001).

In my view, there is a further aspect to the current scenario that is special cause for concern. Unlike even a few decades ago, population control has fully entered middle-class 'common-sense', for whom it is the single most critical problem facing the country. One could cite numerous instances to substantiate this, but I will mention just two: Even as eminent a personage as Justice Ventakatachaliah, who gave up his chairmanship of the Human Rights Commission to convene the controversial review committee of the Constitution of India, has gone on public record to state that it is precisely in the face of the most burning problems of the country, such as the population problem, that a constitutional review is required. School textbooks have also not been spared. Since 2001, the proposed revision of school syllabi by the National Council of Educational Research and Training (NCERT) has been much in the news because of the surreptitious alterations made in the history syllabus to advance right-wing agendas. Less commented upon in all the debate and opposition are other changes and additions. For instance, in the proposed English syllabus for Class V

---

[12] In a recent study of women councillors in the municipalities of the metropolitan city of Delhi and the small town of Karnal in rural Haryana, one of the questions put to the councillors was their response to the recent order in both the states debarring those with more than two children from standing for election. Much to the surprise of the interviewers, they found the councillors in both contexts unanimous in their support of the policy. The interviewers' final comment was that with such widespread consent, it was feminist opposition to such policies that was clearly misplaced (Marg 2001).

primary school children, population growth and gender equality are to be taught together as part of 'population education'.[13]

The women's movement thus finds itself in a climate where population reduction is no longer a relatively marginal matter of covert and coercive 'excesses' but enjoys widespread and far-reaching consent.[14] The situation has been further complicated by new divisions and differences within the movement. Those who draw upon the perspectives of public health initiatives and the need for improvements in the economy in order to address women's health needs are deeply suspicious of the contemporary language of women's reproductive rights. They see this as yet another ploy by both international agencies and the state to advance an older agenda of population control. Imrana Qadeer has critiqued feminist approaches that 'place reproductive health centre stage' with its narrow biological and medicalist focus on a woman's life-cycle (Qadeer 1998b). Others, however, do not see how the annexation of the rhetoric of reproductive health per se diminishes the legitimacy of addressing this sphere of women's lives. Instead, they have argued for broadening the scope of population policies by creating the necessary 'enabling conditions' and 'social rights' within which women could make more genuine reproductive choices (Ravindran 1993; Sen *et al.* 1994). Suffice it to say, therefore, that the entire problematic being covered in the name of population control—with women's reproductive and sexual 'choices' now at its heart—has become one of the hardest areas for the women's movement to confront, where older strategies forged during the development era serve feminists poorly under the present dispensation.[15]

Let me now shift to the third entry-point for approaching questions of poverty, namely its place in relation to the big questions of globalization and liberalization. In a recent article reviewing India's 'micro-movements' from the 1970s to the present, D.L. Sheth has argued that the very onset

---

[13] This is mentioned in the National Council of Educational Research and Training (2001: 30).

[14] Middle-class consensus over population control has also been bolstered by stoking fears regarding the unbounded multiplication of Muslims. This became manifest when 1991 Census data on the break-up of the population by religion—which showed that Muslims had grown slightly faster than Hindus in the 1981–91 decade—was used as 'proof' in numerous newspaper articles and public exhortations soon after it was published in 1995 that Muslims practise polygamy, resist contraception, and are swamping the Indian nation with Islam. Interestingly, high levels of poverty among Muslims (especially in urban areas) were not part of these discussions.

[15] For further discussions of these dilemmas, see Tharu and Niranjana 1996), John (1998), and Mukherjee (2002).

of globalization has revitalized the entire spectrum of social movements (many of which had become moribund or routinized after the initial elan of the 1970s), and is even producing a 'high degree of convergence on a wide range of issues concerning globalisation' (Sheth 2004: 47). There are many fascinating and informative aspects to Sheth's account. However, having rightly seen how the entry of globalization has become the new frame of reference and target for numerous social movements (including the women's movement), this slides into the problematic claim that a 'counter-discourse' of converging positions is consequently in the making. The multiple strands of the women's movement illustrate the extent to which divergent and contrary positions have actually been hardening in recent years. Even when allowance is made for the fact that these positions often focus on different dimensions of liberalization and globalization, their range is truly remarkable, while they are all feminist and committed to social justice. Compared to the extensive debates within the movement on issues such as the question of a uniform civil code, or over reservations for women in local self-government and in Parliament, similar public debates have not taken place over the immensely critical nature of the new conjuncture of 'globalization'. Whether positions are being adopted unequivocally or with considerable uncertainty, it is time that they are reflected on at greater length. No discussion of poverty takes place today without reference to globalization, its discourses, policies, and institutional restructuring.

The most frequently heard and strongest voices within the women's movement have condemned and attacked the New Economic Policies right from their inception a decade ago. Their basis is that globalization can only inaugurate a widening of disparities across and within nations and regions, leading to a deepening of processes of impoverishment for the majority. The special sufferers here will be poor women, for such women will have to increasingly bear the disproportionate burdens arising from the unequal allocation of resources and poorer self-care, even as they work harder to make up for falling real incomes, reductions in social welfare, and the privatization of services. As women take on multiple jobs, their daughters will either follow them or take charge of the household, thus being debarred from an education. Greater levels of stress will also lead to a worsening of men's ability to cope, which then takes such forms as growing violence or increased desertions. Following this line of argumentation, large sections of the women's movement, not only those coming from the left, have been mobilizing repeatedly against economic reform, whether it be over disinvestment of the public sector, conditions of work in export processing zones, or food security subsidies.

In order to show how seriously they viewed the announcement of the New Economic Policies in 1991, the Indian Association of Women's Studies devoted its sixth national conference in 1993 (a three-day event held every two years with plenaries and simultaneous sessions) entirely to the theme of the 'New Economic Policy and Its Implications for Women'. While numerous consultations have followed, actual in-depth studies of the consequences of the new policies in the lives of women are just beginning to appear. One of the earliest efforts was by activists and scholars in Bombay, who questioned claims in favour of the feminization of the labour force during structural adjustment, by showing that major manufacturing industries in the city of Bombay have in fact been retrenching women at unprecedented rates since the 1980s (Shah *et al.* 1994). A parallel critique of the feminization thesis has been levelled by Nirmala Banerjee.[16]

Less visible in the concerted attacks against liberalization have been the frameworks and perspectives being deployed by those who oppose the current regime. In my view, the absence of self-reflexivity about their ideological frames of reference constitutes a major impediment that is blocking the advancement of such oppositional agendas. As I mentioned earlier on, it is never enough, especially not today, to think that facts somehow speak for themselves. What, then, are the ideological subtexts fuelling current opposition, and whom do they address? The major problem here is that these oppositional voices invariably speak from positions that have precisely lost their authority in the present climate. They either stem from the era of developmentalism and economic nationalism that has lost out in the current conjuncture, or hark back to an even earlier time, to a cultural past free from all forms of capitalist and imperialist domination. This has also led to the situation where Marxists, whose frameworks continue to be pinned to state-centred welfare and socialist planning, share a common platform with eco-feminists such as Vandana Shiva, whose opposition to multinational capital arises from a fundamentally different worldview, one based on the desire to preserve the indigenous local knowledges and pre-modern relationship to nature that she imputes to Third World women

---

[16] Banerjee has also opposed a tendency to generalize about the relationship between new work opportunities for women and their empowerment or subordination, advocating a more contextual approach instead. See Banerjee (1997).

farmers.[17] As the result of the coming together of such incommensurable frameworks, there is a definite air of eclecticism in some of the current oppositional rhetorics being deployed. This adds to the problem of coming across as speaking not from the present but from the past.

In comparison, the voices of those who have offered some kind of qualified acceptance to globalization, though often couched in a more tentative or speculative language, nonetheless appear to gain simply by virtue of being more rooted in the present. Here again, positions are quite diverse. A figure like Madhu Kishwar, for example, seems to be basing her assent to the current economic regime less out of any careful assessment of its claims than from her opposition to any state-centric—or what she identifies as Western-inspired—worldview, whether of development or women's empowerment.[18] From a very different perspective, the Marxist-feminist Rohini Hensman views the greater integration of the world economy as a necessary stage in the evolution of global capitalism. She goes further to assert that this demands a correspondingly international level of intervention and struggle, whether through the promotion of coordinated class actions by globally disenfranchised workers or by taking advantage of international standards such as the highly controversial World Trade Organization (WTO) directive to link trade with labour standards in developing nations like India. The anti-globalization agenda does not make sense for groups like women workers in Third World contexts, she goes on to argue, who have potentially more to gain through 'concerted action to shape the global order in accordance with a women's agenda for justice and equity as well as caring and nurturing.... Can a socialist feminist vision of an ideal world include national boundaries maintained by nationalism, with its potential for developing into fascism, imperialism and war?' (Hensman 2004: 1034; see also Hensman 2000). The weakness in her otherwise cogent account has to do with her

---

[17] Vandana Shiva's analyses can be gleaned from lectures such as Shiva (1996) and in essays such as Shiva (1998). A series of phases of globalization—colonization by Europe; the universalization of production and consumption in the name of 'development'; and, finally, the current trade treaties focused on biodiversity and genetic resources—are opposed to the potential of 'decentralized agricultural communities', which, like pre-modern paradigms of the 'home' are somehow without hierarchies—whether of ecology and economics, domestic or commodity production, natural or human economies, or relations of gender.

[18] In a set of proposals canvassed in *Manushi*, Madhu Kishwar wishes to set in motion a 'freeing up of the entrepreneurial skills of the people', especially women, who have been made dependent and prevented from taking their place in the public sphere of the economy due to an over-bloated, over-centralized bureaucracy, and a larger culture of criminalization and violence (Kishwar 2001).

audience—neither the international working class nor transnational feminist groups are particularly visible today. (It is the anti-globalizers who seem to be steadily gaining in global visibility—most recently at the third social summit organized in Mumbai, India, in January 2004, which included several feminist organizations. And yet, there have been some telling reformulations in the rhetoric deployed at these meetings—calls for a movement of 'counter-globalization' and opposition to 'imperial globalization' rather than direct opposition to globalization per se may well be indicative of a nascent political formation critical of both nationalisms and certain versions of globalization.)

The third example of qualified support to globalization comes from the work of Gail Omvedt, and is surely the most provocative. Omvedt has argued that globalization and the new economic order may actually help those very groups whom the development era effectively marginalized. Her analysis is based on the expectation that globalized markets will, on the one hand, rein in the Indian bourgeoisie, its unviable monopolies, and the inefficient upper-caste state bureaucracy, and, on the other hand, give the small farmer a better global price for produce which was previously under-priced due to state intervention. As she has put it polemically, 'if the choice is between a high caste capitalist Indian economy with a highly privileged all-male workforce ... producing steel or automobiles, and a relatively labor-intensive multi-national linked company in a rural area employing women [or lower castes, in leather trades, fruit and vegetable production and so on] then we will prefer the multinational' (Omvedt and Gala 1993: 15). This argument (which shares common ground with some feminization arguments elsewhere) begs as many questions as it raises, the most important of which would be the following: Are these hitherto marginalized groups—peasants, Dalits, backward castes, and women—socially positioned to take advantage of globalization, and on what basis can we expect the hitherto dominant urban classes and castes to lose out in the current realignments taking place?

My final example of a different voice is that of the Self-employed Women's Association (SEWA), as mediated by its leaders Ela Bhatt and Renana Jhabvala. The history of SEWA goes back to the early 1970s, and grew out of its founder Ela Bhatt's formative experience as a Gandhian with the Textile Labour Association in Ahmedabad. SEWA describes itself as a trade union of poor, self-employed workers, and has a membership of over 200,000 women. Its main centres are in Gujarat, though there are newer ones in a few other states as well. Their approach to women's issues is one of economic empowerment—the 'second freedom' Bhatt (1998) believes is India's struggle after political freedom was won in 1947—by providing the necessary economic and financial security to women workers in the informal or unorganized sector, through a system of cooperative banking, maternal and child care, and most recently through an insurance programme set up in collaboration with insurance companies. I would call their response to liberalization one of pragmatism. Recognizing that the living standards of the poor may well have declined after structural adjustment was initiated and that the hitherto secure entitlements of the organized sector may also get eroded, they wish to take the 'positive' approach of creating the necessary social security systems that could potentially address the needs of the vast majority of the country's workers. In contrast to the public sector and the private sector (the backbone of India's experiment with a mixed economy during the development era, and towards whom all national policies have been aimed), they have mooted the concept of 'the people's sector'—unorganized labour and self-employed producers in rural and urban India, subjects of neglect yet on whom the economy effectively depends (Jhabvala and Subrahmanya 2000). With their emphasis on women's economic agency, processes of decentralization, increased levels of financial and managerial participation by the 'beneficiary' population, and the reduced role of the state, it is perhaps not surprising that SEWA has been picked up as a model by international agencies such as the World Bank—and not just for Third World countries, but even for First World nations who are themselves seeking to dismantle their welfare systems in favour of neo-liberal policy orientations. SEWA is therefore at the hub of a number of highly contentious issues. What are the elisions underwriting the liberal concept of women's 'economic agency' and greater efficiency in managing poverty, and what dangers does this portend for the future?[19]

III

This chapter has attempted to identify some of the major challenges posed by the contemporary conjuncture to feminist politics in ongoing battles against poverty. I have in particular concentrated on the effects of a shift in paradigm from the once dominant era of state-led development planning (within which a new phase of the women's movement emerged) to the

---

[19] For further discussions and criticisms see World Bank (1991), John (1996), Carr *et al.* (1997), and Vasavi and Kingfisher (2003).

current rise to dominance of ideologies of liberalization and globalization. Contrasting perspectives—the new hegemonic location of population control for reducing poverty; problems of sustaining local struggles; and the diverse positions in the women's movement towards globalization—have been presented. Of course, there is a great deal more that needs to be examined on all of these, and I have done no more than skim the surface.

If one can venture to say anything with some degree of confidence, it is that the state has been steadily abdicating from its own role, in the past decade not even setting much store by its own agendas for the eradication of poverty. This may be why the erstwhile 'think tank' for the government, the Planning Commission, has provided such optimistic estimates of current trends. If the projections of the recently concluded Ninth Plan are to be believed, poverty in India should have declined from an estimated poverty ratio figure of 29.2 in 1996–7 to 18 in 2001–2 (to drop further to 9.5 in 2006–7 and 4.3 in 2011–12) (Planning Commission 1999a: 33). It is not so much that others have disputed these estimates as being quite off the mark, but that we have entered an era where extensive and serious debates on poverty are increasingly confined to journals such as the *Economic and Political Weekly*. The government, on its part, has been far more concerned to interface with the middle classes, business interests, and the media through the tax proposals of its annual budgets. Why else has the Tenth Plan (2002–7), due to begin in April 2002, received practically no public attention?

But instead of lamenting the failures of planning, the purpose of this concluding section is to take note of other emergent processes whose significance in the years to come is likely to grow. Ironic as it might seem, and in considerable contrast to the divergent—indeed, somewhat chaotic—responses to 'globalization', the one subject of growing consensus today is the re-significance of the 'local'. Obviously, different conceptions of the local abound. But the version that everyone subscribes to is the need for greater political decentralization and local autonomy, a cause espoused by those who might otherwise be pro- or anti-state, liberalizers, or leftists. The revival of local self-government in the late 1980s, after widespread institutional neglect following independence, coupled with a reservations policy granting one-third seats for women in village panchayats and urban municipalities (passed without any debate, let alone opposition, by Parliament during 1993 and 1994), clearly constitutes an unprecedented opportunity: more than a million women representatives across the country are now in a position to tackle local problems, not by waiting to be served from distant centres of power, but right at the grassroots.

There is little question of the radical potential of this revival. The journey, however, has barely begun. The only state where a major devolution of power in financial and developmental terms has taken place is Kerala. It is a telling comment on the extent of the masculinization of politics and political parties in that state, however, that women representatives have yet to make a real difference, all the positive social and educational indicators among Kerala women notwithstanding.[20] In most other states, the burden has been to demonstrate that women elected to local bodies are not mere 'rubber stamps' for more powerful male relatives, and that they can function in spite of patriarchal constraints. The danger today is that unless genuine powers are vested at these local levels, the new energies will become moribund and get dissipated.[21] Furthermore, the somewhat narrow focus by feminists and others on the alleged advantages or disadvantages of women representatives (Are they less corrupt? Are they more vulnerable? and so on)[22] has been at the cost of shying away from the institutional consequences that accompany the participation of women in 'governance'. On the one hand, the 'autonomy' of major sections of the women's movement from political parties has been something of a founding principle. On the other hand, the rise to dominance of right-wing parties such as the BJP, boasting prominent support from women, has been a major source of crisis. Active, vigorous, and accountable 'good governance' cannot be separated from direct involvement in the institutions

---

[20] Indeed, one of the major architects of Kerala's decentralization process has candidly admitted the following in a discussion of women political representatives: 'Most of them were young, educated only up to matriculation or below, from poor or lower middle class backgrounds and without prior experience in elected office. Forty percent of them did not have any previous exposure to public activity. They had to work in an unfriendly social environment and often faced slander and gossip. This triple burden of work, family duties and responsibility as an elected representative gave rise to family tensions, although they were within manageable limits' (Isaac and Franke 2000: 227). Unfortunately, the largely uncritical if not celebratory approach that has been adopted towards the 'empowered' women of Kerala, at least till recently, has been at the severe cost of any nuanced understanding of contemporary practices and gender relations in that complex state.

[21] A genuine contradiction is evident in the means whereby decentralization is to be implemented, since it depends on the 'giving up' of power by the higher tiers of the state apparatus. The contradiction involved is even sharper than it would have been during the development era, because, if anything, political power and regional autonomy among individual states in relation to the Centre have increased in the last decade.

[22] There is a growing literature on the subject, mostly in the form of case studies and training manuals by NGOs. Some examples would be Kaushik (1993); Institute of Social Sciences (1995), Datta (1998), and Buch (2000).

that promote the political process. What, then, might be the relations between party politics, women in power, and the politics of feminism?

If the participation of women in the electoral process brings new opportunities and dangers, the rise of a politics based on caste and minority status also poses radical questions to the women's movement. We have come a considerable way from the reductive and technicist battles over the determination of poverty during the 1970s that focused on the appropriate measurements of calorie intake for determining below poverty line (BPL) populations. And yet, the power of economic ideologies is such that material concepts of disadvantage, lack of entitlements, and unmet basic needs continue to dominate contemporary debates. Furthermore, there has been a tendency during the last decade to uphold struggles over poverty in opposition to those being raised in the name of so-called 'identity politics', especially in the wake of the re-emergence on the national stage of the politics of caste and community. Such misgivings have been voiced in the women's movement as well. To my mind, this polarization blocks the chance of actually transforming our understanding of poverty itself. It could be argued, and I am going to do so here, that one of the failures of the developmental era was its inability to account for inequalities and hierarchies such as those based on caste and community, other than as residues of the past. It therefore required major national crisis points—the anti-Mandal agitation of 1990 against the implementation of reservations for the Other Backward Castes in administration and higher education, the demolition of the Babri Masjid in 1992 and the anti-Muslim riots that followed, and the rise of new regionalisms, among others—for hitherto largely invisible structures of disparity based on caste, community, and region to gain some measure of recognition in their own right. One of the potential gains of the last decade, therefore, would be to acknowledge that the *multiple inequalities of the present* must be taken into account (rather than transcended or sought to be bypassed) in ongoing struggles against poverty.[23] For the women's movement—already accused of having 'divided' prior struggles by introducing questions of gender—the way forward may not be easy. But it is not for nothing that contemporary studies of poverty have begun to notice that Dalits, major sections of the backward castes, tribals, Muslim minorities, and female-headed households

---

[23] For an early effort in this direction, see John (with K. Lalita) (1995).

practically exhaust the categories of the poor. Feminists will have to play their part to turn such lists into live zones of coalition building.[24]

The diversity in the experiences and forms of poverty in India today may thus require unlearning inherited ways of conceptualizing our underdevelopment, which the women's movement can ignore only at its peril. Perhaps this is still less controversial than the final issue I would like to raise, one that is bound to be more debatable since it involves going beyond the 'poor'. To put it most provocatively: Has the heavy emphasis on representations of poverty—at the cost of a parallel understanding of class dynamics—also become one of the weaknesses of the women's movement? Poverty and class continue to be conflated with one another (not unlike the conflation of women and gender), and to the detriment of *both*. Class analysis—that is to say, analysis that focuses on the non-poor as well as the poor—has seen no significant advancements in the last few decades. The mode of deployment of class in campaigns and struggles within a movement such as the women's movement has suffered considerably, and operates to a remarkable degree within a social and epistemological vacuum. At least two dimensions of class analysis need much more attention. The first is the strategic location of the Indian middle classes and their key role in articulating the hegemony of the ruling bloc. They have arguably been at the heart of the major 'critical events' of the decade of the 1990s—liberalization, 'Mandal', and 'Ayodhya' (Deshpande 1997). And yet we do not even have a minimal sense of the social composition of this class, its degree of heterogeneity, and its ideological functions (Sheth 1999). Moreover, leadership of the women's movement has

---

[24] It would, however, be exceedingly naive to suppose that the deprivation and marginalization experienced by these groups would somehow act as a natural magnet drawing them together as a majority, whether socially or politically. It is not for nothing that recognition of the 'cultural' dimensions of poverty is emerging at a time when the nation has witnessed the revival of a very different majoritarian project, that of Hindutva. Recent developments in states as different as Uttar Pradesh and Gujarat are but an indication of how the most vicious conflicts can take place between groups adjacent to one another in strictly economic terms. Moreover, there is a longer history of anti-reservation *resentment* whereby the small but never invisible members of lower castes within the middle classes have not been allowed to forget who they are, a strategy that has been reproduced to deadly effect in the successful destruction of lives and livelihoods of all classes of Muslims in Gujarat. The current agenda of the Hindu Right to produce a Hindu Rashtra by incorporating sections of the most backward castes, Dalits, and tribals within its fold cannot be countered by purely economistic conceptions of deprivation. And yet, as the extraordinary results of the Lok Sabha elections of 2004 indicated, the aggressively marketed 'India Shining' campaign of the BJP, which—more than anything else—sought to make the poor invisible if not irrelevant, backfired in a way no one predicted beforehand.

invariably arisen from this class, whose mandate has therefore been one of *representation*, understood in all its various aspects.

The second aspect of class analysis that is urgently in need of redressal centres on the intermediate classes and castes, which, for lack of a better description, I will call the non-poor. An indispensable dimension of such analysis would include patterns of mobility across class fractions, processes that enable some groups to move out of poverty and possibly gain some measure of prosperity while others strategize to prevent themselves from 'falling'. Is it not curious how little we wish to know of such trends? Now it could of course be argued that since a movement must have its priorities, the problems of the non-poor cannot be expected to figure very highly. However, such a short-sighted approach has come home to roost today. As far back as the first shocked discovery of the prevalence of dowry murders among urban lower middle class families almost three decades ago, there has been evidence of *greater* gender biases in families beyond the pale of dire need. In more recent years, considerable anxiety has emerged over the worsening of female–male sex ratios, which are sharpening outside the classes of poor, leading to speculations of the 'paradox' of the 'prosperity effect' (Harriss-White 1999), the negative effects on women of fertility decline (Das Gupta and Mari Bhatt 1998), and the mismatch between measures of 'backward' districts according to economic and gender indicators (Rustagi 2000). The results of the 2001 Census in particular, where child female/male ratios in the 0–6-year age group have dropped precipitously in many districts of the most economically advanced states of the country, especially in urban areas, have led to dystopic speculations of various kinds. (The worst state averages for 2001 are Punjab [793], Haryana [820], Gujarat [879], and Himachal Pradesh [897], and the all-India figure is 927 girls per 1,000 boys.) There is every reason to believe that these are not isolated patterns but a potential sign of things to come, as men and women make 'choices' under conditions of limited gains and potential losses in an expanding, increasingly competitive economy. And yet, analysis is still largely impressionistic, mobilization quite weak and often not sufficiently sensitive to the genuine problems involved.[25] The women's movement often appears caught in a kind of cleft

---

[25] To date, the main reason advanced for the falling numbers has been the burgeoning practice of prenatal sex determination tests followed by the selective abortion of female foetuses, frequently called 'female foeticide'. Although such sex determination tests have been banned by law as far back as 1986 (as the result of feminist campaigns), unscrupulous doctors and radiologists are said to be making enormous profits with their ultrasound machines in cities, towns, and relatively more prosperous rural areas. Thus far, not a single

stick—denouncing poverty and the 'evils' of the new consumerist culture in one and the same breath. Sometimes the question is posed: If poverty is bad for women, could prosperity be worse?

Perhaps, then, the way forward may have little to do with actually getting the right perspective on 'globalization'. Nor can we rest content with celebrating 'local' initiatives. A marginal presence barely two decades ago, feminists surely have good reason to feel vindicated as more and more institutions address the constituency of 'women'. Today, however, this very gain in legitimacy could result in the stagnation of the movement. And yet, it need not. For feminism to retain its constitutive force and to believe that it can be a part of social transformations, the task is nothing less than to go beyond certain inherited constructs of 'poor women' in order to contest existing accounts of social change as such. Feminism must, on the one hand, realize that its future is tied up with the multiple languages of poverty and disparity that are straining to be heard. On the other hand, even at the cost of overload, there are no stopping places where gender loses its urgency—'success' stories in class terms are not being mirrored in the egalitarian life-chances of sons and daughters.

Above all else, the future of the women's movement will depend on its ability to rejuvenate itself. It cannot simply rely on older strategies devised during the development era. This is by no means an argument in favour of the 'retreat of the state', but simply to note that the state itself should be one of many sites of contestation. The strength of the women's movement in India—as this chapter should have made amply clear—has derived from its capacity to take on new challenges, to break out of narrow definitions of patriarchy and gender oppression. Today these qualities will be needed more than ever before. If it is the exclusiveness of the emergent social order that is blocking democracy in our times, broadening the terrain on which battles of gender and poverty must be fought may well be a risk worth taking.

REFERENCES

Agarwal, Bina (1986), 'Women, Poverty and Agricultural Growth in India', *Journal of Peasant Studies*, 13(4).

---

doctor has been apprehended, and the practice continues more or less secretly. However, much more information and understanding are required at the level of family practices across different classes and social groups before any further explanations, let alone interventions, can be offered.

Agnihotri, Indu and Vina Mazumdar (1995), 'Changing Terms of Political Discourse: Women's Movement in India', *Economic and Political Weekly*, 30(9): 1869–78.

Anveshi (1993), 'Reworking Gender Relations, Redefining Politics: Nellore Village Women against Arrack', *Economic and Political Weekly*, 16–23 January, pp. 87–90.

Banerjee, Nirmala (1997), 'How Real Is the Bogey of Féminisation?' *The Indian Journal of Labour Economics*, 40(3): 427–38.

—— (1998), 'Whatever Happened to the Dreams of Modernity? The Nehruvian Era and Women's Position', *Economic and Political Weekly*, 28(17): WS 2–7.

Basu, Amrita (1993), *Two Faces of Protest: Contrasting Modes of Women's Activism in India*. Berkeley: University of California Press and New Delhi: Oxford University Press.

Bhatt, Ela (1998), 'Doosri Azadi: SEWA's Perspectives on the Early Years of Independence', *Economic and Political Weekly*, 15 April–1 May, pp. WS 25–7.

Buch, Nirmala (2000), 'Women's Experience in New Panchayats: The Emerging Leadership of Rural Women', Occasional Paper No. 35, Centre for Women's Development Studies.

Carr, Marilyn, Martha Chen, and Renana Jhabvala (eds) (1997), *Speaking Out: Women's Economic Empowerment in South Asia*. New Delhi: Vistaar.

Das, Maitreyi (1991), *The Women's Development Programme in Rajasthan: A Case Study in Group Formation for Women's Development*. Washington, DC: The World Bank.

Das Gupta, Monica and P.N. Mari Bhatt (1998), 'Intensified Gender Bias in India: A Consequence of Fertility Decline', in Maithreyi Krishnaraj, Ratna Sudarshan, and Abusaleh Shariff (eds), *Gender, Population and Development*. New Delhi: Oxford University Press, pp. 73–93.

Das Gupta, Monica, Lincoln Chen, and J.N. Krishnan (1995), *Women's Health in India: Risks and Vulnerabilities*. New Delhi: Oxford University Press.

Datta, Bisakha (ed.) (1998), *And Who Will Make the Chapatis? A Study of All Women Panchayats in Maharashtra*. Calcutta: Stree.

Desai, Neera (1986), 'From Articulation to Accommodation: Women's Movement in India', in Leela Dube, Eleanor Leacock, and Shirley Ardener (eds), *Visibility and Power: Essays on Women in Society and Development*. New Delhi: Oxford University Press, pp. 287–99.

Deshpande, Satish (1997), 'From Development to Adjustment; Economic Ideologies, the Middle Class and Fifty Years of Independence', *Review of Development and Change*, 11(2): 294–318.

Forbes, Geraldine (1996), *Women in Modern India*. Cambridge: Cambridge University Press.

Gandhi, Nandita and Nandita Shah (1992), *The Issues at Stake: Theory and Practice in the Contemporary Women's Movement in India*. New Delhi: Kali for Women.

Government of India (1994), *Draft National Population Policy*. New Delhi: Ministry of Health and Family Welfare.

Government of India (2000), *National Population Policy*. New Delhi: Ministry of Health and Family Welfare, Government of India.

Harriss-White, Barbara (1999), 'Gender-Cleansing: The Paradox of Development and Deteriorating Female Life Chances in Tamil Nadu', in Rajeswari Sunder Rajan (ed.), *Signposts: Gender Issues in Post-Independence India*. New Delhi: Kali for Women, pp. 124–53.

Healthwatch Update (2000), Issue 11, September–December.

Hensman, Rohini (2000), 'World Trade and Workers' Rights', *Economic and Political Weekly*, 8–14 April, pp. 1247–54.

—— (2004), 'Globalisation, Women and Work', *Economic and Political Weekly*, 6 March.

Institute of Social Sciences (1995), *Women and Political Empowerment: Proceedings*. New Delhi: Institute of Social Sciences.

Isaac, T.M. Thomas and Richard Franke (2000), *Local Democracy and Development: People's Campaign for Decentralised Planning in Kerala*. New Delhi: LeftWord.

Jain, Devaki and Nirmala Banerjee (eds) (1985), *Tyranny of the Household: Investigative Essays into Women's Works*. New Delhi: Shakti Books.

Jhabvala, Renana and R.K.A. Subrahmanya (eds) (2000), *The Unorganised Sector: Work Security and Social Protection*. New Delhi: Sage Publications.

John, Mary E. (with K. Lalita) (1995), *Background Report on Gender Issues in India*. Sussex: Bridge, IDS and ODA, UK.

John, Mary E. (1996), 'Gender and Development in India, 1970s–1990s: Some Reflections on the Constitutive Role of Contexts', *Economic and Political Weekly*, 23 November.

—— (1998), 'Globalisation, Sexuality and the Visual Field: Issues and Non-Issues for Cultural Critique', in Mary E. John and Janaki Nair (eds), *A Question of Silence? The Sexual Economies of Modern India*. New Delhi: Kali for Women, pp. 368–96.

Kaushik, Susheela (1993), *Women and Panchayati Raj*. New Delhi: Har-Anand.

Kishwar, Madhu (2001), 'Laws, Liberty and Livelihood: Towards a Bottom-Up, Woman Friendly Agenda of Economic Reforms', *Manushi*, January–February, 122: 8–12.

Kishwar, Madhu and Ruth Vanita (eds) (1987), *In Search of Answers: Voices from Manushi*. London: Zed Press.

Krishnamurthy, J. (ed.) (1989), *Women in Colonial India: Essays on Survival, Work and the State*. New Delhi: Oxford University Press.

Kumar, Radha (1993), *A History of Doing: An Illustrated Account of the Movements for Women's Rights and Feminism in India, 1800–1990*. New Delhi: Kali for Women.

Lalita, K. (1988), 'Women in Revolt: A Historical Analysis of the Progressive Organisation of Women in Andhra Pradesh', in Saskia Wieringa (ed.), *Women's Struggles and Strategies*. Aldershot: Gower.

Maheswari, Uma (1999), 'Anti-arrack Movement, Prohibition and After: *Eenadu's* Strategic Support and Silence', *Journal of Arts and Ideas*, Special Issue on 'Gender, Media and the Rhetorics of Liberalisation', 22–3: 73–86.

Marg (2001), *Daughters of the 74th Amendment: A Study of Delhi and Karnal*. New Delhi: Marg.

Mehra, Rekha (1983), 'Rural Development Programmes: Neglect of Women', in Rekha Mehra and K. Saradamoni (eds), *Women and Rural Transformation—Two Studies*. New Delhi: Concept Publishing House.

Menon, Nivedita (ed.) (1999), *Gender and Politics in India*. New Delhi: Oxford University Press.

Mitra, Asok (2001), 'Implications of Declining Sex Ratio in India', in Vina Mazumdar and N. Krishnaji (eds), *Enduring Conundrum: India's Sex Ratio; Essays in Honour of Asok Mitra*. New Delhi: Rainbow, pp. 143–98.

Mukherjee, Vanita Nayak (2002), 'Gender Matters', in 'Beyond Numbers: A Symposium on Population Planning and Advocacy', *Seminar*, 511: 67–75.

Nanda, B.R. (ed.) (1976), *Indian Women from Purdah to Modernity*. New Delhi: Vikas Publishing House.

National Commission of Women (1996), *The Sathin as an Agent of Women's Development*. New Delhi: Government of India.

National Council of Educational Research and Training (2001), *Guidelines and Syllabi for Primary Stage*. New Delhi: National Council of Educational Research and Training.

Omvedt, Gail (1980), *We Will Smash This Prison/Indian Women in Struggle*. London: Zed Books.

Omvedt, Gail and Chetna Gala (1993), 'The New Economic Policy and Women: A Rural Perspective', *Economic Review*, October.

Planning Commission (1999a), *Ninth Five Year Plan 1997–2002, Volume I: Development Goals, Strategies and Policies*. New Delhi: Government of India.

Planning Commission (1999b), *Ninth Five Year Plan 1997–2002, Volume II, Thematic Issues and Sectoral Programmes*. New Delhi: Government of India.

Qadeer, Imrana (1998a), 'Maternal Health in India', in Maitreyi Krishnaraj, Ratna Sudarshan, and Abusaleh Shariff (eds), *Gender, Population and Development in India*. New Delhi: Oxford University Press, pp. 270–90.

Qadeer, Imrana (1998b), 'Reproductive Health: A Public Health Perspective', *Economic and Political Weekly*, 33(41): 2676–8.

Rao, Mohan (2001), 'Population Policies: States Approve Coercive Measures,' *Economic and Political Weekly*, 21 July, pp. 2739–41.

Ravindran, T.K. Sundari (1993), 'Women and the Politics of Population and Development in India', *Reproductive Health Matters*, 1: 26–38.

Ray, Bharati (ed.) (1995), *From the Seams of History: Essays on Indian Women*. New Delhi: Oxford University Press.

Ray, Raka (1999), *Fields of Protest: Women's Movements in India*. Minneapolis: University of Minnesota Press and New Delhi: Kali for Women.

Report of the Sub-committee (1947), *Women's Role in a Planned Economy*. Bombay: Vora and Co.

Rustagi, Preet (2000), 'Identifying Gender Backward Districts Using Selected Indicators', *Economic and Political Weekly*, 25 November, pp. 4276–86.

Sangari, Kumkum and Sudesh Vaid (eds) (1989), *Recasting Women: Essays on Colonial India*. New Delhi: Kali for Women.

Sathin Karamchari Sangh (n.d.), 'The Sathin Issue: A Collective Strategy, the Need of the Hour', unpublished pamphlet.

Sen, Gita, Adriane Germaine, and Lincoln Chen (eds) (1994), *Population Policies Reconsidered. Health, Empowerment and Rights*. Cambridge, MA: Harvard University Press.

Sen, Ilina (ed.) (1990), *A Space within the Struggle: Women's Participation in People's Movements*. New Delhi: Kali for Women.

Shah, Nandita, Sujata Gothoskar, *et al.* (1994), 'Feminisation of Labour Force and Organisational Strategies', *Economic and Political Weekly*, 30 April, pp. WS 39–48.

Sharma, Kumud (1989), 'Shared Aspirations, Fragmented Realities: Contemporary Women's Movement in India, Its Dialectics and Dilemmas', Occasional Paper No. 12, Centre for Women's Development Studies, New Delhi.

Sheth, D.L. (1999), 'Secularization of Caste and Making of New Middle Class', *Economic and Political Weekly*, 34(34–5): 2502–30.

—— (2004), 'Globalisation and New Politics of Micro-movements', *Economic and Political Weekly*, 3–9 January.

Shiva, Vandana (1996), 'Trading Our Lives Away: Free Trade, Women and Ecology', Durgabhai Memorial Lecture, Council for Social Development, New Delhi.

—— (1998), *Globalisation of Agriculture, Food Security and Sustainability*. New Delhi: Research Foundation for Science, Technology and Ecology.

Sinha, Mrinalini (2000), 'Refashioning Mother India: Feminism and Nationalism in Late-Colonial India', *Feminist Studies*, 26(3).

Srivastava, Kavita and Jaya Sharma (1991), *Training Rural Women for Literacy*. Jaipur: Institute of Development Studies.

Stree Shakti Sanghatana (1989), *'We were Making History'…Life Histories of Women in the Telangana People's Struggle*. New Delhi: Kali for Women.

Tharu, Susie and K. Lalita (eds) (1991), *Women Writing in India: From 600 B.C. to the Present, Vol. 1*. New York: The Feminist Press and New Delhi: Oxford University Press.

—— (1993), *Women Writing in India: From 600 B.C. to the Present, Vol. 2*. New York: The Feminist Press and New Delhi: Oxford University Press.

Tharu, Susie and Tejaswini Niranjana (1996), 'Problems for a Contemporary Theory of Gender', in Shahid Amin and Dipesh Chakrabarty (eds), *Subaltern Studies IX: Writings on South Asian History and Society*. New Delhi: Oxford University Press.

Vasavi, A.R. and Catherine P. Kingfisher (2003), 'Poor Women as Economic Agents: The Neoliberal State and Gender in India and the U.S.', *Indian Journal of Gender Studies*, 10(1): 1–24.

Visaria, Pravin (1969), 'The Sex Ratio of the Population of India', *Census of India 1961, Vol. 1*, Monograph no. 10.

The World Bank (1991), *Gender and Poverty in India*. Washington, DC: The World Bank.

CONTRIBUTORS

BINA AGARWAL is Professor and Director, Institute of Economic Growth, Delhi.

FLAVIA AGNES is a legal scholar and a practising advocate of the Mumbai High Court and co-founder of Majlis.

UMA CHAKRAVARTI is a historian, retired from Miranda House, University of Delhi, Delhi.

AMRITA CHHACHHI is Senior Lecturer in Women, Gender and Development, Institute of Social Studies, The Hague, Netherlands.

LAWRENCE COHEN is Professor, Department of Anthropology, University of California, Berkeley.

SHOHINI GHOSH is Sajjad Zaheer Professor, AJK Mass Communication Research Centre, Jamia Milia Islamia, New Delhi.

MARY E. JOHN is Director, Centre for Women's Development Studies, New Delhi.

KALPANA KANNABIRAN is Professor of Sociology, NALSAR University of Law, Hyderabad.

SUMI KRISHNA is an independent scholar and researcher based in Bangalore.

RADHA KUMAR is Professor and Director, Nelson Mandela Centre for Peace and Conflict Resolution, Jamia Milia Islamia, New Delhi.

SABA MAHMOOD is Associate Professor, Department of Anthropology, University of California, Berkeley.

NIVEDITA MENON is Professor, Centre for Comparative Politics and Political Theory, School of International Studies, Jawaharlal Nehru University, New Delhi.

JANAKI NAIR is Professor, Centre for Historical Studies, School of Social Sciences, Jawaharlal Nehru University.

KALPANA RAM is Senior Lecturer, Department of Anthropology, McQuarie University, Australia.

RAKA RAY is Sarah Kailath Chair of India Studies and Professor of Sociology and South and Southeast Asia Studies at the University of California, Berkeley.

TANIKA SARKAR is Professor, Centre for Historical Studies, School of Social Sciences, Jawaharlal Nehru University, New Delhi.

ILINA SEN is co-founder of Rupantar, a non-governmental organization in Chhattisgarh.

MRINALINI SINHA is Alice Freeman Palmer Professor of History, Department of History, University of Michigan.

PATRICIA UBEROI is Honorary Fellow, Institute of Chinese Studies, Delhi.